The Legislative Drafter's Desk Reference

sunwater
INSTITUTE

The Legislative Drafter's Desk Reference

Best Practices in Drafting Federal and State Laws and Regulations

THIRD EDITION

Sandra L. Strokoff
Lawrence E. Filson

The Legislative Drafter's Desk Reference, Third Edition

Hardback ISBN: 979-8-9896992-4-7

Paperback ISBN: 979-8-9896992-2-3

Ebook ISBN: 979-8-9896992-3-0

Cover and interior design: Andy Meaden, meadencreative.com

sunwater
INSTITUTE

The Sunwater Institute is a nonpartisan, nonprofit think tank based in North Bethesda, Maryland. Its mission is to strengthen the foundations of liberal democracy through interdisciplinary science, technology, and open dialogue.

The Sunwater Institute believes Congress's performance as an institution is critical to the wellbeing of the nation and democracy worldwide. It conducts theoretical and applied research aimed at improving Congress's institutional knowledge, processes, and efficiency. The Sunwater Institute strives to convert lessons from its academic research projects into tools, analytics, datasets, publications, and trainings that are leveraged by governments, businesses, academia, media, and nonprofits.

Sunwater.org
Legis1.com

CONTENTS

List of Figures and Tables

Preface

The primary purpose of *The Legislative Drafter's Desk Reference,* first published in 1992, is to present solid drafting principles while recognizing and addressing the problems that the typical legislative drafter faces every day.

For many people, how a bill is drafted remains a mystery, engendered in no small part by the guarded anonymity of the professional "ghost writers" of Federal legislation—in the Offices of the Legislative Counsel of the U.S. House of Representatives and the Senate. A legislator who introduces, sponsors, or supports a bill, or even an outsider who promotes it, is almost certain to claim authorship of the bill; most people are unaware that what is being claimed is an authorship of ideas only.

But how is the actual language of a bill created? What exactly does the writer do to make the words appear, and how do the writer's activities fit into the overall legislative picture? This book sets about answering these questions, clarifying the responsibility of the drafter: to convert the sponsor's initial generalities into specifics; to fill any gaps in the proposal as it was originally presented; to raise and have answered any substantive, legal, administrative, and technical questions that may arise; to arrange the bill's elements in a way that will effectively communicate its message to the intended audience; to do all these things without leaving any loose ends; and to convert the end product into the proper legislative form and style.

Legislative drafting should be thoroughly understood by anyone with a serious interest in how the legislative process works. It is a highly specialized form of writing, and a demanding one, but it is a skill that can be acquired. This book attempts to ease the learning process.

Some individuals draft bills on a regular basis as an integral part of the legislative process, but many others also participate. Officials in the executive branch, as well as lobbyists and other outside groups, for example, frequently need to formulate legislative proposals or at least be able to understand and evaluate proposals already on the table. And drafters at the State and local levels need a familiarity with the ins and outs of drafting at the Federal level, because State objectives can often be best achieved through modifications of the Federal law (or can be achieved, through modifications of the State law, only after particular changes have been made in the Federal law). In addition, the drafting principles in this book can easily be applied or adapted to drafting of State or local law.

The ability to draft well will increase one's ability to identify problems in legislation and to comprehend legislative language, important skills for anyone who needs to understand what a particular legislative proposal would do to or for some group or interest and who wants to know how to enhance the proposal's prospects.

Anyone who needs to understand legislation, whatever the reason, can benefit from a better understanding of the drafting process, and providing that is what *The Legislative Drafter's Desk Reference* is all about.

The primary objective of this book is to provide an all-purpose drafting reference text for individuals who may be called upon to draft legislation, and to serve the needs of those individuals without regard to their background, the setting in which they operate, and the extent (if any) of their previous training. This book is meant to be used by experienced and occasional drafters alike.

A second, but perhaps equally important, objective is to paint a realistic and meaningful picture of what legislative drafting involves and how it fits into the legislative process as a whole. In this sense, it is intended for individuals who simply have a serious interest in government and

are seeking a better understanding of the overall process as well as for individuals who actually draft bills.

This edition has updated the examples and models used in the previous edition to illustrate the drafting process while ensuring that the rules, procedures, forms, references, and principles upon which the examples and models are based remain in effect.

The primary objective of these updated editions is to expand upon the solid drafting principles set forth in the first edition. One way I have done this is by providing more statutory examples and case studies, at times in a politically charged environment, to illustrate those drafting principles or to illustrate how the drafting of the examples can be improved by applying the drafting principles. Another is by updating statutory requirements that have widespread application (for example, provisions in title 5, United States Code, that apply to all executive branch agencies). A third is by discussing additional issues, not before addressed, that most drafters commonly face (as in the section on civil and criminal sanctions in chapter 12).

The major addition, however, lies in the recognition of the role of the courts in statutory drafting. Viewed one way, the legislative and judicial branches of government are in an ongoing dialogue with each other—the judicial branch is called upon to interpret legislation, and the legislative branch may respond by amending a law to address a judicial interpretation (whether based on the Constitution or otherwise). The courts apply certain principles in interpreting statutes and reach decisions after deliberating possibilities that the legislature, in the interests of political expediency, may not have considered. Because of these realities, the drafter's ability to anticipate how a court may approach a statute when the statute is being drafted may obviate litigation or at least indicate to the courts how to interpret a provision of law should it come before them.

Therefore, throughout these editions are citations to court decisions directly relevant to the way a statute is drafted: the discussion of the RICO statute in chapter 4 and the discussion of "willful" in criminal statutes in chapter 12 are two examples.

In addition, chapter 28 discusses principles of statutory construction, and chapter 29 discusses significant Federal court cases that have a direct bearing on how statutes should be drafted. This new edition reflects significant changes in jurisprudence that have occurred since the second edition was published, changes that directly affect the way statutes are drafted.

The second edition and this edition also address some of the concerns of the nonfederal drafter—whether at the State or local level—that arise by virtue of State constitutional requirements and the relationship between the Federal Government and the States under the Constitution of the United States. A separate chapter (35) on drafting nonfederal law has been included, in addition to references to State requirements in other chapters.

Finally, to illustrate how the drafting principles in this book can be applied to the drafting of regulations, chapter 36 attempts to do so by example, critiquing regulations issued pursuant to a Federal statute, the Foreign Narcotics Kingpin Designation Act.

The first edition was published before the widespread availability of documents in electronic format and the explosion of sources of information on the Internet, and much has changed since the publication of the second edition. These changes are reflected in this new edition.

Several useful texts on legislative and legal drafting are cited throughout the book in the discussion of its drafting principles, including:

(1) *The Fundamentals of Legal Drafting*, by Reed Dickerson (to be cited as *Dickerson*), Little, Brown (1986).

(2) *Drafting Federal Law*, by Donald Hirsch (to be cited as *Hirsch*), published for the Department of Health and Human Services, Office of the General Counsel, Legislation Division (1980), and (with revisions) for the use of the Office of the Legislative Counsel, U.S. House of Representatives (1989).

(3) *House Legislative Counsel's Manual on Drafting Style* (to be cited as *HOLC*)—the everyday working manual of the Office of the Legislative

Counsel, U.S. House of Representatives, published by that office in 1989, 1995, and 2022.

(4) *Legislative Drafting Manual, Office of the Legislative Counsel, United States Senate* (to be referred to as *SOLC*)—the everyday working manual of the Office of the Legislative Counsel, U.S. Senate, published by that office in 1997.

Two additional books are cited numerous times:

(1) *The Legislative Drafter's Deskbook: A Practical Guide,* by my former colleague Tobias A. Dorsey, published by TheCapitol.Net, 2006.

(2) *Legal, Legislative, and Rule Drafting in Plain English,* by Robert J. Martineau and Michael B. Salemo, published by Thompson/West, 2005.

These works are referred to for the views they espouse about drafting, although they may not agree with one another or with the views expressed in this book; however, the reader should have the opportunity to see what others have to say about the subject.

The main portion of this book, that is, everything after the introductory material contained in Part 1, consists of eight parts:

Part II (chapters 4 through 6) deals with the preliminary stage of any drafting operation—the things that have to be done before the actual writing begins: pinning down the sponsor's problem and its intended solution, identifying and dealing with any collateral questions that the solution may raise, and organizing the bill.

Part III (chapters 7 through 9) discusses some of the broader considerations that bear upon legislative form and style—the mechanics of good writing, the Roman rule, and the quest for readability.

Part IV (chapters 10 through 13) begins the more specific treatment of the writing process, enumerating the different provisions that might be found in a typical freestanding bill, discussing their form and style, and the alternatives available to the drafter.

Part V (chapters 14 through 18) deals with the writing of amendatory bills, addressing the basic amendatory forms and styles, the proper organization and arrangement of amendments, and a number of problems unique to the amendatory approach.

Part VI (chapters 19 through 27) covers legislative style and usage generally, setting forth a list of the drafting rules, principles, and techniques that would normally apply without regard to the type of bill involved or its setting.

Part VII (chapters 28 and 29) deals with the role of the courts in legislative drafting, addressing rules of statutory construction and significant case law that the drafter should be mindful of in drafting legislation.

Part VIII (chapters 30 through 34) addresses matters of form, style, and procedure that are important in Federal bill drafting but could not appropriately be included in the preceding parts because of the wide variety of circumstances and requirements in the different States.

Part IX (chapters 35 and 36) addresses drafters of nonfederal law and regulations specifically.

When reading this manual, you should keep in mind the following points:

(1) In a number of instances the same point is made, or the same steps in the legislative process are retraced, in two or more places. This redundancy is intentional; it is done so that readers who are interested only in the subject covered by a particular chapter can get the full picture without having to look elsewhere.

(2) Each of the examples and models in this book is intended to illustrate a particular point. Each should be read as addressing only that point and should not be taken as an endorsement or criticism of anything else.

(3) If an example or model used becomes obsolete because a law changes, it is hoped the point of the example or model will still be valid.

In legislative drafting, as in other forms of prose composition, any standard dictionary, read in conjunction with *The Chicago Manual of Style* or its equivalent, should be regarded as the basic authority on editorial style. Editorial style primarily involves such things as spelling, capitalization, hyphenation, and punctuation, as well as the uses of words and numerals in particular circumstances.

When a more specialized manual on the writing or printing of public documents in the context involved (such as the *United States Government Publishing Office Style Manual* or one of its State counterparts) provides a different rule, however, that rule should be followed instead.

And when the unique needs of legislative drafting demand the application of a rule that is different from any of the cited authorities, that rule should be applied even if it violates otherwise established practices.

The style in which this book is written—like the style in which legislation would normally be written—reflects this hierarchy of choices. It generally follows the dictionary and the *Chicago Manual,* but it deviates from them (for example, by capitalizing governmental terms such as State, Federal, and President) when that is what the *GPO Style Manual* does. It deviates from all of the cited authorities whenever that is the only way to meet the drafter's overriding need for absolute clarity and precision (see chapters 21, 22, and 27 for examples).

In an ideal world you would always be able to draft under circumstances that give you every opportunity to do it correctly and comprehensively, with plenty of time and resources and with no possibility of having overlooked anything important. As a practical matter, however, this does not occur often.

For reasons quite beyond your control you must often be satisfied with doing the best you can in the hope that your efforts will be sufficient to accomplish the desired result. Always remember that you will almost never have the option to flatly refuse to assist a sponsor simply because the task appears to be impossible, so you need to know how to face those problems cheerfully and with some hope of success. This book will try to suggest ways of handling the difficulties you are likely to encounter.

There are horror cases, of course—you may find yourself responsible for a massive and complex piece of legislation, or floundering in the middle of a legislative storm, or dealing with frantic sponsors going in opposite directions—but this book should help you get through the ordeal. In most cases the outlook is not so forbidding; most of your drafting assignments will likely involve one-shot proposals of limited scope, being developed in friendly territory.

The legislative process is designed to be self-correcting in the sense that there should be opportunities to take care of early mistakes and technical shortcomings in the later stages. However, since these opportunities may not present themselves, you should do the best drafting job you can at each stage.

Acknowledgments

Many individuals have contributed to this book. My deepest gratitude goes foremost to Larry Filson, my former colleague in the Office of the Legislative Counsel of the U.S. House of Representatives, who created the stellar text with which I had the opportunity to work and who taught me a great deal about approaching legislative drafting.

I thank my colleagues in the Offices of the Legislative Counsel of the House and the Senate, who always responded when I asked their advice about particular passages—Ira Forstater, Rosemary Gallagher, Mark Synnes, Wade Ballou, Bob Weinhagen, Paul Callen, Doug Bellis, Jim Grossman, Greg Kostka, and Susan Fleishman—as well as my longtime Senate counterpart and "partner in crime" on trade law, Polly Craighill. Special thanks are due to Larry Johnston, who reworked the many outdated passages from the Social Security Act, and Ed Leong and Steve Cope, both of whom waded through many chapters and provided invaluable suggestions.

I am deeply grateful to Charlie Johnson, former House Parliamentarian, and Muftiah McCartin, former Assistant Parliamentarian, for their assistance on the matters of procedure addressed in the book.

I also thank Frank Burk, former Legislative Counsel of the U.S. Senate, who was my inspiration for the chapter on significant case law for the drafter.

Many thanks to my friend of 60 years, Betsy Raburn, who patiently read through the entire text from "across the pond" and offered countless useful suggestions to improve it.

I am also deeply grateful to Professor Lou Rulli, of the University of Pennsylvania Law School, whose assistance was invaluable, particularly on chapters 4, 28, and 29.

Special thanks also to Pope Barrow, former Legislative Counsel of the U.S. House of Representatives, and my predecessor, for working tirelessly to create a collegial, supportive work environment to ease the demands of the legislative process.

For their constant love and support, I wish to thank my husband, Jay Gordon, and my children, Jennifer Matsumoto and Jonathan Gordon. Special thanks to Jay, who was extremely helpful in updating the case law in this edition, and to Jonathan Gordon and Polly Craighill, who helped review the final version of the edition.

PART I
GENERAL OVERVIEW

1. Approaching the Subject
2. What is Legislative Drafting?
3. The Drafting Process Itself

1. Approaching the Subject

1.1 The approach in general

Reed Dickerson quoted Middleton Beaman, the first Legislative Counsel of the House of Representatives, as having once said that a legislative drafter must be an intellectual eunuch, and added that the drafter must be an emotional oyster as well.[1] Each of them had a point, but overstated the case considerably. Almost anyone with writing ability and a modicum of analytical judgment can become a respectable legislative drafter and need not secede from the human race to do it.

When reduced to its simplest terms, legislative drafting is nothing more than the process of converting ideas into language that will effectively carry them out—not altogether different from other kinds of writing. The fact that it is writing of a highly specialized and uniquely demanding nature means only that the skills needed to do it properly, and a realistic understanding of what it involves, may be somewhat harder to acquire.

To help you develop those skills and that understanding, this book consciously endeavors to do the following:

(1) It treats legislative drafting as the highly pragmatic activity it is rather than as a merely academic exercise, without minimizing the intellectual and journalistic aspects of the craft.

(2) It places special emphasis upon the problems of the occasional drafter, without "writing down" to the reader (and thereby minimizing its usefulness to more experienced drafters).

(3) Without apologizing for its emphasis on *Federal* legislative drafting, it recognizes the needs of individuals whose interests or drafting activities lie in nonfederal areas and includes material relevant to those needs whenever possible.

A word of warning, however: neither this book nor any other can turn you into an accomplished drafter; only experience, and the imitation of good models under expert guidance, can do that. What this book can do is give you some basic rules and teach you an approach that will equip you with techniques to solve drafting problems for yourself as you encounter them.

1.2 The importance of understanding the rules, and of knowing when to ignore them

Most of the rules and principles that you should follow in drafting a bill would be self-evident to any good writer, and many others would become evident upon a little reflection, simply as a matter of common sense. However, good drafting also involves the application of specialized rules, unique to that form, which would not be likely to occur spontaneously to a nondrafter; it is important that you understand what they are and why they matter.

It would be possible, of course, to apply these rules without having learned anything about them in advance, simply by using this book or its equivalent as a reference manual and consulting its index frequently whenever you sit down to draft. Yet knowing something about the rules *before* sitting down to draft is important if you want to do the job properly.

Without some understanding of the purpose of these rules, you may not recognize a drafting problem when it stares you in the face, nor will you always know what to seek in the index. More importantly, you can seldom afford to spend a lot of time on the mechanics of a drafting job when you need that time to deal with the substantive and legal aspects of the proposal. The mechanical aspects of legislative drafting—approach, organization, form, style, and technique—should become second nature, simply so you can forget about them when you need to focus on other problems.

It is important, however, to remain flexible. In real life the drafter often must choose between conflicting rules or find the lesser of several evils. No drafting rule is written in stone; there are cases where not applying one of the time-honored rules will in fact increase clarity or otherwise improve the product. When the application of one stylistic rule would conflict with another that is more important, the rule in question, however useful and sensible it may otherwise be, must give way.

1.3 Terminology

A number of concepts involved in legislative drafting will surface over and over again in this book, as will several frequently used terms to which somewhat arbitrary meanings are necessarily assigned. Fairness to the reader requires that these terms receive special mention at the outset. Although they relate to the introduction and enactment of a bill, the drafting principles involved can be applied to other vehicles, like regulations (addressed in chapter 36).

To keep things as simple as possible, the following definitions and conventions are used throughout the book:

Classification of drafters. It will often be necessary or desirable to distinguish individuals who draft bills regularly, and should already be thoroughly familiar with legislative drafting and its problems, from those who only occasionally draft bills and consequently may need special help.

The term "professional drafter" will be used to refer to an individual, such as an employee of a legislative body, executive agency, or private organization, whose job-related duties consist wholly or primarily of drafting bills. All others will be arbitrarily referred to as "occasional drafters", with full recognition that some of them may be highly skilled.

Types of legislative vehicles. Except when otherwise indicated, the term "bill" will be used broadly to refer to any measure designed to be introduced in and acted upon by a legislative body, including joint, concurrent, and simple resolutions as well as actual bills, and also to refer to any amendment (or other isolated piece of language) designed to be incorporated into a bill. With respect to the latter, the term "introduced" should be read as meaning "offered" or "proposed".

Policy. The term "policy" will be used to refer primarily to the sponsor's basic objective in introducing a bill and seeking its enactment (the "main thrust"), but it also includes the sponsor's intent with respect to any subsidiary or collateral questions that may be involved in achieving the basic objective.

A policy question that is not part of the sponsor's main thrust will be described as "subsidiary" if—

(1) it is integral to the basic policy and must be answered, one way or another, in order to make the bill complete and coherent, or

(2) it involves matters so closely related to the main thrust that failure to address it would leave an obvious gap in the bill.

A policy question will be described as "collateral" if the bill would be complete and coherent (though not necessarily correct) if it were not addressed at all; the most common examples involve the way in which existing laws would affect how the bill operates and vice versa. Subsidiary policy questions are discussed in chapter 4, collateral questions in chapter 5.

The principle that policymaking and drafting are separate functions applies even in those cases where (because of the nature of your position) you can afford the luxury of being your own policymaker. However, the objectivity required for good legislative drafting may be jeopardized when you are also an open advocate for the intended policy, unless you remember that you are wearing two quite different hats and that opponents of the policy will be looking for flaws in your drafting.

Sponsors. The term "sponsor" (with respect to a bill) will be used to refer to the individual or entity who requests the drafter to prepare the bill, who determines its policy, and who will be responsible for proposing or introducing it.

If you work for the legislature itself, the sponsor is usually a legislator or a committee. If you work for any other agency or organization, the sponsor is usually an official of that agency or organization (although when the bill is drafted and turned over to a legislator for introduction, the latter becomes the sponsor insofar as subsequent drafters are concerned).

Normally the terms "sponsor" and "policymaker" are synonymous. From your point of view as a drafter, however, there is often a distinction. When you deal with a member of the sponsor's staff rather than directly with the sponsor, you are entitled to treat the staff member as the policymaker. A sponsor may instruct you to take the policy from a third party outside the legislative process, such as a consultant, a lobbyist,[2] or a constituent. In this situation, however, it is important to verify that the sponsor thoroughly understands the policy presented by this third party.

If you are acting as your own policymaker, you probably have a sponsor in the wings, or are looking for one.

Setting and context. The terms "setting" and "context" (except for the discussion of context in statutory construction in chapter 28) will be used to distinguish the physical situations in which different drafters operate—an acknowledgment that at least some of the circumstances you will face, and at least some of the factors that bear upon how you should do your job, will be unique to your particular situation. The distinction is often critical because the external factors that determine your choices as a drafter—institutional structure, procedural rules, constitutional provisions, and all manner of long-standing practices both substantive and stylistic—differ widely from one jurisdiction to another, from one legislative entity to another within the same jurisdiction, and even from one time to another within the same entity.

Audience. The term "audience" (with respect to a bill) will be used to refer to the particular people or entities to whom the bill is primarily directed and who will have to read, understand, and apply it. Thus a bill revising the benefit formula under some existing program (though its primary effect would, of course, be upon the intended beneficiaries) normally consists of what amounts to instructions to the administrators responsible for calculating the benefits involved, while a bill making specified conduct unlawful is normally addressed directly to the individuals who might be tempted to engage in that conduct. The differences between an audience consisting of administrators and an audience consisting of the affected individuals can be important to you as a drafter.

Tobias Dorsey, stressing the importance of knowing principles of statutory interpretation, contends that in drafting Federal law the most important "audience" (other than the sponsor) is the courts, in particular the Supreme Court of the United States, because when conflicts arise the courts will interpret what the law means.[3] This reasoning would apply as well to the drafting of not only Federal statutes but State and local statutes as well, and to regulations issued by agencies pursuant to those statutes to the extent that courts in any jurisdiction are charged with interpreting the laws of that jurisdiction. While the drafter should always be aware of the role of the courts (chapter 28 addresses statutory construction), in this book the term "audience" has the narrower meaning of the preceding paragraph.

Robert Martineau and Michael B. Salerno object to drafting a legal document designed to affect a particular group as though only that group is concerned with its content, because other persons are affected (for example, by the actions of government officials) or otherwise concerned with the document, as an argument for using common words that all can understand.[4] The difficulties of attaining this goal when drafting complex concepts are addressed in 2.2 and 9.3.

Readability and clarity. Language is "readable" if it can be read comfortably and comprehended with a minimum of effort. Language has "clarity" if it says precisely what it is supposed to say, leaving no doubt about what it means. Both qualities are virtues but, as will be stressed later (especially in chapter 9), either may exist without the other.

Readability is desirable, but clarity is indispensable.

Notes

1 *Dickerson,* p. 11. Dickerson cited the Beaman statement as having been made during hearings on H. Con. Res. 18, 79th Congress, 1st Session (1945), 413, 416.

2 The term "lobbyist" refers generally to a person retained by another party to communicate with a legislator or executive branch official for the purpose of influencing that legislator or official to adopt a particular position on an issue when action is taken on that issue.

3 Tobias Dorsey, *Legislative Drafter's Deskbook: A Practical Guide* (Alexandria, Va.: TheCapitol.Net, 2006), 62.

4 Robert J. Martineau and Michael B. Salerno, *Legal, Legislative, and Rule Drafting in Plain English* (St. Paul, Minn.: Thomson/West, 2005), 57–58.

2. What Is Legislative Drafting?

2.1 In general

The terms "legislative drafting" and "bill drafting" are commonly used to describe simply the act of writing legislation. Used more accurately, however, they describe the entire process of taking raw ideas, refining them and developing the language to carry them out, and then organizing that language so as to achieve the sponsor's objective exactly—a process in which analysis and perspective are immeasurably more important than style.

The final product must address any problems, omissions, and ambiguities that may have existed in the sponsor's original proposal or that may subsequently arise as a result of refinements in the sponsor's policy. It must be cast in language that is clear, consistent, legally effective, technically sound, administrable, enforceable, and constitutional; is correct in form and style; and is as readable and aesthetically pleasing as possible. Furthermore, it must not inadvertently create any new problems or cause any unintended consequences.

Although legislative drafting does not include the origination of the ideas to be incorporated in the bill, a major part of your work as a drafter does consist of helping to clarify the sponsor's concepts and raising policy issues that the sponsor may not have considered. The drafting process thus involves far more than simply writing; in many cases it actually provides the principal mechanism for developing substantive policy.

Your efforts to convert the sponsor's general policy objectives into specific legislative language often constitute the best way—and sometimes the only way—to identify the aspects of that policy needing further refinement.

Too many people miss the point completely and regard legislative drafting as only packaging language in "legalese", thereby minimizing all that it involves. This view is enhanced when a sponsor presents a draft prepared by a lobbyist or other outside group and, assuming all the work has been done because words are already on the page, asserts that all the legislative drafter need do is simply "put a bill-head on it".

At the other extreme are those who still confuse drafting with policy-making; news accounts may refer to a government agency or official, a legislator, or even a private organization, in sponsoring or publicly supporting a particular bill, as the "drafter" of that bill or one of its major provisions. This misuse of terms is probably harmless, but it illustrates a common misconception.

HOLC (page 4), with characteristic succinctness, summarizes the basic skills of the trained drafter this way:

(1) Finding out what the client[1] *really* wants to do;

(2) Analyzing the legal and other problems involved;

(3) Helping the client come up with solutions to those problems that will—

  (a) be administrable and enforceable, and

  (b) keep hassles and litigation to a minimum; and

(4) Getting the client's message across.

There are many simple bills, of course, that involve little more than *HOLC*'s first step followed immediately by the actual writing; but even then your decision to bypass the other preliminaries must be a conscious one, and must be made before you start to write.

2.2 Legislative drafting as a unique form of writing

Many people regard legislative drafting as just another kind of writing, like a term paper, office memorandum, or business letter, except for its subject matter and format. They understand that there may be a few specialized requirements of style and form, but they assume that any good writer's instincts will be sufficient for the task, at least with the aid of an elementary drafting manual. After all, term papers, memoranda, and business letters need to be carefully phrased too.

Others believe that it is an arcane skill that should be undertaken, and can be mastered, only by a select few.

Neither view is completely realistic. Legislation does resemble other forms of written communication in most important respects, but there are differences that are sufficiently critical to require that the drafter possess special qualifications and training and to demand of the drafter a significantly different approach.

First and foremost, legislative drafting seeks a "degree of precision and internal coherence rarely met outside the language of formal logic or mathematics" (*Dickerson,* page 4), and the attention to structure and detail that it demands is unique. The differences in degree are so great as to constitute practical differences in kind.

Statutory language is frequently criticized and caricatured by learned commentators as well as by the citizenry at large because it is too "complicated". In some cases the critics are right—there are plenty of laws that could have been written more simply. But for the most part these critics fail to appreciate the difficulties that any language would face in attempting to carry out policies that—necessarily or unnecessarily—are complex and convoluted themselves to begin with (see chapter 9).

Laws that are inherently and inescapably complex are, of course, favorite targets—the Internal Revenue Code (one of the most skillfully written laws on the books) has been reviled for its "colossal nebulosity and impenetrable density",[2] and the Social Security Act has been described as a statute that "might have been less confusing if it had been written in Arabic"[3]—but less complicated laws regularly suffer as well.

Efforts to require that laws, regulations, and other legal documents be written in "plain English" are useful to the extent that language can be expressed directly and simplified by avoiding excess words and stilted grammar. But, to the extent that those efforts set out rules that should always be followed, they fail to take into account the fact that complex and poorly thought-out policies at times require language that may appear burdensome but is necessary to reflect those policies.

Second, legislative language is intended to become the law of the jurisdiction involved and must coexist amicably with the other provisions of that law. This means that (in order to make sure it is written correctly) it must be developed with one eye firmly fixed on the existing law in the field involved and in related fields, and also on the existing law in more general areas whose provisions impose administrative, budgetary, procedural, constitutional, or other requirements affecting substantive rights and duties across the board. Meanwhile, in order to make sure it will work after it is written, the other eye must be focused on the possible legal consequences of the specific words the drafter plans to use.

A related point is that while some laws may be totally self-executing, most cannot be; and as a drafter you must keep in mind that regulations will probably have to be written by the agency responsible for administering your product. Future regulations are something over which you have no control, of course; but you must recognize the areas in which administrative discretion will be required and try to make life as easy as possible for both the regulation-writers and the regulation-readers.

Major legislation is invariably crammed with complications of this kind, and failure to identify and deal with them may affect the rights of large numbers of people for decades. Every drafter must learn to recognize them instinctively.

Third, nearly all of the bills with which you may be concerned as a drafter are general in their application, but more often than not the problems that caused them to be proposed in the first place were highly specific—the sponsor has simply become aware of a situation in which the operation (or nonapplicability) of some existing law or program is adversely affecting a particular individual or group in which the sponsor is interested.

But no matter how narrowly the bill is written (unless it is cast in the form of a private relief bill), it will unavoidably cover many people in addition to those whose specific problems triggered the proposal. Most of them usually should be covered (because their situations are sufficiently similar to the triggering situation), but it is easy to overlook the differences and to cover some people whose situations are really dissimilar enough to warrant quite different treatment (see 4.5).

These questions arise even when the proposal involves a matter of broad public policy like a general tax increase or funding reduction. A broad impersonal proposal of this kind will almost always affect different people and situations in different ways, and the legislature will not have done its job unless it considers whether and to what extent the proposal should be modified in order to deal with specific cases. Efforts to amend the proposal for this purpose will almost certainly be made, and some drafter will have to face the problem after all.

Unlike the typical practicing lawyer who looks at specific legal controversies during or after the fact, as a drafter you must look before the fact at all of the possible situations to which the bill might conceivably apply and all of the possible variations that might exist in the types and contexts of those situations. *Dickerson* (page 55), quoting Middleton Beaman, noted that the contingencies a lawyer faces in a will or contract, for example, "while sometimes numerous, are mere flyspecks compared to the contingencies that must be considered in the context of a statute". In many cases addressing all the contingencies is an impossible task, and therein lies the critical importance of a transparent legislative process after a bill is introduced, so that hearings, committee and floor consideration, and other input from affected parties can articulate problems that may then be addressed before the bill is enacted into law.

Fourth, legislation has its own form and style as well as its own specialized vocabulary, and every drafter must learn to use them correctly. Form and style usually have no substantive effect, but they can be critically important nonetheless. Consistently following the proper form and style will aid in organizing the legislative product, achieving precision, and reaching the intended audience as well as create consistency in the law when bills using the proper form and style become law.

There is no excuse for not getting the form and style right, even without a drafting manual such as this book. It may require a little effort, but just observing the standard forms and following the past practice will usually guarantee a respectable product.

Learning the terminology of the field in which you are working, however, can be more demanding. Drafters and other legislative technicians frequently refer to key provisions of existing law by their alphanumeric designations and to key concepts in colloquial, descriptive terms. Such references are an indispensable form of verbal shorthand—convenient "terms of art" precisely alluding to complicated statutory provisions. They are completely unambiguous to the technicians who must work with and talk about the concepts involved (and should not be confused with the casual descriptive terms that are commonly and often misleadingly used in news accounts); but their meaning and significance will almost never be clear at the outset to anyone not already familiar with the field involved.

Finally, the setting in which legislation is considered and enacted is like nothing else on Earth, and you as a drafter must always have in mind the forces that will affect your product as it moves through the legislative process. Writers of other kinds of documents are usually aware of the factors that will determine how their words will be understood and evaluated; they can adjust those words to fit the situation, and remain more or less in control. Drafters cannot, and they must always be on the lookout for ways to protect themselves against unexpected amendments and adverse procedural turns.

Sometimes legislative language that effectively carries out the desired policy will be totally nullified by parliamentary or procedural restrictions if written in one way, but will survive unscathed if written in another. The latter option may not be available in a particular case, of course, for any one of a number of reasons; but it is your job as a drafter to find it if it is.

2.3 Getting the policy right

The bulk of this book does concern itself with matters of form and style; these are, after all, the aspects of bill drafting on which special instruction seems most necessary. But it cannot be stressed enough that using correct form and style is meaningless unless you get the policy right. If a choice must be made between form and style on the one hand and policy-related aspects on the other, the policy-related aspects of drafting *are* more important. As mentioned earlier, the technical aspects of drafting are straightforward objective matters, but getting the policy right is how drafters justify their existence. The ability to effectuate policy, rather than mere stylistic facility, is what defines a skilled drafter.

A bill may be full of stylistic and technical shortcomings, but if it clearly and correctly carries out the desired policy (without creating new substantive problems), it is far better than a beautifully crafted piece of work that does not.

2.4 Nonpartisanship and impartiality

A professional drafter who serves legislators of differing political persuasions must present a nonpartisan and nonpolitical image, and must maintain an impartial attitude concerning the policies to be converted into legislative language.[4]

However, the typical drafter (operating outside of the congressional drafting offices and the corresponding offices in State legislatures) is more likely to serve a single person or entity who consistently advocates particular partisan policies. Obviously, that drafter cannot be expected to be nonpartisan or nonpolitical, or to maintain an impartial attitude about the wisdom of the policies.

Nonetheless, all drafters must maintain an impartial attitude about their tasks in the sense that their professional concern with any assignment is solely to make sure that the bills they write will accurately reflect the sponsors' policies and will work. If you are an active player in a partisan environment, you must always remember, when wearing your drafter's hat, to be scrupulously objective in implementing that concern.

None of this should be taken to mean that the drafter has no part at all to play in the policy area, of course. As indicated earlier (and expanded upon in 4.7), helping to develop and refine the sponsor's policy is an integral part of your job as a drafter; the problem is how to do it without imposing your own substantive views upon the sponsor. The line is often fine, but it is always there.

2.5 Confidentiality and privilege

Any legislative drafter who is an attorney and serves policymakers in an attorney-client relationship must of course treat everything that transpires between them as absolutely privileged and confidential. The attorneys in the congressional drafting offices and in nearly all of the corresponding State drafting offices fall within this category.

However, not every drafting relationship involving an attorney is attorney-client in nature, and many legislative drafters are not attorneys at all. Although every drafter is subject to some requirement of confidentiality, at least part of the time, the requirement is most often imposed simply as a means of protecting the sponsor's interests and promoting trust between sponsor and drafter.

Any strict requirement of confidentiality, of course, requires the drafter to ask the permission of the sponsor before seeking information from any other person, and is likely to limit the drafter's access to needed information. But if the sponsor refuses to permit an outside contact because the source of the information would be hostile, is considered untrustworthy, or would be a possible "leak", the drafter must live with it.

Because most professional drafters are subject to some requirement of confidentiality, they develop what is often described as a "passion for anonymity". If you are working on a bill but are forbidden to reveal what provisions it contains or to talk to anyone about your dealings with the sponsor, you are much better off (and can work more efficiently) if no one knows who you are; in order to avoid bombardment by partisan interests seeking to influence legislation, professional drafting offices are wise to try to keep their participation in particular legislative activities from becoming public knowledge. In reality, however, because of this guarded anonymity, lobbyists and other partisans soon realize the fruitlessness of trying to influence professional drafters.[5]

Notes

1 The "client" is the sponsor.

2 L. Karlton Mosteller, "Income Taxation: Administration Procedures," *American Bar Association Journal* 42 (1956): 1119, 1177.

3 John R. Stark, "Social Security: Its Importance to Lawyers," *American Bar Association Journal* 43 (1957): 319.

4 Section 502 of the Legislative Reorganization Act of 1970 (2 U.S.C. 281a) requires that the attorneys in the Office of the Legislative Counsel of the U.S. House of Representatives be impartial with respect to policy.

5 This has been the experience of the Offices of the Legislative Counsel of the U.S. House of Representatives and the Senate.

3. The Drafting Process Itself

3.1 Preliminary comments

The typical bill starts on its way because someone—usually a legislator or an agency official—believes that there is a problem that can be solved by legislation, and turns to a drafter for help. Whether the proposal is simple or complex, the drafter has a number of steps to take before actually writing a bill that will accomplish what the sponsor has in mind. This chapter offers only a general outline of the overall process—the details come later, beginning in part II with the preliminary steps—but a couple of comments are in order at the outset.

The first is that this book (except when addressing specific practical problems) assumes what might be called the ideal drafting situation—

one in which the sponsor provides a clear policy along with all necessary background information, the sponsor and the drafter can fully discuss the issues, and the drafter has carte blanche to write the bill in the way that seems best.

Unfortunately, except in States where all introduced bills are required to be drafted by the legislature's own in-house professional drafters (and such a requirement is not imposed by Congress or by most State legislatures), any sponsor may write a bill without calling upon a drafter at all. Or the sponsor may limit the drafter's function to a quick review of form and style—an unsatisfactory assignment for the drafter, who will usually detect more serious problems during the process. Obviously, in such cases the ideal situation does not exist.

The second is that most bills don't go anywhere after they are introduced, and their sponsors are usually realistic enough to understand this. Very few introduced bills are actually considered by a committee or subcommittee. But you should never use this as an excuse for sloppy drafting, because sponsors want to make their points effectively and, more significantly, because you can never know which bills will become law regardless of how unlikely that may seem. In some cases, an introduced bill will be added at a late stage in the legislative process to another legislative vehicle, without any committee or floor consideration. This is the strongest argument for preparing the best possible product for introduction.

3.2 Bill drafting as a multistep operation; a checklist

Drafting any bill can be viewed simplistically as a continuous process divided into successive steps. Viewed this way you would—

(1) make sure you understand the factual and legal problems to be dealt with—the problems that led the sponsor to seek legislative relief in the first place;

(2) make sure you understand the main thrust of the sponsor's policy—how the sponsor proposes to deal head-on with those problems;

(3) explore with the sponsor the possible ways of achieving the goal, pointing out the alternatives and their consequences;

(4) identify and deal with any related questions that the implementation of the sponsor's policy may create, giving particular attention to any provisions of existing law that may already deal with the subject and to the bill's effective date if it would play a significant part in implementing that policy;

(5) decide upon the general approach to be taken in drafting the bill—whether it should be broad or narrow in scope, and whether it should be self-executing or rely in varying degrees on administrative discretion and regulation;

(6) decide upon the organization of the bill—what provisions need to be included, and how should they be arranged;

(7) take account of the legislative context—the type of vehicle to be used and the effect of any parliamentary or constitutional restrictions; and

(8) write the bill.

The tasks described in steps (1) through (5) might be regarded as primarily policy-related, and those described in steps (6) through (8) as primarily technical.

As you work through these steps, keep in mind that in order for a bill to be effective, it must answer the following four questions:

(1) To whom or what will the bill apply?

(2) Who will administer the bill, for example, the head of an administrative agency?

(3) How will the bill be enforced? Just because Congress or another legislature directs something to be done does not guarantee that those directed will comply.

(4) When and how will the bill take effect? The effective date may be the thorniest issue to deal with.

3.3 Bill drafting as a two-stage operation

It may be helpful to view the drafting process as simply a two-stage operation, consisting of a preliminary (or preparatory) stage and a final (or writing) stage. The two stages can usefully be thought of as consecutive, even though they almost always overlap. This overlap is addressed in 10.5 (When and how the writing should begin).

The preliminary stage of any legislative drafting effort involves the things you must do before beginning to write. This is usually the most important and demanding stage, encompassing all of the matters set forth in steps (1) through (7) of the checklist in 3.2; and the quality of the final product seldom rises above the quality of the work done at this stage.

These matters (which are the subject of chapters 4, 5, and 6) can often be disposed of quickly and easily, of course, but in major bills they constitute the heart of the drafting process. Needless to say, they are seldom addressed in any precise or preestablished order; and in many cases they can be dealt with more or less simultaneously.

Besides making certain that you correctly carry out the sponsor's policy, you must always remember that the bill is an effort to communicate that policy to a particular audience, and the nature of the audience has a great deal to do with the concepts you choose and the way you arrange them. A bill whose message is addressed primarily to government officials may need to be written differently from one addressed to the public, and a bill addressed to a specialized segment of the public (such as a particular industry) may need to be written differently from one addressed to the public at large. (As indicated earlier, in some fields it is often necessary to treat the relevant government officials as the audience even though the bill is being written for and about particular individuals or groups.) And you must often make a distinction between audiences even within a single bill. Keep in mind, however, that many more groups other than the targeted audience will want to read and understand the statute.

Finally, you should constantly ask yourself, "If this were a statute addressed to me, how exactly would I go about carrying it out?", putting yourself in the shoes of the person who will have to administer the bill once it becomes law. Be aware, however, that the administrators may be subject to requirements about which no drafter could be expected to know; and even professional drafters occasionally write bills that are unworkable simply because existing procedures (of which they were unaware) make it impossible for anyone to take the actions needed to achieve the desired result. If you do not understand the administrative ins and outs of the field you are working in, seek the permission of the sponsor to reach someone who can supply the answers you need.

The final stage is of course the actual writing. It is obviously a critical stage, since the words once written do constitute the entire result of the process. No matter how sound the concept or how brilliant the analysis and treatment of the problems involved, the cause is lost if the language as finally drafted is inadequate to carry out the policy or is otherwise unsuitable (for example, on procedural grounds). (And it goes without saying that the writing itself, like any other kind of writing, can present major problems in terms of how to start, what to say, how to say it, and how to finish it off.)

You should never forget that although your main objective—clarity—is primarily a matter that is achieved in the preliminary stage, it cannot be finally realized without careful attention to form and style. The two stages blend imperceptibly, because substance and form cannot be functionally divorced. The shift is mainly in emphasis. You will continue to be interested in substance up to the last minute, particularly since you will want to take full advantage of the substantive improvements that a systematic attention to matters of form and style inevitably makes possible. And you must avoid becoming so style-conscious that the more fundamental matters of substance are neglected; indeed, any sharp distinction between form and substance can do more harm than good, because it diverts attention from the fact that clarity and simplicity are more than sentence-deep.

In any event, despite the blurred nature of the line between the two drafting stages, this book will continue to emphasize the very real difference between them. But it is important to remember that the really crucial parts of a bill are often concocted hastily at the last minute, and that sometimes the greatest contribution you can make during both of the stages is just to provide a workable framework for them.

3.4 An institutional drafter's perspective

This book generally treats the drafter-sponsor relationship as one in which the drafter is responsible to an individual sponsor, such as a Member of Congress, a State legislator, or a specific agency official, but in many (perhaps most) cases the potential reader will be an institutional drafter, responsible to an agency or organization as a whole. Everything that has been said about drafting for individual sponsors normally applies in institutional cases; but the institutional situation has a special flavor along with some unique problems that result from the hydra-headed nature of the sponsor.

If you are an institutional drafter, you receive your initial marching orders from an individual official of the agency or organization for which you work and are entitled to think of that official as the primary policymaker; but before you are finished you will have had to deal with a number of different policymakers, and there is often no single source to which you can turn to mediate their conflicting positions. Although the policy specifications at the outset are usually no more vague and incomplete than the typical initial request of an individual sponsor, the drafter-sponsor relationship can become quite unmanageable when there are multiple policymakers to satisfy.

Since the policy comes from a number of different sources, some parts of the specifications may be more complete and precise than others, which may make resolving conflicts in policy positions more difficult for the drafter. In addition, at least some of the policymakers—those who had nothing to do with originating the proposal but who will nonetheless be called upon to sign off on the part that concerns them—may have little or no enthusiasm for the project and are likely to be significantly less helpful (and less accessible) than the others.

Institutional drafters do have two advantages over their noninstitutional counterparts, however: their policymakers almost always know the subject and understand the agency's probable position on it, and they are likely to have easier access to the future administrators.

3.5 The drafter at different stages of the legislative process

The drafter's basic objective—carrying out the sponsor's policy accurately and effectively—is the same regardless of the stage of the legislative process; but the way the drafter functions, and the problems and difficulties likely to be encountered, may differ significantly from one stage to another. Indeed, for many drafters the ability to participate at all will diminish and may disappear altogether in the later stages.

In theory, working on a bill to be introduced should provide sufficient time to produce a quality product because nothing has yet been fed into the legislative mill. In reality, however, the drafter's need for time and information frequently succumbs to political pressures that impose unreasonable deadlines even at this stage. Even when the drafter explains that such a deadline will cause the quality of the draft to suffer, the drafter in most cases has no control over these deadlines.

After the bill is introduced, the drafter begins working on amendments to be offered to the bill in subcommittee, in full committee, on the floor, or in conference. The work is likely to be fraught with time requirements, hidden agendas, and external factors over which no one has complete control.

Policymaking in committee or in conference is a collective operation; in a sense drafters become more "institutional" and their chief function is often simply integrating suggestions that have been hastily thrown on the table, rather than analyzing and refining any one sponsor's ideas. This is especially true when the committee is trying to operate on the basis of "consensus" rather than sheer political muscle.

Computerization likely plays a part in the constant time pressures placed on drafters. The speed and versatility of word processing programs may give the impression that producing a bill (or regulation) is simply a matter of executing a few keystrokes to access the correct form in the computer's memory and filling in the blanks. Certainly converting language prepared by an outside group into legislative format is an easy electronic process. The speed of computers, however, masks the careful thought that is the essence of the drafting process.

The point, then, is for the drafter to take advantage of whatever time is afforded, at any stage of the legislative process, to produce the best draft possible. It will give the drafter an advantage throughout the rest of the process.

3.6 Easing the task

An experienced drafter regularly uses a number of techniques to make the job of planning, organizing, and writing a bill easier and less time-consuming. Some of these have been mentioned already (and all of them will be dealt with more fully later); but a few that are particularly useful can be summarized as follows:

Working drafts and outlines. If a bill is lengthy or at all complex, you should make an outline or working draft at the earliest possible moment. It need not be complete or include language on all the matters to be covered, as long as it leaves a slot for each provision that (so far as you can tell at the time) will eventually have to be included. Working from an outline or rough draft not only helps you arrange and integrate your materials properly, it also protects you against oversights and saves time.

Revisions. You should expect to revise the working draft as often as may be necessary in order to perfect the language already written, correct your mistakes, fill in the empty slots, and otherwise keep things current; and you should plan your work on the basis of that expectation. Multiple revisions (with gradually increasing accuracy and completeness) are the hallmark of a sound drafting operation and should never be regarded as a cause for embarrassment or an indication of incompetence.

When you go through a series of discrete revisions, it is a good idea to designate each version as a "Tentative Draft", "Working Draft", or "Discussion Draft", with a number or date to indicate its place in the succession (if your computer does not already do so). Be sure to save a copy of each version and maintain a system to retrieve it; not only will a complete collection of successive working drafts help you answer questions about where particular provisions came from, but sometimes provisions that were stricken in earlier revisions will be restored in later ones.

Definitions. Whenever a bill repeatedly uses a crucial term that might be unclear or ambiguous, you should define it, placing the definition where it may most easily be found—at the place where it first occurs or in a special section or subsection devoted exclusively to definitions. This will not only clarify the meaning of the term; it also will help you express complex thoughts in an understandable way and make the bill shorter and less repetitious and its language less cumbersome.

Although a number of writers have expressed reservations about the excessive use of definitions in statutes, you should use them whenever the occasion arises. Definitions are crucial in answering the question "to whom or what will the bill apply?" The types and uses of definitions in drafting (along with the reservations of the doubters) are fully addressed in 11.7 and 23.2.

Cross-references. In spite of the current tendency to make fun of legislative language that contains frequent incorporations by reference or purely informative cross-references, you should use them freely. There is no rational reason why a drafter who wants to invoke or refer to a particular provision by name or number should not do so. Used correctly, cross-references save time, shorten the bill by avoiding repetition, and promote internal consistency. They are addressed more fully in 22.4 and 23.3.

Tables and tabulation. You should freely use columnar tables to show relationships between numerical quantities, tabulated lists to enumerate items, and tabulated sentences in provisions that necessarily include several interrelated concepts or elements. These devices are among your most useful tools for dealing with complex concepts and avoiding ambiguity. They are discussed in depth in chapter 23.

Headings. Headings for sections, subsections, and other subdivisions are highly visible when flipping through the pages of a draft and aid the reader in understanding the arrangement of the bill. They can also be of great value to you as a drafter, giving you an excellent road map that will help you locate provisions quickly and thereby save time and irritation, and helping you organize the bill by forcing you to provide logical places in advance for all the pieces. Chapter 20 contains a detailed discussion of headings and how to construct them; and chapter 33 sets forth literal examples of the types of headings used in all of the different Federal drafting styles.

Models and boilerplate forms. In a surprising percentage of drafting assignments you will be able to find a previously written law, bill, or draft that (in its entirety or in one or more of its key provisions) is similar enough to what you are working on to serve as a useful model. The extent to which it will have to be modified before it can be used will differ from case to case, of course, but a good model can get you started and be your salvation in a difficult situation.

Both as a time-saver and as an accuracy-promoter, you should develop and maintain a reasonably complete folder on your computer or elsewhere, based on your own previous efforts and other sources, of all the recurring forms you are likely to find useful in the field or fields in which you work (10.4 addresses the subject in detail).

Compilations and similar resource documents. When you work regularly in a particular field you should have available at all times, for easy reference, a reliable compilation or other up-to-date version of the relevant law in that field. You should never have to stop what you are doing and go elsewhere to find a literal copy of a crucial provision if you can avoid it. 5.5 discusses finding aids for compilations.

In addition, when your work involves a particular provision of existing law, you will frequently need to know what other provisions of law may affect or be affected by it. A good cross-reference table that lists all the places (both within and without the statute involved) where that provision is cited can be a real lifesaver.

When a published compilation or cross-reference table is not available in your field, you would be well advised to make your own and keep it current (see 31.6). The time and effort required will repay you many times over.

Checking and polishing the draft. Needless to say, you should double-check your work periodically, and go through it one final time (after you are sure it is substantively correct) for the sole purpose of smoothing out any rough edges. It is particularly important that you look it over carefully each time you complete a major revision, checking the new or revised portions against the unchanged portions to make sure that the revision itself has not created any new internal inconsistencies. An absolutely perfect provision can sometimes be rendered inaccurate or inappropriate by new or revised language in a totally different part of the draft, and this is a kind of error that is very easy to miss.

Getting specialized help. When you need technical or other specialized assistance, you should seek it from any source that is readily available to you. And you should never hesitate to seek help on specific *drafting* problems—all experienced drafters do. But avoid group drafting sessions, as *Dickerson* (page 67) emphasizes:

> [W]riting by conference ... wastes time and talent. Groups can mull over ideas, they can criticize, and they can give or withhold approval, but they cannot compose concisely, consistently, or clearly.

If you are required to participate in a group drafting session, you will have to devote additional time afterwards to check for drafting errors and internal inconsistencies.

The value of a nonspecialized sounding board. Totally apart from any technical or specialized needs you may have, as you go through the drafting process you should periodically seek someone who can serve as a sounding board. It is not necessary that the person be an expert on what you are trying to do; for everyday working purposes it is sometimes better not to have an expert, since what you are looking for is someone to help you see the forest as well as the trees. If need be, try to verbalize the issues even without an audience; the sound of your own voice explaining an idea can call its gaps and flaws to your consciousness.

Most of the suggestions contained here are just matters of common sense. It is true that a few of them—devices such as tabulated provisions, cross-references, and inter-related definitions—may occasionally intimidate people who are not used to reading statutes. But the target audience of most bills consists of administrators and legislative specialists, and they are used to reading statutes. For them these devices will actually improve readability. And since clarity is your prime objective, others will be able to put the pieces together.

PART II

THE FIRST STAGE: PREPARING TO PUT PEN TO PAPER

4. Defining the Problem and Its Solution

4.1 In general

A sponsor who is a legislator, when seeking a drafter's help, is probably acting simply as a matter of personal philosophy or party policy, or as the result of a constituent's request. A sponsor who is an official of an agency or organization is more likely acting to carry out an institutional policy (and will have to find a sympathetic legislator to introduce the bill and take over the role of primary sponsor).

In either case the problem may be broad (like the need for a new national program) or narrow (like the need for an additional Assistant Secretary), or anything in between. But most bills taken seriously in any legislative forum are simply designed to clear up difficulties that have come to light in the everyday administration of an existing law or program. The impetus for such a bill, which might be viewed as being essentially a "housekeeping" measure even though it can have major substantive impact, usually comes from the agency that administers the program involved and is responsible for making it work properly, from a legislator who serves on the committee that is responsible for monitoring its operation, or from a private organization whose interests are affected.

Occasionally the "problem" is not really a problem at all, but simply a perceived need to make a statement of some kind, to give recognition to some person or circumstance, or to call attention to some situation, or just to tidy up the law. Common examples are resolutions expressing the sense of Congress (or of one House of Congress) on an issue, bills changing the names of existing public buildings, and bills providing for new national holidays.

Your job as a drafter, of course, is to help the sponsor put into legislative form what the sponsor wants in substance, and to accomplish it as smoothly and effectively as possible. Your first instinct (after receiving the sponsor's request) may be to reach for a pencil, but experienced drafters know that the first instinct *should* be to look for questions to ask. In many cases the sponsor's substantive ideas are imperfectly formed, providing no more than a set of general objectives; and you must help to refine those objectives before you can hope to develop a practical means of carrying them out.

You ideally should be brought into the picture long before the writing begins, in order to find out as much as possible about what the sponsor is trying to accomplish and about how the sponsor wants to attack the problem. You must be fully informed on both the underlying policy and its factual setting in order to discharge your central responsibility.

You must often engage in a continuing exchange of ideas with the sponsor or the sponsor's staff in order to be sure that your understanding is correct and complete and that the sponsor can live with the consequences. You must help the sponsor think the problem through, pointing out any substantive inconsistencies and any administrative, legal, constitutional, and practical difficulties that the sponsor's proposal may bring.

In addition, since you may need more information than can be supplied by the sponsor, you must often pick the brains of whatever expert advisers (legislative, executive, or nongovernmental) may be available to you (with the permission of the sponsor) in order to fill in the substantive, legal, and technical gaps.

As statute law becomes more and more complex, you are almost *required* to develop a good working knowledge of the substantive field in which you are working. You must know the statutory environment, just as an architect must know the building site, so that what you draft will fit smoothly and workably in that environment.

More often than not the initial stage of your work on any bill requires a thorough examination and analysis of the laws already on the books in the field involved, with the objective of making absolutely certain that all of your legal ducks are neatly in a row before the actual writing begins. In most well-run legislative drafting offices each drafter specializes in a limited number of substantive areas, because that is the only way to develop the necessary substantive expertise.

The drafter's relationship with the sponsor in the process of learning about the problem and working out the desired solution is the most critical element in the drafting of any bill. It is the purpose of this chapter to examine some of the things that are commonly involved in that process (4.2 and 4.3 address the subject head-on; 4.4–4.9 deal with specific aspects of the subject that deserve separate mention).

4.2 Recognizing the problem

In most cases you will have no trouble grasping what the problem is and what you are supposed to do about it. The sponsor simply says in effect "here is my problem—fix it"; and in its broad outlines, at least, the challenge seems clear. But in many cases a little thought reveals that it is not clear at all.

If the proposal is very broad or the subject matter is unusually complicated, so that only a specialist would be likely to understand all the ramifications, the remedy is plain (if the sponsor is willing): find someone who does understand them and pick that person's brains.

However, when the sponsor is acting on a complaint or suggestion from someone else and simply passes the matter along to the drafter with a request for legislation to take care of the situation, life can be more difficult. In most such cases neither the sponsor nor the drafter questions the facts as presented; but surprisingly often the drafter's analysis raises doubts about what the facts really are. The approach that immediately suggests itself, of course, is to keep badgering the sponsor until you are satisfied that you have all the facts—the sponsor will usually have better access to them than you do—but unfortunately this is not always feasible or politic.

Uncharitable persons may be tempted to say that sponsors should do their homework better before disturbing the drafter's repose, but this would not be entirely fair. Legislators and agency officials are not specialists, investigators, or drafters, and within limits they are entitled to rely on those who are to deal with the details involved in carrying out their objectives.

In many cases the situation as presented to them will have been incomplete, misunderstood, or misstated by the complainant or other source, or at least "edited" by someone so as to characterize the situation in the light most favorable to the complainant's case.

Making sure of the factual situation that gives rise to a particular proposal is critically important, however, both for the sponsor (who wants to avoid subsequent regrets about having taken on the project) and for the drafter (who needs to be sure the problem has actually been solved). What can you do when there is a question about the correctness of the information you have been given?

Obviously, you should not proceed without doing whatever you can as a practical matter to make sure (through conversations with the sponsor or the sponsor's staff, consultations with experts, contact with the persons on whose behalf the sponsor is acting, or otherwise) that you have the true picture. If circumstances prevent a full investigation, you may have no choice but to accept the facts as given to you, despite your suspicions about their incompleteness or possible distortion. At a minimum, however, you should alert the sponsor to these suspicions so that the matter can be looked into further, making it clear that the bill as you propose to write it, based on the information at hand, may in fact not achieve its intended purpose.

4.3 Understanding the policy

Types of policy questions. As indicated in 1.3, a sponsor's basic policy (which defines the general objective) is only part of the policy picture; it often presents the drafter with questions of subsidiary policy and collateral policy that can be equally troublesome.

In a proposal to provide for the establishment of a commission to study fraud and abuse in a major Federal program, for example, the question of just what should be studied and the question of what should be done with the information gathered would of course constitute "basic" policy questions; but such things as the makeup and organization of the commission, the compensation of its members, the timing of the study, and whether the Federal Advisory Committee provisions in chapter 10 of part 1 of title 5, United States Code[1] apply are policy questions as well.

The questions about makeup and organization, compensation, and timing are "subsidiary" policy questions for our purposes because (although they are not part of the main thrust of the basic policy and may not even matter to the sponsor) they are integral to the basic policy and must necessarily be answered in the bill, one way or another, in order to complete it. They cannot simply be ignored.

The question about the application of the Federal Advisory Committee provisions is "collateral", since the basic policy would seem to be complete and coherent even if the question were totally overlooked—those provisions would simply apply or not apply in accordance with its terms. (Note, however, that that Act could so integrally restrict the functioning of the commission if it did apply that the question takes on a strongly "subsidiary" flavor.)

Extracting the policy. Once the problem is clear, the next order of business is its solution. And it goes without saying that, since the policy to be carried out (basic, subsidiary, and collateral) is the sponsor's choice, the drafter must look to the sponsor in order to understand it.

The typical drafting operation involves a colloquy between the drafter and the sponsor or the sponsor's staff that may take a matter of minutes or may continue over a period of days, weeks, or months, resurfacing intermittently as new questions arise. If the subject or its factual setting is highly technical and complicated, and the sponsor is willing, most of the colloquy may turn out to be with experts and specialists. The process should continue until everything is clear, however long that takes.

Actually, the drafter will seldom experience any difficulty understanding the basic policy to be carried out in a bill, since a sponsor typically does not seek drafting help to solve a problem without a reasonably firm idea of what the solution is. The sponsor's main thrust is the one thing you will always be told about up front; and a few well-chosen questions will almost always clear up any ambiguity.

However, being clear about the subsidiary and collateral policy issues, which can be extremely important to sponsors (once they are raised), is not quite so automatic. Usually sponsors are preoccupied with the main thrust, and often do not even think about these issues until prodded, either because it never occurs to them to do so or because they assume that the drafters will identify and present them for consideration in due time.

Since the subsidiary and collateral issues are easy for sponsors to overlook or postpone, drafters must focus on them; and doing this is frequently their most important single contribution. These issues generally fall into one of three categories:

(1) Questions about the individual pieces of the puzzle—the separate elements that combine to make up the basic policy as a whole. Examples are the questions about makeup, organization, compensation, and timing in the study commission case discussed earlier.

(2) Substantive questions that result from what the basic policy does. When you tamper with any provision of law that affects another provision of law, for example, it is likely that changes in the other provision will be needed to repair the damage; and when you write any totally new provision, there may be existing provisions that will be rendered ineffective or inconsistent (or will prevent the new provision from working in the intended way) unless they are changed to reflect the new provision. The changes involved are often of a purely technical and conforming nature, but many of them involve serious substantive considerations as well.

(3) Questions involving breadth and specificity. These are discussed more fully in 4.5.

An example of the intricacies addressed in point (2) can be found in Public Law 108-419 (the Copyright Royalty and Distribution Reform Act of 2004, enacted November 30, 2004), which changed the procedures under which royalty rates and terms under the different statutory licenses[2] under title 17, United States Code, were to be determined. The primary change in the law was that the proceedings for determining the rates would be conducted by three Copyright Royalty Judges, U.S. Government employees appointed by the Librarian of Congress, instead of ad hoc copyright arbitration royalty panels appointed for each proceeding from among arbitrators in the private sector. The provisions regarding the proceedings of the panels were generally governed by chapter 8 (sections 801–803) of title 17. The law, therefore, rewrote all of chapter 8, providing for the appointment, functions, and staff of the Copyright Royalty Judges, procedures for the different proceedings conducted by the judges, the schedule for beginning different types of proceedings, and the treatment of agreements voluntarily made among parties (for example, the copyright owners and users).

Every section of title 17 that provided for a statutory license referred to the arbitration panels in the context of the particular proceedings governing the rates and terms for that statutory license. These would seem to require only mechanical technical and conforming changes. However, given that chapter 8 vested more responsibilities in the Copyright Royalty Judges than had been given to the ad hoc arbitration panels, a decision had to be made in every one of those sections regarding whether functions that had been vested in the Librarian of Congress (instead of the ad hoc arbitration panels) should be transferred to the judges. In addition, the new chapter 8 revised the timetables and procedures for the different rate-making proceedings. The other sections in title 17 had provisions tied into the procedures being replaced, so that these sections had to be amended to be consistent with the new timetables and procedures. As a result, of the 30 pages of the law (118 Stat. 2341–2371), almost one-third consisted of these "technical" amendments that were crucial for the bill to work.

Policy alternatives. It is certainly true that many problems might be rationally addressed in any one of several ways. A particular kind of undesirable conduct could be flatly prohibited and made subject to criminal or civil penalties, for example, or regulated, subjected to strict licensing requirements, or taxed. Or abstinence from that kind of conduct could be made a condition of eligibility for related benefits. Or a study commission could be established to look into the problem and make recommendations (thereby postponing the implementation of one of the other alternatives).

If you think a particular approach might carry out the stated objective better than the one suggested by the sponsor, you should diplomatically make sure that the sponsor understands the alternatives. Remember that different approaches can have different consequences, and make sure that the sponsor is aware of them. A prohibition is a prohibition, but whether the penalty is criminal or civil has a good deal to do with how enforceable it is. And attacking undesirable conduct by licensing or taxing it, or rewarding abstinence, may discourage that conduct by making it more expensive but has the effect of legitimizing it.

A case study of what can happen when the problem is complicated, and the possible consequences of the policy adopted are not fully thought out, is presented in 4.9.

Lack of policy altogether. The message contained in the preceding paragraphs is, of course, that the actual writing of a bill cannot progress very far (and sometimes cannot even be properly begun) until the sponsor has made the policy clear.

The hard practicalities of political life, however, often make it more important for the sponsor to have something on paper that can be waved about—an "idea draft" setting forth the main thrust without frills—than for all of the policy questions to be resolved immediately. And when the sponsor demands that a bill be drafted immediately to accomplish some vaguely described objective, you cannot simply abdicate but must do the best you can.

If the sponsor wants to introduce a bill or offer an amendment primarily to make a political point (and does not care whether it is technically correct), or to introduce the bill or offer the amendment immediately for tactical or procedural reasons and let others clean it up at a later stage, the sponsor may be quite unwilling (or unable) to accommodate the drafter's needs. It is sad but true that gaps and defects in a bill (unless they would defeat the main thrust or are highly visible) do not usually matter as much to the sponsor as they do to the drafter. The sponsor appreciates technical perfection, of course, but is well aware of the fact that the media will support the effort, and give credit, on the basis of the main thrust alone; technical shortcomings are not very newsworthy (at least until the bill becomes law and some spectacular misfire occurs). The reality is that proper timing and political support are the things that make a bill move. Hopefully, the necessary perfecting can be done at a later stage.

Some sponsors seem to believe that simply asking a drafter for a bill will automatically produce one on their desk the same day, as if by magic or, more accurately, by a few keystrokes on a computer. But even those who understand full well what the drafter faces, when tormented by tight time schedules or tactical dilemmas, sometimes say in effect "You're the drafter, and I've told you what I want to do—just give me a bill I can use and don't worry about all these trivial questions". It happens quite frequently.

What do you do? Sometimes you must simply resign yourself (if you want to keep your job) to being a scribe instead of a good legislative drafter. Often, though, you can still do a creditable job by following these suggestions:

(1) If the unanswered question is collateral in the sense that it can be ignored without making the bill incomplete or internally inconsistent (even though you think the sponsor might regard it as important), ignore it.

(2) If the unanswered question leaves a gap that would make the bill incomplete or inconsistent, and you can fill the gap with language that is fairly neutral and is commonly used in similar situations, do so. With any luck you can find a respectable model to use. However, make sure the sponsor knows you are simply offering that language for consideration as one of several possible rational approaches—not recommending it.

(3) If the gap is one that could conceivably be filled by administrative fiat and there is an appropriate administrator in the picture somewhere, explicitly leave the matter to that administrator's regulations.

In any event you should make absolutely certain that the sponsor is aware of what you have done, and why; and for your own protection, when you deliver the bill, you should document your misgivings (as in an e-mail or memo) unless you are completely secure about your lines of communication and about how the sponsor will handle the bill. It is not a bad idea to designate the bill itself a "TENTATIVE DRAFT" even though it is as "final" as you can make it, and let the sponsor cross out those words if it is introduced or otherwise made public without first resolving its problems.

4.4 Clarity, consistency, and organization

The one overriding requirement of all good legislative drafting is clarity, and there are two basic principles or techniques that are of particular importance in achieving it:

(1) You must relentlessly strive for complete internal consistency in all respects—form, style, terminology, expression, and arrangement. Nothing will do more to obscure the intended meaning than failure to do this. The subject is addressed in more detail in chapter 7.

(2) You must make certain that the bill—both in its overall contours and in particular sections, subsections, and paragraphs—is organized and arranged in a systematic and logical manner, so as to clearly indicate the nature and relative position of each element in the hierarchy of the sponsor's ideas. This is the subject of chapter 6.

Each of these techniques facilitates comparison and recognition, making it easier for you to uncover substantive problems and policy considerations that would otherwise have been missed and enabling you to exert the constructive influence on policy formulation described in 4.7.

4.5 Approach, breadth, and specificity

When sponsors mull over the approach they ought to take in solving a problem through legislation, they are thinking about the main thrust: what exactly should the proposal accomplish?

On the other hand, when you, the drafter, are considering the approach to be taken, you already know what the sponsor's basic policy will be. What you should be thinking about is the way in which you might best carry out that policy: Should the bill be broad or narrow in its coverage? Should it be general or specific in its administrative details? How should it be organized? Should it amend existing law or be freestanding? These are questions that have a technical flavor, since the sponsor's policy can be effectively carried out regardless of how they are answered, and they can fairly be considered to be (at least concurrently) within the drafter's province; but they themselves may raise a new and totally different set of policy questions.

Questions of this kind pose a common dilemma for the drafter, who may legitimately participate in the process of answering them but (as always in the case of policy questions, even minor ones) must still leave the final decision to the sponsor unless it is certain that there are no substantive or tactical overtones. Every drafter should be conscious of them, and it may be worthwhile to examine a few of them briefly.

How broad or narrow? Some bills are broad or narrow in their scope as a matter of necessity. A bill to establish a comprehensive system for reducing the Federal deficit across the board cannot be approached narrowly, while a bill to simply extend some expiring Federal program for one additional year (without making substantive changes) is narrow and specific by its very nature. In these cases the scope of the bill is conclusively determined by the sponsor's main thrust, and neither the sponsor nor the drafter has to face a decision on whether the approach should be broad or narrow.

Many proposals, however, present both the sponsor and the drafter with a wide range of possible choices. As indicated earlier, in most instances a bill is triggered by a very specific case but will nonetheless be general in its application, so that a decision has to be made about the extent to which the bill's coverage might be extended to other cases that are similarly situated. This in turn requires a decision about which similarities are sufficiently important to warrant the extension—that is, a decision about what "similarly situated" means (which is a matter of the sponsor's policy).

Assume, for example, that the sponsor requests a bill to overhaul the appeals procedure in disability cases based on mental illness under the Social Security program. The request almost certainly arises out of the denial of one specific mentally ill individual's claim for disability benefits under that program, but several questions of breadth immediately suggest themselves:

(1) Should the bill also cover appeals involving other kinds of disability under the same program? Maybe; it would probably depend on the

specific grounds for the denial—that is, on the nature of the alleged procedural defects that caused it. Some kinds of defects would be unique to mental disability cases, some would not. (And some kinds of defects might be uniquely related to the particular kind of mental disorder involved in the constituent's case, creating the possibility that the bill should be narrowed instead.)

(2) Should consideration be given to extending the bill to include appeals in disability cases under the Supplemental Security Income (SSI) program? Probably yes, because the administrative provisions of the two programs are similar and, in many respects, identical (and in fact are largely shared, with one administrative determination being effective under both programs).

(3) What about including appeals under still other disability-related programs—railroad retirement, Medicare, Medicaid, and various programs under the public health laws? Probably not; although the railroad retirement and Social Security programs are closely interrelated in many ways (including disability determinations), there is very little symmetry in the other cases. In addition, the inclusion of any of them would raise serious questions of which committees in Congress would have jurisdiction of the bill. The sponsor would probably not want to extend the bill's coverage that far unless the alleged defect is thought to be so widespread that an across-the-board attack is justified despite the jurisdictional problems.

Keep in mind that all of this may be only the beginning, since cost, politics, tactics, and strategy, which in many cases could be important considerations to the sponsor, have been ignored.

In any event, the bill could be written narrowly to cover only cases exactly like the sponsor's case—limiting it to a single type of disability under a single set of circumstances within a single program—or it could be written more broadly so as to cover other cases (few or many) that are similar but not identical. The former would be easier to draft (and probably to get through Congress) but might create an entirely new and different set of problems by providing discriminatorily different treatment for substantially similar cases. The latter might be more equitable but would cost more, raise jurisdictional questions, and risk covering at least some situations that ought to be governed by quite different considerations.

As a drafter you cannot make these decisions for yourself, since they would have very real substantive consequences. But you must always make sure that the sponsor is aware of the choices and their rationales and understands the consequences. And when the sponsor's decision is based on cost or on political considerations, you must of course take that into account in any advice you give.

Specific or general? An apparently similar but actually quite different dilemma (also briefly mentioned earlier) involves the degree of specificity with which you should describe how the proposal is to work in practice.

On the one hand, you cannot possibly provide a specific answer to every question that could conceivably arise under the bill—indeed you cannot even identify them all—and the harder you try the more likely it is that you will introduce impediments to sensible administrative judgment.

On the other hand, if the sponsor's policy has been well crystallized, most of the individually important questions that will arise often enough to be significant can usually be foreseen; and the bill can (if the sponsor so desires) spell out in detail exactly how the administering agency is to carry it out, specifying such things as the standards to be applied, the procedures to be followed, and any organizational changes within the agency that may be required.

There are several factors to consider. Some situations are best left to future administrative (or judicial) determination. And if the sponsor's policy has intentionally or unavoidably been left in general terms, the development of more specific guidelines may have to be left to the administering agency. In addition, elaborate legislative structures almost always require complex administrative procedures to give them effect, and the more these are expressly included in the bill the less likely the bill is to work as the sponsor intended. It may be desirable to phrase the bill in general (and even deliberately vague) terms, simply telling the agency what it is supposed to accomplish and leaving the specifics to its regulations and administrative practices.

The general approach is easier and less time-consuming to draft, covers a multitude of sins (it is particularly useful when there is no time to work out the details) and avoids interfering with flexible good faith administration by imposing too many restrictions. Most legislators, however, feel that undue reliance on administrative discretion is dangerous, and they generally prefer to see most of the necessary standards and procedures (to the extent they can agree on them) spelled out. In the end, most bills result in a compromise of these approaches (as they do on the question of breadth discussed earlier). It is important to keep in mind that the greater the level of administrative or other details spelled out in the legislation means that even a minor adjustment in those details that becomes apparent once the law is administered will have to be made by another Act of Congress, rather than an administering agency.

4.6 Different bills, different challenges

Bills come in all sizes, shapes, and textures, and all policies are not equally burdensome to the drafter. The way in which you approach your task can differ markedly from one assignment to another depending on the nature and scope of the proposals involved; and naturally enough the differences are most significant during the preliminary stage, while you are trying to figure out just what to put into the bill and how to arrange it.

The policy involved in a relatively straightforward and specific proposal is likely to be quite clear, with few subsidiary or collateral problems; but the policies involved in a broader or relatively nonspecific proposal, or one that intimately affects or is affected by a complicated body of existing law, may be another story altogether. Drafting assignments range from one extreme to the other, of course, but most of them fall easily into the somewhat arbitrary hierarchy of difficulty that follows.

One-shot proposals of limited scope, without predictable complications. In such a proposal the policy is likely to be quite clear; there may be problems to deal with, and there may be a few collateral questions, but there should be nothing that cannot be handled with relative ease.

Assume, for example, that you are asked to draft a bill to provide a one-year authorization of funds for an existing program. The basic policy is perfectly clear, and its factual background is almost immaterial. You are presumably told the amount to be authorized and the fiscal year involved, and you can easily locate the provision of law that contains the program's existing authorization of funds. Normally all that remains is to make a simple amendment to that provision.

If for example the authorization provision is located in section 8(c) of the ABC Act and currently reads:

> (c) AUTHORIZATION OF APPROPRIATIONS.—To carry out the program under this Act, there is authorized to be appropriated—
>
> (1) $1,000,000 for fiscal year 2023; and
>
> (2) $2,000,000 for fiscal year 2024.

Your amendment might read something like this:

> **SEC. ____. AUTHORIZATION OF APPROPRIATIONS.**
>
> Section 8(c) of the ABC Act is amended—
>
> (1) by striking "and" at the end of paragraph (1);
>
> (2) by striking the period at the end of paragraph (2) and inserting "; and"; and
>
> (3) by adding after paragraph (2) the following new paragraph:
>
> "(3) $3,000,000 for fiscal year 2025".

The only other thing you would normally need to do is make sure there are no time-related or amount-related provisions in the ABC Act that might be affected by what you have done—for example, a specific cutoff date for the filing of applications, or a provision limiting the amount of any grant to a specified percentage of the funds currently available (in which case your amendment taken by itself could result in an increase in the maximum grant amount). You should scan the rest of the Act; and if you find any such provision you should either conform it or (if your course is not clear) raise the question with the sponsor.

One-shot proposals of limited scope, with predictable complications. The complications most often arise because the proposal must be woven into a statutory tapestry that is already complicated and the various parts of which are extensively interrelated. The subsidiary policies are likely to be only partially clear, and you must be especially wary of collateral problems.

Assume that you are asked to draft a bill increasing Social Security benefits for widows by a specified percentage. Superficially the request sounds quite straightforward; but in fact it is not clear at all.

Aside from a few esoteric questions involving mathematics and computation formulas that must normally be left to the specialists, there are a number of policy questions (basic, subsidiary, and collateral) on which you need to inform yourself at the outset. For example:

(1) What kind of widows are we talking about? Probably the sponsor has had complaints from one or more widows receiving "widow's insurance benefits", which are derivative benefits payable to widows (on the work records of their deceased husbands) because they are aged or disabled. But there are also widows (age and physical condition immaterial) who receive derivative benefits—called "mother's insurance benefits"—because they have minor children in their care.

There may also be a question about whether the sponsor means to include women who are receiving nonderivative benefits (as retired workers or otherwise) and who just happen to be widows, as well as individuals receiving derivative benefits because they are widows.

Most sponsors would probably limit their proposals to the first category of widows—aged or disabled widows receiving "widow's insurance benefits"—since that is what most people mean when speaking of widows under Social Security.

(2) What about widowers and their benefits? This is a collateral question, of course, but as the Supreme Court has made the equal treatment of widows and widowers under the program a matter of constitutional necessity, it needs to be raised. Most sponsors would include them.

(3) What about the effect of the proposal on the rest of the widow's family? The "family maximum" provisions in the Social Security law place a ceiling on the total amount of monthly benefits that can be paid (to all family members) on the basis of any one individual's work record. Thus if you increase the widow's benefits but the family includes other beneficiaries who are eligible on the same work record, she will indeed get more but the others will get less—since the total would have to remain the same—unless you do something about it.

Once you are clear about what you are supposed to do and who you are supposed to do it to, the actual writing should present no major problems.

(Granted that Social Security is a complicated and specialized field, and you could not be expected to recognize these problems without developing more expertise in it than you have any use for. But the problems it presents are typical of the approach you must frequently take before beginning to write midsized bills in many fields—nothing is truly simple anymore.)

One-shot proposals of broader scope, within a single statutory area. Such a proposal normally involves several different basic policies—the typical "reform bill" is a good example—rather than being limited to just one or two specific points. Although the general objectives are usually clear, the specific policy is likely to be fuzzy everywhere, with related collateral problems in abundance.

Assume that you are asked to draft a bill establishing a major new program in an area not covered by any existing law. This is not necessarily more difficult just because it is broader; but it is demanding because you will be starting from scratch, with no existing framework in which to put it, and you will need many questions answered before you can begin:

(1) The most basic questions involve the main thrust itself, of course: what is the purpose of the program, and how is it supposed to work? For example:

(A) If it is a loan or grant program, who can qualify for assistance, and how do they go about getting it? For what activities can the proceeds be used? How should you set the amount of the assistance? What should the other terms and conditions of the assistance be?

(B) If it is a construction program, what exactly is to be built, and where? Who is to do it? What should the specifications, cost limits, and time requirements be? How should the work be contracted for, and what should the contracts contain?

(C) If it is a regulatory program, who is to be regulated, and what activities? How is the regulatory process to be conducted? Are there constitutional difficulties, and if so, what can be done about them?

(2) The new program will obviously need funding: How much should be authorized to be appropriated, and for what period? If it is a loan program, should repayments (and interest earned) be available for making new loans, through a revolving fund or otherwise?

(3) There will be a number of subsidiary and collateral policy questions that involve organization and administration: Who will administer the new program? If an existing officer or agency is to do it, are the existing administrative procedures adequate, should new offices or positions be created, and how will the new functions fit into the agency's existing framework? If a new agency is to do it, what organizational and operating characteristics should it be given?

4) It is important that the administering officer or agency possess the capacity to actually carry out the functions conferred: What general powers and operating authorities should that officer or agency be given? If the program is placed within an existing agency, will that agency's existing enumeration of general powers (which would automatically apply) be sufficient? And if a new agency is to be created to run the program, what everyday operating powers should it have? (Since enumerations of agency powers typically have an element of boilerplate in them, a good model would be particularly useful here, and one can generally be found.)

(5) The new program must actually work, of course: How will it be monitored and its requirements enforced? Should beneficiaries or other participants be required to give specified assurances before qualifying, or report periodically on their use of the funds made available to them? Should the administering officer or agency be required to report periodically on the operation of the program generally or on the extent to which it is achieving its objectives? Should there be penalties (over and above any existing penalties that may apply automatically) for misuse of funds or failure to comply with the applicable requirements?

This is a sampler only, of course, because the variations among programs are wide even when they are of the same general type, and obviously every bill creating a program of any substance will require provisions that are unique to that program. Thus a bill involving scientific research or a new technology (like the activities of the National Aeronautics and Space Administration [NASA]) will normally contain provisions relating to patents, while a bill involving particularly sensitive subjects (like defense or nuclear energy, or commercial trade secrets) is likely to contain provisions relating to matters of security. And a bill establishing any kind of Federal-State operating arrangement (under State plans or otherwise) must of course spell out the details of that arrangement.

Multipurpose and omnibus bills. Such a bill combines proposals in totally different statutory areas and typically consists entirely of individual segments (related or unrelated), each of which falls into one of the other three categories. As a drafter you would normally treat each of those segments as a separate project. For the many States whose constitutions require that a bill deal with only a single subject, the question becomes: when does a bill become multipurpose and therefore prohibited (see chapter 35)?

Note that most bills that are taken seriously at the Federal level are amendatory rather than freestanding, and that the amendatory approach itself will often involve special problems even in bills that are otherwise uncomplicated (see part V).

It is not always possible to predict the specific problems that will surface in any drafting assignment—collateral policy questions are particularly elusive—but anyone who drafts regularly soon learns to sense the probable difficulties that will be involved in the assignments that come along. Many bills are relatively uncomplicated, but be careful—some of the simplest-looking assignments turn out to be riddled with problems.

4.7 The drafter as a participant in policy formulation

The repeated emphasis upon the distinction between policymaking and drafting may give the impression that neither has anything to do with the other, but in reality, the two are intertwined.

How far can you, the drafter, be legitimately concerned with substantive policy? You do not make the policy, of course, but you can properly influence it in many ways.

While it would be wrong to intrude yourself into matters of policy that are the sponsor's prime responsibility, it would be equally wrong to let yourself be relegated to the status of a mere stenographer. In practice there is a considerable gray area.

A request from a sponsor usually focuses on the main thrust; it seldom includes everything that you need to know about the specifics of the proposal, and one of your most important functions as a drafter is the questioning that is necessary to complete the picture. The questions you ask, no matter how neutrally they are phrased, inevitably have the effect of suggesting (without actually recommending, of course) policy positions for the sponsor to take. This is particularly true if you are presented with a draft prepared by someone else and asked to "clean it up". If you are not in a position to start from scratch, you must question each provision in the draft in order to draw out the policy.

In addition, it is your professional obligation as a drafter to advise the sponsor on the workability of the proposal as well as to devise the language to carry it out; most sponsors find it hard to visualize the impracticability of a favorite proposal or to recognize and evaluate all the problems it raises. You must always be prepared to confront the sponsor with the legal and practical consequences of the proposal.

You must do these things, of course, in a way that does not encroach upon the sponsor's prerogatives; you cannot inject your own substantive views into the sponsor's policy formulation, and must act with scrupulous objectivity to carry out the sponsor's purpose even when you strongly disagree with it. And if in some respects you find yourself leading the sponsor, you must always be sure you are leading in the direction in which the sponsor wants to go.

There are some risks, of course, in playing the devil's advocate to sponsors who are accustomed to having their own way without question. It requires a high degree of tact and diplomacy. But you must always be sure both that you understand what the sponsor is trying to accomplish and that the sponsor understands the problems. Be deliberate and do not be afraid to ask questions. What you are seeking is a meeting of the minds, enabling you to "fill in the chinks" without overstepping your proper function.

People who are accustomed to black-and-white choices may be uncomfortable with the drafter's peculiar shade of gray; but it is important to understand that your contributions, especially during the initial stages, can have a salutary effect on the sponsor's policy formulation even though you are not a policymaker yourself. Always remember that your specialized approach, training, and experience will often enable you to discover fundamental problems (substantive, legal, administrative, or practical) that the sponsor has overlooked. The important thing is this: simply asking sensible questions at the outset and then using good drafting practices—complete consistency and rational arrangement above all—will do more to uncover ambiguities, contradictions, gaps, and other policy-related discrepancies in a proposal than all the mental gymnastics in the world.

4.8. Some ever present real-life drafting problems

When you, as a drafter, find that you are prevented by circumstances beyond your control from doing the job properly, you either do not understand the policy or are facing one or more of the following problems (which may, of course, be the reason why you do not understand the policy):

Lack of substantive expertise. Government at every level generates vast quantities of legislation in areas that were left untouched in the past, and it is increasingly complex, specialized, and interrelated. And the number of court cases and regulations interpreting and implementing that legislation has risen by an even greater degree.

In order to work effectively in any substantive field, you need a reasonably good knowledge and understanding of the existing law (statutes, court cases, and regulations) in that field; without it you can never be certain that you have identified and understood all the problems and have found all the cross-references and interrelated provisions in the relevant existing law. This is true whether the bill you are writing is amendatory or freestanding.

It is difficult to work in an unfamiliar field or amend an unfamiliar statute, regardless of your qualifications. But if you actually read the relevant laws and seek expert help wherever you can find it, you should survive. And if all else fails and you must simply do the best you can, you should cling to the thought that you are not alone—most bills when introduced have gaps and flaws that have to be corrected later. This is what the legislative process is for. It is only when it breaks down that the gaps and flaws remain uncorrected. In any case, be sure to warn the sponsor of any potential problems that you know about.

Lack of legal training. Legal and constitutional questions do, of course, come up in the drafting process, and when they arise you must confront them. You must always be certain that the legal effect of the words you use is the desired effect, and that those words will not cause unnecessary litigation or other avoidable legal problems in the future. Naturally, attorneys have an advantage over nonattorneys in this area, but being an attorney is not always required.

On the one hand, many bills do not involve any significant legal or constitutional questions at all. A bill to establish a new national holiday is unlikely to have any problems of this kind, while a bill to revise the antitrust laws would almost certainly be full of them. The challenge to the drafter is to be able to recognize which bills raise legal or constitutional questions and which do not. If the drafter is not an attorney but has access to legal help within the drafter's agency or organization, the drafter should seek out that help. Even if a nonattorney does not have reason to suspect legal complications, it is wise to have an attorney with expertise in the area review draft legislation (or regulations) for potential legal problems.

On the other hand, since they tend to be the thorniest problems that a drafter faces, legal problems in a bill (unless they are very simple) are the ones that even professional drafters may have to leave unresolved, to be worked out at a later date by the legal staff of the committee to which the bill is referred.

Finally, just being an attorney does not automatically give a drafter complete mastery over the legal aspects of a bill. An attorney-drafter who is a specialist in one field may still be totally unfamiliar with cases and legal principles that are important in another, and thus face the same disadvantages as one who is not an attorney.

Lack of time. Drafting bills in a fraction of the time needed is the story of the drafter's life in far too many cases. Drafters do not control legislative schedules; bills are introduced, taken up, and acted upon when the legislators themselves think it best, and they have no choice but to be ready when the gavel falls.

If what you have been called upon to prepare is a bill for introduction, there is often a deadline because of committee schedules or simply because the sponsor (for political or tactical reasons) wants the bill to burst upon an unsuspecting public on a certain day or in connection with a certain event. If it is a revision of a bill that has already been introduced and is due for consideration in a committee or on the floor, or it is an amendment to such a bill, it must of course be ready by the time that bill is taken up. And legislators are notoriously prone to wait until the last minute before asking the drafter to prepare a bill.

When the sponsor must have a draft of a bill within a specified but insufficient period, you should make sure the sponsor understands the time problem, do the best you can within the limits imposed, inform the sponsor about any known problems that may remain unsolved (with a warning that others may exist), and be willing to continue with the project after the draft is delivered by preparing any necessary amendments.

A substantial percentage of the bills in Congress (and presumably in State legislatures) have serious substantive, legal, or practical problems in them when they are introduced, usually left there because of lack of time and with the knowledge of both drafter and sponsor. The conscious expectation is that the difficulties will be taken care of "in committee" or just "at a later stage"; and they can be if (it bears repeating) the legislative *process* works.

Lack of closeness to the legislative process. Even if a bill has been perfectly drafted by every other standard, the job has not been done properly if it collapses because it violates some procedural rule of the legislative body involved, or because its timing is wrong, or because it does not take into account any one of a number of other factors that control the way in which bills and amendments are considered in that body.

These matters have their greatest importance when you are working on amendments to be offered to a bill already moving through the legislative process. But you should always make a conscious effort to foresee the parliamentary and procedural obstacles prior to the bill's introduction, since the contents of the original bill often determine whether or not such obstacles will exist (and it may be too late to do anything about them when they are actually confronted).

The relevant procedural rules and statutory provisions are available in published form (including on the Internet) and are more or less permanent, and even an occasional drafter can keep abreast of them with a little effort. But the temporary rules and procedures that govern the way in which a bill will be taken up and considered on the floor of the legislative body involved are equally important; they can be critical to the drafter of an amendment since they may determine the form it should take (or even whether it can be offered at all).

In the House of Representatives, for example, the way in which particular bills are to be considered is governed by ad hoc "special rules" (see 34.3). The corresponding decisions in the Senate are usually made by unanimous consent, or simply by leadership action. In either case the decisions involved are frequently made at the last minute. However, even these special rules are posted immediately on the Web pages of the Committee on Rules and the House of Representatives. The unanimous consent agreements of the Senate may be more difficult to access immediately, unless you are watching the proceedings on the Senate floor at the time they are announced. They are available the next day in the Calendar of the Senate and the *Congressional Record*, both of which can be found on congress.gov (*www.congress.gov*), along with the text and information relating to every bill that is introduced. Be aware also that, in the unlikely instance in which a bill is considered under an "open" rule in the House of Representatives (that is, a rule under which the amendments to the bill are not restricted), a unanimous consent agreement could be reached in the House to limit further debate on that bill while the bill is being considered. In that case, you can access the current floor proceedings of the House on those Web pages as well.

If you are unable to keep up with these matters on a minute-by-minute basis, you should do your best to establish a connection with someone who does. And you must at least be certain that the sponsor of the bill or amendment you are working on is aware of any possible procedural problems and is prepared to modify it, or switch to a different approach, if necessary.

4.9 Case study of a policy gone awry

As a means of putting some flesh on the bones of what has been said in this chapter, it may be instructive to look briefly at a well-known Federal statute that is operating today, for better or worse, in a way that seems to bear little resemblance to the way it was originally intended to operate.

In the 1960s the nation was preoccupied with organized crime, and Congress undertook to do something about it. There was no consensus on just what constituted "organized crime", but it was generally agreed that it involved such things as drug dealing, prostitution, and extortion and was carried on primarily by labor bosses, racketeers, and other undesirable individuals.

Under the Constitution most crime is a State responsibility, but a basis for Federal action was found in the assumption that organized crime crosses State lines, requiring a centralized effort to coordinate the fight in a manner analogous to the antitrust laws (which had also involved the Federal Government in matters previously left to the States). The result was the addition of a new chapter 96 in title 18, United States Code, entitled "Racketeer Influenced and Corrupt Organizations" (RICO) (18 U.S.C. 1961–1968).

The findings of the statute enacting this new chapter (title IX of Public Law 91-452; 84 Stat. 923; 18 U.S.C. 1961 note) addressed only "organized crime",[3] and the stated "purpose of the Act" was—

> to seek the eradication of organized crime in the United States by strengthening the legal tools in the evidence-gathering process, by establishing new penal prohibitions, and by providing enhanced sanctions

and new remedies to deal with the unlawful activities of those engaged in organized crime. (18 U.S.C. 1961 note)

Based on the findings and purpose provisions, the intent of Congress appeared to be to limit the scope of the law to "organized crime".

The relevant provisions of title 18 enacted by Public Law 91-452 are section 1962 of title 18, which sets forth the prohibited activities, and section 1961 of title 18, which contains the applicable definitions. In a nutshell, section 1962 makes it unlawful—

(1) for a person who receives income derived from "a pattern of racketeering activity" to use or invest the proceeds in, or establish or operate, an "enterprise" in interstate or foreign commerce;[4]

(2) for a person through a "pattern of racketeering activity" to acquire or maintain an interest in or control over an "enterprise" which is engaged in, or the activities of which affect, interstate or foreign commerce;

(3) for a person employed by or associated with an "enterprise" engaged in, or the activities of which affect, interstate or foreign commerce, to conduct or participate in the conduct of the enterprise's affairs through a "pattern of racketeering activity"; and

(4) to conspire to violate (1), (2), or (3).

On its face, the statute appears to address organized criminal activities. However, the terms used in section 1962, which are defined in section 1961 of title 18, tell a different story.

The term "racketeering activity" is defined as any of a long list of criminal offenses, including a number of criminal offenses under State law. In addition to offenses like murder, bribery, extortion, counterfeiting, embezzlement, drug trafficking, fraud relating to identification and other documents, sexual exploitation of children, and trafficking in persons are offenses like mail and wire fraud and criminal infringement of copyright (18 U.S.C. 1961(1)).

The term "person" is defined as "any individual or entity capable of holding a legal or beneficial interest in property" (18 U.S.C. 1961(3).

The term "enterprise" is defined to "include" any "individual, partnership, corporation, association, or other legal entity, and any union or group of individuals associated in fact although not a legal entity" (18 U.S.C. 1961(4)).

The term "pattern of racketeering activity" requires "at least two acts of racketeering activity, one of which occurred after the effective date of this chapter [October 15, 1970] and the last of which occurred within ten years (excluding any period of imprisonment) after the commission of a prior act of racketeering activity" (18 U.S.C. 1961(5)).

In addition, in order to supplement the criminal penalties for violations of the law and to aid in enforcement, RICO added a civil remedy (in section 1964 of title 18) allowing any person "injured in his business or property by reason of a violation of section 1962" (except for securities fraud cases) to sue for treble damages, plus court costs and attorney's fees (18 U.S.C. 1964(c)). Because it is a civil remedy, the standard of proof would be a "preponderance of the evidence", a lower standard than the "beyond a reasonable doubt" standard that would apply in a criminal case. In a civil RICO case, the defendant need not be criminally convicted (with the "beyond a reasonable doubt" standard) before a civil plaintiff can sue for treble damages under RICO; "racketeering activity consists not of acts for which the defendant has been convicted, but of acts for which he could be". *Sedima, S.P.R.L. v. Imrex Co.*, 473 U.S. 479, 488 (1985). Under section 1964(b), the Attorney General may also institute proceedings to prevent or restrain a violation of section 1962..

Given the definitions in section 1961, the substantive provisions of the statute, despite the findings and purpose of the statute, are extremely broad. The language alone indicates that a "pattern of racketeering activity" under these provisions would seem to be established by proving two offenses listed as a "racketeering activity" over a ten-year period. The Supreme Court has, however, interpreted this language to require that there be a showing that the "racketeering predicates are related, and that they amount to or pose a threat of continued criminal activity".[5] Despite this narrowing of the definition by the Court, the definition covers a broad range of activities.

For example, because one of the "racketeering predicates" is mail fraud and because the mails are used for all types of transactions, it would be possible to characterize almost any wrongdoing as mail fraud under the statute. Another of the predicates is criminal copyright infringement, which covers (among other activities) the reproduction or distribution, by electronic means, of one or more copies of copyrighted works having a total retail value of more than $1,000, even if no financial motive or gain is involved. Thus arguably a group of students who set up a system of "sharing" copyrighted files (file sharing infringes copyright) with other students through e-mails might be a target of a civil RICO suit by copyright owners.

Much of the litigation under RICO has involved civil actions brought for a violation under section 1962(c). To establish a claim under this provision, the plaintiff would have to prove that (1) a defendant person (2) was employed by or associated with an enterprise (3) that engaged in or affected interstate or foreign commerce and that (4) the defendant person operated or managed the enterprise (5) through a pattern (6) of racketeering activity, and (7) the plaintiff was injured in its business or property by reason of the pattern of racketeering activity.[6] Remember that it need only be proved, by a preponderance of the evidence, that the defendant could be convicted of the underlying criminal activity, not that the defendant had been convicted. In addition, in *Sedima,* 473 U.S. at 495–496, the Court held that the "injury" is harm only from the predicate acts; no specific "racketeering" injury need be proved.

Since these provisions of title 18 do not premise a violation on proof or allegations of any connection with organized crime,[7] actions under the RICO statute have been maintained on the basis of a defendant's use of mail and wire communications in furtherance of a wide variety of fraudulent acts in everyday business ventures and financial transactions having no connection to "organized crime", like misrepresenting the defendant's ability to provide immediate commercial financing (*Diamonds Plus, Inc. v. Kolber,* 960 F.2d 765, 769 [8th Cir. 1992]); using the mails to sell computer components when the defendant was required to destroy the components (*Digital Equipment Corp. v. Currie Enterprises,* 142 F.R.D. 16, 23–25 [D.

Mass. 1992]); and using the mails to fraudulently obtain a settlement of a lawsuit (*Turkish v. Kasenetz,* 27 F.3d 23, 27–28 (2d Cir. 1994), on remand 964 F.Supp. 689 [E.D.N.Y. 1997]).

In 1999 the Federal Government sued the tobacco industry under civil RICO on the basis that the tobacco companies used the mails and wire communications to lie to the American people about the effects of tobacco, asking for injunctive relief (one of the remedies under 18 U.S.C. 1964).

In a nearly 1,000 page opinion, the U.S. District Court for the District of Columbia held that the tobacco companies had conspired to violate, and did violate, the provisions of RICO by fraudulently misrepresenting adverse health effects of active smoking, the addictiveness of nicotine and cigarette smoking, the health risks attached to light and low tar cigarettes, and the adverse health effects of second hand smoke, and by their manipulation of cigarettes' nicotine content and their marketing to youth; the court prohibited the companies from engaging in specific acts, and required them to take certain remedial actions, in the future. *United States v. Philip Morris USA Inc.*, 449 F. Supp. 2d 1, 938–41 (D.D.C. 2006), *aff'd in part & vacated in part*, 566 F.3d 1095 (D.C. Cir. 2009) (*per curiam*), *cert, denied*, 561 U.S. 1025 (2010).[8]

Civil RICO has also been used to bring lawsuits against political activists. In *National Organization for Women, Inc. v. Scheidler,* a case that was in the court system for twenty years, a civil RICO action was brought against named individuals and organizations that engage in pro-life, antiabortion activities, on the basis of acts done at health care facilities performing abortions. While the Supreme Court held that the RICO statute does not require proof that the pattern of racketeering activity was motivated by an economic purpose (*National Organization for Women, Inc. v. Scheidler,* 510 U.S. 249, 262 [1994]), it ultimately determined that the predicate criminal statute upon which the pattern of racketeering activity alleged in the case was based did require such proof.[9]

It is noteworthy that Congress also included in the law that enacted these provisions of title 18 a provision stating that "the provisions of this title [enacting chapter 96 of title 18] shall be liberally construed to effectuate its remedial purposes".[10] Even though the purpose stated in the law was limited to organized crime, the courts have relied on this liberal-construction language to justify a broad reading of the statute. See, for example, *United States v. Turkette,* 452 U.S. 576, 587 (1981), in which the liberal-construction language justified construing the statute to cover legitimate as well as illegitimate enterprises.

Suffice it to say that the RICO statute has been used for many purposes other than prosecuting and suing those connected with organized crime. Given the history of the statute, it is unlikely Congress took fully into account the implications of defining "organized crime" so broadly, or of inserting a civil remedy in the criminal statute.

Notes

1 Chapter 10 of part 1 of title 5, United States Code, known as the Federal Advisory Committee Act before its enactment as positive law by Public Law 117-286, establishes procedures that all Federal advisory committees must follow and provides for the automatic termination of those committees (with some exceptions). Under chapter 10, a Federal advisory committee is defined generally as any committee or similar group, made up in whole or in part of private individuals, that is established in the interest of obtaining advice or recommendations for the President or one or more agencies of the Federal Government.

2 A "statutory" or "compulsory" license under title 17, United States Code, refers to a provision that creates an exception to copyright infringement for certain uses if the user (under most circumstances) pays royalties to the copyright owners at rates and terms determined under the applicable provision of title 17. For example, cable operators and satellite carriers provide television programming to their subscribers under a statutory license.

3 The findings were as follows:

The Congress finds that—

(1) organized crime in the United States is a highly sophisticated, diversified, and widespread activity that annually drains billions of dollars from America's economy by unlawful conduct and the illegal use of force, fraud, and corruption;

(2) organized crime derives a major portion of its power through money obtained from such illegal endeavors as syndicated gambling, loan sharking, the theft and fencing of property, the importation and distribution of narcotics and other dangerous drugs, and other forms of social exploitation;

(3) this money and power are increasingly used to infiltrate and corrupt legitimate business and labor unions and to subvert and corrupt our democratic processes;

(4) organized crime activities in the United States weaken the stability of the Nation's economic system, harm innocent investors and competing organizations, interfere with free competition, seriously burden interstate and foreign commerce, threaten the domestic security, and undermine the general welfare of the Nation and its citizens; and

(5) organized crime continues to grow because of defects in the evidence-gathering process of the law inhibiting the development of the legally admissible evidence necessary to bring criminal and other sanctions or remedies to bear on the unlawful activities of those engaged in organized crime and because the sanctions and remedies available to the Government are unnecessarily limited in scope and impact.

4 The link to interstate commerce would be a constitutional hook on which to place a provision like this; see chapter 29.

5 *H. J. Inc. v. Northwestern Bell Telephone Co.*, 492 U.S. 229, 239 (1989). The court, in reaching this result, looked into the legislative history to determine the meaning of "pattern". The court in *Sedima* (473 U.S. at 496, n. 14) relied on the language of the statute, that is, that a pattern of racketeering activity "requires" at least two acts of racketeering activity, not "means" two such acts, to conclude that while two such acts are necessary, they may not be sufficient. The Supreme Court has also limited RICO by holding that the "injured ... by reason of" clause of section 1964(c) demanded "some direct relation between the injury asserted and the injurious conduct alleged". See *Holmes v. Securities Investor Protection Corporation,* 503 U.S. 258, 268 (1992).

6 See Jeffrey Grell, "Rico in a Nutshell", *www.ricoact.com*. The court in *Reves v. Ernst & Young,* 507 U.S. 170, 184–185 (1993) held that the phrase "conduct, or participate in the conduct" of an enterprise's affairs (in section 1962(c)) requires that the defendant must participate in the operation or management of the enterprise itself, although the involvement was not limited to upper management (an outside auditor making misleading financial statements of an enterprise did not participate in the conduct of the enterprise itself). The court in *United States v. Turkette,* 452 U.S. 576, 583 (1981) held that the enterprise had to exist separately from the pattern of racketeering activity in which it was engaged.

7 *Moss v. Morgan Stanley, Inc.*, 719 F.2d 5, 21 (2nd Cir. 1983), cert. denied, *Moss v. Newman,* 465 U.S. 1025 (1984); *Bennett v. Berg,* 710 F.2d 1361, 1364 (8th Cir. en banc 1983), cert. denied, *Prudential Insurance Company of America v. Bennett,* 464 U.S. 1008 (1983). In *United States v. Turkette,* 452 U.S. 576, 587, the Supreme Court held that the term "enterprise" encompasses both legitimate and illegitimate enterprises.

8 Some modifications and clarifications to the corrective actions required of the defendants have been made in the District Court for the District of Columbia. *United States v. Philip Morris USA Inc.*, United States District Court, District

of Columbia June 2, 2014 [2014 WL 2506611] [Only the Westlaw citation is currently available.] *United States v. Philip Morris USA Inc.*, United States District Court, District of Columbia, April 19, 2016 [WL 3951273][Only the Westlaw citation is currently available.]

9 *Scheidler et al. v. National Organization for Women, Inc. et al.*, 547 U.S. 9, 23 (2006). The statute involved was 18 U.S.C. 1951(a): "Whoever in any way or degree obstructs, delays, or affects commerce" by (1) "robbery", (2) "extortion", or (3) "commit[ting] or threaten[ing] *physical violence to any person or property in furtherance of a plan or purpose to do anything in violation of this section...*" (emphasis added). The court held that the last phrase required that the physical violence be related to robbery or extortion.

10 Section 904(a) of Public Law 91-452.

5. Searching Out the Collateral Questions

5.1 In general

When you are clear about what the problem is and about how you are supposed to solve it, you are theoretically ready to write a bill that is complete and coherent. But bills do not exist in a vacuum; as often as not there are provisions of existing law that bear upon or would be affected by what your bill purports to do and that could result in consequences that the sponsor did not intend. Although these "collateral" questions can be ignored without affecting the internal coherence of the bill, you cannot be said to have carried out the sponsor's policy correctly (and you may be putting the sponsor at some risk) if you do ignore them.

Thus collateral questions should not be treated as poor relations. It will often be critically important to the sponsor that you recognize them, and deal with them in a way that promotes the intended policy or at least minimizes the damage. And simply recognizing that one exists is often harder than figuring out what to do about it.

Chapter 4 unavoidably addressed collateral questions along with "subsidiary" questions in its general treatment of policy development (see especially 4.3)—there is obviously overlap between the two. And the "real-life drafting problems" mentioned in 4.8 often involve collateral questions. They come in infinite varieties, so this chapter will attempt only to give you an idea of how to identify collateral questions and some guidelines for handling them.

5.2 Collateral questions within the substantive area involved

The easiest collateral questions to identify in connection with any bill are those that relate more or less directly to the subject matter of that bill, because you have already had to become familiar with that subject matter and with the relevant existing laws in order to deal with the sponsor's basic policy.

Easiest of all, of course, are questions arising under the very law that you are amending or the law that governs the field involved. Questions that arise under related laws may be a little harder to pinpoint, but the necessity of looking for them should be obvious. A couple of brief examples should suffice to illustrate the point:

(1) In the hypothetical bill increasing Social Security benefits for widows that was used as an example in 4.6, the questions involving widowers and the "family maximum" limitation are collateral questions arising under other provisions of the same law; you ought to be aware of them, or at least suspect their existence. You might not know whether there are any collateral questions in the SSI (the Supplemental Security Income program), Medicare, or railroad retirement laws, but you would know that those laws are interrelated with the Social

Security law in many ways and accordingly check out the possibilities.

(2) If you were called upon to draft a bill establishing a new form of assistance under the Foreign Assistance Act of 1961 to address, as is usually the case, an international event or situation, then you would need to look elsewhere in that Act for definitions of different types of assistance, like "foreign assistance", "United States assistance", and "humanitarian assistance", to determine whether your new program should or should not be included in those definitions. Likewise, if your new program is similar to another form of assistance that is referenced elsewhere in that law, you would need to check those references to see whether your new program should be added.

5.3 Collateral questions elsewhere

Identifying collateral questions that arise in areas totally unrelated to the main thrust is harder, because you may have no reason to suspect they even exist. But there are some general guidelines that may be helpful:

(1) The nature of the main thrust will often suggest the possibility of collateral questions in other areas. For example, a bill establishing a new antipoverty program might reasonably be expected to raise questions under the TANF (Temporary Assistance to Needy Families), SSI, food stamp, and housing laws. And a bill regulating the interstate transportation of potentially disease-bearing insects might be expected to have ramifications under the public health and agriculture laws. In the second example cited in 5.2, you could expect to make the same checks in other laws that you make within the Foreign Assistance Act of 1961, for example, looking for references to "foreign assistance" and "United States assistance" that may need to be modified to address the new form of assistance created in the bill.

(2) The more administrative actions are required for the bill's implementation (whether or not you propose to spell them out in the bill itself), the more likely it is that the APA (Administrative Procedure

Act) provisions of title 5 of the United States Code,[1] which establish procedures for agency rulemaking and adjudications and judicial review of agency action, and other laws affecting administrative procedures generally[2] will be involved.

(3) A bill establishing a new executive department or agency, or transferring functions between departments or agencies, will involve all laws referencing the department or agency whose functions are being transferred or otherwise modified.

(4) Laws of general applicability—such as those involving interstate commerce, the budget, and criminal and judicial procedure as well as the regulatory laws, for example, depending on the nature of the proposal—should be regarded as potential candidates.

You may be able to find a suitable model, in another similar bill or in an existing law, that addresses some of the otherwise-hidden collateral questions (see 10.4). Or you may find that the collateral provisions are actually cited in related existing laws, which would automatically lead you to them (see 5.5).

Remember, however, that you will seldom know in the beginning whether there are any collateral questions of this kind to worry about. If you suspect that such questions exist but cannot identify them, you should seek out a specialist—ideally one with practical operating experience in the field involved. But if you are pressed for time and there is no obvious reason to suspect a problem, save your energy. Any collateral questions that do exist will surface eventually (and can be dealt with then).[3] Do not waste your time rummaging through Federal statutes looking for them now.

5.4 Technical and conforming changes

In theory, technical and conforming amendments are never substantive—they are merely the device the drafter uses to clean up the inconsistencies in the law created by the substantive things the bill does. And since they involve no policy questions, they do not need to be thought about in the early stages of drafting. They may raise collateral questions, but not collateral policy questions.

When a bill repeals or renumbers a section referred to in another provision of existing law, the reference to that section becomes meaningless or incorrect and must be either eliminated or conformed. So, if a section being repealed is referred to in twenty other provisions of law, the bill must include (at a minimum) twenty "technical and conforming amendments" eliminating those references and possibly making further conforming amendments to compensate for their elimination. And if the bill adds a new section that needs to be taken into account under another law, or does anything that constitutes a hidden or implied exception or addition to a general rule set forth in another law, the insertion of an appropriate cross-reference in the other law is clearly indicated.

Amendments of this kind are usually simple, mechanical, and purely technical—but not always. In a surprising number of cases, cleaning up the inconsistencies in the law raises its own substantive and tactical problems.[4]

When your bill has the effect of repealing or nullifying a section of existing law, for example, and an unrelated provision of law contains a cross-reference to that section, simply striking the now obsolete cross-reference is not enough if the unrelated provision *depends* upon that cross-reference for its effectiveness. Unless you also want to repeal or nullify the unrelated provision, you will have to rewrite it so as to incorporate specifically what was formerly incorporated only by reference. This can involve real tactical difficulties, and even raise new substantive issues, requiring full-blown collateral policy decisions just as serious as the decisions involved in carrying out the main thrust.

Consider a fairly simple example—a bill to repeal the "earnings test" under the Social Security program. That test reduces or eliminates the benefits to which an individual is otherwise "entitled" if that individual still works and earns more than a specified amount. The earnings test has never been a popular provision, and before the law was amended in 2000 to restrict the earnings test to those who have not yet attained full retirement age, bills repealing the earnings test in its entirety made regular appearances during each new Congress. (The fact that the law was amended in 2000 has not stopped similar bills from being introduced since to further liberalize the earnings test.)

One might assume that simply repealing the earnings test outright would be a simple proposition. The earnings test occupies only a single subsection in the law (section 203(b) of the Social Security Act), and it takes only two lines to repeal it.

But cleaning up the inconsistencies in the law resulting from the elimination of that one subsection requires many pages of technical and conforming amendments—about forty in all in the typical version of the bill. Most of these amendments are purely technical (eliminating provisions that exist only for the administration of the earnings test, redesignating to close gaps, and striking old cross-references), but some have substantive policy overtones:

(1) Two of them repeal the "noncovered employment" test for individuals working outside the United States. This test is the overseas counterpart of the domestic earnings test, and its repeal is generally regarded as a purely conforming amendment. But the considerations and mechanics involved are quite different, and some sponsors might want it left alone (or rewritten, possibly with modifications, as an independent provision).

(2) One of them writes into the SSI law—another law altogether—a detailed definition of the critical term "wages", now handled in that law simply by a cross-reference to the definition that applies to the earnings test provision. This is just a matter of replacing the cross-reference with the verbatim language from the stricken provision; but that language (which is long and complicated, and contains some controversial items) will now become highly visible and attract attention, and the sponsor (or anyone else who notices it) may have second thoughts.

(3) One of them involves a provision in the Social Security law (section

223) that is substantively unrelated to the earnings test but depends for its effectiveness on the way that test (whose critical levels change annually under a cost-of-living formula) applies to the individual involved. Assuming that sponsors do not want to change the effect of that provision, drafters have usually substituted for the present cross-references to section 203(b) a new concept: the way in which the earnings test *would* have applied to the individual if it had not been repealed. This is cumbersome and would require difficult hypothetical calculations; it is done in desperation, and a better approach would have to be found if such a bill ever began to move through the legislative process.

(4) And one of them repeals the corresponding earnings test under the Railroad Retirement Act, which does not spell it out but just picks up and applies the Social Security earnings test by a cross-reference. There is probably no other way to get the ball rolling (and you cannot simply ignore the effect of the bill on the railroad retirement test), but the substantive and jurisdictional problems are obvious.

The lesson to be learned is that if you tamper with existing statutory language, expressly or impliedly, you will probably need technical and conforming amendments. And some of these amendments may themselves present substantive and tactical problems.

Technical and conforming amendments are discussed further in 12.11, which deals primarily with their proper placement in a bill. These amendments are discussed here only to emphasize that, although most of them are purely mechanical, those that are not deserve to be treated as a part of the policy development process. If you can identify the collateral questions early, your job will be much easier from start to finish.

5.5 Finding aids

Even if you become an expert at sensing collateral questions, some will still escape your attention; they seem to hide in unexpected places. But if the provision that raises a particular collateral question actually cites the provision with which you are involved—and it will do that as often as not—there is hope.

The United States Code on the website of the Office of the Law Revision Counsel (*http://uscode.house.gov*) has a search feature with which you can find all references to a particular provision in the U.S. Code (in both its positive-law and nonpositive-law titles). The *United States Code Annotated* (*USCA*, published by West Publishing) and the *United States Code Service* (*USCS*, published by LexisNexis), though lacking the imprimatur of the Law Revision Counsel of the U.S. Congress, are other sources.[5]

There may be a published table of cross-references to provisions of the major laws in the field in which you are working. If there is such a table in your field, or if you have made one of your own (see 3.6), it will refer you to all the places in the covered statutes where the provision you are working on is expressly cited, thereby identifying nearly all of the purely technical and conforming amendments you must make and most of the other collateral questions you need to address as well.

The value of the cross-reference tables in the U.S. Code is not limited to the quest for collateral questions, of course, but is greatest when they are used for that purpose. They will lead you to problems the existence of which neither you nor anyone else working with you has suspected, and their use will enhance your reputation for omniscience.

Notes

1 Subchapter II of chapter 5 of title 5, U.S.C. (5 U.S.C. 551 et seq.); 5 U.S.C. 701–706.

2 See, for example, chapters 6 (analysis of regulatory functions) and 8 (congressional review of agency rules) of title 5, U.S.C.

3 This is not always the case. In 2002, the bill establishing the Department of Homeland Security (the Homeland Security Act of 2002) was enacted into law at record speed. The bill transferred to the Department of Homeland Security functions of dozens of departments and agencies, creating countless collateral questions that time prevented answering. In the case of the Secretary of the Treasury, any function vested in the Secretary under the Tariff Act of 1930 (a long, complex statute relating to customs and imports of goods into the United

States) was split; the revenue responsibilities remained with Treasury, and responsibilities involving protection of the borders went to Homeland Security. The result is that although the Tariff Act of 1930 still states that the Secretary of the Treasury performs all the functions under that Act, in reality the Secretary of the Treasury does not. The technical and conforming amendments in this case would require going through each of the hundreds of references to the "Secretary of the Treasury" and deciding how to express the split, depending on the particular function involved—a gargantuan task.

4 See footnote 3 and the discussion of Public Law 108-419 in 4.3.

5 *USCA* and the *USCS* are also useful for their notes of court decisions that construe each section of the law, as well as provisions of the Code of Federal Regulations that implement that section and law review articles and other legal treatises that discuss it.

6. Organizing the Bill

6.1 In general

The basic principle governing the arrangement of a bill can be stated very simply (paraphrasing *HOLC*, pages 1–2): every bill should be consciously organized, usually the most important thoughts should come first, and the organization should help convey the sponsor's message.

Hirsch (page 21) says pretty much the same thing, in an equally down-to-earth fashion:

> ...you should divide your bill into bite-size chunks, and ...arrange those chunks in some digestible way [with the aim of creating] a framework that others can readily understand, remember, and retrace, and that future drafters can conveniently amend.

In most cases, you should organize the bill in a hierarchical arrangement so that the location of the various items shows their interrelationships and relative importance. However, there are situations in which somewhat different considerations may apply:

(1) In a bill involving a sequence of actions and reactions between the administrators and the persons covered by the bill, a temporal arrangement—describing the relevant events in the exact order in which they are to occur—will sometimes make the connections clearer than a hierarchical arrangement.

(2) In some amendatory bills, following the arrangement of the law being amended rather than the hierarchical principle will serve the reader better. This is discussed in detail in 17.1.

6.2 Organizing a bill substantively

The drafter's principal objective in organizing a bill is to ensure that the final product will be as clear and accurate as possible, with the relationship between the main and subordinate ideas made readily apparent, and that the subjects to be covered are arranged so that they can be found, understood, and referred to with the least possible effort.

No one arrangement is ideal; what is best in one situation may not be the best in another. You should of course keep the bill's structure as simple as possible, arrange its elements in a logical sequence, and follow the principle of "modular construction" (see 6.5); but you must also make sure that you are presenting the ideas in a way that effectively reaches the intended audience.

Provisions relating primarily to the conduct, rights, privileges, or duties of the persons substantively affected by the bill should be arranged from the viewpoint of those persons; while provisions relating primarily to administration should be arranged from the viewpoint of the prospective administrators. You should always identify the audience in your own mind before you start drafting.

A number of legislative drafting manuals specify an optimum arrangement of sections that a drafter should normally follow in structuring a bill, based on the nature, importance, and permanence of the sections that might typically be included. This approach can be moderately instructive and serve as a useful guide in your early discussions with the policymaker (see 4.6 for some examples of the kinds of questions it might lead you to ask). But it should be taken with a grain of salt and used as a safe starting point only, since different bills impose different demands.

Hirsch (page 23), for example, suggests the following as a possible model for most freestanding bills:

1. Short title
2. Findings and purpose
3. Definitions
4. Principal operating provisions, which also specify the bill's scope
5. Subordinate operative provisions
6. Prohibited acts (and related exclusions from prohibited acts)
7. Sanctions for commission of prohibited acts or other offenses
8. General administrative authorities and procedural rules
9. Jurisdiction of courts
10. Relationship of the [A]ct to other statutes
11. Administering agency's report to Congress
12. Appropriations authorization
13. Savings provisions
14. Effective dates

SOLC[1] (page 5) provides a similar breakdown, but points out that this organization template applies only to a bill addressing a single subject, which is a requirement in most States (see the discussion of "senior components" in 20.4 for organization of bills covering multiple subjects):

SECTION 1. SHORT TITLE; TABLE OF CONTENTS; REFERENCES.

SEC. 2. FINDINGS AND PURPOSES.

SEC. 3. DEFINITIONS.

SEC. 4. BASIC PROGRAM AUTHORITY OR ESTABLISHMENT OF OFFICE.

SEC. 5. ADMINISTRATIVE PROVISIONS.

SEC. 6. REGULATIONS.

SEC. 7. CIVIL PENALTIES.

SEC. 8. CRIMINAL PENALTIES.

SEC. 9. REPORTS.

SEC. 10. AUTHORIZATION OF APPROPRIATIONS.

SEC. 11. CONFORMING AMENDMENTS.

SEC. 12. TRANSITION RULES AND SAVINGS PROVISIONS.

SEC. 13. EFFECTIVE DATE (AND TERMINATION OF AUTHORITY, IF APPLICABLE).

HOLC (page 17) reaches a somewhat similar result from a somewhat different direction, stating that, before choosing an organization for a draft, the drafter should determine to what extent it could appropriately fit into the following arrangement:

(1) *General rule.*—State the main message.

(2) *Exceptions.*—Describe the persons or things to which the main message does not apply.

(3) *Special Rules.*—Describe the persons or things—

(A) to which the main message applies in a different way; or

(B) for which there is a different message.

(4) *Transitional rules.*—Describe the rules that are transitional and either are especially important or will have effect for a relatively long period of time.

(5) *Other provisions.*—Any other matters.

(6) *Definitions.*—

(7) *Effective date.*—

Note that paragraph (5) (Other provisions) would include whatever administrative provisions, technical and conforming amendments, and collateral provisions that may be necessary or appropriate to clean up any inconsistencies in the law brought about by implementing the main message.

Dickerson (page 90) adds several helpful rules of thumb:

(1) General provisions normally come before special provisions.

(2) More important provisions normally come before less important provisions.

(3) More frequently used provisions normally come before less frequently used provisions.

(4) Permanent provisions normally come before temporary provisions.

(5) Technical and "housekeeping" provisions normally come at the end.

There are of course many cases in which one or more of these rules of thumb should be ignored; common sense is your best guide. If the bill has a short title or table of contents, or contains a statement of findings and purpose, that provision will normally appear at the very beginning of the bill (ahead of the key operating provisions). *HOLC*'s definitions appear at the end, but, particularly in a longer bill, placing a section on definitions (or a highly visible cross-reference to it) at the beginning of the bill avoids confusion in the audience.

In addition, the category into which a particular type of provision falls may not always be the same; an authorization of appropriations, for example, is treated as a "housekeeping" provision in most bills (since it simply provides funding and otherwise has no substantive content), but would have the flavor of a key operating provision (and should appear up front) in a grant-in-aid bill whose main purpose is to make funds available to meet a particular need and then allocate them among applicants who qualify.

All four of the cited sources emphasize the need to subordinate the less important provisions. If those provisions are isolated and minor, of course, there is no architectural problem; they can be woven into the main body of the key operating provisions as separate sentences or parenthetical phrases. Even when they are major, if there are only a few of them (one or two short exceptions to the general rule, for example), they can often be handled the same way.

Regardless of the nature of the subordinate provisions, however, if there are many of them, they will usually be easier to handle if they are collected in separate sections or subsections, after the key operating provisions (with appropriate headings if stylistic considerations permit). So long as the relationship between the key operating provisions and the subordinate provisions is made clear, placing the subordinate provisions in a separate section also promotes readability, especially if they are long or complicated.

There is only one architectural rule that is always applicable: Give prominence to the more important thoughts, and downplay the others, but keep their relationship clear.

6.3 Structuring a bill stylistically

When you are drafting a straightforward bill of limited scope, structuring it stylistically is not a problem. It will consist of a relatively few numbered sections, appropriately subdivided when necessary, and the correct arrangement will be obvious. (Chapter 20 discusses how to structure a bill at the Federal level and provides guidance for structuring a bill at the State level.)

If you are drafting a bill that contains provisions that are logically separate or that addresses several different subjects, however, you need to make some choices and do some advance planning. Should the bill be divided into titles, parts, or chapters in order to provide logical places for different subjects or for related groups of provisions? Is it long or complicated enough to justify dividing those titles, parts, or chapters into subtitles, subparts, or subchapters (for the same reason)? Are there political or tactical reasons for keeping some of the matters involved totally separate from the others?

Again, there is no single correct answer. Your objective should be to use a stylistic arrangement (as well as specific stylistic devices such as section headings) to help readers find and distinguish the substantive provisions they are interested in, just as your substantive organization (discussed in 6.2) is designed to help readers understand the content and relationship of those provisions once they are found. Whatever stylistic structure will best accomplish that result is the one to use.

6.4 A look at structural problems generally

Dickerson (pages 81–91)—crisscrossing the line between substantive and stylistic structure—divides the problems that a drafter faces in organizing a bill into three kinds—division, classification, and sequence. Each of these raises its own set of questions:

1. *Problems of division.* Into what main segments or parts should the bill be divided? Should this division be based on relative importance, chronology of events, or other considerations? Should the bill simply consist of sections, or should it be broken down into titles and then further broken down (into subtitles or parts and then sections, or just into sections alone)?

   A subsidiary breakdown of the same kind may be needed in some or all of the main segments of the bill (depending on the breadth of the categories represented by those segments). A section of a bill is broken down into subsections and paragraphs for the same reasons and subject to the same logical considerations as those that apply in breaking down the bill as a whole into titles, subtitles, parts, and sections.

Thus, if a section's central theme is most readily understood when analyzed into its component themes, it should be divided into subsections, each developing a single idea that is readily distinguishable from (and ordinarily not logically subordinate to) the ideas developed in the other subsections; and subsections can be further subdivided in the same fashion.

SOLC (page 8) more formalistically states that a section "contains some or all of the following provisions and is organized as follows:"

SEC. 101. SECTION HEADING.

(a) DEFINITIONS.—

(b) GENERAL RULE.—

(c) EXCEPTIONS.—

(d) SPECIAL RULES.—

(e) TRANSITION RULES.—

(f) EFFECTIVE DATE.—

(2) *Problems of classification.* Once you have decided how to divide the bill, you must decide which pieces will go in each of the segments resulting from that division. For the most part this is easy—the nature of the segment will normally determine its contents. But in some cases (where the divisions are very broad or involve subjects that fall partly under one heading and partly under another, or where there are recurring situations that differ just enough to prevent their treatment at a single point in the bill) your ingenuity may be taxed.

(3) *Problems of sequence.* The remaining problem is to arrange the segments or elements of the bill (at every level) in the most logical sequence. In general, the sequence should enable a reader to understand the bill by reading its provisions consecutively, like chapters in a novel. But there is no one right way to do it; as stressed earlier, the way that most effectively communicates the sponsor's message is always the best way.

6.5 Modular construction

Good drafting calls for "modular construction" (*Hirsch*'s term, pages 11–13), which means that each component and subdivision of the bill should be dedicated to a single subject and contain (or at least refer to) all of the substantive provisions that readers will need to understand that subject. Reasonable drafters might differ about the precise modules into which any particular bill should be divided, but in the interest of both clarity and readability and for tactical reasons as well (see below), the modular principle should always be at the center of your architectural planning.

The basic division of any statute is of course the numbered section. Ideally, each section should be devoted to a topic that is conceptually distinct from the topic of any other section; and it should always be possible for the reader to tell which sections deal with which subjects. In order to achieve this objective you should have a logical plan for allocating material among sections and be consistent in applying it.

Normally you should strive to create sections each of which deals comprehensively with a single idea or topic, making it possible for the reader to find within that section not only the basic idea but also every rule that is logically subordinate to it.

It is acceptable, however, to create sections that contain ideas or topics logically subordinate to those contained in other sections, so long as the logical hierarchy of those ideas or topics (or the relationship of the sections involved) is clear; remember that, if two integral ideas are not combined, there is always a risk that one of them when read alone will imply that the other does not exist. Again, it must always be possible for the reader to identify what each section does and to understand its relationship to the rest of the bill.

Theoretically your efforts to get the sponsor's message across clearly to the intended audience will be best served by following two basic principles:

(1) For coherence, combine any ideas that are closely related or integral to each other.

(2) For clarity, separate any ideas that are inherently distinct.

Unfortunately, the two principles often push the drafter in opposite directions, sometimes with strange results. Many existing statutes embody a mixture of both principles that can only be explained by the drafter's lack of time for planning and organization (or by the fact that different drafters, at different times, resolve the problem in different ways).

However, knowing when to separate ideas and when to combine them in a single section involves the balancing of intangibles in ways that no rules can cover. Suffice it to say that many times a set of related provisions could sensibly be combined in a single section or could just as sensibly be placed in separate sections. You can only rely on your experience and best judgment in determining which is best.

In addition to promoting understanding, modular construction has definite tactical advantages. It aids a bill's consideration in committee or subcommittee, because bills are normally read for amendment section-by-section and the Members and staff who are considering a bill are bound to have difficulty following (and dealing with) a single concept that is spread among widely scattered provisions. It also simplifies your task if and when the committee or subcommittee chooses to reject some of the bill's provisions, since the removal of one module from a bill does not usually require much redrafting of the remainder.

In any case, grouping the provisions of a bill by subject (however you choose to define "subject") is essential. It makes their purpose clear, helps to distinguish the main ideas from the subordinate, and promotes reader comprehension.

6.6 Split provisions and split amendments

A common violation of some of these rules is the so-called "split provision" or "split amendment", which is a provision or amendment that in effect has two parts. One section makes an apparently unequivocal statement (that is, it appears on its face to be unconditionally effective), but another section (as the reader discovers much later in the bill) conditions the effectiveness of that statement on satisfying some previously undisclosed requirement.

The inspiration for a split provision is usually the drafter's desire to avoid cluttering up the key operating provisions of a bill with exceptions and special rules that may be distracting to the reader (a subject discussed in detail in 12.3). But in avoiding this clutter the drafter risks misleading the reader, since the key operating provisions themselves then paint only a partial picture.

You should always include a specific cross-reference to the later provision in the earlier one in order to avoid this confusion, if possible, unless the context makes the situation clear without one.[2] However, there is at least one common type of split provision that does *not* call for a cross-reference; it involves effective dates and deserves special mention.

If a bill amends a provision of existing law, the effective date for that amendment should not be included in the amended language, but in a separate freestanding provision of the bill. Some may object to the practice of placing the effective dates in amendatory bills outside of the substantive provisions to which they relate, because they feel that this conceals important information from future readers of those provisions and that every substantive provision in the law should reveal on its face exactly when and how it originally became effective. This is nonsense.

In the first place, most major laws are amended frequently, and provisions that are now merely hard to read would become incomprehensible if they contained a statement of when each of the various pieces became effective. Section 210(a) of the Social Security Act, which consists of a single 40-page sentence with more than 100 tabulated subdivisions, was enacted in 1950 and is now largely the product of the several hundred separate amendments that have been made to it since then; a 40-page sentence that is only barely comprehensible is bad enough, but if it had to include 300 different effective-date provisions (many of which are far from simple) it would become a 500-page sentence largely composed of deadwood, making the present provision a lost cause.

In the second place, most effective-date provisions become immaterial to anyone but a historian shortly after the substantive provisions to which they relate go into operation. If an individual is a historian, or is involved in one of those relatively rare cases where the effective date of an old law actually retains its significance, it is not unreasonable to ask that individual to do a little research. The United States Code, in the notes following every section, provides the dates and substance of every amendment that has been made to that section. And up-to-date tables of the United States Code, available online, show every section that has been affected by the most recent enactments.

Finally, although most major laws set forth their effective dates explicitly, some do it without mentioning any specific date ("This Act shall take effect 60 days after its date of enactment", for example), and some do not contain any explicit effective-date provision at all (relying on the "default" effective date—see chapter 26). It is hard to imagine how the critics would propose to handle this.

Effective-date split amendments are one case where balancing avoidance of clutter against full information to subsequent readers is easy, especially in major bills that contain numerous effective dates and involve laws that are frequently amended; avoiding clutter wins. Keeping substantive provisions free of effective-date language that will quickly become executed (and of cross-references to effective-date provisions as well) is one of the best ways—and sometimes the only way—to keep them both clear and readable.

6.7 The virtues and self-evidence of good architecture

There is some overkill in the preceding text. For relatively short and simple bills you can usually solve the organizational problems in your head; a bill that does just one specific thing and is not part of a broader legislative tapestry can often be written as a single section, requiring at most a few technical or conforming amendments and perhaps an explicit effective date.

And for long and complicated bills, such as omnibus and "reform" bills and bills establishing broad new programs, the right organization will almost force itself upon you.

Most of the bills that you are likely to face in your everyday work, however, fall somewhere between the two extremes, and it is for them that this chapter is written. They are of relatively limited scope (like the first category), but are sufficiently complex or multifaceted (like the modular segments of broader bills in the second) to require that you give conscious thought to their architecture.

As stressed earlier, good organization and arrangement (though it may appear on the surface to be primarily a technical or mechanical matter) can produce real substantive benefits. And it will enable your reader (whether a judge interpreting the law or a high-school civics student on assignment) to understand clearly and quickly what the bill does and the relative importance of its various provisions.

But its most tangible contribution may well lie in what it will do to ease your mechanical burdens as you work your way through the writing process. A concrete plan of organization and arrangement made in advance is indispensable when the bill is complicated or massive. It forces you to think your problems through, and allows you to subdivide the project into smaller and more manageable parts that can be worked on separately. It is one of the most important devices for easing the drafter's burden; and if it is done early it also saves time, since readjustments in basic arrangement become more difficult later and the risk of error increases.

In many ways the organization of a bill is like the organization of a novel; if the reader can get into the context early and follow the plot through to the end, it is a success. Remember that your main objective in organizing a bill is to promote clarity, accuracy, and comprehension. If the bill presents no apparent structural problems, do not try to invent any, but always stop and think about it first. And if that leads you to believe that there may be organizational questions after all, do not proceed until you have taken steps to resolve them.

Notes

1. *Legislative Drafting Manual,* Office of the Legislative Counsel, United States Senate, 2017.

2 Note, again, *SOLC*'s structure of a section in 6.4 that includes the exceptions and special rules within the same section.

PART III
WRITING THE BILL: PRELIMINARY CONSIDERATIONS

7. The Mechanics of Good Writing

7.1 In general

When you have learned all that you need to know about the sponsor's problem and its intended solution and have decided how to handle it—matters that were dealt with in part II—all that remains is to convert the intended solution into legislative language that will do the job effectively.

Many of the tools that you will need for this purpose are specialized tools, in that they are unique to legislative writing; but the most basic among them is not specialized at all—it is simply the ability to write clearly and effectively, without regard to the kind of writing involved. And it goes without saying that good legislative language, like all good writing, should be mechanically sound in grammar, punctuation, and word usage—subjects discussed fully in chapters 21 and 22.

Good writing in and of itself promotes the fundamental virtues of clarity and readability, of course; but it has another important legislative virtue as well. The drafter's audience will always include those who really care about the finer points of good prose composition—the technicalities of proper punctuation, grammar, word usage, sentence structure, and conceptual arrangement—and those people will be bothered if they find anything that does not measure up. Nothing threatens your credibility as much as the appearance of illiteracy, but errors in punctuation, grammar, and sentence structure can also have legal significance if they create ambiguity.

Innumerable books and articles have been and continue to be published on the subject of good writing. They range from simple grammar textbooks to profound philosophical inquiries about human communication. Most of what they have to say is as valid for legislative drafting as it is for other forms of writing. H. W. Fowler, long considered a leading authority on English usage, might have been addressing today's legislative drafters some 95 years ago, for example, when he offered what recent commentators have described as his five basic commandments—prefer the familiar word to the farfetched, the concrete to the abstract, the simple word to the circumlocution, the short word to the long, and the Saxon word to the Romance—and then added that circumstances may sometime justify exceptions.[1]

Many of these books and articles, however, give advice not appropriate for legislative drafters. They devote considerable attention to such things as "how to vary sentence structure for emphasis and variety", "how to amuse and arouse curiosity", and "how to bring the reader up short"—bits of advice that may be useful in fiction but not in legislative drafting. There is certainly nothing wrong with emphasis and even occasional amusement in statutes; but from a drafter's point of view variety is incompatible with consistency (see 4.4), and language that arouses curiosity or results in sudden surprises for the reader strongly implies either lack of clarity or poor organization, or both.

This book emphasizes the part that the principles of good writing play in good legislative drafting and in the development of good drafting habits. What follows is a discussion of a few of the fundamental principles from the drafter's point of view.

7.2 Using everyday English

Since any law is intended to communicate a message to its readers, it ought to be written in language familiar to those readers. It is not always possible to write a bill in a way that will be readily understood by everyone—complicated ideas and highly technical concepts cannot easily be expressed in language that the average person can grasp quickly—but you should always make the effort. You should use everyday English (American style) whenever you can.

Drafters generally agree in theory that conversational language is best, and that there is no legitimate reason why the structure of sentences in statutes should be any different from the structure of everyday speech. This makes sense, but only so long as the sentence involved is equal to the task of expressing its idea with the clarity and precision required for legislative purposes.

Individual words, like sentences, should ideally be part of everyone's everyday vocabulary; you should generally choose the simpler word over a synonym that is unfamiliar, awkward, or less well understood. Do so with caution, however, since many words that are usually thought of as synonyms are not or (because of their derivation or past usage) convey a different shade of meaning. Choose *dog* over *canine*, but only if you want to exclude foxes and wolves; choose *cat* over *feline*, and if you want to exclude lions and tigers add the adjective *domestic* (although even then you may be covering an occasional pet ocelot). Choose the word that is most accurate. Use the dictionary, and get feedback from colleagues; what a word means to you in a particular context may not be what it means to someone else.

Old laws were usually written in an obscure, stilted, ponderous, and even pompous style, but what was right for Benjamin Franklin or Alexander Hamilton is not necessarily appropriate today (indeed, a few visionaries—notably Thomas Jefferson—did not think it was appropriate then).

While it is undoubtedly true that over time the drafter's use of archaic words and phrases has lessened, archaic forms are still with us, especially among lawyers, and every drafter should be on guard against them.

The determination of when and how to back away from archaic forms is not altogether clear-cut, however. Most of them are totally gratuitous; you would never use them in everyday speech, and should never use them in legislation either. Others (although you might not use them in everyday speech) have redeeming virtues because they represent a form of verbal shorthand that aids readability, and the need for them (or their less archaic equivalent) actually arises frequently. In the middle are a number of forms that you should avoid most of the time but which you should feel free to use selectively when special circumstances exist. Chapter 22 attempts to sort them out.

In addition to specific terms and expressions, there are archaic usages of all kinds to watch out for. Their fault lies mainly in their verbosity. For example, Federal laws in the past would typically vest a function in an official by saying that the official "is hereby granted authority, and is hereby directed, to [take some specified action]"; today, no drafter should even consider saying anything but that the official "shall [take that action]". Drafting legislation is not a contest to see who can use the most words to express a simple idea.

You should avoid Latin terms and expressions except when it is necessary to use them in referring to a document, judicial procedure, or legal concept that is known primarily by its Latin name. *HOLC* (page 5) observes that even "[t]hose few people who have had Latin in school can't agree on pronunciation".

To sum up, use a modern term or expression if at all possible. However, if an archaic form suits your purpose exactly and does not sound stilted or awkward to you, use it without apology. Remember that achieving the desired substantive result is always more important than stylistic perfection.

7.3 Short sentences, pro and con

It is a well-known principle of good writing (and good legislative drafting) that long sentences should be avoided. Using two or three sentences to make a point is better English (other things being equal) than using one long and possibly convoluted one.

In declaring that most compound sentences should be broken down into two or more separate sentences, *HOLC* (page 5) claims that a "recent listener survey" found "[t]he median listener [or reader] tunes out after the 12th word", and that the offending sentence often conceals one or more unresolved policy issues or contains both a general rule and one or more exceptions or special rules that would be better handled separately.

For the most part this is the case, and unless the context makes it impossible your sentences should be as short and crisp as you can make them without interfering with the flow of your thoughts.

However, tight compression of language in separated compartments does not always promote the supreme objective of maximum clarity, and *HOLC's* median listener may not be part of your intended audience; conciseness does not ensure clarity, and sometimes prevents it. You should condense your sentences only to clarify the meaning and help your reader's understanding. Ambiguity may often be reduced and both clarity and readability increased by using a longer compound sentence instead of two or three short sentences when the relationship of the ideas involved is particularly elusive or complex, and might be more readily grasped by a reader or a court if those ideas are contained within a single sentence where each "and", "or", "except that", and "subject to" can be expressed rather than only implied.

Consider for example the following hypothetical (and deliberately simplified) provision:

> The individual shall be paid a benefit computed under subsection (c). If the individual is over 55 years of age the benefit shall be computed under subsection (d) instead. The benefit shall be reduced by 20 percent if the individual is not enrolled in an approved rehabilitation program. A benefit shall not be paid while the individual is outside the United States.

The four short sentences do paint the picture, but only when read together; three of them would be incorrect or at least misleading if taken out of context. Since it is a single concept (benefit entitlement) that is being expressed, a single sentence approach might be better—no less readable and definitely clearer, especially if the provision were surrounded by other (unrelated) sentences:

> The individual shall be paid a benefit computed under subsection (c) (or under subsection (d) if the individual is over 55 years of age); except that the benefit so computed shall be reduced by 20 percent if the individual is not enrolled in an approved rehabilitation program, and a benefit shall not be paid while the individual is outside the United States. [2]

(See chapter 23 for some special ways of handling unavoidably long sentences, and 9.5 for an example that indicates some of the considerations pro and con.)

Note that the same principles apply to subsections and paragraphs, each of which ideally should also be short and limited in scope but some of which (especially in amendatory cases) may need to be longer and more compound in order to fit properly within the bill, or within existing law, at the place where the sense of that bill or law requires it. Any drafter writing an amendment to section 210(a) of the Social Security Act (the 40-page sentence cited in chapter 6 as an example of nonstop writing) really has no choice but to perpetuate the flaws and make the situation even worse, simply because it is unavoidable mechanically.

The basic rule is to keep each of the various elements of your bill as short, simple, and readable as you can. You should not, however, carry it to such an extreme that you run the risk of missing your substantive target; clarity and precision are more important.

7.4 Directness and economy of expression

Novelists strive for tone, mood, and flavor in their writing, and use as many words as may be necessary to achieve them; after all, their primary aim is to involve the emotions of the reader. The drafter's primary interest is very different; it is to produce language that will achieve the prescribed statutory objective fully and accurately while avoiding language that may involve the emotions and consequently have different flavors for different readers.[3]

Flamboyance and wordiness may serve the novelist's purposes well, but directness and economy of expression are the hallmarks of good legislative writing. As *Dickerson* (page 44) states, "Every word should pay its own way." A few briefly stated principles should suffice to illustrate the point (which will be discussed in more detail later):

(1) Always try to express your ideas positively rather than negatively, use the active rather than the passive voice, and avoid unnecessary modifying adjectives or explanatory phrases. An approach that is direct and untrammeled by editorial comment not only has more "punch"—it is less ambiguous.

(2) Always go straight to the point. And after you have made that point, leave it alone; once is enough. Circumlocution too often suggests that a point intended to be unequivocal is in fact subject to qualifications or exceptions; while redundancy, instead of emphasizing a point, usually diminishes its force. And most important of all, a court reviewing a statute will look for meaning in all the words used (see chapter 28).

(3) When you have found the right word to express a particular idea or concept in a bill, use that word and only that word every time you express the idea or concept again, even at the cost of drabness in style. As *HOLC* (page 6) puts it, "[y]our English teacher may be disappointed, but the courts and others who are straining to find your meaning will bless you".

The use of synonyms to express the same idea or concept within the same provision—a practice known as "elegant variation"[4]—should be avoided. Again, a reviewing court will seek to assign a distinct meaning to each word used, and the results may not be what the sponsor intended. "In the world of [statutory] construction, there is no elegant variation, only substantive variation."[5] And when a particular word has two different meanings and is used both ways in the same provision—a practice known as "utraquistic subterfuge"[6]—it is even worse, since the ambiguity is actually built into the words themselves.

7.5 Organization that gets the message across

It is not necessary in writing legislative language to "capture the attention of the reader", since no one reads statutes for recreational purposes. But it is necessary to get the substantive message across, and to organize the legislative product in such a way as to make that message clear and help ensure that all readers will extract it in the same way.

Chapter 6 addressed this point in detail in connection with the overall organization and arrangement of a bill and its component parts. It is mentioned again here only to emphasize that these considerations are a particularly important part of good legislative writing. The thoughts you express must flow in the same rational way for all readers.

Thus, if concept A is dependent on concept B or does not make sense without a prior awareness of concept B, the reader cannot be expected to understand it if it appears in the text before concept B has been addressed. This can cause problems when concept A is more fundamental and should logically be addressed first; but the legislative drafter (unlike the novelist) can easily handle them by simply including language in concept A that warns the reader of concept B and directs attention to it—for example, "(as described in section ____ [the place where concept B appears])", "(subject to section ____)", or "(unless section _____ applies)". The use of cross-references for this purpose is more fully discussed in 22.4.

7.6 Stylistic consensus and consistency

The importance of stylistic consensus. Unfortunately (see *HOLC*, page 13), good legislative drafting cannot be reduced to a cookbook-style process in which items from lists of standard ingredients are combined to produce a bill. To believe otherwise creates a false sense of security, because the diversity of individual drafters makes a complete consensus on structure and style impossible.

Although you should use the drafting conventions described in this book as extensively as possible, you should not feel compelled to do so in circumstances where (because of the lack of stylistic consensus among the various drafters working on the project) insistence on the use of a particular convention would interfere with the drafting process or lead to an inconsistent legislative product.

Nevertheless, a general agreement on as many of these conventions as possible is one of your most valuable assets as a drafter simply because (even when the consensus is not complete) it makes the all-important quality of consistency easier to achieve.

The importance of stylistic consistency. The importance of substantive consistency in your drafting has already been stressed and will be mentioned again; but the specific virtues of stylistic consistency as an aid to the everyday drafter deserve special mention. (The following discussion paraphrases *HOLC*'s treatment of the subject [pages 9–11]).

The consideration and enactment of legislation occurs in the midst of constantly changing circumstances and demands, indeed often in the midst of chaos. Style (despite variations from one legislative setting to another) should be one of the steady, predictable elements that drafters can use to reduce that chaos to order, and not one of the fluctuating factors that contribute to it.

A well-defined and uniformly applied style will make life easier in many ways for the drafter, for the legislators who will have to deal with the legislative language, and for subsequent administrators and interpreters of that language. *HOLC* tells why:

(1) Stylistic consistency provides a stable framework for analyzing the legal and other problems of a legislative proposal and for organizing and expressing the proposal rationally, and thereby promotes consistency of substantive expression.

(2) It permits the best use of the drafter's time by permitting two or more drafters working on the same job to concentrate on substantive

matters rather than on conforming style, and by permitting one drafter to substitute for another (or draft from another's work product) without stylistic complications.

(3) It helps to communicate the sponsor's message by enabling the reader to concentrate on that message without being distracted by mere stylistic differences, particularly where they might be thought to have legal significance (under the doctrine that variations within a law are designed to have substantive meaning).

(4) And it satisfies people's need for (or expectation of) orderliness in the expression of ideas.

Courts pay close attention to the stylistic aspects of a law in their quest for its true meaning; but very few of them seem to understand a fundamental feature of the legislative process—the fact that stylistic inconsistencies in a law result from time pressures, tactical limitations, and the participation of different drafters much more often than they do from congressional intent or poor drafting.

However, a bill that deals with one subject and contains noticeable variations in structure or style, whatever the reason, cannot be called an example of good legislative writing even if it meets every other test. Such variations not only interfere with the communication of the sponsor's message; they give ammunition to people who are looking for grounds to misinterpret the language or to criticize the product or process involved.

It must be noted, however, that the ever increasing tendency at the Federal level to enact massive bills in very short time frames, such as a budget reconciliation bill (to which every committee must contribute cost-saving provisions) or an omnibus appropriations bill that incorporates not only many separate appropriations bills but substantive provisions as well from different sources, inevitably results in many inconsistencies among the different parts, and the drafters involved in the different pieces cannot be faulted for those inconsistencies.

The importance of having a list of rules. In any form of writing there are often two or more correct ways of expressing an idea or relationship. In most forms they can be used interchangeably, but in legislative drafting the need for internal consistency requires that one of them be routinely favored.

For this reason, every drafter ought to have a list of specific stylistic rules—stylistic "dos and don'ts"—in hand or in mind. Part VI (chapters 19 through 27) is intended to provide this list.

Very few of the items on that list are unequivocal mandates or prohibitions—most of them merely express with varying degrees of forcefulness a preference for one usage or form over another. However, you are urged to take the list seriously, both because it incorporates what most professional drafters would consider the best choices and because its uniform application will help you avoid the unpleasant necessity of making stylistic decisions on a case-by-case basis as you draft.

Notes

1 Paraphrased from H. W. Fowler, *A Dictionary of Modern English Usage* (Oxford: Clarendon Press; London: H. Milford, 1926); H. W. Fowler, *A Dictionary of Modern English Usage*, 2nd ed., rev. Sir Ernest Gowers (New York: Oxford University Press, 1965).

2 Applying the principles in chapter 33, this sentence, written in modified revenue style, would look something like the following:

SEC.____. ENTITLEMENT TO BENEFITS.

(a) Computation and Eligibility for Benefit.—

(1) Computation in general.—Subject to paragraphs (2) and (3), the individual shall be paid a benefit computed—

(A) under subsection (c); or

(B) under subsection (d), if the individual is over 55 years of age.

(2) Reduction of benefit.—A benefit computed under paragraph (1) shall be reduced by 20 percent if the individual is not enrolled in an approved rehabilitation program.

(3) Ineligibility for benefit.—A benefit [shall] [may] not be paid to an individual under this section while the individual is outside the United States.

3 It may be the sponsor's objective, nonetheless, to choose one word over another because of its connotation and the desire to evoke a certain emotion in the reader. Conversely, the sponsor may direct the drafter not to use a certain word, even if

it achieves the most clarity, because of its connotation; in such a situation it is the drafter's job to come up with a suitable alternative.

4 Fowler, *Dictionary on Modern English Usage*, 2nd ed., 148.

5 Robert J. Martineau and Michael B. Salerno, *Legal, Legislative, and Rule Drafting in Plain English* (St. Paul, Minn.: Thomson/West, 2005), 60.

6 Charles K. Ogden and Ivor A. Richards, *The Meaning of Meaning: A Study of the Influence of Language upon Thought and of the Science of Symbolism*, 8th ed. (New York: Harcourt Brace, 1946), 134.

8. The Roman Rule, Modified

8.1 The rule defined

The Roman rule ("When in Rome, do as the Romans do") has been a rule of thumb encouraging every drafter working in a particular setting to use the traditional form and style of that setting—the form and style that is most familiar and acceptable to the people who will be reading, considering, and acting on the drafter's legislative product as well as to those who will have to live with it after its enactment.

This book lays down a multitude of rules and principles governing legislative form and style and urges their adoption because they promote clarity or have other identifiable virtues; but in fact legislative forms and styles differ from jurisdiction to jurisdiction. A drafter for whom one form or style is second nature will often feel like a stranger in a foreign land when faced with another, and the Roman rule (in such a situation) reminds the drafter to learn the language. Doing so will almost always expedite the drafter's work, since it guarantees that the legislators, staffs, and administrators involved will pay no attention to how the bill is drafted and can proceed without distraction to what it does.

The fundamental thought that the Roman rule expresses is that a bill that amends an existing law, or is intended to become a part of the existing body of laws in any statutory field, should fit within that law or that field—it should look like it belongs there. The purpose of the bill is to implant something new in the permanent law, and the consistency of the permanent law (once the bill is enacted) is far more important than the transitory vehicle—the bill itself—by which the implantation is effected.

Thus, for a bill making changes in the crop-subsidy laws, the Roman rule might be paraphrased to read, "When drafting a bill to amend a crop-subsidy law, do as the drafters of the existing crop-subsidy laws have done."

The Roman rule has two subrules—one for the setting in which the drafter's product will be considered and enacted (for example, in committee and on the floor of the legislative body) and one for the setting in which it will be carried out and administered (under the law being amended).

There would be no occasion for a Roman rule if all legislative forms and styles were the same or were equally good. The application of the rule becomes an issue when you believe that one form and style is significantly better for the purposes involved than the one the rule asks you to adopt.

Certainly if you are in a jurisdiction that mandates (by law) that all legislation be drafted in a prescribed format, you lack the discretion to stray from the Roman rule. Otherwise, the Roman rule should give way, to the greatest extent possible, to the goal of achieving maximum clarity.

As reflected in their manuals, both *HOLC* and *SOLC* have adopted a drafting style that encourages maximum clarity by applying good drafting principles in an organizational structure that uses headings for subdivisions of a section (described in 33.4 and 33.5 as "revenue" and "modified revenue" style; referred to in this chapter as "office" style) over the "traditional" style (the predominant style in use before 1990; see 33.2). The use of headings is more likely to ensure that each subdivision deals with a single subject and makes the organization of the bill much easier to ascertain.

The office style is expected to be applied to all freestanding legislation. In the case of amendatory legislation, the question then becomes, when amending a statute originally drafted in another style, do you continue that style or use the style that promotes more clarity? As stated in *HOLC* (page 12):

> It is a goal that, in time, all Federal law will be in office style. It is also a goal that uniformity of style be maintained within a statute, at least as required for consistency of interpretation. In amending existing law, attorneys should pursue both goals. That is, the attorney should look for appropriate opportunities to apply the office style in ways that do not cause the goals to conflict.

HOLC (page 12) goes on to say that the attorney might consider such things as (1) how much does office style vary from the style of the amended law, and would conforming and technical amendments to the existing provisions also be justified; (2) how separate would the new matter be from the existing matter, both structurally and functionally; and (3) what impacts will using the office style have on the legislative process.

Simply stated, the laws on the books will never achieve greater clarity if the Roman rule is always applied. The exercise becomes how to avoid confusion and internal inconsistency in attempting to apply a clearer style to an existing law.

The answer is to apply the Roman rule selectively.

There are some obvious cases for the literal application of the Roman rule. If, for example, you are to amend a provision of law that has unusual designations of its subdivisions (for example, using letters instead of numbers for paragraphs), you would obviously conform any addition to these subdivisions by using the same designations (unless you were to change all the designations—see 8.5). This has to do with the stylistic framework within which particular legislative ideas are presented.

In addition, the Constitution is a document that is sacrosanct. In a joint resolution proposing an amendment to the Constitution, the Roman rule applies and the proposed amendment should look like all the other amendments to the Constitution.

An extreme example at the Federal level is the Harmonized Tariff Schedule (HTS) of the United States, a huge document that is compiled and maintained by the United States International Trade Commission but by law has the status of a statute. The HTS comprises complex tariff tables (arranged by chapters) for all goods that are imported into the United States, plus sets of "notes" that apply to the entire schedule and to each chapter. The tables and notes have a unique designation and formatting system. Needless to say, a bill to amend the HTS, whether by modifying a tariff table or amending the notes, would have to follow the Roman rule religiously in order to avoid confusion.[1]

However, following an odd designation system or stylistic framework in a less extreme example would still not prevent you from organizing those legislative ideas in a clear fashion, which could include the use of headings.

Another case in which the Roman rule applies involves out-of-the-ordinary definitions and usages of key words and phrases, especially where the odd definition or usage (in the jurisdiction or setting concerned) is not limited to only the particular statute with which the drafter is working.

The positive law titles of the United States Code have an established system for the organization and typography of chapters and section headings. The ultimate goal is that all titles will be enacted as positive law titles with this system. Therefore, amendments to these titles should follow that organization and typography. However, you can easily maintain this system and achieve the greater clarity by applying the favored structural style to the substance of the sections within a chapter (for example, starting out with the main message, inserting headings for subdivisions, and continuing with other aspects of that structural style).

There are countless examples of statutes that now incorporate provisions drafted in the "office" style discussed above, and no confusion in the law has surfaced.[2]

Certainly if you are adding a new title, chapter (in the case of an amendment to a positive law title of the United States Code), or other separate unit dealing with a new and separate subject matter, the decision to use the clearer style is easy.

But it need not stop there. Title 17, United States Code (commonly referred to as the "Copyright Act"), was reenacted in 1976. The drafting was done primarily by the United States Copyright Office, and no professional drafters were involved. The result was an abundance of long, complex sentences, heavy in the use of provisos, and internal references that were inconsistent with other Federal statutes.[3] Amendments to title 17 since the end of the 1980s have increasingly applied the drafting principles discussed in this book, including the organizational principles that use headings for subsections and other subdivisions (whether as part of a new chapter, section, or subsection), and the internal references are now generally consistent with usage in other Federal statutes.[4] The approach has been that whenever a section is amended, it is an opportunity to clean up the other provisions of that section that are flawed, rather than perpetuate mediocre drafting. One caveat, however: sometimes even poorly drafted language has assumed a particular meaning through case law or regulations, so that making changes may be perceived as intended to change the meaning of the case law or regulations. In this case it is possible to insert language clarifying that the intent is not to change the meaning of the statute as interpreted before the bill's passage, but there may be resistance to changing a law that has with it so much interpretive baggage.

Even if other provisions surrounding the new provision are not changed, the clearer style can be applied if a new provision is inserted. There is nothing wrong with, say, an amendment to a section that adds a new subsection and uses the clearer style for that subsection (for example, by using headings for all its subdivisions), even if the remainder of the section does not, particularly if the new subsection is long or complex. The ideal goal in this situation would be to insert headings for the other subsections and subdivisions as well, if possible.

Be sure, however, that when you add a provision to an existing law in a different style, you do not create internal inconsistencies affecting the interpretation of the law.

And remember that even if you feel that you simply must apply the Roman rule and perpetuate an old law's unusual style of section designation, for example, you can almost always avoid using the archaic "wherefores", "abovementioneds", and "hereinbefores" since they serve no purpose and nobody is likely to miss them.

8.2 Amendments to bills under consideration

Another time when you should apply the Roman rule (or, rather, the first subrule) is if you are drafting an amendment to a bill under consideration; in that case, you would draft the amendment in the same style as is used in the bill—the form and style adopted by the legislative forum considering the bill. For example, at the Federal level, the Committees on Appropriations of both Houses of Congress use the same format for all their appropriations bills—funds are appropriated under headings with no designations, provisos are used to set aside amounts for specific purposes, and general provisions are drafted in traditional style. So an amendment to set aside an amount for a new purpose (assuming the amendment is procedurally in order) would be done by inserting a new ": Provided, That", or ": Provided further, That", and an amendment adding a new general provision would use the traditional style used in the bill.

8.3 Form and style in amendatory bills

You should always keep in mind that an amendatory bill is only a vehicle for making amendments to existing law. Every amendatory provision may be thought of as having two parts: the vehicular part (the introductory language, "outside the quotes"), which makes the amendments but has no other substantive significance, and the amendments themselves. As discussed in 8.2, you would apply the Roman rule to the vehicular part; and you would have to determine whether to apply the Roman rule to the amendments themselves (the parts "within the quotes"), that is, whether to follow the traditional form and style of the law being amended.

8.4 Form and style in freestanding bills

As stated above, the presumption in freestanding bills is to use the form that produces the greatest clarity. An argument can be made, however, that nearly every major substantive field is governed by a tapestry of laws, and a new law in any field, even if it is freestanding, will become a part of that tapestry as soon as it is enacted; that the people who administer those laws or are affected by them will tend to read them all together, as part of a larger whole; and that those people may be uncomfortable working with the new law if it looks strange or seems inconsistent with the others. But again, if greater clarity is to be achieved by using a particular drafting style, the tapestry of laws will begin to achieve greater clarity too.

8.5 Case study

The following provision of the Telecommunications Act of 1996 (Public Law 104-104) provides a clever example of how not to surrender to the Roman rule in the interest of updating archaic usages and adopting a clearer drafting style, without rewriting the entire section.

Prior to the enactment of the Telecommunications Act of 1996, section 3 of the Communications Act of 1934, containing the definitions used in that Act, assigned the separate paragraphs containing the definitions as (a), (b), (c), and so forth, rather than numbered paragraphs, without any headings to help the reader find a particular defined term. Section 3 of the Telecommunications Act of 1996 added a series of definitions to the end of section 3 of the Communications Act of 1934, assigning them numbers, with headings, for example—

> (33) Affiliate.—The term "affiliate" means a person that (directly or indirectly) owns or controls, is owned or controlled by, or is under common ownership or control with, another person. For purposes of this paragraph, the term "own" means to own an equity interest (or the equivalent thereof) of more than 10 percent.

Then in the same section that added the new definitions was the following provision:

> (c) Stylistic Consistency.—Section 3 (47 U.S.C. 153) is amended—
>
> (1) in subsections (e) and (n), by redesignating clauses (1), (2), and (3), as clauses (A), (B), and (C), respectively;
>
> (2) in subsection (w), by redesignating paragraphs (1) through (5) as subparagraphs (A) through (E), respectively;
>
> (3) in subsections (y) and (z), by redesignating paragraphs (1) and (2) as subparagraphs (A) and (B), respectively;
>
> (4) by redesignating subsections (a) through (ff) as paragraphs (1) through (32);
>
> (5) by indenting such paragraphs 2 em spaces;
>
> (6) by inserting after the designation of each such paragraph—
>
> (A) a heading, in a form consistent with the form of the heading of this subsection, consisting of the term defined by such paragraph, or the first term so defined if such paragraph defines more than one term; and
>
> (B) the words "The term";
>
> (7) by changing the first letter of each defined term in such paragraphs from a capital to a lower case letter (except for "United States", "State", "State commission", and "Great Lakes Agreement"); and

(8) by reordering such paragraphs and the additional paragraphs added by subsection (a) in alphabetical order based on the headings of such paragraphs and renumbering such paragraphs as so reordered.

In this one provision, the drafter accomplished the following:

(1) Amended those definitions designated with a letter that had subdivisions designated as numbers, and converted those subdivisions to subparagraphs.

(2) Redesignated all the existing definitions designated with a letter as paragraphs, and indented them as appropriate for paragraphs.

(3) Inserted a heading in a descriptive manner, consisting of the defined term, followed by the words: "The term".

(4) Fixed the capitalization ambiguity (that is, changed upper case to lower case for words not normally capitalized) that arises by beginning a definition with the defined word capitalized (because it is the first word in the sentence).

(5) Directed that all the definitions in the existing law plus the new paragraphs added in the first part of this section of the Telecommunications Act be placed in alphabetical order.

What followed were a few conforming amendments made necessary by the redesignations.

These amendments organized section 3 of the Communications Act of 1934 in a way that would easily accommodate all future amendments to the section.

8.6 Summing up

Professional drafters apply the Roman rule routinely in many cases, without ever thinking about it or giving it a name, in order that every bill should fit comfortably within its context. However, the rule does perpetuate questionable drafting practices.

Professional drafters may disagree about the subject, perhaps differing on the question of just how bad a drafting practice needs to be before a violation of the rule is justified or on the question of whether the structural situation involved makes it acceptable. Their answers to these questions are largely based on personal preferences and other subjective considerations.

This chapter has championed clarity as the primary reason to sidestep the Roman rule. A drafter adopting a new style in amending an existing law cannot control the input of other drafters to the same provision that would result in stylistic inconsistency. But it is a risk worth taking. Eventually the merits of the clearer style will prevail.

Notes

1 Another example is the Rules of the House of Representatives and the Senate (although they are not strictly laws). The designation system is inconsistent with that used in bills and laws.

2 This has included inserting new sections entirely in "office" style (including the section headings) in a law drafted in traditional style (that has a different format for section headings).

3 For example, paragraphs are referred to as "clauses".

4 These amendments have been drafted by or with the assistance of the Office of the Legislative Counsel of the House of Representatives or the Senate, or both. The extent to which office style has been applied has, of course, been affected by factors beyond the drafter's control—primarily time pressures.

9. Readability

9.1 In general

Producing legislative language that any literate person can easily read and comprehend is of course one of the drafter's major objectives. After all, when a bill becomes law it not only creates rights, liabilities, and obligations but must also inform the intended audience about them in a way that can be understood, so that the affected persons will know where they stand, and the future administrators will know what is expected of them.

Thus the way in which you use words and structure sentences is just as important in the interest of readability as it is in the interest of clarity and precision. Unless it is absolutely necessary for the accurate expression of an unusual or complex idea, any language that could confuse or bewilder the reader is suspect even though it may be technically correct, and you should seek an acceptable alternative. The best drafting expresses its ideas in as easy and natural a way as the subject matter allows.

Of course simplicity and readability do tend to promote clarity in turn. The avoidance of unnecessary complexity will help readers grasp the intended meaning; and in addition it will help ensure that the drafter is not the only person who is capable of following the threads, so that later drafters of reasonable skill can easily adjust the words to fit changing circumstances.

Make no mistake about it. Every drafter should consciously strive to produce language that makes it possible for any serious reader to extract the message without undue effort. However, this is sometimes easier said than done; and the rest of this chapter addresses the reasons why.

9.2 Archaic usages

One barrier to readability in the law, of course, is the widespread use of archaic or excessively legalistic terminology, style, and form (see also 7.2 and chapter 22)—largely a bequest from earlier times but still prevalent among lawyers and (regrettably) among drafters. Except in the relatively few cases where a particular archaic usage still has demonstrable value, you should always try to avoid it.

Unfortunately, many archaic practices have become so embedded in existing statutes that the drafter of an amendment may simply have to perpetuate at least some of the old forms and structural anomalies in order to maintain internal consistency. For example, if a provision of law is set out as one sentence, to which a number of provisos are appended that are linked to the main message as conditions, and the sponsor wants to add another condition, you will not have much choice but to add another proviso. Another approach might be to add a new sentence, but then your condition would not be linked to the main message of the preceding sentence without restating it.

The cleanest solution is to rewrite the old law entirely, eliminating the archaic forms and obsolete provisions first and then amending it. This is not normally a viable option, however. It would necessitate the restatement and reenactment of provisions that have nothing to do with the sponsor's proposal. For that reason alone, the sponsor will be unlikely to sanction it. Such an approach would not only obscure the sponsor's policy but also almost certainly cause legal and practical problems by gratuitously opening old issues. Another reason objections may be raised to doing this is that the existing language may have developed a considerable body of case law, and rewriting it may raise concerns about the continued validity of that case law. You could counter this argument by adding a provision in the bill stating that the nonsubstantive changes (which you would have to carefully identify) are not intended to modify the interpretation of the provisions amended as they were in effect before the enactment of the bill (this was addressed in 8.1).

As an aside, it should be noted that the process of rewriting old laws to eliminate archaic forms and obsolete provisions on a broad scale—known as "codification" or "code revision"—has long been under way in the States as well as at the Federal level. However, it is not an easy task, or one that can be done quickly. Congress has been continuously revising the United States Code for many years with the objective of enacting the revisions into positive law, title by title; but the job is far less than one-half completed and most of the more difficult titles have not even been touched (see 31.4).

If a particular usage or form sounds outdated and is one that you would not use in everyday speech or ordinary prose composition, it is suspect. But an occasional lapse does not diminish readability much, and there are many borderline cases along with a number of uniquely legislative practices that look out of date but are quite legitimate. All you can really do as a practical matter is scrupulously avoid any usage or form that is clearly an outmoded relic of an earlier age and make your judgment on a case-by-case basis in all doubtful situations.

9.3 Complexity

In spite of your efforts to write clear and present-day English and avoid archaic usages and forms, there is a more basic barrier to reader comprehension in many cases—complexity. The growing impenetrability of legislation is not wholly, or even primarily, the fault of its drafters; in the words of *Hirsch* (page 1), it simply—

> mirrors the increasingly complicated ways in which government intervenes in private and public activity; ... [A]s statutes grow longer, the main impediment to their intelligibility is the poorly organized, convoluted, or otherwise slovenly treatment [by the policymakers themselves] of concepts that demand precision.

Laws are more complex because life itself and the legislative policies necessary to deal with it have become increasingly complicated. Any policy that treats everyone exactly alike, without any qualifications, conditions, or exceptions, can always be written simply and readably, but it will almost certainly result in unfairness, because people's circumstances differ; it is the qualifications, conditions, and exceptions—not the basic objectives—that produce the complexity. If the policy of the Social Security program, for example, had been simply to pay a fixed benefit to everyone at age 65, the law would be only a few pages long, but the actual policy decreed that the benefits should be work-related rather than fixed, that dependents, survivors, and disabled people should be covered (under separate formulas), that eligibility must be proved, and so forth—which accounts for the several hundred additional pages and almost all of the complexity.

Faced with these problems in the real drafting world, readability must frequently take a back seat to more important objectives. Remember that readability is not the same thing as clarity. For proposals that are highly complex or technical or are addressed primarily to specialists, or the basic thrust of which is determined largely by long-established judicial pronouncements, readability may actually be incompatible with clarity, and it may hardly be worth the drafter's time to seek it.

When readability and clarity are incompatible, it is invariably because there is a fundamental difference between the nature and purpose of legislative language on the one hand and the nature and purpose of ordinary communication between human beings on the other.

Everyday conversations between ordinary people are full of generalizations and imprecise terminology, but it usually does not matter. If one person speaking to another uses a word that describes 95 percent of what it is supposed to describe or makes a statement that would be true 95 percent of the time, and can reasonably assume that the listener understands in general what the speaker is trying to say, any further effort to spell out the special conditions, qualifications, and circumstances that might define the 5 percent exception would be regarded by both of them as unnecessarily pompous and inappropriate. The speaker can use simple everyday terms, without dotting each i and crossing each t, and the listener will get the message.

In a statute, however, every contingency must be covered. If the language used would get the wrong result (or would simply not apply) in 5 percent of the situations that it was intended to address, the drafter has committed an unforgivable sin. And if covering every contingency means using unfamiliar or technical words, or adding a string of conditions, qualifications, exceptions, and special rules, the drafter must give up the quest for simplicity and easy reading, or at least make it secondary to the quest for precision.

Experienced drafters use the tricks of the trade discussed in chapter 23 every chance they get, not only because those devices promote clarity but because, although they may make the statutory language less readable than everyday prose, they make it significantly more readable than if they were not used (see 9.4).

There are many types of bills and fields of law that are relatively simple in their scope and content, of course, and a drafter working on such a bill or in such a field has a fighting chance to keep the product readable. There are probably just as many, however, that are not simple at all, and cannot be made simple.

No bill amending the Internal Revenue Code or the Social Security Act, for example, is likely to be simple and readable, even if the basic policy is completely straightforward. Given their inherent complexity and the endless interrelationships of their provisions, the drafter should not waste too much time seeking a simple and readable way to amend them, since the straightforward basic policy still has to be woven into the existing tapestry and in the process will become unavoidably hard to follow for anyone but a specialist.

Even James Craig Peacock—a well-known commentator on legislative drafting who is hardly an ardent admirer of modern-day drafting practices—admits, in his *Notes on Legislative Drafting*, that

> legislation dealing with technical subject matter cannot be couched in the ordinary language of the street. Neither is there ordinarily any occasion … to direct either phraseology or other phases of a draft to maximum comprehensibility at that level.[1]

He does go on to say (correctly) that

> [this] does not mean that a [drafter] should ever relax [the effort] to put [the] draft into the most convenient and intelligible form which is possible under all the circumstances. For judges and lawyers and administrators are human, and even though as a group they may have become more experienced in … legislation, their work should not for that reason be made any more difficult than is absolutely necessary.

A final consideration (addressed more fully elsewhere) is that as laws become more complicated and technical, they are simply not intended to be read by the casual public at all. When this book says that good drafting should result in statutory language that can be comprehended by anyone (as it does frequently), the word "anyone" should be read as meaning "anyone who is a member of the intended audience, or who is interested enough to expend the effort needed to become familiar with legislative language in general and with the concepts in the field involved in particular". It makes no more sense to expect a casual reader to grasp all the implications of a complicated law (no matter how hard the drafter works) than it would to expect a casual viewer of soap operas to understand how the television set manages to produce its picture.[2]

For members of specialized audiences and serious students of legislation, legislative language is readable only if it is clear, accurate, and precise.

9.4 Maximizing readability in the face of adversity

That a statute is hard to read and understand is not necessarily a compelling criticism of the drafter. What the drafter should be ashamed of is needlessly making a statute hard to read and understand. There are ways of approaching difficult drafting assignments that can eliminate many unnecessary complexities.

You can achieve a respectable level of readability in most cases, and learn how to recognize (and forgive yourself for) the cases in which you cannot, if you follow the precepts laid down in this book (particularly chapter 6 and part VI), even in bills that are inherently quite complicated. Nearly all of the drafting rules and principles recommended in this book have the effect of promoting readability even if that is not their primary purpose.

Admittedly, there are circumstances in which it may not be possible to achieve the degree of readability you would like. These circumstances generally involve cases in which the application of all the book's precepts would be impossible, undesirable, or at least impractical because—

(1) the underlying structure of the statute being amended (or in some cases the Roman rule) does not permit it;

(2) the overriding objective of maximum clarity unavoidably calls for a more technical (and less readable) approach; or

(3) the substantive problems involved are so complex or esoteric that nothing could make their solution readable.

If you ever find yourself in one of these situations, resign yourself to it—you cannot go on fruitlessly looking for some ideal that does not exist. But you usually can apply at least some of the precepts, and you should always try to improve readability by applying as many of them as you can. Partial readability is better than none at all. Give special attention to the techniques for handling complexity that are recommended in chapter 23. These techniques intimidate many people, probably because they often make the provisions involved look a bit like exercises in arithmetic or geometry, but once mastered they are anything but intimidating.

Columnar tables are actually quite easy to read and follow, if the headings and relationships of the columns are clear and adequately descriptive. And a good table, like a computer spreadsheet, can say with complete precision in half a page what it would take 10 convoluted pages to say in words.

Tabulated sentences sometimes do have a frightening appearance, but their only real drawback is that they have to be read slowly and with extra care, with special attention to the conjunctions and punctuation—not that they are actually hard to follow.

And incorporations by reference can be made more understandable by including "relating to" clauses—brief parenthetical descriptions of what the referred-to provisions do; for example, "... under section 216(i)(3) (relating to insured status for disability benefit purposes)", or "... in chapter 9 (relating to protection of semiconductor chip products)". Such clauses are regularly used in the tax laws, and ought to be used more widely by drafters in every field.

In any event, when the intended audience is a specialized one, the problem tends to go away—specialists in any field quickly learn to use these devices in their everyday work, simply because it makes the work easier. You should always remember that you are not comparing the readability of statutory language that includes these devices with the readability of a gothic novel—you are comparing it with the readability of statutory language that does not use them at all, which is a very different proposition.

As a drafter, you simply cannot ignore the virtues of these devices just because they have a superficial appearance of complexity. To the contrary, they eliminate complexity, they shorten a bill by removing mountains of convoluted language, and they make it easier for everyone—you, your coworkers, and your eventual readers—to talk about, analyze, and remember the ideas and concepts involved. With a little effort they can quickly become second nature; and the result will be statutory language that (in addition to being clearer and more precise) may astonish you by turning out to be simpler and more readable as well.

You should make that effort, and you should not hesitate to ask your readers to make it too.

9.5 Short sentences versus tabulation—a case study

Hirsch (page 52), in gently chiding *HOLC* for its insistence on short sentences in legislation, uses as an example a provision from the (now repealed) Medicare Catastrophic Coverage Act of 1988, which consisted primarily of one long tabulated sentence (and which, as it happens, was written in the very office that produced *HOLC*). It may be instructive to repeat that example here.

The provision as enacted read as follows:

> (A) IN GENERAL.—Except as provided in subparagraph (B), for drugs dispensed in—
>
> (i) 1990 or 1991, the administrative allowance under this paragraph is—
>
> (I) $4.50 for drugs dispensed by a participating pharmacy, or
>
> (II) $2.50 for drugs dispensed by another pharmacy; or
>
> (ii) a subsequent year, the administrative allowance under this paragraph is the administrative allowance under this paragraph for the preceding year increased by the percentage increase (if any) in the implicit price deflator for gross national product (as published by the Department of Commerce in its *Survey of Current Business*) over the 12-month period ending with August of such preceding year.
>
> Any allowance determined under clause (ii) which is not a multiple of 1 cent shall be rounded to the nearest multiple of 1 cent.

Hirsch's experimental rewrite of the provision in the short-sentence mode was as follows:

> (A) IN GENERAL.—For 1990 or 1991, the administrative allowance under this paragraph is $4.50 for drugs dispensed by a participating pharmacy. It is $2.50 for drugs dispensed by another pharmacy. For a year subsequent to 1991, the administrative allowance for drugs dispensed under this paragraph is the preceding year's administrative allowance under this paragraph, adjusted. Make that adjustment as follows. Compute the increase, if any, in the implicit price deflator for gross national product over the 12 months ending with August of such preceding year. Then raise the preceding year's allowance by that increase. Finally, round the allowance to the nearest multiple of 1 cent. For purposes of the computation, use the gross national product established by the Department of Commerce in its *Survey of Current Business.*

None of the eight sentences in the rewritten version is longer than 25 words and most are considerably shorter, as compared with the 100 or so words in the first sentence of the original. And each of its sentences is certainly more "readable" than the corresponding piece of the original. But the rewritten version as a whole is slightly longer than the original, the apparent moral (depending on your point of view) being either that length has nothing to do with simplicity or that too many sentences garble the message.

You must be your own judge, of course, about which version is more "readable" as a whole. The original (tabulated) version, however, has several advantages over the short-sentence version:

(1) Because its different components are tabulated and have specific alphanumeric designations—for example, "(i) 1990 or 1991" and "(ii) a subsequent year", or "(I) $4.50" and "(II) $2.50"—they can be more easily cross-referred to at other points in the statute.

(2) For the same reason, its components can be more easily and intelligibly amended—for example, by breaking down the formula into three or four levels instead of just two—if that should become necessary later.

(3) And its structure makes both drafting and statutory construction easier. The "except" clause at the beginning, for example, warns the reader that the allowances established by the provision may not actually apply in all cases (a warning that is relatively trivial in this case but could be quite important in slightly different circumstances), while the many sentences used in the rewritten version do not lend themselves to the use of a single qualifying clause.[3]

The example given is not intended as an attack on the short-sentence principle, which in most cases is the right way to go, or as a definitive demonstration of readability; and the differences described in the preceding paragraph are not always important. It does, however, explain, at least in part, why drafters so often use long sentences—even drafters who tell us we must use short ones.

Notes

1 James Craig Peacock, *Notes on Legislative Drafting* (Washington, D.C.: National Republic Pub. Co., 1961), 7.

2 As mentioned in 1.3, Robert J. Martineau and Michael B. Salerno, in *Legal, Legislative, and Rule Drafting in Plain English* (St. Paul, Minn.: Thomson/West, 2005), challenge the "complexity" argument by insisting that by focusing on the reader (they define "audience" [page 58] much more broadly to include ordinary citizens interested in the proper functioning of government) the drafter's obligation is, like the advocate writing a brief, to take complexity and organize it in a way that is easily understood by readers (page 11) of "average intelligence, education, and experience" (page 59). However, anyone working in complex statutory areas will, for the reasons stated, frequently find this to be an illusory goal.

3 Of this example, *SOLC* (page 9) would say to avoid using flush language (in this case, the sentence at the end ["Any allowance determined under clause (ii) ..."]) after a cut in (the tabulated language that precedes it) because doing so makes it difficult to amend the provision later.

PART IV
WRITING THE PROVISIONS OF A PROTOTYPICAL BILL

10. General Considerations

10.1 Organization

The organization of a bill—the determination of which provisions need to be included and the way they should be arranged—is a matter that you would normally decide upon before the actual writing begins. This subject was discussed in some detail in chapter 6, but it may be worthwhile to revisit it briefly.

All bills do not present the same organizational problems, of course. In very simple bills organization is not even a factor, and in more complicated bills it may have to be treated as tentative (and subject to modification as the work progresses). For the most part the succeeding chapters will assume that you are working on a midsized bill, of moderate substance and manageable proportions; but no matter what kind of bill is involved you should not bother to start writing until you are sure that you have some kind of overall framework into which your words can be fitted.

HOLC's general principle—that the most important thoughts should come first—is a good starting point. And *Dickerson*'s rules of thumb—that the general provisions precede the specific, the more important provisions precede the less important, the more frequently used provisions precede the less frequently used, the permanent provisions precede the temporary, and the "housekeeping" provisions come last—are worth keeping in mind as you work.

The order of a bill's "typical" provisions recommended by some legislative drafting manuals (see 6.2) can be moderately helpful, but it can mislead the unwary drafter since no two bills are identical and no one arrangement fits all situations; the organization of a bill in real life is never quite that straightforward. Most bills of any substance, for example, contain introductory provisions that should normally be placed ahead of the key operating provisions, superficially violating several of the general rules. In addition, the category into which a particular type of provision falls is not always the same, but may depend upon the nature and scope of the bill in which it appears.

However, the underlying thread in all cases is very simple: give prominence to the more important thoughts and downplay the others, but keep their interrelationship clear.

This part does not pretend to tell you how you should organize and write any particular bill. It does list and discuss the types of provisions that might be included, taking them in the order in which they would most often appear and indicating some of the considerations involved in writing them. But you will seldom encounter a drafting assignment in which all of these provisions would be included, or in which all of the recommended organizational rules would make sense; and in connection with any particular assignment you should just ignore the provisions that do not apply.

10.2 Stylistic considerations

Like the overall organization of the bill you are working on, the statutory format you will use in actually writing its provisions should be clear in your mind before you start. Neither is something to be worked out as you write.

In this context the term "statutory format" describes only the external appearance of your provisions—the mechanical framework within which your thoughts are presented—and has nothing to do with the way in which the provisions themselves are phrased or what they should contain. (The term "drafting style" as used generally in this book—see especially chapter 33—is broader, including both statutory format and the internal phrasing of provisions.)

Statutory format involves such things as: How will you break down the bill into its various components? What system will you use for designating them? What system (if any) will you use for indenting inferior subdivisions? Will any or all of the bill's components have headings, and if so, how and where will they be set on the page?

Every jurisdiction has one or more accepted statutory formats. The Federal Government has several, with "revenue" style or "modified revenue" style the preferred format of the Offices of the Legislative Counsel of the House of Representatives and the Senate (see chapter 8). These formats are discussed and evaluated in chapter 33; if you have not read that chapter yet (and are working at the Federal level) you might be well advised to do so out of order, since the style and format you use often shapes the decisions you make. And sometimes, even within the same jurisdiction, the accepted statutory format in one field is different from the accepted format in another.

It is your obligation as a good drafter to know the accepted statutory format of the jurisdiction in which you are working (and in the field in which you are working if it makes a difference). If you work regularly in that jurisdiction (and field) it should be second nature to you, so that you never have to stop and think about it at all. In any other case you should do whatever is necessary to become familiar with it before starting to work, using some properly drafted bills or existing laws of the jurisdiction as models or consulting a manual if one is available. In addition, you must be aware of constitutional provisions of the jurisdiction with respect to the enactment of statutes (such as title, enacting clause, and single-subject requirements). See 11.1 and chapter 35 if you are drafting at a level other than the Federal level.

10.3 Parliamentary considerations

In every jurisdiction there are parliamentary rules and precedents that impose restrictions at different points in the legislative process.

Most of these restrictions are purely procedural and involve the way in which (or the stage at which) a bill may be considered after it has been introduced; they do not directly concern the initial drafter of the bill. But some of them actually limit what a bill may do, how it may do it, or what it may contain; and needless to say these concern the drafter at any stage.

Because there are so many parliamentary variations in different legislative settings, any detailed enumeration of parliamentary restrictions is beyond the scope of this book. But you should remain alert to the possibility of their existence, and you should do what you can to identify at least the most obvious ones. Drafters working at the Federal level should pay special attention to chapter 34 (which deals specifically with the subject).

10.4 Using models

In general. There is no limit to the variety of bills you could conceivably be called upon to draft. Some are very short and to the point (which does not necessarily mean they are insubstantial—a two-line bill simply changing a date can affect millions of people in important ways). At the other extreme, a few are so demanding in terms of their size, scope, and complexity (or the number of different subjects involved) that they would intimidate any drafter. Most bills fall somewhere in the middle, being substantial enough to require serious attention to structure and form without posing insurmountable problems.

You as a drafter must often approach your subject head-on, straightforwardly saying what needs to be said and not worrying about whether some previous drafter may have said it differently. But many bills, and many provisions within bills, occur frequently or fall into recognizable categories—some bills are introduced over and over again in each Congress, by Members who want to get onto some bandwagon or other, with little or no variation in form or substance.

You should take advantage of this and categorize the provisions you are working on whenever you can. You will be able to treat already introduced bills or previously enacted statutes containing similar provisions (or isolated pieces of such bills or laws) as models. Using existing examples in this way can get you started when you are otherwise at a loss as to how to proceed, by helping you decide upon the approach you should take and by reassuring you that you have not forgotten to address any of the topics that need to be dealt with. Experienced drafters are constantly on the lookout for this kind of help.

Boilerplate. In addition to the more generalized models, there are many provisions that appear over and over again in the laws of any jurisdiction. Some of them are almost always exactly the same (for example, the limitation on attorneys' fees that is required under congressional rules for all private relief bills making cash awards);[1] these are colloquially known as "boilerplate" forms. Others are always similar and have the same overall structure, but the operative terms, dates, dollar amounts, and other specifics may differ (for example, bills creating study commissions, most of which are structured in more or less the same way and differ from each other only in such areas as the description of the problem to be studied and the membership of the commission); these may be viewed simply as boilerplate forms with a few blanks to be filled in.

Boilerplate forms are such good models that they hardly constitute models at all. In fact, they can often be inserted into a draft verbatim, without the painstaking modification that accompanies the use of models in other cases.

As you become aware of the boilerplate forms that recur in the field or fields in which you work, you should preserve them in an accessible file or folder and use it regularly. Such a file or folder will be a great time-saver; and it will promote accuracy as well if you are careful, since the use of language that has stood the test of time in similar situations avoids the inadvertent creation of new problems and furthers uniformity in the law.

Particular provisions. The complexity of a provision, in and of itself, is usually not what creates the need for help in the form of a model—it is the fact that the provision involves a specialized area of law in which you are not a specialist, or a subject with which you are unfamiliar.

Thus in writing the opening provisions of a bill (discussed in chapter 11), you will not normally derive any benefit from the use of a model; the provisions are usually simple, the ground to be covered is clear, and even when one of them (such as a definition section) is complex, the complications are likely to be related to the substantive area in which you are working (and with which you may be presumed to be reasonably familiar) rather than to the specific type of provision it is. The same thing is true of provisions authorizing appropriations, which are more central but seldom present difficulties.

However, in writing most of the other provisions of the bill—the central or operating provisions (discussed in chapter 12) and the closing provisions (chapter 13)—you would frequently be well advised to cast about for a suitable model, either because those provisions are specialized (as in the case of administrative, judicial review, and penalty provisions) or because they are unusual enough to be outside your everyday drafting arsenal (as in the case of savings provisions and severability clauses). Being knowledgeable in the substantive field in which you are working is not enough; collateral issues of this kind will often present you with your most difficult drafting problems.

If you need to include any of these provisions in your bill, the corresponding provision in an existing law or a previously drafted bill can be of help as a model even if the subject matter of that law or bill is totally different from yours. It could not be copied into your bill verbatim, of course—the difference in subject matter would make that impossible—but the specialized approach is what you are looking for, and that approach (along with its format) would usually be the same or at least quite similar.

Program models. All that has been said so far has had to do with specific types of provisions that might appear in any bill. But there is a much broader approach that experienced drafters often take in easing their task through the use of models.

When you are asked to draft a bill to establish a new program you may be able to find (and you should usually try to find) one or more existing laws or previously drafted bills that establish similar programs—not necessarily similar in terms of their specific purpose but in terms of their scope, the nature of the benefits they confer, and the kind of administrative structure they use to accomplish it.

Most loan programs, for example, require many of the same kinds of provisions—those relating to eligibility, application, amount, terms and conditions, funding, and monitoring—regardless of the different classes or types of recipients and the different purposes for which the loans involved are to be made. The same is true of most grant programs, most benefit programs, and most construction programs, as well as of most bills establishing new agencies or new entities within existing agencies. And most regulatory laws possess the same general set of specialized provisions. Usable models are available everywhere.

State plan programs. If a bill is intended to establish an assistance program that could appropriately be administered by the States (or other entities), instead of being wholly federally run, there are many models to choose from. The Child Abuse Prevention and Treatment Act (42 U.S.C. 5101 et seq.) has several.

Section 106 (42 U.S.C. 5106a) provides for grants to States for child abuse and neglect prevention and treatment programs:

> Subsection (a) provides that the Secretary of Health and Human Services "shall make grants to the States, from allotments made

under subsection (f) for each State that applies for a grant under this section, for purposes of assisting the States in improving the child protective services system of each such State" in a number of areas listed in succeeding paragraphs.

Subsection (b) provides that to be eligible to receive a grant, a State must prepare and submit to the Secretary a plan specifying the areas of the child protective services system listed in subsection (a) that the State intends to address with amounts received under the grant. In addition, there are requirements that the State "has in effect and is enforcing a State law, or has in effect and is operating a statewide program, relating to child abuse and neglect" that meets a detailed list of requirements set out in subsection (b)(2).

Subsection (c) requires each recipient State to establish citizen review panels to ensure (among other things) compliance with the State plan.

Subsection (d) requires each recipient State to report to the Secretary on a list of matters covered by the grant.

Section 107 (42 U.S.C. 5106c) provides for grants to States for programs relating to the investigation and prosecution of child abuse and neglect cases. The structure is similar to section 106 (that is, contains eligibility requirements and a requirement of a State task force, composed of professionals with appropriate expertise, with certain responsibilities relating to the grant), but the operative language is "The Secretary, in consultation with the Attorney General, *is authorized to* makes grants to the States ..." (emphasis added). The funding for this program is to be provided from funds made available under another statute (section 1404A of the Victims of Crime Act of 1984).

On its face, section 106 looks like a State that meets the requirements set out in that section is *entitled* to a grant, and in section 107 the Secretary's authority to make a grant is discretionary, even if a State meets the requirements.

However, the funding for *both* programs (in addition to the funding source under section 107) is only authorized to be appropriated (under section 112 [42 U.S.C. 5106h]). Even though section 106 says that the Secretary "shall" make the grants, the Secretary can do so only if the money is actually appropriated by another law.[2]

Some programs do authorize and appropriate the funds in the same statute. Part A of title IV of the Social Security Act (Block Grants To States For Temporary Assistance For Needy Families) replaced the comparatively simple structure of the AFDC (Aid to Families with Dependent Children) program with a program providing for grants to States that meet lengthy requirements set out in the statute:

> Section 402(a) (42 U.S.C. 602(a)) sets out requirements for a State to be an "eligible State".
>
> Section 403(a)(1)(A) (42 U.S.C. 603(a)(1)(A)) provides that "Each eligible State shall be entitled to receive from the Secretary … a grant in an amount equal to the State family assistance grant" (which is an amount determined under a formula). Then (in section 403(a)(1)(C)) there is an appropriation: "Out of any money in the Treasury of the United States not otherwise appropriated, there are appropriated for each of fiscal years 2017 and 2018 $16,566,542,000 for grants under this paragraph."[3]

The last example is one of an entitlement, but only to the States. Section 401(b) (42 U.S.C. 601(b)) clarifies that "This part shall not be interpreted to entitle any individual or family to assistance under any State program funded under this part."

In programs such as these, there are provisions placing restrictions on the use of the funds. The amount of a grant may be based on a formula. There are usually provisions penalizing a State that does not comply with the requirements. They do not impose the usual civil or criminal penalties, but provide for a system for withholding of funds depending on the type and extent of the violation.

In sum, if you need to establish a grant program, you should consider (based on the policy choices) including provisions relating to the following:

(1) Who are eligible recipients (States or otherwise)?

(2) What are the conditions for eligibility (like a State plan)?

(3) Should the official making the grants be required to do so if an applicant is eligible or has discretion in the matter?

(4) Is there a formula for determining the amount of a grant?

(5) What are the requirements with which recipients must comply, including restrictions on what a recipient may do with the grant or with other funds of the recipient?

(6) Are there reporting requirements with which recipients must comply, and any other enforcement mechanism (like the citizen review panels mentioned above)?

7) What are the sanctions for recipients who fail to meet program requirements?

(8) What will the authorization of funding for the grants be and will there be an appropriation of funds to ensure that funds for the program are available?

(9) Should the recipient coordinate this program with other programs, if appropriate?

Hirsch (page 33) asserts that "State plan provisions give federal statutes a bad name". But State plan provisions usually start off fairly simply and become complicated later because of two things—the need to accommodate the Federal law to the divergent situations in 50 States (plus the District of Columbia) (a need whose specifics only gradually become apparent after the program gets under way) and the inevitable recognition of initial omissions in the list of requirements that any State plan should contain.

A note on terminology. When the same bill is introduced in both the House and the Senate—usually on the same day, and usually done because the proponents in the two bodies wish to present a united front—the two are said to be *companion* bills. If you are unable to locate a bill that you need as a model, its companion (if it has one) can serve your purposes equally well.

When a particular bill is separately introduced by two or more Members in the same body, the bills are not called companions since the introducers are less likely to have acted in concert.

In either case you must exercise caution, however, because many bills that are publicly touted as companion bills, or as the same bill, are not—they have minor differences that may be unimportant to most people but could be critical for a drafter.

A warning. The use of models is one of the drafter's most valuable devices when the models are good ones and they are selected correctly and relied upon with discretion, but it is one of the most dangerous when they are not. Some of the worst horror stories in legislative drafting history involve cases where the drafter selected an inappropriate model or used it carelessly. What is right for one policy may be totally wrong for another, even though they may seem to call for similar structural approaches.

When using a model, keep in mind that you do not necessarily know who drafted it.[4] If a nonprofessional drafter did the drafting, you need to analyze the language carefully. You also will not know the policy behind a particular use of language or the circumstances (for example, time constraints, or the insistence of the sponsor to include certain language that is unnecessary or unworkable) under which it was drafted. For these reasons, it is always a good idea to look at several models and compare them. If there are differences in language among them (and there inevitably are), you will need to understand those differences in order to know which path to follow.

Every experienced drafter is familiar with requests for bills creating programs that are "exactly like the ABC program except ...". Almost invariably the exceptions multiply as the project receives further thought, until it becomes obvious that what is really wanted is a different animal altogether.

A simple substitution of one term or concept for another is almost never the answer. One of the most fun-filled afternoons in author Filson's professional drafting career was spent trying to explain to the staff of the select committee that eventually produced the NASA Act just how ludicrous it would be to start from the Atomic Energy Act of 1954 and simply substitute "space" for "nuclear energy" wherever it appeared (which was the staff's preferred approach at the time).

However, models can serve you well if you keep the possible pitfalls in mind. And perhaps most important of all, the use of a model can get you started when you do not know which way to turn at the beginning of a drafting job that involves unfamiliar territory. It will raise issues that you will need to address. Even if your more deliberate consideration of the similarities between the model and your project leads you to the conclusion that the model cannot actually contribute much, you are ahead of the game and you have a picture of what needs to be done that you would not otherwise have had at such an early stage.

10.5 When and how the writing should begin

It should be evident by now that in most drafting assignments a good deal of work has to be done before the actual writing begins, but there is no objective rule for identifying when to begin. It depends in any case upon the particular circumstances in which you are working: Is the policy completely clear? Do you have all the information you need? Are there time pressures? Will the sponsor leave you alone while you work, or keep looking over your shoulder until you finish?

There are some general principles that may help you determine when the time is ripe for starting to write, and the most basic among them is this: having faithfully served the sponsor's needs in the process of determining what to write, you should now serve your own (to the extent possible) in determining when and how to do it.

The sponsor's initial policy statement to the drafter represents a set of legislative specifications to be carried out; and you must ask yourself at every stage whether you understand those specifications well enough to draft from them:

(1) Are they clear? Can you understand each specification well enough to convert it into a legal requirement?

(2) Are they complete? Does the set of specifications include an instruction on every item that needs to be included in the bill?

(3) Are they administratively feasible? On a mechanical level, will the bill work? If you were the future administrator at the operating level, would you know how to carry out the bill's directives?

As a practical matter you will normally begin working on some of the specifications as soon as you receive them, but you may have to seek further guidance on others. In extreme cases the specifications may be so incomplete or ambiguous as to be unusable; most of the time, though, they will be sufficient to enable you, after clarifying a handful of issues, to write a first draft that contains at least something on every item with which they deal. Experienced drafters tend to develop a fairly reliable sense of what unresolved questions they should initially try to answer for themselves.

Needless to say, dividing the drafting process into discrete steps or stages (as described in 3.2 and 3.3) is an oversimplification in the real world. Unless the basic thrust of the policy is totally unclear or involves a subject about which you have no prior knowledge, you will almost always begin writing before all of the preliminary questions have been resolved. Preparing a rough working draft as soon as possible saves time in the long run, helps unearth some of the important questions that you may have overlooked, and is often the best way to smoke out the problems and stimulate the policymaker to face them.

Many experienced drafters prefer to begin writing immediately upon receiving a reasonably concrete drafting request, simply guessing at obscurities, arguing that the best test of whether they understand an idea is whether they can write a provision expressing it. After all, during the writing itself you can expect to discover gaps and ambiguities even in policies that at first seemed complete and clear.

This approach may seem at odds with what has been said earlier about the care that should be taken in carrying out the sponsor's policy exactly. And, admittedly, it might be more efficient to remove all uncertainties before beginning to draft. But a draft bill—even one that is incomplete or in very rough form—is a marvelous instrument for concentrating the policymaker's mind; it usually precipitates changes in the sponsor's policy (especially the subsidiary and collateral policies) that might not be thought of otherwise. Policy in its early stages is typically fluid, and today's decisions hastily made are tomorrow's decisions hastily reversed.

There are advantages to beginning the writing early. The writing has a way of crystallizing additional questions that the sponsor will need to address. In this way you can have a continuous dialogue with the sponsor while you are writing your first draft. *Dickerson* (pages 74–75) describes this process of writing, even before all of your research is done, as "talk-back", that is, letting the draft "talk" to you in order to sharpen "the sense of the relevant".

In most cases you will need to produce a first draft quickly, before the sponsor has answered all the questions. Policymakers are an impatient breed; they ordinarily prefer to review an imperfect draft bill rather than put up with the delays that are sure to attend the drafter's effort to resolve all policy issues before writing anything.

It is sad but true that the time reserved for the drafter has often been eroded by the sponsor's delays in reaching final decisions on the policy issues. Sometimes the waffling on questions of policy would not end at all except that over the horizon there comes into view some event—a presidential message, a committee meeting, or a major political event—that forces meditation to yield to action.

But when the time has arrived to begin writing, how and where do you start? As a general rule it makes no difference—the different sections of your working draft can be written in whatever order is most convenient and assembled in the proper order later.

If the bill will be massive and complicated, however, you may face a dilemma. On the one hand, the bill's main provisions (which are likely to take the most

time) will almost certainly require policy review by the sponsor; ideally the initial draft of those provisions should be done first, to allow adequate time both for the sponsor's review and for the redrafting that will inevitably result from it. On the other hand, as *Hirsch* (page 8) puts it, "when one confronts a hungry lion, one throws to it whatever meat is handy". Boilerplate and routine administrative provisions are often voluminous but nevertheless easy to write quickly; and if the sponsor is insisting on seeing something on paper you may be well advised to dash off these provisions first, creating the appearance of great efficiency and at the same time giving yourself an opportunity to draft the really important provisions at your comparative leisure.

If the policy is obscure on a very basic aspect of the proposal (such as the main thrust itself), however, especially if it would be unusually time-consuming or otherwise hard to draft, you should generally seek more guidance before writing anything at all. And in any other case what you do should depend upon the time you have available, your feeling for what the sponsor is most likely to want, and the sponsor's accessibility.

In the last analysis, there is no one best way that fits all cases. You should begin writing when you think you are ready; and where you should begin is up to you. Unless a particular approach is absolutely required (or strongly indicated) because of external circumstances, whatever will make the overall operation easiest for you and ensure the most efficient use of your energies, while keeping the sponsor happy, is the right way.

Notes

1 The rules require only that all bills carrying an appropriation (that is, a cash award) must include a provision "limiting any attorney's fees to not more than 10 percent". There is nothing to require that the language read the same way in every bill; in reality it usually does.

2 See 12.6 for a discussion of entitlements.

3 The funding for this program has been continued beyond fiscal year 2018 through separate enactments.

4 The Office of the Legislative Counsel of the House of Representatives maintains a database of all bills drafted by attorneys in the Office. Obviously a resource like this in any organization is invaluable; it pinpoints who should be consulted about the policies and use of language in a model.

11. The Introductory Provisions

11.1 Long titles

The "long title" of a bill is the general description of what it does. It appears on the first page, just after the heading "A BILL" (or the corresponding heading in the case of a resolution) and just before the enacting or resolving clause. Every bill has one.

Some States have specific requirements for what the title of a bill must contain; the constitutions of many States require that a bill contain only one subject, and some of those require that the subject be clearly expressed in the title. What follows addresses titles if no specific requirements apply. This is the case at the Federal level.[1]

A long title should be accurate and relatively brief (although that is often easier said than done, of course). In theory at least, it should not read like a press release—that is, it should not describe the reasons for the bill or set forth any of the sponsor's arguments, and it should not contain extraneous material or bombast.

It should always describe the bill's main thrust, of course, and if there are other miscellaneous, minor, or unrelated items in the bill they are usually handled by simply adding ", and for other purposes" just before the period at the end of the title.

If the bill contains several major ideas or components, it is appropriate either to mention them specifically in the long title or to leave the title quite general, stating the broad objective of the bill without specifically addressing any of its components. Thus the title of a bill designed to eliminate fraud and abuse in the Medicare program might read:

> To amend title XVIII of the Social Security Act to eliminate fraud and abuse in the Medicare program by improving accounting procedures, penalizing persons who file fraudulent applications for benefits, and requiring periodic reviews of eligibility in long-stay cases, and for other purposes.

or it might simply read:

> To eliminate fraud and abuse in the Medicare program.

or even:

> To improve the administration and cut the costs of the Medicare program.

Although you should always strive to make your titles both accurate and informative and to emphasize the sponsor's main objective, it really does not matter much what a bill's long title contains.[2]

In the first place, laws today are almost never cited or referred to by their long titles, which for the most part are ignored after their enactment. In the second place, parliamentary maneuvering sometimes results in bills whose long titles bear little or no relationship to the substantive provisions they contain—the 63-page Balanced Budget and Emergency Deficit Control Act of 1985 (the Gramm-Rudman-Hollings law; Public Law 99-177) was tacked onto the end of a six-line joint resolution "Increasing the statutory limit on the public debt", and was enacted that way.

And finally, long titles (at the Federal level at least) have no legal significance. The long title of a law precedes the enacting clause and thus is not actually a part of what is enacted. Therefore, the long title of a law is not even subject to change by subsequent amendatory legislation, no matter how obsolete or misleading it becomes with the passage of time.

Keep in mind, however, that a court may look to the title as an aid to interpreting a statute, so the drafter should ensure that the title accurately reflects what the bill does (see 28.4).

And remember that if you are drafting at the State level, the State constitution may specify what the title of the bill must contain. Failure to comply with such a requirement will have legal significance.

Long titles are written in a "hanging style" (first line flush[3], remaining lines indented). All of them start with "To" and proceed with whatever descriptive statement the drafter (or the sponsor) wants to make, like the examples given earlier—except in a few specific cases:

(1) In an amendatory bill that consists primarily of amendments to a single law, the title should normally begin "To amend [that law] to provide for ..." instead of just "To provide for ...". You should not have as a title that simply says "To amend the XYZ Act.", since that would say nothing about what the bill purports to do.

(2) In a joint resolution (or any other resolution), the title should normally begin with a gerund—"Providing for ..." instead of "To provide for ...".

(3) In a private relief bill, the title should read simply "For the relief of John Doe [the name of the person or persons to whom the bill provides relief]".

A bill's heading (which is often read as if it were a part of the long title) changes from "A BILL" to "AN ACT" as soon as one House passes it; but this is an arbitrary stylistic change that affects the heading only—the measure remains a bill from the drafter's point of view until it is enacted into law.

11.2 Enacting and resolving clauses

Every bill in Congress begins (after the long title) with an enacting clause, or (in the case of a resolution) with a resolving clause. Chapter 2 of title 1 of the United States Code prescribes the form of these clauses.

An enacting clause, always set in italic type, reads:

> *Be it enacted by the Senate and House of Representatives of the United States of America in Congress assembled,*

and a resolving clause in a joint resolution uses the single word "*Resolved*" in place of "*Be it enacted*". The resolving clauses in concurrent and simple resolutions (which do not become law because the President does not sign them) are somewhat different—see chapter 32 for examples.

In the case of a joint resolution proposing a constitutional amendment (which requires the approval of a two-thirds majority in both Houses), the words "(*two-thirds of each House concurring therein*)" are inserted before the final comma.

Note that a bill or joint resolution is "enacted" when the President signs it or takes no action within a specified period (or when it is passed over his veto). A simple resolution is "adopted" when it is agreed to by the House involved; and a concurrent resolution is "adopted" or "agreed to" when both Houses have passed it.

The drafter does not actually have to write the enacting or resolving clause in most cases. In the Offices of the Legislative Counsel of the House of Representatives and the Senate, for example, these clauses are embedded in the word processing programs used by those offices, once the drafter has selected the appropriate form. In addition, if a draft bill is presented for introduction ("dropped into the hopper") without an enacting clause, the official who receives the bill will automatically supply one. It is probably a good idea, however (if the form is not already present in electronic format), to at least indicate the enacting clause in any draft so that disoriented readers will know what kind of document it is; many experienced drafters start out every rough draft with a condensed version of the clause—"*Be it enacted, etc.*"—for this reason.

11.3 First sections

In the early days of the Republic, the text of a bill was considered a continuation of the enacting clause, so it was thought necessary to give every section of the bill its own separate enacting clause, followed immediately by "That …". The sections were not numbered. This practice gradually disappeared, and today title 1 of the United States Code (section 103) provides that "no enacting or resolving clause shall be used in any section of an Act or resolution of Congress except the first". As a result, a bill has only the one enacting clause; and all sections are given section numbers, with the following exception.

A *resolution* (simple, concurrent, or joint) that has only one section and no heading to that section may properly begin with the word "That" (run in at the end of the resolving clause, on the same line) instead of being paragraphed and having a number (and beginning on the following line).

In this case the beginning of the resolution would look like this:

> *Resolved,* That it is the sense of the House of Representatives …

In this case, the single section should never be divided into subsections. If there is a need for separate subdivisions, then they should be converted into separate sections as is done in every bill.

In every other case, the first thing after "*in Congress assembled*" (despite the fact that it results in an apparent discontinuity in the text), is the section number (and its heading), on a new line.

However, many laws on the books have been drafted in the "traditional" style (see chapter 33). In these cases, the first section of the law will appear as follows:

> *Be it enacted by the Senate and House of Representatives of the United States of America in Congress assembled,* That this Act may be cited as ...;

although, the succeeding sections will be paragraphed and have numbers. Whenever the first section of a law or resolution appears in the traditional style, subsequent references to it must be made to "the first section of" the law or resolution rather than to "section 1". You need to remember this if you are drafting a bill that amends the first section of a law written in this style.

Note that section 1 of a bill is the only place where the section designation itself is spelled out; you say "**SECTION 1.**", but you abbreviate the word and use the form "**SEC. ___.**" at the beginning of all succeeding sections. (When used in a statutory cross-reference to any section, of course, the word "section" is never abbreviated and never capitalized except when it is the first word of a sentence.)

11.4 Short titles

Major statutes need names by which they can be easily cited and referred to—their long titles are much too cumbersome for this purpose, and their public law numbers are too uninformative—so they are typically given "short titles". If the sponsor of a major bill has forgotten to ask for a short title, the drafter can quite appropriately suggest that one be included. You should not invent your own, however, since a short title has public relations consequences that are better left to the sponsor, except in those rare cases where the right short title is altogether obvious.

There is no reason to have a short title for narrow bills, designed to deal with particular problems or to meet particular needs, with one exception. If a bill amends a provision of law, and you need to clarify in the amended language that it is effective on the date of enactment of the bill (as opposed to the date of enactment of the law being amended), then the bill needs a short title to refer to. For example, if your bill amends the ABC Act by inserting a new sentence at the end of a subsection, which will change how that subsection will apply, you might give your bill a short title like "This Act may be referred to as the 'XYZ Act' ". The amendatory provision might read something like the following: "Section 3(b) of the ABC Act is amended by adding at the end the following: 'Any application filed under this subsection on or after the date of enactment of the XYZ Act shall be considered under the following criteria:' ".

While the drafter, as diplomatically as possible, would do well to discourage short titles in insignificant bills, it has become the norm at the Federal level for sponsors to insist on a short title for most bills.

A bill's short title customarily appears in the first section of the bill, immediately after the enacting clause (although in a few substantive fields it is traditionally placed at the end of the bill instead).[4] Its basic form is simple:

SECTION 1. SHORT TITLE.

This Act may be cited as the "ABC Act".

Note that the word "the" is not a part of the short title, and should not be included within the quotes.

Variations in this form do occur. If the bill is one of a series of comprehensive revisions of existing law that are enacted every year or two in the substantive field involved, the short title should reflect the bill's place in the series by mentioning the year of its enactment; the text of the section containing the short title should read "This Act may be cited as the 'ABC Act of [2025]' ". (Note, however, that you should not normally include the year of expected enactment in the short title when it is not necessary to distinguish among a series of laws; having to remember and restate that year will be a nuisance to everyone who has to cite the law.[5])

If the bill consists primarily of amendments to one or more existing statutes, it is appropriate (but not necessary) to insert "Amendments" before "Act" in the short title; thus "... the 'ABC Amendments Act [of 2025]' ".[6]

It has become common for sponsors to request separate short titles for some or all of the principal components of a major bill, even though the bill itself has a more comprehensive short title. This practice should generally be avoided; for citation and cross-reference purposes "title II of the ABC Act" is just as convenient as a separate short title for the component involved, and is much less confusing.

However, a separate short title for an individual component of a major statute that has its own comprehensive short title may be both appropriate and desirable—

(1) if that component is unrelated to the rest of the statute, so that the statute's comprehensive short title would completely misrepresent it (or would at least be misleading as applied to it); and

(2) in the case of an omnibus bill (such as a budget reconciliation bill) that consists of unrelated proposals that would otherwise constitute individual pieces of legislation.

The Congressional Budget and Impoundment Control Act of 1974 has separate short titles for its two major components. The "Congressional Budget Act of 1974" is the short title for the first nine titles of the Act (which relate to the congressional budget process). Title X is divided into three parts: the short title for parts A and B (which relate to Presidential impoundments) is the "Impoundment Control Act of 1974"; the short title for part C is the "Line Item Veto Act of 1996".[7]

One final comment. A short title should be short—it loses its value as a convenient handle if it is not. It should simply describe the field that the bill covers rather than going into detail about what the bill does. The Social Security Act, the National Housing Act, and the Internal Revenue Code of 1986 meet the test. At the other end of the spectrum are real stylistic horrors—consider for example the "Microenterprise for Self-Reliance and International Anti-Corruption Act of 2000" (Public Law 106-309), and the " 'Satellite Home Viewer Extension and Reauthorization Act of 2004' or the 'W. J. (Billy) Tauzin Satellite Television Act of 2004' " (title IX of Division J of Public Law 108-447).[8]

The last example given is bad on two other counts. The "short" title winds up having two short titles, which defeats the purpose of having a short title. You should resist naming the sponsor in the short title; leave it to posterity to give the sponsor the desired (and maybe even deserved) recognition. Note that the colloquial sponsor-related names often given to laws after their enactment, for easy reference, like the "Robinson-Patman Act", are both convenient and proper even though they cannot be used in statutory citations (except parenthetically, in an explanatory way). And, with the enactment of the Sarbanes-Oxley Act of 2002 (Public Law 107-204), it obviously became more important that the title reflect the sponsors than the subject matter of the law! It is not uncommon, in the Federal arena, to name bills in honor of or in memory of a Member of Congress or, on occasion, even a staff member or private individual.[9]

Needless to say, if the sponsor has a pet short title, you have no choice but to include it. And if a short title is actually taken up and considered in committee or on the floor and has to satisfy all of the legislators' conflicting public relations needs, almost anything can happen; you just have to live with it.

If you cannot come up with a short title that is short, simple, and easy to say, at least try to come up with one that has a pronounceable acronym (but always watch out for short titles whose acronyms, when read or pronounced, might seem derisive, suggestive, or otherwise inappropriate). More often than not, the sponsor will insist on a specific short title *because* of its acronym. It seems as though, among sponsors and their staffs, coming up with a short title that has a catchy acronym has become not only the norm but almost a competitive sport. And sometimes the acronym is *included* in the short title. High on the list is the "Uniting and Strengthening America by Providing Appropriate Tools Required to Intercept and Obstruct Terrorism (USA PATRIOT ACT) Act of 2001)" (Public Law 107-56) and the " 'Prosecutorial Remedies and Other Tools to End the Exploitation of Children Today Act of 2003' or 'PROTECT Act' " (Public Law 108-21). Note that because the acronym "(USA PATRIOT ACT)" Act was not placed in separate quotes, any reference to the law would have to cite the entire short title, including the embedded acronym (the PROTECT Act did not have this flaw). This flaw was remedied by an amendment to the short title, enacted in 2006 (Public Law 109-177), to separate the two:

> SEC. 101. REFERENCES TO, AND MODIFICATION OF SHORT TITLE FOR, USA PATRIOT ACT.
>
> (a) REFERENCES TO USA PATRIOT ACT.—A reference in this Act to the USA PATRIOT Act shall be deemed a reference to the Uniting and Strengthening America by Providing Appropriate Tools Required to Intercept and Obstruct Terrorism Act (USA PATRIOT Act) of 2001.
>
> (b) MODIFICATION OF SHORT TITLE OF USA PATRIOT ACT.— Section 1(a) of the USA PATRIOT Act is amended to read as follows:
>
> "(a) SHORT TITLE.—This Act may be cited as the 'Uniting and Strengthening America by Providing Appropriate Tools Required to Intercept and Obstruct Terrorism Act of 2001' or the 'USA PATRIOT Act'. ".

It helps if the short title is one that can intelligibly be shortened for conversational purposes. The Congressional Budget and Impoundment Control Act of 1974 is usually called simply the "Congressional Budget Act" (even though, as indicated earlier, it consists of two parts that have manageable short titles of their own), while any law whose short title specifies the year of its enactment can be conversationally referred to as "the [2025] Act" when the context is clear. Note that the administrative procedure and judicial review provisions in chapters 5 and 7 of title 5 of the United States Code are still commonly referred to (collectively) as "the Administrative Procedure Act" even though the latter Act was repealed and replaced by the title 5 provisions many years ago.

11.5 Tables of contents

If a lengthy bill has internal headings and is broken down into a large number of separate sections, particularly if it deals with several subjects and is also broken down into major components such as titles, subtitles, chapters, or parts, it should have a table of contents listing the headings of the sections and major components. And if the major components are lengthy, a subsidiary table of contents at the beginning of each of them should also be considered. This will greatly assist readers in finding their way through the morass (and will also serve as a working outline for the drafter while the bill is being developed).

Conversely, if a bill consists simply of a relatively few numbered sections—say sections 1 through 9—there is normally no good reason for a table of contents at all.

The table of contents should be located in the first section of the bill, immediately after the short title if there is one. Its style and form are not important, although there is a more or less standard form that should be followed in many jurisdictions; like the standard formats of bills and resolutions, it saves time if the format for the table of contents is included in the word processing program you are using. If not, using a model will help you here.

Note that although published compilations invariably contain tables of contents of the laws involved, these tables are often supplied by the compilers, and you cannot assume they are included in the laws themselves. If you are drafting a bill that adds a new section to one of these laws, you need to find out whether the table of contents is part of the law in order to know whether to include an amendment to the table of contents as well.

If the bill contains a provision adding a number of new sections to an existing law (such as a completely new title or chapter), it may be useful to show those sections in the table of contents along with the vehicular provision, adopting a format (such as indenting the items referring to those sections and surrounding them with quotation marks) that will distinguish them from the sections of the bill itself. See 16.5 for an example.

One word of caution. Section numbers are often changed, and headings are often revised, during the course of the drafting process; and the drafter should remember to conform the table of contents whenever that happens. If your word processing program enables you to rerun a table of contents at any point, this is a great time-saver. Otherwise, waiting until the bill is finished and then proofreading the table of contents against the numbers and headings of the bill's provisions (though a desirable final double check) isn't good enough, because there is too often no time to do it (or it is just plain forgotten) in the final rush.

11.6 Statements of findings and purposes; whereas clauses

The practice of preceding the substantive portion of a bill with a statement of legislative findings and purposes or a statement of legislative policy, or both, is becoming increasingly popular. Sponsors seem to like the approach because it gives them a way to make their arguments and speeches right there in the legislation. In an extreme case, a bill could have nothing in it except a dozen or so pages of findings, purpose, and policy, followed by a six-line substantive provision simply directing the designated official, in effect, to "carry out the purpose of this Act".

You should diplomatically discourage this practice. In most cases statements of findings and purpose are without legal significance; and in addition they are matters that are more appropriately (and more safely) dealt with in the different committee reports that will accompany the bill. The proper function of a bill—whatever the sponsor's reasons for it—is to do what the sponsor wants to do.

Note that there is no set form for statements of findings and purpose in a bill.

"Whereas clauses"—technically called the "preamble"—are used in resolutions to do what statements of findings and purpose do in bills. They appear before the resolving clause (and are therefore not part of the resolution proper) and are written in a "hanging" style rather than being paragraphed like normal bill provisions. They are punctuated as a list or series in the regular way (see chapter 21) and lead into the resolving clause with ": Now therefore be it" in place of a final period. For example:

> Whereas serious problems have recently arisen in the ABC program;
>
> Whereas something ought to be done about them; and
>
> Whereas time is of the essence: Now therefore be it
>
> *Resolved*, That [the designated official] should take immediate action to …

If the sponsor insists on including a statement of findings, purpose, or policy in a bill, or a series of whereas clauses in a resolution, you should ask the sponsor to submit draft language for your review, as these are statements of policy by the sponsor. You, in reviewing and editing the draft language, can raise issues with the sponsor, pointing out that all the factual statements and quoted material included in the findings must be accurate (errors are frequently apparent). You can usually pare down lengthy findings or whereas clauses editorially. You should also point out that, in the case of lengthy findings (or whereas clauses), readers of the bill (or resolution) may lose interest before getting to the main message of the bill (or resolution).

A word of caution about statements of findings and purpose: if the bill is enacted into law, a reviewing court may look to them (and will, before consulting committee reports) in interpreting the meaning of the law. Therefore, as the drafter, you should never treat them as extraneous.

There is a case in which including findings may be appropriate *because* a court may review the law: if a court is construing a regulatory law or other law affecting commerce when the constitutional basis for the Federal action may be open to question, a finding stating the constitutional basis for the bill can guide the court. The Supreme Court has affirmed that, in evaluating constitutionality under the Commerce Clause, it will consider legislative findings (and even congressional committee findings) regarding effect on interstate commerce (*United States v. Lopez,* 514 U.S. 549, 562 [1995]). In that case, however, there were no congressional findings; the statute in question (making it a Federal offense for "any individual knowingly to possess a firearm at a place that the individual knows, or has reasonable cause to believe, is a school zone") was held not to be within Congress's power to regulate commerce. However, in *United States v. Morrison*, 529 U.S.

598 (2000), a case in which there were congressional findings, the Supreme Court nonetheless held against the constitutionality of the statute involved ("the existence of congressional findings is not sufficient, by itself, to sustain the constitutionality of Commerce Clause legislation") (529 U.S. at 614).[10]

Suffice it to say that when drafting a bill to govern, for example, the intrastate manufacture and distribution of a particular article, you should be amenable to a congressional finding that the manufacture and distribution of that article "affects" and is a "burden" on interstate commerce (and therefore is subject to regulation under the Commerce Clause of the Constitution), and also to language that includes a basis for the court's determining the "substantial" effect on interstate commerce, even though findings cannot make a bill constitutional.

11.7 Definitions

11.7A In general. Whenever a bill repeatedly uses a term that may be unfamiliar, unclear, or ambiguous (even if only when taken out of context), or uses a term in a sense that differs from its dictionary meaning, you should define it in the bill. A formal declaration that "as used in this Act [or section], the term 'A' means 'XX' " effectively dispels all doubt about the term's meaning.

The corollary is that a definition should never recite the obvious. A term that is familiar, clear, and used in its dictionary sense should never be formally defined (unless there are special circumstances that call for reassurance to the reader)—it would be unnecessary and might create doubts about the meaning of other familiar words in the bill. For example, the term "State" should be defined if you want to include the District of Columbia or Puerto Rico (or any other territory or possession of the United States), but not if you mean to include only the 50 States. Definitions help answer the question to whom or what does the bill apply.

The proper use of definitions in a bill does more than simply clarify the meaning of its crucial terms, however. It promotes internal consistency by assuring that those terms are given the same meaning regardless of their context, it avoids clutter, and it promotes readability and drafting economy by making the bill shorter and its language less cumbersome. In short, the purpose of definitions is to achieve clarity and consistency without burdensome repetition.

Of equal importance is the fact that definitions can reduce complexity by allowing the bill's key operating provisions to be stated simply, even when the concepts they involve are extremely complicated. Dealing with those concepts in a separate definition section does not actually eliminate the complications, of course, but it segregates them from the operating provisions and makes them easier to handle (see 23.2). It must be admitted, however, that the intensive use of definitions in this way usually entails putting at least some of the substantive rules in the definitions—a practice that has powerful enemies (and about which the views expressed in this book may not reflect the majority position among drafting commentators). See the discussion of definitions containing substantive rules ("stuffed definitions") below.

11.7B Placement of definitions. In general, definitions should be placed where they can be most easily found, and where they will be most helpful to the reader. Thus the definition of a term used in only one section of a bill should always be included in that section, while the definitions of terms used throughout the bill should always be grouped in a separate section (usually headed simply "Definitions") that normally appears early in the bill. The individual definitions in such a section are usually arranged in descending order of importance, although sometimes they are arranged alphabetically. (The problem with alphabetizing is that the addition of a new definition will require the redesignation of all the paragraphs appearing after the point where the new definition is inserted, often with extensive conforming changes elsewhere.[11])

Admittedly, definitions stacked at the beginning of a bill can be tedious and will delay the reader in coming to the bill's operative provisions. But their placement up front serves an important purpose: It gives the reader an early warning of any terms that may be obscure or technical or that are to be used in ways that differ from their dictionary definitions, and it ultimately makes the bill's operative provisions easier to comprehend.

If you do not want to confront the reader with a series of long and complicated definitions at the outset and prefer to place them instead in a later section of the bill—*HOLC* (page 20) takes the position that definitions should never precede the main message unless there are "strong organizational or tactical reasons" for it—you should at least include an unmistakable early cross-reference to that section. For example:

> ( ) Definitions.—For definitions of terms [or "the principal terms"] used in this Act, see section _____.

Sometimes the defined terms in a bill include one or two basic terms along with a number of others that are less important. In such cases, according to *HOLC* (page 21), it is appropriate to define each of the important ones in a separate section (headed "**XX DEFINED**") and the others in another section (headed "**OTHER DEFINITIONS**").

Whether or not the bill contains a separate section or subsection devoted exclusively to definitions, if there is a recurring term (for example, an organizational name or title such as "Agency" or "Secretary") that could use a short definition, it is quite proper (despite the apparent violation of the rules given above) to simply insert the definition parenthetically after the first mention of that term. Thus:

> **SEC. 2. RESPONSIBILITIES OF THE SECRETARY OF HOUSING AND URBAN DEVELOPMENT.**
>
> (a) IN GENERAL.—The Secretary of Housing and Urban Development (in this [Act, section, or other provision] referred to as the "Secretary") shall …

And if a defined term is used ahead of the definition and it is particularly important in the context to warn the reader that the term has a specially prescribed meaning, a specific (though technically unnecessary) parenthetical warning—"(as defined in section _____)"—can be inserted immediately after the term where it is first used.

11.7C Forms of definitions. Except as noted later under this heading, the basic form for every definition is as follows:

( ) DEFINITIONS.—In this Act [or section], the term "A" means ...;

or, in a section or subsection containing a list of definitions (see part VI for more about punctuation and style):

SEC. ______. DEFINITIONS.

In this Act:

(1) A.–The term "A" means ....

(2) B.–The term "B" means ....

The advantage of this format is that each definition has a heading and is easy to find. It is, however, acceptable to use the following as well:

SEC. ______. DEFINITIONS.

In this Act—

(1) the term "A" means ...; and

(2) the term "B" means ....

The lead-in language of any definition may properly take either of the forms used in the models just given; in addition, it may say "As used in this Act" or "For purposes of this Act". These three forms are interchangeable for all practical purposes, although the one that begins "For purposes of" may be slightly broader; in theory at least it could conceivably get a different result when two interrelated laws with different definitions are involved (and it works better when it precedes a list that includes both definitions and other things).

You should always include the modifying phrase "the term" in any definition. This avoids possible confusion over initial capitalization of the defined term, and in addition permits the later use of the construction ", except that such term does not include...".

If it is inevitable that the defined term will sometimes be used in the bill in a different sense, it is permissible to add the phrase "(unless the context requires otherwise)" after "As used in this Act". Examples include definitions of terms like "Secretary" or "Commissioner"— referring to the Federal official who will administer the bill—in cases where other officials with the same word in their title will be mentioned as well. It is better, however, to avoid the phrase, and to state the exceptions (by cross-reference) within the definition itself, unless they are too numerous. As a practical matter, if you spell out the full titles of the other officials each place they are mentioned, and never refer to any of them as just "the Secretary" or "the Commissioner", the problem solves itself. And the difficulty with "Unless the context requires otherwise" is that it becomes unclear *when* the context requires otherwise.

If a defined term contains two or more terms that are themselves defined but are used only in the compound term, the definitions of those terms should be made subsets of whatever provision defines the compound term.

When you use a defined term, use it in the same form as that contained in the definition. If you defined the word "produce", then do not use "production". If you are going to use both "produce" and "production", then "production" should be included in the defined term (for example, the terms "produce" and "production" refer to ...). Do not use introductory language like "In this Act, the following terms *and their variant forms* mean the following:". Define terms in the singular. If you use the plural in the bill, there is no confusion about whether you mean more than one of the defined term.

Consider the following definition in section 101 of title 17, United States Code:

> "Copies" are material objects, other than phonorecords, in which a work is fixed by any method now known or later developed, and from which the work can be perceived, reproduced, or otherwise communicated, either directly or with the aid of a machine or device. The term "copies" includes the material object, other than a phonorecord, in which the work is first fixed.

The first difficulty is that by not using "the term" before the definition, "Copies" is capitalized. Because of this, every time that word is used in title 17, it should be capitalized (note that the second sentence begins with "The term 'copies' ...". Because the definition has no designation (as in a paragraph number), the only way to refer to this definition is "the definition of 'copies' contained in section 101 of title 17, United States Code".[12] Second, the term is used in the plural, when the description is talking about the fixation of a single work. (See 21.2 on the virtues of using the singular.) This would technically mean that a single work can only be fixed in multiple copies, not a single copy. Then the second sentence says that the term "copies" includes *the* material object. Again, this looks like the material object can only be fixed in multiple copies, not one copy. And worst of all, the term "copy" is used throughout title 17, including in other definitions. There is no reason for not defining "copy" instead of "copies". Also, because there is both a "means" and "includes" in the definition, it would be clearer to separate them out. (As another drafting matter, using "now or later developed" is an unclear temporal statement. If "now" was the date on which the provision was enacted, it should say so.) A redraft could look like this:

> The term "copy"—
>
> (1) means a material object, other than a phonorecord,[13] in which a work is fixed by any method known on the date of enactment of this title or developed on or after that date, and from which the work can be perceived, reproduced, or otherwise communicated, either directly or with the aid of a machine or device; and
>
> (2) includes the material object, other than a phonorecord, in which the work is first fixed.[14]

Any use of "copies" in title 17 would then clearly mean more than 1 copy.[15]

If a term to which reference is made is not defined in existing law, but is defined by an officer in the executive branch under express or implied authority given by law (*SOLC* [page 18]), you can say the term "(as defined *under* section 123 of the ABC Act (YY U.S.C. ZZZ))". If a term used in statute is not defined in the statute or by regulation, but a meaning has evolved through administrative or judicial decisions (*SOLC* [page 18]), you can say the term "(*within the meaning of* section 123 of the ABC Act (YY U.S.C. ZZZ))".

11.7D "Means" and "includes". In definitions, the word "means" is used to establish the complete meaning of a term, and the word "includes" is used when the purpose is to make it clear that the term encompasses some specific matter. To put it in a slightly different way, one thing means another when the two are identical or synonymous, and one thing includes another when the second is a part of the first.

The word "means" is seldom misused, but the word "includes" is frequently found where it should not be or is accompanied by language that prevents it from playing its part as the dictionary intended (see 22.5 and 22.15, which address some common instances of the latter).

11.7E Invented words. If there is no right word to describe a concept or relationship frequently referred to in a bill, or if the available words carry with them too much baggage, you should feel free to invent a word or term and then define it. Most cases of this kind involve complex concepts or relationships for which a short, simple, and fully descriptive term—at least one that is free of emotional content and partisan disadvantage—simply does not exist in the English language.

The point is that if you are going to have to refer frequently to a complicated concept or relationship, you need to give it a manageable name; and if one is not otherwise available you may have to make one up. It need not be clever or imaginative; consider the defined term "section 306 stock" and the term "S corporations" (for businesses that are covered by subchapter S), in the Internal Revenue Code of 1986 (which even invents and defines "C corporations" to refer to businesses that are not covered by subchapter S).

Or consider how the drafters of the Medicare law, unable to come up with a descriptive name for the key period of time against which Medicare entitlement is calculated, finally settled for "spell of illness" despite the fact that the period's main component is a spell of nonillness, apparently on the theory that the term is so folksy that no one could expect it to be accurately descriptive.

In all fairness it should be noted that some commentators have reservations about using invented words, as a matter of principle. *Hirsch* (page 44) claims that "innovation in devising new meanings for words is a flaw, not an asset, in a [drafter]", and goes on to say that "[c]ertainty of meaning largely depends on the [drafter's] unbendingly conservative use of language".

If you do invent a term, just be sure that it points in the right direction and will not look silly in your bill, and then define it to mean exactly what you want it to mean.

11.7F Partial definitions. In many cases it is best to assume the dictionary meaning of a term and merely clarify its penumbra. For example, if you want to include osteopaths in a grant program on the same basis as physicians (the latter being a term that is reasonably clear on its face), you need not redefine "physician"—you can simply provide that "the term 'physician' includes an osteopathic practitioner as determined under the law of the State in which the practitioner is practicing".

To take another example, there is a world of difference between "The term 'State' means the District of Columbia" on the one hand and "The term 'State' includes the District of Columbia" on the other. The former (which is ridiculous on its face) is a true definition in every sense; while the latter (which is thoroughly rational) is considered a definition only because it is convenient to do so.

The use of the word "includes" in this sort of construction normally indicates that something that is not really within the defined term is to be treated as though it were; it is a "partial definition", and assumes that what is within the defined term is clear enough to need no definition. So long as this is so, the use of "includes" is quite proper and even desirable—it saves having to restate (in the previous example) the self-evident fact that the 50 States are really "States" before going on to say that the District of Columbia should be treated as though it were a State too. But in any other situation "includes" should be avoided.

11.7G Definitions containing substantive rules. Sometimes a general term that occurs frequently in a long bill will be used in a slightly different way in particular circumstances or will have a slightly different application in particular types of cases. In this situation, building the necessary exceptions, exclusions, conditions, and even expansions into the definition of the general term instead of into the operating provisions themselves (in effect stating the substantive rules in the definition) is often the best and easiest way to accomplish what would otherwise require a whole series of "special rule" provisions throughout the bill. For example:

> ( ) DEFINITION.—As used in this Act, the term "A" means XX; except that—
>
> (1) when used in sections ___ and ___, it means YY, and
>
> (2) whenever used to describe [a particular kind of relationship], it also includes ZZ.

As indicated earlier, many professional drafters frown upon this practice as a matter of principle. *Dickerson* (pages 151–152) uses the term "stuffed definitions" to describe definitions that include substantive rules, and describes them as not only inartistic but dangerous; he feels that the practice, which the authors approve primarily because it simplifies key operating provisions, in fact has quite the opposite effect because it makes it harder for the reader to fit the pieces of the puzzle together and makes the key operating provisions themselves unclear. He suggests that a good working test of whether a substantive rule and its accompanying definitions are properly stated is whether the reader can get a generally accurate and complete impression of the substantive rule without referring to the definitions at all.

And *Hirsch* (page 31) points out that the practice "may mislead one who reads only the bill's substantive sections, which have thereby been rendered deceptively simple. The reader may believe that he has grasped the bill's essential rules, when unknown to him a body of them is elsewhere."

Hirsch cites as an example the definition of "new animal drug" (before it was amended in 1988) under the Federal Food, Drug, and Cosmetic Act, which regulates new animal drugs but authorizes the Secretary of Health and

Human Services to exempt any such drug from regulation if the Secretary finds that it is generally recognized as safe, effective, and pure; however, this exemption authority was included in the definition itself instead of being stated as a substantive provision, so that the provision containing the Secretary's authority to regulate the drugs paints an incomplete picture. The 1988 amendment struck this part of the definition, perhaps proving Hirsch's point.

It is true that a reader would not instinctively expect to encounter substantive rules in definitions; and it is one of the drafter's objectives to help the reader find all the pieces. In a rational world all definitions would be sterile and totally devoid of substance; and you should normally keep your substantive rules in the operating provisions where they belong.

But placing substantive rules within a definition is often the fastest and easiest way to dispose of them, which makes the practice a valuable one for drafters facing time pressures. In addition, the most important objective is to keep the key operating provisions of the bill free of unnecessary clutter and complexity; and if burying some of the substantive complications in a definition section will promote that objective the practice will as often as not promote clarity as well as readability. And a reader who fails to look at the definitions in concert with the main provisions will not understand the bill in any case. See 23.2 for a further discussion, along with some examples.

11.7H Artificial definitions. Defining the term "State" to include the District of Columbia and the territories and possessions of the United States for purposes of some Federal program does create a fiction, but it is a rational way (and usually the best way) of saying that the District and those possessions should be treated the same as States under that program. After all, they are governmental entities like States, and possess many of the attributes of States; and in addition the practice avoids the need to repeat throughout the bill a litany of entities such as "a State, the District of Columbia, the Commonwealth of Puerto Rico, Guam, the Virgin Islands, American Samoa, the Commonwealth of the Northern Mariana Islands, and any other territory or possession of the United States". The convenience of the practice quite properly overcomes the reservations of the purists.

On the other hand, if a term is given a meaning that is too different from its dictionary meaning or from common understanding, the drag of its original meaning may lay a trap for the reader and even the drafter, who may have difficulty later in remembering the artificial usage (especially in a lengthy bill). *Dickerson* discusses the psychological basis of the link between language and communication that is learned. He states that "[t]he lawyer who defines 'wheat' as including 'rye' is laying a trap not only for his readers but for himself"; and he goes on to say (pages 143–144):

> Even a legislature is powerless to repeal the psychological law on which this is based. Like ghosts returning to a haunted house, established connotations return to haunt the user who attempts to banish them ... [When a fiction is actually necessary] the [drafter] should continue to use ... words in their normal senses and label the fiction plainly by using "as if" [for example, by saying "X shall be treated as if it were Y" instead of "the term 'X' means (or includes) Y"].

As an example of the practice at its worst, *Dickerson* cites (page 141) a series of bills (in the 1950s) that defined "September 16, 1940" to mean "June 27, 1950" in a shorthand effort to apply some of the World War II rules to military personnel engaged in the Korean conflict. And *Hirsch* (pages 17-18) cites the case of a bill (which actually passed Congress twice) that defined "poultry" to include domesticated rabbits and "feathers" to include their pelts; this one is described more fully later.

Definitions of this kind, which *Hirsch* calls "definitional roulette" and *Dickerson* calls "Pickwickian" or "Humpty-Dumpty" definitions (the latter in reference to Mr. Dumpty's assertion of his freedom to make words stand for whatever he pleased), are unnecessarily artificial and completely irrational. They might be technically effective (in theory at least) but they guarantee confusion and invite massive administrative problems.

As a drafter, you should not feel that you should never define terms in ways that conflict with normal understanding—properly used the practice is too often the best way to solve a difficult problem—although much of what these commentators have said has merit. Extremely artificial definitions should always be avoided, and even moderately artificial ones should be used with special care. Some slight stretching of a term's meaning is often acceptable, especially when there is a reasonable relationship between the content of the term as defined and its content in normal usage, but if you stray too far from reality your sponsor may have to pay the price.

11.7I Across-the-board statutory definitions. In identifying the terms that need defining in a bill and in developing the definitions, you should be aware of any definitions and other rules regarding terminology that may be contained in the permanent law of the jurisdiction involved. Such definitions and rules (which are found in both Federal and State law) are often written so as to apply to all of the laws of that jurisdiction.

Most of the across-the-board Federal instances are found in chapter 1 of title 1 of the United States Code; these include definitions of such terms as "person", "officer", "writing", "county", "vessel", and "vehicle", along with various rules of construction (such as that the singular includes the plural and vice versa, the masculine includes the feminine, and the present tense includes the future). The pertinent part of the text of chapter 1 is set forth in 19.5.

But others appear elsewhere—the Congressional Budget Act of 1974, for example, included a Government-wide definition of the term "fiscal year", so that it is now correct to say simply "fiscal year [2025]" instead of "the fiscal year [ending September 30, 2025]" (see also 22.8).

The existence of across-the-board statutory definitions may render unnecessary (or require modifications in) some of the definitions that you would otherwise have to include in a bill. A word of caution, however. A later Congress can override, even by implication, what an earlier Congress has done, and if you think your bill (because of its special characteristics) might be judicially determined to have overridden one of these definitions, you might consider including an explicit citation to the definition involved to make your meaning absolutely clear.

Notes

1 There is one exception. Section 105 of title 1, United States Code, specifies the title for any Act making appropriations, as follows: "An Act making appropriations (here insert the object [for example, for foreign operations]) for the year ending September 30 (here insert the calendar year)." *SOLC* (page 12).

2 Sometimes a sponsor dictates the wording of a long title, perhaps to avoid stating specifically what the bill does, or to state a broad policy objective that does not reflect what the bill does (a bill that, for example, increases penalties for bribery might read, "A bill to clean up corruption").

3 "Flush" indicates that the sentence is to be printed without the first line indented, as you would in a new subdivision. See 30.2.

4 At the Federal level, the short titles of the appropriations bills appear at the very end of the bills.

5 Unfortunately, most sponsors at the Federal level insist on including the year in the title; there is, at least, the virtue of knowing for historical purposes when bills were enacted.

6 It would be unwise to give such a bill a short title like the "ABC Amendments of 2025". If a later bill had to refer to this law, the grammar would become sticky: would you say the "ABC Amendments of 2025 are amended" or the "ABC Amendments of 2025 is amended"?

7 Part C was declared unconstitutional in 1996 as a violation of the Presentment clause of the U.S. Constitution.

8 Public Law 117-103, The Consolidated Appropriations Act, 2022, is an example of the mammoth omnibus bills (1067 pages) that are enacted at the Federal level, covering multiple subjects (in addition to appropriations).

9 Note, for example, the Admiral James W. Nance and Meg Donovan Foreign Relations Authorization Act, Fiscal Years 2000 and 2001.

10 For a further discussion of *Lopez and Morrison*, see chapter 29.

11 This is true whether a definition is added during the drafting process or whether you have to add a new definition to a law with definitions in alphabetical order. To be consistent, you would insert the new definition where it belongs alphabetically and then have to check the rest of that law and all other laws to ensure that cross-references are accurate. To avoid these technical difficulties, you can simply add the definition at the end and not worry about the alphabetical scheme. This has happened in a number of statutes.

12 At least the definitions in section 101 are in alphabetical order, so the reader knows where to look for a particular definition.

13 The definition of "Phonorecords" in section 101 of title 17, United States Code, has the same flaws as the definition of "copies".

14 If this were an amendment to section 101 of title 17, you would not be able to assign a number to this definition of "copy" without assigning numbers to all of the other definitions. This is a case in which the Roman rule applies. See chapter 8.

15 Section 1 of title 1, United States Code, (title 1 has across-the-board definitions for Federal law discussed at the end of this chapter) says that words importing the singular "include and apply to several persons, parties, or things". Although that section also says that "words importing the plural include the singular", the example shown is evidence of the ambiguity that can arise from this practice.

12. The Central Provisions

12.1 Preliminary comments

This chapter lists and briefly discusses the different provisions or types of provisions that you might reasonably expect to encounter in the central part of any bill—the part that actually carries out the sponsor's basic policy.

However, keep in mind the following:

(1) No two bills are the same, and only a very massive bill is likely to contain all of the provisions discussed in this chapter. However, the list in this chapter should not be considered exhaustive either; many bills will require additional central provisions to serve some special purpose.

(2) The majority of introduced bills, and nearly all amendments offered to bills, are "one-shot" in nature. The former typically consist of "key operating provisions" only (with perhaps one or two other "central" provisions to make them work), while the latter (which typically attack or append a single item or element in the bill under consideration) are likely to be even narrower.

(3) Any of the provisions discussed in this chapter can be either freestanding or amendatory. Part V discusses the two forms, along with the reasons you might have for selecting one form over the other.

(4) Although all of the provisions discussed in this chapter after 12.2 are treated as independent "supportive" provisions only, they are often written as a part of (that is, integrated into) the key operating provisions rather than being stated separately; and in special-purpose bills, they may actually be the key operating provisions.

Please note that the order in which the "central" provisions are presented should be regarded as no more than a rough approximation of the order in which they normally appear in a bill. Different bills use different systems of arrangement, and all are acceptable so long as the principles laid down in chapter 6 are observed.

12.2 The key operating provisions

The key operating provisions of a bill are the provisions that carry out the bill's principal objective; they state the basic policy or main thrust, and might include most of the subsidiary and collateral policies as well. These provisions can take many forms because what they do and how they do it will depend upon the nature and scope of the bill's principal objective and upon the kinds of things that have to be done in order to achieve it.

They may be the only purely substantive part of the bill, with any supportive provisions being integrated into them (as would often be the case when the supportive provisions are short, simple, and few in number); or they may constitute no more than a statement of the main thrust in its broad affirmative outlines, leaving some or all of the necessary supportive provisions to be handled separately in later sections. (Note that exceptions and special rules of the type discussed in 12.3 should always be thought of as part of the key operating provisions even when they are set forth separately.) Sometimes, when the focus of the sponsor's objective is narrow enough, the key operating provisions may constitute the entire bill.

In a bill intended to improve the everyday operation of some existing program, the key operating provisions may consist entirely of administrative provisions (which in most bills would be supportive only—see 12.9) or structural provisions (see 12.4). In a bill designed to improve enforcement under an existing program, they may consist entirely of criminal provisions or other sanctions (see 12.10). Indeed, any of the supportive provisions discussed in this chapter can turn out to be key operating provisions instead.

The key operating provisions of a bill are its centerpiece, of course— they are highly visible, always substantive, and frequently bulky—but they can be short and simple even in a major bill. The National Aeronautics and Space Act of 1958 (even before it became laden with extraneous subprograms) was anything but short and simple—it took a lot of words to create NASA and to deal with the many novel space-related problems—but its basic key operating provision occupied only a few lines:

> (a) The Administration, in order to carry out the purpose of this Act, shall—
>
> (1) plan, direct, and conduct aeronautical and space activities;

The statement of the Act's purpose (which took a few pages) and the definition of "aeronautical and space activities" (which took about half a page) completed the picture; they were located elsewhere, of course. (Note that here, as in the similar cases mentioned in 11.6, the meat of the bill is not contained in the operating provisions at all; this approach may occasionally work, but you should try to avoid it.)

Needless to say, no matter how many of the supportive provisions you feel free to develop on your own, close collaboration with the sponsor on the key operating provisions is a must.

12.3 Exceptions and special rules

The key operating provisions of a bill incorporate what drafters call the "general rule"—the sponsor's main thrust or primary purpose— but there are almost always persons or things to which the general rule does not apply ("exceptions") and there are often persons or things to which it applies but in a different way ("special rules").

In one sense the broadest exceptions are usually incorporated into the general rule—sometimes in the form of exceptions (clauses beginning with "except that" or "unless") but often simply in the form of descriptive language (characterizing the rights and duties involved) that has the effect of "excepting" anyone who does not fit the description.

It would be possible, of course, in the case of a bill that is to apply only to citizens of the United States, to phrase the general rule so that it applies to everyone in the world, and then add a specific exception for anyone who is not a citizen of the United States. But it is easier (and better) to begin the general rule with "Every citizen of the United States shall ...", thereby excluding aliens at the outset. (This is not quite as farfetched as it may sound; in the 1950s the Railroad Retirement Board, in an attempt to do something about the growing number of bereaved spouses who were concealing the deaths of their husbands in order to continue cashing the latter's benefit checks, seriously proposed legislation creating a rebuttable presumption that every beneficiary had died at the end of each month.)

In a similar but slightly more realistic vein, a provision designed to impose a special reporting requirement on people who claim trade or business expense deductions on their income tax returns should obviously begin "Any individual who claims a deduction for the taxable year under section 162 [of the Internal Revenue Code of 1986] shall file a report …". It should not impose the requirement generally and then add a special exception for people who do not claim such a deduction.

Even narrower exceptions and limitations can be written into the general rule instead of being separately stated. Thus (in the example just given), if the sponsor wants to exempt smaller businesses from the reporting requirement, one way to do it would be simply to insert the words "of more than $25,000" (or other dollar figure consistent with the sponsor's policy) immediately after "deduction" in the general rule.

All of this should be self-evident. The point is, of course, that narrowing the scope of the bill by identifying at the outset the persons or things to whom it applies helps the reader, as long as the necessary language is not so lengthy and cumbersome that its inclusion makes the general rule harder rather than easier to read. You can usually invent a term that fits the main target and then define that term at the appropriate place in the bill, including the limitations or exceptions within the definition; the language of the example given might then simply read "Every small-business taxpayer shall file a report …", with the term "small-business taxpayer" defined separately.

Exceptions and special rules are often too long and complicated to be appropriately included within the general rule itself, or too obviously substantive to be included in a definition without incurring the wrath of the purists. It then becomes necessary to put them in a provision of their own, couched in language that clearly indicates just what it is they are exceptions to.

This also should be self-evident, and needs no detailed discussion here. If you feel compelled to create a separate provision for exceptions or special rules, there are only two questions that need to be addressed:

(1) Where in the bill should the exceptions or special rules be placed?

(2) To what extent should you include explicit cross-references to indicate the relationship between the general rule and the exceptions or special rules?

The answer to question (1) is clear. Exceptions and special rules are just as substantive as general rules even though somewhat narrower in scope, and they often constitute an extremely important part of the sponsor's basic policy. They should accordingly be treated as a part of the key operating provisions of the bill, and should usually appear immediately after the general rule—either in a separate subsection of the section in which the general rule appears or in a separate section immediately following that section.

The answer to question (2) is more difficult, and (assuming that your exceptions and special rules are clearly recognizable as such) you have a choice.

Assume, for example, that you are working on section 2 of a bill to require that visitors to national parks pay admission fees (or higher admission fees) with full knowledge that section 16 of the bill will exempt senior citizens or reduce the fees on legal holidays. Section 16 will be effective in any case—under principles of statutory interpretation[1] it would be read as providing an exception to the general rule, so there is no actual need for any cross-reference at all. However, an express acknowledgment of the relationship between the two sections (by a simple cross-reference in section 2 or even in section 16) might help the reader get the whole picture.

The considerations that might be involved in making this kind of choice are discussed in 22.4, but keep in mind the following:

On the one hand, maximum clarity would be served by including explicit cross-references at every opportunity, both in the general rule and in the exceptions and special rules. After all, if they were included within the general rule itself their relationship to that rule would be explicitly indicated by prepositional or conjunctive phrases such as "except that the individual may not …", "unless the individual is …", or "but any action taken under this section shall not apply to …"; and there seems no valid reason to be less explicit simply because the provisions involved are separated.

On the other hand, multiple cross-references do tend to interfere with readability, at least for people who are not used to statutory language. In addition, if the exceptions and special rules are carefully written, they will not only be readily recognizable as such but will also apply correctly, and reach the intended result, whether or not they show on their face the designation of the general-rule provision they affect.

In most bills of any substance there are many interrelationships between provisions, ranging from blatant inconsistencies to the subliminal; an argument can be made that if you decide to include explicit cross-references for the important ones but not for the others you may have trouble deciding where to draw the line.

In drafting, you should attempt to make the relationship between a bill's provisions apparent to its readers. If the general rule and the exceptions are placed so that they can be read more or less as a unit—in successive subsections or successive sections—and especially if the provision containing the exceptions can be clearly labeled "Exceptions" (this is an example of why using headings is so important), you should feel free to omit the cross-references. In other cases, however, you ought to include them if you think it might help the reader.

12.4 Institutional structure

In a significant number of bills the sponsor's basic policy cannot be properly effectuated without making changes in the structure, personnel, or procedures of the administering agency, or in its relationship to other agencies or programs. Sometimes it is even necessary to create a totally new office or agency. At other times the sponsor's basic policy involves no new substantive functions at all, but is simply designed to improve the administration of an existing program through changes in institutional structure or procedures or through a reallocation of existing functions. (In the latter case, of course, the institutional changes are the key operating provisions.)

Structural changes in an existing agency, and changes in existing functions and procedures, must usually be made through amendments to the existing law. However, the creation of a new office or agency can often be done by either a freestanding or amendatory bill. If the basic policy plows totally new ground, the provision creating it would normally be freestanding (unless the entire bill is amendatory), but if it will operate in a field that is already covered by comprehensive legislation the provision likely would amend that legislation.

Drafting structural provisions is normally quite straightforward. Such provisions usually are boilerplate; after all, every agency must have a name, a staff, some functions, a fairly standard collection of powers, a fairly standard collection of administrative procedures, a source of funds, and other attributes that are common to all organizations (along with whatever unique attributes may be appropriate for that particular agency in light of its mission).

Your best approach is to seek out one or two examples of existing laws that create Federal agencies of similar scope or provide for their operation, and to pattern most of your structural provisions on the corresponding provisions in those laws—always remembering that your project will be different enough to require modifications in many of the provisions of those laws before you can use them as models.

Note that if your bill creates a new agency that replaces an existing one in whole or in part, or provides for the exercise of existing functions by a new or different agency, an explicit transfer of the existing functions may be required. The transfer of the principal substantive functions is often inherent in the key operating provisions, with the transfer of any administrative and other supporting functions along with related property and personnel being accomplished in a separate section (that could be titled "Administrative Transfers and Other Provisions") toward the end of the bill. There will almost

certainly be amendments to laws administered by the agency or agencies from whom the functions are transferred. Bills of this nature frequently have provisions stating that any reference in any provision of law to the [agency from which functions are transferred] shall be deemed to be a reference to the [agency to which the functions are transferred] to avoid these technical amendments. The provisions of law need to be checked nonetheless, because this one-size-fits-all approach does not work in every case.

12.5 Funding

It would be hard to imagine a law that costs no money at all. Even laws that involve no identifiable expenditures (for example, a law simply honoring some individual or group, or a private law permitting a named alien to remain in the country) will eventually require the use of some pens and paper clips, some printing, and the expenditure of some time by salaried employees. Most laws, of course, indicate their cost in a way that is much more obvious. And in almost all cases the necessary funds are obtained through appropriations.

Every appropriation must be authorized in advance, but the authorization may be either express or implied. If an explicit authorization provision is required it will seldom involve any drafting difficulties; 13.1 discusses the factors you should consider and lists the forms you should follow.

In most cases the authorization of appropriations simply provides the funding necessary to carry out the key operating provisions—it is substantive in that it determines the size of the program but has no other substantive content. For this reason it normally appears at the end of the bill (for the detailed discussion of the subject see 13.1). Sometimes, though, it is a key operating provision itself; in a program that accomplishes its objective by creating a supply of money and then allocating it among designated recipients, the authorization of appropriations is not only a key operating provision but is often the first one set forth.

There are ways of funding Federal programs, in theory at least, without the need for separate appropriations; and a few words about some of them follow.

For many years major programs were often funded by simply permitting the administering agencies to issue bonds and then directing the Secretary of the Treasury to purchase them. This device was called "Treasury borrowing" or (less charitably) "backdoor financing", and it enabled the legislative committees of Congress to control the size of the programs over which they had jurisdiction, to the exclusion of the appropriations committees (which might have whittled down the funding). But the turf battle between the two types of committees was long ago resolved in favor of the appropriations process. Under current congressional rules and precedents, funds can still be obtained by an agency through Treasury borrowing, but such funds can only be spent to the extent approved, in advance, in an appropriations Act.

As another example, the administrators of some of the older Federal trust funds were permitted to spend money from those funds without limit for their designated purposes, regardless of how that money got there. Under the current practice, money appropriated into a trust fund can still be spent that way; but money from any other source must be appropriated out of the trust fund before it can be spent.

Programs that generate revenues of their own (such as license or admission fees, or receipts from loan repayments) almost always have specific statutory limits on the extent to which those revenues can be retained and used for operating purposes.

Thus the old ways of obtaining funds from sources outside the direct appropriation process are still available, but they have lost their luster, since they can no longer be used to avoid the ordeal of "selling" a program twice—once to the legislative committees and once to the appropriations committees. As a practical matter, the appropriation process cannot be circumvented; and it is no longer realistic for sponsors to seek ways of doing it.

For this reason, drafters seldom have occasion to even consider any funding mechanism other than the straightforward authorization of appropriations.

12.6 Entitlements

Every drafter needs to understand what "entitlement" means, because sponsors may ask that their proposed programs be written as entitlement programs.

The true entitlement program is one in which the designated beneficiary (which may be a State or other public entity as well as an individual or other private entity) is legally entitled to a statutorily determined amount of assistance, whether or not the necessary funds are appropriated. In other words, the size of the appropriation does not govern the size of the program, since Congress is legally obligated (under the full faith and credit clause of the Constitution) to appropriate all the funds that are necessary.

You will sometimes hear "entitlement" inaccurately applied to a program under which the designated beneficiaries are legally entitled to a statutorily determined share of the program's appropriations. However, such a program does not actually create any entitlement in the current budgetary sense; Congress remains free to vary the appropriation from year to year as it pleases, and the designated beneficiary (though technically entitled to something) may in fact wind up with little or nothing when funds for the program are reduced or withheld. No matter what the specified share is, it equals zero if the amount appropriated is zero.

The significance of all this for the drafter is twofold. If the sponsor seeks to establish an entitlement program:

(1) The authorization of appropriations, if there is one, should be for an indefinite amount and should not be limited to any particular fiscal year or years. For example, a provision might read as follows: "There are authorized to be appropriated for each fiscal year such sums as are necessary to carry out the purposes of [the program]."

(2) There must be language in the bill that clearly establishes the entitlement. This is not difficult—it requires only the use of English words in their everyday sense. The phrase "Every [designated beneficiary] shall be entitled to receive a monthly payment in the

> amount of ..." or its equivalent will do the job. Do not add "from appropriations made therefor" or anything like it; that would create only the pseudoentitlement mentioned earlier. And be careful—the common phrase "The Secretary shall pay to every [designated beneficiary] ...", being addressed to the administering official rather than to the beneficiary, should not be regarded as creating an entitlement.

Entitlement language that governs an isolated situation within a nonentitlement program occasionally creates a narrowly limited entitlement, but more often it creates a pseudoentitlement at best because of its context.

The idea of a true entitlement may appeal to a sponsor, because it guarantees that the beneficiaries of the bill will actually receive the intended assistance. However, be aware (and warn the sponsor) that the Congressional Budget Act of 1974 imposes several parliamentary barriers, and prohibits Congress from even considering entitlement proposals under some circumstances (see chapter 34).

A full explanation of Federal budgetary concepts is beyond the scope of this book; 34.7 outlines some parliamentary considerations. You need a good grounding in budgetary concepts if you are to properly translate the sponsor's decisions not only on entitlements but also on such esoterica as "budget authority", "obligations", "outlays", "spending authority", "advance appropriations", and "credit authority". You should always have access to the most current Budget and should pay particular attention to the part dealing with "The Budget Systems and Concepts"; looking at the definitions in section 3 of the Congressional Budget Act of 1974 may also be helpful.

12.7 Federal mandates

It is worth mentioning here the Unfunded Mandates Reform Act of 1995,[2] which imposed certain requirements on the Congress and Federal agencies with respect to bills and laws containing Federal mandates. A Federal mandate refers to a provision in legislation, a statute, or a regulation that would impose an enforceable duty on a State or local government or the private sector.

The law establishes parliamentary hurdles to the consideration of any bill containing a Federal mandate without providing adequate funding to carry out that mandate. For example, section 425 of the Congressional Budget Act of 1974 (2 U.S.C. 658d) provides that it is not in order in the Senate or the House of Representatives to consider a bill or joint resolution carrying a Federal mandate without providing funding for the mandate (at levels specified under the law).

The Unfunded Mandates Reform Act also requires agencies to address unfunded mandates in the promulgation of rules.

You need to be familiar with this law so that you can advise the sponsor of the hurdles to be overcome if a bill you are drafting contains an unfunded mandate. And if you are drafting regulations, you need to be aware of the procedures imposed by the law in the rulemaking process. See 12.9.

12.8 Reports

It is common to require officials to make periodic reports (usually annually) on the functions or programs for which they are responsible. A provision requiring such a report is usually quite straightforward and might look something like this:

SEC. ____. REPORTS.

The [Secretary] shall, not later than ___ of each year, submit a report to Congress on the program under this Act. Each such report—

(1) shall include [specified items];

(2) shall indicate the progress that has been made during the preceding year toward achieving the objectives of this Act; and

(3) shall set forth in detail the [Secretary's] plans for carrying out the program during the ensuing year.

The items required by the report are often spelled out in considerably more detail, but this is a matter for the sponsor. Your concern with the additional details is very much like your concern with the specific declarations to be included in a statement of findings or purpose (see 11.6)—unless you have a model you can use without significant modification, simply take what the sponsor gives you and recast it in the proper form.

There are several other items worth noting and perhaps mentioning to your sponsor:

(1) It is wise to include a specific reporting date, either to ensure that each report will be made in time to be taken into consideration in the annual budget process or will otherwise fit properly into existing procedures, or to ensure the accountability of the reporting official (to the Congress or State or local legislature) for failing to file the report, or filing it late. Simply requiring an "annual" report, without a date certain, creates ambiguity about when the report is due.[3]

(2) The laws establishing departments and agencies of the Federal Government require the heads of those departments and agencies to make annual reports to Congress on the activities and programs under their jurisdiction. If the administering official in your bill is subject to that requirement, a special reporting requirement may be unnecessary, except to the extent your bill requires specific items to be addressed. One caution, however: at the Federal level, many general reporting requirements have been eliminated by law, so you need to make sure that if you are relying on a reporting requirement elsewhere, the requirement still exists. If your administering official is a subordinate officer within a department or agency, you might want to require that the report be made to the head of that department or agency (for inclusion in the regular annual report) instead of directly to Congress.

(3) You may find provisions in another bill (or law) that require reports from program administrators to be made both to the President (or chief executive of a State or local government) and to the Congress (or State or local legislature). There is nothing wrong with this practice, although it is probably unnecessary; the President (or chief executive) presumably is aware of the operations of agencies in the executive branch. The one exception at the Federal level, however, would be in the case of independent agencies (like the various "Commissions"—the Federal Communications Commission (FCC), Federal Trade Commission (FTC), Securities and Exchange Commission (SEC), and International Trade Commission (ITC)—that are designed to operate independently of the President as they are headed by multiple "commissioners" appointed to a fixed term of years from both political parties, instead of serving at the pleasure of the President.

Note that reports to Congress should in general be addressed to Congress—that is, your reporting provision should require that they be made "to Congress" or "to the Senate and House of Representatives", and not to the particular committees having jurisdiction over the matters involved. Requiring that the reports be made directly to the committees is unnecessary, since the presiding officers of both Houses will automatically rerefer the reports to them anyway; it may, therefore, antagonize the leadership officials of both Houses (who feel that it is their right and duty to receive and refer all executive communications), to the probable detriment of the sponsor. There may be reasons, however, to specify the committee to which the sponsor wants the report to go: it may be unclear which committees would have jurisdiction over the report; the sponsor may want a committee to see the report despite not having primary jurisdiction; or the sponsor may want to exclude primary referral to other committees (for example, the sponsor may want the authorizing committee, but not the appropriations committee, to see the report first).

12.9 Administrative and judicial review provisions

Every program has to be administered by someone. As a drafter you have a special responsibility to ensure that, mechanically at least, the bill's directives can be followed. Otherwise, you can be left with beautifully written statutory provisions that for purely administrative reasons cannot be given effect.

As the drafter you need to think about the inclusion of some "administrative" provisions in your bill to make sure the program is carried out the way in which the sponsor wants it.

Many things contribute to the administrative climate in which your bill will operate—the particular official or agency you choose to run the show, the institutional structure you create, and the nature and scope of the program itself, for example, as well as the extent of the administrative discretion that the sponsor wishes to allow.

You can prescribe whatever rules and procedures you like, of course, but unless you are an incorrigible innovator or an accredited expert on administrative law, you will probably do what most drafters do— leave the details to the so-called Administrative Procedure Act (APA) (now spread over several chapters of title 5 of the United States Code). Every drafter needs to become well-grounded in these provisions (or comparable provisions in the jurisdiction for which you are drafting). The following are several potential trouble spots in the APA you should know about.

Rulemaking. If you are silent on the question of rulemaking (unless you are amending a statute that provides its own rulemaking procedures), any regulations to be issued by an agency under your bill will be subject to the informal rulemaking procedures set forth in section 553 of title 5, United States Code. At a minimum, the public will have to be given an opportunity to present written views before a rule is adopted; and the issuance of regulations will in most cases require several stages—notice of proposed rulemaking (including the terms or substance of the proposed rule or a description of the subjects), an opportunity for public comment, and final publication (at least 30 days before the effective date of the rule). You should be aware, however, of the exceptions to these general requirements. Section 553 does not apply at all if a military or foreign affairs function is involved, or "a matter relating to agency management or personnel or to public property, loans, grants, benefits, or contracts".[4] The notice requirement and 30-day final publication requirement do not apply in certain circumstances. The point is that if the rules in your bill fall within an exception and the sponsor wants to ensure that APA procedures apply, your bill will have to specify those procedures.

Judicial review of this process will be available (under chapter 7 of title 5); the courts will set aside agency action under this process if it is "arbitrary, capricious, an abuse of discretion, or otherwise not in accordance with law" (5 U.S.C. 706(2)(A)), or for other reasons set out in the law.[5]

Sponsors frequently want to make it clear in the bill that interested persons will have an opportunity for a hearing. You can make this mandatory, without otherwise affecting the process; but if you do it by providing that the rule involved is to be "made on the record after opportunity for an agency hearing" you will have subjected it to the APA's formal rulemaking process, which involves a trial-type hearing (sections 556 and 557 of title 5, United States Code) and invokes a different standard of review by the courts, namely, that the courts will overturn agency action under this process if it is "unsupported by substantial evidence" (5 U.S.C. 706(2)(E)).

Adjudication. Unless your bill provides otherwise, or provides for a de novo judicial hearing, the adjudication of any claims or disputes that may arise under the bill will be a formal process (sections 556 and 557 of title 5, United States Code), and subject to the substantial evidence test upon judicial review. (The term "adjudication" [defined in section 551 of title 5] refers to an agency process leading to an agency decision in a matter other than rulemaking; an example of an adjudication might be a determination of an individual's benefits or a determination of whether to issue a license.) Thus if it seems more desirable to give an agency (or a State, in the case of a State grant program) the flexibility to design its own adjudicative procedures, based on program experience, than to reassure beneficiaries of their rights by extending them specific statutory protection, you must say so explicitly.

This point is most important in the case of a State grant program. The APA does not extend hearing rights to the beneficiaries of such a program, so any such rights must come either from the Federal assistance statute or from State law.

Authority to issue rules. Presumably you always want to be sure, when you vest a function in some Federal agency, that the agency head has the necessary authority to issue whatever rules[6] may be required to carry out the duties of that office under the bill. You should check to see whether this authority is already covered in a generic statute on the books. If so, you need not include it in your bill.

Look, for example, at section 301 of title 5, United States Code, which provides—

> The head of an Executive department or military department may prescribe regulations for the government of his department, the conduct of its employees, the distribution and performance of its business, and the custody, use, and preservation of its records, papers, and property....

This provision would seem to cover an agency head's power to govern the conduct of agency affairs. However, you also need to know what the terms "Executive department" and "military department" cover. These terms are defined in sections 101 and 102, respectively, of title 5. A military department, as you would expect, means the departments of the Army, Navy, and Air Force. An Executive department is each of the departments (like State, Treasury, and Defense) in the President's cabinet. You will notice that section 103 of title 5 defines a Government corporation as a "corporation owned or controlled by the Government of the United States"; section 104 defines an "independent establishment" as an "establishment in the executive branch ... which is not an Executive department, military department, Government corporation, or part thereof, or part of an independent establishment";[7] and section 105 defines an "Executive agency" as "an Executive department, a Government corporation, and an independent establishment". Section 301 of title 5, then, would not give general regulatory authority to independent establishments (that is, an agency other than a department [or part thereof]) or Government corporations. In fact, statutes creating the so-called "independent" agencies, like the SEC and the FCC, spell out the authority of those agencies to issue regulations; in the case of the SEC, that authority is limited to specified issues.

Therefore, if you are creating a new department, section 301 covers the general regulatory authority, and you need not provide this authority in your bill. If you are creating a Government corporation or a new agency (that is, an "independent establishment"), you should.

What about establishing an entity (its name might use the word "agency", "office", or "bureau", for example) "within" a department? Section 301 gives the authority to issue regulations to the head of the department, and not the head of the entity, although presumably the head of the department would delegate the authority to the head of the entity being created. Still, giving this authority to the head of the agency obviates any need for specific delegation of authority by the head of the department.

Addressing this minor issue, which is unlikely to be on the radar screen of the sponsor, exemplifies the analysis required for every issue: finding out what the law is, what it means, and how your bill fits into the existing statutory fabric.

The power to interpret the new statute is inherent in the statute's mandate that the agency head administer it, so you need not give the agency this power.

If you want to give the agency head substantive rulemaking authority—the power to issue a regulation imposing penalties, for example, or to issue any other regulation that would have the effect of law— you must say so explicitly in your bill. The best way to do it is to express the desired power directly ("The Secretary may prescribe fines ..."); doing it indirectly by granting "substantive rulemaking authority", or authority to issue regulations "for the efficient enforcement of this Act", may be too obscure to withstand a court challenge.[8]

Other administrative provisions. You should be aware of any other generic provisions that apply to agencies. Section 552 of title 5, United States Code, commonly referred to as the "Freedom of Information Act," establishes procedures under which agencies are required to make information available to the public. Section 552a of title 5 requires agencies to protect from disclosure records maintained on individuals. Section 552b of title 5 requires agencies to conduct open meetings. Sections 561 through 570a of title 5 authorize negotiated rulemaking by the affected parties. Sections 571 through 584 of title 5 provide for alternative dispute resolution to resolve controversies in administrative programs. Chapter 6 of title 5 (5 U.S.C. 601 et seq.) requires agencies issuing rules to do a regulatory flexibility analysis of the impact of those rules on small businesses and other small entities. One of the consequences of not doing the analysis can be deferred enforcement of the rule in question. And chapter 8 of title 5 (5 U.S.C. 801 et seq.) delays the effective date of any "major" rule (that is, a rule with significant economic impact as defined in 5 U.S.C. 804) while Congress reviews it and a required agency report on the rule.

In addition, the Unfunded Mandates Reform Act of 1995 requires agencies to address the impact on State and local governments and the private sector of Federal mandates imposing significant financial burdens. These include identifying and considering the least costly, most cost-effective, or least burdensome regulatory alternative for State and local governments and the private sector.[9]

Of course, all of the requirements discussed have exceptions to them, and you need to be aware of the requirements and exceptions in these provisions. If a provision of your bill conflicts with any of these provisions, you will need to address the conflict by creating an exception, special rule, or other provision in accordance with the sponsor's policy.

12.10 Sanctions

When drafting a bill that provides benefits for persons who can qualify for them (like the Social Security and railroad retirement programs), imposes duties on specified classes of persons (like the Federal Food, Drug, and Cosmetic Act and most other regulatory programs), or requires States to meet specified conditions in order to receive Federal funds (like most formula grant statutes), where the likelihood of attempts at evasion is relatively great, you should raise with the sponsor the inclusion of explicit sanctions to promote compliance and assist in enforcement. And certainly if a bill imposes a prohibition on a person, providing a sanction for violating the prohibition gives the prohibition "teeth". Presumably without a specific sanction, the only relief obtainable would be seeking in an appropriate court injunctive relief to stop a prohibited activity or a writ of mandamus to require an official to carry out mandates in a statute.[10]

There are several kinds of sanctions that are frequently used in Federal legislation; which one is right in a particular case will largely depend on the nature of the activity or program you are establishing. Some of the more common sanctions are briefly discussed below.

Criminal penalties. Any criminal provision usually contains the following basic elements:

(1) The persons subject to the provision.

(2) The actions made unlawful.

(3) The associated penalties (fine, imprisonment, or both).

(4) The malefactor's state of mind (if it matters).

Note that the persons subject to the provision need not be specifically described if anyone who engages in the prohibited actions is covered—most criminal statutes begin simply "Whoever ..." or "Any person who...".

The first three elements are relatively straightforward, and sponsors understand them perfectly well; but most sponsors tend to overlook or underestimate the intricacies of the fourth. You should always direct the sponsor's attention to the question of the malefactor's state of mind. Is it to be an element of the offense, and (if so) how is it to be characterized? There are three main choices:

(1) An offense may be established without any criminal intent, so that lack of any intention to commit the prohibited act (or even of any knowledge that it was being committed) is no defense. This is called "strict [or absolute] criminal liability", and is most common in regulatory laws such as the Federal Food, Drug, and Cosmetic Act. The typical way to draft a strict liability provision is to simply say that "Any person who violates [this Act or section, or a specified regulation] shall be [punished ...]".

(2) An offense may require a "generalized" criminal intent, which merely means that the individual must have actually intended to commit the prohibited act and was personally involved in it in some way, whether or not the individual knew the act was prohibited. This kind of intent is usually signaled by characterizing the prohibited conduct as action that is performed "knowingly".

(3) An offense may require a specific criminal intent, so that the individual must not only have intended to commit the prohibited act but must have done it for a specific unlawful purpose. For example, many provisions of law provide that a person who commits an act "with the intent to defraud" or with the intent to achieve some other goal, is imprisoned or fined, or both. In such a case, the prosecutor must prove beyond a reasonable doubt both the act committed and the intent.

Ignorance of the law is usually not a defense. If you intend to impose a penalty on an individual for specified conduct only if the individual knows that it is prohibited, you should say so.

Beware of the word "willfully". Many criminal statutes provide penalties for persons who "willfully" carry out a specific act, and many are under the impression that the word creates a specific intent that needs to be proved.

But the courts have not consistently interpreted the word this way, or any way, for that matter. The United States Supreme Court has said that the term "willful" can have many meanings, depending on its context.[11] "Willful" has been interpreted as meaning an act done with a bad purpose or an evil motive,[12] or that the person only had the "purpose to disobey the law",[13] or only that the person had done the forbidden act in question "deliberately and with knowledge", even without proof of evil intent.[14] And these are not the only interpretations. Consequently, using "willfully" in a bill is ambiguous and it should not be used. Instead, you need to describe what elements of the crime need to be proved to find a violation.[15]

Title 18 of the United States Code (which is positive law) is the general repository of Federal criminal provisions. Although in it the word "willful" appears from provisions enacted in the past, there are good models for criminal provisions that state the prohibited conduct and the circumstances under which it is a criminal offense.[16]

If you propose to include a criminal provision in your bill, you would ideally do it through an amendment to title 18. However, many criminal provisions remain outside of that title. As a practical matter, it makes more sense to include the violation provision in the vehicle that contains the requirements that are the subject of the violation. The alternative is to have a provision in title 18 that says, "Whoever violates the ___ Act shall be imprisoned etc...". In that case, you would need to look at two separate provisions of law to understand the violation. Note that the House and Senate Judiciary Committees (which have jurisdiction over crimes in general and title 18 in particular) can claim jurisdiction and have your bill referred to them for consideration, whichever way you do it.

You also need to be aware that title 18 (18 U.S.C. 3551 et seq.) provides the guidelines for sentencing a defendant found guilty of an offense in any Federal statute. The amount of a fine is linked to the length of imprisonment, subject only to a larger amount provided in the statute creating the offense (18 U.S.C. 3571(a)). In other words, if a bill (or law) provides a punishment of up to three years in prison and a fine of $50,000, then under the terms of title 18—

—imprisonment of less than 5 years but more than 1 year is a class E felony (18 U.S.C. 3559); and

—the fine for a felony is up to $250,000 for individuals and up to $500,000 for organizations (18 U.S.C. 3571), or alternatively, a fine can be based on pecuniary gain or loss.

Therefore, the fines in the bill or law would be the higher amounts in title 18, unless the bill or law specifically exempts the applicability of section 3571 of title 18 (18 U.S.C. 3571(e)). In *Legislative Drafter's Deskbook: A Practical Guide* (pages 257–260), Dorsey discusses whether one Congress can bind another with a provision like 18 U.S.C. 3571(e). To the extent of any ambiguity, you should address this issue, where a conflict may present itself, as any other. If the policy is to create an exception to section 3571, state the exception and leave no doubt. If the policy is to accept the statutory framework in title 18, it is best to say the following:

> Whoever [commits the offense] shall be imprisoned ____ years, fined under title 18, United States Code, or both.

In any case, avoid the intermediate word "punished" (as in "... shall be punished [by a fine or imprisonment]"; it is unnecessary.

Before you write any criminal provision, you should look at title 18 to see whether there is already a provision that covers your case; title 18 contains a number of provisions that punish such things as fraud and misrepresentation in a Federal program (18 U.S.C. 1001). In addition, provisions in title 18 already penalize persons for such things as aiding and abetting,[17] or conspiring with,[18] others in the commission of an offense, so you know that these elements will already be included in your offense.

Civil penalties. Civil penalty provisions frequently appear in statutes along with criminal penalties. Civil penalties may take the form of fines imposed by agency heads for violations of laws administered by them, may provide for injunctive or other equitable relief, may provide for the forfeiture of property that is the subject of the violation, or may simply subject violators to a civil penalty of not more than $_____, which would be prosecuted by the Justice Department. With civil penalties the offense need be proven only by "a preponderance of the evidence" instead of by the stricter "beyond a reasonable doubt" standard that applies in criminal cases. A sponsor may want a civil penalty to be enforced by the administering agency (rather than by the Justice Department, which is charged with representing the United States in cases arising under *all* statutes) because of the greater likelihood of prosecution and the greater likelihood of finding liability because of the lower standard of proof.

Be aware, however, that civil penalties have been challenged in court as being criminal in nature and, therefore, subject to the protections of the Fifth and Sixth Amendments to the Constitution (for example, double jeopardy rights, the right against self-incrimination, and the rights to a jury trial and to assistance of counsel). The Federal courts treat this issue as a matter of statutory construction, looking first to whether Congress indicated either expressly or impliedly a preference for whether a penalty be treated as civil or criminal.[19] In drafting a civil penalty, therefore, it is extremely important to state that a civil penalty is what is intended. The courts then consider whether Congress, "despite its manifest intention to establish a civil remedial mechanism, nevertheless provided for sanctions so punitive as to 'transfor[m] what was clearly intended as a civil remedy into a criminal penalty' ",[20] applying a seven-prong test to determine whether a civil penalty is in fact criminal.[21]

In determining what the civil penalty should be, keep a possible court challenge in mind, although it may be difficult to determine when a civil penalty is "too punitive".[22] In any case, however, you can find many models for civil penalty provisions.

Note that in *SEC v. Jarkesy*, 144 S. Ct. 2117, 603 U.S. (2024), the Court found that when the Securities Exchange Commission seeks civil penalties against a defendant for securities fraud, the Seventh Amendment entitles the defendant to a jury trial and therefore the SEC must bring the action in Federal court. The *Jarkesy* decision raises the question of whether *any* Federal regulatory agency—not just the SEC—can bring in-house proceedings to enforce civil penalties. The legislative drafter should raise this new constitutional requirement with the sponsor when civil penalties are to be included in the sponsor's bill.

Termination or withholding of funds. In formula grant programs the preferred sanction for violations of program requirements is the termination or reduction of Federal assistance.

So, for example, if a State's plan under such a program is changed so as to impose a prohibited requirement or the State fails to comply with a required State plan provision, the head of the Federal agency would have the authority to withhold or reduce the amount of funds otherwise payable to the State under the plan (or funds ticketed for the affected portion of the State program) until the violation ceases. As a practical matter, however, in a program like Medicaid, for example, the consequence of applying this sanction would be the termination or reduction of aid to vast numbers of needy individuals; but the threat of using the sanction should, in theory, be sufficient to bring a State into compliance. (See 29.5 on the spending power.)

These provisions are complicated but largely boilerplate. If you need to draft a program of this kind, you might use the Medicaid sanctions (section 1904 of the Social Security Act) as a model.

Note that no special provision is needed to recover amounts spent by a State for purposes outside the scope of the program (since such expenditures are simply not subject to Federal financial participation), and that a court may compel a State to comply with its plan conditions as long as it remains in the program.

Note also that a number of provisions in chapters 37 and 38 of title 31, United States Code (Money and Finance, a positive law title of the Code), authorize Government agencies to collect funds already paid to recipients of Federal grant funds who become ineligible for or violate the terms of the grant. These include 31 U.S.C. 3729-3733 (liability for false claims; the so-called "False Claims Act"; 31 U.S.C. 3801-3812 (recovery of false claims by administrative agencies); and 31 U.S.C. 3711 et seq. (collection of claims of the U.S., including assessment of interest and penalties, authority to hire private parties to collect debts owed the Government, and reduction of tax refunds). Since these authorities are already in the law, you should not provide them in your bill unless the policy is to modify those authorities or provide new ones.

12.11 Technical and conforming amendments

More often than not, especially when a bill does something that directly affects or is affected by existing law, the enactment of the key operating provisions (whether freestanding or amendatory) leaves some technical inconsistencies in its wake. And even the subordinate provisions can have that effect.

The amendments required to clean up these inconsistencies, universally referred to as "technical and conforming amendments", were discussed in chapter 5 in connection with the treatment of collateral policy questions. As indicated in that chapter, they are usually just mechanical—simply correcting, eliminating, or adding cross-references in other provisions of law to reflect what the key operating provisions have done—although sometimes they can raise serious substantive or tactical questions of their own.

The technical and conforming amendments in your bill should always be given a place of their own. Either put all of them in a separate section toward the end of the bill, or put those that relate to any particular substantive section in a separate subsection toward the end of that section. The former is most appropriate when the number of amendments is large; but the latter is usually preferable when the number is small or when they can be readily divided according to the substantive provisions involved (since it keeps them within their own "modules" and facilitates committee and floor amendments). In either case the amendments to any particular existing law should generally be grouped together, arranged within each group in the order of the provisions amended, and identified by appropriate headings whenever possible.

As an alternative, you can group technical and conforming amendments to other provisions of the law to which the associated substantive amendment was made (or which is otherwise most directly affected by the associated substantive provision) with the substantive provision, and use a separate section (titled "Other Technical and Conforming Amendments") for all of the technical and conforming amendments to other laws.

One final word of caution. There is often a gray area between substantive provisions on the one hand and technical or conforming amendments on the other. Be careful not to characterize any amendment as "technical or conforming" if it could have substantive significance.

If your sponsor insists on calling a provision "technical" when you know it is not, you have an ethical problem to solve in your own way. At a minimum, be sure the sponsor understands that you do not regard the provision as technical, and that you would have to say so to anyone who requests your professional opinion under circumstances in which you can legitimately respond (but never challenge the sponsor publicly and always observe the applicable requirements of confidentiality [see 2.5]). Of course, if some other legislator or staff member erroneously characterizes a substantive provision as "technical" in your presence you do not have the same problem, although you may still have a diplomatic one.

As the drafter you are traditionally regarded as the expert in distinguishing between the substantive and the technical—legislators and committees will usually take your word for it and often will not even look at amendments that you characterize as purely technical or conforming. Nothing harms your credibility as much as being caught in the act of slipping in a substantive provision among the technical and conforming amendments.

12.12 Substantive amendments to other laws

Substantive provisions in a bill that bear no relationship to the bill's main message are comparatively rare. They can be included in the introduced bill if the sponsor so desires—a tax reform bill, for example, could include military construction, crop subsidy provisions, or low-income housing—but they would cause parliamentary problems, primarily in requiring referrals to more than one committee and in reconciling the different versions reported by the committees before consideration of the bill by the whole House of the legislature.[23] (These provisions cannot be added later by amendment in committee or on the floor, since they would not be "germane".) If unrelated substantive provisions are included, they should be kept altogether separate from the main message.

It is quite common, though, for a bill dealing primarily with one subject and extensively amending one law to include substantive amendments to other laws when an appropriate relationship exists.

The Social Security program, for example, is closely related to the SSI program (in the administrative area), to the railroad retirement program (in the benefit computation area), and to the Medicare program (in the eligibility area); and the Medicare program is closely related to the Medicaid program. It would not be irrational to include amendments to all of them in a comprehensive Social Security bill; these amendments would in many cases be almost (but not quite) like technical and conforming amendments, and the parliamentary complications would be less troublesome because the several committees involved are accustomed to working with one other.

Related substantive amendments to other laws should be appropriately grouped by subject or target law and clearly identified, especially when their inclusion would vest concurrent or consecutive jurisdiction in other committees. They are usually placed just before the technical and conforming amendments; but they can be located earlier in the bill if they constitute a sufficiently important part of it.

Needless to say, in an omnibus bill, or any other bill with multiple main messages, the treatment and arrangement of the major elements is a matter for the policymakers and tacticians rather than the drafter, because it involves judgments about the relative importance of those elements. Their order of precedence in the bill becomes in effect a basic policy question.

12.13 Appropriations bills and riders

Bills and amendments in general. Most drafters seldom get a chance to work on an appropriations bill as such. The big annual appropriations bills in Congress are written in the Appropriations Committee and are not introduced until they are reported in the House of Representatives. They have a form and style of their own, and often bear little resemblance to anything in this book.

However, sponsors do quite often ask for amendments that they can offer to appropriations bills (and drafters in executive agencies and lobbying organizations spend a good deal of time developing language to be submitted to the Appropriations Committees). The parliamentary rules that apply, even to amendments that simply change a dollar amount, are complex. In the case of other amendments, for example to earmark funds[24] or to limit the uses to which an appropriation may be put, drafting an amendment that will be in order under parliamentary rules is even more challenging.

Sponsors do occasionally introduce special-purpose appropriations bills, seeking funds (or additional funds) for particular programs in which they are interested, although these seldom go anywhere. The text of such a bill should read like the first sentence of the form for authorizing appropriations set forth in 13.1, but with the words "authorized to be" omitted.

If you must draft a bill to make an appropriation or amend such a bill, and you are unsure how to proceed, try the following.

Get a copy of a recently enacted annual appropriations Act that includes the substantive area in which you are interested and find an appropriation that resembles the one you are proposing to make in both its purpose and scope; then pattern your language after that appropriation. However, if you are drafting a separate bill rather than an amendment, you must be sure to specify the fiscal year for which the appropriation is being made. The provision you are using as a model will not do that, since by definition all of the appropriations in an annual appropriations Act are for the upcoming fiscal year and that year is specified only in the Act's general introductory language. And always remember that no appropriation can be made unless it has previously been authorized (see 13.1 and 34.5).

Finally, a word may be in order about "continuing resolutions", the desperation method of funding the Government that Congress uses when it is deadlocked on one or more of the regular annual appropriations bills. The stated purpose of such a resolution is simply to continue the current level of appropriations until the new appropriations bills are passed (although in practice such resolutions tend to become primarily "Christmas trees" full of substantive goodies). It is substantially the same sort of vehicle as an appropriations bill from the drafter's point of view except for two things: it is extremely unlikely that you will ever be called upon to write one, and such resolutions are usually adopted in an atmosphere of great haste so that there are far fewer opportunities to offer amendments.

Appropriations riders. Neither an appropriations bill nor an amendment to an appropriations bill can include "legislation"—that is, it cannot include any language that would have the effect of changing existing law. However, in fact a great deal of substantive legislation does originate in appropriations bills, and is enacted in appropriations Acts and continuing resolutions, notwithstanding the rules that forbid it. The parliamentary difficulties are considerable (they are discussed in detail in chapter 34); but if your sponsor proposes to seek the stated objective through an "appropriations rider"—a legislative amendment to an appropriations bill or a continuing resolution—you should know a bit about it.

As *Hirsch* (page 40) puts it—

> For an ... individual Member, the single most potent legislative tool—the device with the largest return for the lowest investment in time and energy—is the appropriations rider... [I]f an appropriations subcommittee accepts it, the rider is almost certain to be accepted also by the parent committee and passed by the House to which it is reported. [And] whatever may be the fate of other bills, the enactment of an appropriations bill, or a continuing resolution embracing its text, can be relied upon.

If the parliamentary prohibition were absolute, and were uniformly applied, appropriations riders could hardly exist. In fact, however, legislating through appropriations riders has long been a common practice, based largely on the so-called principle of "limitation", which provides in essence that, since Congress is not obliged to appropriate anything just because there is an authorization on the books, it is permissible for Congress to limit the use of any appropriation it does make to selected purposes. It is not as easy as it used to be to legislate this way, but it is still being done. For example, the Legal Services Corporation, the Federal corporation that funds legal aid programs throughout the United States, has not been "authorized" to operate, under the statute that created it, since 1980. It continues to operate only by virtue of annual appropriations bills that are laden with restrictions, not included in the underlying statute, on the use of the funds appropriated.

The more detailed discussion of appropriations riders will be reserved for chapter 34, since their special problems are all parliamentary in nature. They are mentioned here because they are really just freestanding legislative provisions couched in appropriations terminology, and because they often offer the sponsor (for the reasons given by *Hirsch*) the best chance to achieve a legislative objective.

Every drafter should learn how to write appropriations riders that will stand up against parliamentary challenges, and should know enough to advise sponsors on whether that approach in a particular case would or would not be feasible (34.6 deals explicitly with the subject).

12.14 Provisions involving congressional procedures

Provisions that call upon Congress to perform specified functions in connection with the operation of a statute are not uncommon, and they often include changes in congressional procedures in order to ensure that the functions involved can be effectively carried out. The procedural changes are sometimes accomplished by direct amendments to the rules of the House and Senate; but more often the provisions are freestanding, with the changes being either directly stated or merely implied as matters of necessity.

When the specified congressional function is the adoption of a resolution approving or disapproving some impending executive action, or setting forth a finding to serve as a trigger for some executive action or process, the provision usually attempts to expedite the performance by Congress of the specified function by eliminating at least some of the omnipresent procedural obstacles to quick congressional action. These typically involve discharging a committee that has not acted on the measure within a specified time period, limiting floor debate, and precluding amendments to the measure.[25]

Or such a provision may be necessary because the existing House and Senate rules and procedures would actually prevent or seriously inhibit the performance of the specified function.

Consider, for example, the President's authority under the Constitution to enter into agreements with other countries. If these agreements require legislation to implement them, then Congress can add provisions to the implementing legislation that have the effect of modifying or nullifying the agreement. This would be fatal in the case of a complex agreement that may have involved years of negotiation with other countries.

Over the years, different statutes have provided that if the President, during a specified period of time, enters into trade agreements with other countries and complies with certain procedures (such as frequent consultation with Congress) regarding those trade agreements, then implementing legislation that the President transmits to Congress with the agreement will be subject to expedited procedures spelled out in section 151 of the Trade Act of 1974 (19 U.S.C. 2191) that will not permit amendments to the legislation and that require Congress to act within specified periods, thereby ensuring a vote on the legislation.[26] The effect of these statutes has been that if the legislation is enacted, the agreements are not modified. Without such statutory provisions, any amendment to the legislation could change the agreement, which would then have to be renegotiated with the country or countries involved.

Or it may be simply that the congressional presence is unavoidably involved in everything the statute aims to do, so that a massive procedural facelift is necessary. The Congressional Budget Act of 1974 consists almost entirely of provisions requiring congressional participation.

There is nothing wrong with changing congressional rules and procedures by statute, and the changes made are perfectly valid as long as they are in effect; but they exist on shaky ground because they can remain in effect only as long as both the House and Senate want them to. Section 5 of Article I of the Constitution provides that "Each House may determine the rules of its proceedings", and no mere statute can take away that constitutional right. Thus, either House can unilaterally revoke such changes at any time (insofar as that House is concerned) in spite of the fact that they were duly enacted into law. This in fact happened in April 2008 when the House exercised its constitutional right and waived a procedural requirement in the law that in effect delayed a vote on the United States-Colombia Free Trade Agreement.

If you are faced with the necessity of drafting this kind of provision, you should do the following:

(1) Make sure the sponsor knows that the provision can fail if either House becomes disenchanted.

(2) Make sure that your provision clearly states the legislative vehicle that will trigger the special procedures. For example, "For purposes of this [section], the term 'joint resolution' means a joint resolution of the two Houses of Congress, the matter after the resolving clause of which is as follows: 'That the Congress [approves] [does not approve] the [determination of the President relating to [the subject] submitted to the Congress on ______', with the blank space being filled with the appropriate date.".

(3) If you are amending the rules of the House or Senate (or a State legislative body), follow the Roman rule religiously by adopting the form, style, and terminology of the rules you are amending regardless of the form and style in which the rest of the bill is being written.

(4) Note that although there are good models for this type of provision, the procedures can be modified to achieve different results. See, for example, section 125 of the Uruguay Round Agreements Act (19

U.S.C. 3535), which cross-references (in subsection (c)(2)(B)) certain subsections of the expedited procedures of section 152 of the Trade Act of 1974, but then has a different provision (in subsection (c)(2)(C)) relating to discharging a committee from considering the measure.

(5) Consider the inclusion of an explicit statement recognizing that the provision represents a statutory usurpation of the constitutionally protected congressional rulemaking powers. Such a statement is pure boilerplate, and should read like this:

> ( ) The provisions of this [title or section] [other than . . .] are enacted by the Congress—
>
> (1) as an exercise of the rulemaking power of the House of Representatives and the Senate, respectively, and as such they shall be considered as part of the rules of each House, respectively, or of that House to which they specifically apply, and such rules shall supersede other rules only to the extent that they are inconsistent with them; and
>
> (2) with full recognition of the constitutional right of either House to change such rules (insofar as they relate to that House) at any time, in the same manner and to the same extent as in the case of any other rule of that House.

The preceding language is viewed by some as nothing more than an attempt to be honest with the reader, since the result (being constitutionally required) would be the same without it; but it is important to include it when the procedural changes involved are accomplished by simply overriding the existing rules rather than explicitly amending them. The intent that these provisions become part of the rules of each chamber should be clear. In each Congress the House of Representatives adopts its rules (since the Senate is a continuing body, it does not need to do this). In recent Congresses, the language of the resolution adopting the rules provides that "the rules of the House of the preceding Congress, together with such concurrent resolutions and statutes which constituted the rules of the House at the end of that Congress, are hereby adopted as the rules of the new Congress..." followed by whatever changes will apply in the new Congress. Inclusion of the boilerplate language ensures that the resolution covers the provisions involved.

Keep in mind that any bill that has the effect of modifying the rules of the House of Representatives will raise the additional procedural hurdle of being referred to the Committee on Rules, in addition to the committee with jurisdiction over the substantive matter in the bill.

A different sort of statutory provision involving congressional participation in the administration of laws is the so-called "committee veto". Since about 1960, a number of congressional committees had experimented with ways to prevent the executive branch from initiating and carrying out projects for which funds are legally available but that the committees have not specifically considered (or to which they may simply be opposed).

A broader "legislative veto" provision would attempt to prevent the executive branch from carrying out some other act unless Congress had a chance to first review it.

The early legislative and committee veto provisions required the executive official involved to notify the Congress (or the relevant congressional committees) before engaging in a specified activity, and then either (1) flatly forbade that official from engaging in the activity unless either the Congress (or the committees) (by resolution) approved, or (2) gave the Congress (or either House of Congress) (or those committees) a set period (usually 30 days) in which to veto it (by resolution). These provisions were declared unconstitutional in 1983[27] because they violated the separation of powers of the legislative and executive branches under the Constitution.

The replacement for the legislative and committee veto is to require the executive official to notify the Congress or relevant committees of Congress and then wait [a period of] days before engaging in the activity, the theory being that if the Congress (or committees) wish to prevent it they will have enough time to introduce, report, and secure the enactment of legislation to do so. This approach is almost certainly constitutional because the veto, if exercised at all, is exercised through a duly enacted statute rather than just by action of one or two legislative committees.

Such a provision is largely boilerplate, and normally reads something like the following:

> Funds under this [section] [subsection] may not be transferred or obligated until a period of [30] days has passed after the [Secretary] [Administrator] has transmitted to the Committee [of jurisdiction] of the House of Representatives and the Committee [of jurisdiction] of the Senate a written report describing the nature of the [project for which the funds will be used], its cost, and the reasons for the [project].

Sometimes provisions are added so that a measure introduced to approve or disapprove the executive action will be considered under expedited procedures discussed above.

If you are asked to include a provision like this requiring congressional review in a bill, make sure the sponsor understands that you both are walking on the edge of a constitutional precipice. You are probably on safe ground if you use the form just given, but you should never feel totally comfortable with any provision that allows the legislative branch (without enacting a new statute) to second-guess the executive on the everyday administration of the laws after the authority has been granted and the funding has been made available.[28]

Notes

1 The courts will read a statute to give effect to every provision, and more specific provisions will be given effect over more general ones. See chapter 28.

2 The law appears in the United States Code at 2 U.S.C. 1501 et seq. The amendments in the law to the Congressional Budget and Impoundment Control Act of 1974 can be found at 2 U.S.C. 658 et seq. and 2 U.S.C. 602.

3 See the discussion of "shall" in 22.2 regarding the effect of language directing an official to act.

4 An agency may, however, choose to follow the APA procedures anyhow.

5 Section 706 of title 5 reads as follows:

§706. Scope of review

To the extent necessary to decision and when presented, the reviewing court shall decide all relevant questions of law, interpret constitutional and statutory provisions, and determine the meaning or applicability of the terms of an agency action. The reviewing court shall—

(1) compel agency action unlawfully withheld or unreasonably delayed; and

(2) hold unlawful and set aside agency action, findings, and conclusions found to be—

(A) arbitrary, capricious, an abuse of discretion, or otherwise not in accordance with law;

(B) contrary to constitutional right, power, privilege, or immunity;

(C) in excess of statutory jurisdiction, authority, or limitations, or short of statutory right;

(D) without observance of procedure required by law;

(E) unsupported by substantial evidence in a case subject to sections 556 and 557 of this title or otherwise reviewed on the record of an agency hearing provided by statute; or

(F) unwarranted by the facts to the extent that the facts are subject to trial de novo by the reviewing court.

In making the foregoing determinations, the court shall review the whole record or those parts of it cited by a party, and due account shall be taken of the rule of prejudicial error.

6 The terms "rules" and "regulations" are interchangeable; to say "rules and regulations" is redundant.

7 This is an obvious example of a circular definition: an independent establishment is an establishment that is not a part of an independent establishment.

8 5 U.S.C. 558(b) provides that a "sanction may not be imposed or a substantive rule or order issued except within jurisdiction delegated to the agency and as authorized by law".

9 The requirements that agencies must meet under the Unfunded Mandates Reform Act appear generally in title II of that Act (2 U.S.C. 1531 et seq.).

10 In that case there would be the issue of whether the person bringing the action would have standing to do so.

11 *Spies v. United States,* 317 U.S. 492, 497 (1943).

12 *United States v. Harris,* 185 F.3d 999, 1006 (9th Cir. 1999).

13 *Ratzlaf v. United States,* 510 U.S. 135, 141–142 (1994).

14 *United States v. Carrier,* 654 F.2d 559, 561 (9th Cir. 1981).

15 Thanks to Ellen Lin and Michael Volkov (former counsel, Subcommittee on Crime, Committee on the Judiciary of the House of Representatives) for the research on which this paragraph is based.

16 See, for example, 18 U.S.C. 2332b (acts of terrorism transcending national boundaries).

17 18 U.S.C. 2 provides that whoever "commits an offense against the United States or aids, abets, counsels, commands, induces or procures its commission, is punishable as a principal" or "willfully causes an act to be done which if directly performed by him or another would be an offense against the United States, is punishable as a principal". A principal refers to the person who commits an offense.

18 18 U.S.C. 371.

19 *United States v. Ward,* 448 U.S. 242, 248 (1980).

20 Ibid., 249, citing *Rex Trailer Co. v. United States,* 350 U.S. 148, 154 (1956).

21 The seven prongs are: (1) whether the sanction involves an affirmative disability or restraint, (2) whether it has historically been regarded as a punishment, (3) whether it comes into play only on a finding of *scienter,* (4) whether its operation will promote the traditional aims of punishment—retribution and deterrence, (5) whether the behavior to which it applies is already a crime, (6) whether an alternative purpose to which it may rationally be connected is assignable for it, and (7) whether it appears excessive in relation to the alternative purpose assigned. *Kennedy v. Mendoza-Martinez,* 372 U.S. 144, 168–169 (1963).

22 In this regard, Federal law has without a doubt "pushed the envelope". The Foreign Narcotic Kingpin Designation Act (21 U.S.C. 1901 et seq.), a law that prohibits transactions in property interests of certain designated foreign narcotics traffickers, allows the Secretary of the Treasury (who administers the law) to impose a civil penalty of up to $1,000,000 for any violation of any license, order, or regulation issued to carry out the law.

23 It is possible, however, that a sponsor may want an unrelated provision included in order to ensure the bill's referral to a particular committee (presumably a committee on which the sponsor serves).

24 There was considerable media attention given to "earmarks" before 2007, but no definition of the term (at the Federal level) before the 110th Congress. The House of Representatives amended its rules in January 2007 to require disclosure in legislation of congressional earmarks (Rule XXI, clause 9), defined as a provision (or report language) included primarily at the request of a Member of Congress or Senator, providing, authorizing, or recommending a specific amount of funds for a contract, grant, loan, or other expenditure with or to an entity, or targeted to a specific State, locality, or congressional district, other than through a statutory or administrative formula-driven or competitive award process.

25 There are many models. Sections 151 and 152 of the Trade Act of 1974 (19 U.S.C. 2191 and 2192) are examples.

26 The most recent statute allowing this procedure was the Bipartisan Congressional Trade Priorities and Authorities Act of 2015 (19 U.S.C. 4201 et seq.), which expired in July 2021.

27 *Immigration and Naturalization Service v. Chadha,* 462 U.S. 919, 959 (1983).

28 An example of "legislative veto" provision from the Consolidated Appropriations Act, 2022 (Public Law 117-103) is the following:

> "SEC. 225. None of the funds made available for 'Construction, Major Projects' may be used for a project in excess of the scope specified for that project in the original justification data provided to the Congress as part of the request for appropriations unless the Secretary of Veterans Affairs receives approval from the Committees on Appropriations of both Houses of Congress.".

13. The Caboose

13.1 Authorizations of appropriations

Provisions authorizing appropriations were mentioned briefly in chapter 12 because of their relationship to a bill's key operating provisions, but in most bills they appear at the end (just before the effective-date provision if there is one) because they simply provide funding and are not actually part of what the bill does substantively. People who are accustomed to reading legislation will expect to find them at the end of the bill, and you should not vary this placement without good reason.

At the Federal level, before any appropriation can be made it must be authorized in a "legislative" provision—that is, in a law that came through the legislative committees of Congress rather than through the appropriations committees and is totally separate from (and enacted before) the law actually making the appropriation.

However, an explicit statutory authorization of the appropriation is not required unless it is desired to limit that appropriation in some way. It is well established that the enactment of legislation providing for the performance of a function or for the establishment or expansion of an agency or program, or authorizing or directing any other action or thing that requires money to accomplish, is in and of itself an authorization of whatever appropriations may be necessary for that purpose—without limitation as to amount or time. (See 34.5.)

Thus the only legitimate purpose of a provision authorizing appropriations is to place a ceiling on their amount, or to limit the period for which they may be made or within which the money appropriated may be spent.

Although a provision authorizing the appropriation of "such sums as may be necessary" is almost always unnecessary, some legislators feel uneasy when they cannot see the authorization of appropriations in a bill. You should make it your practice to avoid unnecessary "such sums" authorization language, which promotes inconsistency and possible confusion; but, if your sponsor is unhappy without it, go ahead and put it in—it won't do any real damage.

There is one case in which a "such sums" authorization is needed. When a bill intends to authorize the appropriation of a definite amount for one or more specified fiscal years and an indefinite amount thereafter, it should say so. Otherwise there is a strong implication that nothing is authorized after the period for which the definite appropriations are authorized.

For example, a provision simply reading "There is authorized to be appropriated $1,000,000 for fiscal year 2025." is inadequate if the sponsor wants a 3-year program with no maximum appropriation during the last two years. The provision should include the phrase ", and such sums as may be necessary for each of the 2 succeeding fiscal years" just before the final period.

The authorization of an appropriation customarily states the purpose of the appropriation, the agency or official to receive the appropriation, the amount, the fiscal year or years involved, and any restrictions that may apply. All else being equal, these items should be stated in the order given. For example:

> ( ) AUTHORIZATION OF APPROPRIATIONS.—For grants under section ______, there is authorized to be appropriated to the Secretary the sum of $1,000,000 for fiscal year 2025. Of the amount appropriated pursuant to this subsection, the Secretary shall obligate …

If the policy is that the amount appropriated be available indefinitely (that is, until it is used up), you may omit the reference to fiscal year 2025 or replace it with the phrase "to be available without fiscal year limitation" (the so-called "no-year money"). You should be aware, however, that the law actually making the appropriation will almost certainly override your provision, since the appropriations committees like to keep control by limiting the availability of appropriations to a specified amount (which may or may not be the amount the legislative committees wanted), and to a single fiscal year, regardless of what the legislative committees have said.

Note that even if authorizing legislation requires that an annual authorization for a continuing program be enacted into law before an appropriation can be made for the program, an appropriations bill need only "notwithstand" the authorization provision to get around this requirement. Note also that if a requirement in authorizing legislation that a minimum amount of funds appropriated for a program be used for a specified purpose, that requirement will not be nullified if the total amount appropriated is less than the amount authorized to be appropriated for the program. See 28.8 for rules of statutory construction for appropriations Acts.

13.2 Effective-date provisions

An "effective-date provision" is a provision in a bill—it may be a section, subsection, paragraph, sentence, or clause—that specifies exactly when and how the bill or the substantive provision involved is to go initially into effect. Many State constitutions specify when a law will go into effect, usually some defined period after enactment, subject to specific exceptions. A bill in such a State would not need to specify its effective-date unless such an exception applies.

At the Federal level, if the bill is to go into effect immediately upon its enactment, there is usually no need for an explicit effective-date provision at all.

There is a need for an effective-date provision, however, if—

(1) the sponsor wants the bill or any part of it to become effective at a time other than the time the bill is enacted (at the Federal level); or

(2) the effectiveness of the bill (or any of the substantive provisions involved) cannot be stated in terms of time alone, or left unstated, but instead must be tied to one or more specific events to which it will relate.

Occasionally an effective-date provision can pose a real challenge; in a massive bill requiring interrelated effective dates for different provisions it can become very complicated, and often turns out to be the most controversial provision in the entire bill. However, most effective-date provisions are relatively simple, consisting largely of boilerplate.

Chapter 26 deals in detail with the specifics of the subject—when explicit effective-date provisions are needed, the forms they should take in different situations, and some of the collateral considerations that may be involved—but a few more general comments are in order here.

The question of when and how a bill is to go into effect upon its enactment sounds technical and nonsubstantive, but it is often one of the most troublesome policy questions you will face. The effective date determines the universe of cases to which the bill will apply, and often determines its cost and budgetary impact as well.

It is certainly true that in most cases the effective date of a bill has nothing to do with the sponsor's substantive policy decisions, and can safely be dealt with at the last minute. It is also true that sometimes the effective date is such an integral part of the sponsor's final tactical decisions that it must be left until the last minute. But in a significant number of cases the substantive policy and the effective date are part of the same package, in that early decisions made about either one will affect the other; and you must always be alert to this possibility as you plan your work.

Although the decision on what effective date to adopt is ultimately the sponsor's, the date that should be chosen will often be obvious to the drafter. In such a case you may feel quite safe about making the decision yourself if you have heard nothing from the sponsor, but you must always remember that it is a policy decision you are making on the sponsor's behalf, and when there is any doubt you should always inform the sponsor about what you propose to do.

You should also be aware that many bills contain special provisions indirectly or selectively involving their effective dates—the most common being transitional provisions, savings clauses, and sunset provisions. These are dealt with in the rest of the chapter.

13.3 Transitional provisions

Sometimes the abrupt substitution of new law for old causes hardship or creates inequities for some or all of those affected, but the sponsor does not wish to exempt anyone altogether by including one or more explicit exceptions (or by using a savings provision—see 13.4).

"Transitional provisions" are the means used to make the changeover more gradual and give time for adjustment, while not unduly postponing the effective date of the new law as a whole; in theory at least that is all they do (although there is regrettably much substantive abuse in practice). They can apply to everyone covered by the new law, or (like savings clauses) they can apply only to classes of people for whom the adjustment would be particularly difficult. But they always differ from savings clauses in one significant respect: after the transitional period is over, the new law will apply to everyone according to its terms.

Thus if the sponsor of a bill raising specified rates or charges by 30 percent wants to phase in the increase over a three-year period in order to ease the adjustment, the drafter (instead of putting the whole thing in the key operating provisions) might impose the full 30 percent increase effective immediately but then add language somewhere else (usually toward the end of the bill) that partially overrides the effective date by limiting the increase (in some or all cases) to 10 percent in the first year and 20 percent in the second.

A different sort of example (and invariably a more complicated one) might be a regulatory bill that imposes a series of new requirements effective immediately, but includes a provision waiving or softening (during a specified transitional period) the ones that require the most time to prepare for, or waiving or reducing (during that period) the penalties imposed for noncompliance.

Most transitional provisions can be placed either inside or outside of the particular substantive provisions to which they relate, depending upon their length and complexity and to some extent upon past practice in the field involved.

In tax bills (where they are most frequently used), and in regulatory bills, transitional provisions are invariably complicated and are almost always placed after the operating provisions. They are sometimes the most difficult and controversial provisions in the entire bill (usually because the bill could not pass if the Members' constituents were required to face the new burdens "cold turkey"). In areas that are relatively uncomplicated, however, they are more likely to be found within the affected substantive provision itself. Thus in the first example given above, the temporary 10 percent and 20 percent rates could very well be prescribed along with the final 30 percent rate in the substantive provision, although in drafters' parlance they would then be "transitional" in the dictionary sense only, since they would be part of the basic rate structure and no one would think of them as part of a transitional "provision".

A transitional provision placed within the substantive provision itself has the disadvantage of complicating the permanent law with material that will soon become obsolete, while placing it elsewhere results in a "split" provision that may cause confusion (see 6.6); each case must be decided on its own merits. Section 215 of the Social Security Act (42 U.S.C. 415) reflects transitional provisions (enacted in 1977 and covering a five-year period) that were integrated into the underlying statute. The resulting complexity of the provision is frightening. (*Hirsch* [page 39] suggests that anyone who thinks this solved the split amendment problem should look at the result in section 215 of the Social Security Act [42 U.S.C. 415], a section "that looks like the drafter's version of *Finnegan's Wake*".)

Unless a transitional provision is clearly straightforward (like the rate increase example), it should be treated as though it were a separate piece of legislation with all of the policy problems and collateral issues that are involved in drafting a stand-alone bill from scratch.

13.4 Savings clauses

Regulatory statutes and other statutes that impose burdens on the affected persons often create a perceived need to "save" the rights that some of those persons had under prior law, either permanently or for a longer period than a transitional provision would normally allow. Meeting this need in a bill calls for the inclusion of a "savings clause", which is not a clause at all but is usually a full-scale section or subsection, and which in theory at least (like the typical transitional provision) is nothing more than an effort to be fair. Savings clauses are sometimes called "grandfather clauses", after the post–Civil War practice in some States of extending the right to vote only to individuals whose grandfathers had been eligible to vote.

A savings clause allows specified persons or groups already operating in the area covered by the bill to continue their established operations as though the bill had not been enacted, or addresses particular problems that those persons or groups might face in adapting to the new rules. Like transitional provisions, savings clauses can be placed either within the substantive provisions involved—sometimes a straightforward exception or special rule (or even a simple qualifying phrase) is really a savings clause in disguise—or in separate provisions of their own after the operating provisions. For example, if you are imposing new requirements on interstate carriers, but wish to exempt existing carriers whose long-established infrastructure would be unduly disrupted by those requirements, you might say (in the substantive provision) that "Every interstate carrier, other than a carrier that has been continuously operating as such for at least 10 years on the date of enactment of this Act, is required ..."; or you might simply say "Every interstate carrier is required ..." and then add a formal savings clause toward the end of the bill:

> **SEC. _____. SAVINGS PROVISION.**
>
> The requirements imposed by section ____ shall not apply to an interstate carrier that has been continuously operating as such for at least 10 years on the date of enactment of this Act.

As with transitional provisions, the former has the disadvantage of complicating the statute with material that will soon become obsolete, while the latter results in a "split" provision that may cause confusion. Again, you must decide. The longer and more complicated savings clauses are almost always placed in separate provisions of their own (as would be the case in the example just given, for instance, if the exemption were to be available only upon the carrier's satisfying specified alternative requirements). In a major bill requiring a number of savings provisions, they are customarily collected in a single section toward the end of the bill.

Savings clauses are generally thought of as exceptions to effective-date provisions, though they are more substantive than that. They have elements of boilerplate in them, but every case is different and there is no standard form. You should try to acquire a feeling for what a typical savings clause looks like—it will help you decide upon your approach—but when you are ready to proceed you will be faced with the same kinds of problems you would face if you were drafting a separate bill.

13.5 Preemption provisions

The Supremacy Clause of the Constitution (Article VI, clause 2) makes the Constitution and Federal law the "supreme" law of the land; therefore, valid Federal law supersedes inconsistent State law. But the Tenth Amendment to the Constitution reserves to the States powers not delegated to the Federal Government. The courts are left to resolve the tension between the two provisions. If a Federal law is silent on the extent to which the law preempts State law, the courts' task is more difficult. You as the drafter should, therefore, always consider whether your bill will affect State law and, if so, suggest to the sponsor the inclusion of a provision in your bill that states whether, and the extent to which, the bill is intended to preempt State law. The Unfunded Mandates Reform Act of 1995 (discussed in 12.7) added a provision to title IV of the Congressional Budget and Impoundment Control Act of 1974 (section 423(e); 2 U.S.C. 658b(e)) requiring each authorizing House and Senate committee to include, in the committee report accompanying any bill or joint resolution, an explicit statement (if relevant) on the extent to which the bill or joint resolution is intended to preempt State, local, or tribal law, and, if so, an explanation of the effect of the preemption.

State law is preempted if it interferes with, or is contrary to, Federal law.[1] Congress may preempt State law expressly[2] (express preemption). But even in the absence of express preemptive text, Congress's intent to preempt an entire field of State law "may be inferred where the scheme of federal regulation is sufficiently comprehensive to make reasonable the inference that Congress 'left no room' for supplementary state regulation" (field preemption).[3] State law is also preempted if it is a physical impossibility to comply with both provisions[4] or if the State law "stands as an obstacle to the accomplishment and execution of the full purposes and objectives of Congress" (conflict preemption).[5]

In any case it will be the court's job to determine congressional intent to preempt State law. Into which category of preemption a law falls may depend on the subject matter. On the one hand, the Supreme Court has held that a

State law restricting the authority of the State's agencies to purchase goods and services from companies doing business with Burma (Myanmar) was preempted by a Federal law imposing sanctions on Burma by giving the President discretion to control those sanctions.[6] The Federal law had no express preemption provision, but was held to "occupy the field". Note that this case involved a foreign affairs issue, a distinctly Federal function under the Constitution.

On the other hand, the court may find that some State law is not preempted even when there is an express preemption provision in the Federal statute. In such a case, the court will apply the rules of statutory construction to the words of the statute to determine whether a particular State law or regulation is preempted.[7]

Including a provision in a bill regarding preemption avoids the necessity of a court determining whether preemption exists. But there are obvious variations, depending on the policy, in the wording of preemption provisions. For example, a provision that says "This Act preempts the laws of any State to the extent such State laws are inconsistent with this Act" would tell the courts that Congress does not intend the Federal law to become the sole governing law in the substantive area addressed by the Federal law, but the courts would then have to decide the extent to which State laws are inconsistent. Or if you have a preemption provision, but create exceptions for laws relating to specific areas, the courts would have to decide which laws fall within the exceptions. If a State's laws are more restrictive than the Federal law, are the State's laws then "inconsistent" with the Federal? You can address this issue as well in a preemption provision.

Note that the preemptive effect of a statute may appear as a savings clause, as in "compliance with this Act or regulations issued under this Act does not relieve a person of liability under State law".

If a bill providing that a regulation issued (by the appropriate administrator) under the bill's provision preempts any State law or regulation on the same subject, an issue may arise as to whether the administrator's decision *not* to issue a regulation under this bill preempts State law or regulations as well. In *Sprietsma v. Mercury Marine*, 537 U.S. 51 (2002), at issue was the following provision (section 10 of the Federal Boat Safety Act of 1971): "a State ... may not establish, continue in effect, or enforce a law or regulation establishing a recreational vessel ... performance or safety standard ... that is not identical to a regulation prescribed" by the Secretary of Transportation under the Boat Safety Act. The Court held that the decision by the Secretary of Transportation not to prescribe a safety standard for propeller guards did not preempt State common law claims (for injury from propellers without propeller guards). The Court analyzed the words of the preemption clause and found that the natural meaning of the words "law or regulation" was to limit them to enacted State laws or regulations and not to apply them to the State's common law. The fact that the Boating Act has a savings clause providing that compliance with the Boating Act "does not relieve a person from liability at common law or under State law" was found by the Court to "buttress the conclusion" as to the common law limitation of the preemption clause in this instance.[8]

If a bill covers more than one subject, particularly in separate titles, any preemption provision should be clear about to which of those subjects the provision applies.

Because preemption has national impact, it is important to raise the preemption issue and explicitly state the relationship of a bill to State law, with as much specificity as possible.

13.6 Sunset provisions

A "sunset provision" is a provision in a law—usually at the end—that terminates all authority to carry out that law (or to spend money under that law) at some specified future time. The idea is not to repeal the law automatically, but to suspend its operation after a suitable period so as to enable Congress to review it to determine whether it is still needed and whether it is being overfunded or underfunded. The expectation is that Congress will in effect reenact the law with whatever changes may be needed based on that review.

There is nothing complicated about writing a sunset provision—anything that will effectively bring the law to a halt at the desired time (without actually repealing it) is sufficient. It might read:

SEC. ______. SUNSET.

The Secretary may not make any loan under this Act [take any action to carry out this Act] [enter into any contract or obligation under this Act] after September 30, 2028.

or

SEC. ______. SUNSET.

The Secretary may not obligate budget authority under this Act for any fiscal year beginning after fiscal year 2028.

Sunset provisions are becoming increasingly popular, and Congress has periodically considered bills to subject a broad range of government programs (or even all government programs) to sunset review. However, they still do not appear in most bills, chiefly because there are more traditional ways for Congress to retain control.

To begin with, Congress can always review and amend an existing law, no matter what that law says; in any event the same result can be achieved on the face of a bill without a separate sunset provision. The operating cutoff date can be expressed internally, as a part of the bill's substantive provisions (instead of using the first type of sunset provision shown above). The funding cutoff can also be accomplished by limiting the authorization of appropriations to the desired period (instead of using the second type).

In one situation, however, there may be a difference. A subsequent "continuing resolution" (see 12.13) would preserve the law and its funding beyond the termination date if the cutoff were accomplished simply by limiting the authorization of appropriations, but would not do so if it were accomplished by a sunset provision (or by an internal cutoff); this could be significant because of the increasing use of continuing resolutions by Congress.

A sunset provision in a bill that makes amendments to existing law is problematic. If the provision says "This Act and the amendments made by this Act cease to be effective on ______", and the termination date passes, what happens to the laws that were amended? They would still contain the text of the amendments, but the inserted provisions would not be effective. The result would be particularly bizarre if the amendments merely inserted words into a sentence. If a provision adds something like "and all laws amended by this Act shall be effective as if this Act has not been enacted", it is still unclear how those laws are to read, since the provision does not actually amend the law to its previous state. If the sunset provision attempts to revert the law to read as it read on the day before enactment, that would not take into account any intervening amendments that may have been made to the law. Reinstating prior law after a specified period can also result in the law existing in different forms for different groups of people. This has been the consequence of reinstating prior law in the trade adjustment assistance program (chapter 2 of title II of the Trade Act of 1974 (19 U.S.C. 2271 et seq.), which provides certain assistance to workers whose employment is displaced because of trade agreements with other countries. The law applies in different forms for different beneficiaries, a very confusing state of the law for anyone to figure out.

The preceding paragraph illustrates the policy problems with sunset provisions in general. However, there will be times when they are necessary politically to gain support for the measure or to meet some other objective.

13.7 Severability clauses

A severability (or separability) clause is a provision declaring that if any part of the statute in which it appears is found to be unconstitutional, the rest of that statute is not to be affected. The inclusion of a severability clause is a questionable practice; it is debatable whether such a clause can affect the outcome of a judicial determination, or indeed (in most cases) whether you would want it to.

The court that invalidates a particular provision of a law is in a better position than anyone else to say what should happen to the remaining provisions of that law. It is foolish to suppose that the legislature— which after all cannot normally predict exactly what part of its product might be invalidated or on what grounds the invalidation might be based—really intends that everything not specifically struck down will be automatically preserved however interrelated the provisions may be, or that all of the statute's collateral provisions will remain active after the key operating provisions are gone.

In any case, the courts will always have the last word regardless of what the legislature says. As *Hirsch* (page 38) puts it:

> If a court finds some part of a statute unconstitutional, it may be expected to leave the rest of the statute untouched, even without the clause, unless its decision has left the statute in tatters. If so, one would expect the court to strike down the entire statute, notwithstanding a severability clause. If a court finds the application of a provision unconstitutional, it may ordinarily be expected to narrow the provision to valid applications without the clause's help.

The Supreme Court has made it clear that invalid portions of statutes are to be severed (and the remaining portions left alone) "[u]nless it is evident that the Legislature would not have enacted those provisions which are within its power, independently of that which is not" (*Immigration and Naturalization Service v. Chadha,* 462 U.S. 919, 931 (1983); *Buckley v. Valeo,* 424 U.S. 1, 108 (1976). But see *Reno v. ACLU,* 521 U.S. 844 (1997), in which the Court took notice of a statute's severability clause, although it said that a severability clause "requires textual provisions that can be severed" (521 U.S., *supra,* 882) and did its own analysis of how much of the statute could survive without the unconstitutional provisions.

A typical severability clause is pure boilerplate. It should be placed as near the end of the bill as possible—just before the general effective-date provision if there is one—and in its basic form it reads as follows:

SEC. ____. SEVERABILITY.

> If any provision of this Act (or the application of that provision to particular persons or circumstances) is held invalid [or found to be unconstitutional], the remainder of this Act (or the application of that provision to other persons or circumstances) shall not be affected.

If you must include such a clause in a bill, try to modify this language so as to specify which provisions are to fall, and which are not to fall, if a specified provision is held invalid. At the very least a court will recognize such a provision as not purely boilerplate.

The only good thing about a severability clause is that (if it is relatively specific) it could conceivably help the Court in one of those relatively rare cases where legislative intent is a crucial constitutional factor. This would certainly be the case if a "nonseverability" clause (that is, a provision that says that if any provision of the law is held invalid, the entire law is invalid) appeared in a law. See *Gmerek v. State Ethics Commission,* 807 A.2d 812, 819 (2002); because of a nonseverability provision in a lobbying disclosure law, the Supreme Court of Pennsylvania struck down an entire lobbying disclosure law even though it was unconstitutional (under the Pennsylvania Constitution) only with respect to lawyers because it impermissibly regulated the practice of law.

13.8 Sources of ambiguity

The Federal Courts Study Committee, which was established within the Judicial Conference of the United States under title I of Public Law 100-702 to examine problems and issues facing the Federal courts, included in its recommendations a checklist for legislative staff to use in reviewing proposed legislation for technical problems. The purpose was to avoid common ambiguities in legislation.[9] The Committee urged drafters to consider, for all bills, the following:

- The appropriate statute of limitations;
- Whether a private cause of action is contemplated;

- Whether preemption of State law is intended;
- The definition of key terms;
- The mens rea requirement in criminal statutes;
- Severability;
- Action would be removable to Federal court;
- The types of relief available;
- Whether retroactive applicability is intended;
- The condition for any award of attorney's fees authorized;
- Whether exhaustion of administrative remedies is a prerequisite to any civil action authorized;
- The conditions and procedures relating to personal jurisdiction over persons incurring obligations under the proposed legislation;
- The viability of private arbitration and other dispute resolution agreements under enforcement and relief provisions; and
- Whether any administrative proceedings provided are to be formal or informal.[10]

The points raised come from those who are tasked with interpreting statutes and who face them repeatedly. While some may not be relevant to most bills (for example, attorney's fees), it is not a bad idea to keep a checklist like this handy.

Notes

1 *Gibbons v. Ogden,* 22 U.S. 1 (1824).

2 *Hillsborough County, Fla. v. Automated Med. Labs, Inc.,* 471 U.S. 707, 713 (1985).

3 Ibid.

4 *Florida Lime & Avocado Growers, Inc. v. Paul,* 373 U.S. 132, 142–143 (1963).

5 *Kewanee Oil Co. v. Bicron Corp.,* 416 U.S. 470, 479 (1974), quoting *Hines v. Davidowitz,* 312 U.S. 52, 67 (1941).

6 *Crosby v. National Foreign Trade Council,* 530 U.S. 363, 366 (2000).

7 See *Empire Healthcare Assurance, Inc. v. McVeigh*, 547 U.S. 677, 696-699 (2006) (a preemption clause providing that the "terms of a contract [for Federal health care] … which relate to the nature, provision, or extent of coverage of benefits … shall supersede and preempt any State or local law … which relates to health insurance or plans" did *not* preempt the State law relating to subrogation and reimbursement rights of insurance carriers and therefore did not create jurisdiction in Federal court of an action by a Federal health plan administrator seeking reimbursement of benefits from a health plan enrollee awarded damages in a State personal injury case).

8 The Court, in essence applying the rule against surplusage discussed in chapter 28, found a way to give effect to both the preemption and savings clauses. The Court also determined that Congress had not "preempted the field" of boat safety.

9 Ambiguity in language is addressed in 19.4.

10 The list is discussed in Gregory E. Maggs, "Reducing the Costs of Statutory Ambiguity: Alternative Approaches and the Federal Courts Study Committee," *Harvard Journal on Legislation* 29 (1992): 123.

PART V
WRITING AMENDATORY PROVISIONS

14. General Considerations

14.1 Freestanding and amendatory bills compared

Much of the time this book deals with matters of form and style as though all bills were entirely freestanding. Many are, of course, but most bills that are taken seriously and progress beyond the introduction stage are amendatory in nature.

A substantial part of all Federal statutes (about half of the active titles of the United States Code) has been codified and enacted into positive law, and in most States the law is entirely codified. If the subject matter of the sponsor's proposal falls into a statutory field already covered by a positive-law title of the Code, there is seldom any choice; the bill must amend that title of the Code, which after all was enacted for the express purpose of putting in one place the entire body of Federal law in the field.

Most major statutory fields not yet covered by positive-law titles of the Code are nonetheless already blanketed by comprehensive laws into which nearly anything on the subject involved could appropriately be placed. When a drafting project falls in such a field, the sponsor's objective can almost always be rationally accomplished either by a bill amending the existing law or by a freestanding bill. You have a choice, and there is no difference in legal effect between the two approaches. However, if a place can be found in the existing law where the proposal would logically fit, it is usually better to amend that law rather than to draft a freestanding bill, for at least two reasons.

First, the amendatory approach places the sponsor's proposal in the midst of its relatives, where it naturally belongs and where future researchers would normally expect to find it, and avoids the all-too-common occurrence of separate laws that have to be somehow fitted together and read as a unit in order to get the full picture of what the current law is.

Second, many of the structural, administrative, and procedural provisions that may be required to make the sponsor's proposal work will already be contained in the existing law and will automatically apply to any newly added piece of that law, enabling you to keep your bill shorter and simpler. (Note, however, that if the sponsor's proposal is one that requires structural, administrative, or procedural provisions substantially different from those that are generally applicable in the law being amended, you would have to add special exceptions and conditions, possibly making the amendatory approach longer and more complicated instead.)

Drafting an amendatory bill is not fundamentally different from drafting a freestanding bill. All of the steps that precede the actual writing are the same, the organizational principles set forth in chapter 6 will normally apply, and nearly all of the drafting rules and principles set forth in parts IV and VI will apply in the same way.

There are, however, a number of drafting rules and principles that are especially or uniquely applicable to amendatory bills. Some of them simply involve special application of the general rules and principles discussed elsewhere; others are totally different. Because, as previously mentioned, the drafting of amendatory provisions is probably the most important single aspect of any drafter's work, these rules and principles deserve special attention; they are examined in depth in this part.

14.2 Hybrid bills

For purposes of this book, a bill is considered amendatory if it uses amendments to existing law to accomplish its basic objective and freestanding if it does not. However, many bills in fact are neither entirely freestanding nor entirely amendatory. Indeed, most bills of any consequence that are essentially freestanding contain at least a few substantive amendments to existing laws, and almost all of them contain technical and conforming amendments. These bills might be called hybrid, or partially amendatory.

The rules and principles set forth in this part will normally apply to the amendatory portions of hybrid bills in the same way as they do to bills that are wholly amendatory.

14.3 Vehicular language

Every amendatory provision has two parts—the one that serves as the vehicle by which the amendment is made and the one that comprises the amendment itself.

If a section of a bill reads

> **SEC. 12. AMENDMENTS TO ABC ACT RELATING TO ______.**
>
> The ABC Act is amended by adding at the end the following new section:
>
> **"SEC. 4...".**

the new section 4 is the amendment itself, while everything that precedes it (that is, the language by which it is added to the ABC Act) is purely "vehicular"; section 12 is a provision of the bill, and has no relationship (other than vehicular) to that Act.

When the bill is enacted, the amendment itself—the part that is "within the quotes" or is otherwise identified as material to be added to or stricken from the law being amended—becomes a part of the permanent law. The vehicular language does not; since it is a part of the bill only, it is completely executed once the bill is enacted. It does its job—striking or inserting, or both—and then disappears.

14.4 Interaction of amendments

There are two principles of modular construction that apply uniquely to amendatory bills. They are best combined and thought of as parts of a single amendatory principle, which might be stated as follows:

Early amendments should not anticipate later ones; but later amendments should assume the enactment of earlier ones.

Assume, for example, that section 2 of a bill you are working on makes an amendment to section 123(a) of the ABC Act, and that section 15 of your bill makes another (quite different) amendment to section 123(a). Section 2 of the bill should ignore what section 15 does, and should address section 123(a) of the ABC Act as though no other change in it were anticipated, while section 15 should address section 123(a) as though it already contained the amendment made by section 2. If the two amendments involve the same language in section 123(a) or are otherwise related, however, section 15 should indicate parenthetically that it is the revised version of section 123(a)—the version that would result from the enactment of section 2—that is being addressed.

Thus if section 123(a) contains three numbered paragraphs, and section 2 of your bill inserts a new one after the existing paragraph (1) while section 15 inserts another new one after the existing paragraph (2), section 2 should read:

SEC. 2. AMENDMENTS TO ABC ACT RELATING TO _______.

Section 123(a) of the ABC Act is amended by redesignating paragraphs (2) and (3) as paragraphs (3) and (4), respectively, and by inserting after paragraph (1) the following new paragraph:

"(2) ...";

and section 15 should read:

SEC. 15. AMENDMENTS TO ABC ACT RELATING TO _______.

Section 123(a) of the ABC Act (as amended by section 2 of this Act) is further amended by redesignating paragraph (4) as paragraph (5), and by inserting after paragraph (3) the following new paragraph:

"(4) ...".

The point is that anyone interested in the amendatory bill will normally read it from the beginning, will understand an amendment that refers to what has come before, but may be quite mystified by an amendment that assumes something not yet seen. If sections 2 and 15 had made unrelated amendments to totally different parts of section 123(a), you would not need to acknowledge in section 15 the earlier amendment (by including the parenthetical reference to section 2), but you should do so if there is the slightest chance of confusion.

Needless to say, in those relatively rare cases where organizational or tactical considerations require a reversal of the amendatory principle stated earlier (so that the earlier section has to assume the enactment of the later), you must give the reader adequate warning; in the example given, since section 15 would then be treated as having been enacted first, section 2 (the earlier section) would have to contain the phrase "(as amended by section 15 of this Act)".

14.5 Problems for the occasional drafter

Aside from the mechanical differences that are discussed later in this part, the chief difference between the freestanding and the amendatory approach from the drafter's point of view is that the amendatory approach involves one additional step—fitting the pieces properly into an existing statute. Since under either approach the drafter's words must coexist rationally with the words already contained in the relevant law, this is largely a mechanical step; but it can be a very difficult one if the statute is massive and complex, and it can pose a serious problem for the occasional drafter.

There is seldom any practical way for a drafter not intimately familiar with the operation of a complex law to acquire the competence to draft amendments to it in the time available. There are a number of things you can do to help yourself, however, and they are all variations on one simple theme: first, actually read the law or laws involved, and if that is not possible, or does not work because you find yourself confronted with a 700-page monster, then consult an expert to direct you to the most relevant provisions and possibly even to the specific provisions you will need to amend.

And whether or not this resolves your initial drafting problems, you should always have some knowledgeable person waiting in the wings to review your draft, if possible, when it is finished.

14.6 Amending a bill in Congress

Before proceeding with the business of drafting amendments to laws that have already been enacted, we should digress for a moment to consider drafting amendments to be offered to bills in committee or on the floor.

The considerations involved in amending a bill are important, because the number of amendments to bills that a typical legislator offers is usually much greater than the number of bills the same legislator introduces, and the chances of having an amendment actually adopted are much greater than the chances of having an introduced bill passed.

Amendments to bills are usually easier to write than amendments to provisions of existing law. They are most often short and present no major technical problems; and since they usually address a single proposition, many of the more complicated drafting problems (such as those involving modular construction) do not normally arise.

There are, however, two principal differences in form and style that you should keep in mind:

(1) The vehicular language is always written in the imperative mood in an amendment to a bill, rather than in the indicative mood as in an amendment to existing law. In essence that language is merely an instruction to the legislative clerk who will enroll the bill, indicating how the bill is to be changed, so (as discussed more fully later) you can sometimes take liberties with it; if the clerk understands what you mean it is sufficient.

(2) The place where the amendment is to go is usually identified simply by a page-and-line reference in an amendment to a bill, rather than by a descriptive reference to the target provision (by its section number or otherwise) as in an amendment to existing law. If, however, you have the text of the bill but the page and line numbers are uncertain, you will need to do the amendment descriptively (see 32.7).

Thus an amendment to a bill might simply read "Page 3, line 6, strike 'XX' and insert 'YY' ", while an amendment to existing law doing the same thing in a bill would read "Section 123(a) of the ABC Act is amended by striking 'XX' and inserting 'YY' ". For a fuller discussion see 32.7, which also gives examples of the proper form.

15. The Basic Amendatory Tools

15.1 In general

Every amendment to existing law does one of three things—it eliminates something old, it adds something new, or it does both. If it does both, what it adds is most often simply a changed version of what it eliminates (as in the case of an increase in a dollar figure or a change in a date).

It can be accomplished either by a "cut-and-bite" approach (addressing only the specific language that is to be stricken, added, or changed), or by a "restatement" or "substitute" approach (striking the entire provision in which that language appears or will appear and substituting a revised version with all changes shown in place).

It is always stated in the indicative mood, since amendatory bills are drafted on the assumption that their amendments are self-executing and do not require intervening action by anyone else.

These concepts, and the other terms, concepts, forms, and usages involved in drafting amendments to provisions of existing law are defined and discussed later in this chapter and in chapters 16, 17, and 18.

15.2 Cut-and-bite amendments

A cut-and-bite amendment is an amendment that achieves its purpose by attacking specific language—eliminating, adding, or changing that language by direct reference to it—in the text of the provision of law affected.

The keyword for eliminating something is "striking", and the key word for adding something is "inserting" (unless the addition occurs at the very end of the provision affected, in which case it would be "adding"). As more fully discussed later, a "repeal" has the same legal significance as a "strike", but should generally be reserved for the elimination of whole sections or larger units.

The following are examples of all of the basic cut-and-bite amendment forms you will ever be likely to need:

> ( ) Section 101 of the ABC Act is amended by striking "XX".
>
> ( ) Section 101 of the ABC Act is amended by striking "XX" and inserting "YY" [or by striking "XX" and inserting the following: "YY"].
>
> ( ) Section 101 of the ABC Act is amended by inserting "XX" before/after "YY" [or by inserting before/after "YY" the following: "XX"].
>
> ( ) Section 101 of the ABC Act is amended by adding at the end the following: "XX".
>
> ( ) Section 101 of the ABC Act is repealed.

Note that in these examples the terms "XX" and "YY" could represent anything from a single word or figure to a full subsection, and that in the first three examples the addition of the words "each place it appears" would permit the single cut-and-bite amendment to make multiple changes (when the term involved appears repeatedly in the section).

The last example could of course have read "Title I of the ABC Act is amended by striking section 101" instead of just repealing the section. At the Federal level at least, there are considerations both pro and con. Amending a larger component of a bill than is necessary just to strike a piece of it (which is what you would be doing if you amend title I of the ABC Act to strike section 101) sometimes creates parliamentary problems, at least in a reported bill (see 16.1, 32.8, and chapter 34). But it often promotes clarity, and also enables you to use serial amendments (see 17.2) in cases where striking that piece is only one of several changes that have to be made in the larger component. For example:

( ) Title I of the ABC Act is amended—

(1) by striking sections 101 and 103;

(2) by striking the fourth sentence of section 107(b); and

(3) by adding at the end of section 111(c) the following new paragraph:

"(5) ....".

Cut-and-bite amendments are most often used when the changes to be made are relatively few and can easily be isolated. They have both advantages and disadvantages.

On the one hand, they highlight the particular changes being made so that the reader can identify and focus on them (unless the number or complexity of the changes is so great that it would be overwhelming). They also avoid the risks that might be created by including unchanged language; only the changes themselves are opened up to public view. (There may be highly controversial language in the unchanged portions of the provision involved, but anyone who is looking for an opportunity to challenge that language must look elsewhere—the amendments themselves will not serve as a reminder.)

On the other hand, in many cases cut-and-bite amendments (on their face) tell the reader absolutely nothing about what they are trying to accomplish or how they propose to accomplish it. For the reader to understand their effect, a redline of the law showing the amendments, or another side-by-side comparison of the amendments and the provisions of law affected, is required.

One useful technique for making a cut-and-bite amendment more understandable is to strike (and then reinsert) a few more words than necessary, and you should always consider this approach whenever the additional words would help provide a context.

For example, if existing law provides that a specified official "shall pay a benefit to individuals who qualify under section 6" and your sponsor wants to make that benefit available also to individuals who qualify under section 7, an amendment simply inserting "or 7" after "6" would be legally sufficient but probably meaningless to the reader. Striking "section 6" and inserting "section 6 or 7" instead would be an improvement—at least it would tell the reader that the numbers involved are section numbers—and striking four additional words and inserting "individuals who qualify under section 6 or 7" would be better yet; but striking the whole phrase and inserting "shall pay a benefit to individuals who qualify under section 6 or 7" (though going this far would not be necessary in most cases) would be most informative of all.

15.3 Amendment by restatement

An amendment made by restatement sets forth the entire section, subsection, paragraph, or sentence in which you want to make changes, with those changes incorporated into its text but without any specific indication of what they are.

The classic form for an amendment by restatement is as follows:

> ( ) Section 123 [or title I, or the fourth sentence of section 201 (a) (4)] of the ABC Act is amended to read as follows:

Note that a cut-and-bite amendment that strikes an entire section, subsection, paragraph, or sentence and inserts a revised version of it is in effect an amendment by restatement (of that section, subsection, paragraph, or sentence), and will be so treated in this part. The second example set forth in 15.2 ("Section 101 of the ABC Act is amended by striking 'XX' and inserting the following: 'YY' ") would be one of these if XX were a complete subsection.

Amendments by restatement are most often used when there are multiple changes to be made in the provision affected; obviously restating a whole three-page section to reflect the insertion of a single word (or even a single new sentence) would make no sense. The restatement form might, however, be appropriate even though only a single substantive change has to be made, if it necessitates conforming changes in areas such as indentation and paragraph designation; the alternative might be a couple of dozen cut-and-bite amendments to effectuate the single substantive change, and that makes no sense either.

Amendments by restatement also have both advantages and disadvantages—the exact opposites of the advantages and disadvantages of cut-and-bite amendments.

On the one hand, since an amendment by restatement shows the sponsor's changes already firmly fixed in their proper places, it gives the reader a clear picture of what the revised provision as a whole will look like and aids in understanding its effect. An amendment by restatement can also incorporate additional nonsubstantive changes in the law that improve its readability or correct errors. Of course these can also be done as cut-and-bite amendments; the downside is that the cut-and-bite amendments become more cumbersome.

On the other hand, an amendment by restatement tells the reader absolutely nothing about what specific changes have been made (so that a redline or side-by-side comparison of the amendment and the existing provisions of the law affected is still required in order for the reader to locate those changes). In addition, it results in the unchanged portions of the affected provision appearing in the bill, which is often tactically unacceptable, has the legal effect of reenacting the unchanged language,[1] and invites further amendments to that language. If there are people ready to bleed and die about language that is contained in the unchanged portions of the provision involved, the amendment will gratuitously invite them to the fray.

There may be circumstances in which a sponsor has many amendments to a block of text, which would make the restatement approach simpler to draft and easier for readers to understand, but chooses the cut-and-bite approach because the sponsor may oppose the policy underlying the text being amended and, therefore, does not want to convey the impression of validating the underlying language.

Note that the restatement form (both versions) should be reserved for cases in which the amendment will produce a revised version of the original. It should not be used when the intent is to repeal one provision and insert a totally unrelated provision in its place; if that is what you want to do, you should strike the old provision and insert the new in two distinct steps, using the cut-and-bite approach. Using the classic restatement form would strongly imply a nonexistent relationship between the two provisions, and might cause confusion at best and judicial misinterpretation at worst. Ideally you should strike or repeal the old provision at one place in the bill and insert the new provision at a later place; but if you must do the whole job at once, at least modify the basic strike-and-insert form to make it clear that two unrelated steps are involved. For example,

> ( ) Title I of the ABC Act is amended by striking section 123, and by inserting after section 122 the following new section:

instead of using either of the two more usual forms.

As a drafter, when you are confronted with the necessity of drafting an amendment or series of amendments on the borderline between cut-and-bite and restatement, you can only balance the advantages and disadvantages of each and use your best judgment.

15.4 Other approaches; State requirements

Needless to say, if the jurisdiction for which you are drafting *requires* that amendments be drafted in a specified manner, you do not have the discretion to choose.

A State may require that a bill amending the text of an existing provision of law must first make the amendments in a cut-and-bite fashion and then restate the text of that provision in its entirety, showing the amendments in place. As an example, assume that the text of section 10 of the ABC Act provides (in its entirety) that "Benefits under this Act shall be payable only to a child, and only for periods beginning on or after January 1, 2025.", and that your sponsor (before 2025) wants a bill covering disabled people as well as children but delaying the key date for a year. In a State that requires that the amendment be shown both ways, the operative section of the bill would read something like this:

SEC. ____. ELIGIBILITY FOR BENEFITS.

Section 10 of the ABC Act is amended by inserting "or a disabled individual" after "child", and by striking "2025" and inserting "2026", so that the section will read as follows:

"SEC. 10. ELIGIBILITY FOR BENEFITS.

"Benefits under this Act shall be payable only to a child or a disabled individual, and only for periods beginning on or after January 1, 2026.".

The changes are shown both by cut-and-bite amendments and by restatement.

This approach embodies all of the virtues of both amendment forms, and its only vice is the inclusion of unchanged language. It works very well in an isolated case that is short and simple like the example given. But it becomes a potential horror when the changes are numerous or the affected provisions are long. One two-word change in a provision that is three pages long—the kind of amendment normally made by a simple five-line cut-and-bite amendment—would take over three pages of text in the sponsor's bill.

The typical bill making major revisions in a broad field of Federal law (such as taxes, housing, welfare, education, or defense) contains hundreds of separate amendments and involves existing provisions that tend to be lengthy to begin with; the use of the combined approach, or even the restatement approach alone, would result in a bill that could hardly be lifted from the table, let alone read through. Even worse, nearly every page would consist primarily of unchanged language, with all the hazards that entails.

The only way to make the combined approach workable at the Federal level would be to sharply limit the number and scope of the amendments that can be included in a single bill. On the House side, this would have to be done by an ad hoc special rule (see 34.3) or by unanimous consent. The Senate can limit debate only by unanimous consent.

If, however, a State that uses the combined approach also has a constitutional requirement that legislation be limited to a single subject (which is the case in most States), such a requirement would presumably limit the process (that could be problematic at the Federal level) and therefore avoid an overly burdensome bill.

Without these limitations, the increased clarity that might result from the combined approach would be more than offset by the sheer bulk and surface complexity that would tend to hide the sponsor's changes and obscure their effect, much more than using either the cut-and-bite or the restatement form.

Some States require that amendments be done not simply by restating the amended provision, but by showing the stricken words with a line through them (this is referred to as "linetype") and the new material in italic (or bold or other specified font). This approach leaves no doubt as to what is being changed and how the existing law would look as changed. It has the benefits of both the cut-and-bite and restatement approaches. It is interesting to note that at the Federal level, the rules of the House of Representatives and the Senate require committee reports that accompany bills reported by the committee (before the bill is considered on the floor of the House or the Senate) to show the changes to existing law that would be made by the bill in the same way (that is, with linetype and italics)[2], but do not require that the bill as enacted do the same. The logic here is elusive; one has a better understanding of what a bill does before it goes to the floor of the House of Representatives or the Senate than after is enacted.[3]

15.5 Repealers

As indicated in 15.2, the "repeal" of a provision accomplishes the same result as "striking" it, and has the same legal significance, but is usually reserved for the elimination of entire sections or larger statutory units. Thus you would "repeal" a section, chapter, or title of a bill if you wanted to get rid of it, but you should "strike" a subsection or pargraph; in other words, say "Section 6 of the ABC Act is repealed" but say "Section 6 of the ABC Act is amended by striking subsection (c)".

However, there is a difference between the two. When a provision is repealed, it is so noted in the United States Code (whether in a positive-law or nonpositive-law title); when it is stricken, it disappears from the United States Code (you may find it in the notes after the relevant section appears). Technically, when you strike a provision (section, subsection, paragraph, and so forth), you should redesignate the provisions that remain to ensure the logical sequence of the statute. When you repeal a provision, you do not redesignate the remaining provisions. Therefore, if by redesignating you risk error in not making all conforming changes to other laws, or if redesignating would cause confusion because the stricken provision had a "life of its own", repealing the provision is preferable, even if it is a subsection or paragraph. An example of a provision that has a "life of its own" is section 501(c)(3) of the Internal Revenue Code of 1986. So, if (as in the example above) a provision says "Section 6 of the ABC Act is amended by striking subsection (c)", where there is a subsection (d), and you do not redesignate, it would appear in the United States Code as follows:

§[2406]. Section heading

(a) Text.

(b) Text.

(d) Text.

If the provision says "Section 6(c) of the ABC Act is repealed", it would appear in the United States Code as the following:

§[2406]. Section heading

(a) Text.

(b) Text.

(c) Repealed.

(d) Text.

The first result looks simply like a drafting error. The second result tells the reader immediately what happened.

A repealer is the device of choice for disposing of programs that have expired, are no longer being funded, or are being superseded. The following are some of the collateral points that you should keep in mind when you are deciding whether or how to remove an old law from the books:

(1) An existing law can be effectively eliminated without actually repealing it, by simply adding to it a provision terminating its key operations.

(2) An existing law can be repealed for some purposes but not for others. This can mean a law is repealed and a new provision is enacted to replace it, but the old law continues to apply for some purposes; there are in fact two parallel laws in existence, although it may be difficult to find the old law. This is perhaps a strong argument against repealing the old law; an alternative would be to keep the old law, clarify its limited applicability, and then append to the law the new provisions that are to apply to everyone else. When the old State-plan welfare programs for the aged, blind, and disabled were replaced by the SSI

program in the 1960s, they were expressly repealed; but another provision of the law repealing them made the repeal inapplicable in Puerto Rico, Guam, and the Virgin Islands, which continued to operate under the old law. (There are still two title XVIs in the Social Security Act, although only the one containing the SSI program can be found in most compilations.)

(3) The repeal of an existing law does not wipe out or disturb any of the continuing legal obligations or liabilities that were incurred under it (unless the repealer expressly so provides). This rule is stated in section 109 of title 1 of the United States Code.

(4) When the law to be eliminated is one that has been extensively amended over the years and under which there may be continuing obligations and liabilities, it is often better to insert a termination provision and leave the law on the books rather than repeal it. The law in its most recent pretermination form then remains available in the Code and in compilations, so that anyone who is affected by those obligations and liabilities can find the relevant provisions.

(5) The repeal of a law that itself repealed a predecessor law does not revive the predecessor law; a repealer is "executed" upon its enactment, and its work is still not undone when it is itself wiped from the books. This rule is stated in section 108 of title 1 of the Code.[4]

A repealer should always be specific—you should never say that "all laws in conflict with [or inconsistent with] this [provision] are repealed". Such a provision would tell no one which laws are or are not repealed. If you do not have the time to identify the particular provisions of law that need to be eliminated, you could include a section that expresses the intent of Congress that the bill supersede any inconsistent law as a guide to courts, which may be tasked with construing the statute. If you say nothing, the courts will try to give effect to all the provisions of law affected because the courts do not favor repeals by implication (see 18.2 and 28.7).

Notes

1 A court may interpret this "reenactment" as incorporating every judicial and administrative interpretation of the law that preceded this reenactment. See 28.7.

2 This is according to the "Ramseyer" rule; see 32.8.

3 At the Federal level programs are becoming increasingly available to show changes to existing law made by bills, and to show changes to freestanding provisions of bills, at different stages of consideration—for example, introduction, committee consideration, and floor consideration. The House of Representatives has, in recent Congresses, directed its standing committees and officials to "continue efforts to broaden the availability and utility of legislative documents in machine readable formats" in furtherance of "enabling all House staff to produce comparative prints showing the differences between versions of legislation, how proposed legislation will amend existing law, and how an amendment may change proposed legislation". *H. Res 5,* 118th Congress, adopted January 9, 2023.

4 But there is a way around this. The Equal Access to Justice Act (Public Law 96-481), which amended titles 5 and 28 of the U.S. Code to provide for fees and costs to be awarded to certain parties against whom the United States brought administrative (5 U.S.C. 504) or judicial (28 U.S.C. 2412) proceedings, also contained a provision repealing these amendments to titles 5 and 28 as of October 1, 1984. Congress was working on a bill renewing (and amending) the provisions of the Equal Access to Justice Act when the repeal took effect, and Congress adjourned sine die. In the next Congress, the renewal bill was reintroduced and subsequently enacted (Public Law 99-80); but rather than reenacting all the provisions that had been repealed (which would have otherwise been required), the law provided as follows:

> (Section 6 of Pub. L. 99-80)
>
> "(a) Revival of Certain Expired Provisions.—Section 504 of title 5, United States Code, and the item relating to that section in the table of sections of chapter 5 of title 5, United States Code, and subsection (d) of section 2412 of title 28, United States Code, shall be effective on or after the date of the enactment of this Act [Aug. 5, 1985] as if they had not been repealed by sections 203(c) and 204(c) of the Equal Access to Justice Act [Pub. L. 96481]".

16. Amendatory Form and Style

16.1 Amendatory terminology

Most of the stylistic rules and principles set forth in the other parts of this book apply equally to freestanding and amendatory bills, but there are a number of rules that are uniquely applicable to amendatory drafting. Following these rules (some of which have already been mentioned in a more general way) will help both you and your readers by eliminating archaic usages and surplusage and by promoting consistency. These unique rules are the subject of this part; what follows here is a concentrated look at the terminology of amendatory drafting.

Striking and inserting. Material is eliminated by simply "striking" it. Do not use "striking out" (the "out" is surplusage). And do not use the archaic "deleting" unless you are drafting for a State legislature that still uses it.

Material is "inserted" when it is being placed within the text of an existing provision, and "added" when it is being placed at the end of the provision. Do not use the archaic "inserting in lieu thereof" when replacing existing matter (the "in lieu thereof" is surplusage if the insertion is being made at the place where the striking occurred).[1]

The words "strike" and "insert" may also seem somewhat archaic (deriving as they do from the lingo of typesetters and scribes), but at the Federal level the terms are so widely used that substituting other terms would create stylistic inconsistency, most obviously in bills with input from multiple sources.

In common use until recent decades, "striking out" and "inserting in lieu thereof" had been the standard amendatory form for 200 years, and some drafters (outside the Offices of the Legislative Counsel in the House of Representatives and the Senate) may still use them. In any case, when what you are drafting will be a part of a larger product that has input from other sources and you cannot control its final form and style (either by persuading the other contributors or by editing the draft at the last minute), you should try to make your style consistent with the prevailing style of the bill.

Narrowing the target. Any amendment to an existing law should be addressed to the smallest possible subdivision of that law. If your objective is to strike a word in the fourth sentence of section 5(b) of a lengthy law, it would be legally sufficient to do it by saying "The ABC Act is amended by striking 'XX' " (at least if the word does not appear anywhere else in that Act); but a reader would find it nearly impossible to locate the offending word, and there might be parliamentary complications resulting from the overly broad approach (see 32.8 and chapter 34).

Addressing the amendment directly to section 5 would be better, addressing it to section 5(b) would be better still, and addressing it to the fourth sentence of section 5(b) would be best of all. It should read either "The fourth sentence of section 5(b) of the ABC Act is amended by striking 'XX' ", or "Section 5(b) of the ABC Act is amended in the fourth sentence by striking 'XX' ". The latter form has the advantage of directing the reader first to the narrowest designated unit in the law, and then to the appropriate sentence in that unit.

You may have to be creative when the words to be stricken are not located in a part of the section that can easily be referred to by its alphanumeric designation. Thus if section 5(b) consists of a single tabulated sentence beginning with a few lines of "lead-in" language and followed by 20 indented numbered paragraphs and then by a few unindented valedictory lines (a fairly common format), and the words to be stricken are located in the lead-in or valedictory language rather than in one of the numbered paragraphs, the amendment should indicate that location. It ought to read "Section 5(b) of the ABC Act is amended, in the matter preceding paragraph (1) [or in the matter following paragraph (20)], by striking 'XX'. ".

Descriptive characterizations. Any descriptive characterization of material that is to be stricken, added, or changed (such as "the word ...", "the number ...", or "the phrase ...") and that is only part of a sentence is surplusage and should be omitted if the material itself is set forth. Say simply "Section 5(b) is amended by striking 'eligible on that date' "; do not say "... is amended by striking the phrase 'eligible on that date' ". However, when striking an entire statutory unit (such as a title, section, subsection, paragraph, or sentence), or amending it by restatement, the existing text should never be set forth in the amendment; it should simply be referred to by its proper name—"... by striking section 301", "... by striking subsection (b)", or "... by striking the fourth sentence".

When inserting or adding an entire new statutory unit, the preferred form would be "... is amended by inserting after 'XX' the following new [title, section, subsection, paragraph, sentence]:". However, all of the language after "following" and before the colon is actually unnecessary; and many professional drafters choose to omit it. (Note that you should always omit it if what you are inserting or adding is less than a full sentence.) Some drafters adopt the preferred form in substance but omit the word "new" on the grounds that it is surplusage (which it is). An advantage of omitting the language and saying only "the following:" is that if the designations of the material being inserted change in the drafting process (for example, if what were originally added as subsections have to be changed to paragraphs), you will not risk error by having to go back and change all the prefatory language.

Headings and designations. The heading of a section or other subdivision (if the section has a subdivision) and its designation ("**SEC. 3.**" or "SEC. 3."[2] in the case of a section or "(a)", "(1)", of "(B)" in the case of an inferior subdivision) are a part of that section or subdivision. Thus if you amend a section "to read as follows" and fail to reinsert its heading, you have repealed the heading; you can avoid the problem, of course, by amending only the "text" of the section. In the "traditional" style (see 33.2) the heading appears above the section designation.

However, you should remember that the designation of a section is not a part of any of its subsections. Thus if you amend section 3(a) "to read as follows" you must of course reinsert the designation "(a)", but you must not insert the designation "SEC. 3." or "**SEC. 3. HEADING.**" In the traditional style the two designations appear together on the page. If you do insert the designation, you will have two "SEC. 3."s or "**SEC. 3. HEADING.**"s. You will be less tempted to do this if you start out by saying "Subsection (a) of section 3 is amended to read as follows".

Adding new material after cut-in paragraphs. If you need to add a new and separate sentence at the end of a section or subsection that contains nothing but some lead-in language followed by several indented ("cut-in") paragraphs, you need to make sure that using the usual form—simply saying that the provision involved "is amended by adding at the end the following new sentence:"—will not result in the new sentence appearing in the last cut-in paragraph instead of after it.[3]

Use the expanded phrase "is amended by adding at the end (after and below paragraph (6)) the following flush[4] sentence:". And start the new sentence on the next line—not right after the colon—being careful to indent it properly; give it the same indentation as the lead-in language, not the indentation of the cut-in paragraphs.

Look, for example, at section 106 of title 17, United States Code, which sets forth the rights of a copyright owner:

> **§106. Exclusive rights in copyrighted works**
>
> Subject to sections 107 through 122, the owner of copyright under this title has the exclusive rights to do and to authorize any of the following:
>
> (1) to reproduce the copyrighted work in copies or phonorecords;
>
> (2) to prepare derivative works based upon the copyrighted work;
>
> (3) to distribute copies or phonorecords of the copyrighted work to the public by sale or other transfer of ownership, or by rental, lease, or lending;
>
> (4) in the case of literary, musical, dramatic, and choreographic works, pantomimes, and motion pictures and other audiovisual works, to perform the copyrighted work publicly;
>
> (5) in the case of literary, musical, dramatic, and choreographic works, pantomimes, and pictorial, graphic, or sculptural works, including the individual images of a motion picture or other audiovisual work, to display the copyrighted work publicly; and
>
> (6) in the case of sound recordings, to perform the copyrighted work publicly by means of a digital audio transmission. [5]

If, for example, you needed to add a sentence to ensure that these rights were subject to some other provision of law, you would say

> ( ) Section 106 of title 17, United States Code, is amended by adding at the end the following flush sentence:
>
> "The rights set forth in this section are subject to the limitations set forth in section _ of the ABC Act.".

You could avoid using this formulation by designating the existing text of section 106 as subsection (a) and then adding a new subsection (b) ("The rights set forth in subsection (a) etc."), but this is an example of a provision of law that has been so widely referenced, not only throughout title 17 but in case law and the copyright community as well, that changing the designation of the existing text would create inconsistency in the law and confusion among those conversant with copyright law (see 18.1).

"Place" rather than "time". The word "place" has to do with location, and the word "time" with chronology. Thus when changing a word or phrase that appears more than once in a provision, "place" is better than "time" as a way of referring to its various locations. For example, say "Section 10 is amended by striking 'XX' each place it appears [or the first and third places it appears if you want to leave it alone at its other locations] and inserting 'YY' ". ("Wherever" can be substituted for "each place" if you prefer the sound of it.)

If you think it is clearer to be explicit that "YY" is to be inserted each place "XX" is stricken (since literally the phrase "each place it appears" or "wherever it appears" modifies only "by striking 'XX' "), it is permissible (though unnecessary) to add the words "in each instance" before the final period.

"That Act" or "such Act". The first time an Act, a section, or any other designated subdivision is amended in a section of a bill, it is always cited by its full name—"the ABC Act", "section 5(b) of the ABC Act", or "paragraph (3)(C) of section 5(b)". If that same Act, section, or subdivision is subsequently amended one or more times in the same section of the bill (without any intervening provisions that refer to some other Act, section, or paragraph), the customary practice is to cite it as "that (or such) Act", "that (or such) section", or "that (or such) paragraph". (See also 24.11.)

"Immediately". Avoid the use of "immediately" in conjunction with "after" or "before" to identify the place at which new language is to be located; the intended meaning is invariably clear without it. Say that the provision involved is amended "by inserting 'XX' after 'YY' ", not that it is amended "by inserting 'XX' immediately after 'YY' ".

"Thereof". The use of "thereof" in the description of the matter being amended is redundant. Say that the provision involved is amended "by adding at the end [or after subsection (d)] the following:", not that it is amended "by adding at the end [or after subsection (d)] thereof the following:".

Consolidated reference convention. In a lengthy bill consisting mostly or entirely of amendments to one particular law, having to refer to that law by name over and over again (in the process of amending it) can be an irritation to both drafter and reader. One good way of avoiding these repetitive references is to use the following convention (placing it at or near the beginning of the bill):

> ( ) [Except as otherwise specifically provided,] whenever in this Act [or title] a section or other provision is amended or repealed, the amendment or repeal shall be considered to be made to that section or provision of the ABC Act.

Using this convention eliminates the necessity of specifying, each time an amendment is made, the Act in which the provision being amended is located. The drafter can say "Section 5(b) is amended ..."—anywhere in the bill—instead of "Section 5(b) of the ABC Act [or of that Act] is amended"; and the reader will know that the law being affected is the ABC Act since the convention would not be used if the bill also contained amendments to other laws. (See also 24.10.)

Actually, a few scattered amendments to other laws in the bill would not prevent the use of the convention—those laws would of course be cited by their full names in the usual manner, and the "except" clause in the suggested language (as stated above) would take care of them. But if there are more than a few the reader might become confused, and the convention should not be used. An alternative is simply to use "the Act" throughout the bill to identify the law in which the provisions being amended are located, after first defining the term to mean that law (for example, "References to 'the Act' in this Act [or title] are to the ABC Act").

16.2 Amendatory punctuation

Quotation marks in general. It goes without saying that when a bill adds language to an existing law, or specifies language in an existing law for the purpose of defining the location of an amendment, that language appears in regular quotation marks ("double quotes"). The same is true when the bill strikes language from an existing law if that language is expressly set forth. When the quoted language being added or stricken itself includes quoted material, the marks surrounding that material are converted to "single quotes".

There is only one possible exception to these rules. When the material being added or "amended to read as follows" is very lengthy (such as a complete new title) and constitutes substantially all of the bill, it is permissible and often desirable to show it without quotation marks. In a case of this kind the possibility of confusing the reader (by omitting the quotes) is minor, and the omission of the quotes will save a lot of work, promote readability, and minimize errors in drafting and in the bill's enrollment and printing.

"Following"; Colons. A cut-and-bite amendment inserting language can be stated in either of two ways—"… is amended by striking 'XX' and inserting 'YY' ", or "… is amended by striking 'XX' and inserting the following: 'YY' ". The former approach is best when the material being inserted is short and can be run in without indentation, while the latter should always be used when the material is long or a particular indentation is required.

An amendment by restatement always includes the words "… is amended to read as follows:" or "… and by inserting the following:".

In a tabulated list (such as a provision making serial amendments—see 17.2), if the numbered paragraphs are to end with periods (instead of with commas or semicolons as they would in a true tabulated sentence—see 23.5), the lead-in language usually winds up with "… is amended as follows:" or "… shall include the following [things]:".

Whenever "as follows" or "the following" appears this way (in lead-in language), use a colon, not a dash or some other device. And for the sake of clarity keep those terms as close to the colon as possible—say that the provision involved is amended "by adding after 'XX' [or at the end] the following:", not that it is amended "by adding the following after 'XX' [or at the end]:".

Periods and quotation marks. Never include any part of the vehicular punctuation inside the quotes along with the language of the amendment.

When inserting, adding, or striking quoted material, any punctuation that is to be included at the end of (and as a part of) the quoted material must appear within the quotes, and any final punctuation that is a part of the vehicular sentence (and not a part of the quoted material itself) must appear after the closing quotation marks. (This will be stressed again in chapter 21.)

Most journalists can get away with placing the final punctuation mark of a sentence or clause before a closing quotation mark—editors generally endorse this practice, as does the Government Printing Office in everything except bills—but a legislative drafter cannot. There must be no confusion in a bill about whether or not a final punctuation mark was meant to be part of the quoted material.

The material inside the quotes is being inserted into an existing statute, after all; and if the vehicular sentence's own final period is placed within the quotes, as is customary in expository writing, that period will also wind up in the statute—where it does not belong—even though you merely used it in a vehicular way. And the reader of your words will often have no way (short of doing a comparative check of the statute being amended, and sometimes not even then) of knowing what you intended. Leave the vehicular period outside the quotes, where it can do its job properly.

If the quoted material does end with a period (and the amending sentence goes no further), there should be another period after the closing quotation marks to serve as the final punctuation mark of the amending sentence itself. Letting the period within the quotes serve also as the final period of the amending sentence would leave the reader and the courts confused in some cases about your meaning (just as it would in the reverse case mentioned in the preceding paragraph). Admittedly, a sentence that appears to end with a double period, one outside the closing quotation mark and the other just inside it, will strike many people as strange looking (21.6 gives an example); but the device is critically important in the interest of clarity and precision. It would be unforgivable to hide your punctuational intent.

In either case, if the result is contrary to the conventional editorial rules for final punctuation in sentences containing quoted material there is a good reason for it: Those rules do not penalize lack of precision the way legislative drafting rules do.

Needless to say, these considerations also apply when the quoted material is in the middle of a sentence and is followed by a comma or semicolon rather than by a period.

Punctuation marks by themselves. A punctuation mark all by itself within quotes (such as ",", ";", or ".") is confusing and can easily be misread. Always call it by its name rather than quoting it. Thus do not say "… is amended by striking ',' and inserting ';' "—say instead "… is amended by striking the comma and inserting a semicolon". And in a similar vein, do not say "… by inserting 'X' before ','—say instead "… by inserting 'X' before the comma".

16.3 Being literal

There is one requirement of amendatory form that is so obvious that it should need no mention, but in practice is so often ignored that it deserves special emphasis. It might be called the "amendatory Roman rule".

When drafting an amendment that actually shows (in quotes) the matter being inserted or added, that matter must be shown exactly as it should appear in the law upon its enactment. This goes beyond merely designating it properly and writing it in the proper style, and addresses its external parameters—how it will look on the page in the statute.

If it should be paragraphed in the permanent law, it must be paragraphed in exactly the same way in the bill. If it should be indented in the permanent law, it must be indented the same way in the bill. And any capitalization or punctuation that you want to see in the permanent law must appear in the bill.

Too many drafters seem to assume that somewhere along the line someone—the enrolling clerk, the printer of the bill, or the publisher of the Statutes at Large—will somehow convert the external parameters of their provisions into the correct form. But enrolling clerks, printers, and publishers cannot and will not do this—they are not qualified to judge the drafter's intent, and anyway they are bound by law to follow the provision's words and arrangement literally. Do not make this mistake.

16.4 Special forms

"Metes and bounds" references to long material. When faced with the necessity of removing large chunks of language, especially when showing all of it would not aid the reader in understanding what the bill is doing or would be tactically unacceptable, you can delineate the language to be removed by simply identifying its beginning and ending. (The beginning or ending of the language can be implicit if it coincides with the beginning or ending of the unit being amended.)

The following are examples of "metes and bounds" references:

> ( ) Section 101 of the ABC Act is amended by striking "XX" and all that follows through "YY".
>
> ( ) Section 101 of the ABC Act is amended by striking "XX" and all that follows through the end and inserting a period.
>
> ( ) The first sentence of section 101 of the ABC Act is amended by striking all that precedes "XX" and inserting "YY" [or by striking all that precedes "XX" and inserting the following: "YY"].
>
> ( ) So much of section 101 of the ABC Act as appears after "XX" and before "YY" is amended to read as follows: "ZZ".

Note that the first example given uses the phrase "all that follows through 'YY' "—a fairly common string of words in amendatory language. For many years it was customary in this situation to say "all that follows down through 'Y' "; the word "down" is pure surplusage and should not be used.

A word of caution: Remember that when you strike part but not all of a sentence and do not substitute anything for the part stricken, you must repair the damage. Thus if the part stricken includes the beginning of the sentence, you must go one step further and capitalize the first remaining word (which has now become the first word of the sentence); and if the part stricken includes the end of the sentence you must reinsert the period (see the second example given above).

Similarly, if you are to amend a provision by inserting words at the beginning of a sentence, remember to change the capitalization of the existing text accordingly, as in the following example:

> ( ) Section 101 of the ABC Act is amended by striking "The Secretary" and inserting "Subject to the provisions of section X, the Secretary".

Margin and alignment amendments. The traditional method for converting an unsubdivided, unindented subsection (or other provision) into an indented paragraph solely to make it possible to add an additional (indented) paragraph, or for correcting the margin or indentation of the provision, is simply to replace the existing provision with a new provision containing the same words but written in the proper form, with the desired new margins, indentations, and designations.

This can take the form of a cut-and-bite amendment (striking the existing provision and reinserting it in the desired form, including the new paragraph) or an amendment by restatement (amending the existing provision "to read as follows:"). Either one does the job; but each of them displays the entire unchanged text of the provision on the face of the bill, with all of the tactical hazards mentioned earlier. This is particularly undesirable in a "technical correction" provision where no substantive changes are made to the existing law.

At the Federal level efforts have been made to address this kind of problem without repeating the text of the provision involved; and many have been enacted into law (note the case study in 8.5). An example is section 2004(a)(12) of Public Law 108-429[6]:

> (15) Section 583(c)(1) of the Tariff Act of 1930 (19 U.S.C. 1583(c)(1)) is amended by moving the matter preceding subparagraph (A) and subparagraphs (A) through (K) 2 ems to the right.

Another example is in section 2004(d)(5)(A) of the same Public Law:

> (5) Section 337(a) of the Tariff Act of 1930 (19 U.S.C. 1337) is amended—
>
> (A) in paragraph (1), by aligning the text of subparagraph (E) with the text of subparagraph (D); and

The sole purpose of this type of provision—which includes printers' jargon—is to realign the margins of existing text, and the first example, in particular, would be difficult for most people to understand; but no one except the drafter and an occasional technician pays any attention to it, and it works. However, no two cases are the same, and no standard approach has been developed. If you are in a position where you need to use it, you should seek out and study two or three examples of the approach and then try to write a similar provision that will fit the facts of your particular situation. But be careful—it is tricky.

You need to be sure that your approach will result in making the corrections you want. Assume, in the following example (section 202(a) of the International Emergency Economic Powers Act [50 U.S.C. 1701(a)], that you wanted to change the existing text to a new paragraph (1), add a new paragraph (2), and add headings to the subsection and paragraphs, requiring each of the numbered paragraphs to be indented:

> (a) Any authority granted to the President by section 203 may be exercised to deal with any unusual and extraordinary threat, which has its source in whole or substantial part outside the United States, to the national security, foreign policy, or economy of the United States, if the President declares a national emergency with respect to such threat.

Supposing you said the following:

> ( ) Section 202(a) of the International Emergency Economic Powers Act (50 U.S.C. 1701 et. seq.) is amended—
>
> (1) by striking "(a) Any authority" and inserting
>
> "(a) Basis of Authority.—
>
> "(1) In General.—Any authority"; and
>
> (2) by adding at the end the following:
>
> "(2) Notice.—The President may exercise the authority under paragraph (1) only after notifying the Congress.".

The result would be that only the first two words of the existing subsection (a) would actually be indented along with the new paragraph designation for paragraph (1). The rest of the text would technically remain as it is in the law—and not indented.[7] This is another example of the importance of being literal when you do amendatory instructions.

Moving provisions around. Occasionally it becomes necessary to move a provision of existing law from one location to another, with or without substantive changes. There is no reason why you cannot do this, and it does not require complicated or esoteric language. A typical provision of this kind might read:

> ( ) Title I of the ABC Act is amended by moving subsection (b) of section 123 to the end of section 124 and redesignating it as subsection (g) [and by appropriately redesignating the remaining subsections of section 123].

But remember that when you change the location or designation of the provision involved you must watch for any cross-references to it that may need to be conformed, and you must be sure you are aware of any more general provisions that may become automatically applicable to it in its new location.

16.5 Specific usages that vary from the freestanding

There are several specific provisions that may appear in bills of any kind but that are handled in a slightly different fashion when they appear in amendatory bills. Most of them have been mentioned elsewhere, but it may be worthwhile to repeat them in the present context.

Long titles. When a bill's primary purpose is to make changes in a particular existing law, the long title should begin "[A BILL] To amend the ABC Act so as to provide …", instead of simply beginning "[A BILL] To provide …" as it would in a freestanding bill.

Short titles. When a bill's primary purpose is to make changes in an existing law and it is broad enough to warrant a short title at all, it is appropriate (and probably desirable) for the short title to read "ABC Amendments Act [of 2025]" instead of "ABC Act [of 2025]" as it would if it were freestanding.

Tables of contents. When a bill contains a section or other provision adding a number of consecutive new sections to an existing law (such as a new title or chapter), it may be useful to show those sections in the bill's table of contents if it has one.

Thus if section 2 of a bill adds a new title to the ABC Act or broadly revises one of that Act's existing titles, the table of contents for the bill would show the heading of section 2 in the usual manner but might follow it with a table of contents for the new or revised title. The latter should be artificially indented (to distinguish its elements from the elements of the bill itself), and should be surrounded by quotation marks (to indicate that its elements do not refer to subdivisions of the bill itself but rather to something added by the bill). For example:

Sec. 2. Revision of title IV of the Public Health Service Act.

"TITLE IV—NATIONAL RESEARCH INSTITUTES

"Part A—National Institutes of Health

"Sec. 401. Organization of the Institutes.

"Sec. 402. Appointment and authority of Director.

"Sec. 403. Report of Director."

Sec. 3. Technical and conforming amendments.

Amendments to tables. The elements of a table of contents, or any other table, are generally referred to as "items" for amendatory (or cross-reference) purposes, as in "the item relating to section 401 in the table of contents of the ABC Act is amended…". Once again, if you are amending an item "to read as follows" or inserting a new item, make sure that the item is printed exactly as it is to appear in the table you are amending.

Note that whenever you add a new major component (such as a title, chapter, or section) to an existing law that has a table of contents, you must make a conforming change to that table of contents. (Be careful, however, if you are working from a compilation; many compilers of major statutes that have no table of contents add their own tables of contents as a convenience to readers, and since these do not actually appear in the law they should of course not be conformed.)

Effective dates. If a bill makes amendments to existing law and an explicit effective date is required for those amendments, it should be stated in terms of the amendments rather than in terms of the bill itself.

Thus, if sections 4 and 6 of a 10-section bill consist of amendments to existing law that require explicit effective dates, the bill's effective-date provision should say that "the amendments made by sections 4 and 6 take effect …", adding that "the remaining provisions of this Act take effect…". Even if the remaining provisions do not require explicit effective dates, for clarity you may want to specify the "default" effective date of the jurisdiction: "The remaining provisions of this Act take effect on the date of enactment of this Act" (at the Federal level). Relying on the traditional effective-date provision ("This Act takes effect…") is often unclear in its application to amendments, and relying on it is chancy. See chapter 26.

Notes

1 An argument can be made that "in lieu thereof" is not surplusage, that simply saying "inserting" does not tell you where the language is to be inserted. However, at the least at the Federal level, "in lieu thereof" is no longer used. If the concept were still in use, "instead" (recommended by *Hirsch*) is certainly less archaic.

2 See chapter 33 for a discussion of the different drafting styles.

3 See 23.5 for a discussion of tabulated sentences.

4 "Flush" indicates that the sentence is to be printed without the first line indented, as you would in a new subdivision. See 30.2.

5 Note that this section (17 U.S.C. 106) does not observe the convention that each item in a tabulated list following a colon should start with a capital letter and end with a period.

6 The Miscellaneous Trade and Technical Corrections Act of 2004.

7 As a practical matter, the Law Revision Counsel, when inserting the provision in the U.S. Code, would indent all of the text as the probable intent of Congress, but because there is a precise way to describe how the text is to appear, it is better to use it.

17. Organization of Amendments

17.1 Sequence of amendments

How should an amendatory bill be structured? As indicated in chapter 6, the basic organizational rule is that all bills should set forth their provisions in the relative order of their importance or at least in some rational arrangement of subject matter, whether they are freestanding or amendatory. The key operating provisions should come first, housekeeping provisions last, and so forth.

However, serving the objective of orderly arrangement is often not as clear-cut in the case of an amendatory bill as it is in the case of a freestanding bill, since you may feel somewhat limited by the preexisting arrangement of the law you are amending. If, for example, the basic operating provisions of that law are to be found after its housekeeping provisions for some reason, you may be tempted to follow the same approach in your (amendatory) bill and make any necessary housekeeping amendments first.

In most cases you should firmly resist this temptation. You should group your amendments by subject ("modular construction"), and arrange the subjects as you would if you were writing a freestanding bill. You should normally acquaint the reader with any changes in the existing law's key operating provisions first, and then with any changes that may be needed in its definitions, before going on to deal with collateral matters. Any imperfections in the arrangement of the existing law you are amending will be perpetuated—you will rarely have the opportunity of totally overhauling that law's organization—but your bill (the vehicle by which the amendments are being made) will have internal coherence.

This approach will avoid unnecessary confusion, facilitate the bill's consideration as it goes through the legislative mill, and simplify the redrafting process if some but not all of the amendments are rejected. Your primary aim should be to place the various amendments in the sequence that makes their substantive impact most understandable, even when the provisions being amended are not in that sequence.

It is only fair to point out, however, that there are certain areas in which the recommended sequencing approach is not followed. In some fields of Federal law that are governed by positive-law titles of the United States Code or by one or two comprehensive statutes and that are routinely subject to periodic reauthorizations or comprehensive revision—such as the annual National Defense Authorization Acts[1] and the education laws—the amendatory bills customarily make their changes in the exact order of the provisions of the law being amended, without regard to whether or not that results in a rational arrangement for the amendatory bill itself.

There is a logic to following the exact order of the law being amended, as a matter of course, whenever that law is massive and the amendments cover many topics (so that they are not all part of a single theme), especially when those topics would be regarded by most of the players as approximately equal in importance. Proponents of this approach would regard it as foolish, for example, in a comprehensive reauthorization bill for educational programs, to deal with the title IV student aid programs before the title I provisions just because the title IV provisions carry the "main message"; the argument here is that following the order of the law being amended helps the reader to find items of interest and avoids having to deal with conflicting ideas about which provisions are "more important".

There are sometimes mechanical considerations (not present in a freestanding bill) that are inescapable. For example, when you must redesignate some of the numbered paragraphs in a list in order to create a space at the proper point in the list for a new paragraph (3), you should do it before you add that paragraph even though it is a trivial detail; if you insert the new paragraph first you are risking ambiguity and confusion, because you will (temporarily) have two paragraph (3)s; when you do get around to redesignating the remaining paragraphs, the reader may not be able to tell which of the two is to become paragraph (4). (See the first example in 18.1.)

One final word. Everything that has been said here has addressed the subject of sequence in terms of amendatory bills taken as a whole; but the same considerations apply, in exactly the same way, if all of the amendments involved are made in separate subdivisions of a single section instead of being made in separate sections of the bill.

17.2 Serial amendments

If you want to make several cut-and-bite amendments to the same provision of law, and your analysis has determined that they are of approximately equal importance or are interrelated, you can put them in a single subdivision of your bill (a section, subsection, or paragraph) instead of putting them in sepa¬rate subdivisions, one for each amendment. However, you should not take this approach as an expedient way to avoid careful analysis of the relative importance of provisions, which the organizational principles set forth in chapter 6 would require. Treating each amendment separately with an appropriate heading will almost always be easier for the reader to follow.

The serial format sets forth the amendments as a list, with a separately numbered cut-in paragraph for each of them, and is an example of the basic form of a "tabulated list". The lead-in language is followed by a dash rather than a colon, and is read as a part of each numbered paragraph. Each paragraph begins with a lower-case letter and ends with a semicolon (except the next-to-last paragraph, which ends with "; and", and the last paragraph, which of course ends with a period). This may sound complicated, but it is not; it will actually be easier for most readers to wade through and understand than stating the amendments in separate provisions. You should read 23.4 and 23.5 to make sure you understand the mechanical details.

As a simplified example, assume that you want to make several amendments to section 123 of the ABC Act. If you use the serial approach, your amendatory provision might look something like this:

( ) Section 123 of the ABC Act is amended—

(1) in subsections (a) and (b), by striking "XX" and inserting "YY";

(2) in subsection (c), by inserting "PP" after "QQ";

(3) in subsection (d), by adding at the end the following new[2] sentence: "________________."; and

(4) by adding after subsection (e) the following new subsection:

"(f) APPLICABILITY.—Subsections (a) through (e) shall apply…".

You have made five separate amendments in a single sentence. (Note that the word "by" is repeated in each of the numbered paragraphs rather than being stated only once just before the dash; see 23.4.)

A close relative involves lead-in language that ends with a colon instead of a dash (and represents the second kind of tabulated list described in 23.4); it is not actually an example of the true serial amendment format but might be called a modified serial approach. Each of the numbered cut-in paragraphs begins with a capital letter, ends with a period, and consists of one or more sentences.

If it were drafted in the modified serial format, the example given above would read like this:

( ) Section 123 of the ABC Act is amended as follows:

(1) Subsections (a) and (b) are each amended by striking "XX" and inserting "YY".

(2) Subsection (c) is amended by inserting "PP" after "QQ".

(3) Subsection (d) is amended by adding at the end the following new sentence: "______________________.".

(4) The following new subsection is added after subsection (e):

"(f) Applicability.—The preceding provisions of this section shall apply…".

Some drafters prefer this approach because each numbered paragraph is a self-contained unit (that is, the subject of the sentence need not be imported from the lead-in language), and because it is easier to make subsequent additions to or deletions from the list (since there would be no punctuational complications).

Either serial approach has the advantage of gathering together in one place all of the amendments that involve the subject under consideration and are related to the particular provision of existing law that is being amended, clearly indicating that relationship to the reader.

Note that under both approaches the new language in quotes is shown in exactly the form in which it is to appear in the law being amended (as it must be—see 16.3), with the correct paragraphing and indentation, even though it may make the amendatory provision itself look strange or untidy. The new subsection (f) that is added by paragraph (4), for example, seems to be out of alignment with the rest of the provision, but there is a reason for it; it is indented less than the four amendatory paragraphs because that is how it will appear in the law being amended.

As with any drafting device, the serial format should be used with discretion. You can legitimately use it many times in the same bill, but you should make sure each time that the amendments involved are reasonably localized. A set of serial amendments that begins "The ABC Act is amended—" or "Title 28, United States Code, is amended—" would be too broad; the individual amendments would be too scattered, too hard to find, and too likely to produce parliamentary problems.

17.3 Cumulative amendments

When amendments are made at several different places in a bill to the same provision of existing law, especially when those amendments add new paragraphs or subdivisions sequentially, the amendatory language for each of the later amendments must take into account what the earlier amendments have done, and should embody one of the following formulations:

> ( ) Title I of the ABC Act is amended by adding after section 123 (as added by section 5 of this Act) the following new section:
>
> **"SEC. 124....**
>
> ( ) Section 123 of the ABC Act (as amended by sections 6 and 7 of this Act) is further amended by striking [quoted language including part or all of the language previously inserted by sections 6 and 7] and inserting the following: [new quoted language]
>
> ( ) Section 123(a) of the ABC Act (as amended by the preceding provisions of this Act) is further amended [this assumes that the preceding provisions added new paragraphs (12), (13), and (14), for example]—
>
> > (1) by striking "and" after the semicolon at the end of paragraph (13);
> >
> > (2) by striking the period at the end of paragraph (14) and inserting "; and"; and
> >
> > (3) by adding after paragraph (14) the following new paragraph:
> >
> > "(15) ....".

In the case of cumulative amendments of this kind the earlier amendments should never anticipate the later ones—it would be unforgivably confusing to the reader. But (as you will note in each of the examples just given) the later amendments assume that the earlier (preceding) amendments have been executed. And remember, when the amendment adds a new paragraph at the end of a tabulated series of paragraphs, you must clean up the punctuation; the third example given above illustrates this.

Cumulative amendments would not be necessary in a rational world. But the various amendments to the single provision involved are usually designed to accomplish quite different objectives; and they are often offered and adopted at different times and at different stages of the legislative process. However, because of the confusion to the reader, the drafter should, if it is possible from a political and tactical point of view to do so, take the opportunity to combine them.

17.4 Organizing amendments to support legislative strategy

When organizing a group of provisions to amend an existing law, your primary aim is to place them in the sequence that makes their purpose the clearest; the order in which you put them will not usually alter their legal effect. Sometimes, however, the order of your amendments, or how you organize them, may have tactical implications bearing on their enactment.

As a general rule, proposed changes that depend on each other should be combined in a single section or other subdivision of the bill, so that they can be considered together; if one of them falls they will probably all fall, but that is as it should be. Conversely, amendments that are not interrelated should usually be kept separate enough so that if one is rejected the others will not be affected. Amendments should normally be arranged so as to facilitate their consideration by the legislative body involved.

There are times, however, when unrelated amendments should be combined, and made to appear as interdependent as possible, usually to serve tactical needs. This would be the case, for example, when one of them is strong enough or popular enough to provide coattails upon which the less popular ones can ride to enactment. (This is very similar to the practice of attaching riders to appropriations bills or unrelated amendments to bills that are likely to pass in some form [for example, a bill increasing the debt limit] and therefore become vehicles for otherwise unpromising proposals—see 12.13.) Of course in a State whose constitution requires bills to cover only a single subject, combining arguably unrelated amendments runs the risk of a court challenge.

As a drafter, you are not expected to be a parliamentarian or a political tactician—these are matters for the sponsor exclusively. You should organize your amendments in the recommended manner unless there is an obvious reason to do otherwise—the sponsor (or some other person who is wise in political or tactical matters) will let you know if some other course is indicated.

Notes

1 See, for example, Public Law 117-81.

2 Remember that "new" is not necessary but is commonly used.

18. Amendatory Cautions

18.1 Redesignations

It is desirable when adding or striking provisions of an existing law to make certain that the existing law will appear (and function) as it would if the amendments had been incorporated into the law as originally enacted. In other words, any new provisions should be where they logically belong, consecutively numbered or otherwise designated; the scheme of the law should remain rational and consistent; and there should be no gaps between sections or other subdivisions.

Ideally, the reader of the amended law should not be able to tell (except possibly by their subject matter) which provisions were a part of its original factory equipment and which are optional extras that were added later.

One way to accomplish this objective is by appropriately redesignating any of the provisions of the existing law so as to create a slot for new provisions and close gaps resulting from the elimination of old ones. This involves simply changing the alphanumeric designations of the provisions involved, without making any other change in them.

To take a simple example, when a new definition is being inserted in a section of existing law that already contains a list of 20 consecutively numbered definitions in strictly alphabetical order, you would normally insert the new definition where it belongs alphabetically and renumber the succeeding paragraphs to create an opening for it. If the new term begins with the letter "p" and would be the 16th term in the alphabetical listing, you might say

( ) Section ___ of the ABC Act is amended—

(1) by redesignating paragraphs (16) through (20) as paragraphs (17) through (21), respectively; and

(2) by inserting after paragraph (15) the following new paragraph:

"(16) ....".

Or, when subsection (d) of a section already containing five subsections is being stricken in its entirety, you would normally close the resulting gap by saying

( ) Section ___ of the ABC Act is amended—

(1) by striking subsection (d); and

(2) by redesignating subsection (e) as subsection (d).

In either case you must of course be careful to correct any cross-references that may be rendered erroneous by the redesignation. If any other existing provision of law refers explicitly to paragraph (16), (17), (18), (19), or (20) in the first example, or to either subsection (d) or (e) in the second, you would have to make a conforming change in that other provision as well.

If internal amendments have to be made in any of the existing paragraphs that appear after the point where the new paragraph is to be inserted and that consequently will have to be redesignated, it is often desirable (when it would not interfere with the flow of the bill) to make those amendments before inserting the new paragraph and making the redesignations. This approach avoids awkwardness—otherwise each of those amendments would have to indicate specifically that the designation given for the paragraph being amended is its new one ("Paragraph (7) of such subsection, as redesignated by paragraph (1) of this subsection, is amended ...", for example). It also makes it easier for readers to execute the amendments to the law they have in front of them, especially when the bill will contain a number of cumulative ("piggy-back") amendments of the type discussed in 17.3.

As discussed in 15.5, however, a provision whose section number or other designation has become inextricably linked to its substance in the public eye should never be redesignated. If that section number or other designation alone is widely used as its name, by the public or in nonstatutory literature, redesignating it would result in more confusion than benefit.

And if there would be too many redesignations (and cross-reference corrections) to deal with in the time available, you should not hesitate to forget about some or all of them (and hopefully address them later in the process). In the first example given above you could just place the new definition nonalphabetically at the end of the section (or call it "paragraph (16A)"). In the second example, you could just leave the gap (which produces no adverse legal effects, but does result in an untidy law) or, as suggested in 15.5, repeal the provision (because the repeal will be noted in the United States Code at the exact place in the law where the provision appeared).

You should never, in desperation, use the old scatter-gun approach—specifically redesignating a section or subsection and then providing that "all cross-references thereto" are amended "accordingly"—just to save time. It leads to chaos and confusion. Although in some cases the changes may be purely technical and obvious, in others "accordingly" will be ambiguous or even meaningless.

Redesignation has long been a favorite target of writers on the subject of legislative drafting, who complain about the "burdens" that redesignation places upon users of the statute and of other materials making reference to the statute, and the undue demands that are consequently placed upon their time, with resulting great possibility of error. James Craig Peacock[1] called redesignation an "abominable practice … contributing to [the law's] so unnecessary complexities", and stated flatly that it "should be totally scrapped as a legislative drafting technique". *Dickerson* (pages 251–255) also complains about the proliferation of amendments that redesignation causes, stating that it is only appropriate "rarely",[2] and suggests substitutes.[3]

These complaints fail to recognize the very real virtues of keeping the permanent law tidy, and ignore the realities of the drafter's situation. In addition, although it is true that a recent redesignation may make the provision involved a bit harder for a student or practicing lawyer to locate, there are always clues to what has happened. And the primary burden on users of the statute (which the complainants do not mention at all) arises from recent substantive changes that alter what the amended provision does.

In major statutory areas that are subject to frequent broad revision, frequent redesignation is an absolute necessity. If nothing had ever been redesignated in the Social Security Act, for example, that Act would today be many thousands of pages long, with 90 percent of it consisting of gaps with "repealed" notations and most of the rest consisting of intermediate designations from "(aaa)" to "(zzz)" and beyond—and even that would be better than the hodgepodge that would have resulted if no effort had been made at all to keep its provisions in some logical order. In statutory areas of this kind, redesignation is absolutely essential to keep the law reasonably usable.

In taking the middle ground (as every drafter should, at least in theory), *Hirsch* (page 17) stresses on the one hand "the desirability of having a bill's provisions in the sequence that best ensures their being found and understood, and having their designations logically reflect that sequence"; but he recognizes on the other that the renumbering or relettering of provisions of existing law can cause confusion and sometimes mislead readers—especially readers of other laws that contain cross-references to the redesignated provisions, pointing out that if a redesignated provision is referred to in other laws, the drafter who fails to correct those references will invariably mislead the users of those laws. (Needless to say, if there will not be enough time before the bill is enacted to identify and correct all relevant cross-references or to assure yourself that there are none, you should not redesignate.)

Do not shy away from redesignations; just be aware of the responsibilities involved in using them correctly.

18.2 Amendments in substance but not in form

A special word of warning may be in order about implied and hidden amendments, chiefly to remind you that they are very common and very real while stressing that they do not actually belong in this part. They are mentioned here (although they are not cast in amendatory form) in the hope that a better understanding of what they are and what they do may help you recognize the problems they create, and encourage you whenever possible to eliminate or solve those problems by using express amendments instead.

Inconsistent enactments. What happens when two legislative enactments are inconsistent? It is logical to assume that when two statutes are inconsistent, the later enactment governs because it constitutes an "implied amendment" of the earlier one. However, the Supreme Court has stated a number of principles against repeals by implication: First, there is the "cardinal rule ... that repeals by implication are not favored" (*Posadas v. National City Bank*, 296 U.S. 497, 503 [1936]; *Morton v. Mancari*, 417 U.S. 535, 549 [1974]; *Watt v. Alaska*, 451 U.S. 259, 266–267 [1981]; *J. E. M. Ag Supply, Inc. v. Pioneer Hi-Bred Int. Inc.*, 534 U.S. 124, 146–147 [2001]).[4] "In the absence of some affirmative showing of an intention to repeal, the only permissible justification for a repeal by implication is when the earlier and later statutes are irreconcilable" (*Morton v. Mancari, supra*, 550). "The rarity with which [the Court has] discovered implied repeals is due to the relatively stringent standard for such findings, namely, that there be an irreconcilable conflict between the two federal statutes at issue" (*Matsushita Elec. Indus.*

Co., Ltd. v. Epstein, 516 U.S. 367, 381 [1996] [internal quotation marks omitted]). "[W]hen two statutes are capable of coexistence, it is the duty of the courts, absent a clearly expressed congressional intention to the contrary, to regard each as effective" (*Morton v. Mancari, supra,* 551).

A common situation in which this issue arises is in the conflict between a specific and a general statute. In such a case, the courts frequently reconcile the conflict by finding that the specific statute is a limited exception to the general, but the general statute otherwise remains in effect. "Where there is no clear intention otherwise, a specific statute will not be controlled by a general one, regardless of the priority of enactment" (*Morton v. Mancari, supra,* 550–551; *Radzanower v. Touche Ross & Co.,* 426 U.S. 148, 153 [1976]).

Suppose law A says that "every citizen of the United States shall be entitled to [some specific monetary benefit]", and law B as subsequently enacted says that "no person convicted of an offense under this section may receive any payment from the United States". Would law B amend law A by implication? Maybe, or maybe not. The court would try to give effect to both; it might depend on whether the court read law B as more specific than law A or vice versa. If the two provisions cited in the example given had been contained in sections 3 and 7 of a single law instead of in two separate laws, the same dilemma would arise.

Other rules of statutory construction may apply, but this is an example of how a simple statement in the law expressing the relationship between two provisions avoids an ambiguity of what that relationship is.

The main problem is not really the necessity of interpreting the interrelationship between two provisions in order to eliminate an inconsistency between them; it is rather that their interrelationship has to be implied because it does not show on the face of either of the provisions involved.

Hirsch (page 18) cites the provisions of law (in effect before 1983) for determining the maximum interest rate on FHA-insured home mortgages. Section 203(b)(5) of the National Housing Act—the basic law on the subject since 1935 and the place where any intelligent person then seeking to learn that rate would have looked for it—had for years fixed the rate unambiguously at 6 percent. But memorizing that section in its entirety would not have told you that Public Law 90-301 (an obscure statute enacted in 1968 to amend the veterans' home loan program) contained a section directing the Secretary of Housing and Urban Development to fix the maximum rate at whatever the mortgage market required; and as any homebuyer would have known, the rate fluctuated continuously.[5]

The point is that if the drafter (in any of the examples given) had taken the trouble to make an express amendment—even a simple cross-reference in one or both of the affected provisions—the problem would not exist.

Hidden extras. One law may expand or restrict the scope of another "from a distance"—without expressly amending it, and without doing anything that would objectively qualify as an "inconsistency"—by simply providing (for example) that the affected law shall include a new function or be administered in a new way. The difference between this case and the "inconsistency" case is that here there is no problem of interpreting what the laws (taken together) will do—the result is perfectly clear, at least to anyone who is aware of both laws, and the problem is simply finding them.

Hirsch (page 17) cites a spectacular example. In the late 1970s Congress undertook to require the inspection of domesticated rabbits slaughtered for human food, and in the process "enacted (twice) what is surely one of the most peculiar bills ever vetoed (twice) by an American President". The drafter used the Poultry Products Inspection Act, but did not amend it, use it as a model, or repeat its provisions. The drafter simply wrote a short freestanding bill stating in effect that the Poultry Act applies to rabbits, and that all poultry-related terms (when used in that Act) are "deemed" to refer to rabbits as well as poultry, even going so far as to deem domesticated birds to be domesticated rabbits, and feathers to be pelts.

Extremely artificial usages of this kind are always undesirable (see 11.7H) even when they work. In this case, the least of the bill's sins was the quaintness of its definitions. Far more serious was its failure to amend the statute expressly. Had the bill actually become law there would be no whisper of a suggestion in the Poultry Act to warn the reader that its scope had been expanded to include rabbits.

The moral is that some amendatory techniques—particularly the use of implied and hidden amendments—can make it very difficult for anyone to understand exactly how the affected statute would operate. In the example given, the operation of the Poultry Act (even with the inclusion of invisible rabbits) is comparatively straightforward; techniques of this kind are most commonly used in the more complicated statutory fields, where they make the situation far less penetrable.

When you are drafting any bill, you should constantly be aware that your provisions may impliedly amend other laws—indeed the possible effect of your words on other laws (and vice versa) is one of the most frequently occurring "collateral questions" discussed in chapter 5.

Other things being equal, it is almost always better to use an express amendment—one making an appropriate cross-reference at the very least—if there is an inconsistency that is both clear and significant or if there is a hidden extra, simply because that makes it easier for a person who may be subject to the affected law (or a court charged with interpreting the law) to understand and cope with the situation.

"Notwithstanding" clauses. Another questionable type of provision is one that begins with the words "Notwithstanding any other provision of law, ...". When taken with care this approach can be moderately useful; it can serve as a warning to the reader that there may be conflicting provisions somewhere and (if indeed there are any) as an indication of how to resolve the conflict.

What it really says, however, is that the drafter was unable (perhaps from lack of time or the exigencies of the political process) to integrate the bill with whatever other statutes might be relevant. *Hirsch* (page 18) says that this drafter "is a little like the hunter who fires at anything that moves and then checks to see what he has killed... [and] who uses an intangible bullet and thus leaves no visible wound on his victim as evidence to others of his marksmanship".

As with any other provision, a court may have to interpret what the phrase means in a given context, whether reading a "notwithstanding" clause with respect to other provisions of the same statute or other statutes. The court will first try to determine if the plain language of the statute is decisive and, if not, it will apply rules of statutory construction to reconcile the provisions.[6] Courts have held that a law having a "notwithstanding any other provision of law" clause overrides both prior-enacted laws[7] and laws enacted subsequently.[8] But a "notwithstanding any other provision of law" clause is not always effective in overriding other statutory requirements. Courts have adopted narrow constructions of the scope of a "notwithstanding" clauses, focusing on congressional intent while attempting to reconcile seemingly conflicting statutory principles.[9] If there are two conflicting provisions, both of which say "notwithstanding any other provision of law", then the principles discussed (earlier in this subdivision) on implied repeals would come into play: the specific controls the general, and if the conflict is irreconcilable, the later enactment would prevail.

The phrase "notwithstanding any other provision of law" rarely means what it literally says; that is, the intent is not to disregard every law on the books. For example, a provision that gives an official the authority to enter into contracts "notwithstanding any other provision of law" is probably saying that other requirements regarding competitive bidding do not apply, not that the official can accept bribes to award contracts, for example. The job of the court would be to decide which laws are *not* disregarded.

To some extent the phrase has become boilerplate, so that *not* using the phrase would raise questions among the persons charged with carrying out the provision. In trade law, the phrase is always used in bills that direct the Secretary of the Treasury or U.S. Customs and Border Protection of the Department of Homeland Security to "liquidate[10] or reliquidate" customs entries under a rate of duty different from that under which the entries were or would be liquidated. The provisions always begin with "Notwithstanding section 514 of the Tariff Act of 1930 or any other provision of law …" or "Notwithstanding sections 514 and 520 of the Tariff Act of 1930 or any other provision of law …". Sections 514 and 520 include the procedures for persons to file protests of decisions of U.S. Customs and Border Protection[11] and for that agency to pay refunds of duties, including time limits for doing so. The purpose of the "or any other provision of law" in this case is to pick up any extraneous provision of law that might impose a similar procedural conflict on the government official directed to carry out the action required. One could view this as a corollary to the textual canon of statutory construction "eiusdem generis": interpret a general term to be similar to more specific terms with which it is associated (see 28.4). The point here is that if you are going to use "notwithstanding any other provision of law", it is helpful to identify the types of provisions of law contemplated by the phrase.

Note that making the "notwithstanding" clause more specific is somewhat better, but does not solve the problem. Saying "Notwithstanding section 123 of the ABC Act" puts the explicit provision in the wrong place; the implied amendment is still only implied or at least hidden, unless of course you also indicate the interrelationship by a cross-reference in section 123.

18.3 Amendments to amendments

There is almost never any reason to amend a provision of existing law that was itself an amendatory provision, because an amendatory provision (being only a vehicle for making changes, with no substantive content of its own) is fully executed and becomes surplusage for most purposes—it does its job and then melts away—as soon as its amendments become effective. It remains on the books but is of historic interest only; the amendments that it made to the permanent law, on the other hand, are fully operative in accordance with their terms. Subsequently repealing it may remove it from the face of the law, but does not invalidate those amendments.

You should always amend a provision of permanent law directly, not by addressing the amendatory provision that added it to the permanent law.

However, there are a few exceptions to this rule, usually involving the vehicular portion of newly enacted amendatory provisions rather than the amendments themselves.

One such exception involves a previously enacted provision with a delayed effective date that has not yet arrived. The most common reason for wanting to amend such a provision is a desire to further delay its effectiveness, and the easiest way to do that is to go back to the amendatory provision and simply change its original effective date— for example, by striking "Effective one year after the date of enactment of this Act, the ABC Act is amended ..." and inserting "Effective two years after [that date] ...". Obviously, this could not be done (or at least could not be done without causing serious problems—see 26.4) if the provision were already effective.

If you want to make a substantive amendment to a provision of law after it is enacted but before it has become effective, you should do so directly—by amending the provision itself and not by going back to the law that added it—since it is in fact an existing statute despite its delayed effective date. But you must always make it completely clear whether or not you want the amendatory law's own effective date to apply to your changes.

You must always remember that administrative and other actions may already have been taken in reliance on the provision in its original form even though the provision is not yet effective, and you might have to undo those actions or deal with their consequences—a task that is always thorny and sometimes impossible.

Another type of exception occurs when the previous amendatory provision, through inadvertence or typographical error, added a new sentence or other undesignated new language to the wrong subdivision of the law—to subsection (e) of some section, for example, when it should have been to subsection (b). The necessary correction can be most easily made, whether the substantive provision has already become effective or not (at least if its enactment was fairly recent), by going back to the vehicular language of the amendatory provision, striking "is amended by adding at the end of subsection (e)", and substituting "is amended by adding at the end of subsection (b)"— with the correct effective date, of course.

In some cases, because of technical error in the vehicular language, the amendment cannot be executed at all. This may arise if two bills that are enacted virtually simultaneously amend the same provision of law in different ways. The amendments in the bill that is signed into law first would be executed, changing the provision amended. The second bill signed into law will amend a section that is already changed by the first bill so that the amendatory instructions no longer work. Here you have no choice but to amend the vehicular language (with the correct effective date) or draft a new bill from scratch with the correct vehicular language (and effective date).

Most readers will never have to face challenges of this kind. If your problem concerns the substantive content of the changes made by the amendatory provision (or concerns the erroneous placement of a designated subdivision such as a subsection or numbered paragraph), and the changes made by that provision have become effective as a part of the permanent law, you should ignore the amendatory provision altogether and address the problem directly by amending that law.

In an erroneous placement case, for example, you might say something like this:

> ( ) Subsection (f) of section 123 of the ABC Act, as added by section 456 of the XYZ Act, is redesignated as subsection (e).

The exact form would depend on whether the erroneous placement resulted in a gap (as in the example just given) or in a duplication (in which case you might have to rearrange some of the other provisions as well).

18.4 Amending the wrong law

As indicated earlier, when the sponsor's subject matter falls within a Federal statutory field that is already covered by a positive-law title of the United States Code, your bill must be amendatory in nature and must amend that title. But the converse is equally important; when the statutory field involved is not yet covered by a positive-law title (and you decide that your bill should be amendatory in nature), you must amend the underlying statute and not the nonpositive-law title of the Code in which that statute is codified.

That a nonpositive-law title of the Code can never be directly amended should be abundantly clear (see chapters 24 and 31), but it deserves special emphasis because inexperienced drafters (and regrettably even some experienced ones) regularly overlook the point and try to amend the wrong thing. Do not do it.

18.5 Annual authorization amendments and other quantitative changes

A relatively minor but occasionally perplexing drafting problem involves the question of how to draft an amendment to a provision of existing law that authorizes annual appropriations for a particular program or specifies other periodically changing quantitative values. If an authorization provision already authorizes specific amounts for one or more prior fiscal years, for example, and you are asked to draft an amendment providing an authorization for the upcoming fiscal year, do you simply add your new authorization at the end of the existing list or do you replace the existing authorizations with your new one?

Assume that you are asked to draft a provision authorizing appropriations of $40,000,000 for fiscal year 2025 to carry out the ABC Act, and that section 123(d) of that Act (the authorization section) presently reads as follows:

> (d) AUTHORIZATION OF APPROPRIATIONS.—For the purpose of carrying out this Act, there is authorized to be appropriated—
>
> (1) $10,000,000 for fiscal year 2022;
>
> (2) $20,000,000 for fiscal year 2023; and
>
> (3) $30,000,000 for fiscal year 2024.

You could strike everything after "authorized to be appropriated" and insert "$40,000,000 for fiscal year 2025.", on the theory that paragraphs (1), (2), and (3) are executed and thus no longer necessary; or you could simply add a new paragraph (4) (with conforming punctuational changes) setting forth your 2025 authorization, on the theory that the retention of the previous years' authorizations has historical value as a description of the program's scope and growth.

The same sort of question—when successive quantitative values are involved, do you save the old ones and add to them or do you replace them with the new?—arises in areas other than just annual authorizations.

Under the Social Security program, for example, the "earnings base"—which is the maximum amount of a worker's earnings that is covered each year for both tax and benefit purposes—was increased by statute from $3,600 to $13,200 in eight separate steps between 1950 and 1975 (when automatic annual adjustments took over). Most of the Social Security coverage provisions are the same in both the tax provisions and the benefit provisions, but with the earnings base they differ; every time the earnings base was increased to a new dollar amount the tax provisions were amended to eliminate the old figure and substitute the new (since tax changes are prospective only), while the benefit provisions added the new dollar amount prospectively and retained the old ones (since benefit levels are based on the worker's lifetime covered earnings and the earnings for past periods therefore remain relevant).

And in section 427A of the Higher Education Act of 1965 (20 U.S.C. 1077A) are the different interest rates on student loans over the past few decades. Although retaining all the old interest rates does lead to more clutter in the statute, having the information retained in the statute is relevant for those who have extant loans from a prior time and gives a context to current legislators and staff making new policy in this area. The statute serves as its own institutional memory.

If you have no guidance at all on a question of this kind the choice is yours. But you should consider what approach the institutional establishment might prefer; in the annual authorization example, the fact that the existing section 123 contains three different prior-year authorizations suggests that someone in the past has appreciated their historical value (especially if the 2023 and 2024 authorizations were added after the original enactment of the section) and that you should probably keep those authorizations in the law. You would not have that clue to guide you, however, if the section contained only a single prior-year authorization.[12]

You should always consider the possibility, before eliminating the existing values, that (as in the Social Security earnings base example) there may be a rational reason for retaining them.

18.6 Case study: The cost of a drafting error

The following case illustrates what can happen when an amendment is made to an existing law but fails to include the necessary conforming changes to the law as well.

In *Koons Buick Pontiac GMC, Inc., v. Nigh,* 543 U.S. 50 (2004), the issue involved the interpretation of a provision of the Truth in Lending Act (section 130(a)(2)(A); 15 U.S.C. 1640(a)(2)(A)). Before being amended in 1976, the relevant provision read as follows:

> (a) [A]ny creditor who fails to comply with any requirement imposed under this chapter ... with respect to any person is liable to such person in an amount equal to the sum of—
>
> > (1) any actual damage sustained by such person as a result of the failure;
> >
> > (2)(A) in the case of an individual action twice the amount of any finance charge in connection with the transaction, except that the liability under this subparagraph shall not be less than $100 nor greater than $1,000.. ."

An amendment in 1976 added a new clause relating to consumer leases. The provision in paragraph (2)(A) then read as follows:

> > (2)(A)(i) in the case of an individual action twice the amount of any finance charge in connection with the transaction, or (ii) in the

> case of an individual action relating to a consumer lease ..., 25 per centum of the total amount of monthly payments under the lease, except that the liability under this subparagraph shall not be less than $100 nor greater than $1,000...

Following this amendment, the courts consistently construed the clause limiting liability "under this subparagraph" to apply to both clauses (i) and (ii).

In 1995, Congress amended the language again, by adding a new clause (iii) *at the end* of subparagraph (A), so that the provision then read as follows:

> (2)(A)(i) in the case of an individual action twice the amount of any finance charge in connection with the transaction, (ii) in the case of an individual action relating to a consumer lease ..., 25 per centum of the total amount of monthly payments under the lease, except that the liability under this subparagraph shall not be less than $100 nor greater than $1,000, or (iii) in the case of an individual action relating to a credit transaction not under an open end credit plan that is secured by real property or a dwelling, not less than $200 or greater than $2,000...

The question before the Court was whether the words "under this subparagraph" applied only to the consumer lease provision in clause (ii) or also to the cases covered under clause (i). The addition of clause (iii) at the end of the provision created the ambiguity, because now the provision no longer had a parallel structure. The Court (in a plurality opinion), citing this book, *HOLC*, and *SOLC* in order to determine the meaning of "subparagraph", and noting the silence on this issue in the legislative history, decided that "common sense" dictated that Congress did not intend to change the meaning of clause (i) when it added clause (iii) and that "this subparagraph" applied to both clauses (i) and (ii).

Even though a majority of the Court reached the result (that is, that "this subparagraph" applied to clauses (i) and (ii)), the reasoning that got them there was not uniform. There were three separate concurring opinions.

In his dissent, Justice Scalia, also quoting from this book ("If a section or other statutory unit contains subdivisions of any kind, it should never contain subdivisions of any other kind unless they are parts of one of those subdivisions"), relied on the statutory language to find that "subparagraph" applied only to clause (ii). He found the dropping of "or" between clauses (i) and (ii) as one indication of congressional intent to segregate the three clauses, but he also said that it was not the Court's job to "rescue Congress from its drafting errors, and to provide for what we might think is the preferred result". 543 U.S. at 76 (dissent), quoting *Lamie v. United States Trustee,* 540 U.S. 526, 542 (2004).

Needless to say, the Court struggled with the ambiguity created in the law. This case could have been avoided altogether if the provision had been drafted properly. The drafter added a clause (iii) and failed to make a change to the existing language referring to "subparagraph".

The easiest way to clarify the language of the statute would have been to change "subparagraph" to "clause" and insert the phrase inside of clause (i), as follows (the new language is in italics):

> (2)(A)(i) in the case of an individual action twice the amount of any finance charge in connection with the transaction, *except that the liability under this clause shall not be less than $100 nor greater than $1,000,* (ii) in the case of an individual action relating to a consumer lease ..., 25 ~~per centum~~ *percent*[13] of the total amount of monthly payments under the lease, except that the liability under this ~~subparagraph~~ *clause* shall not be less than $100 nor greater than $1,000, or (iii) in the case of an individual action relating to a credit transaction not under an open end credit plan that is secured by real property or a dwelling, not less than $200 or greater than $2,000 ...

Another way would be to break out the paragraph as follows:

> (2)(A)(i) in the case of—
>
> (I) an individual action, twice the amount of any finance charge in connection with the transaction, or
>
> (II) an individual action relating to a consumer lease ..., 25 ~~per centum~~ percent of the total amount of monthly payments

under the lease,

except that the liability under this ~~subparagraph~~ *clause* shall not be less than $100 nor greater than $1,000, or

(ii) in the case of an individual action relating to a credit transaction not under an open end credit plan that is secured by real property or a dwelling, not less than $200 or greater than $2,000 …

In this way, the $100/$1000 limitation clearly applies to both the first two categories of actions.

Attention to details in drafting is a must. *Koons Buick* shows how costly is the failure to do so.

Notes

1 James Craig Peacock, *Notes on Legislative Drafting* (Washington, D.C.: National Republic Pub. Co., 1961), 37, 44.

2 At opposite ends of the spectrum: either in the case of a "drastic overhaul" of a statute, or (quoting *Hirsch*) if redesignating a paragraph or subparagraph in a recently enacted statute with which the drafter is familiar. But see the case study in 8.5 as an example of reordering and editing a long section of definitions without having to restate the entire section.

3 One suggestion *Dickerson* (page 254) makes is, in the case of alphabetized material, not to use designations at all. This approach sacrifices precision in subsequently referring to the undesignated provision. You would have to say (in the case of alphabetized definitions) "the definition relating to '_______' contained in _____ of the ABC Act is amended… ". You would have to ensure that your reference could only be to one place in the law. But what if there were a secondary definition made necessary by the primary definition? Logically this should appear with the primary definition (see 11.7C), but with no designations, how would the secondary definition be referred to? If the secondary definition were placed alphabetically with the other definitions, then you create confusion about why the secondary definition appears; it is no longer "secondary".

4 Similar rules apply with respect to State law. See 82 C.J.S. Statutes § 325 (Implied Repeal, Generally): "An implied repeal must be recognized and accorded effect where it is apparent that it was intended. Conversely…[i]n the absence of clear legislative intent, a construction of a statute will not be adopted which has the effect of nullifying or repealing another statute" (footnotes omitted).

5 In 1983, section 203(b)(5) of the National Housing Act (12 U.S.C. 1709(b)(5)) was amended to strike the provisions regarding a maximum interest rate and to read "[shall b]ear interest at such rate as may be agreed upon by the mortgagor and the mortgagee" and the provision in PL 90-301 was repealed. (There is now

no maximum rate set either by law or by the Secretary of Housing and Urban Development).

6 See chapter 28.

7 See, for example, *Crowley Caribbean Transport, Inc. v. United States*, 865 F.2d 1281, 1284 (D.C. Cir. 1989) (in which a "notwithstanding" provision of the Foreign Assistance Act of 1961 authorizing disaster relief assistance to be furnished overrode an earlier cargo preference law requiring that shipments of U.S. goods to foreign countries be made on U.S. flag vessels).

8 See, for example, *New Jersey Air National Guard v. FLRA*, 677 F.2d 276, 282 (3d Cir. 1982), cert. den. 459 U.S. 988 (1982) (a more specific earlier enactment containing a "notwithstanding" clause was not overridden by a later, more general statute).

9 *Conono, Inc. v. Skinner*, 970 F. 2d 1206, 1224 (3d Cir. 1992) (in which a "notwithstanding" clause was held *not* to override other requirements in the same statute; "courts must discern the meaning of 'notwithstanding' from the legislative history, purpose, and structure of the entire statute".

10 Liquidation is the process under which U.S. Customs and Border Protection makes a final determination of the value of, and the amount of duties owed on, goods imported into the United States.

11 Most of the provisions of the Tariff Act of 1930 actually refer to the "Customs Service"; in 2003 the Department of Homeland Security renamed it the "Bureau of Customs and Border Protection", and later (effective March 31, 2007) "U.S. Customs and Border Protection"; the Trade Facilitation and Trade Enforcement Act of 2015 (Public Law 114-125) amended section 411 of the Homeland Security Act of 2002 (6 U.S.C. 211) to establish the agency by law as "U.S. Customs and Border Protection".

12 A minor point: if you take the first approach (striking the authorization of appropriations for prior years and substituting the new one), and the bill were to be enacted into law before the beginning of fiscal year 2025, it would have stricken the authorization for the fiscal year still in effect (2024); if for some reason additional funding were needed for fiscal year 2024, the amendment could be construed as either removing *any* authorization of funds for fiscal year 2024 (creating a procedural hurdle in an appropriations bill that would then not have an underlying authorization [see 12.5 and 34.5], or, alternatively, as removing any limitation on the amount of funds that could be appropriated for that fiscal year (and thus removing the authorizing committee from the funding process). If the prior authorizations are not stricken in the amendment, this issue does not arise.

13 If the opportunity arose to amend the statute, then "percent" could replace the archaic "per centum".

PART VI
STYLE, FORM, AND USAGE GENERALLY

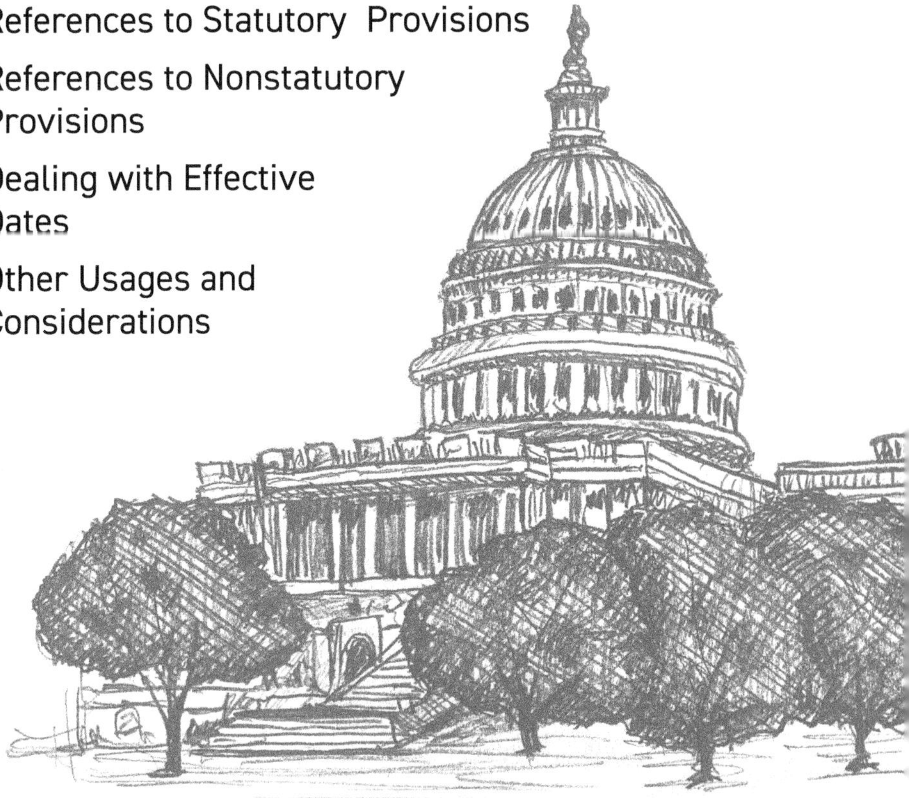

19. General Considerations

19.1 Using this part

Part VI is primarily intended as a reference document for use by drafters during the writing process. It represents an effort to bring together and discuss, in one place, substantially all of the drafting rules relating to style, form, and usage that have not already been discussed in detail (although some points may be addressed here that have already been treated in depth in one of the previous chapters).

Part VIII will add some basic stylistic information for those of you working at the Federal level. Chapter 33 describes in detail the specific drafting styles you might use, and the other chapters in that part discuss the legislative context in which you will be using them.

19.2 Common complaints

By and large, people who are not particularly familiar with legislation have one general complaint about it (in addition to their dislike of specific substantive policies, of course): laws are too complicated, and too hard to read and understand. Up to a point they are right, but for the most part (as emphasized earlier) they just do not understand the kinds of problems that both drafters and policymakers face.

Many writers and commentators who are familiar with legislation also complain about complexity and lack of readability, but they add a variety of more specific complaints about the drafting techniques and practices that they believe produce those undesirable characteristics. Most of their complaints fall into several recurring categories:

(1) *Long sentences.*

(2) *Excessive subdivision.* Several commentators have actually taken the trouble to count the number of different statutory subdivisions—subsections, paragraphs, subparagraphs, clauses, and the like—that are contained within selected sections of carefully chosen statutes, recoiling in horror when they manage to find one in which the number seems excessively high.

(3) *Legalese.* This includes such things as provisos, archaic words, stilted usages, Latin expressions, cross-references, and interlocking definitions.

(4) *Overcomplicated construction.* This includes the high incidence of exceptions and qualifications, the use of "broken verbs" (that is, sentences whose subjects and predicates are interrupted by substantive matter that ought to have been placed elsewhere), and sentences laden with parentheses and commas.

(5) *Bureaucratic words.* Among the targets are "effectuate", "institute", "finalize", "facilitate", "coordinate", and "input".

(6) *General failure to use conversational language.*

Long sentences should generally be avoided but are necessary (and even desirable) in many situations. Intensive subdivision looks intimidating, but it is one of the drafter's most valuable tools in dealing with complicated ideas. Legalese and bureaucratic terminology should be avoided, but such things as multiple exceptions, broken verbs, and the intensive use of parenthetical expressions and commas are highly valuable parts of the drafter's arsenal. And the quest for language that resembles conversational speech, though a worthy objective in theory, can be fruitless and even inappropriate in many cases.

The substantive aspects of these complaints (and the reasons for the authors' opinions on them) were dealt with more fully in parts II and III (see especially chapter 9); and the stylistic considerations that bear upon the matters complained of are given special attention in this part.

19.3 Consistency

The need for consistency in drafting has been mentioned many times earlier, but it is so essential that it deserves to be reemphasized here. The style and arrangement of your bill should never vary internally, and should be as consistent as possible—or at least be capable of comfortably coexisting—with the style and arrangement of other laws in the same field.

The way you break down the bill and its major components into lesser subdivisions, your paragraphing, your indentation, your sentence structure, your typography, and the particular drafting style you adopt—whether or not it is one of the recognized Federal drafting styles—should be uniform throughout the bill.

The words you use to express a particular idea or concept should always be the same regardless of the number of times it appears, and regardless of the availability of words that might otherwise be regarded as synonyms in everyday speech.

And the words you use to express a particular idea or concept should never be used to express any other idea or concept. As *Hirsch* (page 43) puts it:

> It is an elegant bit of poetry for Shakespeare's Berowne to declaim, "Light, seeking light, doth light of light beguile", but it is an inelegant model for the legislative drafter.

Failure to observe these rules does more than make your end product look untidy. A bill that contains unwanted or inadvertent variations in style cannot be called an example of good legislative writing, whatever its other virtues. Such variations not only interfere with the communication of ideas and concepts to the intended audience; they almost guarantee that your bill will contain substantive ambiguities, they give aid and comfort to people who are looking for grounds to misinterpret the language or to criticize the product or process involved, and they invite both courts and administrators to get the wrong result in close cases.

Indeed some of the rules of statutory construction used by the courts (addressed in chapter 28) are based on consistency. Examples are the "whole act rule" (the court will look to the whole statute in interpreting a particular word, phrase, or other provision); the presumption that every word and phrase adds something to the statutory command; and the presumption that the same meaning is implied by the use of the same expression throughout an Act.[1]

19.4 Ambiguity, vagueness, and generality

Dickerson (pages 31–44) describes ambiguity, overvagueness or overprecision, overgenerality or undergenerality, and obesity (that is, prolixity, circumlocution, avoidable redundancy, and other unnecessary verbiage) as "the major diseases of [legislative] language". He and a number of other writers have devoted considerable attention to the apparently widespread confusion between them.

A term is ambiguous if it is capable of more than one legitimate interpretation. *Dickerson* discusses semantic ambiguity (for example, does the term "residence" refer to a place of abode or one's legal home), syntactic ambiguity (uncertainty about what a word modifies or refers back to), and contextual ambiguity (for example, a bill imposes a requirement on "persons" in one section and on "residents" in another, with no apparent reason for the different terminology).[2] Ambiguity is the bane of legislative language, and the use of an ambiguous term is always bad (unless, of course, the sponsor affirmatively wants ambiguity for tactical reasons). Many of the stylistic rules and principles discussed in this part serve primarily as weapons in the battle against ambiguity.

As indicated in the preceding paragraph, ambiguity may be the policy for any number of reasons; one may be that using ambiguous language is the only way for the legislature to reach agreement on a piece of legislation. The potential for litigation is obvious. However, if there is an administering agency that will have to interpret the statute in regulations, the agency's interpretation of an ambiguous term (as with a vague term [*infra*]) may provide a solution, given the deference the courts accord agency interpretations of statutes under chapter 7 of title 5, United States Code (see chapter 12), and under *Skidmore v. Swift & Co.*, 323 U.S. 134 (1944) (see chapter 29). Note, however, that with the Supreme Court's decision in *Loper Bright Enterprises v. Raimondo*, 144 S. Ct. 2244, 603 U.S. __ (2024), which overruled *Chevron U.S.A., Inc. v. Natural Resources Defense Council*, 467 U.S. 837 (1984), the courts will decide questions of statutory ambiguity and will no longer defer to a "permissible construction of the statute" (the standard of deference under *Chevron*) by the agencies on those questions.

The context in which language appears can create ambiguity as well. The *Koons Buick* case discussed in chapter 18 is an example of contextual ambiguity created by a drafting error. It is possible that a drafting error will be so plain that the court will recognize it as such and decide that there is no ambiguity. See *Chickasaw Nation v. United States,* 534 U.S. 84 (2001) (insertion of a reference in a parenthetical that was not illustrative of the language outside the parenthetical did not create ambiguity, but was simply a drafting mistake), and *Lamie v. United States Trustee,* 540 U.S. 526 (2004) (a statute rendered awkward and ungrammatical does not make it ambiguous). Needless to say, as a drafter your goal is to avoid a court ever having to decide the issue.

A term is vague, according to *Dickerson* (page 39), if it is "uncertain in its application to a number of particulars"; that is, vagueness is uncertainty resulting from the broadness of a term (like "student" or "employer").[3] A term is general if its application is not limited to entities that are specifically identifiable. Martineau and Salerno limit general words to nouns that describe a class of persons or things (parent, child, animal, plant) to distinguish a general from a vague word, which can be descriptive (near, reasonable, handicapped), an action (give, sell, conspire), or a concept (freedom, beauty, art).[4] The use of a vague or general term is good if it reaches the result the drafter is seeking, and bad otherwise. A drafter may seek a degree of vagueness because of the sponsor's policy or for the express purpose of giving the administering agency room to exercise judgment consistent with the sponsor's objective; but precision and specificity are highly desirable in most cases and a drafter must never be vague inadvertently. Vagueness in a criminal statute raises constitutional flags. In *Lanzetta v. New Jersey,* 306 U.S. 451 (1939), the Supreme Court invalidated a law as too vague that made it a crime to be a "gangster", defined as one who (among other things) was "known to be a member of any gang consisting of two or more persons". This is admittedly an extreme case, but you get the point.

The use of undefined modifying adjectives, though as essential to drafting as it is to other forms of writing, risks creating either ambiguity or vagueness or both and can cause endless legal difficulties if done carelessly (see 22.5). *Hirsch* (page 45) points out that every modifier used in a bill will eventually call for some sort of administrative judgment, and expresses the view that, other things being equal, the fewer the modifiers, the better the bill.

Readers with a scholarly bent may wish to dig into these matters more deeply; others should simply avoid ambiguous terms and obesity to the extent possible, and make sure that their choice of words helps achieve, with minimal difficulty, the sponsor's objective.

19.5 Rules of statutory construction

Chapter 28 addresses rules of statutory construction applied by the courts. However, statutes themselves have rules of construction. They usually read like definitions; some are specifically intended for application only to the law in which they appear, while others apply across the board to all statutes in the jurisdiction involved. The most important of the latter at the Federal level appear in chapter 1 of title 1 of the United States Code, the very first section of which (for example) provides in part that "In determining the meaning of any Act of Congress, unless the context indicates otherwise—

> words importing the singular include and apply to several persons, parties, or things;
>
> words importing the plural include the singular;
>
> words importing the masculine gender include the feminine as well;
>
> words used in the present tense include the future as well as the present; …
>
> the words "person" and "whoever" include corporations, companies, associations, firms, partnerships, societies, and joint stock companies, as well as individuals; …

It should be obvious that one or more of these rules will significantly affect nearly every bill you ever write. You need to be aware of all of the definitions in chapter 1 (or comparable provisions in State law) because you need to know when a general definition will apply to a bill you are drafting so that you can modify it if necessary to carry out the policy involved. The terms defined in chapter 1 include "oath", "signature", "writing", "county", "vessel", "vehicle", "company (or association)" (as including successors and assigns), and "marriage"[5].

Sometimes a "rule of construction" in a bill can serve as a quick fix to an otherwise technical nightmare. Public Law 109-115 joined together two separate appropriations bills, one designated "Division A" and the other

"Division B". Because the bills had been considered separately in the Congress, there was a multitude of references to "this Act" in the general provisions of the first appropriations bill limiting the use of funds in that bill. To avoid having to change every reference to "this division" and to avoid the construction of the limitations extending to the second appropriations bill contained in the Act, the following provision was added to division A:

> SEC. 847. Except as expressly provided otherwise, any reference to "this Act" contained in this division shall be treated as referring only to the provisions of this division.

Suffice it to say that rules of construction, whether those already on the books, or ones you create, can save you time (if the policy fits).

19.6 Contributing to the legislative history

The legislative history of a statute encompasses the full array of all the things that happened to it while it was still just a bill making its way through the legislative process, along with all the things that were said about it in the accompanying legislative documents.

To the extent that the courts look at the legislative history to derive the meaning of a statute, what that history says is important. The Federal agency that has to administer a law pays close attention to the relevant committee reports and other aspects of its legislative history in trying to determine just what Congress intended.

No drafter can control a bill's legislative history, of course. But, if you are strategically placed, you may be able to contribute to some of its more important parts, specifically the committee reports that accompany the bill when it is being sent to the floor in the House and Senate, and the statement of managers that accompanies the conference report when the bill is approaching final passage.

A committee report or statement of managers is the vehicle by which the standing committee or committee of conference that considered the bill explains what has been done, why it was done, and what is expected to occur as a result. A large part of it typically consists of language designed to clear up ambiguities and to specify what is supposed to happen under the bill in particular cases; and much of that language might otherwise have been included in the bill itself.

Every committee understands full well that it has choices of this kind, and (since it knows that the administering agency will treat the directions contained in the committee report or statement of managers almost as though they were contained in the law) it will seldom hesitate to move legislative language out of the bill and into the report or statement when tactical, political, or other considerations indicate that that would be expedient. Many heated arguments about controversial amendments are amicably settled by a simple agreement to "handle the problem in the committee report" (or the statement of managers).

When this happens, the strategically placed drafter may be called upon to assist the committee staff in the writing of the report or statement since the language involved, being intended to achieve a legislative result, needs the same kind of careful attention to soundness and detail that it would receive if it were part of the bill itself. This is particularly true of a "section-by-section analysis" or comparable description of what each provision of the bill purports to do.

Note that a committee report or statement of managers lends itself to use by courts in decisions based on legislative history because it is a required step in the legislative process—a formal document with an officially assigned number. A subcommittee report is not such a document—it can normally take any form or even be bypassed altogether—and therefore it is not as likely to be so used; but the same considerations would apply insofar as the drafter is concerned.

However, as will be seen in chapter 28, because the courts will always look first at the language of a statute and may not look beyond the language in the statute, you as the drafter should encourage the committees involved to clarify the meaning in the statute itself and *not* to rely on committee reports to do this.

Notes

1 William N. Eskridge Jr., Philip P. Frickey, and Elizabeth Garrett, *Cases and Materials on Legislation: Statutes and the Creation of Public Policy* (St. Paul, Minn.: West, 2007), 862–868.

2 Martineau and Salerno, in *Legal, Legislative, and Rule Drafting in Plain English,* pages 77–78, discuss these three types of ambiguity.

3 Ibid., 79.

4 Ibid., 80.

5 Public Law 117-228, the Respect for Marriage Act" (enacted December 13, 2022) redefined marriage in section 7 of title 1, United States Code, so that "an individual shall be considered married if that individual's marriage is between 2 individuals and is valid in the State where the marriage was entered into or, in the case of a marriage entered into outside any State, if the marriage is between 2 individuals and is valid in the place where entered into and the marriage could have been entered into in a State".

20. Breakdown, Designation, and Headings of Subdivisions

20.1 General considerations

A rational system of subdivisions and subdivision designation in a bill, uniformly followed, not only helps the drafter in composing the bill and promotes clarity and precision, it also aids in orienting the reader and makes legislation easier to follow and understand.

Every jurisdiction has its own established system for breaking down a bill into subdivisions and designating them. If there is more than one system, the Roman rule may govern what you should do (see chapter 8), because there are few jurisdictions, outside of those States whose statutory law is completely codified, in which the established system is applied universally and without exception.

If you are drafting for a State or other jurisdiction, you will need to follow the system of designation adopted by that jurisdiction for the particular vehicle you are drafting. This should include looking not only at compilations of previous legislation found in codes, but also at the documents that preceded the compilation—the bill as originally introduced, the act or ordinance as enacted by the legislative body, and the substantive provisions as incorporated into the code of laws of the jurisdiction.[1]

Because Federal statutes are written in different formats (see chapter 33), it might appear that no general statements about breakdown and designation can be made in the Federal area; but fortunately this is not so. As indicated in 10.2, the Federal formats manage to coexist more or less amicably, largely because their breakdown and numbering systems are nearly identical. The differences between them lie almost entirely in the external characteristics of the individual subdivisions—the headings, the placement of designations, the indentation, and the typography.

It is important to remember that the way in which a bill is broken down into subdivisions has nothing to do, directly at least, with the contents of the bill's subdivisions or the style in which they are written. It is only the external format of the subdivisions that varies according to the drafting style being used.

Note that when this chapter describes the mechanical and typographical attributes of the different subdivisions of a bill, it employs many of the technical and colloquial terms that both drafters and printers use in their everyday work, such as "full measure" in contrast with "cut-in", "flush" in contrast to "paragraphed" (or "indented"), and "paragraphed" in contrast to "run in". All of these terms are defined and discussed fully in chapter 30; if you have any trouble with them you should consult that chapter before reading this one. And most of what is said in this chapter will obviously be repeated, and expanded upon, in chapter 33.

In any event, when reading what follows you should keep in mind that this chapter is narrowly focused, and (except for 20.5, which deals specifically with headings) concerns itself only with two things: how a bill is broken down into its component pieces and what those pieces are called.

20.2 The basic section

The fundamental division of all statutes—Federal and State—is the numbered section. Some simple bills have no other divisions of any kind, while bills that are more complicated invariably include both broader divisions—the "senior components", of which the numbered sections are a part—and narrower ("inferior") subdivisions into which the sections themselves are broken down. Most bills have at least some of the narrower subdivisions.

A section is always a self-sufficient unit, in that its text (after the heading, if any, and the designation) starts with a capital letter, ends with a period (no matter how many sentences or inferior subdivisions it contains) and is grammatically complete without any help from what precedes or follows it. Every section is designated by an Arabic numeral (not enclosed in parentheses), and its text always appears on the page as a "full-measure" paragraphed subdivision.

In a bill without any senior components, the sections are numbered consecutively beginning with section 1. In a bill divided into titles, however—

(1) the sections in each title are numbered consecutively beginning with section 101 in the case of title I, section 201 in the case of title II, and so forth (so that the first digit in any section number reflects the number of the title in which it appears); except that

(2) if a particular title is further subdivided into subtitles, chapters, or parts, appropriate gaps are normally left in the numbering of the sections so as to leave space for the future addition of new sections—if title II of a bill were divided into subtitles A, B, and C, for example, the sections in subtitle A might be numbered consecutively beginning with section 201, those in subtitle B with section 211, and those in subtitle C with section 221.

In extremely lengthy bills, particularly "omnibus" bills covering many subjects, the numbering of titles frequently begins with four digits, for example, 1001 for title I, 2001 for title II, and so forth, to accommodate the large numbers of sections. Massive bills may have titles of five digits.

20.3 The inferior subdivisions

In Federal statutes—regardless of the style in which they are written—sections that need to be subdivided are always broken down successively into—

(1) subsections (starting with subsection (a)),

(2) paragraphs (starting with paragraph (1)),

(3) subparagraphs (starting with subparagraph (A)),

(4) clauses (starting with clause (i)),

(5) subclauses (starting with subclause (I)), and

(6) items (starting with item (a)(a)) and subitems (starting with subitem (A)(A)).

Items and subitems should be avoided whenever possible, because the successive subdivisions become very difficult to follow.[2] If in drafting a bill you find you have reached down to the item level, you should rethink the organization of the bill.

Note that if you have a subsection (a), you must at least have a subsection (b); if you have a paragraph (1), you must at least have a paragraph (2), and so on for each inferior subdivision.

Each subdivision is always referred to by its proper name and alphanumeric designation—for example, a subdivision designated "(a)" is always called "subsection (a)", and a paragraphed subdivision designated "(1)" is always called "paragraph (1)" whether it is a self-sufficient unit or just an element in a tabulated sentence or series.

However, there is one case where it is not necessary to mention the name of the subdivision to which you are referring at all—it arises when more than one level of subdivision has to be specified in order to identify the target subdivision. For example, the second subdivision in paragraph (4) of subsection (c) (in any given section) could properly be referred to as "subparagraph (B) of paragraph (4) of subsection (c)", since it is a subparagraph, of course, but it could also be properly referred to as "paragraph (4)(B) of subsection (c)" or as "subsection (c)(4)(B)"; the more compact form is usually preferred if the location of the reference permits it. For further guidance in cases like this, see the discussion of "multiple breakdown" or "composite" references in 24.8.

A subsection, like a section, is always a self-sufficient unit in that its text (after the designation) starts with a capital letter, ends with a period (no matter how many sentences or inferior subdivisions it contains), is grammatically complete without any help from what precedes or follows it, and always appears on the page as a "full-measure" paragraphed subdivision.

Paragraphs, subparagraphs, clauses, and even subclauses (and items and subitems) can also be self-sufficient in this sense, but they are just as often used as grammatically incomplete parts of a tabulated list or series, or a tabulated sentence, separated by commas or semicolons rather than periods. In the latter case, there is a temptation to call them all by the generic name "clauses". Some drafters yield to this temptation, but you should not. The virtue of having a consistently designated hierarchy of inferior subdivisions greatly outweighs any momentary confusion that the occasional use of one of them in a slightly different way might cause.[3]

There is one important exception to this hierarchy, however. Since subsections must always be self-sufficient and full measure, they can never be parts of an indented list or series that depends on lead-in language for its completeness. Thus if a section that is not divided into subsections contains lead-in language followed by a list or series of designated items (such as a definition section that begins "For purposes of this Act—"), those items become numbered paragraphs just as they would be if they were part of a subsection, and the subsection stage of division is simply omitted.[4]

Finally, here are a few things to watch out for:

(1) If a section or other statutory unit contains subdivisions of any kind, it should never contain subdivisions of any other kind unless they are parts of one of those subdivisions. Thus if a subsection has to contain two separate lists of items (which ought to be numbered in the same way since they occupy the same level of subdivision but which obviously cannot both be numbered starting with "(1)"), you should not number one of them starting with "(1)" and the other starting with "(A)"; you must find a way to give each list its own paragraph designation (that is, create lists "(1)" and "(2)") and then designate the items on each list—which will now be located in its own separate statutory unit—as subparagraphs starting with "(A)".

(2) You should create all the subdivisions you need in order to separate your ideas and indicate their hierarchy, of course, but you should avoid carrying the technique to extremes (as mentioned above regarding items and subitems).

(3) Never use undesignated subdivisions above the sentence level. Every paragraphed subdivision of a bill must be given its own alphanumeric designation, in accordance with the system you are using. Failure to do this makes it impossible to refer to the provision later in a sensible way.

A good example of the difficulties created by the undesignated subdivision and unorthodox designation system could be found in section 231 of the Foreign Assistance Act of 1961 (22 U.S.C. 2191), establishing the Overseas Private Investment Corporation (in effect from 1969 to 2018), prior to the repeal of the provision when the Corporation was replaced by the United States Development Finance Corporation in Public Law 115-254. The provision read substantially as follows:

> SEC. 231. CREATION, PURPOSE AND POLICY.—To mobilize and facilitate the participation of United States private capital and skills in the economic and social development of less developed countries and areas, and countries in transition from nonmarket to market economies, thereby complementing the development assistance objectives of the United States, there is hereby

created the Overseas Private Investment Corporation (hereinafter called the "Corporation"), which shall be an agency of the United States under the policy guidance of the Secretary of State.

The Corporation, in determining whether to provide insurance, financing, or reinsurance for a project, shall especially—

(1) be guided by the economic and social development impact and benefits of such a project and the ways in which such a project complements, or is compatible with, other development assistance programs or projects of the United States or other donors;

(2) give preferential consideration to investment projects in less developed countries ...; and

(3) ensure that the project is consistent with the provisions of section 117 ..., section 118, and 119 of this Act ..., and consistent with the intent of regulations issued pursuant to section 118 and 119 of this Act.

In carrying out its purpose, the Corporation, utilizing broad criteria, shall undertake—

(a) to conduct financing, insurance, and reinsurance operations on a self-sustaining basis, taking into account in its financing operations the economic and financial soundness of projects;

(b) to utilize private credit and investment institutions and the Corporation's guaranty authority as the principal means of mobilizing capital investment funds;

(c) to broaden private participation and revolve its funds through selling its direct investments to private investors whenever it can appropriately do so on satisfactory terms;

(d) to conduct its insurance operations with due regard to principles of risk management including efforts to share its insurance and reinsurance risks;

(e) to the maximum degree possible consistent with its purposes—

(1) to give preferential consideration in its investment insurance,

reinsurance, and guaranty activities to investment projects sponsored by or involving United States small business; and

(2) to increase the proportion of projects sponsored by or significantly involving United States small business to at least 30 percent of all projects insured, reinsured, or guaranteed by the Corporation;

(f) to consider in the conduct of its operations the extent to which less developed country governments are receptive to private enterprise, domestic and foreign, and their willingness and ability to maintain conditions which enable private enterprise to make its full contribution to the development process;

(g) to foster private initiative and competition and discourage monopolistic practices;

(h) to further to the greatest degree possible, in a manner consistent with its goals, the balance-of-payments and employment objectives of the United States;

(i) to conduct its activities in consonance with the activities of the agency primarily responsible for administering part I[5] and the international trade, investment, and financial policies of the United States Government, and to seek to support those developmental projects having positive trade benefits for the United States;

(j) to advise and assist, within its field of competence, interested agencies of the United States and other organizations, both public and private, national and international, with respect to projects and programs relating to the development of private enterprise in less developed countries and areas;

(k) (1) to decline to issue any contract of insurance or reinsurance, or any guaranty, or to enter into any agreement to provide financing for an eligible investor's proposed investment if the Corporation determines that such investment is likely to cause such investor (or the sponsor of an investment project in which such investor is involved) significantly to reduce the number of his employees in the United States because he is replacing his United States production with production from such investment which involves substantially the same product for substantially the same market as his United States production; and (2) to monitor conformance with the representations of the investor on which the Corporation relied in making the determination required by clause (1);

(l) to decline to issue any contract of insurance or reinsurance, or any guaranty, or to enter into any agreement to provide financing for an eligible investor's proposed investment if the Corporation determines that such investment is likely to cause a significant reduction in the number of employees in the United States;

(m) to refuse to insure, reinsure, or finance any investment subject to performance requirements which would reduce substantially the positive trade benefits likely to accrue to the United States from the investment; and

(n) to refuse to insure, reinsure, guarantee, or finance any investment in connection with a project which the Corporation determines will pose an unreasonable or major environmental, health, or safety hazard, or will result in the significant degradation of national parks or similar protected areas.

Note that this section begins with an undesignated paragraph (which should be a subsection (a)). Then a second undesignated paragraph begins, under which are three designated paragraphs (1), (2), and (3). This is followed by another undesignated paragraph, under which are a number of lettered paragraphs. These are not subsections because they are not independent units, but to refer to them as paragraphs is confusing because of the first set of paragraphs. The references would have to read something like "paragraph (1) of the second undesignated paragraph of section 231"; and "paragraph/subsection (e) of the third undesignated paragraph of section 231". Note that paragraph/subsection (e) has its own paragraphs (1) and (2); paragraph/subsection (k) has two numbered subunits also, but because they are not paragraphed, they are referred to as "clauses". This example illustrates the value of giving each unit a designation and using a uniform system of designation.

20.4 The senior components

If the bill you are working on deals with two or more separate major topics, or is so massive that it must be broken up somehow in order to be manageable, you will have to consider dividing it into pieces that are broader than mere sections.

Each drafting style has its own rules for doing this, of course. Just to get the ball rolling, here is the way you might conceivably divide and subdivide a monumentally large and complicated bill into senior components (at the Federal level) if you are using "revenue" style:

(1) Divide the bill into titles (beginning with title I).

(2) If any title needs to be further broken down into senior components, divide it into subtitles (beginning with subtitle A).

(3) If any subtitle needs to be further broken down, divide it into chapters (beginning with chapter 1).

(4) If any chapter needs to be further broken down, divide it into subchapters (beginning with subchapter A).

(5) If any subchapter needs to be further broken down, divide it into parts (beginning with part I).

(6) If any part needs to be further broken down, divide it into subparts (beginning with subpart A).

(7) And finally, divide each subpart (or the lowest senior component you wound up with) into the individual sections you were aiming for in the first place. A senior component is always divided at least into sections.

This is the way the Internal Revenue Code of 1986 is structured (except that it treats itself as a single title and begins the subdividing process with step

(2)); the authors know of no other Federal statute that actually has so many levels of senior components. (The nonrevenue drafting styles prescribe similar but not identical forms for the hierarchy of senior components—see 33.6.)

The trouble with all this is that only the first operation—the division of the bill into titles—is universally used. Every bill that is divided into senior components at all is divided into titles, whether or not it is further subdivided (and regardless of the drafting style being used). But if it is further subdivided all bets are off—in actual practice the next lower components may be subtitles, chapters, or parts. In most cases it seems to depend on how many levels of senior components are going to be required.

As the example of a rule of construction in 19.5 demonstrated, bills can have larger subdivisions than titles, namely "divisions", a unit that grew out of the practice of combining many bills into one at a late stage of the legislative process, or otherwise coagulating "omnibus" bills covering a multitude of subjects.[6]

The United States Code—a special case—is itself divided into titles, and every title is divided into chapters (whether or not it is first divided into subtitles or parts). The chapters (as originally codified) are odd-numbered, in order to leave space for the future addition of new ones. [7]

If two levels of senior components are all you will need, you could simply go to subtitles (and then sections), or divide the titles into parts (and then sections), omitting the steps in between. When amending an existing law, you simply follow the system of designation in that law for the senior components.

One final comment: sections, not senior components, are the vehicles that carry the substantive freight. From the drafter's point of view, titles and other senior components of a bill are nothing but defined spaces within which related sections can be grouped—they are empty receptacles for holding the substantive provisions. And except for their designations, those provisions (the sections themselves) are written and structured in the way they would be written and structured even if the bill were not divided into senior components.

Thus when drafting a new section, giving it a heading and a number is only a trivial preliminary—the real work has barely begun—but when creating a new title the job is finished as soon as you have inserted its designation and heading at the appropriate place in the bill. As a consequence, the only stylistic decision you have to make in creating a title or other senior component involves its heading.

20.5 Headings

For your own good as well as for the edification of your eventual readers, you should make maximum use of headings for all of your paragraphed subdivisions. This rule applies whether or not the bill you are working on is divided into broader segments such as titles, chapters, and parts (which always have headings).

As a general rule, headings should be as short as possible, but informative enough to be of help to the reader; they need not (and indeed should not try to) exhaust the ideas expressed in the text. They should be accurately descriptive, should a court choose to take a heading into account when interpreting the law.

Chapter 33 sets forth literal examples of all of the types of headings that are used in the different Federal drafting styles.

Headings for sections and inferior subdivisions. Headings for sections, subsections, and further subdivisions are highly visible when flipping through the pages of a draft. They orient the readers, and help give an understanding of the overall organization of the bill as well as the purpose of each of its provisions.

In the early stages of a lengthy draft, headings can be particularly useful to you as a drafter. They give you an excellent road map of your product, enabling you to locate provisions quickly and saving you time and irritation; language hastily inserted while putting together a rough working draft is often hard to find later without them. Headings also help you plan the architecture of the bill, since they give you a built-in working outline and force you to provide logical places in advance for all the pieces.

At least as important is the fact that the necessity of inventing headings (especially when they are used for the lower-level subdivisions) makes you think about what you are doing. It is amazing how often your efforts to come up with an appropriate heading for a section, subsection, paragraph, or other subdivision will reveal to you for the first time that you have been guilty of trying to combine ideas that do not really go together, or of failing to combine ideas that do.

As a rule, the harder it is to come up with a heading that is both succinct and illuminating for a particular section, subsection, paragraph, or other subdivision, the more likely it is that some further thought is needed. The provision involved may cover too much territory (and need to be further divided), or the whole scheme of division for the bill (or for the part of the bill in which that provision appears) may need to be reconsidered.

When sections fall into logical groupings, it is sometimes helpful to give each section in a group a compound heading stating first the common idea and then the subject of the particular heading, with the parts separated by a colon. For example, in a bill dealing with traffic safety you might have a section headed "Speed of motor vehicles: passenger cars", followed by sections headed "Speed of motor vehicles: trucks and buses" and "Speed of motor vehicles: motorcycles".[8]

When you put several coordinate subjects in the same section you can quite properly use a compound heading with the parts separated by semicolons, for example, "Appointment of Commissioner; tenure; removal for cause".

Although whenever possible you should try to include headings for a bill's sections and inferior subdivisions (see chapter 8 on the Roman rule), the extent to which you do so may depend on the context in which you as the drafter are operating (for example, at the Federal level, amendments to appropriations bills or to the Rules of either House would not have headings for section subdivisions). But if headings are used at all in a bill for subdivisions of a particular kind—sections, subsections, paragraphs, or subparagraphs—then all subdivisions of that kind in the bill should have headings.

To the extent that you must follow a particular format at the Federal level, the following guidelines may be useful. The "traditional" or "classic" style permits headings for sections but does not require them, and generally does not use them at all for inferior subdivisions. "U.S. Code" style requires headings for sections and, until relatively recently, did not use headings for inferior subdivisions. This has changed with the move, in the Offices of the Legislative Counsel of both the House of Representatives and the Senate, toward using headings to the maximum extent possible (again, see chapter 8). The "modified revenue" style requires both section and subsection headings and recommends (but does not require) paragraph and subparagraph headings as well. And the full-blown "revenue" style requires headings at every level—sections, subsections, paragraphs subparagraphs, clauses, and subclauses. In the traditional style, the section heading (if there is one) is centered and appears by itself on a separate line; the designation appears at the beginning of the text. In all the other styles the section's designation and heading are combined on the same line, just above the text, and are not centered. The heading for any lesser subdivision in both the revenue and modified revenue styles is "run-in"—it appears within the text, immediately after the designation.

Thus a section dealing with criminal penalties written in U.S. Code style would begin

§123. Criminal penalties

(a) IN GENERAL.—Any person who …

while in revenue or modified revenue style it would begin

SEC. 123. CRIMINAL PENALTIES.

(a) IN GENERAL.—Any person who …

and in traditional style it would begin

CRIMINAL PENALITIES

SEC. 123. (a) Any person who …

(The typographical details are spelled out in chapter 33.)

Headings for senior components. All senior components have headings (called "superior" headings in this book), even when the sections and subsections they contain do not. As has been indicated, in one sense they consist of nothing but their headings. And all superior headings are "centered" on the page (in combination with the associated component designations) even when the bill has section and subsection headings that are "flush".

Each of the accepted Federal drafting styles has its standard rules for superior headings, but in practice (as in the case of the rules for subdividing a bill generally—see 20.4) they are not always followed. The only thing you can say with certainty is that a bill's superior headings should be prominent, consistent, and consistent with the Roman rule. Read 33.6 for guidance—it contains a tabular comparison of the rule prescribed for superior headings under the different drafting styles. But if you remain in doubt, just follow the best models you can find.

Notes

1 Robert J. Martineau and Michael B. Salerno, *Legal, Legislative, and Rule Drafting in Plain English* (St. Paul, Minn.: Thomson/West, 2005), 123.

2 This may be unavoidable when amending a complex law that has already been broken down into many subdivisions, particularly if the policy is to expand the subject matter covered by a clause or subclause.

3 As will be seen in chapter 36, Federal regulations refer to every subdivision of a section as a paragraph, making internal references challenging.

4 Some laws on the books are not drafted in this way, that is, the lead-in language is followed by units designated (a), (b), and so forth. See, for example, section 1 of the Foreign Agents Registration Act of 1938, as amended (22 U.S.C. 611). If you have to amend a provision like this by adding a new definition, the Roman rule would require you to follow suit by also using a letter designation (unless you were to change all the subdivisions to numbered paragraphs and all cross references to these subdivisions). It is unclear whether these subdivisions with letter designations would be referred to as "paragraphs" or "subsections".

5 This was a reference to the Agency for International Development of the Department of State.

6 The National Defense Authorization Acts (enacted each year) are divided into divisions.

7 An example was the addition (by Public Law 107-273 (in 2002)) of a chapter 16 to title 28, United States Code, relating to judicial discipline.

8 An example of this appears in chapter 1 of title 17, United States Code. Section 106 lays out the exclusive rights of the copyright owner. Of the sections that follow in chapter 1, many have the heading "Limitation on exclusive rights:" followed by the subject matter of the limitation covered by the section.

21. Grammatical Considerations

21.1 Preliminary comments

Good legislative language must be mechanically sound in terms of grammar, punctuation, word usage, and arrangement. As indicated in chapter 7, this usually involves nothing more complicated than the application of the everyday rules governing good writing of any kind.

Of the differences that do exist between legislative writing and other forms of prose composition, very few are actually clear-cut matters of right and wrong. Mostly they involve choices between alternative usages that are matters of personal preference or subjective judgment, where either usage would adequately serve a novelist's purposes but one is demonstrably better than the other for the drafter.

However, it cannot be repeated too often that legislative language has an overriding need for clarity and precision; and you must always apply (or not apply) the established rules of grammar and punctuation in the way that will best meet that need. It is the purpose of this chapter to help you do it.

21.2 Number

The clearest expression of an idea or concept uses singular rather than plural nouns, if for no other reason than that it cuts out one unnecessary layer of possible relationships; it avoids the question of whether the plural applies to each individual member of the class or only to the class as a whole. The phrase "Any employee who ..." works the same as "Employees who ...", but it eliminates the risk that a reader or a court will erroneously interpret the statement to mean that at least two employees must be involved before any employee is covered, or that it only applies to groups of employees as such.

The use of the plural is a major source of ambiguity in legislative language. *Hirsch* (page 43) offers the following as a typical example of a provision that raises unnecessary questions:

> ( ) The Secretary shall not[1] award grants, or enter into contracts, in excess of $25,000 without the approval of the National Advisory Committee.

Does the $25,000 restriction limit the aggregate amount of the grants that may be made or merely the size of each individual grant? Does it limit the aggregate amount of the contracts that may be made or merely the size of each individual contract? Or does it perhaps seek to limit the combined aggregate amount of both? Read literally, it seems to limit each of them separately, although that is clearly not what it intended. Simply substituting "a grant" for "grants", and "a contract" for "contracts", would remove all doubt (unless, of course, an aggregate limitation was intended, in which case that fact should be explicitly stated).

A statute speaks to each person who is subject to it, and should be drafted that way. The singular is not limiting (see 19.5). You should avoid the use of plural nouns in the interest of clarity; and if there is any reason in a particular case to think that a singular noun might be read as not applying to every person in the group you are trying to cover, use "each" or "every" instead of "a", "an", or "any".

(Note that where number is a matter of indifference, you can often avoid both the singular and the plural by using the generic, as in "Proof of hardship may be by affidavit".) If you must begin a sentence by describing the individuals covered in the plural, remember that it is almost always possible to switch over to the singular in mid-stream—before you get to the part that requires precision—by saying (for example) "individuals who …" and then starting a new sentence beginning "Any such individual". Or, in the case of the example given above, by simply inserting "(in the case of any recipient)" after "$25,000". But remember also that the reverse approach—describing the covered individuals in the singular and then switching to the plural when the situation demands it—would have been easier.

21.3 Tense

Whenever possible, use the present tense rather than the past or future tense. As *HOLC* (page 5) puts it, a statute is a movable feast—that is, it speaks as of whatever time it is being read rather than as of the time when it was drafted, enacted, or put into effect. The use of verbs in the past or future tense may raise unnecessary (and misleading) questions about who or what is being covered.

It is true that, when expressing time relationships in a law, there may be cases in which it is appropriate to use the present tense for facts contemporary with the law's operation and then the past (or future) tense for facts that must precede (or follow) its operation. But even in those cases it is preferable whenever possible to keep the main verb in the present tense throughout and to express the temporal relationships explicitly. In this context phrases such as "An individual who is or has been a member of a subversive group is not eligible ..." and "If having been convicted of a felony, an individual is found to be ..." are quite proper.

The use of the passive past participle when referring to past events can be particularly troublesome. The phrase "an individual who was married on January 1, 1986", for example, can be read as meaning either an individual who got married on that date or an individual who was a married person on that date (depending on whether the intended verb is "was" or "was married"). Unless the context clearly resolves the ambiguity, the phrase should be recast.

Note that the use of the auxiliary verb "shall" in the imperative mood—as in "The Secretary shall award a grant ..."—should not be regarded as a violation of the rule laid down here. And even if you agree with the view that the use of "shall be" in a phrase like "This Act shall be effective ..." constitutes use of the purposive future tense (see 21.5), you should treat it as a permissible exception to the rule laid down here. In the authors' opinion, the use of "shall", like the use of "may", is completely compatible with that rule.

21.4 Voice

Use the active voice rather than the passive voice unless the actor cannot be identified or the statement is intended to be universal. It not only gives your language more "punch", it also identifies much more clearly who is to do what.

The use of the passive voice in a sentence invariably leaves one or more of its material elements unspecified. In a provision reading "Proceeds derived from such sale shall be used for [some specified purpose]", for example, it obscures whose proceeds are covered and quite possibly (depending on the context) leaves some doubt about whose responsibility it is to use them in the required way.

In a sentence granting a power or privilege or imposing a duty, the use of the active voice helps to avoid vagueness by forcing the drafter to name, as the subject of the sentence, the person in whom the power or privilege is vested or upon whom the duty is imposed.

There may be times when using the passive is appropriate. Penalty provisions are a good example ("Whoever violates this Act shall be fined", or "shall be imprisoned"). In this case other law makes clear who orders the punishment (that is, the courts) and the emphasis is rightfully on who is committing the act.[2] In other cases, if you have already identified the actor and the action in one provision (for example, "(a) A person who receives a grant under this section shall submit a report to the Secretary"), in a subsequent provision you can refer to the "report submitted under subsection (a)" without any confusion as to what is intended.

21.5 Mood

Any provision that is intended to make something happen or to force someone to take an action—a provision imposing a duty or requirement, for example, or a provision creating a function or establishing an agency—should be written in the imperative mood, with the auxiliary verb "shall" accompanying the main verb. If you mean to issue a command, you should write it as a command.

A provision that is intended to confer a right or privilege, or to describe a statutorily mandated state of affairs, can usually be written either in the imperative mood ("A qualified applicant shall be entitled to receive ..." or "This Act shall take effect on [a specified date]") or in the indicative mood

("A qualified applicant is entitled to receive ..." or "This Act takes effect ..."). Many experienced drafters prefer the indicative, because it seems less stilted and artificial, and because it better expresses the present tense flavor; and a number of major Federal laws use it as a matter of course.

In a similar vein, *Dickerson* (page 126)—contending that the use of "shall" (and "shall not") merely to declare a legal result rather than to prescribe a rule of conduct (as in "A qualified applicant shall be entitled to receive ...") constitutes a "false imperative"—feels that it is not only unnecessary but involves a circumlocution in thought, because the purpose of the provision is achieved by the very act of declaring the legal result; *Dickerson* recommends that the indicative rather than the imperative mood should always be used in any declaratory (that is, self-executing) provision.

The authors understand the point but do not totally agree. Logically it may seem that there would be no exceptions to using the indicative mood. But as a practical matter phrases like "shall take effect" and "shall be entitled" are so widely used, probably because of a strong desire to avoid any ambiguity regarding an effective date or an entitlement, that they have taken on a life of their own.

Simply be sure of what you mean when you say "shall". *Dickerson* is correct in cautioning against using "shall" to confer a right when the recipient is the subject of the sentence, for example, instead of "The Director shall receive compensation of $____ per year", say "The Director is entitled to receive $____ per year." See the discussion of "may" and "shall" in 22.2.

The problem with saying you should "always" use the indicative mood is that many statutory expressions in the indicative mood look suspiciously like mere descriptions of the existing state of affairs, without any apparent legal or substantive effect; in extreme cases they can look positively silly, and sometimes (in theory at least) they run the risk of being misinterpreted, especially when the imperative mood is used elsewhere in the law involved. But using the imperative mood for commands and in noncommand situations where the indicative just does not look right, while using the indicative mood in most non-command situations, will inevitably produce a widespread and very obvious stylistic inconsistency in your bill, with all the potential problems that entails.

If you develop a preference for the indicative approach, go ahead and use it. But make sure that you have a rational criterion for distinguishing the situations in which you use it from the situations in which you do not, that you apply the criterion consistently, and that your readers will be able to understand the lines you have drawn.

21.6 Punctuation

In legislative drafting, even more than in other forms of writing, proper punctuation is critical because of the tremendous contribution it can make to the drafter's twin objectives of clarity and readability. Courts will inevitably rely upon punctuation in interpreting laws (as they should); and the right punctuation helps to ensure the right interpretation.

For the most part, the generally accepted rules of punctuation apply with equal force to punctuation in legislative language. The drafter should depart from the accepted rules only when maximum clarity demands it; and that does happen, of course, but only when those rules—

(1) would result in language that is insufficiently precise to serve the special needs of legislation, or in language that makes it unnecessarily hard for the intended audience to extract and understand the message;

(2) would be unequal to the task of handling a particularly complex concept within a confined space; or

(3) would not adequately deal with a particular form or usage that is unique to statutory language.

As will soon become clear, the chief offender is the comma—an indispensable writing tool but unfortunately one that can easily produce ambiguity or otherwise mislead the reader if used carelessly.

It should not be necessary to belabor the subject further. As a drafter, you need to know the accepted rules of punctuation and religiously follow them in most cases, but you must also learn to recognize the situations in which a departure from (or special application of) those rules may be justified for one of the reasons just cited. For illustrative purposes (and at the risk of repeating things that have already been said) there are several specific punctuational points that arise frequently and deserve mention here.

Commas in series. When setting forth a series of items in a sentence either in conjunctive or disjunctive form, the last two items in the series, like the earlier items, should always be separated by a comma; for example, "A, B, and [or] C"—never just "A, B and [or] C". The omission of the final comma in the series—a common practice in expository writing—sometimes invites the misreading that the last item is part of the preceding one (that is, that B and C, together or as alternatives, are a single item), and sometimes even suggests that the last item is not a part of the series at all but is rather a part of what follows it.

Commas used parenthetically. Use commas to set off clauses that describe a subject already identified (as in "The Administrator, who shall be appointed as provided in section 103, may …"), but not clauses that themselves identify the subject (as in "A disbursing officer who is responsible under section 507 may …"). In the latter case the "who" clause is defining or restrictive while in the former it is not—the same distinction that is made between the relative pronouns "that" and "which" in 21.8.

Colons and dashes. When the words "as follows" or "the following" are used in making an amendment or as lead-in language for a list or description, or for any similar purpose, they should always be followed by a colon (with the first word after the colon capitalized)— never by a dash. Dashes should be reserved for language that could be read (with or without the punctuation) as a continuous sentence.

Lists. As will be discussed more fully in chapter 23, it is often necessary or desirable in a bill to set forth a list of items—definitions, rules, powers, functions, or just plain descriptive nouns—and the most practical all-purpose approach is to tabulate the list, with appropriate lead-in language and a separate indented paragraph for each item. There are two ways of doing this.

If the lead-in language ends with a dash—

(1) each item should be paragraphed and its margin indented 5 spaces (with any further subdivision being indented an additional 5 spaces);

(2) the first word in each item should begin with a lowercase letter (unless it is a proper noun);

(3) each item other than the last item should end with a comma or semicolon; and

(4) the conjunction "and" or "or", which determines whether the items on the list are collective or separate, should appear at the end of the next-to-last item only.

If the lead-in language ends with a colon, on the other hand, the following guidelines would apply:

(1) Each item should be paragraphed and indented as though the lead-in language ended with a dash.

(2) The first word in each item should be capitalized.

(3) Each item should end with a period.

(4) The collective or separate nature of the items is expressed in the lead-in language itself.

(It is hopefully unnecessary to point out that each of the two foregoing statements is written so as to embody the stylistic approach it describes. Additional examples can be found in 23.4.)

Periods and quotation marks in amendatory legislation. When a sentence amends existing law, and sets forth the language being inserted or added (or literally repeats the language being stricken), any punctuation that is a part of that language must appear within the quotes; and the sentence's own punctuation that follows—whether a final period or an internal comma or semicolon—must be kept outside them.

Thus, if the language being inserted or added ends with a period, just put that period inside the quotes where it belongs and leave the amendatory sentence's final period outside the quotes where it belongs, despite the odd appearance of the double period. For example:

> ( ) Section 123 (a) of the ABC Act is amended by striking ", except that" and all that follows and inserting "but shall not include minors.".

These rules, which were addressed at some length in 16.2, are contrary to the accepted practice in expository writing; but they are important and should be followed consistently. You must never leave the reader (or the courts) in any doubt as to whether or not the punctuation within the quotes is really meant to be added to or taken away from the existing law.

Commas after dates. The rule for punctuating a date such as "January 1, 2009", is the same in legislative drafting as it is in expository writing—add a comma after the year as well as after the day (unless of course the date is the last thing in the sentence and is followed by a period). The point is mentioned here only to provide a vehicle for two comments:

(1) Commas after dates are an abomination to the drafter, and are placed there only to satisfy a completely arbitrary convention the reason for which is unknown to the authors. A comma traditionally indicates a pause in the sentence, but dates are like single words and their final commas do not indicate pauses except when the date involved would be followed by a comma even if it were a single word. Placing a comma after a date not only brings the reader up short at a point where (in most cases) no pause is intended—it also promotes confusion and ambiguity in many cases because the reader has no way of knowing whether or not the pause is intended (and the presence or absence of a pause can sometimes make a real substantive difference). Most drafters would love to see the general adoption of the military system of expressing dates—day, month, and year, totally unpunctuated, instead of month, day, and year with two commas.

(2) In the authors' opinion you should abide by the convention, but only because if you do not it would look like a typographical error to

most people (so that they still would not know what you intended). If the sentence is already complicated and you think that the arbitrary comma would cause undue damage to its clarity and readability, you will be forgiven (by the authors at least) for any contortions you may have to go through in order to omit or relocate the date.

Hyphenated words. The rules for determining whether or not you should hyphenate the two words making up a compound noun are clearly prescribed by dictionaries and style manuals, and you should normally follow those rules religiously. But when there would be the slightest doubt about whether the two words are a compound noun or about what their combination means, you should always hyphenate them regardless of what the authorities say. The term "cross-reference" means a reference that crosses subdivision lines, but if you omit the hyphen as many dictionaries recommend, it could just mean any reference that is made angrily; "cross-reference" is clearer.

21.7 Capitalization

The accepted rules of capitalization in statutes vary from jurisdiction to jurisdiction, but there is a hard core from which you can start. In the first place, there are the basic rules of proper English composition that are observed everywhere; it is assumed that all readers of this book are familiar with them. In the second, every jurisdiction has a style manual for governmental documents (like the *U.S. Government Publishing Office Style Manual*, available at *govinfo.gov*), which should be followed in legislation unless there is a compelling reason to do otherwise. Insofar as they involve capitalization, the conventions established by these rules and manuals are almost always completely consistent with good legislative drafting.

Once again, however, you must remember that legislation has special needs. When these needs are not adequately served by the generally accepted stylistic rules (of capitalization, punctuation, or anything else), you should ignore them if you can get away with it or else use whatever devices may be available to circumvent them. (An everyday example of the latter is the inclusion of the modifying phrase "The term" in all definitions—see 11.7—to circumvent the requirement [which cannot be ignored] that the first word in a sentence must always start with a capital letter; beginning a definition with that phrase guarantees that the capitalization or noncapitalization of the term itself will be the same in the definition as it is in the text.)

Government style manuals differ in their specifics from jurisdiction to jurisdiction, of course, and you must become familiar with (and follow) the one that governs documentary writing in the particular jurisdiction in which you are working. In general, however, capitalization should be used sparingly. For those who work at the Federal level, here are a few rules of capitalization (from the *U.S. Government Publishing Office Style Manual*) that ought to be second nature but in fact are often violated by both occasional and experienced drafters:

(1) The term "Federal" is always capitalized when used as an adjective, as is the term "Government" when used as a noun referring specifically to the government of the United States, or of a foreign country, as an institution. The term "federally" is not capitalized, nor is the term "government" when used as an adjective.

(2) The term "State" is always capitalized (whether used as a noun or an adjective) when referring to one of the 50 States. (The term "possession" is never capitalized.) The term "state" is not capitalized when referring to a foreign country.

(3) The terms "Act" and "Public Law" are always capitalized when referring to a specific statute, but the term "public laws" when used generically is not.

(4) Terms such as "title", "chapter", and "section" are never capitalized when referring to a subdivision or component of a statute (even though they are capitalized, initially or as a whole, when used as designations at the beginning of the provisions involved).

(5) Official titles such as "President", "Secretary", "Administrator", and "Governor" are always capitalized.

(6) The terms "Department" and "Agency" are capitalized when referring specifically to governmental entities whose official names contain that term, but not when referring to a "department" or "agency" generically.

(7) The first word following a colon is always capitalized, whether it is a single item on a list or the beginning of what would otherwise be a complete sentence in and of itself (unless, of course, it is an uncapitalized word in quoted matter).

21.8 The relative pronouns "that" and "which"

A common grammatical question that drafters face involves the choice between the two relative pronouns "that" and "which". For example, should you say "a benefit under this section that is payable by reason of disability shall be reduced…", or should you say "a benefit under this section which is payable by reason of disability shall be reduced…"? This choice presents itself to the drafter about once every half dozen lines of text, and consequently it deserves special mention.

Many people use the two interchangeably; but grammatically there is a distinction. When properly used, the pronoun "that" is defining—it prefaces a relative clause that limits or restricts its antecedent (and is almost never preceded by a comma). The pronoun "which", on the other hand, is nondefining—it prefaces a relative clause that explains or gives a reason, or adds a new fact, but does not limit or restrict the antecedent (and it is almost always preceded by a comma).

To put it another way, use "that" if the relative clause is needed to complete the thought being expressed, but use "which" if it is informative only and the thought would be complete without it.

Thus the answer to the question in the first paragraph depends on what you are trying to say. The first alternative (using "that") would be correct if the section involved providing benefits in nondisability as well as disability cases and you wanted to limit the proposed reduction to the latter. The second, with commas before "which" and after "disability", would be correct only if the section provided benefits in disability cases alone and you simply wanted to note that fact or to indicate the reason for the reduction.

Note, however, that the second alternative without the commas would be ambiguous on its face. Most likely it would be read as defining—that is, as though the "which" were a "that"—but you would be better off (other things being equal) if you used the terms properly and eliminated all doubt.

H. W. Fowler, after making a plaintive plea for proper use of the two relative pronouns, admitted that "it would be idle to pretend that [their proper use] is the practice either of most or of the best writers".[3] And he went on to acknowledge that there are sometimes legitimate practical reasons for choosing the less-preferred term:

(1) The defining "that" must always be the first word of the relative clause, and if a preposition is needed it must often follow at quite a distance, while the nondefining "which" is easier to work with because it can be preceded by its governing preposition ("of which", "to which", or "from which"). Indeed, the use of "which" becomes a necessity when you are writing a series of terms and one or more of those terms has to be stated prepositionally (as in "... a benefit which is paid to a widow, and the amount of which is calculated ...").

(2) The defining "that" can often be omitted and still be operative ("the dog you saw", for example, is equivalent to "the dog that you saw"), while the nondefining "which" must always be expressed—it cannot be omitted without altering the sense of the sentence.

A few less scholarly observations may be in order. The use of the word "that" as a relative pronoun is clearly closer to everyday speech, but it has disadvantages to the drafter because it is also used in so many other senses—adverbially, adjectivally, and as a demonstrative pronoun or conjunction. The word "which" avoids most of these disadvantages.

Conversely, using both "which" and "that" (as relative pronouns), even within the same sentence, is sometimes the only practical way of avoiding the appearance of a series (despite the fact that it constitutes a form of elegant variation you would normally shun).

The best advice is to use the two relative pronouns in their proper grammatical senses as much as you can—reserving "that" for defining clauses and "which" for nondefining clauses—simply because that is the correct way to do it. But when the various "thats" begin to proliferate, or you have special series-related needs, or you just think it would improve readability, follow your instincts and choose the pronoun that seems best in the circumstances. Fowler's rules may sometimes sound like they are written in stone, but he always recognized the need for flexibility in special circumstances, and if he had been addressing legislative language specifically, presumably he would have agreed.

21.9 The relative pronouns "who" and "whose"

As a general rule, the relative pronouns "who" and "whose" are used to refer to particular individuals, while "that" is used to refer to individuals generically and "which" is reserved for things (or nonhuman "persons").

There is one case, however, in which the use of the relative possessive pronoun "whose" to refer to things is such a convenience (and so improves readability) that it has become acceptable even among grammatical purists and legislative drafters. When it is necessary to enumerate the attributes of a particular thing, it is permissible to substitute "whose" for "of which" if the alternative would be too awkward or cumbersome. Thus you can respectably say "an agency whose head is appointed by the President and most of whose employees occupy professional positions", for example, instead of "an agency the head of which is appointed by the President and most of the employees of which occupy professional positions".

There is another case in which any pronoun chosen would be partially inappropriate. When the subject is a "person" in the broadly defined legal sense, you need "who" for situations where the person is an individual and "that" or "which" for situations where the person is a corporation or other nonhuman entity; but you cannot have it both ways. The best advice is to use "that" unless the provision's impact on individuals is significantly greater and more obvious than its impact on nonhuman entities. Note, however, that title 18 of the United States Code generally uses the formulation "Whoever does XX shall be imprisoned ___, fined under this title, or both", when it is clear in most instances that "whoever" covers nonhuman entities as well as individuals. In some cases this is even clarified. Section 921 of title 18 (which defines terms for the succeeding sections relating to firearms) defines "person" and "whoever" to include "any corporation, company, association, firm ..." as well as any individual, but then uses the phrase "any person who" throughout the sections to which the definition applies. This may be a case in which using the instinctual "person who" can be forgiven even if it is not always grammatically precise.

21.10 The conjunctions "and" and "or"

Everyone learns at an early age that the words "and" and "or" have totally different meanings, but it is amazing how often drafters use them carelessly. You should never forget that using the wrong conjunction (or using the right conjunction in the wrong way) can lead to a result that is diametrically opposed to the one you want.

As both *Dickerson* and *Hirsch* point out, simply distinguishing "and" from "or" is not the whole story; each of the two terms is itself semantically ambiguous, and can be used in two quite different senses.

The phrase "A and B" may mean A and B jointly and severally (so that the provision involved applies to either or both of them), or it may mean A and B jointly but not severally (so that the provision applies to both or not at all). And the phrase "A or B" may mean A or B or both (so that the provision involved can apply inclusively to either or both of them), or it may mean A or B but not both (so that the provision can apply only to one of them).

Thus the use of "and" between paragraphs (18) and (19) of a 19-paragraph list means one of two quite different things with respect to, say, paragraph (2) of that list—either that the section applies in every case described in the list and therefore always applies in the case described in paragraph (2), or that it applies in the case described in paragraph (2) only if it also applies to all of the cases described in the other 18 paragraphs. The use of "or" between paragraphs (18) and (19) also means one of two quite different things—either that the section applies in the case described in paragraph (2) without regard to any of the other paragraphs, or that it can apply in that case only if it does not apply in any of the others.

In each instance the effect of the conjunction depends upon the lead-in language of the list—often separated from the conjunction itself by many pages—which is one reason why it is so easy to be careless about it. Normally "and" is used in the joint and several senses and "or" is used inclusively, but if any doubt exists in a particular case you should deal with it explicitly in the lead-in language or in language placed immediately after the list. There is no set formula for doing this—any combination of words that makes your intent clear will serve. Do not fall back on the ancient "and/or" approach; it is a sloppy device and does not solve the problem in most cases.

A variant that is particularly important for the everyday drafter to understand is the relatively common case, involving the enumeration of two or more persons or entities, in which it may be unclear whether the linkage produced by the "and" or "or" is meant to apply to the enumerated persons or entities themselves or to their characteristics.

On its face, for example, the phrase "every husband and father" could be read as meaning "every person who is either a husband or a father" or as meaning "every person who is both a husband and a father". And the phrase "every husband or father" could be read as meaning "every person who is either a husband or a father" or as meaning "every person who is a husband or a father or both".

In every such case—and this is the most important point in the whole discussion of "ands" and "ors"—the desired meaning can be unambiguously expressed by using either "and" or "or", without any difference in substance, by simply making it clear whether it is the persons or entities themselves or their characteristics to which the term applies. Whether you use "and" or "or" then depends upon whether you choose to identify the affected persons by enumerating the classes into which they fall or by defining them as a single class, and then enumerating their qualifying characteristics. Thus a provision reading:

( ) A payment shall be made under this section to—

(1) each person who is 70 years of age or older, and

(2) each person who is physically disabled.

is the exact equivalent of a provision reading:

( ) A payment shall be made under this section to each person who—

(1) is 70 years of age or older, or

(2) is physically disabled.

The word "and" is necessary to the first version because it enumerates two separate classes of persons each of which must be included, whereas "or" is necessary to the second because it names a single class of persons by enumerating its two alternative qualifications for membership.

For you as a drafter, it need not be this complicated. Look hard at what it is that you are trying to do, and choose explicit clarity over compactness if there is the slightest doubt about what your "ands" and "ors" would accomplish.

21.11 Questionable practices that can help

There are a number of grammatical practices which may be maligned by the purists, but which nevertheless may often represent the easiest and most natural way to express a particular thought. A few of them deserve comment here.

What should the drafter's attitude be about such things as using split infinitives and ending sentences with prepositions? On the one hand these practices do not detract from clarity, and it is often hard to find an alternative that is not cumbersome or confusing; but on the other they are likely to be jarring for many readers.

Although most grammar textbooks frown upon these practices, many do not; and highly literate authors from time immemorial have engaged in them without apology. They are simple, direct, and forceful; they are never ambiguous; and the contortions a writer has to go through in order to avoid them often result in awkward sentences that border on the ludicrous.

H. W. Fowler said of split infinitives that, although they are not desirable in and of themselves, they are "preferable to … real ambiguity, and to patent artificiality".[4] He described sentence-ending prepositions as "a valuable idiomatic resource" and "an important element in the flexibility of the [English] language".[5] (Fowler claimed that the only reason for the traditionalists' distrust of sentence-ending prepositions in English is that they were never used in Latin.) And Winston Churchill once made the point somewhat more sarcastically, in responding to a noisy critic of the practice, by declaring that "This is the sort of pedantry up with which I will not put".

Another common practice of expository writers that is widely questioned by the textbooks is that of beginning sentences with conjunctions ("And", "Or", or "But"). They engage in the practice for one very simple reason—it is a useful way of indicating how successive thoughts are intended to fit together, without having to combine them into long sentences or to include cumbersome explanations of their relationship. In theory at least, this practice could obviously have value in legislative drafting for the same reason.

How should you as a drafter sort out all these considerations in your everyday work? There is of course a presumption that you should not use any practice that may be frowned upon by a substantial segment of your intended audience, since making it easy for that audience to read and understand your words without distraction is one of your primary objectives. But you should not risk distorting your language simply to follow convention either.

The best and most conservative advice is to follow the majority view (thereby offending the smallest number of readers), unless you think clarity and precision are compromised. The following guidelines may prove useful:

(1) You should feel free to use a split infinitive whenever it seems natural and clear to you. The effort involved in making your sentence "correct" is seldom worth it, and the alternatives will make your sentence worse (from a drafting point of view) as often as they make it better. Reversing the order of the verb and the offending adverb, for example, will indeed eliminate the "split", but it usually results in an awkward or jerky sentence, and it sometimes leaves the reader in doubt about whether the adverb applies to that verb or to a later one. (See the discussion of "squinting modifiers" in 22.5.)

(2) You should be willing to end a sentence with a preposition whenever the situation seems to call for it, but you should do it with caution. When a preposition strays very far from the verb to which it relates, there is always a possibility of losing it in the shuffle, with resulting confusion or ambiguity.

(3) You should avoid sentences that begin with conjunctions. There is usually a simple alternative (such as using "In addition," instead of "And") or some other easy way to make the relationship between sentences clear; and in many cases the sentences involved could be combined.

(The authors have not avoided sentence-starting conjunctions in this book, as you will have noted, but have almost never used them in statutory language. You too should feel free to use them if you write a book; just do not put them in statutes.)

Fowler's general conclusion about sentence-ending prepositions is a good statement of principle for determining what the drafter's approach should ideally be to any grammatical practice:

> Follow no arbitrary rule, but remember that there are often two or more possible arrangements between which a choice should be consciously

made. If the final preposition that has naturally presented itself sounds comfortable, keep it; if it does not sound comfortable, still keep it if it has compensating vigour, or when among awkward possibilities it is the least awkward.[6]

Notes

1 See 22.2 for the discussion of "shall" and "may".

2 Tobias Dorsey, *Legislative Drafter's Deskbook: A Practical Guide* (Alexandria, Va.: TheCapitol.Net, 2006), 189.

3 H. W. Fowler, *A Dictionary of Modern English Usage,* 2nd ed., rev. Sir Ernest Gowers (New York: Oxford University Press, 1965), 627.

4 Ibid., 581.

5 Ibid., 474.

6 Ibid., 475.

22. Word Usage in General

The power of language

In an episode of the Simpsons, Marge is trying her hand at selling real estate. She is not selling any homes, apparently because she is being too candid about the condition of the houses on the market. Her boss (the voice of Phil Hartman) has a talk with Marge, in which he explains that "Marge, there is the truth, and then there is the TRUTH". He shows her pictures of a number of houses and asks her to describe them. Marge describes the first as "cramped"; the boss says no, the house is "cozy". She describes the second as "dilapidated"; he says no, it's "rustic". Of the third house, Marge declares "This house is on fire"; he replies, "motivated seller".

22.1 Preliminary comments

Most of the commonly occurring usages and forms that legislative drafters need to know about are addressed elsewhere in this book—either along with the general subjects to which they primarily relate or in a special place set aside for usages and forms of the particular type involved. But there is a residual body of commonly occurring usages and forms—not set forth or adequately addressed anywhere else in this book—that may be worth your attention.

Many of these usages and forms are relatively trivial, and involve matters of preference rather than matters of right or wrong, but some (see for example 22.2) are fundamental. The purpose of this chapter (along with chapter 27) is to complete the picture by touching upon them briefly.

22.2 Use of "shall" and "may"

In general. When requiring that some action be taken, use "shall" rather than "is directed to" or "must"; and when permitting some action to be taken, or granting a right, privilege, power, or authority, use "may" rather than "is authorized [or empowered] to". To distinguish the case in which authority granted elsewhere is required to be exercised by the provision at hand, the provision can read "shall, under section ___, take [the action involved]". In everyday English, "shall" and "may" can be ambiguous: "shall" can express a prediction or intention as well as a command, and "may" can express capability or possibility as well as authority.[1] And "must" may be ambiguous because the word implies more obligation than command.[2] (The drafting manual of the *Federal Register* [the *Document Drafting Handbook*], which is used in drafting regulations, says to use "must" instead of "shall").

To the extent that there is ambiguity in these terms, the context in which you use either word should convey your meaning. One way to do this could be to include, in every law that imposes a command, a consequence for failing to comply.[3] Certainly this is true for any law imposing a requirement on the citizenry. But laws also routinely direct officials in other branches of government to perform acts, like issuing regulations or reports, frequently within specified periods of time; although imposing a consequence for failing to comply is possible, the questions become what would it look like and does the sponsor want it? *Dorsey* (page 141) cites one example—barring an executive official from spending certain funds until a certification required by the law was made—but pulling the purse strings in every case would arguably be micromanaging the exercise of an official's responsibilities and would fail to take into account obstacles the official inevitably encounters in trying to meet deadlines, especially competing ones.

A consequence of a government official's failure to comply is answerability to the legislative branch when it exercises oversight over the official. Arguably there is also a basis for a mandamus action in a court (to direct the official to act), if there is someone with standing to do so. In addition (at the Federal level), an "aggrieved" party with standing could seek judicial review under section 706(1) of title 5 of the United States Code if the agency action is "unreasonably withheld or unlawfully delayed".[4] But "if a statute does not specify a consequence for noncompliance with statutory timing provisions, the federal courts will not in the ordinary course impose their own coercive sanction".[5]

If a law requires a government official to act within a specified time period and the deadline passes, does the authority to do the act after the deadline remain intact? At the Federal level, the answer is, in most cases, yes. The Supreme Court, in *Brock v. Pierce County*, 476 U.S. 253, 260 (1986), stated its reluctance "to conclude that every failure of an agency to observe a procedural requirement voids subsequent agency action, especially when important public rights are at stake". In reaffirming this position, the Court, in *Barnhart v. Peabody Coal Co.*, 537 U.S. 149, 158 (2003), noted that the Court had not, since Brock, "construed a provision that the Government 'shall' act within a specified time, without more, as a jurisdictional limit precluding action later".[6]

However, if the issue of whether jurisdiction to act after a deadline is passed is not settled law in the jurisdiction in which you are drafting, the legislative language will have to clarify the intent.

When prohibiting an act, should you say "may not" or "shall not"? *HOLC* (page 47) says to use "may not" when denying a right, privilege, or power, and "shall not" when directing that an action not be taken. Arguably a distinction exists that "shall not" speaks to the person subject to the prohibition and is silent as to whether an act done by a person in violation of the prohibition is nevertheless valid (particularly as to a third party), whereas an act done in violation of a denial of a power to act is void as to all parties. But there is nothing in the words themselves that would convey this meaning. An issue relating to the legality of an act done in violation of any prohibition should be specifically addressed in the legislative language (as recommended by *HOLC*). One could also argue that "A person shall not" literally means that a person does not have a duty to act,[7] but still has the discretion to act.

The controversy over questions of mood—whether to use the imperative or indicative mood when granting or denying a right, privilege, power, or authority, and the undesirability of using the "false imperative" to simply declare a legal result—was addressed in 21.5 and will not be further discussed here.

Imposing duties. The best way to impose a duty on an individual is through the use of a sentence, in the active voice, whose subject is that individual and whose main verb is accompanied by the auxiliary verb "shall"—for example, "The Secretary shall pay to any qualified applicant…", or "An applicant shall file with the Secretary…". This form should not be unnecessarily varied or embellished.

Note, however, that to state as a command what is intended only as a condition precedent often creates ambiguity. Thus "Any appointee shall be a citizen of the United States" might (in some contexts) be read as merely requiring an individual to become a citizen if he is appointed rather than as limiting the class of individuals eligible for appointment, or perhaps (as *Dorsey* suggests) somehow bestowing citizenship on an individual upon appointment.[8]

Be careful not to use "shall" to express an obligation to act in a certain manner ("a pleading shall be filed with the clerk") or to impose a limitation on a grant of discretionary act or grant of authority ("an aggrieved party shall file an appeal within 30 days after judgment is entered"). Martineau and Salerno point out that these uses of "shall" are incorrect because they appear to create a duty to act when none exists. In the examples given, a pleading is not required to be filed, but if one chooses to file a pleading, it is required to be filed with the clerk; and an aggrieved party is not required to file an appeal, but is required to act within 30 days if the party chooses to appeal.[9] You can avoid using "shall" by saying "A pleading may be filed only with the clerk" and "An aggrieved party may appeal a judgment only by filing a notice of appeal within 30 days after the judgment is entered".

Conferring rights. The best way to confer a right, privilege, power, or authority upon an individual is through the use of a sentence, in the active voice, whose subject is that individual and whose main verb is accompanied by the auxiliary verb "may"—for example, "Any individual who has attained age 65 may file an application...". This form should not be unnecessarily varied or embellished either.

But the granting of a right should not leave the reader in any doubt about who has the option. Sometimes a simple "shall"—as in "A member of the commissioned corps shall receive transportation"—could be viewed as requiring the individual involved to exercise the right, while a simple "may"—as in "A member of the commissioned corps may receive transportation"—could be viewed as leaving unclear whether the agency involved is obliged to provide it. Substituting "shall be entitled to" or "is entitled to" (for the naked "shall" or "may") will resolve the doubt.

You should not add "in his or her discretion" after "may" because you fear in a particular case that the grant of a power to an official might be construed as imposing on the official a duty to exercise that power. The phrase is implicit in the word "may"; adding it in one place creates a negative inference in every other case where it is not used that "may" is not discretionary.

Imposing prohibitions. *Hirsch* recommends that you always place a prohibition in the verb rather than in the subject, through a sentence, in the active voice, whose subject is that individual and whose main verb is accompanied by the auxiliary verb "may not"—for example, "An individual under the age of 18 may not use the facility" rather than "No individual under the age of 18 may use the facility".

Dickerson disagrees; his preference is the other way around. *HOLC* says "a person may not" is preferable, in logic and grammar, to "no person may", although the latter is often seen in statutes.

The logical problem with a provision that begins with "no person may" is that, literally, it "is not addressed to anyone, when the exact opposite is intended—the provision applies to everyone".[10] This is a strong argument for placing the negative with the action and not the actor.

But even if you do choose to put the prohibition in the subject rather than in the verb, do not combine the negative subject with an affirmative "shall", as in "No individual under the age of 18 shall use the facility"; if the word "shall" is given its dictionary meaning ("is required to") the sentence would then mean that the individual, though not required to use the facility, could do so if the individual wished (the same thing was mentioned in the general discussion of "shall not" above). Say "No individual under the age of 18 *may*...".

22.3 Use of "such"

The use of "such" as a demonstrative adjective to mean "the previously mentioned" (as in "pay such benefit" or "within such agency") is frequently denounced by commentators and scoffed at by critics of legislative style. It is admittedly a somewhat archaic way of referring to an antecedent; many professional drafters flatly refuse to use it, and in most cases a more natural term ("the" or "that") will indeed sound better and work equally well.

However, there are enough situations in which either of those alternatives would be confusing so that the use of the more precise demonstrative "such" to refer to the antecedent is almost indispensable. Sometimes "the" would fail to identify the antecedent unambiguously—if, for example, the word being referred to has multiple modifiers; and sometimes "that" would be confusing or awkward because the provision involved already contains too many "thats" being used in other senses (compare the demonstrative pronoun dilemma described in 21.8). Plus, the use of "such" in legislation is so common (partly for the reason just given and partly from sloth) that it cannot possibly constitute a jarring note for the reader.

The authors would encourage you to use "the" or "that" in place of the demonstrative "such" as long as you can do so consistently and are satisfied that the meaning is clear. In the process, you can often use the word "involved"—as in "pay the benefit involved" or "within the agency involved"—to add a touch of specificity. But you should feel free to use "such" without apology, and you should always use it when you suspect that the alternative would jeopardize the clarity and precision of your product.

(When used with an indefinite article as a synonym, as in "pay such a benefit" or "within such an agency", the word "such" has no similar problems—it is considered quite proper even in everyday speech. The authors note in passing, however, that Fowler (pages 601-602) regards both this and the demonstrative use of the word as "illiterate" although grammatically correct.)

Note that you should *always* shun the extremely archaic expressions "said" (as in "the said agency") and "the same" (as in "calculate the benefit and pay the same to the beneficiary").

22.4 Use of explicit cross-references

If you want to be open and aboveboard, on the face of the bill, about the relationship between two provisions, you should use an explicit cross-reference. In whichever one of the two provisions is most substantive (or in both), cite the other specifically.

Admittedly, multiple cross-references may make the bill seem difficult to read for some people; but usually the lack of readability is caused not so much by the cross-references themselves as by the bulk and internal complexity of the subject matter that made them necessary. (The Internal Revenue Code, often cited as the worst offender in this area, could not exist without them.) Their use saves time, shortens the bill, and (most importantly) promotes clarity, precision, and internal consistency.

Cross-references may have direct substantive impact or be merely informative. They are usually used for one of several specific purposes:

(1) To indicate that another provision of the bill, or a provision of existing law, is to apply also under the provision at hand. For example, "Section 123 applies [in this situation]", "The rules that apply under section 123 also apply [in this situation]", or "as defined in section 123" (where the definition involved would not otherwise apply). These are typical examples of incorporation by reference, a subject discussed in detail in 23.3.

(2) To indicate that another provision is to be read as making an exception to or modification of the rules contained in the provision at hand. For example, "except as provided in section 123", "subject to section 123", or "as computed without regard to section 123". This type of cross-reference, which is not usually necessary but often desirable, was discussed in 12.3.

(3) To simply describe and identify a concept or relationship that is established in another provision. For example, "benefits under section 123", "any action taken under section 123", or "the rates in effect under section 123".

(4) To simply call attention to another provision or to its effect on the provision at hand. For example, "as defined in section 123" (where the definition involved would apply anyway), or "as described in section 123".

The use described in paragraph (1) is substantive; the use described in paragraph (2) can be either substantive or just informative (usually the latter); and the uses described in paragraphs (3) and (4) are primarily informative.

Except in cases in which the cross-reference has real substantive effect (as in the case of an incorporation by reference, where the only alternative is either to restate the other provision verbatim [which would be cumbersome, repetitious, and time-consuming] or to try and paraphrase it [which might be dangerous]), the drafter faces a choice: should the other provision be acknowledged by an explicit cross-reference in the provision at hand, as an aid to readers, or should the drafter remain silent about it and simply let the bill operate according to its terms?

The broader aspects of the problem were discussed at length in 12.3 in connection with exceptions and special rules; the remainder of this subdivision focuses on the mechanics of making the choice—the things you need to take into account before deciding which way to jump.

As indicated earlier, many professional drafters avoid most cross-references as a matter of principle; they feel that, given the unavoidable interrelationships within most statutes, all laws of any substance would soon consist of nothing but "except that", "subject to", and "notwithstanding" clauses if they were allowed a foothold. Others use them liberally, without regard to the clutter, simply because they make those interrelationships clear.

In the authors' view there is a sensible middle ground.

Isolated minor exceptions to (or qualifications of) a basic provision of a bill are to be expected, and everyone familiar with legislation knows this—they need not be flagged in advance. And many other purely informative cross-references actually provide little or no information that the readers would not otherwise have. Since cross-references in these cases contribute nothing substantively to the bill, and are almost never actually necessary, you should feel free to use them or not, as your best judgment indicates; but you should use them consistently if you use them at all, and you should not use them if their number is so great that the bill would look cluttered as a result.

In addition, when the basic provision is closely followed by exceptions or special rules and the format makes their relationship clear (as by the use of consecutive headings such as "General Rule", "Exceptions", and "Special Rules"), the use within the basic provision of internal cross-references to those exceptions or special rules would actually be redundant.

However, there are situations in which the use of "except that", "subject to", and "notwithstanding" clauses is not only permissible but desirable in the interest of both clarity and readability. For example:

(1) When an exception or modification is not minor, but actually changes the thrust of the bill, the drafter should always be up-front and explicit about the hierarchical interrelationship of the provisions involved if there could be the slightest doubt about it.

(2) When there is a genuine question about whether or not one provision is an exception to or modification of another, or whether a definition would or would not apply, the relationship should always be made clear.

(3) When the other provision is contained in an existing law rather than in another section of your bill (and conversely when your bill does something that significantly affects a provision of existing law), the relationship should always be spelled out. While in the case of "equal" inconsistent provisions, the later enactment would supersede the earlier, you need to remember both that courts are reluctant to find a repeal by implication and that they treat specific provisions as exceptions to general provisions when the provisions are inconsistent, regardless of the order of enactment (see 18.2).

Case (3) is of course a subset of case (2), and (unlike the situation in which the two sections involved are contained within the same bill) it depicts a true "split provision".

Remember, however, that "except that" and "subject to" clauses placed in the bill's basic substantive provisions are considerably more useful than "notwithstanding" clauses in the collateral provisions. Being absolutely clear about the scope of the substantive provisions at the outset is more important to the reader than being reminded later that an exception is really an exception.

One final comment: scattergun notwithstanding clauses ("Notwithstanding any other provision of law, ...") should be avoided. If you strongly suspect when writing a bill that there are provisions in existing law that may importantly affect or be affected by what you are doing but you have no time to identify them, and you are willing to gamble by overriding them all without even knowing what they are (thus leaving their identification to the administrators and courts), there may on balance be some slight value in including such a clause as an obscure general warning to readers; but you should never do it routinely as a kind of automatic safety valve. See 18.2.

22.5 Modifiers and explanatory phrases

Adjectives, adverbs, and explanatory phrases enrich the meaning of nouns and verbs, and are as essential to legislative drafting as they are to other forms of writing. But in drafting they can cause endless legal difficulties when used carelessly, because a modifier typically ascribes to a noun or verb a characteristic that it does not precisely define.

Hirsch (pages 44–45) offers as an example the use of the term "serious physical injury" in a hypothetical definition of "domestic violence". He would tolerate the use of the term "physical" even though it is not altogether clear, but regards the term "serious" as

> so vague that it would add to the administrative burden of the agency and otherwise multiply the points of controversy between the agency and those that the statute affects. It would compel the agency to define the term … by regulation, open the agency to legal action to test that definition, and be a constant source of friction between the agency and those whose injuries the agency refuses to consider "serious" despite their seriousness to the victims.

Consequences of this kind are often knowingly accepted by Congress and the administering agency for political or tactical reasons, or as the price of giving the agency the opportunity to exercise flexible judgment in the light of its experience.

Vagueness for reasons of policy is quite proper; vagueness resulting from the careless use of modifiers is not.

Other things being equal, the fewer the modifiers the easier the statute is to administer. Every modifier that you use in a bill is likely at some stage to require an administrative or judicial interpretation (which may or may not accurately reflect the true legislative intent), no matter how aptly it is used or how much it smoothes out the language. Most modifiers in practice are legally unnecessary and are intended only to add flavor; ideally they should be used only to add meaning. Use them, of course, but with discretion.

An inclusionary clause is a special form of modifier—usually parenthetical—that lists some of the more important things that the noun or verb involved is intended to include or affect. It is most often intended simply to indicate the principal targets of the legislation; but this is dangerous because it may strongly imply that anything not listed is not covered. Thus a statement about “domestic animals (including dogs, cats, and horses)”—even though problems involving dogs, cats, and horses may indeed have been the reason for the legislation—leaves the reader in some doubt about its effect on hamsters, canaries, and tropical fish. And the practice of saying “including but not limited to” is a poor solution in most cases for the reasons discussed in 22.15.

You should also avoid the use of modifiers that are merely redundant, like “real”, “true”, “actual”, and “complete”. They may seem useful for purposes of emphasis, but their occasional use in a bill casts doubt on every noun in the bill that is not similarly modified.

Finally, a word of caution. When you do use a modifier, make sure it is completely clear what it applies to. In a sentence that reads “The Secretary shall request the borrower promptly to submit a full report…”, for example, the word “promptly” could be read as applying either backward or forward—that is, either to the Secretary's request or to the borrower's submission; this is called a “squinting modifier” by *Dickerson* (and is usually caused by the drafter's desire to avoid a split infinitive—see 21.11). Also beware of modifiers that immediately precede or follow a series; in the phrase “corporations and partnerships that are exempt from taxation” it may be quite unclear, depending on the context, whether or not taxable corporations are included.

Many years ago a popular song titled “Purple People Eater” was the nation's top-selling recording for many weeks. Most people instinctively thought of the title character as a purple being of some kind who ate people; it took a very careful study of the libretto to discover that he (or it) was simply a being of undetermined hue who ate purple people.

In any of these cases the solution is relatively simple, of course: adjust the context so that the modifier is semantically incapable of modifying anything but the intended term, even if it takes a split infinitive to do it. (Note that the same kind of ambiguity, with the same simple solution, can result from the careless use of “because” or “since” clauses, or of juxtaposed prepositional phrases.)

22.6 Vesting functions in an agency

When you want a function to be exercised by or within a particular department or other Federal agency, vest that function in the head of the agency—not in the agency as such, and not in some subordinate official or branch of the agency even when you expect or intend that the function will be exercised on a day-to-day basis by that official or branch.

Everything that a Federal agency does is by law the responsibility of its head, and for many years it has been the firm policy of the Federal Government to reflect that fact in all statutory provisions conferring functions, powers, or duties upon any department or agency. This gives Congress a single high-level official who is accountable and cannot deny responsibility, and leaves subordinate officials in no doubt about who is in control.

The assumption is, of course, that the agency head will delegate the performance of any function vested in the agency head to the appropriate subordinate official or branch of the agency.

Thus a bill changing the method of calculating Social Security benefits should say "The Secretary [of Health and Human Services] shall compute ...", and a bill providing for the construction of a new space station should say "The Administrator [of NASA] shall construct ...", even though the named agency head would hardly notice the statutory directive as it passed across the agency head's desk on its way to the appropriate operating officials.

There are a few areas in which modern statutory grants of authority appear to violate this rule (those involving relationships between the Secretary of Defense and the Secretaries of the Army, Navy, and Air Force, for example, or between the Secretary of the Treasury and the Commissioner of Internal Revenue), but most instances of this kind are relics from the remote past. If in doubt, you should take the trouble to check existing laws to see how things are done in the area involved.

If it is important from a political or tactical point of view that a particular subordinate official or branch of an agency be formally recognized as the day-to-day administrator of a proposal, there is nothing wrong with mentioning that official or branch in passing—for example, by saying "The Secretary (acting through the Assistant Secretary for Internal Affairs) shall carry out a program ..."—so long as the function itself is clearly vested in the agency head.

You can sometimes address subordinate officials or branches directly when the matters involved are purely administrative or otherwise clearly nonsubstantive, although even then it is better in most cases to apply the usual rule and address the agency head.

22.7 Use of "person" and "individual"

Always use the term "individual" to refer to a person who is a living member of the human race. The term "person" is much broader than that, including corporations and other entities, under the common law as well as under title 1 of the United States Code and corresponding State statutes.

Use the term "person" only when you affirmatively mean to include more than just individuals; and if the other entities you want to include are not the same as those listed in the applicable statutory definition, define the term (for your purposes) to make the difference clear. Note that section 1 of title 1, United States Code, does not include governments in the definition of "person"; if you intend to cover governmental entities when using the term "person", at the Federal level you will need to say so; in any other case you will need to check any corresponding rules of construction in the jurisdiction in which you are drafting to determine whether the term "person" includes governmental entities.

There is one situation in which it is convenient (and permissible) for a drafter to use the term "person" to refer to an individual. When you are describing one individual's relationship to another individual, it is often helpful to call the latter "another person", so as to facilitate subsequent references to "such individual" and "such person" and distinguish them clearly. But you should do this, of course, only when you are absolutely certain that the use of the broader term will not unintentionally expand the coverage of your provision by including corporate and other nonhuman entities along with individuals.

22.8 References to fiscal years

The Congressional Budget Act of 1974, which changed the fiscal year of the Federal Government to its present form—the 12-month period beginning on October 1—also added to the law (section 1102 of title 31, United States Code) a description of the fiscal year of the Treasury. As a consequence, in specifying a particular fiscal year in language authorizing appropriations or in any other context, you should simply call it "fiscal year [2025]"; it is not appropriate to say "the fiscal year ending [September 30, 2025]".

The only choice you have to make is a trivial one—do you say "the fiscal year 2025" or just "fiscal year 2025"? Experienced drafters divide on the question, although the latter form is now preferred (since the former is largely a relic from the days before the term was statutorily defined). Subject to the Roman rule, however, you can use either one.

22.9 Other references to times and time periods

In general. The terms "before", "after", and "at the same time as" are all that you need to express the temporal relationship between events. You should avoid stilted terms like "prior to", "subsequent to", and "concurrent with".

When describing a period after some stated event, such as a period within which some action must be taken, you should say (for example) "within 30 days after [the event]", or "not later than 30 days after [the event]". Do not say "within 30 days of [the event]"; if it is read literally (and sometimes even if it is not) it creates uncertainty about whether the action is to precede or follow the event, or both. And do not say "within [a specified period]" at all unless you really mean it; if you mean "at any time before the end of [that period]" you should say so.

When describing a period by specific reference to its beginning and ending dates, you should make very clear just what those dates are. Do not say "from", "to", "until", or "by" a specified date—those terms create doubts about whether the date specified is included as part of the period; say instead (for example) "any action taken during the period beginning January 1, 2025, and ending March 31, 2025", or "any action taken after December 31, 2024, but before April 1, 2025".

Do not say "any action taken [during the period] between January 1, 2025, and March 31, 2025"; the effect of the term "between" is unclear in most people's minds, but read literally it excludes both of the specified dates.

(Note that a similar ambiguity can exist in describing individuals' ages. The phrase "less than 21 years old" is clear enough, but a phrase like "more than 21 years old" or "between 18 and 21 years of age" is ambiguous.)

The word "year" is normally understood to mean a calendar year; therefore, the term "calendar" should be omitted unless the context requires it. If you mean to refer to a fiscal year the term "fiscal" should always be included, of course. If you mean to refer to any period of 12 consecutive months (regardless of the stage of the calendar year at which it begins) you should always say "12-month period", not "year". And, if you mean to refer to one continuous period where the context might permit the aggregation of shorter periods, you should be explicit about the requirement of continuity: say "two years of continuous service" or "service for a 2-year period", for example, rather than just "2 years' service".

When used to fix the beginning or ending of a period, the word "time" can be read as referring to the exact time of day (or night) when the relevant event occurs. This can cause problems. If you intend (as you almost always would) that the period be measured in whole days, use "day" or "date" instead of "time", as in "90 days after the date on which…". In certain cases, it may be preferable to become even more specific. The Terrorism Risk Insurance Act of 2002 (15 U.S.C. 6701 note), which provides for payments of certain insured losses arising from acts of terrorism, has a rule of construction for dates (in section 102(15)) as follows:

> (15) Rule of construction for dates.—With respect to any reference to a date in this title, such day shall be construed—
>
> (A) to begin at 12:01 a.m. on that date; and
>
> (B) to end at midnight on that date.

References to enactment dates. When referring to the date on which a statute is enacted—whether the reference is internal (like a reference in a bill to the date of its own enactment) or external (like a reference in a bill to the enactment of some existing law)—either "the date of enactment of this Act [or that law]" or "the date of the enactment of this Act [or that law]" is correct. However, be consistent within a bill, except that you should follow the Roman rule when amending an existing law.

Experienced drafters divide more or less evenly on this question; some prefer the former (in which "date of enactment" is a single compound noun) because it is more to the point, while others prefer the latter (which keeps the two nouns "date" and "enactment" separate) because they think it reads better. Most follow whatever usage is prevalent in the statutory environment in which they work. Needless to say, if the reference is to an existing law the actual date of its enactment (being already known) can always be specified instead, although this may leave the reader unclear about the reason for selecting that date.[11]

A bill should never use terms like "now", "present", "already", "heretofore", and "hereafter" in relating events to the date on which it is enacted or takes effect. A law speaks continuously, as of the time it is being read or applied, and to prevent ambiguity you should relate those events involved to that date explicitly, using one of the forms mentioned in the preceding paragraph.[12]

22.10 Indefinite articles

The indefinite articles "a" and "an" are equivalent in effect to the pronominal indefinite adjectives "any", "each", and "every"; accordingly, when referring to a person or thing generically you have a choice. However, the preferred style in most cases (because it is simpler and a bit freer of possible substantive implication) is to use "a" or "an"—for example, "a beneficiary" or "an agency".

The terms "any", "each", and "every" should ideally be reserved for expressions that require unusual emphasis, or for those cases where the use of "a" or "an" might permit the unintended interpretation that the obligation is to be discharged (or the privilege exhausted) by applying it to a single member of the class instead of to all of them. And when you feel the need for such emphasis, use "any" with "may", and "each" or "every" with "shall".

22.11 Deeming, treating, and considering

Deeming is nothing more than a device for claiming that something is so when it is not; it creates a legal fiction, and has many of the same problems as unduly artificial definitions (see 11.7H). Treating something as being so when it is not also creates a legal fiction, although it is more flexible in the sense that it can be used to establish a rule of law as well as to create the fiction unadorned.

Thus the phrases "For purposes of this Act, a tennis racquet is deemed a handgun" and "For purposes of this Act, a tennis racquet shall be treated as a handgun" are equivalent; they both create a blatant legal fiction and do nothing more. But the phrase "For purposes of this Act, the Attorney General shall treat a tennis racquet in the same way as a handgun" creates no fiction; it rather establishes a rule of law under which the designated official is to operate—an approach that is often useful and that avoids many of the problems of the artificial definition.

The term "consider" should be used only to indicate an exercise of judgment or discretion, as in the phrase "For purposes of this subsection, an individual

who satisfies subsection (b) shall be considered qualified even though …";
it should not be used to create a legal fiction.

Note that when you deem or consider something to be so when it is not, or treat something as being so when it is not, you are doing it only for a specific and limited purpose; and (unless the context makes it absolutely clear) that purpose should be explicitly indicated. Whether you say "For the purpose of …", "For the purposes of …", or just "For purposes of …" is immaterial (most experienced drafters seem to prefer the last)—you can choose the one you like best, and you should use that one consistently.

22.12 Directness, informality, and positive expression

In writing legislative language you should always try to express yourself directly and in a positive manner.

Dickerson (pages 187–188) urges the drafter to use "live" words—"finite verbs instead of their corresponding participles, infinitives, gerunds, and other noun or adjective forms"—because they are less artificial and, in most cases, will reach the intended audience better. For example, use "consider" instead of "give consideration to", "applies" instead of "is applicable", "provide for" instead of "make provision for", and "pay" instead of "make payment to".

In a similar vein, a number of commentators have strongly recommended that you always use the simplest and most conversational word available as an aid to readability. For example, use "begin" or "start" instead of "commence" or "institute", "stop" instead of "cease", "before" instead of "prior to", "get" instead of "obtain", "tell" instead of "inform", and "ask" instead of "inquire". This is a good rule as long as it is not carried to an extreme (which of course is a matter of subjective judgment). In the authors' opinion, the first three examples given in the preceding sentence are clearly desirable while the last three sound too conversational to be appropriate in legislation.

And when the same idea can be expressed either positively or negatively, you should do it positively unless what you are expressing is a mandatory prohibition. Say "This section applies only to individuals who have reached age 60", not "This section does not apply to individuals under age 60".

You obviously have a good deal of slack on all of these recommendations—there is nothing really wrong with using the more indirect, formal, or negative form when you think it reads better or is more compatible with neighboring forms—but by and large the advice is good on all counts.

22.13 Circumlocutions and redundancies

In general, you should avoid using pairs of words that have the same effect (such as "each and every", "final and conclusive", "from and after", "full and complete", "force and effect", "null and void", "over and above", and "unless and until"); one of the pair is always unnecessary, and should usually be dropped in the interest of brevity and simplicity.

You should also avoid using pairs of words where one of them includes the other (such as "any and all" and "means and includes"); the broader term can carry the freight alone.

Many such expressions are nothing but relics from older times and should be avoided primarily because the courts look for meaning in every word used in a statute.

22.14 Order of thoughts in a sentence

One way to approach drafting an idea is to state the circumstances in which a rule is to apply before stating the rule itself. For example, "Whenever the Secretary finds it necessary in carrying out section 123, the Secretary shall ...", or "If, after taking the steps described in section 123, the Secretary determines that it is necessary to ... , the Secretary may ...". Any exceptions that may be necessary should normally be dealt with after the rule has been fully stated. The idea, of course, is to avoid cluttering up the statement of the rule itself with collateral matters of either kind.

If the circumstances in which the rule is to apply involve a number of contingencies or conditions, however, it is usually preferable to state the rule first (since otherwise it will be buried too deeply in the middle of the sentence), and to place any exceptions that can be stated briefly ahead of the rule. For example, "Except as provided in section 4, the Secretary shall... ; but the Secretary may do so only if . . .".

These recommendations are obviously aimed at the objective of increasing readability, and they do make sense. But no two cases will be exactly the same, so use your own judgment about whether or not they will promote readability in your particular case.

22.15 Use of "means" and "includes"

One thing "means" another when the two are identical or synonymous, and "includes" another when the second is a part of the first. This rather obvious distinction has its most important application in the case of definitions and was addressed in 11.7.

But "means", "includes", and their derivatives are much more than definitional concepts—they are regularly found in ordinary narrative sentences—and you should be careful to use them correctly. For example:

(1) You should always avoid the phrase "means and includes". It is totally redundant, and its use at any point in a bill (in a misguided attempt to give emphasis, presumably) invites misinterpretations elsewhere.

(2) And you should not shackle the word "includes" with language that changes (or appears to change) its meaning by adding phrases like "but is not limited to". Such phrases have unfortunately become popular in recent years (in a misguided fear that readers may not know what the word means, apparently). Since "includes" is not exhaustive, the additional words are unnecessary—they add nothing to the dictionary definition, and they too invite misinterpretation.

The latter practice can probably be tolerated when the purpose is to make absolutely certain that hostile administrators will not limit the application of the provision involved to just the named items, or when because of the context the word "include" might reasonably be read as meaning "consist of" (as in "The membership of the Commission shall include ..."). Another case in which this construct may be necessary is when the legislative language directs an administrator to take certain action and more, as in specifying that a rule *shall* include certain consequences but *shall* not be limited to those consequences.

In any other case, however, it should be avoided unless it is consistently used in other parts of the bill over which you have no control. If you use "includes, but is not limited to," at all you should use it consistently throughout the bill, since there will otherwise be a strong implication that you do not want "includes" to have its dictionary meaning unless you say so. Unfortunately, "includes but is not limited to" has become so widespread that many sponsors fear that simply using "includes" will be interpreted as excluding all other possibilities. This argument may be particularly strong when the phrase is used repeatedly in a particular area of the law. And, in a case in which you are drafting a bill obviously modeled after an existing law where the phrase exists, not including it in your bill raises the same concern. Nevertheless, your first option should be to stick with the dictionary definition of "includes".[13]

22.16 Use of "insure", "ensure", and "assure"

As synonyms for "make certain", the terms "insure", "ensure", and "assure" are largely interchangeable, but only the latter two should be used in that sense in legislation. And of their noun forms only the term "assurance" should be used when describing an ironclad and enforceable promise that makes something certain.

The term "insure" should be reserved for use in describing what happens under a commercial or government insurance policy, or for use (with "against") in describing generically a form of safeguard or protection that resembles an insurance policy—for example, "regulations to provide insurance against fraud and abuse in the program".

22.17 Use of "by", "under", and "pursuant to"

In general, if the result being sought in a provision you are writing is to be achieved through the operation of that provision itself (without the necessity of some administrator taking a particular action), use "by"—as in "the reduction required by this section".

If the result is to occur through some action that is required or permitted by that provision, or that is required or permitted by some other cited provision, use "under"—as in "an adjustment made under this section [or under section 123]". This assumes that the provision to which you refer establishes reasonably clear rules for the taking of actions of the type involved.

If the provision to which you refer does not establish such rules, or the result is more remotely derived from the authority of the provision you are writing (as it would be if the cited provision is merely a very general authorization of some kind), "pursuant to" is an acceptable alternative—as in "The Secretary shall prescribe regulations pursuant to section 123 for the purpose of ..."[14]—but you should normally avoid "pursuant to" when "under" would do the job.

22.18 Use of "if", "when", and "where"

The terms "if", "when", and "where", when used as conjunctions to mean "in case it happens that" or otherwise to express a condition or supposition, are often treated in expository writing as more or less interchangeable. In legislative drafting there are subtle or not-so-subtle differences; and over a period of time you will achieve a net increase in clarity and precision if you recognize those differences and consistently reflect them in your writing.

"If" has the most universal application; and you will always be safe if you choose it to express a condition based on the existence or nonexistence of a fact or on the occurrence or nonoccurrence of an event. "When" expresses a condition as to time, and should normally be used only for that purpose. In all fairness it must be admitted, however, that in most cases these two terms can be used interchangeably—a fact that may be useful when you are trying to make a complex or difficult sentence readable. "Where" expresses a condition as to place, and should never be used for any other purpose. The concept of "place" can be stretched a bit, however, permitting "where" to be used as a synonym for "in which" in formulations such as "in any case where" or "in any situation where"; in a complicated sentence this can help.

The terms "whenever" and "wherever" are occasionally useful, in places where "when" or "where" would otherwise be used, to emphasize that the clause that they introduce applies no matter how many times the conditioned fact or event occurs.

22.19 "Hereby", "thereof", and their kin

There is a class of adjectives and adverbs each of which consists of "here", "there", or "where" in combination with an ordinary preposition. They can be quite useful in difficult drafting situations because they permit a three-word or four-word thought to be expressed clearly in a single word, but they have a definitely archaic or artificial flavor and constitute the kind of "legalese" that is subject to caricature.

What should your attitude be toward these words? Unfortunately there is no single answer; it depends on a balancing of the value of the word in the case at hand against the degree of artificiality it exhibits. Some are so regularly useful that you should use them without apology, some sound so archaic that you should never use them, and most fall somewhere in between. The following are random recommendations based on the authors' own drafting experience and personal preferences, and should not be regarded as holy writ.

The words “thereby”, “thereof”, and “thereafter” should be part of every drafter’s arsenal. They are highly useful, and the need for them arises with great frequency.

Words like “herein”, “thereto”, and “whereof” should be avoided, simply because their archaic sound outweighs their usefulness (and “herein” is almost always ambiguous). Words like “hereafter” and “heretofore” are undesirable when used to describe the location of a provision in a bill (see 22.21), and simply have no place in legislative language when used in a temporal sense. “Aforementioned” is beyond the pale.

Words like “therefore”, “therein”, “hereunder”, “thereunder”, “whereas”,[15] and “whereby” fall somewhere in the middle. In the last analysis, it’s a matter for your own subjective judgment.

Note that the word “hereby”—as in “section 6 is hereby amended” or “the Secretary is hereby empowered”—is something of a special case. It is suitably descriptive but almost always redundant, and should be used only when necessary to make it clear in a doubtful case (usually arising out of the use of the indicative mood) that the language involved is actually meant to accomplish some result rather than simply to describe the preexisting situation.

22.20 “Respectively” and “as the case may be”

When you want one provision or thing to apply in a particular case and one or more other provisions or things to apply in one or more other cases, and you have to accomplish it (or prefer to accomplish it) in one fell swoop, you can do it by saying “A, B, and C apply to X, Y, and Z, respectively”. The word “respectively” means that A applies to X, B applies to Y, and C applies to Z. Note that the relationships are always concurrent, and the verb is always plural.

One very common example (discussed in part V) involves the redesignation of a series of numbered paragraphs; thus

> ( ) Section 123 (a) of the ABC Act is amended by striking paragraph (6), and by redesignating paragraphs (7) through (10) as paragraphs (6) through (9), respectively.

When you want to say that if one thing should happen one particular provision or thing will apply, and that if one or more other things should happen one or more other particular provisions or things will apply, you can do it by saying "If X, Y, or Z occurs, A, B, or C (as the case may be) applies". The phrase "(as the case may be)", which need not be but usually is parenthetical, means that if X occurs then A applies, or if Y occurs then B applies, or if Z occurs then C applies. Note that in this case the relationships are alternative rather than concurrent, and the verb is singular. (Note also that some experienced drafters consider the phrase too ambiguous, for untutored readers at least, and prefer to spell out the relationships individually.)

22.21 "Above", "below", and "hereafter"

If it is worth taking the trouble to indicate the general direction in which the reader of your bill should turn in order to find a particular item or provision, it is worth going one step further and specifying the place where that item or provision is located.

Thus, unless the context makes the location obvious, you should not say "the individual described above [or below]", or "the program as hereafter established"; the use of these words is imprecise. Say instead "the individual described in paragraph (2)" or "the program established in section 9".

22.22 Percentages

In keeping with the earlier admonition to favor everyday English over Latin, when expressing a percentage you should always use "percent" rather than "per centum".

22.23 A few closing cautions

There are one or two fairly common drafting mistakes that are quite easy to make, and that have not been mentioned earlier.

Wrong placement of negatives. Be careful to place your negatives where they belong. It should not be necessary to belabor this point; however, many an innocuous-looking sentence reaches a result that is altogether different from what was intended simply because the word "not" was incorrectly located. For example, "The Secretary shall appoint not more than 10 assistants" is very different from "The Secretary shall not appoint more than 10 assistants". In the former case the Secretary is limited to no more than 10 assistants but must appoint some; in the latter the Secretary is not legally obligated to appoint any at all.

The undistributed middle. When you divide any thing, entity, or progression into two mutually exclusive parts, be careful not to leave a small piece in the middle that is not included in either of the two divisions.

Probably the most common example of a drafting error that leaves an "undistributed middle" has to do with dates. If you are drafting a provision that will establish one rule until a specified date (say May 1, 2025) and a different rule thereafter, and you provide that the first rule is to be effective "before May 1, 2025" and the second "after May 1, 2025", you have left a 24-hour gap—there is no rule at all on May 1. You should have made the second rule effective either "on and after May 1, 2025" or "after April 30, 2025". Arriving at the correct result is easy, but unfortunately so is overlooking the problem.

As a slightly different example, assume you want to divide all employees into two classes and confer some benefit on one of them but not the other. If the class to receive the benefit is described as

> any employee who is at least 65 years old or has at least 35 years of service,

you cannot describe the second class by just substituting "less than" for each of the "at leasts", that is

> any employee who is less than 65 years old or has less than 35 years of service,

unless you remember to change the "or" to an "and" as well (see 21.10); the result would be to place a number of employees in both classes simultaneously (or in neither). An easier solution (after making sure you have described the members of the first class correctly) is simply to describe the members of the second class as "any other employee".

(Note that still another example involves the rounding of dollar figures for administrative convenience—see 27.5.)

22.24 Case study

Even if you think you have followed all the "rules" of good drafting, such as those laid out in this chapter, you need to be able to step back from the language and make sure that its message is clear.

Consider the following language, which has been added to the Tariff Act of 1930 (section 592; 19 U.S.C. 1592) in the same form by laws implementing free trade agreements—in this case the Dominican Republic-Central America-United States Free Trade Agreement ("CAFTA") (Public Law 109-53). Paragraph (1) makes it unlawful for any "person" to certify falsely that a good qualifies for the preferential tariff treatment[16] under the Agreement as an "originating good" (that is, a product originating in one or more of the countries that are parties to the Agreement under rules set out in the statute). Paragraph (2) appears to create a relief from liability in certain circumstances.

> (h) FALSE CERTIFICATIONS OF ORIGIN UNDER THE DOMINICAN REPUBLIC-CENTRAL AMERICA-UNITED STATES FREE TRADE AGREEMENT.—
>
> (1) IN GENERAL.—Subject to paragraph (2), it is unlawful for any person to certify falsely, by fraud, gross negligence, or negligence, in a CAFTA-DR certification of origin (as defined in section 508(g)(1)(B) of this Act) that a good exported from the United States qualifies

> as an originating good under the rules of origin set out in section 203 of the Dominican Republic-Central America-United States Free Trade Agreement Implementation Act. The procedures and penalties of this section that apply to a violation of subsection (a) also apply to a violation of this subsection.
>
> (2) Prompt and voluntary disclosure of incorrect information.—No penalty shall be imposed under this subsection if, promptly after an exporter or producer that issued a CAFTA-DR certification of origin has reason to believe that such certification contains or is based on incorrect information, the exporter or producer voluntarily provides written notice of such incorrect information to every person to whom the certification was issued.

Paragraph (2) is problematic. It literally says that if any exporter or producer that issues one of these certifications, promptly after having "reason to believe" information in the certification is incorrect, notifies every person to whom the certification was issued, then no penalty is to be imposed under this subsection on any person, ever (remember that the prohibition in paragraph (1) applies to any "person", not just exporters and producers). What is missing is a link between the acts of the exporter or producer and the penalty that would otherwise be imposed. A possible rewrite of paragraph (2) to clarify this might be the following:

> (2) Prompt and voluntary disclosure of incorrect information.—If an exporter or producer that issues a CAFTA-DR certification of origin, promptly after the exporter or producer has reason to believe that the certification contains or is based on incorrect information, voluntarily provides written notice of the incorrect information to every person to whom the certification was issued, then that exporter or producer shall not be subject to any penalty under this subsection because of that incorrect information.

Notes

1 Tobias Dorsey, *Legislative Drafter's Deskbook: A Practical Guide* (Alexandria, Va.: TheCapitol.Net, 2006), 191.

2 Ibid., 192.

3 Ibid., 192–193.

4 Dorsey, in the *Legislative Drafter's Deskbook,* page 141, suggests the judicial review possibility.

5 *United States v. James Daniel Good Real Property,* 510 U.S. 43, 63 (1993).

6 In *Barnhart,* the Court also used the ratification doctrine (mentioned in 15.3) to interpret the intent of Congress. The language at issue in *Barnhart* was a requirement that the Commissioner of Social Security take certain action within a specified time period that had passed. The Court said that since Congress had passed the requirement after the earlier decision in *Brock,* Congress was presumably aware that the Court does not "readily infer congressional intent to limit an agency's power to get a mandatory job done merely from the specification to act by a certain time" (*Barnhart,* 537 U.S. at 160). Therefore, *Brock* has to mean that "a statute directing official action requires more than a mandatory 'shall' before the grant of power can sensibly be read to expire when the job is supposed to be done", since nothing so limiting was found in the subsequent enactment (537 U.S. at 161). See also 28.7.

7 Robert J. Martineau and Michael B. Salerno, *Legal, Legislative, and Rule Drafting in Plain English* (St. Paul, Minn.: Thomson/West, 2005), 50.

8 Dorsey, *Legislative Drafter's Deskbook,* 193.

9 Martineau and Salerno, *Legal, Legislative, and Rule Drafting in Plain English,* 49.

10 Ibid., 42.

11 In the nonpositive-law titles of the United States Code, the Law Revision Counsel substitutes the actual date for any reference in the enacted law to the "date of enactment".

12 One anomaly, however, relates to drafting riders or limitation provisions in an appropriations bill. Since the Comptroller General, in interpreting an appropriations Act, applies a presumption that all the provisions of the Act are effective only for the one fiscal year involved, a limitation that is intended to be permanent should contain words indicating its future effect, such as "after the date of enactment of this Act", or specifically mention future fiscal years ("None of the funds made available in this or any other Act with respect to any fiscal year"). The terms "hereafter" and "henceforth" are also used but are imprecise (see 22.19). However, all of these added words indicating future effect raise a parliamentary hurdle in that they would constitute legislating in an appropriations bill because the provision would apply to funds not provided in the appropriations bill under consideration. See 34.6.

13 The Law Revision Counsel has clarified this point in the U.S. Code. The revision notes following section 31301 of title 46, which was enacted as positive law in 1988 (Public Law 100-710), have the following comment regarding a definition in section 31301(4) that says the term "'necessaries' includes repairs, supplies … for a vessel.": "*As in all codifications,* the term 'includes' means 'includes but is not limited to' and, therefore, is not intended to be an exclusive listing of those items that a court has determined or may determine as falling within the meaning of the term 'necessaries' as contained in current law." (emphasis added).

14 A bill that authorizes appropriations (at the Federal level) commonly refers to "amounts appropriated pursuant to this [section] [Act]".

15 Of course at the Federal level the preambles of all resolutions have "Whereas" clauses instead of findings.

16 Preferential tariff treatment refers to the reduction or elimination of tariffs on goods imported into the United States from a country or countries pursuant to a trade agreement or statutory program.

23. Devices Especially Suited for Coping with Complexity

23.1 Preliminary comments

The ideal way to handle complexity in a drafting project is of course to break the proposed bill down into as many short, simple subdivisions as may be necessary to cover all the different aspects of the problem, and then to arrange those subdivisions rationally so that their interrelationships will be clear. As has been indicated, that course may not always be available as a practical matter; but fortunately there are a number of special approaches and techniques that can help you get the job done in a way that is both clear and readable in spite of it all.

Some of these approaches and techniques are obvious and straightforward; some are not. Most of them have been touched upon earlier in this book, although their special utility in dealing with unusually complex drafting problems may not have been sufficiently stressed. It is the purpose of this chapter, by gathering them together and discussing them in one place, to emphasize both their existence and their special utility.

23.2 Definitions

In many cases, a bill's complexity resides chiefly in the various concepts and terms that have to be used in expressing the drafter's thoughts rather than in the operating scheme itself. When everything that bears upon the meaning of those concepts and terms can be made clear in their definitions, the key operating provisions of the bill often turn out to be relatively simple. Definitions, like mathematical symbols, serve to make complex thoughts easier to express and to understand.

Consider, for example, the concept of "insured status" under the Social Security program. Since insured status is almost always a prerequisite of eligibility for benefits, the terms "fully insured", "currently insured", and "insured" appear innumerable times in title II of the Social Security Act; and the provision defining those terms (which is only moderately complicated on its face) takes up about one page.

But the definition of those terms is based on "quarters of coverage" (which takes six pages to define) and also involves "periods of disability" (another six pages). The term "quarter of coverage" depends in turn upon the definitions of several other terms—"employment", "self-employment", "wages", "net earnings from self-employment", and "self-employment income"—which occupy 60 or 70 pages. With a few minor terms added in, the definitions needed for a clear understanding of insured status would come to nearly 100 pages of highly complicated language.

Keeping the complexities in the definitions away from the key operating provisions permits those provisions to make their point simply and in a straightforward manner. Thus, for example:

> SEC. 202. (a) Every individual who … is a fully insured individual … shall be entitled to an old-age insurance benefit....

And

> (d)(1) Every child … of an individual who dies a fully or currently insured individual … shall be entitled to a child's insurance benefit....

The example given is admittedly an extreme one, but the principle would be the same if the relevant definitions were short and the term defined appeared only a few times in the bill.

The uses and forms of definitions generally (along with the widespread opposition from some sources to what the authors are recommending here) have already been discussed in detail—see 11.7. Suffice it to say again that segregating as many of a bill's complexities as possible in its definition section is one of the first options you should explore when you find yourself wondering if you'll ever see daylight.

You should of course avoid the inclusion of substantive rules in the definitions if you can, as the critics urge, in cases where the reader would have no reason at all to look for them there. But most of the substantive rules that are found in definitions are in fact nothing but elaborations of the concepts and terms used in the operating provisions, and when this is the case you should not hesitate to include them as part of the definitions of those concepts and terms rather than in the operating provisions themselves. Matter in definitions is not hidden, after all—it can readily be found by anyone who needs to know the details, since the serious reader will always expect to encounter detailed definitions of key terms collected at an appropriate location in the bill. And if necessary a few judiciously placed cross-references can lead the way to any definitions that might otherwise be overlooked. In the example of section 202(a) of the Social Security Act, the phrase "(as defined in section 214(a))" follows "fully insured individual".

When you do it this way there is a good chance that your key operating provisions can be kept short, simple, and clear despite the complexities, and without concealing anything from the reader. The technique does not actually eliminate the complications, of course—it just puts them in a place where they can be studied one by one and keeps them from interfering with the expression of the message.

23.3 Incorporation by reference

As indicated in 22.4, one of the main uses of cross-references is to incorporate the substance of one provision into another without having to repeat or paraphrase it. This device is of course particularly valuable when the material to be incorporated is long and complicated, but it simplifies the drafter's task even when it is not.

A good (though relatively trivial) example of what incorporation by reference can do to make a complicated concept short, easy to handle, and relatively readable is the last sentence of section 215(d)(3) of the Social Security Act, which reads (in its entirety) as follows:

> This paragraph shall not apply in the case of any individual to whom subsection (a)(7) would not apply by reason of subparagraph (E) or the first sentence of subparagraph (D) thereof.

This is hardly bedtime reading, but it separates the complications and produces a clear gain in readability. The subsection (a)(7) referred to comprises over five pages of convoluted technical language, and nearly all of it would have to be repeated in order to reach the desired result without cross-references. Why bother? Once is enough.

When the purpose is to achieve parallel results under two provisions—complete uniformity is very important when the same concept or situation repeats itself in a bill—incorporating the substance of one into the other by a simple cross-reference guarantees those results, while restating or trying to paraphrase the language in its entirety, in a totally new and different setting, risks creating unintended problems. And you can use the device even when the two provisions need not be exactly parallel or the two concepts or situations are not exactly the same, by adopting the borrowed language by cross-reference and then modifying it (at the place where the cross-reference appears) to the extent necessary to limit or expand its application at that place. It can still save time, minimize effort, and promote consistency.

If substantive material is incorporated into a provision by reference not to another provision of the bill (or other legal document) being drafted, but to another law (or document) altogether, the question arises whether the incorporated law (or document) is taken only in its current form or whether it includes later changes as well.

There is case law that supports the principle that incorporation of specifically named provisions picks up only current text, unless there is an express intent to the contrary. The Supreme Court stated this principle in *Hassett v. Welch,* 303 U.S. 303, 314 (1938):

> Where one statute adopts the particular provisions of another by a specific and descriptive reference to the statute or provisions adopted, the effect is the same as though the statute or provisions adopted had been incorporated bodily into the adopting statute.... Such adoption takes the statute as it exists at the time of adoption and does not include subsequent additions or modifications by the statute so taken unless it does so by express intent.

Although the Court did not rely upon this principle in its holding, several Federal circuit court decisions have applied the "Hassett rule".[1] The decisions for the most part draw a distinction between the incorporation of "specific" provisions of another statute (by referring to its title or section number), which would not include subsequent amendments, and the incorporation of the "general" law on a subject, which would include such amendments. It is, however, not clear where the line between specific and general is drawn;[2] "facially specific provisions can and sometimes do operate as general legislative references".[3]

There is a conflict between the *Hassett* rule[4] and the specific versus general distinction on the one hand, and, on the other, the assumption and practice among Federal drafters that any reference to another statute automatically adjusts to changes in that other statute.[5] Consequently, one routinely sees in Federal statutes references to a provision of law (including a regulation) "as in effect on" the date of enactment of the law that includes the reference, or some other date, in order to freeze the cross-referenced provision in time, for the express purpose of overcoming the assumption that changes to the incorporated provision are also incorporated by reference.

An example can be seen in section 119 of title 17, United States Code, which provides for statutory licenses (that is, a copyright license granted by statute, along with mandatory royalty rates) for retransmissions by satellite carriers of television broadcasts. The section contains seven references to regulations in various titles of the Code of Federal Regulations. However, only 2 have the words "as in effect on" a specified date. The references without those words would logically mean those regulations as they change over time. This is in effect the opposite of the Hassett rule. Add to that the fact that an earlier version of section 119 also contained the "as in effect on" language, including regarding a statutory provision within the jurisdiction of another committee. The "as in effect" references freeze the provisions in time. The intent was to clarify that the other provisions were being frozen in time because of the presumption that not including the language would have the opposite effect.

What is the drafter to do? If you choose to incorporate by reference, the advantages—uniformity, clarity, consistency, and the saving of space and time—do come with additional risks. The chief danger is that the incorporated language may not exactly fit the case at hand. And this risk is increased because in all likelihood the very pressures that cause the drafter to use the device often preclude a thorough check to ensure that seemingly parallel situations or seemingly identical concepts are in fact so. You should not use the device unless you are absolutely certain that the incorporated material exactly fits your situation, even though screening the material for this purpose may take more time than you would like to give it.

In addition, incorporated language is less likely to be checked by the sponsor (or by anyone else for that matter), which increases the chances of mistake and even deception, since it can obscure what is being done.

And you must always be aware that the incorporated material may not continue to fit your situation if there are future amendments to either of the two provisions involved. For example, if you are drafting a bill to establish a new program dealing with employees and you want the term "employee" to mean the same thing in that program as it means for Social Security purposes, you might include a provision like this:

> ( ) The term "employee" means an employee as defined by section 210(j) of the Social Security Act.

Such a provision should be sufficient to keep the coverage of your new program parallel with that of the Social Security program. But if the nature, scope, or coverage of either program is materially changed by a future law, the "fit" may disappear—the problem then falls into the lap of the drafter of that law, and you can only hope that that drafter will be able to recognize it.

Even if your sponsor believes (for political or tactical reasons, for example) that your program should parallel the Social Security program no matter what changes are made in the future, a court may apply the *Hassett* rule and interpret your reference as a reference to section 210(j) only as it was in effect on the date your bill became law. To allow for this possibility you might add after "section 210(j) of the Social Security Act" the phrase ", as that section may from time to time be amended"; the problem, however, with adding such a phrase is the negative implication it creates for every other instance in which the phrase has not been used,[6] because it has been the convention among Federal drafters for some time that such a phrase is *not* necessary. You as the drafter will have to make a decision, in concert with the sponsor, weighing the risks involved.

As already suggested, if the sponsor believes that future amendments to section 210(j) might not be appropriate for your new program—there is no way of knowing what those amendments would be, of course—you would add instead ", as in effect on the date of enactment of this Act". This would require that those who are interested in the new program after its enactment keep a close eye on what happens to section 210(j) in the future.

You could draft an incorporation by reference in a way that clarifies that you are merely adopting the substance of the other law, and not in effect amending it to extend its coverage, by saying (for example) that an individual "has the same rights or duties" (under the bill) as those prescribed by the other law rather than by saying that the other law "applies" to that individual. *Dickerson* (page 132) recommends this in every case; however, if you clarify the relationship between the two provisions, the "applies to" language should work.

A further consideration for drafters who do not work at the Federal level is that a number of State constitutional provisions (expressly, by implication, or by judicial interpretation and with varying degrees of clarity) forbid or restrict incorporations by reference. A drafter in such a State needs to be familiar with the practical implications of these restrictions; the drafter in this case can use Dickerson's formulation of saying that a person "has the same rights or duties" (under the bill) as those prescribed by the other law.[7]

In summary, incorporations by reference when done correctly will promote accuracy and precision while easing the task of dealing with complex and interrelated concepts, but they must not be used carelessly. Since the cross-reference conceals the text of the substantive provision it invokes, it makes it harder for a reader (and for the drafter) to be certain that the desired result has actually been achieved, especially when revisions are made in the provision that contains it. Every cross-reference in a draft should be periodically checked and rechecked.

23.4 Tabulated lists

Ordinary lists of things are as common and as useful in bills as they are in other kinds of written documents; but the list form has a special utility for the drafter who must deal with complicated concepts in legislative language and whose options are limited by the arrangement or structure of the bill being drafted.

When a bill contains a number of related elements—definitions, rules, powers, functions, limitations, restrictions, or other substantive concepts—that would otherwise have to be dealt with essay-style in separate subdivisions, their relationships to each other and their respective places in the overall scheme of the bill can often be clarified by presenting them as items on a single list instead.

In any event, whether the items involved are substantive concepts or simple descriptive nouns (or are serial amendments as described in 17.2) the listing process can be managed in any one of several ways.

When the items are few in number and each of them is short, they can be set forth as parts of a single unbroken sentence. Thus for example: "The prohibition contained in this section shall not apply to a minor, an alien, or a disabled individual.". (All three terms would of course have to be defined elsewhere.) This form does contain a list, but it is just a common everyday mode of expression and needs no special discussion.

When some of the items are longer and more complicated, however, or when it will be necessary to cross-refer to one or more of them at other points in the bill, the ideal approach would be to deal with each of them individually in a separate freestanding subsection or paragraph. But this is not always possible, especially when you are amending an existing law; space for the necessary subsections or paragraphs may be unavailable because of that law's arrangement, or other structural considerations may prevent it.

The most practical all-purpose approach is to tabulate the list, with appropriate lead-in language (ending with either a dash or a colon) and a separate indented paragraph for each item.

If the lead-in language ends with a dash (the "dashed" form), the whole thing is technically a single sentence and the example given above would appear as follows:

( ) The prohibition contained in this section shall not apply to—

(1) a minor;

(2) an alien; or

(3) a disabled individual.

This has several advantages. It can accommodate items that are relatively long and complicated (note that its items should end with semicolons rather than commas). It can fit most anywhere, since it comprises a single sentence and can even be used as only a part of a larger sentence (in which case it would not begin with a capitalized word or end with a period, of course). And it gives each item its own designation (thus facilitating cross-references). It still requires that the terms be defined elsewhere, however.

If the lead-in language ends with a colon (the "colon" form), the provision can be viewed as consisting of several self-sufficient items or compound nouns listed separately and would look slightly different:

> ( ) The prohibition contained in this section shall not apply to any of the following:
>
> (1) A minor.
>
> (2) An alien.
>
> (3) A disabled individual.

The colon form is even better than the dashed form at handling lists that include long and complicated items, because it allows any of the numbered items to be broken down into two or more sentences (as would be desirable, for example, if you wanted to include the relevant definitions within those items themselves). And it too gives each item its own designation. But it is less flexible than the dashed form, since its use of capitalized initial words and final periods in the indented paragraphs usually prevents its insertion into the middle of an existing provision.

In general, the dashed form should be used when the items on the list are relatively short (or when structural considerations make it necessary) while the colon form is better when the items are more substantial. In both forms proper punctuation is essential; the two examples given above indicate how the punctuation should be handled, and 21.6 sets forth the detailed specifications for doing it right.

In either form the items on the list should always be recognizable for the kind of things they are—that is, it should always be possible to tell (without reference to the lead-in language) whether the items represent verb-type calls for action, noun-type descriptions of things or functions, amendments to existing law, or something else. The dash or colon dividing the lead-in language from the items on the list should always be placed so as to achieve this result, either by making the items complete enough to be recognizable for what they are or by putting the "pause" where it belongs in the sense of the sentence.

In the colon form this result is almost automatic (since each item on the list is a self-contained unit); but in the dashed form you have a choice, and in every case but one you can use your own judgment about where the dash should go. The one exception involves the case of serial amendments (see 17.2) or any other case in which each item is introduced by a preposition ("by", "for", "to", "in", or "with"). In such a case the dash should be placed so that the preposition is repeated at the beginning of each item rather than being stated only once (just before the dash); this puts the pause where it will do the most to make the nature of the items clear even when they are quoted out of context.

Note that subsequently adding a new item to the end of a list will require three separate amendments if the list is in the dashed form (one to strike the "and" (or "or") at the end of the next-to-last existing item, one to strike the existing final period and insert "; and" (or "; or"), and one to actually add the new item), but can be done with a single stroke if the list is in the colon form. (Subsequently inserting a new item somewhere in the middle of the list is just as easy in the dashed form as in the colon form, since in either case the succeeding items have to be redesignated.)

Note also that the lead-in language must apply to all of the items on the list; and when using the dashed form each item must be a logical and grammatical continuation of the lead-in language so that the two can be read together, without regard to the rest of the provision, as a complete grammatical sentence or phrase.

Failure to observe this rule constitutes what *Dickerson* (page 119) calls "the sin of bastard enumeration". He uses the following example: the phrase "the several States, possessions, and the District of Columbia" in the following tabular form commits this sin:

( ) [This section shall apply to] the several—

(1) States;

(2) possessions; and

(3) the District of Columbia.

Paragraph (3) is unresponsive to the lead-in language, both because the word "several" does not belong with "the District of Columbia" and because of the two "the's". The sin is easily removed, however, by transferring "the several" to paragraph (1) and (2) (possibly combining the two into a single paragraph). Actually the best solution in the untabulated version—in real life you would seldom bother to tabulate such a short sentence—is simply to eliminate the "several" (it is unnecessary anyway) and the second "the", or to substitute "and" for the first comma so that the phrase reads "the several States and possessions, and the District of Columbia".[8]

And finally, it is not enough that each item on the tabulated list is a logical and grammatical continuation of the lead-in language—it should also be the same kind of continuation. Consider the following (which is a not uncommon example of what happens in hastily drafted provisions):

( ) In order to qualify for assistance under this Act, a State must demonstrate that it has—

(1) met the eligibility requirements of section 2; and

(2) a State plan approved under section 3.

Paragraphs (1) and (2) are both logical and grammatical continuations of the lead-in language, so there is no bastard enumeration in the strict Dickersonian sense. But the construction is nonetheless undesirable and can result in misinterpretations as a form of utraquistic subterfuge (see 7.4), since the key word "has" must be given two different meanings to make it work; for purposes of paragraph (1) it is a part of the past-tense verb "has met", while for purposes of paragraph (2) it stands alone as a present-tense verb equivalent to "possesses". A little fairly obvious shifting about of the words is all that it takes to repair the damage, of course—the only prerequisite is that you recognize the problem.

23.5 Tabulated sentences

One of the most valuable tools for handling a complex concept or relationship within a confined space—that is, within a single subsection or paragraph (or even as a single sentence within a subsection or para-graph)—is the tabulated sentence, which is in fact nothing but an expanded version of the tabulated list described in 23.4. It includes one or more tabulated lists, and often sublists, just like its relative, but there is one important difference—it treats each of them as just one of its terms or grammatical elements, and does not stop when the listing process is completed.

The simple example given in 23.4 could be written as a tabulated sentence instead of as an ordinary sentence that just happens to contain a tabulated list. It would look like this:

( ) In the case of—

(1) a minor,

(2) an alien, or

(3) a disabled individual,

the prohibition contained in this section shall not apply.

In this form it is indeed a tabulated sentence, because the sentence goes on after the list is finished. (Note that in this case, since the sentence continues after the list, you would use a comma at the end of each paragraph.) But it embodies such a simple policy that most drafters would not normally bother to tabulate either the list or the sentence, and real life is seldom that straightforward. Suppose that the sponsor (after listening to other people express their fears of possible abuse and evasion) decides to limit the provision to the most clearly deserving cases by imposing specific requirements that individuals in each of the three categories must meet in order to be covered, and to limit the total benefits that any such individual may receive as a result of the lifting of the prohibition.

Suppose also that the sponsor (after listening to other people express their astonishment at the omission of various allegedly deserving groups—this scenario is fairly typical of the way laws become complicated) decides to include military and diplomatic personnel as well, but only in times of crisis.

And suppose finally that, for logical or tactical reasons, the drafter cannot afford the luxury of using up a whole section or subsection with a series of individual subdivisions to present the message, but must write the provision as a single sentence in the middle of a single existing paragraph.

Now the tabulated sentence approach becomes the drafter's salvation. The provision, which has by now become a real monstrosity, could be written in any one of a number of ways, but it might look something like this (with the terms deliberately generalized—in actuality the provision would have to be longer and more technically precise):

> The prohibition contained in this paragraph shall not apply—
>
> (A) in the case of—
>
> (i) a minor who—
>
> (I) is regularly attending school, or
>
> (II) is under age 12 and receiving TANF[9] benefits,
>
> (ii) an alien who—
>
> (I) is legally within the United States, and
>
> (II) has no criminal record, or
>
> (iii) a disabled individual who—
>
> (I) is eligible for Medicare benefits,
>
> (II) has been under the same disability for at least 5 years, and
>
> (III) is participating in an approved rehabilitation program, or
>
> (B) in time of war or national emergency, in the case of—
>
> (i) a member of the armed services on active duty, or
>
> (ii) a member of the diplomatic corps serving overseas,

> if such minor, alien, disabled individual, or member files a formal request for an exemption from the prohibition; except that no individual shall be entitled to a benefit by reason of this sentence for any month after the individual has received such benefits for a period of 12 months (or after the termination of the war or national emergency involved, in the case of an individual described in subparagraph (B)).

Note that the indentation tells you exactly what the undesignated portion (beginning "if") applies to, and that the breakdown of the sentence into designated pieces (however intimidating it may otherwise look) actually helps you to follow the thread.

The drafter could theoretically have written the provision in the required single sentence without tabulation, but that would have eliminated any hope of achieving readability, clarity, or precision. Turning it into a tabulated sentence did not make it easy to read, but it did make it possible to read, and it allowed the drafter to achieve maximum clarity and precision. Careful attention to proper punctuation, meticulous distinction between "ands" and "ors", and progressively increasing indentations to indicate the subordination of ideas is what made it possible.

The example given is of course a pure invention, and a ridiculous one at that, but if you ran across it in an actual existing law (and are reasonably familiar with such things) you would not consider it unique or atypical in form.

It bears mentioning that you should use the tabulated sentence carefully and only if no other solution works. As you can see, it is extremely important to get the margins right or the construct will not work. Frequently, if you think about a provision, you can find a way to organize it in a less complex way.

23.6 Parenthetical expressions

Grammatical purists and most expository writers seem to believe that parenthetical expressions in a sentence are only additive—that their sole function is explanatory—and that the contents of any parenthetical expression must be such that omitting it altogether would not detract from what the sentence says.

When confronted with the necessity of writing a complicated sentence in a bill, forget this. For the drafter, parenthetical expressions are the best available device for combining complicated ideas within a single sentence in a way that achieves clarity. Use them in an additive way when appropriate, of course, but do not hesitate to fill them with substance when the occasion arises.

Most parenthetical expressions could just as well be set off by commas instead, of course, and commas are generally better when the sentence involved is short and simple. A sentence that reads "The Secretary may terminate the contract, without giving any advance notice, if [a specified event] occurs" would satisfy anyone; and most drafters would not even think of converting the language between the commas into a parenthetical expression.

But parentheses are generally more reliable than commas in setting off a phrase when there is possible uncertainty as to how the ideas that follow the phrase are linked to those that precede it. And a long sentence tends to be already full of phrases set off by commas, so that as new ones are added it is likely to become harder and harder for the reader to sort out the pieces. If the language within the quotes in the preceding paragraph had appeared in the middle of such a sentence (instead of constituting the entire sentence), any good drafter would instinctively consider using the parenthetical approach rather than the commas.

Substantive parenthetical matter, like parenthetical matter that is purely additive or explanatory, can be skipped over by the reader without making nonsense of the sentence. There is a big difference, however. If purely explanatory parenthetical matter is omitted the sentence still says what it set out to say, whereas the omission of substantive parenthetical matter detracts from the sentence by removing part of its message.

But it is this very fact—that substantive parenthetical expressions can be skipped over by a reader—that makes them so useful to the drafter. The first time through, an overwhelmed reader can ignore the parenthetical expressions and still get a good general picture of what the message is, and then mentally replace those expressions and evaluate them one by one, thereby getting the whole convoluted picture without having to wade through the entire thicket at the outset.

The point is quite straightforward, and it should not be necessary to belabor it. When a sentence is becoming long and complex, and you cannot find a good way to solve the problem by breaking it down into several separate sentences, put some of the substantive ideas—preferably the less important ones—in parenthetical form. At minimal cost to readability, this approach will make it possible for you to pack a sentence with complex concepts and relationships without sacrificing clarity.

23.7 Tables, formulas, and other graphic aids

Columnar tables. Anyone who has ever done any bookkeeping knows that many complex relationships can be described better in columnar tables than in any other way. This is especially true of relationships between amounts that vary with time or with other factors.

A good table can say with complete precision in half a page what it would take 10 pages of convoluted language to say in narrative form.

Columnar tables are widely used in all legislation—Federal, State, and local. There is no standard form, since each table has to be custom designed to fit the particular situation being addressed, but they are almost always easy to construct and they are not intimidating to any reasonably well-informed reader.

The key to a good table lies in the headings of its columns, which should clearly identify each of the concepts whose interrelationships are the subject of the table. In many tables, the headings, when read from left to right across the top of the table, comprise a complete sentence that could have been placed verbatim before the table instead of in it.

Formulas themselves can be complex; in title 10 of the United States Code (relating to the Armed Forces), for example, there are tables with multiple columns that are used to compute retired pay (see chapter 71 [10 U.S.C. 1401 et seq.]). But most tables are short and simple, and much more likely to be useful models for the average drafter. The table from the Higher Education Act of 1965 in Figure 23.7 is an example.

A columnar table guarantees clarity and precision, and (once the right structure and format have been worked out) it eases your task by providing a ready-made resting place for each of the quantities you will have to specify and for any modifications or adjustments you may subsequently have to make in those quantities.

In addition, it eliminates and replaces a great deal of legislative language that might otherwise be very tricky to handle, and makes the bill shorter and simpler. It does not eliminate or replace all of that language, of course—there will still have to be appropriate preliminary language to put the table in context, and the terms used in the headings may have to be defined elsewhere—but the main message is generally shorter, simpler, and more precise than it would be if it were expressed entirely in words. Every drafter should use columnar tables whenever the opportunity arises.

Formulas. Anyone who has made it through one or two years of high school knows that numerical relationships are most readily described through the use of mathematical formulas, which can be either verbal or algebraic. Verbal formulas are found everywhere in the law— whenever the amount of some rate, benefit, payment, or other numerical quantity has to be calculated—while algebraic formulas are much less common.

Adjusted Net Worth of a Business or Farm	
If the net worth of a business or farm is—	Then the adjusted net worth is
Less than $1 ...	$0
$1-$140,000 ...	40 percent of net worth of farm/business
$140,001-$415,000 ...	$56,000 + 50% of net worth over $140,000
$415,001-$695,000 ...	$193,000 + 60% of net worth over $415,000
$695,001 or more ...	$361,500 + 100% of net worth over $695,000

Figure 23.7. Table from section 478(c) of the Higher Education Act of 1965

A verbal formula is just a specialized form of everyday writing. A statement that "an individual's weekly unemployment compensation benefit shall be equal to one-half of the weekly wage the individual was earning when last regularly employed" constitutes a formula, of course, although you might not think of it as such. The current procedure for computing Social Security benefits, on the other hand, is recognizable as a formula by any test:

> (A) The primary insurance amount of an individual shall (except as otherwise provided in this section) be equal to the sum of—
>
> > (i) 90 percent of the individual's average indexed monthly earnings (determined under subsection (b)) to the extent that such earnings do not exceed the amount established for purposes of this clause by subparagraph (B) [the first "bend point"],
> >
> > (ii) 32 percent of the individual's average indexed monthly earnings to the extent that such earnings exceed the amount established for purposes of clause (i) but do not exceed the amount established for purposes of this clause by subparagraph (B) [the second "bend point"], and

> (iii) 15 percent of the individual's average indexed monthly earnings to the extent that such earnings exceed the amount established for purposes of clause (ii),
>
> rounded, if not a multiple of $0.10, to the next lower multiple of $0.10, and thereafter increased as provided in subsection (i) [the annual cost-of-living adjustment].

You may regard this provision (which is a classic example of a properly used tabulated sentence) as unforgivably complicated, but it is actually about as simple as it could be made, given the policy; the real complications are elsewhere. Defining the crucial terms (average indexed monthly earnings, bend points, and cost-of-living adjustments) requires many pages of language that could cause nightmares.

Almost any verbal formula could also be stated algebraically, but the latter has two disadvantages: It entails an extra step—defining the algebraic symbols themselves—and it is intimidating to people who fear mathematics. However, in the right situation it can be clearer and more precise than the verbal form, and it makes the formula far easier to remember and restate (which is a real plus for the drafter while working on it). The formula "$E = mc^2$" is bandied about (and reasonably well understood) in high school science courses addressing the nature of the universe, but far fewer people would develop an interest in such things if Einstein's theories or the Lorentz transformation had to be discussed in verbal terms exclusively.

A good example of the algebraic approach can be found in the Railroad Unemployment Insurance Act, which uses the formula

$$B = 600 (1 + A - 37{,}800/56{,}700)$$

in the computation of an individual's "monthly compensation base", and uses various algebraic formulas, combined with verbal formulas, to determine the applicable "contribution rate". (In each case the meaning of the algebraic symbols is defined in the clause immediately following the formula.)

You should not go out of your way to present your formulas in algebraic terms, or spend a lot of time looking for opportunities to do so; but if you are working on a policy that lends itself to that approach and the situation permits it, you should at least consider the possibility.

One useful approach—a kind of compromise between the purely verbal formulas and the mathematical ones—is the so-called "cookbook" formula, which takes the reader step-by-step through the various determinations and calculations that have to be made, in more or less conversational language. For example:

> ( ) The Secretary shall determine the [quantity sought] as follows:
>
> (1) The Secretary shall–
>
> (A) first determine A and B;
>
> (B) then determine the percentage of B that is equal to A;
>
> (C) then multiply C by that percentage;
>
> ....
>
> (H) then subtract the larger of the two figures determined under subparagraphs (F) and (G) from the figure determined under subparagraph (C).
>
> (2) The [quantity sought] is one-half of the amount determined under paragraph (1)(H).

Note that *Hirsch*'s experimental rewrite in the chapter dealing with readability (see 9.5), though not in tabulated form, is an example of the "cookbook" formula approach.

Other graphic aids. Devices such as graphs, diagrams, and odd charts are very common in supporting documents such as committee reports, but are relatively rare in legislative measures. A number of them, however, have actually been enacted into law (including at least one musical score).

A few jurisdictions actually forbid such things by rule or law; but in most cases the reluctance to use them results from considerations of precedent, or simply from the fact that they look strange to people who are not used to seeing such things in legislation and who want everything written in plain English.

Nevertheless, there are situations in which the use of unusual graphic devices might be the best possible way to achieve clarity and precision while reducing complexity; and you should feel free to give them a chance.

23.8 Summing it up

It is important to understand that most of the approaches and devices described in this chapter—though their best and highest use may be in dealing with complexity—can always be used when appropriate. Even in a relatively short and simple bill, the crucial terms should be defined, and without cluttering up the main message. Cross-references are really the only way to clearly indicate the interrelationship of provisions. Any series of related ideas, things, or other items (for maximum clarity) should logically be set forth in a list of some kind. And the virtues of columnar tables are obvious in any bill dealing with variable numerical quantities.

The others—sentence tabulation and the intensive use of substantive parenthetical expressions—are usually reserved for situations involving both a high degree of complexity and a shortage of maneuvering room. And in those situations their virtues easily outweigh the sensibilities of the purists who are offended by them. But if you are an occasional drafter without much exposure to such things, you ought not attempt tabulated sentences gratuitously—they can be tricky to write, and can create more problems than they solve if done incorrectly or carelessly. Use them when they will make your work significantly easier, of course, but always look for a good model to follow and make sure you understand how its construction can be adapted to serve your purposes.

Notes

1 *United States v. D'Amario*, 12 F.3d 253, 256 (1st Cir. 2005); *Director, Office of Worker's Compensation Programs, United States Department of Labor v. Peabody Coal Co.*, 554 F.2d 310, 322–331 (7th Cir. 1977); *United States v. Smith*, 683 F.2d 1236, 1239 (9th Cir. 1981); *Clark v. Crown Construction Co.*, 887 F. 2d 149, 152–155 (8th Cir. 1989); *U.S. v. Griner*, 358 F.3d 979, 982 (8th Cir. 2004).

2 See *Pearce v. Director, Office of Worker's Compensation Programs, United States Department of Labor*, 603 F.2d 763, 767–770 (9th Cir. 1979).

3 *Peabody Coal, supra,* note 1, 554 F.2d, 324. See also *United States v. Rodriguez-Rodriguez,* 863 F.2d 830 (11th Cir. 1989) (a reference to penalties to be assessed under the Comprehensive Drug Abuse Prevention and Control Act of 1970 is a "general reference" incorporating subsequent amendments [863 F.2d, 831]).

4 The *Hassett* rule is also cited in Norman J. Singer, Shambie Singer, and J. G. Sutherland, *Statutes and Statutory Construction, Statutory Interpretation*, 7th ed. (St. Paul, Minn.: West Group, 2010), sec. 51.7 (commonly referred to as *Sutherland Statutory Construction* after its original author, J. G. Sutherland); in *American Jurisprudence*, 2nd ed., *Statutes* (73 Am. Jur. 2d Statutes §16); in *Corpus Juris Secundum* (82 C.J.S. Statutes §90); and in various State court decisions.

5 Tobias Dorsey, in *Legislative Drafter's Deskbook: A Practical Guide* (Alexandria, Va.: TheCapitol.Net, 2006), 266, refers to this "conventional wisdom" among Federal drafters.

6 See the discussion of canons of negative implication in 28.4.

7 *Dickerson* (pages 131–132) also suggests that if the incorporated language was not enacted by the legislature that the drafter is serving, the inclusion of future changes may jeopardize the constitutionality of the incorporating provision as an unconstitutional delegation of the legislative power to the persons authorized to change the incorporated material.

8 In Federal law, one would not normally see the word "several" modifying "possessions". The word usually is in the singular and appears in the phrase "any territory or possession of the United States", or "any commonwealth, territory, or possession of the United States".

9 TANF refers to the Temporary Assistance for Needy Families program under title IV of the Social Security Act.

24. References to Statutory Provisions

24.1 Preliminary comments

Any reference or citation to a provision of law has two main purposes—to identify that provision briefly and in an unambiguous manner, and to provide a finding aid for readers. The methods suggested in this chapter are consistent with those purposes; they are generally followed in the case of Federal laws, and should serve as useful guides (making allowances for differences in statutory structure and nomenclature) in the case of State and local laws as well.

In most cases, the reference mentions only the provision's alphanumeric designation ("section 123", "paragraph (7) of subsection (c)", or "part B of title III", for example), although it will often include a parenthetical citation to the corresponding provision of the United States Code as an aid to readers if it is not a reference to a positive-law title of the Code itself (see 24.4).

Most of the examples given in this chapter (and chapter 25) are taken from *HOLC*.

24.2 References to laws with positive-law provisions of the United States Code

If the provision to which you wish to refer has been enacted into positive law as part of the United States Code, it should be cited by its Code designation, directly and without parentheses or abbreviations—for example, "section 1234 of title 34, United States Code".

When the provision making the reference is itself within a positive-law title of the Code, however, the words "United States Code" are unnecessary, and should be omitted, so that in the example given in the first paragraph the reference would read simply "section 1234 of title 34" (or "section 1234" if the two provisions are both in title 34).

Because you cannot cite a provision by its U.S. Code designation (except for purely informative purposes—see 24.6) unless it is in a positive-law title of the Code, you must know which titles (or portions of titles) of the Code are positive law and which are not (31.4 and 31.5 contain the information you will need to sort them out, including a complete list of the titles in each category). In addition, each title that has been enacted into positive law so states on its first page.

24.3 References to laws with short titles

If the provision to which you wish to refer has not been enacted into positive law as a part of the United States Code, always cite the statute in which it is contained by its short title if it has one. Showing its Code citation parenthetically, for purely informative purposes, is not actually necessary but should be supplied; for example, "section 345 of the ABC Act (34 U.S.C. 1234)".

24.4 References to laws without short titles

If the provision to which you wish to refer is contained in a law that does not have a short title (and is not within a positive-law title of the United States Code), there are several ways it can be cited:

By public law number. If the law was enacted after 1956 (when the present system of public law designation went into effect), it should usually be cited by its public law number—for example, "section 1234 of Public Law 109-123". (The latter number simply means that the law was the 123rd public law enacted in the 109th Congress.)

Pre-1957 laws also had numbers, of course, but their numbers did not reflect the particular Congresses in which they were enacted, so they are not usually cited by their public law numbers. If you do choose to use that method of citation, you must remember to specify the Congress—thus "section 1234 of Public Law 567 of the 79th Congress".

By long title. If the long title of the law is not too long, particularly when that title's content would be helpful to the reader, you can refer to it as "the Act entitled 'An Act [to ...]', approved [May 6, 1974].".

By enactment date. If the law was enacted before 1957, it can be referred to simply by the date of its enactment, with a citation to the Statutes at Large—for example, "the Act of [January 5, 1945] (33 Stat. 3434)". Note that the parenthetical citation tells the reader where to find the law being referred to, but it gives only the first page of that law; if the reference is to a provision of the law that appears several pages later, it is usually desirable to expand the citation to indicate also the actual page on which the provision appears—thus "(33 Stat. 3434, 3451)". And whenever you cite the older Statutes at Large you should watch out for the relatively rare cases in which there are two Acts beginning on the same page. In such a case the parenthetical citation should be enlarged to include the chapter as well as the page—thus "(33 Stat. 3434; ch. 883)".

Citations to a law by its public law number or date of enactment are excellent candidates for "relating to" clauses aimed at aiding the reader, since the nature of the provision being cited will not be clear from the citation alone—for example, "section 123 of Public Law 91-456 (relating to admission fees in national parks)". And in the case of a law without a short title but with a generally known popular name, the popular name may be included in the parenthetical reference for the same purpose—for example, "section 343 of Public Law 91-353 (commonly known as the Chappell-Bell Act)".

Note that the use of parenthetical U.S. Code citations for informative purposes (as a finding aid) is particularly important when referring to laws in any of the ways described here—each of the examples given should have included such a citation (which was omitted simply to avoid obscuring the points being made).

24.5 "As amended"

The name of an Act invariably remains the same throughout its life, and it speaks as of the time it is being read or applied, no matter how many times it has been amended since its original enactment. It is therefore never necessary (and can be misleading) to attach the phrase ", as amended" when referring to an existing law;[1] and the practice should be avoided. This rule always applies when the law involved is the United States Code or has a short title, and normally applies in any other case as well.

There are a few situations, however, in which a reference to a law by its long title or date of enactment may mislead the reader (because of some quirk in its amendatory history) unless you make it abundantly clear that it is the up-to-date amended version you are talking about. If you believe that you are in such a situation, go ahead and attach the phrase, but do it with regret; and if possible vary the phrase—say "as amended by section 15 of the ABC Act", for example, or "as most recently amended" so the reader will realize it is a special case. (The other side of the coin is, of course, that if for some reason you really do need to address the old unamended version of the law you must always explicitly say so.)

And there is one situation—superficially similar but actually quite different—in which a mention of a previous amendment is always proper. When you must refer to a provision that was amended so recently that the changes made have not had time to be reflected in the Code or in other published sources, it is appropriate to indicate that fact—not for the sake of accuracy but as a warning to readers who may not yet be aware of the changed version. Thus if you want to refer in a bill to section 10 of the ABC Act, which was extensively changed last month by section 234 of the XYZ Act, your citation might properly read "section 10 of the ABC Act (as [recently] amended by section 234 of the XYZ Act)".

24.6 Code citations for purely informative purposes

Most people who read a provision that you have drafted will not have ready access to the slip laws or the Statutes at Large, or to compilations of the laws referred to in that provision. Consequently, when referring to a provision that is not within a positive-law title of the United States Code and that is contained in a law that has no short title, you should always include a parenthetical Code citation after the basic reference—for example, "section 123 of Public Law 91-456 (42 U.S.C. 2983)", or "section 123 of the Act of January 5, 1945 (33 Stat. 3435; 42 U.S.C. 2983)". You owe this to your readers.

(Note that in parenthetical Code citations of this kind "United States Code" is always abbreviated.)

You should also use this device in cases where the law to which you are referring does have a short title, although it is less important in those cases since laws with short titles are easier for the reader to find (both in their literal form and in the Code). The U.S. House of Representatives has, in recent Congresses (prior to the 118th Congress) included, in the resolution adopting its rules at the beginning of that Congress, a provision stating that, to the maximum extent practicable and consistent with established drafting conventions—

> an instruction in a bill or joint resolution proposing to repeal or amend any law or part thereof not contained in a codified title of the United States Code shall include, in parentheses immediately following the designation of the matter proposed to be repealed or amended, the applicable United States Code citation...

Citations to appendices in titles of the United States Code should take the form "(50 U.S.C. App. 660)"; and citations to nonstatutory provisions that are included in the Code as notes (such as treaties and Executive orders) should take the form "(5 U.S.C. 3301 note)".

Public laws beginning with the 94th Congress generally give the U.S. Code citations for all of their substantive provisions, and you can use those citations as soon as the laws involved are enacted. But if the law to which you want to refer was enacted too recently to be reflected in the volumes of the Code that are generally available, it is advisable to use the public law citation as well—thus "the XYZ Act of 2024 (Public Law 118-56; 42 U.S.C. 19683)".

Provisions that are temporary, obsolete, or executed do not appear in the Code at all, so you will have to cite them in the manner described in 24.3 or 24.4 without any accompanying Code citation.

24.7 References within an Act or section

When one section of an Act refers to another section of that Act, or one subdivision of a section refers to another subdivision of that section, it is unnecessary to specify the location of the section or subdivision being referred to. You do not have to say "section 123 of this Act" or "paragraph (6) of this subsection"—just "section 123" or "paragraph (6)" is enough. The reader will assume that both the subdivision containing the reference and the subdivision referred to have the same parent.

An exception may be appropriate, however, when there are also references to other Acts or subdivisions in the vicinity. If you think the shorter approach recommended in the preceding paragraph might be confusing to the reader because of the neighboring references, you should feel free to include the phrase "of this Act", "of this section", or "of this subsection" in the interest of clarity.

24.8 References to components of a section

References based on alphanumeric designations. As indicated in 20.3, a section (to the extent that subdivision is necessary) is broken down into—

(1) subsections (starting with (a)),

(2) paragraphs (starting with (1)),

(3) subparagraphs (starting with (A)),

(4) clauses (starting with (i)),

(5) subclauses (starting with (I)), and

(6) if necessary—

(A) items (beginning with (aa); and

(B) subitems, beginning with (AA),

all of them paragraphed and the lesser ones often indented. (Remember that a provision is "paragraphed" when its first line is indented more than the remaining lines, whether or not the provision as a whole is indented.)

Paragraphed provisions are always referred to on the basis of their class designation—thus paragraphed provisions designated with lower case letters ((a), (b), (c)) should always be referred to as subsections, those designated with Arabic numerals ((1), (2), (3)) as paragraphs, and so forth. However, if the provision is a designated part of a continuous run-in sentence and is not paragraphed, it is always referred to as a clause or subclause, whatever its letter—or number—designation.

Note that a few older laws have systems of designation that differ from the system just described—the Federal Food, Drug, and Cosmetic Act, for example, consistently refers to units beginning "(a)", "(b)", or "(c)" as paragraphs—and you should apply the Roman rule and follow those systems when amending or referring to those laws, unless, as discussed in chapter 8, you are adopting a more uniform style in a discrete part of such a law in a way that will not cause confusion.

Composite references. For the sake of both clarity and brevity, a composite reference such as "section 503(b)(2)(A) of the XYZ Act" is preferred to a "strung-out" reference such as "subparagraph (A) of paragraph (2) of subsection (b) of section 503 of the XYZ Act", although the two are of course identical in effect—see 20.3.

There are, however, a few cases in which this rule should be varied:

(1) *In amendments.* When amending just one piece of what would otherwise call for a composite reference, that piece should be separated out and referred to specifically in order to make clear exactly what is being amended. Thus an amendment to section 503(b)(2)(A) should not use the composite reference but should be stated as an amendment to subparagraph (A) of section 503(b)(2). Experienced drafters always apply this rule when the amendment is being made by restatement (see 15.3), and most of them apply it in the case of cut-and-bite amendments as well.

(2) *For later reference.* When it will be necessary at a later point in the bill (or in some other law) to refer specifically to just one piece of what would otherwise call for a composite reference, that piece should be separated out. For example, saying "subparagraph (A) of section 503(b)(2)" instead of "section 503(b)(2)(A)" will make it possible to say simply "such subparagraph" in the later reference. (See 27.7.)

(3) *Joint references.* When referring simultaneously to two or more pieces of what would otherwise call for a composite reference, those pieces should be separately stated. A reference to "clauses (i) and (ii) of section 503(b)(2)(A)" is easier to understand (and clearer) than a reference to "section 503(b)(2)(A)(i) and (ii)".

Note that a composite reference always uses the generic name of the senior unit involved. Thus if you want to refer to paragraph (1) of subsection (a) of section 5 and you choose (as you normally would) to do so by a composite reference, you should say "section 5(a)(1)" rather than "paragraph [or subsection] 5(a)(1)" even though it is the paragraph you are interested in.

24.9 References to senior components

The senior components of a bill, like the individual sections and inferior subdivisions, should be referred to by their class designations—for example, "title II" or "part C".

The composite approach, however, should be reserved for references to sections and their subdivisions; it should not be used in referring to the senior components of a bill. Thus a reference to subtitle C of title III of a bill or law should read "subtitle C of title III"—not "title III-C".

And remember that the reader normally wants to know the particular sections to which the reference applies. If the senior component being referred to is a title of the bill or of a law the section numbers involved can be easily identified (since the section numbers in a title always begin with the same number as the title—see chapter 20), but if it is a subtitle, chapter, or part it cannot. In the latter case it may be helpful to include a parenthetical indication of the particular section numbers involved—for example, "part C of title I (sections 161 through 175)".

24.10 Consolidated reference convention

In a lengthy bill or title consisting primarily of amendments to a single law, the use of a consolidated reference convention of the type described in chapter 16 is often a desirable alternative to endless repetitions of the law's full citation. By indicating in an early section that all amendments are to that law unless otherwise specified, you can avoid the necessity of naming it every time you want to refer to one of its provisions; you can just say "Section 123(b) is amended ...", for example, instead of "Section 123(b) of the ABC Act is amended ...". The text of such a provision is set forth in 16.1.

24.11 Abbreviated references; use of "such" or "that"

Once a reference has been made in any section to another provision of your bill (or to a provision of some existing law), that provision should be referred to later in the same section simply as "such [provision]" or "that [provision]" rather than by repeating the full citation, unless a reference in that form would be unclear because of the distance between it and the original reference or because of the intervention of references to other provisions. (See 16.1.)

Thus, for example, the first time you refer in a section of your bill to section 123(a) of the ABC Act, you should give it its full name—"section 123(a) of the ABC Act"—but whenever you refer to that section or that Act later in the same section of your bill (unless it would be unclear for one of the reasons given in the preceding paragraph) you can just say "such [that] section" or "such [that] Act".

This practice can do wonders for the smoothness and readability of your prose in any bill where numerous references to other provisions are necessary.

Notes

1 There is at least one law that has the words "as amended" in its short title, so the words would appear there: it is the Foreign Agents Registration Act of 1938, as amended. In that case, the short title was added in 1942, together with other amendments to the 1938 law; presumably the reasoning was that technically the law had become the Act, "as amended".

25. References to Nonstatutory Provisions

25.1 Executive orders

When making reference to a specific Executive order that appears as a notation (along with the provision of law involved) in the United States Code, include a parenthetical citation to the Code along with the order number. For example, "Executive Order 13124 (5 U.S.C. 3301 note, relating to civil service rules)".

If the order does not appear as a notation in the Code, cite directly to the *Federal Register* instead (all Executive orders are printed in the *Federal Register* on the day they are issued)—thus "Executive Order 13124 (64 Fed. Reg. 31103, relating to civil service rules)". And if by reason of amendment the order as currently in effect derives from more than one entry in the Federal Register, you should cite each of them: "Executive Order 13124 (64 Fed. Reg. 31103 and 65 Fed. Reg. 648, relating to civil service rules)".

25.2 Regulations

In most cases, Federal regulations should simply be cited by their section and title number in the Code of Federal Regulations (CFR). For example, "section 76.103 of title 47, Code of Federal Regulations (commonly known as the 'Network Syndication Rule')".

Occasionally a regulation carries with it an identifying name that has greater currency than its CFR section number. In such a case the drafter may refer to it by that name, but with a parenthetical citation to the Code of Federal Regulations. For example, "Federal motor vehicle safety standard numbered 208 (49 CFR 571.208, relating to occupant crash protection)".

Note the potential drafting difficulties in referring to regulations (and even Executive orders), because the legislature does not generally control when an agency can change its regulations. The underlying issue is whether a reference to a regulation is to that regulation as in effect at the time the law referring to it is enacted, or to the regulation as it may be modified by the agency concerned.

The conventional wisdom is that it refers to the latter; if the policy is to freeze the regulation in time, the statutory language should say so: for example, "section 73.658(b) of title 47, Code of Federal Regulations, as in effect on December 1, 2023". If the regulation is not frozen in time, then because an agency generally can modify its regulations at any time, the agency may move a provision to another part of its regulations or change the structure of the regulation so that the statutory reference no longer works. See the discussion of this issue in 23.3.

25.3 Treaties and other international agreements

A treaty or other international agreement should be referred to by its full name (including the names of the countries involved in the case of a bilateral or multilateral agreement), together with—

(1) a reference either to the location and time of its signing or to the time at which it became applicable to the United States (whichever is more appropriate for the agreement and context), and

(2) a finding aid consisting of either a citation to the "United States Treaties and Other International Agreements" (UST), which is comparable with a Statutes-at-Large citation, or a citation to the "Treaties and Other International Acts Series" (TIAS), which is comparable with a public law citation.

Examples of proper references to international agreements are "the Convention on the Territorial Sea and the Contiguous Zone, signed at Geneva on April 29, 1958 (TIAS 5639)" and "the Seabed Arms Control Treaty (entered into force with respect to the United States on May 18, 1972; 23 UST 701)".

If a treaty is published in the United States Code, it would be helpful to include a Code citation—as a hypothetical example, "the Universal Copyright Convention (as revised at Paris on July 24, 1971; 25 UST 1341; 17 U.S.C. 104 note)".

25.4 Legislative rules

The rules of legislative bodies always have their own special systems of organization; their provisions are usually not broken down into sections, subsections, paragraphs, and so forth in the same way that statutes are. The Rules of the House of Representatives, for example, are broken down progressively into—

(1) rules (starting with Rule I [designation not in parentheses]),

(2) clauses (starting with clause 1 ([also without parentheses]),

(3) paragraphs (starting with (a)),

(4) subparagraphs (starting with (1)), and

(5) subdivisions (starting with (A)).

When amending or referring to provisions of these Rules, you should of course reflect this breakdown and system of designation.

25.5 Other public documents

It will occasionally be necessary for you to refer to measures and documents from jurisdictions other than the one in which you are working. A drafter in the Federal context, for example, may sometimes have to refer to a State statute or constitution or a local ordinance, to a State or local rule, regulation, or other executive action, to an interstate compact, or even to a private measure or document that is legislative in nature (such as a corporate charter or the records of a public-service organization).

Needless to say, there is no one rule that covers these things, since each jurisdiction and entity will have its own system for designating and referring to the items involved. The simple answer is to follow the Roman rule if you can find out what it is; but the necessary information about just how the Romans would do it in a particular case may not be available to you as a practical matter. In the absence of that information, all you can do is be as careful and descriptive as possible in making your reference, so that (whether or not it is in the right form) it will lead the reader and the courts to the intended destination.

26. Dealing with Effective Dates

26.1 When an explicit effective-date provision is unnecessary; the "default" rule

At the Federal level and in some States, every law takes effect on the day it is enacted—by default, so to speak—unless some other effective date is specifically provided for. (In general, a bill is "enacted" when the President signs it or fails to act on it within 10 days, or when Congress overrides the President's veto; State constitutions specify what is required for the enactment of a measure into law.) Many States have constitutional or statutory provisions making all laws effective (unless otherwise provided) only at the close of a specified period, or on a specified date, after their enactment or after the close of the legislative session in which they are enacted; the "default" effective date is different but the principle is the same.

As a consequence, it is not usually necessary to include an explicit effective-date provision in a bill that is simply intended to go into effect immediately upon its enactment (or on a comparable default effective date in a State). Except when an event-related approach is required (see 26.4) or other special factors are present (see 26.5), an effective-date provision should be used only to contravene the "default" rule stated in the preceding paragraph.

Under the old common law rule that "the law knoweth not parts of a day", making a bill effective "on the date of its enactment" is exactly the same thing as letting it become effective by default—in either case the bill will apply all day long on the day the President signs it. There is one exception, though; in a criminal bill (one creating a new crime or changing a criminal penalty) the old common law rule is overridden by the constitutional prohibition against *ex post facto* laws, and the bill may not become effective until the split second of its enactment (only after 2:17 p.m. eastern standard time, for example, if that is when the signing occurs) whichever approach is taken.

It does happen from time to time, of course, that a sponsor insists on including a totally unnecessary provision declaring that the bill is to take effect on the date of its enactment, probably just because other bills have it. If not having an explicit effective-date provision seems to worry the sponsor, go ahead and put one in; it causes no real harm, and you should save your energy for more important matters.

26.2 Delayed effective dates

One obvious example of a bill that *does* need an explicit effective-date provision is a bill whose sponsor wants it to become effective only after some time has elapsed following its enactment.

There are several possible reasons for wanting to postpone the effectiveness of a newly enacted statute. The officials who will have to administer it may need time to get the machinery in motion, or the persons who will be affected by it may need time to adjust. If it establishes a new or substantially revised government program, regulations may have to be written and published before that program can work effectively. Or there may be budgetary considerations; after all, a newly established program whose effectiveness is postponed for a two-year period will not cost as much (and cannot cost anything during that period). These are matters for the sponsor; you would not usually volunteer a delayed effective date to take care of them (although if you recognize a possible need for delay you should of course point it out to the sponsor).

The most common cases in which delayed effective dates are used do not really involve intentional delays at all, but merely administrative necessity. There are many programs that operate on a monthly, annual, seasonal, or other periodic basis (Social Security, SSI, Federal salaries, retirement annuities, and crop subsidies, to name a few), and bills affecting those programs should logically become effective at a time (usually the first day of the first month or another relevant period after enactment) that reflects this periodicity and is convenient for both the administrators and the public. If the field of law involved has an established tradition of briefly delaying effective dates for this kind of administrative reason (as many do), you should not hesitate to make the decision on your own.

In any case it is important to remember that the specific changes to be made by the final version of the bill (whether its effective date is strictly time-related or is event-related as described in 26.4) typically remain fluid until the last stages of the House-Senate conference—only a few days before enactment and much too late for immediate implementation.

26.3 Retroactive effective dates

Delayed effective-date provisions are very common, and generally pose no special difficulties for the drafter. But retroactive effective-date provisions, though relatively rare, are full of problems that have to be dealt with if the job is to be done right.

On its face a retroactive effective-date provision is the same as a delayed effective-date provision except that it specifies a past date instead of a future one. The trouble is that during the period between the specified past date and the date of the bill's enactment a number of significant things may have happened.

The sponsor most likely wants retroactivity in order to ratify one or more past actions that were not strictly authorized at the time they were taken, or in order to confer past benefits on some deserving class of people. More often than not the proposal is intended to undo the past effect of regulations that the sponsor regards as ill-advised. Or the sponsor may simply have been fighting to get some statutory provision enacted for a long time and thinks (upon finally succeeding) that, as a matter of principle, it should be effective back to the beginning of the fight.

But remember that if a bill makes retroactive changes in existing law, it wipes out the changed provisions as they were in effect during the retroactive period and substitutes new ones. Benefits that were properly received under the law then in effect may now prove to have been improper (and repayable). Actions that were optional may now turn out to have been mandatory (and vice versa). And actions that were perfectly legal may now turn out to be illegal. Even worse, it is now probably far too late (without a time machine) for anyone to do anything about those benefits or those actions, and if anything could be done about them now, it would probably be inequitable to insist on it.

What are you to do when confronted with a sponsor who wants a retroactive effective date? There are no rules that cover all cases, except that you should always look first to see what might have happened under the provisions that would be retroactively superseded. If you find for certain that nothing significant could have happened (which is quite possibly the case if the sponsor is acting rationally), you are home free, and can just write a regular effective-date provision with an odd-looking date in it.

If, however, you believe that significant actions may have been taken during the retroactive period in reliance on the then-existing law, you are on your own. All you can do is try to identify all of the undesirable consequences that might result from the retroactive feature, point them out to the sponsor, and suggest the kind of language (probably in the form of a savings clause—see 13.4) that might be added in order to deal with them.

26.4 Event-related effective dates

There are a number of situations where the primary effective-date question is not the date on which a bill is to go into effect but rather the events (occurring on or after the chosen date) to which it is to apply.

The "events" involved might be particular months or pay periods, or might be benefits received, applications filed, grants made, offenses committed, or causes of action arising, on or after the chosen date. Occasionally an effective date is tied to the issuance of regulations implementing the statute. And bills involving programs of financial assistance are usually made effective with the beginning of a particular fiscal year or, with respect to appropriations, for a particular fiscal year.

For example, if a bill increasing monthly benefits under some public program were enacted on April 25 without any explicit effective-date provision, what would an individual's monthly benefit check for April look like? Should it be in the old amount or in the new increased amount? Unfortunately, neither would carry out the bill's mandate. What *would* happen, since the bill becomes effective (by default) in the middle of the month, is that the April check would have to be in a prorated amount equal to 24/30 of the benefit computed at the old rate plus 6/30 of the benefit computed at the new rate—an administrative nightmare that would satisfy no one.

Since the program operates on a monthly basis, the bill should have included an explicit provision making it effective with respect to specified monthly events rather than simply at a specified time. The most logical provision would be one making the increase effective with respect to benefit payments, either for months beginning on or after the chosen date (which would in effect defer the increase until May 1 and keep the April checks at the old rate if the chosen date were the date of enactment) or for months ending on or after that date (if the sponsor prefers instead to apply the full increase to the April checks).

Note that simply making the increase effective on April 1 or May 1, or with respect to benefits paid on or after the chosen date (without any reference to the periods for which they were payable), would leave doubts about what is intended and might not get the right result in all cases.

The principle illustrated by this example—using events, rather than just times, to fix effective dates when the bill makes changes that fall in the middle of the very process that it seeks to affect—applies to many different kinds of bills; any quantitative change that affects an ongoing process is normally handled this way. Thus a bill changing income tax rates would be tied to specified taxable years; a bill changing admission fees at national parks would be tied to admissions occurring, or admission tickets purchased, on or after the chosen date; and a bill increasing Federal salaries would be tied to specified pay periods.

And a bill increasing criminal penalties is normally made applicable only to penalties imposed for crimes committed on or after its chosen date. If its effective-date provision specified only a date (which would always fall in the middle of the crime-indictment-trial-punishment process for at least a few people), the increased penalties would literally apply to individuals who, as of that date, have been charged but not yet brought to trial or have been convicted but not yet sentenced, as well as to those who commit the crimes thereafter, with resulting constitutional and other drawbacks. It should be emphasized again that the chosen date in event-related cases need not be the date of the bill's enactment; indeed, delays in event-related cases (as in strictly time-related cases) are the rule rather than the exception.

26.5 Hybrid effective dates

There may be situations in which a delayed effective date, or an event-related effective date, will still need additional provisions to cover the existing playing field. Consider a bill that creates a new court, and the policy is to delay the effective date of the bill for a period of time to allow the court to be up and running. When that effective date arrives, how is the court to get cases to consider under its jurisdiction? If you add to the delayed effective date a simple event-related provision that the bill applies to cases filed on or after the effective date, there will potentially be a long period of time both before the court gets a full docket of cases and before the cases that are pending on the effective date get through the system (which can be years). In such a case, addressing logical places in the litigation process to transfer existing cases (in essence adding in a retroactive provision) to the new court may make more sense. So, for example, the bill may (in addition to new cases) apply to a case filed before the effective date that has not yet gone to trial, or for which discovery has not begun. Note that the bill would also have to provide for the transfer of the case, along with all records and other papers of the case, to the new court. Another possibility is to allow a mechanism whereby a party to the case can transfer it to the new court (although this raises issues of inequity between the parties). There may be certain types of cases that are more feasible to transfer than others, and that can be a dividing line.

Comparable transition issues arise in any proposal that replaces an existing mechanism with something new—it may be a new agency or a new method of resolving administrative disputes. In cases such as these (or any retroactive provision), seeking input from those who will have to administer the effective-date provision should help refine the language to address the complexities.

26.6 Placement of effective-date provisions

A general effective-date provision that applies to the bill as a whole or consists of separate effective dates for all of the bill's various substantive provisions should always be the last section of the bill.

If most but not all of the bill's substantive provisions are to have explicitly stated effective dates, it is still best to group those effective dates in a section at the end of the bill, where most readers would expect to find them. If you fear that readers might be mystified by your failure to mention some of the bill's substantive provisions in the effective-date section, you can fill in the gaps by adding a paragraph or sentence—which would otherwise be unnecessary—to remind them that "the remaining provisions of this Act shall take effect on the date of enactment of this Act".

If some but not most of the bill's substantive provisions are to have explicitly stated effective dates, it is probably better to omit the general effective-date section at the end altogether, and to set forth the effective date for each of those provisions in a separate subsection, paragraph, or sentence at the end of the section (or a separate section at the end of the title) in which that provision appears.

If only a few of the bill's substantive provisions are to have explicitly stated effective dates, or the bill does indeed have a general effective-date section at the end but some of its provisions require an explicitly stated effective date that is different from the one contained in that section, it is perfectly respectable to state each of the maverick effective dates within the text of the provision to which it relates. Normally the effective date in these cases would be placed in a separate subdivision at the end of the substantive provision, in the usual way; but it can just as easily be placed at the beginning—see 26.7.

Whenever you include special effective-date provisions in particular sections of a bill that also has a general effective-date provision, however, you must remember to begin the latter provision with the phrase "Except as otherwise specifically provided,".

It should be emphasized that a "substantive provision" for these purposes need not be an entire title or section; it can be a subsection, a paragraph, or any other subdivision of a bill. Even a single sentence can sometimes require its own unique effective date.

26.7 Form and style in effective-date provisions

Except in those relatively rare cases with complications that require extensive improvisation on the part of the drafter, effective-date provisions are short, simple, and easy to write. Most of them are just different versions of the same boilerplate sentence, of which the following might be regarded as the basic form:

> **SEC. __. EFFECTIVE DATE.**
>
> This Act shall take effect on January 1, 2025.

All of the pieces of this form—the section designation, the subject, the verb, and the adverbial phrase at the end—may be freely varied to fit the circumstances involved and to reflect the kind of effective date that is being prescribed. (In the models that follow, the changed portions of the form are indicated by italics.)

For example, when the effective date applies only to one particular section rather than to the bill as a whole, it would normally be placed in a subsection at the end of that section rather than in a section at the end of the bill, and would read:

> (d) EFFECTIVE DATE.—This *section* shall take effect on January 1, 2025.

Note that these examples depict only two of the many possible variations in the sentence's subject, which describes the substantive provision or provisions to which the effective date is being applied. In the examples just given, "This Act" became "This section"; but it could just as well have become "This paragraph", "Section 101", "Subsection (c)", "The second sentence of section 202(d)(4)", or "Sections 14, 37, and 355".

And if the bill is essentially just a "vehicle" for making amendments to some existing law, the effective-date provision should reflect that fact:

SEC. ___. EFFECTIVE DATE.

The amendments made by this Act shall take effect on January 1, 2025.

The italicized words are not strictly necessary, but including them makes things clearer. Remember, however, that this form technically allows the bill itself to become effective upon enactment (by default) while postponing the effectiveness of the amendments; and if there is anything in the bill that has possible significance other than the amendments themselves you may want to omit those words or use the form "*This Act and* the amendments made by this Act...".

Either "shall take effect" or "shall become effective" (or "takes effect" or "is effective" if you are a devotee of the indicative mood) is proper when the effectiveness of the substantive provision involved is being tied solely to a particular date—they are totally interchangeable. But you should substitute "shall apply to", "applies to", or "shall apply with respect to"—the authors prefer the latter because it deals better with collateral matters—when the effectiveness of that provision is being tied to events. In this case the basic form would become:

SEC. ___. EFFECTIVE DATE.

This Act [or the amendments made by this Act] *shall apply with respect to [events of the relevant type] occurring* on or after January 1, 2025.

It should be noted that in all of the models presented in this subdivision, the use of the indicative mood—"takes effect", "is effective", or "applies" instead of "shall take effect", "shall be effective", or "shall apply"—would be equally correct. Many drafters prefer it, adhering to the rule that "shall" should be used only to impose a duty (see 21.5 and 22.2); the authors, as you will have observed, regard effective dates as permissible exceptions to that rule.

Note that if the effective date is simply intended to tell when an official may begin to exercise some function that the substantive provision vests in that official, or the substantive provision uses an amendment to some existing law to confer that function, it may be more convenient to weave the effective-date language into the text by placing it at the very beginning of the substantive provision instead of at the end (which would make it a first cousin to the "internal" effective dates discussed in 26.8). In the first case, the opening sentence of the substantive provision might then read "*On and after [or with respect to events of the relevant type occurring on or after] January 1, 2025*, the Secretary may…"; and in the second it might read "*Effective January 1, 2025*, the XYZ Act is amended…".

Before leaving the subject of effective-date form and style, there are several points that should be emphasized.

First, it is important to be precise, whatever form you are using. A provision that reads "This Act shall take effect six months after its enactment" invites confusion, especially if the bill will operate on a monthly or other periodic basis. It is always safest to tie a bill's effectiveness to a definite day; for example, "This Act shall take effect *180 days after the date of enactment of this Act*", "This Act shall take effect *at the end of the 180-day period beginning on the date of enactment of this Act*", "This Act shall take effect upon the expiration of *six months after the month in which* this Act is enacted", or "This Act shall take effect *on the first day of the sixth month beginning after* the date of enactment of this Act".

Second, as indicated earlier, special effective dates for particular provisions in a bill (and internal effective dates) are always permissible even though the bill also has a general effective-date provision, if it seems desirable for any reason, so long as the general effective-date provision adequately warns the reader that there are exceptions.

Third, special effective dates at the beginning of the substantive provision involved (instead of at the end) are always appropriate when only a few sections of the bill need explicit effective dates—for example, "Effective January 1, 2025, any person who…". They are particularly useful in writing serial amendments (see 17.2); thus "Effective January 1, 2025, section 123 of the ABC Act is amended—". And they have a special value in cases where the provision involved amends an existing law to phase in a quantitative change (such as an increase in rates or dollar amounts) over a period of time.

In the latter case, for example, if a dollar figure in some existing formula is to be increased by $300 in three equal increments over a three-year period and the entire formula has to be rewritten each time an increment is added, you can simply write the three amendments in consecutive subsections and begin each of them with its own effective-date language; the first could begin "(a) Effective January 1, 2025, section _____ [the formula] is amended…", the second "(b) Effective January 1, 2026, section _____ [the formula] is amended…", and the third "(c) Effective January 1, 2027, section _____ [the formula] is amended…", (with appropriate headings for each) so that each of the latter two, in effect, repeals the preceding one while enacting the new formula.

Fourth, an event-related effective date can always be tied either to events occurring "on or after [the key date]" or to events occurring "after [the day preceding that date]"—for example, either to "applications filed on or after May 1, 2025" or to "applications filed after April 30, 2025". The two forms are totally interchangeable. The only advantage of the "on or after" approach is that it does specify the key date, which may be helpful to the reader.

And finally, no matter what form you use, the adverbial phrase that indicates the time at which the provision or provisions involved will become effective (whether it is time-specific or event-related) need not actually specify a particular date at all. It is a very common practice, especially where the delay is intended simply to give time for adjusting to the new law, to measure the delay by the passage of time after enactment rather than by specifying a date. In such a case, the adverbial phrase in the basic form might read "shall take effect *30 days after [at the end of the 30-day period beginning on] the date of enactment of this Act*" instead of "shall take effect on January 1, 2025".

26.8 Internal effective dates

When it does not matter when the bill as a whole becomes effective, but it is thought desirable to postpone the exercise of some particular function for a while, it is a common practice to place the temporal limitation at the core of the relevant substantive section—not at the beginning or end of that section (or in a separate subsection or paragraph) but at the precise place where the function involved is being authorized. The section then has a built-in or "internal" effective date, without any effective-date "provision" to make it so.

For example, if the sponsor's policy is to make certain specified monthly benefits subject to new deductions, but only beginning with the benefits payable for some future month (say January 2025), the effective date might be handled either—

(1) externally, by stating the substantive rule without any temporal limitations—"there shall be deducted from any benefit…"—and then including somewhere else, either at the beginning or end of the section involved or at the end of the bill, an explicit event-related effective-date provision declaring that "[the section involved] shall apply only with respect to benefits payable for months after December 2024"; or

(2) internally, by including the temporal limitation in the substantive provision itself, stating that "there shall be deducted from any benefit payable for a month after December 2024" instead of simply "there shall be deducted from any benefit".

The two approaches get the same result. Some drafters prefer the separate effective-date provision (option (1) above) because it leaves the permanent substantive law uncluttered by dates that become history almost as soon as they are enacted, while others prefer the internal effective date (option (2)) because it eliminates any necessity for a separate effective-date provision or even because it does show the substantive provision's history on the face of the law. (See 6.6 for a more detailed discussion of the "split amendment" controversy.)

A somewhat different kind of internal effective-date provision involves bills that simply authorize or make appropriations for ongoing programs. Since the fiscal years for which the appropriations involved are being authorized or made are always specified—"There is authorized to be appropriated to the Secretary for fiscal year 2025…", for example—those bills too have built-in or "internal" effective dates.

27. Other Usages and Considerations

27.1 Numerals

When expressing a cardinal number, use figures rather than words—that is, say "12", "36", or "1,375" rather than "twelve", "thirty-six", or "one thousand three hundred and seventy-five". It not only is clearer (and much less cumbersome when the number involved is large), but it also makes it easier for both drafter and reader to find key numbers in a bill. Figures stand out from words in the statutory text when the pages of the bill are rapidly scanned.

And when expressing a number in its ordinal form, do likewise—say "10th" or "150th" rather than "tenth" or "one hundred fiftieth"—for the same reason.

These rules, which apply to fractions as well as to whole numbers, should always be followed when the number involved (or either of the numbers involved, in the case of a fraction) is 10 or more. In the case of numbers below 10, you have some flexibility. Most drafters begin using figures well below that level (partly for the reason given in the first paragraph above and partly because that is the form used in the law or bill being amended), but it is acceptable to spell them out. Small figures in a sentence may look peculiar on the page, and might be confusing because the cardinal "1" would often be just a synonym for "any" and the ordinals "1st", "2nd", and "3rd" are more relational than numerical.

Note the following possible exceptions regardless of the style you choose:

(1) If in a particular instance a number appears at the very beginning of a sentence, it is usually better to use a word (which can be capitalized) rather than a figure (which cannot).

(2) If the number appears in the middle of a provision that contains many section or paragraph references (which of course are numbers also) or a series of short, numbered clauses, it is sometimes confusing to add another figure to the pot, and it may be preferable to use a word instead.

(3) When two or more numbers are stated in a series or grouping that straddles your cut-off point, they should all be expressed in the same form. If you normally start using figures at "10", for example, either "8, 9, 10, or 11" or "eight, nine, ten, or eleven" would be correct—but not "eight, nine, 10, or 11".

One final word about numerals. Legal writers of old liked to express numbers by both words and figures, as in "sixty-five (65) years of age". This is nonsense; once is enough.

27.2 Provisos

Provisos are ancient stylistic devices originally intended for use in expressing conditions in sentences. They are awkward and confusing as well as archaic, and you should avoid them like the plague.

For what it is worth, a true proviso is recognizable by the italicized term *"Provided"*, *"Provided, however"*, or *"Provided further"*, which is always preceded by a colon and followed by the word "That" (always capitalized).

Provisos are commonly used by nondrafters and even by some experienced drafters to express simple exceptions and totally unrelated thoughts as well as conditions, probably because a proviso is an easy way to insert language without having to worry about its interrelationship with the surrounding words. But they make sentences long and cumbersome; and when a proviso is inserted in the middle of a sentence it is often impossible to determine where the proviso ends and the sentence proper resumes. In addition, they signal poor organization and often suggest that the thought expressed was an afterthought which, for convenience, the drafter inserted in the wrong place. The Offices of the Legislative Counsel of the House of Representatives and the Senate do not use them, and the Law Revision Counsel will not use them in the United States Code.

Anything that might be stated as a proviso would be better expressed in a clause beginning with "except that", "if", or "but", or in a separate sentence.

In all fairness, however, it must be admitted that there are one or two situations in which the use of a proviso may be permissible:

(1) When inserting new language into an existing provision that already contains a number of provisos (and there is no other place to put it), you should just grit your teeth and feel free to add another one.

(2) When the specific language you are inserting in a sentence of existing law will have to be cited or referred to in a later provision (and there is no other place to put it), using a proviso gives that language a designation by which it can be identified—the later provision might

then say, for example, "subject to the proviso in the first sentence of section 123".

When your sponsor wants to insert a legislative provision in an appropriations bill—a practice that is forbidden by the Rules of the two Houses of Congress unless the provision constitutes a "permissible limitation" (see 12.13 and 34.6)—the use of a proviso is often the best way to do it. It suggests that the provision involved is indeed only a limitation, and thereby helps (if there is any doubt about whether the limitation is "permissible") to downplay its legislative nature.

Note that the use of "provided that" (lowercase and unitalicized) as a simple conjunction—as in "The Secretary may hold a hearing, provided that adequate public notice is given of the time and place"—does not constitute a true proviso, and might be permissible, although a plain old "if" or "after" would be better English.

27.3 Gender

Codified rules of construction at the Federal (in title 1 of the United States Code) and State levels provide that masculine pronouns are to be read as including the feminine (that is, "he", "him", and "his" are read as meaning "he or she", "him or her", and "his or her", respectively), except where the context requires otherwise; and this rule is universally applied by the courts.

The use of the masculine pronoun alone is therefore legally sufficient, but it reflects a historic gender bias and (other things being equal) is objectionable on that account; and, in order to be inclusive of all individuals, such as those identifying as non-binary, all drafters should be on the lookout for ways to avoid the practice by using gender neutral language whenever possible. As *HOLC* suggests, it is preferable to do this by repeating the noun (or finding a gender-neutral synonym) rather than using personal pronouns (such as "he or she"; "him or her"). For example, if a particular provision leads off with a reference to "an individual" or "a claimant", repeat "the individual" or "the claimant" every place a pronoun would otherwise be used.

Gender bias also exists, of course, in words that use "man" or "men" as a prefix or suffix but are intended to designate people of either sex, so the drafter should be sensitive to these words as well.

Gender-neutral provisions are the goal. But keep in mind that good drafting requires stylistic consistency and clarity. If using a gender-neutral term would create ambiguity or confusion, you may in some instances have to fall back and rely on the classic statutory principle that the masculine includes the feminine unless the context requires otherwise.

27.4 Abbreviations

As a general rule, abbreviations should not be used in statutory language. It would always be a mistake, for example, to refer to a section—say section 5—as "sec. 5" in the text of a bill (even though the abbreviated form is used in the section's formal designation).

As you might expect, however, there are occasional exceptions to this rule. The most common involve parenthetical ("backup") citations to sources or locations of law. Thus, although a direct reference to a positive-law provision of the United States Code always spells out "United States Code", a parenthetical citation to a nonpositive-law provision of the Code for informative purposes (see 24.6) always abbreviates it, as in "(45 U.S.C. 509)".

The same is true in the case of parenthetical citations to the Statutes at Large, the *Federal Register,* the Code of Federal Regulations, and the treaty compilations; for example, "(89 Stat. 123, ch. 44)", "(19 Fed. Reg. 7521)", "(49 CFR 571.208)", "(TIAS 5639)" and "(UST 701)".

Although you may be tempted to abbreviate the term "United States" when using that term as an adjective, as in "U.S. participation in [some international organization]", it is more accurate (and therefore preferable) to say "participation by the United States in [some international organization]".

Using the abbreviation may be forgivable in a preamble to a resolution, or a statement of findings in a bill, both of which carry little substantive weight. Note, however, that you would never use the abbreviation when referring to the United States as a noun.

There is an increasing tendency to use acronyms in statutes, which is understandable and quite appropriate; obviously "NASA" is much more convenient than "the National Aeronautics and Space Administration" if you have to repeat it many times. But an acronym should be used in legislation only as a defined term, and not simply as an abbreviation; if you plan to use one you should use the full name once and define the acronym for subsequent uses, as in "The National Aeronautics and Space Administration (in this Act referred to as 'NASA') shall…".

Needless to say, this is another area in which you should be guided by the style manual of the jurisdiction in which you are working.

27.5 Rounding

Fractional quantities are almost always hard for administrators to deal with, and even harder for the affected persons to remember. In many cases, the application of a formula in calculating such things as benefit amounts, pay rates, or allotments of funds, especially if it involves percentages, results in untidy figures like $75.13 or $237.54 (in a benefit or pay-rate case) or $38,877.26 or $11,361,042.87 (in a per-State allocation case). The usual solution is to round the figure to some nice even quantity so that the odd cents or odd dollars are eliminated.

The rounding might be to a nearby even multiple of 10 cents (if the computed formula figure is very small), or to a nearby even multiple of $1,000 (if the computed figure is very large), or to anything in between. In some programs that start with an annual benefit or pay figure, that figure is rounded to the nearest $12 so that the monthly checks will be in even dollars. Most often the figure involved is rounded to the nearest multiple of $1.

The necessary language of a rounding provision is very simple—it is often just the final part of the last sentence in the formula and is never more than a single short paragraph. There are, however, a couple of things to keep in mind:

(1) Whatever number your sponsor selects for the purpose—10 cents, $1, or $1,000—you can round a figure (up) to the next higher multiple of that number, you can round it (down) to the next lower multiple of that number, or you can just round it to the "nearest" multiple of that number.

(2) If you choose to round it to the nearest multiple, however, you must be careful not to leave an "undistributed middle". Remember that if the computed formula figure is $6.50, for example, $6 and $7 are equally "near", and you must deal with that case specifically.

Section 215 of the Social Security Act (which governs the computation of social security benefits) is a hotbed of rounding provisions and contains all the different varieties in several combinations—you might look at it if you are interested in the subject (although you should disregard everything but the rounding provisions themselves if you want to avoid a headache). Two of those provisions, however, will give you most of what you are likely to need in the way of models:

> [(a)(1)(B)] (iii) Each amount established under clause (ii) for any calendar year shall be rounded to the nearest $1, except that any amount so established which is a multiple of $0.50 but not of $1 shall be rounded to the next higher $1.
>
> (g) The amount of any monthly benefit computed under section 202 or 223 which [after various reductions and deductions] is not a multiple of $1 shall be rounded to the next lower multiple of $1.

The Railroad Unemployment Insurance Act (in connection with the first algebraic formula stated in 23.7) takes a slightly different approach:

> (iii) Rounding Rule.—If the monthly compensation base computed under this formula is not a multiple of $5, it shall be rounded to the nearest

multiple of $5, with such rounding being upward in the event the amount computed is equidistant between two multiples of $5.

One final comment. Obviously you should never even consider rounding if the figures involved must add up exactly to some particular amount (which would be the case, for example, if those figures represented allocations to States from a fund that has only a specified dollar amount for that purpose). In such a case the odd cents and odd dollars must be allowed to stand, whatever the administrative inconvenience.

27.6 Bills and Acts

The term "Act" (with a capital "A") is reserved for legislative measures that have actually been enacted into law, and is the only term that is ever used in a bill to refer to a specific enacted statute.

A bill is headed "A BILL" when it is introduced, and it remains a bill in fact until it is enacted (although by convention the heading changes to "AN ACT" as soon as one house passes it). Thus in speaking and writing about a bill you should call it a "bill" even after one house has passed it and its heading has changed to "AN ACT" (at least until the President signs it); but it should refer to itself as an "Act" even at the moment of its introduction. It should say, for example, "section 8(b) of this Act"—never "section 8(b) of this bill".

Note that a joint resolution (the other type of legislative measure that can actually be "enacted") is headed "H. J. RES." or "S. J. RES." both when it is introduced and after it becomes law—the heading does not change—and it always refers to itself as a joint resolution (lower case).

27.7 Choosing the right antecedents

It frequently happens that a basic term or concept that is expressed early in a section will have to be referred to (once or twice, or many times) later on in that section or in other provisions of the bill; and how you express it the first time often determines how much trouble you will have in referring to it later.

The simplest and most obvious example of a case in which the choice of the right antecedent will make your job easier is a purely mechanical one, involving the way you cite a particular provision of your bill or of existing law. If the provision in which you are interested is subparagraph (A) of paragraph (1) of subsection (b) of section 102, you would normally cite it as "section 102(b)(1)(A)" (see 24.8); but citing it instead as "subparagraph (A) of section 102(b)(1)" will make it possible in later references to say simply "such subparagraph", which is considerably clearer and more precise (though no more accurate) than "such section".

Other examples are less mechanical, but choosing the right antecedent can be just as helpful. Here is a very simple one:

If your intention in a bill is to confer a benefit of some kind on elderly individuals but only when they can demonstrate that they are physically disabled, you might confer that benefit in either of two ways:

(1) The first time you mention the prospective beneficiary in the operative part of the bill (say in section 2), you might describe the beneficiary as "an individual who has attained age 65 and is under a disability", thus covering both requirements up front, as coequal aspects of eligibility.

(2) Or you might describe the beneficiary as "an individual who has attained age 65, subject to section 3 [the section dealing with disability]", thus leaving the requirement of disability to be handled separately as a kind of special limitation.

Either course would do the job—the choice might depend on any of several factors—but a later reference to "such an individual" or to "an individual described in section 2" might have one meaning if you took the former course and another if you took the latter.

There is nothing complicated or esoteric about these thoughts, but you can ease your task (and avoid the necessity of periodically going back and revising the earlier expression) if you keep them in the back of your mind as you write.

27.8 Case study: A reality check

Before moving on to the role of the courts and the idiosyncrasies of Federal forms and styles, this seems an appropriate place to look at the following case, which is a good example of the challenges that the drafter faces when confronted with a problem that appears to materialize suddenly and that legislators rush to address in legislation.

Background. In February 2006 a story broke about a pending takeover by Dubai Ports World, a company owned and controlled by the Government of the United Arab Emirates, of London-based Peninsular & Oriental Steam Navigation (P&O), a British company that at the time was responsible for the operations of six major U.S. seaports. Dubai Ports World would reportedly then take over those port operations. In a matter of days, there arose a national uproar over the threat to the national security of foreign interests controlling the ports and, presumably, the cargo that entered and left the United States. Congressional response was swift; some of the bills introduced on the heels of this crisis are discussed below, together with some of the issues that the drafter would raise with the sponsor to ensure that the policy expressed is what was intended.

Drafting challenges. The major challenges facing the drafter in this case before being able to evaluate a legislative proposal included the following:

(1) What was the legal relationship among the companies and the seaports that would allow Dubai Ports World to take over port operations from P&O? This is an example of a case in which the sponsor should bear some responsibility for providing the facts. In many cases, to the extent that a sponsor's constituency is generating the legislative proposal, the sponsor has better access to the facts. In this case, news accounts, information obtained from port authorities, and the Congressional Research Service were all sources of information.

(2) Could Federal law under the Constitution prohibit this sort of corporate takeover? Was there any law that addressed the issue and, if so, how did it apply in this case?

(3) What objective did the client hope to achieve in the legislation?

Results of research. Research into the matter revealed the following:

(1) The ports, owned by port authorities, themselves quasi-governmental entities, leased operations of the ports under their control to the British company.

(2) By acquiring the British company, the United Arab Emirates company would assume the lease obligations of the British company and, therefore, port operations under the leases.

(3) Although it would seem that no law would prevent one company from acquiring another, there was a provision of law (section 721 of the Defense Production Act of 1950 [50 U.S.C. 4565; in 2006, the citation was 50 U.S.C. App. 2170]) that—

(A) allowed the President or the President's "designee"[1] to make an investigation to determine the effects on national security of proposed mergers, acquisitions, and takeovers, by or with foreign persons that could result in foreign control of persons engaged in interstate commerce in the United States;

(B) required such an investigation if an entity owned or controlled by or acting on behalf of a foreign government seeks to engage in any merger, acquisition, or takeover that could result in control of a person engaged in interstate commerce in the United States that could affect the national security of the United States;

(C) authorized the President to take such action to "suspend or prohibit any acquisition, merger, or takeover, of a person engaged in interstate commerce in the United States … by or with foreign persons so that such control will not threaten to impair the national security"; and

(D) included some time periods for action and factors to consider with respect to national security.

(4) The President's "designee" under the statute (charged with conducting investigations under the statute) was, by Executive order, the Committee on Foreign Investment in the United States (CFIUS), chaired by the Secretary of the Treasury and made up of the heads of a number of other departments and agencies.

(5) No mandatory investigation of the effect on national security had been conducted under the statute of the proposed acquisition of P&O Ports by Dubai Ports World.

A look at the bills introduced. Consider the different approaches taken in several bills that were introduced on this issue over a very short period of time:

(1) *S. 2341* (introduced on February 28, 2006)—directed the President to exercise the authority under section 721 of the Defense Production Act of 1950 to prohibit the merger, acquisition, or takeover of P&O Ports by Dubai Ports World.

Comments: The issues that this bill raises include the following:

(a) The legislation stops the Dubai Ports acquisition but does not prevent similar mergers, acquisitions, and takeovers in the future.

(b) Directing the President to prohibit the deal under the statute may not have been possible, because the timelines for investigation and Presidential action under the statute had lapsed. This issue could have been addressed in additional provisions addressing the particular timelines in the statute that could be construed to prevent taking action under this bill.

(2) *H.R. 4817* (introduced on February 28, 2006)—

(A) prohibited any entity owned or controlled by a foreign government from—

(i) conducting operations at any seaport in the United States; and

(ii) entering into any contract or other agreement to conduct such operations;

(B) directed the President to issue regulations necessary to enforce the prohibitions;

(C) provided penalties for violators of the prohibitions;

(D) defined "foreign government" to include its agencies and instrumentalities and "United States" to include its territories and possessions; and

(E) had an effective date of February 28, 2006.

Comments: Some of the issues this proposal raises are the following:

(a) It is unclear what "conduct operations at any seaport" means; the term could arguably cover any contractor's activities at a seaport—providing food service or trash collection, for example; the result is that the President would have to define it in regulations and therefore determine the scope of the prohibition.

(b) There is no definition of "entity owned or controlled by a foreign government", so the term would mean whatever the regulations say it means.

(c) The prohibition would apply to any entity controlled by any government, even a staunch ally of the United States—a Canadian Government corporation, for example. It is unclear whether the regulatory authority of the President could allow for a definition under (B) that did not cover such a corporation.

(d) The bill would be retroactive if enacted (the effective date was the date on which the bill was introduced) and could potentially cause disruption in the port operations affected.

(3) *H.R. 4839* (introduced on March 1, 2006), had the same prohibitions as those in H.R. 4817, but clarified that—

(A) operations at seaports related to the import or export of cargo by vessel and the movement of cargo in connection with such import or export; and

(B) the prohibitions did not apply to individuals performing operations in the course of employment by another person.

The bill also had a delayed effective date (90 days after enactment) and a clarification that the prohibitions would not apply to contracts entered into before the effective date.

Comments: This bill differs from the others in several ways:

(a) It leaves less discretion to the President than does H.R. 4817 by its clarifications.

(b) It avoids an interpretation that would prohibit foreign nationals working for a U.S. company from being employed at a port.

(c) The delayed effective date addresses the port disruption issue.

(4) *H.R. 4833* (introduced on March 1, 2006, as the "Americans Securing American Ports (ASAP) Act")—

(A) directed the Secretary of Homeland Security to require that only United States persons (defined as U.S. citizens, entities at least 51 percent owned or controlled by U.S. citizens, and State and Federal government agencies and instrumentalities) may control security operations at seaports in the United States;

(B) required the Secretary to conduct background checks of each individual performing security operations;

(C) included regulatory, penalty, and employee exemption provisions as in the other bills; and

(D) had a delayed effective date of 90 days after enactment.

Comments: This bill also differed from others in several ways:

(a) This bill is limited to controlling security operations, but includes no definition of what is covered by "security operations"; this term would have to be defined entirely in regulations.

(b) The prohibition, rather than simply excluding entities controlled by foreign governments, excludes any entity other than a U.S. person from conducting the undefined security operations. In fact, foreign companies (like P&O) at the time conducted operations at U.S. ports, so there could be considerable disruption of port activities depending on how "security operations" was defined, even with a 90-day delayed effective date, because regulations would have to be issued before the bill language is clear.

(5) *H.R. 4807* (introduced on February 28, 2006)—

(A) directed the President (or the President's designee) to conduct an investigation, under section 721(b) (the mandatory investigation) of the Defense Production Act of 1950, of the Dubai Ports World takeover and to suspend any decision already made under the statute regarding the takeover;

(B) required certain elements to be included in the investigation;

(C) required reporting to Congress on the investigation, and briefing certain Members of Congress on the report; and

(D) required the President to prohibit the acquisition if a joint resolution was enacted into law[2] disapproving a determination of the President not to take action on the takeover.

Comments: This bill provides detailed instructions on how to investigate the Dubai Ports World deal but, as with S. 2341, would not address future mergers, acquisitions, or takeovers.

(6) *H.R.* 4814 (introduced on February 28, 2006), *H.R. 4820* (introduced on February 28, 2006), and *H.R. 4842* (introduced on March 1, 2006)—amended section 721 of the Defense Production Act of 1950 in different ways to establish procedures presumably to prevent the approval of a Dubai-type deal without a thorough investigation under that section.

Comments: The primary challenge of these bills would be to ensure the accuracy and consistency of the amendments to the law. For example, H.R. 4842 made procedural changes, with timelines, to the Defense Production Act (there was a technical error referencing the statute—a liability of drafting under pressure) but had a retroactive effective date that would make compliance regarding investigations commenced before enactment (that is, of the Dubai deal) impossible.

H.R. 4814 made changes to the law without an effective date (or more precisely, with the default effective date of date of enactment), so its applicability to ongoing investigations was unclear. However, the policy objectives of bills like this are arguably more forward-looking. A mechanism is in place for the executive branch to review mergers, acquisitions, and takeovers from the perspective of national security, and the purpose of these bills is to hone that mechanism.

As it happened, in the second session of the 109th Congress, both the House and the Senate passed separate bills (H.R. 5337 and S. 3549) amending section 721 of the Defense Production Act of 1950 to modify the procedures for determining the effect on U.S. national security of mergers and acquisitions; however, neither bill was enacted into law. But Public Law 110-49 (in 2007), and Public Law 115-232 (in 2018) substantially amended section 721 to provide detailed procedures for the Committee on Foreign Investment in the United States to follow in certain prospective mergers and acquisitions by foreign persons.

This case study zooms in on "a day in the life of" the drafter. Time constraints obviously prevented careful consideration of all aspects of the Dubai Ports World problem, but the example shows how, even within such extreme time constraints, one can still apply the basic tools of drafting to produce a reasonable work product.

Notes

1. Notice that the term "the President's designee" in section 721 of the Defense Production Act of 1950 is unnecessary, given that the President, under section 301 of title 3, United States Code, is authorized to delegate any function vested in the President by law. Why is this term used? One can speculate that Congress was recognizing that the President had a review process in place before the law was enacted.

2 Such a joint resolution, if it passed both Houses of Congress, would probably have to overcome a presidential veto.

PART VII

THE ROLE OF THE COURTS

28. Statutory Construction

28.1 General Comments

Statutes do not exist in a vacuum, and legislative language does from time to time have to be interpreted. To meet this need there has developed over the years a substantial body of rules, or canons, of statutory construction—rules of thumb that courts (and administrators) can apply in determining legislative intent and attributing meaning to legislative expressions that might otherwise be unclear. These rules determine how statutes are construed by the courts and administrative tribunals. A drafter without any knowledge of these rules runs the substantial risk of drafting legislation that leads to unexpected consequences.

The rules of statutory construction may not reflect the political realities that determine how, and the time constraints under which, a statute is drafted. A court studies the words of a statute that are in dispute, considering multiple possibilities in ascribing meaning to them. The reality may have been that the language was composed hurriedly without the kind of analysis done by the courts. The knowledge that the canons attribute to the legislature (described below) may be lacking, to say the least.

Nevertheless, to say that the drafter need not be concerned with rules of statutory construction because they will be applied only to resolve ambiguities and inconsistencies or supply omissions that should not arise if the drafter has done a good job, is a myopic view.[1] Circumstances arise that the sponsor or the drafter does not or could not foresee. Moreover, later enacted statutes drafted by others create inconsistencies with earlier ones. And the rules are not intuitive. The drafter should have some knowledge of the rules in order to advise a sponsor who may insist on particular language of the likely consequences should a court apply an applicable rule of construction to that language.

The canons of statutory construction are based on assumptions the courts and administrative tribunals make about the legislature. While you may find that these assumptions are inconsistent with your experiences on how the legislative process actually works, these assumptions are so fashioned as means of construing legislation by the courts and administrative tribunals, given the limitations of these bodies in construing statutes based on what is officially set forth as the legislative history. Nevertheless, knowing the canons of statutory construction provides one insight into how the judicial branch might construe the statutes you draft and the accompanying legislative history.

There is a presumption that lawmakers, in enacting a statute, had knowledge of and took into account existing laws on the same subject (*Erlenbaugh v. U.S.*, 409 U.S. 239, 244 [1972]); another rule of construction requires explicit language expressing the intent of the legislature to contravene certain fundamental legal principles.[2] Indeed the Supreme Court assumes that Congress legislates with knowledge of the Court's basic rules of statutory construction (*McNary v. Haitian Refugee Center, Inc.*, 498 U.S. 479, 496 [1991]). The drafter should be aware of what those assumptions are. Certainly in the case of an individual drafting in a State or other jurisdiction in which rules of construction are codified, they need to be part of the drafter's lexicon (see chapter 35).

It is not the intent or within the scope of this book to set forth in detail all of the rules of statutory construction. Major textbooks and treatises and innumerable periodical articles have been written on statutory construction. The leading American treatise is *Statutes and Statutory Construction*.[3] Nevertheless, this chapter will attempt to address the subject in order to give a quick brief on the most salient principles from the drafter's point of view.

Keep in mind the "rules of thumb" aspect of these canons, because they are not necessarily consistent; "[c]anons of construction need not be conclusive and are often countered, of course, by some maxim pointing in a different direction" (*Circuit City Stores, Inc. v. Adams*, 532 U.S. 105, 115 [2001]). Much of the case law involves a battle between the canons. If nothing else, the canons reinforce the responsibility of the drafter to choose each word carefully.

28.2 Theories of statutory interpretation

Legal scholars have posited a number of theories of statutory interpretation to help explain the case law interpreting statutes. Three are *intentionalism*, in which the interpreter identifies and follows the original intent of the drafters of the statute; *purposivism*, in which the interpreter chooses an interpretation that best carries out the statute's purpose; and *textualism*,[4] in which the interpreter follows the "plain meaning" of the statute.[5] However, cases often do not fall neatly into any one of these categories in a specific context.

To the extent that the inquiry into the intent or purpose of a statute goes beyond the language of the statute to other sources, like legislative history,[6] that are often beyond the control of the drafter, the drafter cannot anticipate the inquiry through preemptive language. However, intentionalism and purposivism do underscore the drafter's responsibility to be absolutely certain of what the sponsor's intent and purpose (that is, the policy) is from the get-go, so that the intent and purpose are clearly reflected in the language.

An example of the search for the intent and purpose of a statute, despite what the words say, can be found in *Church of the Holy Trinity v. United States*, 143 U.S. 457 (1892), a case cited for the principle that the courts will not follow the literal language of a statute, including a "scrivener's error" (a drafting error), if to do so would produce an absurd result that the legislature would never have intended.[7] In that case, a law prohibiting anyone from contracting with an alien to pay his transportation to the United States to perform labor *or service* of any kind was held not to apply to a church hiring an alien to serve as a pastor and paying his expenses to bring him to the United States. The Court, in order to reach this result (143 U.S. at 463), looked to the title of the law, "An act to prohibit the importation and migration of foreigners and aliens under contract or agreement to perform labor in the United States, its territories, and the District of Columbia", and decided that

> … the thought expressed in this reaches only to the work of the manual laborer, as distinguished from the professional man. No one reading such a title would suppose that congress had in mind any purpose of staying the coming into this country of ministers of the gospel, or, indeed, of any class whose toil is that of the brain.

It is intriguing to note that the Court based its reasoning on the *title* of the law rather than the text, which specifically covered services in addition to labor. The Court determined that the "evil" the law was designed to remedy was the influx of cheap unskilled labor. The Court based this determination on extrinsic sources, including a district court judge's analysis in another case. "It was never suggested that we had in this country a surplus of brain toilers, and, least of all, that the market for the services of Christian ministers was depressed by foreign competition." (143 U.S. at 464).[8]

Even though in *Holy Trinity* the Court rewrote the words in the statute, the starting point was still the statute. As a practical matter, the drafter should assume that the courts will approach any issue of statutory construction using a textualist analysis. Even if other approaches are followed, the bill's text begins the analysis and, in many instances, ends it as well.

28.3 The basics

The canons of statutory interpretation that courts may apply can be grouped into three main categories:

(1) Textual canons—inferences drawn from the words of the statute at issue, their grammatical placement, and their relationship to other parts of the statute as a whole.

(2) Extrinsic source canons—principles regarding which materials extrinsic to the statute (like other laws, the common law, and legislative history) can be used to interpret the statute.

(3) Substantive canons—presumptions drawn from the common law, other statutes, and the Constitution.[9]

28.4 Textual canons

Since the logical starting point in interpreting a statute is the language itself,[10] the textual canons are obviously very important to the drafter who crafts the language.

Plain meaning rule. If the meaning is clear from the language of the statute, the inquiry ends. The plain meaning rule will be the first rule of statutory construction a court will apply. Or, rather, the rule should be qualified somewhat: "If the statutory language is unambiguous, *in the absence of 'a clearly expressed intent to the contrary,* that language must *ordinarily* be regarded as conclusive'. " (*United States v. Turkette,* 452 U.S. 576, 580 [1981] [emphasis added], quoting *Consumer Product Safety Commission v. GTE Sylvania, Inc.*, 447 U.S. 102, 108 [1980]).

The inquiry then becomes what "plain" means. Words, unless otherwise defined by the statute, will be interpreted consistently with their ordinary, contemporary, common meaning (*Mallard v. United States District Court*, 490 U.S. 296, 301 [1989]; *Schindler Elevator Corp. v. U.S.*, 563 U.S. 401, 407 [2011]). To determine this, the Supreme Court has increasingly relied on dictionaries to determine meaning; as a result, a "junior cottage industry of dictionary shopping by counsel" has arisen.[11] What happens when a word has more than one common meaning?

This book has stressed the importance of using definitions to avoid ambiguity. Beware of using a word with more than one meaning; define the term to clarify which usage of the word is intended.

Specific textual canons. The following are some specific textual canons that can affect the drafter.

Noscitur a sociis—a thing shall be known by its associates. When words of similar meaning but not equally comprehensive are grouped together, the more specific word limits the general. In *Gustafson v. Alloyd Co., Inc.* 513 U.S. 561 (1995), the Court looked at the following definition in the Securities Act of 1933:

> The term "prospectus" means any prospectus, notice, circular, advertisement, letter, or communication, written or by radio or television, which offers any security for sale or confirms the sale of any security.

Applying *noscitur a sociis*—"a word is known by the company it keeps" (513 U.S. at 575)—the Court made the following analysis:

> From the terms "prospectus, notice, circular, advertisement, or letter," it is apparent that the list refers to documents of wide dissemination. In a similar manner, the list includes communications "by radio or television," but not face-to-face or telephonic conversations. Inclusion of the term "communication" in that list suggests that it too refers to a public communication.

The courts rely on the doctrine of *noscitur a sociis* "to avoid ascribing to one word a meaning so broad that it is inconsistent with its accompanying words, thus giving 'unintended breadth to the Acts of Congress.'" (*Gustafson v. Alloyd Co., Inc.*, 513 U.S., *supra*, 575, quoting *Jarecki v. G. D. Searle & Co.*, 367 U.S. 303, 307 [1961]).

Ejusdem generis—of the same kind. "[W]hen a general term follows a specific one, the general term should be understood as a reference to subjects akin to the one with specific enumeration." (*Norfolk & Western Ry. Co. v. Am. Train Dispatchers Ass'n*, 499 U.S. 117, 129 [1991]).[12]

Noscitur a sociis and *ejusdem generis* are statutory construction cousins that guide the search for meaning by looking at words in context; one can ascertain the meaning of a word in a statute by looking at other words with which it is associated. These canons presume that "people use lists to illustrate coherent patterns" and, consequently, broad regulatory duties or exemptions should not be inferred without a clear indication from the legislature.[13] As *Dickerson* (page 49) points out, however, the principle of *ejusdem generis*, for example, will not indicate what falls between the specific term and the general,[14] so here is another case in which the drafter needs to be as specific as possible when creating any kind of list, including lists of duties or exemptions.

Canons of negative implication. If the legislature includes particular language in one section but excludes it in another, the legislature acts intentionally in doing so; and *inclusio [expressio] unius est exclusio alterius* (the inclusion [expression] of one thing suggests the exclusion of all others], or what is not prohibited is allowed). "Where Congress explicitly enumerates certain exceptions to a general prohibition, additional exceptions are not to be implied, in the absence of a contrary legislative intent." [15]

These canons can lead to odd results, depending on the context. The following example illustrates the point:

> If Mother tells Sally, "You can have one cookie and one brownie," Sally is not allowed to have a candy bar, because the instruction reflects a background rule of "no sweets unless authorized." But if Mother tells Sally, "Don't hit,

> choke, or kick your sister," and Sally immediately pinches and pushes her sister, Sally cannot legitimately argue that pinching and pushing were implicitly authorized because they were omitted from the prohibition, notwithstanding *inclusio unius.*[16]

The rule of "negative implication" highlights the importance of using language consistently in drafting. Including words in a phrase in one place and not another can lead to the statutory interpretation that the meaning is not supposed to be the same in both places. An example of this is using the word "including" in one place and the words "including, but not limited to" in another. While the word "including" followed by a list of examples would not, under the dictionary meaning of "including" as indicating a part of a larger whole, be considered to be limited to the matters contained in the list, a court, coupling negative implication with the rule against surplusage discussed in the next paragraph, may determine that the word "including" is meant to exclude anything not listed because the words "but limited to" do not appear with it.

Whole act rule. A court looks at the entire statute in interpreting any part of it. Under this rule, a provision otherwise ambiguous can be clarified by the remainder of the statute. The principle here is to make the whole Act harmonious, a principle that follows from the duty of the courts "to construe statutes, not isolated provisions" (*Gustafson V. Alloyd Co. Inc.*, 513 U.S. 561, 568 [1995]). Presumptions embodied in this principle are that the same word used multiple times in a statute should be given the same meaning, that every statutory term adds something to a law's regulatory impact (the rule against surplusage), that a change in wording denotes a change in meaning,[17] and that the legislature does not want one provision to undercut others.

The courts may, in looking at the "whole act", take into account the title of a bill and section and other subdivision headings if something is otherwise ambiguous (*Brotherhood of R. R. Trainmen v. Baltimore & O. R. Co.*, 331 U.S. 519, 528–529 [1947]):

> [T]he title of a statute and the heading of a section cannot limit the plain meaning of the text... . For interpretative purposes, they are of use only when they shed light on some ambiguous word or phrase. They are but tools available for the resolution of a doubt. But they cannot undo or limit that which the text makes plain.

Remember that in the *Holy Trinity* case discussed above, the Court based its findings in part on the long title of the Act in question. *Brotherhood* appears to narrow *Holy Trinity* by requiring that the language of the statute be ambiguous before looking at the title to interpret the statute. However, the *Brotherhood* case is a warning to the drafter to choose the words for a bill's title and captions carefully.

The whole act rule can create difficulties for the drafter who does not have control over the entire piece of legislation moving forward. The rule is based on the assumption that "the legislature writing a statute is a single-minded and omniscient author", an assumption "strongly at odds with actual legislative practice, where ... duplication occurs for reasons of emphasis or even just oversight, and compromises may yield provisions that are in tension with one another."[18] It is undoubtedly the case, particularly in the U.S. Congress, that much legislation is bundled together, frequently at the last minute, from a variety of sources and drafters, so that looking for consistency in such a megabill would hardly reflect the "intent" of Congress. But the whole act rule does reflect many of the golden rules regarding consistency, word usage, and grammar that the drafter should follow.

28.5 Extrinsic source canons

To interpret a statute, courts may look to sources outside the statute, such as the common law, the statute's legislative history, and an agency's interpretation of the statute. The question here is when these extrinsic sources are to be consulted (see the discussion of theories on statutory interpretation in 28.2). The plain meaning rule seems to say that extrinsic sources should not be consulted unless textual sources cannot provide a clear answer to the matter in dispute.[19] However, there are differences in how a court determines that language is ambiguous and therefore warrants consulting extrinsic sources.[20] And a court may consult extrinsic sources even if the language of the statute is clear on its face "if reliance on that language would defeat the plain purpose of the statute."[21]

The degree to which a court will use legislative history (or other sources) cannot be predicted. The importance of this to the drafter arises when a sponsor chooses to address an issue in a committee report, for example, rather than develop statutory language. In such a case, it is the drafter's responsibility to advise the sponsor that a court will always look to the legislative language first, may never look at the report, and will not favor report language over the language in the statute if there is a potential conflict between the two.

Much discussion has surrounded the statements accompanying the President's signature on legislation. These are statements that express the President's interpretation of the laws that are enacted with the President's signature. The jury is still out on the effect of these statements, particularly on statutory interpretation by the courts. However, to the extent a sponsor wants to craft legislation to nullify one of these statements, the drafter needs to know what is being nullified. This is not to suggest the need to read all of these statements; however, they should be on the drafter's radar screen.

A court may also look to other statutes or the common law in order to determine the meaning of those terms in the statute at issue. This is another compelling reason for the drafter to define terms to the greatest extent possible. It is virtually impossible to be aware of every use, in other statutes and cases, of every word the drafter uses in a bill.

28.6 Substantive canons

Substantive canons "attempt to harmonize statutory meaning with policies rooted in the common law, other statutes, and the Constitution";[22] they may be stated as a presumption or a direction that a particular type of statute be construed liberally or strictly. While all the canons will require some subjective judgment by a court, a direction that something be construed "liberally" or "strictly" requires more. Several of these substantive canons that a drafter may confront on a regular basis follow.[23]

There are a number of rules and presumptions based on the Constitution; a description of some of the *Constitution-based canons* follows.

Avoidance of constitutional problems. An overriding principle is to avoid interpretations that would render a statute unconstitutional, unless the language of the statute is clear. "[W]hen 'a statute is susceptible of two constructions, by one of which grave and doubtful constitutional questions arise and by the other of which such questions are avoided, our duty is to adopt the latter.' " *Harris v. United States,* 536 U.S. 545, 555 (2002), quoting *United States ex rel. Attorney General v. Delaware & Hudson Co.,* 213 U.S. 366, 408 (1909).

Preservation of separation of powers. Corollaries of the preceding canon are the rules of construction relating to the preservation of separation of powers among the three branches of government, that is, the Constitution enumerates and separates the powers of the three branches of government, and the Constitution prohibits one branch from encroaching on the essential prerogatives of another. *Miller v. French,* 530 U.S. 327, 341 (2000), addressing the constitutionality of legislative restrictions on powers of the judiciary. See also *I.N.S. v. St. Cyr,* 533 U.S. 289 (2001): "when a particular interpretation of a statute involves the outer limits of Congress' power, we expect a clear indication that Congress intended that result" (533 U.S. at 299). Note, however, that the principle can be affected by national security concerns. See *Hamdi v. Rumsfeld,* 542 U.S. 507 (2004): "Whatever power the United States Constitution envisions for the Executive in its exchanges with other nations or with enemy organizations in times of conflict, it most assuredly envisions a role for all three branches when individual liberties are at stake." 542 U.S. at 536 (plurality opinion).

Federal sovereign immunity. "A waiver of the Federal Government's sovereign immunity must be unequivocally expressed in statutory text

... will not be implied ... [and] will be strictly construed in favor of the sovereign." (*Lane v. Pena,* 518 U.S. 187, 192 [1996]).

Federal-State relations. There are a number of canons relating to Federal-State relations; examples are rules against Federal preemption of traditional State functions[24] and against Federal abrogation of States' Eleventh Amendment immunity from lawsuits in Federal courts.[25]

Due process canons. There are a number of due process canons; these include the "rule of lenity", which is the rule against applying punitive sanctions if there is ambiguity with respect to criminal liability or a criminal penalty;[26] the rule against imposing criminal penalties absent specific legislative intent;[27] the rule against interpreting statutes to be retroactive;[28] and the presumption in favor of judicial review of agency action. "From the beginning 'our cases [have established] that judicial review of a final agency action by an aggrieved person will not be cut off unless there is persuasive reason to believe that such was the purpose of Congress.'"[29]

Common law canons. Some common law–based canons are the following: a presumption of following the common law usage where Congress has used words or concepts with well settled common law traditions;[30] and the rule against extraterritorial application of U.S. law.[31]

28.7 Additional canons

The following canons are also applied by the courts in interpreting statutory text; they may be applied as textual, extrinsic source, or substantive canons.

Statutory conflicts. There are a number of canons that courts can apply when statutes conflict with one another; these were discussed in 18.2:

(1) Repeals by implication are not favored.[32] A statute that is enacted will not be presumed to repeal a prior-enacted statute that is inconsistent, absent a clear intention by the legislature to the contrary, if the two statutes are "capable of co-existence".[33]

(2) The specific statute controls the general (see the next paragraph). In some cases, however, which of two statutes is general and which is specific may call for a subjective judgment.

(3) The more recent of two irreconcilably conflicting statutes governs. While the Court in Watt v. Alaska, 451 U.S. 259, 266 (1981), recognized this principle in addressing two statutes in apparent conflict regarding distribution of revenues from minerals extracted from certain public lands, the Court declined to find such an "irreconcilable" conflict "without seeking to ascertain the actual intent of Congress" (451 U.S. at 266); the Court then looked to the legislative history of the later-enacted statute and could not find an intent to repeal the prior law by implication. Given the language in *Morton v. Mancari* ("[w]here there is no clear intention otherwise, a specific statute will not be controlled by a general one, regardless of the priority of enactment" [417 U.S. 535, 550–551], and "the only permissible justification for a repeal by implication is when the earlier and later statutes are irreconcilable" [417 U.S. at 550]), a court will probably apply this "primacy of the last enacted statute" principle only as a last resort.

The principles discussed in (2) and (3) can also apply within a statute: The specific provision overrules the general.[34] If there exists a conflict in provisions of the same Act, the last provision in point of arrangement must control.[35]

Role of precedent. What is the role of precedent when courts interpret the text of a statute? Three principles apply, although only the latter two are directly relevant to the drafter:

(1) Under the principle of *stare decisis,* once a statute has been construed by the highest court of a jurisdiction, that precedent affects subsequent interpretations of the statute. Departure from precedent is exceptional; this is especially true where the principle has become settled through "iteration and reiteration over a long period of time".[36] In the case of the Supreme Court, the precedent is to be given an even stronger *stare decisis* effect than other Supreme Court precedents.[37]

The Supreme Court contravened this principle of stare decisis in *Dobbs v. Jackson Women's Health Organization*, 142 S. Ct. 2228 (2022), in which the court overruled its 1973 decision *Roe v. Wade*, 410 U.S. 113 (1973).

(2) If the legislature reenacts, without change, a statute that had previously received long continued executive or judicial construction, the legislature normally can be presumed to be adopting that construction.[38]

(3) If the legislature adopts a new law incorporating sections of a prior law, the legislature normally can be presumed to have had knowledge of the interpretation given the incorporated law.[39]

The second of these presumptions is relevant when amending a statute such that the amendment, even though it makes substantive changes, also in effect reenacts existing language without change, as in an amendment of a provision "to read as follows". In the case of a drafter in a jurisdiction where every bill has to restate the existing law with the changes included, this second presumption is relevant in every case, unless the courts (or statutes) in the jurisdiction do not follow this presumption.

The third presumption is an additional factor to keep in mind when "borrowing" provisions from another statute, since the danger in such a case is that the borrowed language, if the courts have construed it in a certain way, may not fit the policy being expressed.

28.8 Appropriations Acts

At the Federal level, there are a number of specific interpretation issues that arise regarding appropriations Acts and their relationship to authorizing legislation. The following are a few guidelines, although the "canons" are not consistent:[40]

(1) Although congressional rules prohibit "legislating" in an appropriations Act (see 12.13 and 34.6), it does happen, particularly at the end of a session of Congress when appropriations bills may be the "only train leaving the station". There are competing presumptions: on the one hand, there is a presumption that any change in existing law made by an appropriations Act is intended for only one fiscal year; on the other hand, an amendment to a general law is as binding as any other provision of law. In this case it is best to make it clear in the appropriations Act how long the legislation is to apply. See (3) below.

(2) An agency must follow its authorizing statute as much as possible in distributing funds even when amounts appropriated are less than authorized. However, under Federal law, an agency cannot distribute any more funds than those appropriated. Thus, if a certain amount of funds is earmarked in an authorization Act for a certain purpose, even if "subject to the availability of appropriations", and the agency concerned is appropriated less money than requested, but more than the earmark, the directions of the earmark will govern unless in direct conflict with other earmarks or clear language overruling the earmark. An example of this principle is the following:

> Agency A seeks $5,000,000 in appropriations. The authorization Act states, subject to the availability of appropriations, that $1,250,000 shall be used to build a facility at a given location. If Agency A is appropriated $3,000,000, the $1,250,000 must still be used to build the facility, even though Agency A received $2,000,000 less than requested.

(3) An appropriations Act can expressly limit or expand, beyond the authorizing statute, the purposes for which the money can be spent, or the period during which it can be spent.

(4) There is a presumption against the ratification of an agency action by appropriations (that is, the principle that Congress can, by appropriating funds, confer legitimacy on an agency action).

(5) If an appropriations bill clears the parliamentary hurdle of appropriating funds for something not specifically authorized, or authorized for a period shorter than the period of the appropriation, the appropriation provides the authorization for the use of the funds.

(6) If an agency has an appropriation for a specific purpose and a more general appropriation that might otherwise cover the specific purpose, the agency must use the specific appropriation. If an agency has two appropriations for the same purpose (and one not more specific than another), it can choose which appropriation and then must continue using the one it selected.

(7) Unless an appropriations Act specifically provides otherwise, funds appropriated in the Act are available for obligation for only one fiscal year, and unused funds revert to the United States Treasury.

(8) There are a large number of general provisions and specific restrictions that are included in an appropriations Acts and apply to the use of the funds appropriated. Especially since these laws tend to be extremely lengthy, a drafter needs to be aware of what they are or where to look for them.

All of these presumptions are of course rebutted where there is a clear statement by Congress to the contrary.

The drafter of authorizing legislation for an agency, for example, should be aware of appropriations laws that apply to that agency, particularly if there is a conflict between a provision in an appropriations law and the authorizing statute of the agency that may need to be addressed in legislation. In addition, a regulatory drafter should also be aware of the principles addressed in this subdivision, as they may affect programs to which regulations are addressed.

28.9 Facing the canons: Case studies

The drafter who is aware of the canons of statutory interpretation can work to include in the legislation being drafted specific language to address them, within the bounds of the U.S. Constitution (and, if drafting for a jurisdiction within a State, the constitution of that State), particularly to the extent that the sponsor's policy conflicts with the canons.

However, the following two case studies illustrate some of the difficulties in trying to anticipate a court's interpretation of a statute on the basis of the canons of statutory interpretation.

Same law, different holdings. Under the Clean Air Act (42 U.S.C. et seq.), State and local governments are required to develop plans to implement and enforce national air quality standards, and Federal facilities are subject to and are required to comply with these State and local requirements. In *People of California v. United States,* 215 F.3d 1005 (9th Cir. 2000), the Sacramento Air Quality District (SAQD), a local governmental entity, brought an action in State court against a U.S. Air Force base for violating air quality permits issued by the SAQD. The United States then removed the case to Federal court pursuant to the Federal removal statute in section 1442(a)(1) of title 28, United States Code, which allows actions against the United States that are brought in State court to be removed to Federal court. The issue was whether the following language, in section 304(e) of the Clean Air Act (42 U.S.C. 7604(e)), precluded removal to Federal court:

> Nothing in this section or in any other law of the United States shall be construed to prohibit, exclude, or restrict any State, local, or interstate authority from—
>
> (1) bringing any enforcement action or obtaining any judicial remedy or sanction in any State or local court, or
>
> (2) bringing any administrative enforcement action or obtaining any administrative remedy or sanction in any State or local administrative agency, department or instrumentality,
>
> against the United States, any department, agency, or instrumentality thereof, or any officer, agent, or employee thereof under State or local law respecting control and abatement of air pollution.

The court held that the "plain text" of this provision of the Clean Air Act "unequivocally demonstrates that Congress intended to prevent the removal of a covered action to federal court" (215 F.3d at 1011). Focusing on the language of the statute that guaranteed the rights of State and local governments not only to commence an enforcement action against the United States in a nonfederal forum, but to *obtain* judicial remedies and sanctions there, the court went on to say that "it is impossible to obtain judicial remedies and sanctions in state and local courts once an action is removed to federal court", because removal "necessarily divests state and local courts of their jurisdiction over a particular dispute."

The court, in the same case (at 1012), then looked to language in another environmental statute, the Clean Water Act, which was enacted the same year as the language at issue in the Clean Air Act and which had a specific provision allowing removal of actions brought against the United States under the Clean Water Act in State and local courts to be removed to Federal court. By "negative implication", the fact that the language did *not* appear in the Clean Air Act was persuasive that Congress "consciously foreclosed" the removal of actions brought under that Act.

The court also applied (at 1013) the canon that a general statutory provision does not trump a specific provision, holding that "though Congress intended to confer upon the federal government a general right of removal (under 28 U.S.C. 1442(a)(1)), it did not intend for the right to apply to actions brought by state and local governments pursuant to their own air quality laws".

The Eleventh Circuit reached the opposite result in *City of Jacksonville v. Department of the Navy,* 348 F.3d 1307 (11 Cir. 2003). It could not find a clear and manifest intention in the "plain language" of the Clean Air Act to preclude removal. Citing the principle in *Morton* v. *Mancari* that "when two statutes are capable of co-existence, it is the duty of the court ... to regard each as effective", it expressly disagreed with the Ninth Circuit holding. It found the "plain language" of the two statutory provisions not to conflict; therefore, the "specific controlling the general" canon did not apply; State and local governments may bring enforcement actions in State courts under the Clean Air Act, and the United States may remove them to Federal court pursuant to 28 U.S.C. 1442(a)(1).[41]

These cases could have been avoided with specific language in the Clean Air Act regarding removal. Congress, however, apparently had considered the issue; the Ninth Circuit found in the legislative history language precluding removal that was included in an early version of the 1977 amendments to the Clean Air Act but was later stricken. This may have been done for any number of reasons that drive the political process. The consequence was litigation.

The canons and the Constitution. The following case also illustrates the difficulty in trying to foreclose litigation even when following the Supreme Court's instructions with respect to a particular canon of interpretation—especially one rooted in the Constitution.

The Supreme Court, in *Atascadero State Hosp. v. Scanlon,* 473 U.S. 234 (1985), held that Congress "must express its intention to abrogate the Eleventh Amendment [States' immunity from suit] in unmistakable language in the statute itself" (473 U.S. at 243), if the States consent to suit or Congress is acting pursuant to its authority to enforce the Fourteenth Amendment to the Constitution (which prohibits states from abridging the rights and immunities of, or denying due process to, its citizens).[42] Congress wanted to clarify that States could be sued for patent infringement under title 35, United States Code. Congress, using *Atascadero* as its guide, enacted Public Law 102-560 (the Patent and Plant Variety Protection Remedy Clarification Act), which amended title 35, United States Code, by adding the following "unmistakable" language:

> **§296. Liability of States, instrumentalities of States, and State officials for infringement of patent**
>
> (a) IN GENERAL.—Any State, any instrumentality of a State, and any officer or employee of a State or instrumentality of a State acting in his official capacity, shall not be immune, under the eleventh amendment of the Constitution of the United States or under any other doctrine of sovereign immunity, from suit in Federal court by any person, including any governmental or nongovernmental entity, for infringement of a patent under section 271, or for any other violation under this title.[43]

> (b) REMEDIES.—In a suit described in subsection (a) for a violation described in that subsection, remedies (including remedies both at law and in equity) are available for the violation to the same extent as such remedies are available for such a violation in a suit against any private entity. Such remedies include damages, interest, costs, and treble damages under section 284, attorney fees under section 285, and the additional remedy for infringement of design patents under section 289.[44]

The law followed the Court's mandate in *Atascadero.* The Court, however, in *Florida Prepaid Postsecondary Education Expense Board v. College Savings Bank,* 527 U.S. 627 (1999), held the law unconstitutional; the Court's reasoning was that while Congress retains the authority to abrogate State sovereign immunity to enforce Fourteenth Amendment rights (protecting violations by States of the privileges and immunities of citizens [in this case protecting citizens with patent property rights against State infringers]) by "appropriate legislation", the language added to the patent law could not be justified on that basis. Congress failed to "identify conduct transgressing the Fourteenth Amendment's substantive provisions, and must tailor its legislative scheme to remedying or preventing such conduct" (527 U.S. at 639). There was insufficient evidence that "unremedied patent infringement by States had become a problem of national import" (527 U.S. at 641) to justify abrogating the sovereign immunity protections. The Supreme Court was apparently unwilling to abrogate State sovereign immunity, at least to protect patent rights. The lesson for the drafter in this case is to draft carefully with the canons of construction in mind, but that is only one ball in the air among many the drafter must juggle—including the many, and sometimes competing, provisions of the U.S. Constitution.

28.10 Summing up

The purpose of this chapter is to illustrate that the drafter should keep in mind how the courts may interpret statutory language at the time the drafter chooses words for the legislation. Careful drafting goes a long way toward preserving the intent of the legislature (as well as avoiding costly and needless litigation), but no statute is immune from judicial review. Being aware at the outset of the way a court may look at language may ensure an interpretation that the sponsor of the statute intended.

Notes

1 *Dickerson* (pages 47–50), for example, discards many of the rules as "irrelevant" and not helpful in a context different from that in which a statute is construed. However, "[a]s Justice Frankfurter put it in his famous essay on statutory interpretation, correctly reading a statute 'demands awareness of certain presuppositions.' " Some Reflections on the Reading of Statutes, 47 Colum. L. Rev. 527, 537 (1947)." Quote from *Bonds v. U.S.* , 572 U.S. 844, 857 (2014).

2 *Chickasaw Nation v. United States*, 534 U.S. 84, 95 (2001) concerning the canon against interpreting Federal statutes as providing tax exemptions unless those exemptions are clearly expressed; in addition, the substantive canons discussed later in this chapter illustrate this principle.

3 Norman J. Singer, Shambie Singer, and J .G. Sutherland, *Statutes and Statutory Construction,* 7th, and 8th ed. (St. Paul, Minn.: West Group, 2010, 2018) (commonly referred to as *Sutherland Statutory Construction*).

4 During the 1980s there arose the "new textualism", championed by Justice Antonin Scalia among others, which proposed that courts should not try to determine legislative intent, which is an incoherent concept. Scalia states that judges should almost never consult legislative history. For one thing, under the Constitution, legislative history (committee reports, floor statements, and similar materials) was not enacted into law; for another, how does one glean a collective intent of Congress from the varying statements made by different Members of Congress during the statute's consideration? The apparent plain meaning of the statute's text must be the basis of a court's interpretation—the meaning that a reasonable person would give the text. See William N. Eskridge Jr., Philip P. Frickey, and Elizabeth Garrett, *Cases and Materials on Legislation: Statutes and the Creation of Public Policy,* Fourth ed. (St. Paul, Minn.: West, 2001), 778–781, discussing Antonin Scalia, *A Matter of Interpretation: Federal Courts and the Law, an Essay* (Princeton: Princeton University Press, 1997).

5 See Eskridge, Frickey, and Garrett, *Cases and Materials on Legislation,* 849 et seq.

6 Legislative history refers to the record of the deliberation relating to the enactment of a law, including committee hearings and markups, the report of a committee accompanying a bill reported by the committee, floor statements, statements of managers of a conference between the two houses of a legislature to resolve differences on a bill, and even presidential veto and signing statements. This record would presumably also include the fact that a particular issue was not included in the deliberations.

7 This principle from *Holy Trinity* is also referred to as the "golden rule"; see William P. Statsky, *Legislative Analysis and Drafting*, 2nd ed. (St. Paul, Minn.: West Publishing Co., 1984), 81.

8 The drafter should not rely on a court to fix errors in legislation because the court would have to find the result to be "absurd" (not merely unreasonable) before the court would rewrite the words of a statute.

9 Eskridge, Frickey, and Garrett, *Cases and Materials on Legislation*, 848.

10 "Our analysis begins with the language of the statute." (*Lorillard Tobacco Co. v. Reilly*, 533 U.S. 525, 542 [2001]).

11 William N. Eskridge Jr., Philip P. Frickey, and Elizabeth Garrett, *Legislation and Statutory Interpretation*, 2nd ed. (New York: Foundation Press, 2006), 260.

12 The Court in this case went on to say that "[t]he canon does not control, however, when the whole context dictates a different conclusion" (499 U.S. 117 at 129) and found the principle not to apply in the case.

13 Eskridge, Frickey, and Garrett, *Legislation and Statutory Interpretation*, 262. See *Southwest Airlines Co. v. Saxon*, _U.S. _, 145 S. Ct. 1783, 1789-90 (2022) , in which the court applied the "*ejusdem generis* canon, which instructs courts to interpret a 'general or collective term' at the end of a list of specific items in light of any 'common attribute[s]' shared by the specific items."

14 The example *Dickerson* gives is "pines, firs, spruce, or other kinds of vegetation". While the canon will tell you that "other kinds of vegetation" includes vegetation of the same general kind as pines, firs, and spruce, it will not tell you which narrower class is intended; it could be trees, conifers, nondeciduous conifers, or the pine family of evergreens.

15 *Andrus v. Glover Construction Co.*, 446 U.S. 608, 616–617 (1980). See also *O'Melveny & Myers v. F.D.I.C.*, 512 U.S. 79, 85 (1994) ("matters left unaddressed in [a Federal regulatory] scheme are presumably left subject to the disposition provided by state law").

16 Eskridge, Frickey, and Garrett, *Legislation and Statutory Interpretation*, 263–264.

17 Eskridge, Frickey, and Garrett, *Cases and Materials on Legislation*, 866, lists this as a "weaker" presumption.

18 Eskridge, Frickey, and Garrett, *Legislation and Statutory Interpretation*, 271–272.

19 Ibid., 297. This "canon" was expressed in *West Virginia Univ. Hospitals, Inc. v. Casey*, 499 U.S. 83, 98–99 (1991): "The best evidence of [the statutory] purpose is the statutory text adopted by both Houses of Congress and submitted to the President. Where that contains a phrase that is unambiguous—that has a clearly accepted meaning in both legislative and judicial practice—we do not permit it to be expanded or contracted by the statements of individual legislators or committees during the course of the enactment process."

20 Larry Eig, *Statutory Interpretation: General Principles and Recent Trends*, Congressional Research Service, p. 44 (2014).

21 See *Bob Jones University v. United States*, 461 U.S. 574, 586 (1983), in which the revocation by the Internal Revenue Service of the school's tax exempt status under section 501(c)(3) of the Internal Revenue Code of 1954 was upheld because of the school's racially discriminatory policies.

22 Eskridge, Frickey, and Garrett, *Legislation and Statutory Interpretation*, 342.

23 The canons are excerpted from Eskridge, Frickey, and Garrett, *Legislation and Statutory Interpretation*, 392–397.

24 "When considering pre-emption, 'we start with the assumption that the historic police powers of the States were not to be superseded by the Federal Act unless that was the clear and manifest purpose of Congress.' " (*Wisconsin Public Intervenor v. Mortier*, 501 U.S. 597, 605 [1991], quoting *Rice v. Santa Fe Elevator Corp.*, 331 U.S. 218, 230 [1947]).

25 See *Atascadero State Hosp. v. Scanlon*, 473 U.S. 234 (1985) discussed in section 28.9. Congress subsequently amended the statute to overrule the Court's reading of the law in *Atascadero*. See *Hurst v. Texas Dept. of Assistive and Rehabilitative Services*, 482 F.3d 809, 812 (5th Cir. 2007).

26 But see *Chapman v. United States*, 500 U.S. 453, 463 (1991), clarifying that the rule of lenity does not apply "unless there is a 'grievous ambiguity or uncertainty in the language and structure of the Act' " (quoting *Huddleston v. United States*, 415 U.S. 814, 831 [1974]).

27 See *Whalen v. United States*, 445 U.S. 684 (1980): "If a federal court exceeds its own authority by imposing multiple punishments not authorized by Congress, it violates not only the specific guarantee against double jeopardy, but also the constitutional principle of separation of powers in a manner that trenches particularly harshly on individual liberty." (445 U.S. *supra*, 684, 689).

28 See, for example, *Gozlon-Peretz v. United States*, 498 U.S. 395, 404 (1991): "absent a clear direction by Congress to the contrary, a law takes effect on the date of its enactment".

29 *Bowen v. Michigan Academy of Family Physicians*, 476 U.S. 667, 670 (1986) (internal citation omitted). Shortly after *Bowen*, Congress amended the law to address the issues raised in the case.

30 This principle is discussed in *Carter v. U.S.*, 530 U.S. 255, 264–266 (2000) and in *Pasquantino v. U.S.*, 544 U.S. 349, 359–360 (2005), in which the Court clarified that the principle no longer applies if a contrary statutory purpose is evident.

31 *EEOC v. Arabian American Oil Co.*, 499 U.S. 244, 248 (1991): "legislation of Congress, unless a contrary intent appears, is meant to apply only within the territorial jurisdiction of the United States", quoting *Foley Bros., Inc. v. Filardo*, 336 U.S. 281, 285 (1949). One year after *Arabian Am. Oil*, Congress amended the statute (title VII of the Civil Rights Act of 1964) to overrule the Court's interpretation of the law. See also *Hartford Fire Ins. Co. v. California*, 509 U.S. 764 (1993) for a discussion of laws (antitrust) that have overcome the presumption against the extraterritorial application of U.S. law.

32 *Posadas v. National City Bank,* 296 U.S. 497, 503 (1936); *Morton v. Mancari,* 417 U.S. 535, 549 (1974); *Watt v. Alaska,* 451 U.S. 259, 266-267 (1981).

33 *Morton v. Mancari,* 417 U.S., *supra,* 551; *United States v. Borden Co.,* 308 U.S. 188, 198–199 (1939). See also *National Association of Home Builders v. Defenders of Wildlife,* 551 U.S. 644 (2007), applying the canons against repeals by implication to conflicting mandates in two statutes.

34 *Townsend v. Little,* 109 U.S. 504, 512 (1883); *Bulova Watch Co. v. United States,* 365 U.S. 753, 758 (1961).

35 *Lodge 1858, Am. Federation of Government Employees v. Webb,* 580 F.2d 496, 510–511 (D.C. Cir. 1978) (citing cases), *cert. denied* 439 U.S. 927 (1978).

36 See *Randall v. Sorrell,* 548 U.S. 230 (2006) (plurality opinion).

37 See *Hilton v. South Carolina Public Railways Com'n,* 502 U.S. 197, 202 (1991). "Considerations of *stare decisis* have special force in the area of statutory interpretation, for here, unlike in the context of constitutional interpretation, the legislative power is implicated, and Congress remains free to alter what we have done." *Hilton,* 502 U.S., *supra,* 202, quoting *Patterson v. McLean Credit Union,* 491 U.S. 164, 172-173 (1989).

38 See *Lindhal v. Office of Personnel Management,* 470 U.S. 768, 782, note 15 (1985).

39 *Lorillard v. Pons,* 434 U.S. 575, 580–581 (1978).

40 Excerpted generally from chapter V of *Principles of Federal Appropriations Law* (also known as the "Red Book"), a publication of the General Accountability Office, available online at *www.gao.gov/legal/appropriations-law/red-book.*

41 The court also doubted that it was Congress's intent to preclude removal when enacting the provisions of the Clean Air Act at issue in 1977, since at the time the removal statute in title 28 of the U.S. Code had not been amended to allow the United States or its agencies to remove actions to Federal court; hence the reference to "any other law" in the Clean Air Act did not contemplate removal to Federal court. 348 F.3d, *supra,* 1311.

42 This case held that a State had not waived its Eleventh Amendment immunity from suit in Federal court under the Rehabilitation Act of 1973, even though provisions under the Act were addressed to the States. Subsequently Congress enacted Public Law 99-506 (1986) specifically providing that States were not immune from suit in Federal court for a violation of the Rehabilitation Act or other laws prohibiting discrimination.

43 This language was duplicated in section 271 of title 35, United States Code, the provision defining infringers of patents.

44 Title 17, United States Code (relating to copyrights), in Public Law 101-553, and the Act of July 5, 1946 (commonly referred to as the "Trademark Act of 1946") (protecting registered trademarks), in Public Law 102-542, were also amended to include language similar to the title 35 amendments, specifically in section 511 of title 17, United States Code, and in sections 32(1), 40(b), and 43(a)(2) of the Trademark Act of 1946 (15 U.S.C. 1114(1), 1122(b), and 1125(a)(2)).

29. Significant Case Law for the Drafter

29.1 In general

While this book has already cited case law in the course of discussing different topics, the purpose of this chapter is to lay out several significant principles that the United States Supreme Court has adopted and the drafter is likely to encounter. Like chapter 28 on statutory construction, what is presented in this chapter is not exhaustive; it is hoped that it can provide an easy point of reference for the drafter when one of the following issues arises.

29.2 Tensions in the Federal system

The tension between Article VI, clause 2, of the United States Constitution, the "supremacy" clause …

> This Constitution, and the Laws of the United States which shall be made in Pursuance thereof; and all Treaties made, or which shall be made, under the Authority of the United States, shall be the supreme law of the Land; and the Judges in every State shall be bound thereby, any Thing in the Constitution or Laws of any State to the Contrary notwithstanding.

and the Tenth Amendment to the United States Constitution …

> The powers not delegated to the United States by the Constitution, nor prohibited by it to the States, are reserved to the States respectively, or to the people.

was discussed in 13.5 (preemption provisions) and 28.6 and 28.9 (canons of construction). While Federal law is "supreme", it must be justified by a provision of the Constitution.

The justification for many statutes rests squarely on a specific constitutional provision. Article I, section 8, has a long list of Congress's powers; section 9 has a list of what Congress cannot do; and section 10 has a list of what the States cannot do. But it is no secret that Article I, section 8, clause 3, which gives to Congress the power to regulate interstate and foreign commerce, has been proffered as the basis for many other statutes, particularly in areas not previously regulated by Congress.

29.3 The Commerce Clause

The Commerce Clause provides that "The Congress shall have Power … To regulate commerce with foreign Nations, and among the several States, and with Indian Tribes".

Although it looks like the "plain meaning" of the clause would limit

Congress's power to regulate commercial transactions between persons in one State and persons outside that State, the Commerce Clause has become the constitutional basis for a significant number of laws passed by Congress, including laws addressing national social problems.[1]

For many decades in the twentieth century, there seemed to be no limit on what Congress could regulate in the name of "affecting" commerce. In the 1942 case of *Wickard v. Filburn*, 317 U.S. 111 (1942), the Court held that the quota system for agricultural products under the Agricultural Adjustment Act applied to bushels of wheat that were homegrown and personally consumed, because economic activity, regardless of its nature, can be regulated by Congress if the activity "asserts a substantial economic impact on interstate commerce" (317 U.S. at 125). In other words, the effects of individual producers on a commercial market could be aggregated to find a substantial economic impact on interstate commerce.

Beginning in the mid-1990s, however, the Supreme Court handed down decisions that invalidate some statutes as exceeding Congress's power under the Commerce Clause.

In *United States v. Lopez*, 514 U.S. 549 (1995),[2] the Court summarized the three categories of activity that Congress could regulate under the Commerce Clause. First, Congress can regulate the use of the channels of interstate commerce (514 U.S. at 558); also see, for example, *United States v. Darby*, 312 U.S. 100 (1941) in which the Court held that Congress can prohibit the shipment in interstate commerce of goods produced for interstate commerce by employees whose wages and hours of employment do not conform to the requirements of the Fair Labor Standards Act, even if the goods were produced only within one State. Second, Congress can regulate the instrumentalities of interstate commerce (vehicles, for example), or persons or things in interstate commerce, even though the threat may come only from intrastate activities (514 U.S. at 558). And third, Congress can regulate those activities that "substantially affect interstate commerce" (514 U.S. at 558–559).

The Court in *Lopez* then proceeded to strike down as unconstitutional a Federal statute making it illegal for an individual "knowingly to possess a firearm at a place that the individual knows, or has reasonable cause to believe, is a school zone" (an area in and around a public, private, or parochial school). The Court held that the statute fell into none of the three categories, that it covered an intrastate activity that had nothing to do with economic activity, and that it was not an essential part of a larger economic regulatory scheme that would be undercut unless the intrastate activity were regulated (514 U.S. at 561-562). The link between gun possession and a substantial effect on interstate commerce was found to be attenuated. The Court did not accept the Government's arguments that the possession of guns may lead to violent crime, which affects the functioning of the national economy, and that the presence of guns threatens the educational process, which produces a less productive workforce, which in turn affects national productivity.

Lopez was followed in 2000 by *United States v. Morrison* (529 U.S. 598), in which the Court held as unconstitutional section 40302 of the Civil Rights Remedies for Gender-Motivated Violence Act (subtitle C of title IV of Public Law 103-322, the Violent Crime Control and Law Enforcement Act of 1994; 42 U.S.C. 13981),[3] which provided a Federal civil remedy for the victims of gender-motivated violence. Despite congressional findings (which were lacking in the *Lopez* case), the Court held that gender-motivated crimes were not economic activity and rejected the "costs of crime" and "national productivity" assertions in the findings (529 U.S. at 612-613), because to do otherwise would allow Congress to "use the Commerce clause to completely obliterate the Constitution's distinction between national and local authority" (529 U.S. at 615).

The significance of *Lopez* and *Morrison* for the drafter is that the cases underscore the need to keep in mind that there are boundaries, however limited they may be, to what Congress can do under the Commerce Clause. Congress may not "regulate noneconomic, violent criminal conduct based solely on that conduct's aggregate effect on interstate commerce" (529 U.S. at 617). The drafter should keep in mind the three bases for the proper exercise of authority set forth in *Lopez* and, with regard to the third ("substantial effect" on interstate commerce), remember that a statement of jurisdictional basis in the statute and express findings about the effect on interstate commerce are factors a court will look at, but so are whether the regulated activity is economic in nature and whether the link between regulated activity and the effect on interstate commerce is attenuated.

Nonetheless, the precise scope and limits of *Lopez* and *Morrison* are not entirely clear. The Court appears to find a link to interstate commerce that others might question under the standards set in those cases, if the stakes are high enough. Thus, in *Gonzales v. Raich,* 545 U.S. 1 (2005), the Court, finding homegrown marijuana for personal use akin to homegrown wheat in *Wickard v. Filburn*, held that Congress's Commerce Clause authority includes the power to prohibit the local cultivation and use of marijuana in compliance with a California statute. The Court found that Congress can regulate a purely intrastate activity that is not commercial (growing marijuana for personal consumption) if Congress concludes that failing to do so would undercut a regulation of the interstate market in the commodity (in this case the Controlled Substances Act that prohibited commerce in that commodity altogether) (545 U.S. at 18). In addition, the Court said that "the case for the exemption [from the Federal Controlled Substances Act] comes down to the claim that a locally cultivated product that is used domestically rather than sold on the open market is not subject to federal regulation. Given the findings in the CSA and the undisputed magnitude of the commercial market for marijuana, our decisions in *Wickard v. Filburn* and the later cases endorsing its reasoning foreclose that claim." 545 U.S., *supra*, 32-33.

The limits of Congress's Commerce power were tested again in a challenge to a provision of the Patient Protection and Affordable Care Act, enacted in 2010, requiring certain individuals who did not have health insurance to purchase that insurance or be charged a monetary penalty. In *National Federation of Independent Business (NFIB) v. Sebelius*, 567 U.S. 519 (2012), while no single opinion was supported by a majority of justices, a majority of justices appeared to agree that the Commerce Clause could not be a basis for compelling individuals to engage in commercial activity (i.e., purchase an unwanted product), that there must be economic activity to regulate, not inactivity. Therefore, the individual mandate was unconstitutional as an exercise of the Commerce Power. (The mandate did survive constitutional muster as an exercise of Congress's power to "lay and collect taxes". 567 U.S. at 563-564).

29.4 The Spending Power

Congress has the authority to "lay and collect Taxes, Duties, Imposts, and Excises, to pay the Debts and provide for the common Defence and Welfare of the United States". Under this clause, Congress may impose conditions under which Federal funds are accepted by recipients, most notably the States. In this way Congress may achieve "objectives not thought to be within Article I's 'enumerated legislative fields,' ... through the use of the spending power and the conditional grant of federal funds." *South Dakota v. Dole*, 483 U.S. 203, 207 (1987), quoting *United States v. Butler*, 297 U.S. 1, 65 (1936). *South Dakota v. Dole* set forth the parameters of Congress's spending power. Congress can attach conditions on the receipt of Federal funds, subject to the following:

(1) The expenditure must be for the general welfare.

(2) The conditions imposed must be unambiguous.

(3) The conditions must be reasonably related to the purpose of the expenditure.

(4) The conditions do not violate an independent constitutional prohibition.

The law in question—a provision in title 23, United States Code, that a State that did not increase its drinking age to 21 would lose 5% of its Federal highway funds—was held by the Court to meet these four tests.

The question as to when a condition would become unconstitutional under the spending clause remained open, until *National Federation of Independent*

Business (NFIB) v. Sebelius, 567 U.S. 519 (2012), discussed in 29.3. The provision of law in question was a condition that if a State did not adopt the major expansion of the Medicaid program contained in the Affordable Care Act, the Secretary of Health and Human Services had the authority to bar all future Medicaid payments to that State. In this case, the Court held that, in applying the test in *South Dakota v. Dole* of whether the financial inducement offered by Congress was "so coercive as to pass the point at which 'pressure turns into compulsion,' " *South Dakota v. Dole*, 483 U.S. 203, 211 (quoting *Steward Machine v. Davis,* 301 U.S. 548, 590 (1937)), the financial 'inducement' Congress has chosen is much more than 'relatively mild encouragement'—it is a gun to the head." 567 U.S. at 581. In *Dole*, the "penalty" was limited to a 5 percent reduction in highway funding. By contrast, Medicaid spending accounted for over 20 percent of the average State's total budget, with federal funds covering 50 to 83 percent of those costs. *Id.*

The drafter should be aware of these limitations on Congress's spending power; drafting Federal grant and other spending programs can be a major source of the drafter's workload.

29.5 Maintaining the "delicate balance"

The following cases address the relationship between the Federal Government and State governments.

Application of Federal statutes to State governments. Because of the tension between the Federal Government and the States, the Supreme Court is the arbiter of when and the extent to which Federal statutes apply to State governments. Among the canons of statutory interpretation are several relating to Federal-State relations: the rule against Federal encroachment on core State functions, the rule against Federal abrogation of States' Eleventh Amendment immunity from lawsuits in Federal courts, and the rule against Federal preemption of traditional State functions. The Court, in *Atascadero State Hospital v. Scanlon* (473 U.S. 234), said that "Congress may abrogate the States' constitutionally secured immunity from suit in federal court only by making its intention unmistakably clear in the language of the statute" (473 U.S. at 242). Even though *Atascadero* was an Eleventh Amendment case, "a similar approach is applied in other contexts. Congress should make its intention 'clear and manifest' if it intends to pre-empt the historic powers of the States" (*Will v. Michigan Dept. of State Police,* 491 U.S. 58, 65 [1989]). Included in these "state decisions that 'go to the heart of representative government' " is the authority of a State's people to determine the qualifications of their most important government officials (*Gregory v. Ashcroft,* 501 U.S. 452, 462 [1991], quoting *Sugarman v. Dougall,* 413 U.S. 634, 647 [1973]).

At issue in *Gregory v. Ashcroft* was whether a provision of the Missouri Constitution that required State judges to retire at age 70 violated the Federal Age Discrimination in Employment Act of 1967 (ADEA), which made it unlawful for an "employer" to discharge any individual who is at least 40 years of age "because of such individual's age". The term "employer" is defined in the statute to include "a State or political subdivision of a State"; the definition of "employee" specifically excludes elected officials and "an appointee on the policy-making level"; judges are not specifically excluded. The Court, applying the "clear statement" standard, decided that it would not read the ADEA to cover judges unless Congress made it clear that judges were included. While recognizing that "appointee at the policymaking level" would be an odd way to describe a judge, the Court held that the phrase was sufficiently broad that it could not conclude that the statute "plainly covers appointed state judges. Therefore it does not." (501 U.S. at 467).

The lesson of *Gregory* is that when issues of State sovereignty arise, including matters involving core State functions (like determining the qualifications of State officials), a Federal statute will not apply to the States unless the language doing so is crystal clear.[4] The drafter should, in drafting a regulatory scheme, raise with the sponsor not only the issue of the bill's applicability to the States, including State officials, but also the need for a basis in the Constitution for congressional action in the face of the Eleventh Amendment.

State regulatory schemes pursuant to Federal statutes. Another line of cases addresses the extent to which the Federal Government can require State governments to act. The distinction here appears to be that the Constitution confers upon Congress "the power to regulate individuals, not States", and therefore, "even where Congress has the authority under the Constitution to pass laws requiring or prohibiting certain acts, it lacks the power directly to compel the States to require or prohibit those acts" (*New York v. United States,* 505 U.S. 144, 166 [1992]).

Congress can *encourage* a State to regulate in a certain way or offer incentives to influence a State, for example—

- by attaching conditions to the receipt of Federal funds, if the conditions bear some relationship to the purpose of the Federal spending (505 U.S. 144 at 167); and
- by offering States the choice of regulating private activity (if the regulation is permissible under the Commerce Clause) according to Federal standards or having State law preempted by Federal regulation (505 U.S. 144 at 167).

The Court in *New York v. United States* analyzed a Federal statute regulating the disposal of low-level radioactive waste. While the Court upheld two provisions as not compelling the States to take an action, it struck down as unconstitutional under the Tenth Amendment a third provision. This provision offered States a "choice" between regulating according to Congress's direction, or taking title to and possession of the radioactive waste generated within their borders and becoming liable for damages that waste generators suffer as a result of the States' failure to act promptly. The Court found that neither choice, even on its own, would be permissible under the Constitution as an acceptable alternative to accepting congressional regulatory directions—the first in essence a command to State governments to implement legislation enacted by Congress; and the second a command that radioactive waste be transferred from the producers of the waste to the States, thereby compelling a State subsidy of the waste producers, and that the States assume liabilities of certain State residents: "A choice between two unconstitutionally coercive regulatory techniques is no choice at all." (505 U.S. at 176). Either way "the Act commandeers the legislative processes of the States by directly compelling them to enact and enforce a federal regulatory program" (505 U.S. at 176, quoting *Hodel v. Virginia Surface Mining & Reclamation Assn., Inc.*, 452 U.S. 264, 288 (1981).

Similarly, in *Printz v. United States,* 521 U.S. 898 (1997), the Supreme Court held as unconstitutional a provision in section 922 of title 18, United States Code, *requiring* the "chief law enforcement officer" of each State to conduct background checks of persons desiring to purchase handguns; Congress could not circumvent the prohibition on compelling the States to enact or enforce a federal regulatory program by conscripting the State's officers directly (521 U.S. at 935).

The drafter, therefore, in drafting or responding to the directions of any kind of Federal regulatory scheme, has to be sensitive to whether State governments are being compelled to act under that scheme—a result that would be unconstitutional.

29.6 Separation of powers

A number of landmark cases have addressed the balance of power among the branches of the Federal Government. Legislation that infringes on the separation of powers of the Federal Government can be constitutionally challenged.

The legislative veto. In *Immigration and Naturalization Service v. Chadha,* 462 U.S. 919 (1983), the Supreme Court struck down a type of provision in a statute that had become commonplace: the so-called "legislative veto", under which an action by an executive branch official could be invalidated by a resolution adopted by one or both Houses of Congress (*Chadha* involved a one-House veto). The Court held that resolutions like these are "legislative" in nature, because they modify rights and duties of individuals outside the legislative branch; and because they are legislative, they have to be presented to the President for signature or veto. In addition to violating the presentment clause, the one-House veto provision violated the requirement in the Constitution that legislation pass both Houses of Congress.

INS v. Chadha has become such settled law that it seems unlikely that a sponsor would propose a legislative veto-like provision, but it can happen. Many legislative veto provisions remain on the books, although they are ineffective after *Chadha.*[5]

Appointment of individuals performing executive functions. In *Buckley v. Valeo,* 424 U.S. 1 (1976), the Supreme Court held unconstitutional a provision of the Federal Election Campaign Act of 1971 under which the Speaker of the House of Representatives and the president pro tempore of the Senate appointed members of the Federal Election Commission, which was vested with "executive" functions like enforcing the law, conducting litigation, and determining eligibility for public funds. The Court held that under Article II, section 2, clause 2, of the Constitution only the President, with the advice and consent of the Senate, could appoint officers to perform such functions.

Because of *Buckley v. Valeo,* the drafter needs to be sensitive to the types of functions vested in an individual or a government body in proposed legislation if the individual or government body is *not* appointed by the President, by and with the advice and consent of the Senate; if the functions can be characterized as "executive", there is a constitutional problem.

President's authority to remove officers. In *Myers v. United States,* 272 U.S. 52 (1926), the Court held that Congress cannot restrict the power of the President to remove an officer of the United States appointed by the President with the advice and consent of the Senate. The officer who was the subject of that case was a postmaster.

In *Humphrey's Executor v. United States,* 295 U.S. 602 (1935), the Court narrowed the ruling in Myers to apply only to officers carrying out purely executive functions. The Court held that if the officer appointed by the President serves in an independent agency, like the Federal Trade Commission (FTC), charged with performing quasi-legislative or quasi-judicial functions, Congress can limit the grounds for removing the officer.

In reaching this conclusion, the Court analyzed the FTC and the type of functions vested in it. The Court found that the FTC was charged with preventing persons from engaging in unfair methods of competition and exercising judicial-like powers to do this; the Commission also had the power to investigate matters and subsequently report to Congress its recommendations. The Court concluded that the agency was nonpartisan, had to act with impartiality to perform its duties, and required persons as Commissioners who had appropriate expertise but would gain experience by their length of service on the Commission; its duties were neither political (in the sense of carrying out a political agenda of another in the government) nor executive.

One may argue whether there really is a distinction between the FTC's authorities and those of any executive department. For example, executive departments and agencies within them conduct adjudicatory proceedings routinely pursuant to statute; they are frequently required to study an issue and report back to Congress; and logic would seem to dictate that the expertise of an officer in the subject matter of the department or agency to which the officer is appointed would affect that officer's ability to perform the functions of the department or agency.

There is a significant distinction, however, between the FTC and the heads of other departments and agencies in that the statute creating the FTC provides that "[not] more than three of the [five] Commissioners shall be members of the same political party" (15 U.S.C. 41), thereby ensuring at least a bipartisan approach by those at the agency's helm. The Court in *Humphrey's Executor* based its ruling on the independent nature of the FTC in part on the legislative history to determine Congress's intent in creating the FTC.

Other independent agencies are structured like the FTC: the Federal Communications Commission, the Securities and Exchange Commission, and the International Trade Commission, to name a few.

Note, however, that *Humphrey's Executor* was distinguished in *Seila Law LLC v. Consumer Financial Protection Bureau*, 140 S. Ct. 2183 (2020), where a provision limiting the President's power to remove the head of the CFPB was declared unconstitutional. "The New Deal-era FTC upheld in *Humphrey's Executor* bears little resemblance to the CFPB. Unlike the multiple Commissioners of the FTC, who were balanced along partisan lines and served staggered terms to ensure the accumulation of institutional knowledge, the CFPB Director serves a five-year term that guarantees abrupt shifts in leadership and the loss of agency expertise. In addition, the Director cannot be dismissed as a mere legislative or judicial aid. Rather, the Director possesses significant administrative and enforcement authority, including the power to seek daunting monetary penalties against private parties in federal court—a quintessentially executive power not considered in *Humphrey's Executor*." 591 U.S. 207, 140 S. Ct., 2199-2201.

The drafter should, in creating a new commission or agency charged with carrying out a legislative mandate, try to determine whether the new entity is like one of the independent agencies in which the grounds upon which an officer in the entity can be discharged can be limited.

Marbury v. Madison. In *Marbury v. Madison,* 5 U.S. 137 (Cranch) (1803), the Supreme Court articulated the role of the Federal courts: "It is emphatically the province and duty of the judicial department to say what the law is ... If two laws conflict with each other, the courts must decide on the operation of each" (5 U.S. at 177). Furthermore, the Constitution is paramount to any act of the legislature; it is therefore, the role of the courts to determine whether an Act of Congress conflicts with the Constitution (5 U.S. at 177 178).

The judicial review function of the courts is so central that the issue would not seem to be one the drafter would face. Consider, however, the following bill, which passed the House of Representatives, in similar form, in both the 108th and 109th Congresses:

109TH CONGRESS

2D SESSION

H. R. 2389

AN ACT

To amend title 28, United States Code, with respect to the jurisdiction of Federal courts over certain cases and controversies involving the Pledge of Allegiance.

Be it enacted by the Senate and House of Representatives of the United States of America in Congress assembled,

SECTION 1. SHORT TITLE.

This Act may be cited as the "Pledge Protection Act of 2005".

SEC. 2. LIMITATION ON JURISDICTION.

(a) IN GENERAL.—Chapter 99 of title 28, United States Code, is amended by adding at the end the following:

"§1632. Limitation on jurisdiction

"(a) Except as provided in subsection (b), no court created by Act of Congress shall have any jurisdiction, and the Supreme Court shall have no appellate jurisdiction, to hear or decide any question pertaining to the interpretation of, or the validity under the Constitution of, the Pledge of Allegiance, as defined in section 4 of title 4, or its recitation.

"(b) The limitation in subsection (a) does not apply to—

"(1) any court established by Congress under its power to make needful rules and regulations respecting the territory of the United States; or

"(2) the Superior Court of the District of Columbia or the District of Columbia Court of Appeals;[6]".

(b) CLERICAL AMENDMENT.—The table of sections at the beginning of chapter 99 of title 28, United States Code, is amended by adding at the end the following new item:

"1632. Limitation on jurisdiction.".

SEC. 3. EFFECTIVE DATE.

This Act and the amendments made by this Act take effect on the date of the enactment of this Act and apply to any case that—

(1) is pending on such date of enactment; or

(2) is commenced on or after such date of enactment.

This bill would remove from the Federal courts, including the Supreme Court, the ability to interpret or determine the constitutionality of the Pledge of Allegiance as set forth in law (section 4 of title 4, United States Code). Such a bill would appear to conflict with the red-letter law of *Marbury v. Madison* and itself be unconstitutional. Similar jurisdiction-stripping bills relating to same-sex marriage have been introduced, and one (H.R. 3313) passed in the 108th Congress. Needless to say, the issues addressed in *Marbury* 200 years ago *continue* to cross the drafter's desk.[7]

29.7 Agency interpretations of statutes

While section 706 of title 5, United States Code, establishes the standard of review by a court of agency action, the Supreme Court has articulated the level of deference that a court should give to an agency's interpretation of a statute.

In *Skidmore v. Swift & Co.*, 323 U.S. 134 (1944), the Court held that the weight to be accorded an administrative action depended on a number of factors: the thoroughness of the agency's consideration, the validity of its reasoning, its consistency with its other decisions, and "all those factors which give it power to persuade" (323 U.S. at 140).

In *Chevron, U.S.A., Inc. v. Natural Resources Defense Council*, 467 U.S. 837 (1984), the Court created a new standard of deference. It held that—

- if Congress has directly spoken to the issue, and the intent of Congress is clear, then the agency must give effect to the unambiguously expressed intent of Congress (476 U.S. at 842–843), but

- if the statute is silent or ambiguous with respect to an issue, the court does not simply impose its own construction of the statute; rather, the question for the court is whether the agency's interpretation is based on a permissible construction of the statute; if the answer is yes, the court must defer to the agency's interpretation (467 U.S. at 843–844).

After *Chevron,* the Court clarified that administrative implementation of a statutory provision qualified for *Chevron* deference when "it appears that Congress delegated authority to the agency generally to make rules carrying the force of law, and that the agency interpretation claiming deference was promulgated in the exercise of that authority" (*United States v. Mead Corp.,* 533 U.S. 218, 226–227 [2001]), as in formal adjudication or rulemaking. Informal actions were less likely to qualify; in such cases, the standard in *Skidmore* would likely apply instead.

Chevron, the precedent since 1984, was overruled on June 28, 2024, in *Loper Bright Enterprises v. Raimondo*, 144 S. Ct. 2244, 603 U.S. __ (2024), in which the Court held that the Administrative Procedure Act requires courts to exercise their independent judgment in deciding whether an agency has acted within its statutory authority, and courts may not defer to an agency interpretation of the law simply because a statute is ambiguous. Even though the Court ruled that its decision would not overrule prior cases decided under Chevron absent a "special justification" (144 S. Ct. 2273), *Loper* could lead to many new challenges to Federal regulations.

This area of the law is nuanced and is only introduced here. The relevance of these cases to a statutory drafter is that the extent to which legislation details how that legislation is to be carried out by an administering agency needs to be considered in light of the *Loper* decision. And if a sponsor is concerned about whether a specific interpretation of the statute should occur, or not occur the legislation should be clear about that interpretation.

The relevance of these cases to the regulatory drafter is much greater. An agency contemplating the promulgation of a regulation or other agency action needs to determine whether the standard for the action is already set in the statute under which the agency operates; if so, the agency action must conform to that standard. The extent to which the courts will defer to agency regulations interpretating statutes in ambiguous cases will be determined in cases decided after *Loper*.

29.8 Summing up

The cases presented in this chapter illustrate why the drafter has to stay tuned to what the Supreme Court does; its decisions can affect mundane issues the drafter faces. The challenge for the drafter is to fall within the acceptable lines, constitutional or otherwise, that the Court draws.

Notes

1 Kenneth R. Thomas, *The Power to Regulate Commerce: Limits on Congressional Power* (Washington, D.C.: Congressional Research Service, May 16, 2014 (*fas.org/crs/*).

2 See section 11.6 for a discussion of *Lopez* and *Morrison* (infra) with respect to congressional findings.

3 Public Law 103-322, which enacted these provisions, is an example of a law with too many short titles. The short title of the entire Act was the "Violent Crime Control and Law Enforcement Act of 1994"; the short title for title IV was the "Violence Against Women Act of 1994"; then each subtitle of title IV had its own short title. The provisions that were the subject of *U.S. v. Morrison* were in subtitle C. As discussed in 11.4, the value of so many short titles is questionable, and it is unlikely that, without a U.S. Code citation, anyone would find a provision of a law referred to by an "embedded" short title like the ones described.

4 Remember, however, that even when the language is crystal clear, the court will still look for a constitutional basis—like the Fourteenth Amendment—to validate the statute. See the discussion of *Florida Prepaid Postsecondary Education Expense Board v. College Savings Bank*, 527 U.S. 627 (1999), in 28.9.

5 There can be something that looks like a legislative veto provision but really is not. There has been a succession of statutes giving the President authority to enter into trade agreements with other countries and then providing that "fast track" or "trade authorities" procedures will apply to legislation that the President transmits to Congress to implement the trade agreements entered into. (The special procedures allow quick action on the legislation and prohibit amendments to it and were addressed in 12.14.) These laws have provisions stating that "fast track" or "trade authorities" procedures will not apply to an implementing bill if either House adopts a resolution that so provides. This provision passes constitutional muster because only the rules of a House of Congress are being affected, a constitutional prerogative of each House of Congress.

6 The semicolon at this point should obviously be a period.

7 The approach of the U.S. Senate on both issues (no doubt realizing the constitutional problems) was to consider an amendment to the Constitution instead of a bill on these matters.

PART VIII
THE UNIQUELY FEDERAL FORMS AND STYLES

30. Typography and Typographical Terminology

30.1 Preliminary comments

There are many ways in which material can be presented on a page. Some forms of writing involve more specialized typographical devices than others (consider the subscripts, superscripts, and symbols used in scientific writing, for example), but legislative drafting involves relatively few. By and large, legislative drafting (typographically) is just an ordinary form of prose composition.

The special typographical constraints that do exist in legislative drafting involve just two things:

(1) The way in which the various discrete pieces of a bill (the sections, subsections, paragraphs, and other subdivisions) are constructed on the page and located with respect to each other—most importantly their varying degrees of indentation. The specifications for this are set forth in detail in chapters 20 and 33 and are touched upon at several other places in the book; and the terminology is discussed in 30.2.

(2) The nature and placement of the headings to be used, and the characteristics of the type in which they are to be set—its size, font, and face. The specifications are set forth in detail in chapter 33, and the terminology is discussed in 30.3.

When drafting a bill, even though the specifications may be embedded in a computer program you are using (as is the case in the Offices of the Legislative Counsel of the House or Representatives and the Senate), you may need to describe the typographical aspects of what you do to other technicians (committee staff, concerned agency staffs, and other specialists) while you are working on it and after it is finished. Certainly if you are piecing together a bill at the last minute by hand, you will have to accurately convey to the printer how you want the finished product to look. Remember that the public at large never sees your draft, and if the bill is not printed the way you meant it to be no one will ever know what you wanted it to look like.

It is the purpose of this chapter to help you become comfortable with the typographical aspects of bills and laws at the Federal level. Sections 30.2 through 30.5 lay out the rules and symbols involved; 30.6 gives you an example of their practical application; and 30.7 and 30.8 show you how to mark your copy so as to apply them correctly.

30.2 Placement and structure

Centering and the left-hand margin. All headings for a bill's senior components (and section headings in the "traditional" style) are centered on the line or lines on which they appear. Everything else in a bill, regardless of the drafting style being used, is based on the left-hand margin—that is, it begins either at the left-hand margin or at a point that is measured from the left-hand margin. The printer's shorthand mark for centered material is "ctr".

Full measure. A subdivision or any other material in a bill is "full measure" when its left-hand margin coincides with the full left-hand margin of the page on which it appears. All sections and subsections are set full measure (as are most lesser subdivisions in the "traditional" and "United States Code"[1] styles). The shorthand mark is "fm".

Paragraphing and flush material. A subdivision or any other material in a bill is "paragraphed" when its first line is indented 5 spaces (2 ems) from its left-hand margin, whether that margin is full measure or not. It is "flush" if it starts at the beginning of a new line and is not paragraphed, whether the new line is full measure or not. The shorthand marks are a backwards "P" with two stems ("¶") to denote a paragraph and "fl" to denote flush material.

"Cut-in" or indented material. A subdivision or any other material in a bill is "cut in", or "indented" as a whole, when its left-hand margin is moved to the right of the page's full left-hand margin (or the left-hand margin of the matter immediately preceding it) by 5 spaces (2 ems). Indentations of this kind are often progressive; if the material immediately preceding a subdivision is itself cut in "once" (2 ems), that subdivision may be further indented or "cut in twice" by moving its left-hand margin two more ems to the right.

The shorthand mark to denote that material is to be cut in is a small box or circle with a figure inside it indicating the number of ems by which the material is to be indented (placed in the margin alongside that material, and preferably accompanied by a vertical marginal line indicating where the indentation starts and stops); for example, "2" in the case of material to be cut in once, or "6" in the case of material to be cut in three times.

"Run-in" and "dropped-down" material. Material is "run in" when it is a continuation of what precedes it and does not start on a new line. If the language immediately following the run-in material (or any other language for that matter) is to begin on a new line, it is "dropped down". Lines are never left blank, but it is always permissible to mark material "new line" (or even "new page") when necessary to make the arrangement clear. The headings of subsections and other inferior subdivisions in the "revenue" and "modified revenue" styles are always run in (immediately after the subdivision designation); and any designated subdivision that is run in is always called a "clause" regardless of how it is designated.

Placement of marks. As indicated in 30.8, all printer's marks (like regular penciled-in amendments) must be placed in the margin alongside the material to which they relate—not within the text itself—with a line drawn to (or around) the affected material if there could be any doubt about what that material is.

30.3 Characteristics of type

Type size. Type comes in many sizes, of course, and these are measured in "points" (each of which, by the way, is equal to about 1/72 of an inch).

The text of any bill is always printed in 14-point type, and so are the headings except for title and subtitle headings in revenue style (18-point), section headings in revenue or modified revenue style (10-point), and section headings in Code style (12-point). And occasionally the major headings in an omnibus bill are set in even larger type (that is, more than 18-point) in order to allow each of the principal components the full range of normal headings.

It should be emphasized, however, that (regardless of the drafting style involved) the size of the superior headings in a bill does not just gradually increase (and usually does not change at all) as you go up the scale of senior components. The important typographical variations between the several kinds of superior headings in a bill arise out of their different mixtures of large capital letters ("caps"), small capital letters ("small caps"), and lowercase letters and their different uses of boldface and lightface type.

(Note that there are specialized elements of a bill, such as tables of contents and columnar tables, that often use smaller [6-, 8-, or 10-point] type; but there are no established rules for them, and you should feel free to use whatever typographical devices seem appropriate. Note also that very massive bills have on occasion been printed in 8- or 10-point type in their entirety, with the lines set close together instead of double-spaced, in order to save space and avoid the sheer bulk that would be required if they were printed normally; but you are not likely to be confronted with this situation.)

The exact typographical specifications for all of the various headings that might be found in a bill in each of the accepted Federal drafting styles are set forth in chapter 33, along with literal examples.

Caps, small caps, and lowercase letters. At each level of size—14-point, 16-point, and so forth—there are three possibilities for each letter: It can be a full-sized cap (a "cap"), a small cap, or a lowercase letter. Caps at any level are obviously bigger than small caps and lowercase letters at that level (the latter two being of equal size); and caps, small caps, and lowercase letters at any level are obviously bigger than they would be at the next lower level. Numerals are printed the same size as caps.

You will occasionally have to mark your copy to specify the level of type size you want, but normally both you and the printer will know what level of type size is correct for the situation involved and marking for this purpose is unnecessary. It does sometimes become necessary, however, to specify whether you want caps, small caps, or lowercase letters in a particular case—not just in the headings but within the text as well—and the appropriate shorthand mark for a block of material would be "cap" or "caps", "sc", or "lc", or (for combinations of caps and either small caps or lowercase letters) "c + sc" or "c + lc". Single letters and individual words are simply underscored three times to indicate caps and twice to indicate small caps.

Typeface and font. For the most part, all bills are printed in ordinary lightface (roman) type; no marking of the text is ever necessary to indicate this kind of type (except when returning to it after a lengthy segment of some other kind of type).

As has been mentioned and will be more fully discussed in chapter 33, however, headings are often printed in boldface type; and unless the face type required is absolutely clear from the kind of heading that is involved (section headings are always boldface in revenue, modified revenue, or Code style, for example), you should mark it accordingly. The shorthand marks are "lf" and "bf", respectively.

And on those rare occasions when you want something in your draft to be set in italic type you should of course mark it accordingly; the frequently used device of simply underscoring language to indicate italicization would usually work but is too often ambiguous (except in the case of a proviso, where the need for italicizing "*Provided*" is understood by everyone). The shorthand mark is "ital".

Special typographical care is needed when you are working on a reported bill that contains amendments (see 30.7 and 30.8). Matter being eliminated is retained in the bill but printed with a line drawn through it ("linetype" or "cancelled type"), and matter being added is shown in italics, with the unchanged portion remaining in roman type. A bill being reported with an amendment in the nature of a substitute shows the original language in linetype (unless omitted altogether because of its length) followed by the substitute version in italics, which is easy enough. But a bill reported with cut-and-bite amendments often looks like it has measles, with bits and pieces of linetype and italics scattered about indiscriminately; they must be marked ("lt" and "ital") with extreme care.

A bill as set forth in its conference report version has similar problems, although it is printed in "report style" (8-point type) rather than in bill style. The entire bill is shown in italic type in a conference report of the "complete substitute" variety, but heavy black brackets are used instead of linetype to indicate stricken matter in the "numbered amendments" case. When it is of the "numbered amendments" variety, which is highly stylized and can be quite intricate (see 31.7 and 32.10), it must be marked ("bl.br.", "ital", and "roman") with care.

30.4 Other typographical terms and symbols

The printer's mark for deleting something from the copy is a line with a hook or loop at the end, colloquially referred to as a "pigtail"; see 30.8 for examples. Cross out or encircle the word or phrase you want to eliminate, draw a line from it extending into the margin, and end the line with this mark. If you are deleting a large block of material, it is customary to do so by drawing a large "X" totally covering the material and enclosing it within a penciled box or circle, with a marginal pigtail attached to the latter.

When inserting something into the copy, write the material to be inserted in the margin (or staple it to the page if it is long), draw a line from that material (or from a marginal note referring to that material if it is attached) to the place where you want to insert it, and end the line (in the text) with a caret (an inverted "V"). Do not omit the caret; it helps to pinpoint the place of insertion. If the material being inserted is a comma, semicolon, colon, or period and nothing else, put an inverted "V" over it or circle it (and if it is a quotation mark or apostrophe put an upright "V" under it), so it will be recognized as the kind of punctuation mark it is.

The mark for showing that you want a blank space left between two words that have been inadvertently run together (or indeed for showing that you want a blank space left between two of anything) is the pound sign ("#"). And the mark for showing that you want to eliminate one or more blank spaces at some point (for example, to run two words together) looks like two parentheses (which can be of any length) lying on their sides, one over and one under the offending space; see 30.8 for an example.

The mark for reversing the order of two letters (or two words) that have been inadvertently transposed looks like an "S" lying on its side, with one of the offending letters (or words) within each of its curves; see 30.8.

The term "stet", alongside stricken matter, means "please ignore this deletion and retain the original matter".

Anything placed within parentheses is colloquially described as being "in the hole". The alphanumeric designations of the inferior subdivisions of a bill—the subsections, paragraphs, subparagraphs, clauses, subclauses, items, and subitems—are always placed "in the hole". Section numbers, and the alphanumeric designations of the senior components of a bill (the titles, subtitles, chapters, subchapters, parts, and subparts), are never "in the hole".

30.5 The Federal drafting styles

Four different drafting styles are commonly used and accepted at the Federal level, and they are discussed in detail, with literal examples, in chapter 33. They are mentioned now, in passing, simply because the only mechanical differences between them involve the typographical matters discussed in this chapter—their headings and their systems of indentation.

Most of the things you are going to read in chapter 33 will thus be based on (and require a knowledge of) what you have read in this chapter; and conversely this chapter should be viewed as a kind of prologue to chapter 33.

30.6 Using the terminology

As a test of your comfort level in this area and an example of the sort of things that are involved, you might consider the typographical aspects of the following hypothetical provision, the text of which consists mainly of a single tabulated sentence written in "revenue" style (it would be the same in modified revenue style, but would vary somewhat in format if it were written in traditional or Code style):[2]

SEC. 123. BENEFIT PROGRAM.

(a) IN GENERAL.—The Secretary shall make a payment under this section to any individual who—

(1) files an application under subsection (b) and meets the eligibility requirements of section 124, and

(2) on the first day of the period for which the payment is made—

(A) is at least 65 years of age, and

(B) is needy (as determined under section 125),

unless the individual (i) is a dependent of another person receiving payments under this section or (ii) is unable to provide the assurances required by subsection (c).

(b) Procedure for making application.—Any individual who…

Subsections (a) and (b) (like all subsections) are full measure. Paragraphs (1) and (2) of subsection (a) are indented or cut-in; they are cut in "once" (2 ems). Subparagraphs (A) and (B) of paragraph (2) are also indented or cut-in, but they are cut in "twice" (2 more ems, for a total of 4). All of these are paragraphed, of course. The full-measure material beginning "unless" is flush (full measure), and clauses (i) and (ii) are run in.

The revenue-style section heading (which is full measure and flush) is set in 10-point boldface small caps. The subsection headings (which are run in) are set in 14-point (lightface) caps and small caps. Paragraphs (1) and (2) and subparagraphs (A) and (B) have no headings at all, since they are only parts of a tabulated sentence; they would have had run-in headings (set in 14-point small caps) if they were self-contained subdivisions or were prefaced by a colon (see 23.4).

30.7 Reproducing the typography

It should be obvious by now that what you write may actually appear in the printed bill in a number of different typographical formats, involving every conceivable combination of lowercase and capital letters in a dozen different sizes and typefaces along with various degrees of indentation, depending on the drafting style you are using, the complexity of the subject, and other factors. The typographical format that is indicated in any particular case will usually be clear to you after a reading of chapter 33, and you should always be familiar with it.

But unless the typography is embedded in a computer program you are using, there is simply no way that you can reproduce many of a bill's headings and designations correctly on the page; and if you are writing in longhand, even the indentations can be hard to show precisely. And yet you do need to be certain that your bill will be printed exactly the way you want it. Chapter 33 only tells you what to do, not how to do it. What are your remedies?

In many cases, of course, there is no problem; the printer knows what the correct form is, and will get it right no matter what you do. For example, if your bill is clearly written in revenue style the printer will pay no attention to how you type your section headings and simply set them in 10-point boldface caps, full measure flush, because that's obviously what you meant to do. And if you type "Sec. 123." as a section designation in a bill that is clearly written in traditional style, or "(a) Secretary's Authority.—" as a subsection heading in a bill that is clearly written in revenue style, the printer will set it with caps and small caps, for the same reason.

In addition, if you are careful, most of your indentations will speak for themselves—the printer can just count spaces from the left-hand margin if necessary.

But whenever the characters on the page do not accurately and precisely depict the exact typography that you intend, you should mark your copy so that the printer (and anyone else working on the project with you) will have no question about what you have in mind; this is the subject of 30.8 below.

30.8 Marking copy

The best way to mark copy is to use the terminology and shorthand marks described earlier in this chapter. All printers and most legislative technicians understand them. But if all else fails, do not hesitate to write a folksy note to the printer—for example, "Note to GPO: Please make this heading look exactly like the one at the top of the previous page", or "Please indent this paragraph 5 spaces more than the last one". Just do what you must to make your point absolutely clear, with all marks displayed in the margin and connected by lines and arrows to the places within the text where they are to have their effect.

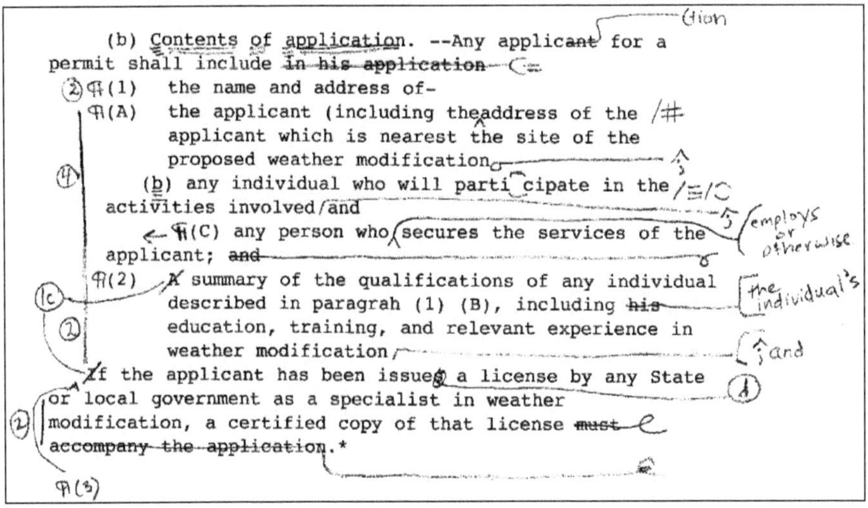

(b) Contents of application. --Any applicant for a permit shall include in his application

(1) the name and address of-

(A) the applicant (including theaddress of the applicant which is nearest the site of the proposed weather modification

(b) any individual who will parti cipate in the activities involved/and

(C) any person who secures the services of the applicant; and

(2) A summary of the qualifications of any individual described in paragrah (1) (B), including his education, training, and relevant experience in weather modification

If the applicant has been issued a license by any State or local government as a specialist in weather modification, a certified copy of that license must accompany the application.*

Figure 30.8. Edited Text with Proofreader's Marks

*This last paragraph could have been made flush left text, but making it a paragraph (3) instead avoids any confusion about what the language applies to.

Figure 30.8 above shows a sample page of draft language, liberally sprinkled with some of the more common typographical marks and showing how it ought to be done.

Notes

1 This is true only of subdivisions of a section that do not have headings; see chapter 33.

2 This example is structured to illustrate the terminology. However, it is better to avoid a construction that has flush text after paragraphed material, especially when that flush text has additional subunits (clauses (i) and (ii)).

31. Locations and Forms of Existing Law

31.1 Preliminary comments

If the bill on which you are working will be amendatory, you must of course locate and understand the relevant existing law in the field involved—in its most up-to-date form—before you can legitimately think about drafting at all. But even when your bill will be totally freestanding you will usually need to learn at least a little about the existing law in the field in order to determine the effect of the words you propose to use (and the effect of the existing law on those words). And very often you will not know until you have studied the existing law whether your approach should be amendatory or not.

In addition, even when there is no direct substantive connection between your bill and any definable body of existing Federal law, it will often be necessary (or at least desirable) that you locate and understand any existing laws that might—

(1) bear upon specific aspects of your bill, such as those dealing with administrative procedures or involving the performance of existing functions by the relevant Federal officials,

(2) overlap or be inconsistent with particular provisions of your bill, or

(3) serve as useful models.

This chapter is designed to familiarize you with the various forms that Federal laws take, and to help you find them.

31.2 Slip laws

The first official publication of any statute is in the form generally known as the "slip law". In this form, each law is published individually—as a separate document or pamphlet. Its heading indicates the public law number, the House or Senate number of the bill that was enacted, the date of enactment, and (since 1976) a citation to the volume and page of the Statutes at Large in which the law will appear.

In addition, each slip law contains marginal notes giving citations to any statutes mentioned in the text, and (since 1974) the U.S. Code classifications of the statute itself so that the reader can immediately determine where each of its provisions will appear in the Code. It also includes (since 1963) an informative guide to the legislative history of the law consisting of the names of the committees that handled it in each House, the committee report numbers, and the dates of consideration and passage in each House (with references to the *Congressional Record* by volume, year, and date). If it was passed over the President's veto or became law without his signature, a statement to that effect is included.

Figure 31.2 is an example of an enacted statute in its slip-law form (it is a short one but contains all the essential pieces).

The slip laws are prepared by the Office of the Federal Register in the National Archives and Records Administration and delivered to the document rooms of both Houses—usually within a few weeks after enactment—where they become available to officials and the public. The Government Publishing Office (*https://www.govinfo.gov*) updates its database to include a new slip law when its publication is authorized by the Office of the Federal Register; the website has all laws enacted from the 104th Congress to the present. Slip laws dating from earlier Congresses are available electronically from *www.congress.gov*. Both websites have a wealth of information about legislation, which can be downloaded. Under section 113 of title 1, United States Code, slip laws are competent evidence (of the laws involved) in all Federal and State courts, tribunals, and public offices.

Under the right circumstances slip laws are your best source of information about existing laws for two reasons:

(1) They give you your earliest opportunity to see the laws in their official form—the first available version of those laws, which contains all the requisite citations and references, and on which you can absolutely rely as to both form and substance.

(2) They are the most convenient of all statutory forms to carry about and work with, since each slip law is a self-contained unit with no extraneous material in it and is of a relatively manageable format (in printed form, a mere 5 1/2 by 8 3/4 inches, like a committee report).

136 STAT. 2204 PUBLIC LAW 117–189—OCT. 10, 2022

Public Law 117–189
117th Congress

An Act

Oct. 10, 2022
[H.R. 5641]

To amend the Robert T. Stafford Disaster Relief and Emergency Assistance Act to increase the threshold for eligibility for assistance under sections 403, 406, 407, and 502 of such Act, and for other purposes.

Be it enacted by the Senate and House of Representatives of the United States of America in Congress assembled,

Small Project Efficient and Effective Disaster Recovery Act. 42 USC 5121 note.

SECTION 1. SHORT TITLE.

This Act may be cited as the "Small Project Efficient and Effective Disaster Recovery Act" or the "SPEED Recovery Act".

SEC. 2. SIMPLIFIED PROCEDURE.

(a) IN GENERAL.—Section 422 of the Robert T. Stafford Disaster Relief and Emergency Assistance Act (42 U.S.C. 5189) is amended—

(1) in subsection (a) by striking "$35,000" each place it appears and inserting "$1,000,000"; and

(2) in subsection (b)(3)—

(A) in the heading by inserting "AND REPORT" after "REVIEW"; and

Reports. Recommendations.

(B) by inserting "and submit to the Committee on Transportation and Infrastructure of the House of Representatives and the Committee on Homeland Security and Governmental Affairs of the Senate a report regarding such review, including any recommendations developed pursuant to such review" after "under this section".

42 USC 5189 note.

(b) APPLICABILITY.—The amendments made by subsection (a) shall apply with respect to any amounts appropriated after the date of enactment of this Act.

Reports.

SEC. 3. AUDIT AND REVIEW.

Not later than 3 years after the date of enactment of this Act, the Inspector General of the Department of Homeland Security shall conduct an audit, and submit to Congress a report, on whether there has been waste and abuse as a result of the amendment made under section 2(a)(1).

Approved October 10, 2022.

LEGISLATIVE HISTORY—H.R. 5641:

HOUSE REPORTS: No. 117–274 (Comm. on Transportation and Infrastructure).
SENATE REPORTS: No. 117–145 (Comm. on Homeland Security and Governmental Affairs).
CONGRESSIONAL RECORD, Vol. 168 (2022):
Apr. 5, considered and passed House.
Sept. 20, considered and passed Senate, amended.
Sept. 28, House considered concurring in Senate amendments.
Sept. 29, prior proceedings vacated; House concurred in Senate amendments.

Figure 31.2. Example of a Slip Law

Their usefulness is somewhat diminished, however, because they show only the statute as it was originally enacted, and they become out of date (from the drafter's point of view) as soon as they are amended by a later law. For this reason, the utility of the older ones is limited.

If you can get your hands on the slip law setting forth the statute in which you are interested, you should choose it as your source whenever you can be sure (either because of its recency or because you have carefully checked and noted any subsequent amendments) that it is still reliable as a representation of the current state of the law. In any other case you should keep it handy and use it for stylistic guidance.

31.3 The Statutes at Large

The United States Statutes at Large constitute a permanent collection of the laws of each session of Congress, printed in bound volumes. Each volume (which is also prepared by the Office of the Federal Register, and usually becomes available several months after the close of the session of Congress to which it relates) includes a complete index and table of contents, along with marginal notes referring to laws in earlier volumes and to other matters in the same volume.

You can think of the Statutes at Large as simply constituting chronological arrangements of slip laws, Congress by Congress. There is no attempt to arrange the laws according to their subject matter or to show the present status of earlier laws that have been amended on one or more occasions—that sort of thing is the function of the United States Code. And if you want to know what the slip law set forth in 31.2 would look like when it is printed in the Statutes at Large, just refer back to 31.2—the two versions are identical, down to the very last detail.

The Statutes at Large are legal evidence of the laws contained in them and will be accepted as proof of those laws in any Federal, State, or local court.

However, their utility for the drafter is limited by two factors:

(1) They are less readily available to most drafters than the other statutory sources because of the lag time after the end of a session of Congress before they are published.

(2) As with slip laws, the usefulness of the Statutes at Large diminishes with the passage of time, since subsequent amendments to the laws are not reflected. And their sheer bulk makes them harder to carry around and work with.

(Needless to say, the current state of any law can be determined from the slip laws or the Statutes at Large, by finding the original version of that law and then modifying it to incorporate all subsequent amendments as shown in later slip laws; but this can be a tedious and time-consuming process that is usually worth the effort only if you are preparing or updating a compilation for regular personal use in the field of your specialty [see 31.6].)

In addition, you obviously need to know the particular Congress in which the law you are seeking was enacted in order to find that law quickly in the Statutes at Large, even if you do have a complete desk-side set, because of their Congress-by-Congress arrangement.

31.4 The United States Code—positive-law titles

The United States Code contains a consolidation and codification of the permanent laws of the United States, arranged according to subject matter under 54 title headings (although title 53 is marked "reserved" for future content). It sets out the current version of those laws without repeating the vehicular language of the statutes that enacted or amended them. Its purpose is to present the laws in a concise, usable, and up-to-date form without requiring recourse to the many volumes of the Statutes at Large that might otherwise be involved.

For you as a drafter (whether or not the title you are interested in has become positive law), the Code has three great advantages over the slip laws and the Statutes at Large:

(1) Its provisions are arranged by subject matter and are comprehensively indexed, so that the provision being sought can readily be found.

(2) It is kept up-to-date online on an ongoing basis, so that all amendments to existing provisions are incorporated as rapidly as possible after they are enacted. The currency date of each section of the Code is displayed above each section, noting any pending updates.

(3) It is the most widely available, and by far the most accessible, of all the possible sources.

The Code is prepared by the Law Revision Counsel of the House of Representatives. New editions (each of which contains many very large volumes) are published not more often than every five years (1 U.S.C. 202(c), with cumulative supplements published after the conclusion of each regular session of Congress. As a practical matter, however, accessing the U.S. Code on the Law Revision Counsel's website (*http://uscode.house.gov*) ensures an up-to-date, accurate version of the law, greatly diminishing the value of the printed volumes regarding currency of the law. The Code is available online from subscription and other sources as well, but the wealth of historical and other information included in the notes following each section of the Code at *uscode.house.gov* is invaluable (this is also true for the nonpositive-law titles of the U.S. Code).[1]

(The annotated version of the Code (the U.S.C.A.), which is the same sort of document but also contains references to relevant court cases and administrative rulings, is prepared and published by the West Publishing Company (and available online through Westlaw). Its main body occupies well over 54 volumes—one or more volumes for each title of the Code except in the case of a few of the shorter titles (which may be combined), so each volume is smaller and more manageable than its official counterpart—and it is kept more up-to-date than the hard copy of the official U.S. Code with releases, annotated pamphlets, and annual pocket parts. One advantage of the annotated Code (in addition to the annotations themselves) is that you can buy any of its volumes (with updates) individually, which makes ownership feasible if most of your work is done within a single area.) Another annotated code service is the United States Code Service (published by and available online through LexisNexis).

Originally the United States Code was intended simply as a convenience to individuals who might need to find, read, and understand particular provisions of existing law—it was not itself the law (although it has always been treated as "prima facie evidence" of the law, a treatment that is currently specified in section 204(a) of title 1, United States Code). However, over the years selected titles have been revised and enacted into positive law, in a manner reminiscent of what was done in the Revised Statutes during the 1870s; and the process is continuing under the direction of the Law Revision Counsel.

But only 27 of the titles have been rewritten and enacted into positive law, leaving the Code in a current state of considerable disarray; and work on some of the most difficult and lengthy titles has not even begun. Recent codifications enacted into positive law are title 51 (National And Commercial Space Programs) and title 54 (National Park Service And Related Programs), and other codification projects (described on the Law Revision Counsel's website) are underway.

In addition, title 26—the title dealing with revenue and taxation—is identical to the Internal Revenue Code of 1986 for all practical purposes (and indeed is entitled "Internal Revenue Code") although it has never actually been enacted as positive law. It is the hope of the Law Revision Counsel that eventually all of the titles of the Code will be enacted into positive law, and thereafter kept up-to-date by direct amendment.

If you are working from the United States Code (as most drafters must necessarily do, at least some of the time), it is critical that you know the status of the particular title in which you are interested (and of any other Code provisions to which you may have to refer). A positive-law title of the Code can be treated as gospel because it is the law—you can amend and cite it directly (ignoring the now-immaterial statute that enacted it), and you can absolutely rely upon its designations, style, and form. But if you are not sure you must be careful, since the titles that have not been enacted into positive law (and thus cannot be amended or relied on) have the same general appearance in the Code as those that have.

Continued on next page

Figure 31.4 contains two examples of provisions in positive-law titles of the United States Code.

These provisions reflect the "Code style" (see chapter 33); the second example reflects a more recent enactment that uses headings for subunits of the section. When amending a positive-law title, you would follow the formatting of the section heading, and you would have the flexibility of using headings for the subunits. This format is used nowhere else in Federal statutes, and should not be used in *vehicular* language even when that language is adding a new section to a positive-law title of the Code.

For those who may be interested, table 31.4 shows a complete list of the titles of the United States Code, as of this writing. On the website of the Law Revision Counsel, the positive law titles of the United States Code are indicated with an asterisk (*).

Section 204(a) of title 1, United States Code, provides that positive law titles of the Code constitute legal evidence of the law.

31.5 The United States Code—other titles

As indicated in 31.4, many of the titles in the United States Code have never been enacted into positive law and are still primarily just a convenience to individuals seeking statutory provisions—they constitute prima facie evidence of the law (under section 204(a) of title 1, United States Code) but are not themselves the law. However, they remain invaluable to drafters (and others) because of the same three factors (arrangement by subject matter, regular updating, and ready availability) that apply to the positive-law titles.

Even though the seeker must usually go further and consult more reliable sources (the Statutes at Large, the slip laws, or a literal compilation) when the title involved has not been enacted into positive law—an additional step not required in the case of the positive-law titles—they do provide a starting point, which is frequently half the battle.

Example 1: 11 U.S.C. 324

§324. Removal of a Trustee or examiner

(a) The court, after notice and a hearing, may remove a trustee, other than the United States trustee, or an examiner, for cause.

(b) Whenever the court removes a trustee or examiner under subsection (a) in a case under this title, such trustee or examiner shall thereby be removed in all other cases under this title in which such trustee or examiner is then serving unless the court orders otherwise.

(Pub. L. 95–598, Nov. 6, 1978, 92 Stat. 2562; Pub. L. 99–554, title II, §208, Oct. 27, 1986, 100 Stat. 3098.)

HISTORICAL AND REVISION NOTES

SENATE REPORT NO. 95–989

This section permits the court, after notice and a hearing, to remove a trustee for cause.

EDITORIAL NOTES

AMENDMENTS

1986—Pub. L. 99–554 amended section generally, designating existing provisions as subsec. (a), substituting "a trustee, other than the United States trustee, or an examiner" for "a trustee or an examiner", and adding subsec. (b).

STATUTORY NOTES AND RELATED SUBSIDIARIES

EFFECTIVE DATE OF 1986 AMENDMENT

Effective date and applicability of amendment by Pub. L. 99–554 dependent upon the judicial district involved, see section 302(d), (e) of Pub. L. 99–554, set out as a note under section 581 of Title 28, Judiciary and Judicial Procedure.

Continued on next page

Figure 31.4. Provisions in Positive-Law Titles (title 11 and title 28) of the United States Code

Example 2: 28 U.S.C. 597

§597. Relationship with Department of Justice

(a) Suspension of Other Investigations and Proceedings.—Whenever a matter is in the prosecutorial jurisdiction of an independent counsel or has been accepted by an independent counsel under section 594(e), the Department of Justice, the Attorney General, and all other officers and employees of the Department of Justice shall suspend all investigations and proceedings regarding such matter, except to the extent required by section 594(d)(1), and except insofar as such independent counsel agrees in writing that such investigation or proceedings may be continued by the Department of Justice.

(b) Presentations as Amicus Curiae Permitted.—Nothing in this chapter shall prevent the Attorney General or the Solicitor General from making a presentation as amicus curiae to any court as to issues of law raised by any case or proceeding in which an independent counsel participates in an official capacity or any appeal of such a case or proceeding.

(Added Pub. L. 95-521, title VI, §601(a), Oct. 26, 1978, 92 Stat. 1872; amended Pub. L. 97-409, §2(a)(1)(A), Jan. 3, 1983, 96 Stat. 2039; Pub. L. 100-191, §2, Dec. 15, 1987, 101 Stat. 1306.)

Editorial Notes

Amendments

1987—Pub. L. 100-191 amended section generally, substituting provisions relating to relationship with Department of Justice for substantially similar provisions.

1983—Pub. L. 97-409, §2(a)(1)(A), substituted "independent counsel" for "special prosecutor" wherever appearing.

Figure 31.4. Continued

STATUTORY NOTES AND RELATED SUBSIDIARIES

EFFECTIVE DATE OF 1987 AMENDMENT

Amendment by Pub. L. 100-191 effective Dec. 15, 1987, and applicable to proceedings initiated and independent counsels appointed on and after Dec. 15, 1987, see section 6 of Pub. L. 100-191, set out as a note under section 591 of this title.

Figure 31.4. Continued

In form and style the nonpositive-law titles of the Code are the same as the positive-law titles—a provision of one is indistinguishable on its face from a provision of the other. You could not tell just from looking at it, for instance, whether the first example given in 31.4 is or is not positive law[1] (which is why, in order to avoid serious drafting mistakes in connection with any Code provision that you are dealing with, you must always check to confirm the category into which the provision falls if you do not already know).

Table 31.4. Titles of the United States Codes

Title 1	*General Provisions	Title 28	*Judiciary And Judicial Procedure; and Appendix
Title 2	The Congress	Title 29	Labor
Title 3	*The President	Title 30	Mineral Lands And Mining
Title 4	*Flag And Seal, Seat of Government, And the States	Title 31	*Money And Finance
Title 5	*Government Organization And Employees; and Appendix	Title 32	*National Guard
Title 6	Domestic Security	Title 33	Navigation And Navigable Waters
Title 7	Agriculture	Title 34	Crime Control And Law Enforcement
Title 8	Aliens And Nationality	Title 35	*Patents
Title 9	*Arbitration	Title 36	*Patriotic And National Observances, Ceremonies, And Organizations
Title 10	*Armed Forces	Title 37	*Pay And Allowances Of The Uniformed Services
Title 11	*Bankruptcy; and Appendix	Title 38	*Veterans' Benefits
Title 12	Banks And Banking	Title 39	*Postal Service
Title 13	*Census	Title 40	*Public Buildings, Property And Works
Title 14	*Coast Guard	Title 41	*Public Contracts
Title 15	Commerce And Trade	Title 42	The Public Health And Welfare
Title 16	Conservation	Title 43	Public Lands
Title 17	*Copyrights	Title 44	*Public Printing And Documents
Title 18	*Crimes And Criminal Procedure; and Appendix	Title 45	Railroads
Title 19	Customs Duties	Title 46	*Shipping
Title 20	Education	Title 47	Telecommunications
Title 21	Food And Drugs	Title 48	Territories And Insular Possessions
Title 22	Foreign Relations And Intercourse	Title 49	*Transportation
Title 23	*Highways	Title 50	War And National Defense; and Appendix
Title 24	Hospitals And Asylums	Title 51	*National And Commercial Space Programs
Title 25	Indians	Title 52	Voting And Elections
Title 26	Internal Revenue Code	Title 53	[Reserved]
Title 27	Intoxicating Liquors	Title 54	*National Park Service And Related Programs

* This title has been enacted as positive law. However, any Appendix to this title has not been enacted as part of the title.

There is one difference between positive-law and nonpositive-law sections of the Code (in addition to the difference in their legal effect) that should not be overlooked. The parenthetical citations at the end of each section in a positive-law title of the Code, which refer to the statutes that enacted and amended it, are of historical interest only; but the corresponding parenthetical citations in a nonpositive-law title are critical—they tell you where to look to find the actual law that the provision involved reflects (and where to look to find all of the amendments that may have been made to it).

Consider, for example, the nonpositive-law section from title 22 of the Code in figure 31.5.

The parenthetical citations at the end of the section tell you that it came from section 571 of Public Law 87-195 (you would need to look up that statute to find its short title, the "Foreign Assistance Act of 1961"), and the section was added by Public Law 98-151, and has since been amended by Public Law 104-164 in 1996. Citations to all of these are given. In the notes that follow, you are told what the source of the language is, what the amendment did, the effective date of the provision, and the Executive order under which the President delegated authority under this section.

These are critical pieces of information, because as a drafter you must go beyond the Code provision in your quest. Not only will a nonpositive-law provision's own section number always be wrong (2349aa instead of 571 in this case), but such things as indentation, internal cross-references (note the section here refers to other noncodified provisions of title 22), and some of the key terminology will also have been changed (to fit the Code format) from the way they actually appear in the law.

You can (and should) use the nonpositive-law titles of the Code as convenient road maps, but you cannot amend them, and you cannot rely on them for drafting purposes. When you have found what you want to do you must almost always turn to the positive law to make sure that you do it right. Take the time to read the notes immediately following the provision involved—they will advise you of any other provisions of law (by reference to their Code citations) that may be relevant. And consult the table of internal references discussed in 5.5 (Finding aids).

It is noteworthy that, because the United States Code is the resource most readily available to individuals who are looking for any provision of law, the House of Representatives, in some recent Congresses, has included in its rules a directive that "[t]o the maximum extent practicable and consistent with established drafting conventions, an instruction in a bill or joint resolution proposing to repeal or amend any law or part thereof not contained in a codified title of the United States Code shall include, in parentheses immediately following the designation of the matter proposed to be repealed or amended, the applicable United States Code citation (which may be a note in the United States Code), or, if no such citation is available, an appropriate alternative citation to the applicable law."

> **§2349aa. General authority**
>
> Notwithstanding any other provision of law that restricts assistance to foreign countries (other than sections 2304 and 2371 of this title), the President is authorized to furnish, on such terms and conditions as the President may determine, assistance to foreign countries in order to enhance the ability of their law enforcement personnel to deter terrorists and terrorist groups from engaging in international terrorist acts such as bombing, kidnapping, assassination, hostage taking, and hijacking. Such assistance may include training services and the provision of equipment and other commodities related to bomb detection and disposal, management of hostage situations, physical security, and other matters relating to the detection, deterrence, and prevention of acts of terrorism, the resolution of terrorist incidents, and the apprehension of those involved in such acts.
>
> (Pub. L. 87-195, pt. II, §571, as added Pub. L. 98-151, §101(b)(2), Nov. 14, 1983, 97 Stat. 972; amended Pub. L. 104-164, title I, §121(a), July 21, 1996, 110 Stat. 1428.)

Figure 31.5. Provision in a Nonpositive-Law Title of the United States Code

EDITORIAL NOTES

CODIFICATION

Section 571 of Pub. L. 87-195 is based on section 201 of title II of H.R. 2992, Ninety-eighth Congress, as reported May 17, 1983, and enacted into law by Pub. L. 98-151.

AMENDMENTS

1996—Pub. L. 104-164 substituted "Notwithstanding any other provision of law that restricts assistance to foreign countries (other than sections 2304 and 2371 of this title)" for "Subject to the provisions of this part".

STATUTORY NOTES AND RELATED SUBSIDIARIES

EFFECTIVE DATE

Section 203 of title II of H.R. 2992, as enacted into permanent law by Pub. L. 98-151, §101(b)(2), Nov. 14, 1983, 97 Stat. 972, provided that: "This title [enacting this part and amending sections 2304 and 2403 of this title] shall take effect on the date of enactment of this Act [Nov. 14, 1983]."

EXECUTIVE DOCUMENTS

DELEGATION OF FUNCTIONS

For delegation of functions of President under this section, see Ex. Ord. No. 12153, Sept. 29, 1979, 44 F.R. 56673, as amended, set out as a note under section 2381 of this title.

Figure 31.5. Continued

31.6 Compilations and loose-leaf services

You can always rely upon the United States Code for information about the current status of an existing law, because the Code on the website of the Law

Revision Counsel is current, and notes the status of pending amendments in each section of the Code; but, without question, the most valuable statutory source for everyday use by a drafter—although it is not an official source like the others—is the "literal" compilation.

A compilation of a statute shows that statute in its most up-to-date form; that is, it incorporates into the original statute all of the changes that have been subsequently made, with the amendments in place and the repealed provisions omitted (and it usually indicates in footnotes or otherwise the places where those changes appear). It is a "literal" compilation if it shows the statute exactly as it would appear in the positive law, faithfully reproducing its format, indentations, type sizes, typefaces, and its other stylistic features (including misspellings and typographical errors).

Compilations of significant Federal laws, which can be found in most major legislative fields, are prepared by the Office of the Legislative Counsel of the House of Representatives and are available to the public by the Government Publishing Office on *https://www.govinfo.gov*. Compilations prepared by other federal agencies, committees, or other organizations may or may not be "literal" (depending on whether its primary intended use is by drafters and other technicians or by policymakers), and may include a number of different laws when the field involved is broad. The Library of Congress website (*www.loc.gov*) has links to numerous legislative and statutory resources in its Law Library as well.

The compilations prepared by committees or agencies may be regarded by them as "in-house" working documents that are not generally available to the public. But most of the important ones can be obtained simply by asking the committee or agency for a copy (which would be free) or by purchasing one from the Government Publishing Office (which would be relatively inexpensive). Remember, however, that such a compilation will lose its currency as soon as the law involved is amended again, and you should be prepared to keep it up-to-date yourself until the next updated version is available.

Even better are the various commercially produced compilations that are frequently available. The Commerce Clearing House and Prentice-Hall loose-leaf services, for example, are best known for their compilations of the tax laws, but they produce similar compilations in many other fields. Along with the relevant statutes themselves (which are always presented in "literal" form) their compilations contain all of the relevant regulations, administrative rulings, and court decisions. And their compilations are kept more current than any others; subscribers typically receive their replacement pages within days after the enactment of amendatory legislation, even when that legislation has made massive changes in the statute or statutes involved. They tend to be bulky and expensive; but if you have access to such a service within your agency or organization you should use it.

Finally, you can of course make and maintain your own compilation, first by obtaining an accurate version of the original statute and all amendments to it from some reliable source, executing the amendments yourself and then keeping your compilation up-to-date yourself whenever the law is amended in the future. (Most professional drafters do this; in the two Legislative Counsel's Offices of Congress each drafter maintains a personal compilation of the laws with which that drafter most often deals, and the Offices themselves (even though they subscribe to a broad spectrum of loose-leaf services) maintain compilations of all major Federal statutes that they bring up-to-date as they are amended. As indicated above, these are available on *govinfo.gov*)

Bear in mind, however, that keeping any compilation current involves two separate activities—keeping abreast of any changes in the statute (which is not always as simple or clear-cut as it sounds), and then incorporating those changes (by executing them exactly as they are enacted) into the compilation—and either can consume a good deal of time and effort.

In any case, if you must deal regularly with an existing statute your first choice should be to work from a literal compilation if you can arrange it.

31.7 Interim sources

One of the times when it is most crucial to know just what form a newly amended statute has taken is immediately after its enactment. At that time, however, nothing official has yet been published and the relevant compilations have not yet been updated. And the enrolled bill (the one the President actually signs) is almost never publicly available (although the enrolled version of the bill will become available online relatively quickly on *www.congress.gov*. What can you do?

Needless to say, if the bill has passed both Houses in exactly the same form, any copy of the bill as it passed either House will serve your purposes reasonably well. You can treat it as though it were the public law and take it from there.

If the final version of the bill resulted from a conference agreement of the complete substitute variety (see 32.10), the conference report, which is printed in both the House and the Senate and is available on *congress.gov*, will set forth that version verbatim.

In any other case, until the final version is available (online or otherwise), you must reconstruct it yourself:

(1) If the final version of the bill resulted from a conference agreement of the numbered amendments variety (see 32.10), you will have to assemble a set of three documents—the bill as it passed the House in which it originated; the bill as it passed the other House (which will not be in bill form at all, but rather in the form of amendments to the first House's bill); and the conference report (which will show the action taken on each of the second House's amendments). By modifying the first House's bill to reflect all of the conference actions, you will arrive at the final version; this is not difficult in most cases, but it can be quite tedious.

If some of the second House's amendments were "reported in disagreement" in the conference report, and left to be dealt with on the floor of each House after the conference report is agreed to, you will need a fourth document—the record of the action taken on those amendments. For this you must turn to the *Congressional Record*; and you must take what you find there with a grain of salt, since the *Congressional Record* (because of its multicolumn format) is not a reliable guide in matters of form and style and (because of its overnight printing) frequently contains typographical errors.

(2) If the bill was never sent to conference and its final version resulted simply from amendments made on the floor of one or both of the two Houses—sometimes a bill bounces back and forth between the House and Senate several times before there is complete agreement—you can consult the *Congressional Record* to see what was done (bearing in mind the caveat stated in the preceding paragraph). The final version will consist of the bill as it passed the House in which it originated, modified to reflect all of these amendments. The different versions of each bill are also available on *congress.gov*.

Note that the only official version of what passed either House is the "engrossed" bill (or "engrossed" amendments) of that House—see 32.9. If you need a copy of a bill as it passed the House in which it originated but for some reason cannot obtain the engrossed version, a copy of the bill as initially referred to committee in the other House can be safely treated as the exact equivalent of the first House's engrossed bill.

Finally, on a somewhat different level, you should be aware that the *U.S. Code Congressional & Administrative News* (which is prepared by the West Publishing Company and consists of a series of softcover pamphlets that are published monthly) not only sets forth the text of the laws as they are enacted but includes periodically updated appendices that list all of the sections of the United States Code (positive law and nonpositive law) that are changed or otherwise affected by those laws. If you need to learn whether a particular provision of existing law has been recently amended (since your compilation was last brought up-to-date, for example), and you know the Code citation of that provision, a quick glance at those appendices will tell you. And if it has been recently amended, they will also direct you to the public law that did it. Of course, as has already been said, this information is also available online; the classification tables of the U.S. Code show sections of the U.S. Code that are affected by recent enactments; with that information, you can look up the Public Law that affected those sections of the Code.

31.8 Omnibus, appropriations, and reconciliation Acts

The task of learning whether or not a particular provision of existing law has been recently amended, and locating the amendment if it has, is often complicated by the growing tendency of Congress to enact laws in bunches—multiple laws contained within a single bill.

Omnibus laws have always been with us, but until fairly recently they consisted of collections of provisions amending only related statutes and establishing only related programs. Today, however, a significant percentage of all Federal substantive legislation is enacted in omnibus bills that do not limit themselves to particular legislative areas. These take the form of appropriations bills (especially continuing resolutions) that are loaded down with substantive provisions and reconciliation bills (which are theoretically intended simply to bring the Federal budget into line but typically accomplish this by changing the scope and coverage of substantive programs).

The substantive provisions in appropriations bills and continuing resolutions have nothing to do with the appropriations process, of course, and many of the provisions in reconciliation bills actually have little or nothing to do with the budget process.[2] They are put there in any particular case because time is running out and the appropriations or reconciliation bill is a convenient vehicle, because of political or intragovernmental divisions, or just because including them improves the sponsor's odds (since any such bill is almost certain to be enacted, in some form at least).

This is not the time or place to discuss the appropriations process or the budget process in depth. Suffice it to say (and it is the purpose of this subdivision simply to point out) that the increasing use of these omnibus bills makes it difficult for people in general and drafters in particular to know exactly what has been enacted—or even whether or not something has been enacted at all—until long after the fact. These bills are always massive, they are invariably enacted under extreme time pressure, and they can include anything under the sun. And their lack of any rational order or stylistic consistency often makes it difficult to find what you are looking for even when you know it is there.

In the case of reconciliation bills you have a fighting chance, since there is some order to them—the separate titles are at least arranged according to committee jurisdiction. And they are typically assembled by the Legislative Counsel's Offices, using material provided by the specialized committee staffs. But in the case of appropriations bills and continuing resolutions there is usually no order at all, since there is only limited participation by professional drafters and the specialized staffs of the legislative committees; there is no way that is both easy and practical to know what they contain, although if you are looking for a particular provision, you can try to search the document for keywords when it becomes available online. You would risk your sanity if you tried to read one of these monster bills from cover to cover. (The bright side is that the Law Revision Counsel cannot avoid doing this, and once that office has completed its work you can get your answer by simply consulting the United States Code.)

All you can do is remain alert to the fact that bills of this kind may contain material that changes or otherwise affects the laws you are working with, and be ready to look for it should the need become apparent.

31.9 Federal regulations

Occasionally a sponsor may ask you to draft a bill to "undo" the effects of some government regulation. More often, the existence of a government regulation will have caused the problem you are being asked to solve, or simply needs to be taken into account in solving that problem. Whatever the reason, every drafter must from time to time consult government regulations, and it is important that you have a reasonably clear idea of how to find them.

Regulations formally prescribed by a Federal official, like Executive orders, first appear in the *Federal Register* (which is published more or less daily). They are subsequently codified in the Code of Federal Regulations (CFR), which is a multivolume set that is updated at least once a year and constitutes prima facie evidence of the text of the original documents. The 50 titles of the CFR (which represent broad areas of Federal jurisdiction but unfortunately are not numbered to conform with the numbering of the titles of the United States Code) are divided into chapters each of which usually bears the name of the issuing agency involved; and each chapter is subdivided into parts covering specific substantive areas. The subject index, which is revised annually as of January 1, appears in a separate volume entitled *CFR Index and Finding Aids.*

The CFR is kept up-to-date by the individual issues of the Federal Register; thus the two publications must be read together if you need to find the latest version of any given rule or regulation. To determine whether a CFR volume has been amended since its most recent revision you should consult the *List of CFR Sections Affected* (LSA), which is published by the Office of the Federal Register, and the *Cumulative List of Parts Affected*, which is published daily in the *Federal Register.* The two lists will provide you with the page number in the *Federal Register* of the latest amendment to any given rule or regulation. The Government Publishing Office's website, on *govinfo.gov*, has all this information as well as the CFR in electronic format. The electronic version is updated when the printed versions are published. *Govinfo.gov* also has a wealth of other helpful information on the CFR, and has The Electronic Code of Federal Regulations (eCFR), which provides a way of exploring the Code of Federal Regulations as it exists at different points in time. The eCFR allows you to:

- browse the Code of Federal Regulations as it existed at any point in time;

- compare the regulations as they existed on any two dates;
- view a timeline of how the CFR content has changed;
- search for specific terms; and
- subscribe to changes in the regulations.

The eCFR is not an official legal edition of the CFR.

31.10 Equipping yourself for the job

As a drafter you will have to refer frequently to provisions of existing law, whether you are planning to amend that law (in which case you need a literal copy) or simply want a general understanding of it (in which case a nonliteral copy such as a nonpositive-law title of the United State Code is usually enough). And in either case you should be able to find what you want without bringing your other drafting activities to a grinding halt—that is, you need to know in advance where and how you will look for it.

What all of this means might be summarized as follows:

(1) Having on-hand at all times an up-to-date literal compilation of the laws to which you most often need to refer is the best way to avoid the necessity of looking further or of maintaining a large library and will allow you to work with a document that is thoroughly familiar to you.

(2) If the particular provisions in which you are interested are located in a positive-law title of the United States Code (see 31.4), you must know where to find it. As mentioned in 31.4, you must check for recent enactments that have affected sections of the Code.

(3) In any other case, even though you will normally start with the United States Code, you should always check the Statutes at Large or the relevant slip laws (or at least look at a recently enacted law that amends the statute containing the provisions you are interested in) to ensure that the form and style you are using is the correct one.

> Remember that half of the titles of the Code are not positive law and never reflect the correct form and style of the laws they contain.

Beyond this, as a precautionary measure, you should make sure you know in advance how to get your hands on any of the documents discussed in this chapter on short notice—you never know when you will need them. And if you will not be able to download them and print them, you should know where you can make photocopies, bearing in mind that some of them will require a machine that can handle large bound volumes.

Notes

1 In the second example, the typeface of the subsection headings is different from what would appear in nonpositive-law titles.

2 In the Senate, however, "extraneous" matters (that is, matters unrelated to reconciling the budget) are not in order in reconciliation bills (the commonly referred to "Byrd rule").

32. Legislative Vehicles in Congress

32.1 Preliminary comments

There are four basic vehicles that Congress can use to accomplish its legislative objectives—the bill, the joint resolution, the concurrent resolution, and the simple resolution. Each has its own special purpose.

The four basic vehicles are described in 32.2 through 32.5; 32.6 sets forth and discusses the forms in drafting them for introduction; and 32.7 discusses the forms that amendments to them may take. The discussions in 32.2 through 32.7 bear upon what you are likely to be doing in your everyday drafting assignments. What remains in this chapter, 32.8 through 32.14, is largely for informational purposes, since most readers will seldom if ever be called upon to prepare the documents involved; they address the special forms that the basic vehicles may take at later stages of the legislative process (where new and different considerations may apply). In each case examples of the vehicles and forms are given.

Any bill or resolution can originate in either the House of Representatives or the Senate, except for tax bills ("bills for raising revenue"), which are required by the Constitution to originate in the House, and appropriations bills, which traditionally also originate in the House. (These exceptions are more matters of form than of substance, as a practical matter, since the Senate can always propose or concur with whatever amendments it chooses.)

The vast majority of legislative measures introduced in Congress are bills—most of them introduced in the House of Representatives—but all four of the basic vehicles go through the same stages (with a few exceptions that will be noted later) as they move through the legislative process, whether they are bills or resolutions and whether they originate in the House or the Senate.

One word of warning, however: because it is one of the purposes of this chapter to distinguish between the various legislative vehicles, the broad definition of the term "bill" contained in 1.3 will be largely disregarded here—bills will be called bills, resolutions will be called resolutions, and amendments will be called amendments (although it should still be assumed that when reference is made to a House vehicle generically it could just as well have been made to the corresponding Senate vehicle).

32.2 Bills

A bill is the vehicle used for most legislation, whether that legislation is permanent or temporary, general or special, or public or private. Once it is passed by Congress, and is signed by the President (or becomes effective without his signature in a veto-override or failure-to-return case), it becomes the law of the land.

If a bill originates in the House of Representatives it is designated by the letters "H.R." followed by a number, and it retains this designation throughout all of its parliamentary stages; thus the 123rd bill introduced in the House in any Congress is designated "H.R. 123", even when it is being considered in the Senate. (The letters signify "House of Representatives" and not, as is sometimes supposed, "House resolution".) A bill that originates in the Senate is designated by the letter "S." followed by a number indicating its chronological place among the bills introduced in the Senate, but there are no other differences.

Figure 32.2 is an example of the beginning of a bill as introduced in the House. Except for its designation, this bill would look exactly the same if it had been introduced in the Senate.[1] (You will see the same bill again, later on, in its reported, engrossed, conference, and public-law forms.)

Note that the enacting clause is identical in all bills regardless of where they originate, and mentions the Senate before the House even when the bill involved is a House bill.

109TH CONGRESS
2D SESSION

H. R. 4954

To improve maritime and cargo security through enhanced layered defenses, and for other purposes.

IN THE HOUSE OF REPRESENTATIVES

MARCH 14, 2006

Mr. DANIEL E. LUNGREN of California (for himself, Ms. HARMAN, Mr. PEARCE, Mr. THOMPSON of Mississippi, Mr. BOEHLERT, Ms. LORETTA SANCHEZ of California, Mr. MCCAUL of Texas, Mr. DICKS, Mr. SOUDER, Mr. HOYER, Ms. HARRIS, Mr. DEFAZIO, Mr. JINDAL, Ms. JACKSON-LEE of Texas, Mr. SHAYS, Mr. LANGEVIN, Mr. DENT, Ms. NORTON, Mr. SIMMONS, Mr. ETHERIDGE, Ms. GINNY BROWN-WAITE of Florida, Mr. BROWN of South Carolina, Mr. MEEK of Florida, Mrs. BONO, Mr. LARSEN of Washington, Mr. FERGUSON, Mr. RUPPERSBERGER, Mr. GIBBONS, Mr. SMITH of Washington, Mr. PALLONE, Mr. CARDOZA, Mrs. MALONEY, Mrs. NAPOLITANO, Mr. BROWN of Ohio, Mr. SCHIFF, Mr. BERRY, Ms. EDDIE BERNICE JOHNSON of Texas, Ms. LEE, Ms. KILPATRICK of Michigan, Mr. FORD, Mr. PRICE of North Carolina, Mr. MCDERMOTT, Ms. ROYBAL-ALLARD, Mr. BRADY of Pennsylvania, Mr. BISHOP of Georgia, and Mr. WU) introduced the following bill; which was referred to the Committee on Homeland Security

---

A BILL

To improve maritime and cargo security through enhanced layered defenses, and for other purposes.

Be it enacted by the Senate and House of Representatives of the United States of America in Congress assembled,

Figure 32.2. Bill Introduced in the House (First Two Pages Only)

SECTION 1. SHORT TITLE; TABLE OF CONTENTS.

(a) SHORT TITLE.—This Act may be cited as the "Security and Accountability For Every Port Act" or "SAFE Port Act".

(b) TABLE OF CONTENTS.—The table of contents for this Act is as follows:

SEC. 2. FINDINGS.

Congress makes the following findings:

(1) Maritime vessels are the primary mode of transportation for international trade and they carry over 80 percent of international trade by volume.

(2) In 2004, maritime vessels carried approximately 9,700,000 shipping containers into United States seaports at an average of 27,000 containers per day.

Figure 32.2. Continued

32.3 Joint resolutions

A joint resolution may be thought of as the equivalent of a bill, in that each becomes the law of the land upon its final approval. Both are subject to the same requirements and procedures and they are completely interchangeable (with one exception discussed below); statutes that originated as bills can be amended by joint resolutions and vice versa.

In practice joint resolutions are generally (although they are not required to be) used for proposals that are narrower or more limited in scope.

If a joint resolution originates in the House of Representatives it is designated "H. J. Res." followed by its number, and it retains this designation throughout all of its parliamentary stages just like a bill. A joint resolution that originates in the Senate is designated "S. J. Res." followed by its number. The term "joint" does not signify that the resolution must be introduced in both Houses or be simultaneously considered by them.

Aside from their designations there are only a few relatively minor mechanical differences in form between bills and joint resolutions:

(1) A joint resolution has a resolving clause instead of an enacting clause—that is, it begins with the word "*Resolved*" instead of with the words "*Be it enacted*". The resolving clause (like the enacting clause in a bill) is identical in all joint resolutions regardless of where they originate.

(2) The title of a joint resolution customarily begins with a verb in its gerundive form rather than its infinitive form—"Providing for" or "Authorizing", for example, instead of "To provide for" or "To authorize" as in the case of a bill—but this is not a requirement.

(3) A joint resolution can contain a preamble (in the form of "whereas" clauses) if the sponsor wants to lead off with language justifying or explaining the need for the legislation; a bill cannot contain a preamble, and must do its justifying or explaining internally—usually in a separate "findings and purposes" section.

(4) A joint resolution refers to itself internally as a "joint resolution" rather than as an "Act", even though it is "enacted" just like a bill

Figure 32.3 is an example of a joint resolution as introduced in the House. Except for its designation, this resolution would look exactly the same if it had been introduced in the Senate.

110TH CONGRESS
1ST SESSION

H. J. RES. 14

Concerning the use of military force by the United States against Iran.

IN THE HOUSE OF REPRESENTATIVES

JANUARY 12, 2007

Mr. JONES of North Carolina introduced the following joint resolution; which was referred to the Committee on Foreign Affairs

JOINT RESOLUTION

Concerning the use of military force by the United States against Iran.

Resolved by the Senate and House of Representatives of the United States of America in Congress assembled,

SECTION 1. REQUIREMENTS CONCERNING THE USE OF MILITARY FORCE AGAINST IRAN.

(a) RULE OF CONSTRUCTION.—No provision of law enacted before the date of the enactment of this joint resolution shall be construed to authorize the use of military force by the United States against Iran.

(b) REQUIREMENTS.—Absent a national emergency created by attack by Iran, or a demonstrably imminent attack by Iran, upon the United States, its territories or

2

possessions or its armed forces, the President shall consult with Congress, and receive specific authorization pursuant to law from Congress, prior to initiating any use of military force against Iran.

Figure 32.3. Joint Resolution Introduced in the House

There is one situation in which a joint resolution should not be thought of as equivalent to a bill. Joint resolutions are the vehicles used in proposing amendments to the Constitution, and when used for this purpose they require a two-thirds vote in both Houses (a fact that is indicated in their resolving clauses). Upon their approval by such a vote they are signed by the Clerk of the House and the Secretary of the Senate and then sent directly to the Office of the Federal Register in the National Archives for submission to the States for ratification; they are not presented to the President.

32.4 Concurrent resolutions

A concurrent resolution is not actually legislative in character. It deals with matters of concern only to the two Houses of Congress—matters involving their joint procedures or operations, or simply expressing facts, opinions, or purposes (the "sense of Congress") that both Houses want to get on the record.

It has to pass both Houses in identical form in order to be effective, just like a bill or joint resolution, but (unlike the latter) it stops there—it is not presented to the President for signature, it does not become law, and it is not binding on anyone beyond the congressional establishment.

If a concurrent resolution originates in the House of Representatives it is designated "H. Con. Res." followed by its number. A concurrent resolution that originates in the Senate is designated "S. Con. Res." followed by its number. Upon approval by both Houses, it is signed by the Clerk of the House and the Secretary of the Senate and published in a special part of the Statutes at Large. The term "concurrent" does not signify that the resolution must be introduced in both Houses or be simultaneously considered by them.

Figure 32.4 is an example of a concurrent resolution as introduced in the House. Except for its designation and resolving clause, this resolution would look exactly the same if it had been introduced in the Senate. (A House concurrent resolution starts off "*Resolved by the House of Representatives (the Senate concurring)*", while a Senate concurrent resolution reverses the order and starts off "*Resolved by the Senate (the House of Representatives concurring)*").

118TH CONGRESS
1ST SESSION

H. CON. RES. 17

Expressing the sense of Congress that the Federal Government should not impose any restrictions on the export of crude oil or other petroleum products.

IN THE HOUSE OF REPRESENTATIVES

FEBRUARY 17, 2023

Mr. GUTHRIE submitted the following concurrent resolution; which was referred to the Committee on Energy and Commerce

---

CONCURRENT RESOLUTION

Expressing the sense of Congress that the Federal Government should not impose any restrictions on the export of crude oil or other petroleum products.

Whereas the United States has enjoyed a renaissance in energy production, with the expansion of domestic crude oil and other petroleum product production contributing to enhanced energy security and significant economic benefits to the national economy;

Whereas, in 2015, Congress recognized the need to adapt to changing crude oil market conditions and repealed all restrictions on the export of crude oil on a bipartisan basis;

Whereas lifting the restrictions on crude oil exports encouraged additional domestic energy production, created American jobs and economic development, and allowed

Figure 32.4. Concurrent Resolution Introduced in the House

2

the United States to emerge as the leading oil producer in the world;

Whereas, in 2019, the United States became a net exporter of petroleum products for the first time since 1952, and the reliance of the United States on foreign imports of petroleum products has declined to historic lows; and

Whereas free trade, open markets, and competition have contributed to the rise of the United States as a global energy superpower: Now, therefore, be it

Resolved by the House of Representatives (the Senate concurring), That it is the sense of Congress that the Federal Government should not impose—

(1) overly restrictive regulations on the exploration, production, or marketing of energy resources; or

(2) any restrictions on the export of crude oil or other petroleum products under the Energy Policy and Conservation Act (42 U.S.C. 6201 et seq.).

Figure 32.4. Continued

32.5 Simple resolutions

A simple resolution is like a concurrent resolution except that it deals only with matters of concern to the House in which it is introduced—matters involving the procedures or operations of that House, or expressing facts, opinions, or purposes that House wants to get on the record. It is considered only by the House in which it is introduced; as soon as it is approved by that House the job is done, and it has no effect on anyone outside of that House.

The most important uses of simple resolutions involve matters with which the reader of this book is not likely to be concerned:

(1) The organization of the House involved and its committees (at the beginning of each Congress).

(2) The establishment of the formal rules of the House involved (at the beginning of each Congress), and their subsequent amendment.

(3) In the House of Representatives, the establishment of the ad hoc "rules" (see 34.3) under which particular legislation is to be considered on the floor.

A simple resolution in the House of Representatives is designated "H. Res." followed by its number. A simple resolution in the Senate is designated "S. Res." followed by its number. Upon approval by the House involved, it is attested to by the appropriate official (the Clerk of the House or the Secretary of the Senate) and published in the *Congressional Record.*

Figure 32.5 is an example of a simple resolution as introduced in the Senate. Except for its designation and resolving clause (which of course mentions only the House of origin), this resolution would look exactly the same if it had been introduced in the House.

109TH CONGRESS
2D SESSION

S. RES. 456

Expressing the sense of the Senate on the discussion by the North Atlantic Council of secure, sustainable, and reliable sources of energy.

IN THE SENATE OF THE UNITED STATES

MAY 1, 2006

Mr. LUGAR submitted the following resolution; which was referred to the Committee on Foreign Relations

---

RESOLUTION

Expressing the sense of the Senate on the discussion by the North Atlantic Council of secure, sustainable, and reliable sources of energy.

Resolved, That it is the sense of the Senate that—

(1) the President should place on the agenda for discussion at the North Atlantic Council, as soon as practicable, the merits of establishing a policy and strategy for the North Atlantic Treaty Organization to promote the security of members of the Organization through the development of secure, sustainable, and reliable sources of energy; and

(2) the President should submit to Congress a report that sets forth—

Figure 32.5. Simple Resolution Introduced in the Senate

2

(A) the actions the United States has taken to place the matter referred to in paragraph (1) on the agenda for discussion at the North Atlantic Council;

(B) the position of the United States on the matter, as communicated to the North Atlantic Council by the representatives of the United States to the Council;

(C) a summary of the debate on the matter at the North Atlantic Council, including any decision that has been reached with respect to the matter by the Council; and

(D) a strategy for the North Atlantic Treaty Organization to develop secure, sustainable, and reliable sources of energy, including contingency plans if current energy resources are put at risk.

Figure 32.5. Continued

32.6 Using forms

Forms for preparing bills and resolutions in the House of Representatives and the Senate are computer-generated from a program uniquely designed for the demands of drafting legislation.[2] Other widely used word processing programs can, to some extent, copy the format. Chapter 33 (on the different drafting styles) may help in doing this.

Using the bill in figure 32.2 as a model, you will notice that the title is inserted in two places on the title page (below the "H.R. __" [the number is, of course, left blank; see the following paragraph]) and below "A BILL" (or their equivalent in the case of a resolution).

You as the drafter fill in the Congress and session, the title, and the sponsor's name when you complete the draft; the sponsor signs it; the appropriate legislative clerk (at the time of introduction) fills in the date and assigns the bill number; the parliamentarian adds a statement of the bill's committee reference; the printer adds a few mechanical touch-ups; and the deed is done. (Note that you should consult an official list showing the exact name by which each Member prefers to be called, including whether to use "Ms." or "Mrs." in the case of a female Member. It is a good idea to have one of these lists handy.[3])

If there are cosponsors, the blank for the sponsor's name is filled in "Mr. [Ms.] X [the primary sponsor, who introduces the bill], for himself [herself] and [the cosponsors]", although only the primary sponsor actually adds a personal signature. A cautious drafter, having no authority from the cosponsors, may choose to insert "[see attached list]" after the word "and"—not actually naming them—and lets the primary sponsor attach a list of the cosponsors' names before introducing the bill.

The form for a Senate bill is exactly the same (except that the designation is "S." instead of "H.R.").

Bills and resolutions are not required to be submitted in printed format; they can be written out in longhand (although that is not a good idea). You could create a first page for the bill by placing the sponsor's name at the indicated place (upper left), centering the heading "A BILL", locating the title immediately below that heading and the enacting clause (or at least a paraphrase of it, such as "Be it enacted, etc.") below the title. The bill clerk of the House involved will fill in the rest of the blanks when it has been introduced.

32.7 Amendments in committee and on the floor

Woodrow Wilson observed that "Congress in session is Congress on public exhibition, whilst Congress in its committee-rooms is Congress at work."[4] This may be a slight overstatement, but it is certainly true that the most tangible manifestation of Congress's work on legislation is found in the amendments it adopts, and although some will come later, of course, most of them are adopted in its "committee-rooms."

An amendment offered to one of the basic legislative vehicles (a bill or resolution) is itself a legislative vehicle, in the sense that it is the recognized parliamentary device for changing what the basic vehicle does. The basic vehicle's message, more often than not, turns out to be (in whole or in part) the message carried to that vehicle by amendments that were offered to it at various stages of the legislative process.

But in terms of form amendments involve considerations that are quite different from those that apply to the bills and resolutions to which they are offered. As indicated earlier (in part V), there are two principal differences in form and style that you should keep in mind, both having to do with the form of the vehicular amendatory language.

First, an amendment to a bill is really nothing more than an instruction to the legislative official who will assemble and print the final product—the enrolling clerk of the House involved, for example— and is therefore always stated in the imperative mood, while an amendment to existing law in a bill is treated as being self-executing and is therefore always stated in the indicative mood.

Second, in a printed bill or resolution, every line (beginning with the first line of the enacting or resolving clause) is numbered; so the place in the bill where the amendment is to appear is normally identified simply by a reference to the relevant page and line number rather than by a descriptive reference to the provision being amended.

In a sense, the moment a bill or resolution is introduced, it comes into the custody of the House or Senate enrolling clerk, whose job during the legislative process is to keep up with it by incorporating any amendments that may be adopted from time to time. This job is initially handled at the committee stage by the professional staff of the committee involved, but in a practical sense every amendment made to a bill after its introduction is simply a way of telling the enrolling clerk how to make a specified change in it.

What this means to the drafter is that the formal requirements are relatively easy to satisfy. If the enrolling clerk can understand from reading an amendment exactly what you want the clerk to do to a bill, the amendment meets the test. Shorthand devices are quite appropriate; thus, although a bill that inserts a new numbered paragraph in the middle of an existing subsection would have to explicitly renumber the subsequent paragraphs, an amendment that does the same thing in a subsection of a bill need only include the phrase "and renumber [or redesignate] the succeeding paragraphs accordingly". (You can even add the words "and any cross-references thereto" if cross-references need to be conformed and you are short of time, although this is asking a little much of the clerk.)

In the House there is no standard or required form for amendments to bills and resolutions. You can simply indicate the bill's or resolution's number and the Member's name and then state the amendment in page-and-line terms. For example:

Amendments to H.R. 1234

Offered by Mr. [Ms.] X

Page 3, line 5, strike "four" and insert "seven".

Page 6, beginning on line 11, strike "but the Secretary" and all that follows through page 8, line 2, and insert a period.

Page 9, strike the paragraph beginning on line 4 [or strike lines 4 through 10].

In the Senate the form of proposed amendments requires additional information. Figure 32.7 sets forth the amendment form in the Senate.

AMENDMENT NO.____ Calendar No.___

Purpose:

IN THE SENATE OF THE UNITED STATES —119th [*or current number*] Cong., 1st [*or current*] Sess.

[official title of the bill]

Referred to the Committee on __________ and ordered to be printed

Ordered to lie on the table and to be printed

AMENDMENT intended to be proposed by _______

Viz:

At the appropriate place, insert the following:

[amendment-body]

Figure 32.7. Amendment Form in the Senate

Note that in some situations the document being amended has no line numbers (and occasionally no page numbers either), so you cannot use the page-and-line-number approach. Such a situation might involve—

(1) a bill that has not yet been introduced, or a subcommittee or committee substitute to a bill that may undergo further changes prior to consideration that will realign page and line numbers;

(2) an amendment that is to be offered to another amendment already offered by someone else (in the Senate the previous amendment will have sometimes been printed with line numbers prior to consideration on the Senate floor; in the House amendments are never so printed); or

(3) an amendment to the long title of a bill or resolution, or to the preamble of a resolution, since those are matters that appear before the enacting or resolving clause and thus are never given line numbers.

In addition, keep in mind that the text of the bill to which amendments are to be drafted for consideration on the floor of the House or Senate may be available online (in the House, on the website of the Committee on Rules), but in many cases this is before this version is printed. Once printed, the page and line numbers can change; you cannot, therefore, rely on the earlier online version.

In situations described in (1) and (2), and in the situation addressed in the preceding paragraph, you should identify both the section or other provision you are amending and the language you are proposing to amend. For example, instead of

> "Page 3, line 6, strike 'XX' and insert 'YY' ",

you would say

> "In section [2(a)(1)] of the bill, strike 'XX' and insert 'YY' ".

If there is more than one occurrence of "XX" in the provision, you will either have to identify it as "strike 'XX' the [first] [second] place it appears" or identify the XX you are striking by striking more words around it that are unique to that occurrence of XX and reinserting them:

> "strike 'not more than XX but' and insert 'not more than YY but' ".

If the bill amends an existing provision of law, and you want to amend the existing provision, it is trickier. You would have to identify both the provision of the bill and the provision of existing law: "In section 123(a) of the XYZ Act, as contained in section 2(a) of the bill, strike 'XX' and insert 'YY' ".

If the clerk responsible for executing the amendment can understand your instructions, you will have done your job. You may even get away with identifying the provision by its subject matter—"In the provision relating to eligibility…", for example—although again that is often asking a good deal of the clerk.

In situation (3) addressed above, if the amendment is to the long title, you should always state the new and revised title in its entirety (even if only a single word or punctuation mark would be changed):

> Amend the title so as to read: "A Bill to promote good animal husbandry, and for other purposes.".

And if the amendment is to one of a resolution's whereas clauses you simply refer to it by its ordinal number—for example, "Amend the fifth [whereas] clause in the preamble…".

(Note that amendments to the long title or preamble are never offered or considered until all amendments to the text have been disposed of. In the House they are not considered at all in the Committee of the Whole (where the other amendments are considered), but must wait until the Committee has "risen" and the action resumes in the "Whole House"—see chapter 34.)

32.8 Reported bills

The first official printing of a bill is of course the introduced version, and the second official printing occurs when it is reported to the House involved by the committee to which it was referred. The reported version is easy to distinguish from the introduced bill by its report number, its calendar number, and a few other typographical legends that appear at the top of the front page. If the bill is reported unchanged there are no other differences; but if there were committee amendments they are incorporated into the bill.

The committee's amendments are shown in linetype and italic; that is, any part of the introduced bill that would be stricken out is retained but printed with a line through it, and matter that would be added is printed in italic type. All unchanged portions of the bill remain in roman type. There is one exception: if the committee struck all of the text of the introduced bill and inserted a complete substitute and the stricken language was lengthy, the reported bill sometimes omits the stricken language altogether, starting off (right after the enacting clause) with the proposed substitute (entirely printed in italic) and simply referring readers who want to know what was eliminated to the introduced bill.

Note that the committee report itself (which "accompanies" the bill at this stage) will set forth all of the committee's amendments one by one, just as they were shown in the reported bill itself (except of course that they are individually listed by page and line instead of being incorporated into the bill at the places where they appear). However, it is a common practice for a committee (or subcommittee), after making a number of amendments to a bill that was referred to it, either to introduce a completely new bill (with a new number) incorporating all of the amendments and then report that bill without amendment, or to incorporate all the amendments adopted into one amendment in the nature of a substitute (instead of achieving the same purpose by reporting the original bill with amendments). This often simplifies the process and (and in the case of a newly introduced bill) avoids parliamentary problems; and the differences between the two bills or two versions of the bill can be explained in the accompanying committee report.

To get a clearer picture of what the reporting process typically involves, you might take as an example the bill (H.R. 4954 of the 109th Congress) that was shown in its introduced form in 32.2. To see how it looked (the first two pages) as reported with an amendment, see figure 32.8A.

Note the additional legends at the beginning of the reported bill, and the italic treatment of the committee's amendment.

As indicated earlier, the drafter's functions in connection with bills reported from committee may vary widely, depending in any particular case on the committee's procedures, the drafter's personal relationship with the committee's professional staff, and the nature of the project.

The committee staff will always handle the bulk of the accompanying committee report—the committee's findings and recommendations, executive communications, the "bombast" (including the factual background, the reasons and justifications for the committee's actions, and the economics of the proposal), and the various declarations (on matters such as inflationary impact and estimated cost) that have to be included in order to satisfy the rules of the House involved.

As the on-the-scene drafter you would normally have three relatively specific functions:

(1) The preparation of the reported bill itself, properly incorporating all of the committee's amendments.

(2) The preparation of the first part of the accompanying report, which lists those amendments.

(3) The preparation of the part of the report that is necessary to comply with the "Ramseyer rule" (see below) if it applies.

You may in theory also be called upon to do the assembling of the committee's accompanying report—putting together the parts that you have written and the parts that the committee staff has provided if, for example, there are minority or dissenting views whose authors wish to keep the majority from seeing them in time to include an effective rebuttal in the main body of the report. And occasionally you might be asked to write (or review) a section-by-section analysis (as a technician, not as an advocate) for inclusion in the report.

Union Calendar No. 250

109TH CONGRESS
2D SESSION

H. R. 4954

[Report No. 109–447]

To improve maritime and cargo security through enhanced layered defenses, and for other purposes.

IN THE HOUSE OF REPRESENTATIVES

MARCH 14, 2006

Mr. DANIEL E. LUNGREN of California (for himself, Ms. HARMAN, Mr. PEARCE, Mr. THOMPSON of Mississippi, Mr. BOEHLERT, Ms. LORETTA SANCHEZ of California, Mr. MCCAUL of Texas, Mr. DICKS, Mr. SOUDER, Mr. HOYER, Ms. HARRIS, Mr. DEFAZIO, Mr. JINDAL, Ms. JACKSON-LEE of Texas, Mr. SHAYS, Mr. LANGEVIN, Mr. DENT, Ms. NORTON, Mr. SIMMONS, Mr. ETHERIDGE, Ms. GINNY BROWN-WAITE of Florida, Mr. BROWN of South Carolina, Mr. MEEK of Florida, Mrs. BONO, Mr. LARSEN of Washington, Mr. FERGUSON, Mr. RUPPERSBERGER, Mr. GIBBONS, Mr. SMITH of Washington, Mr. PALLONE, Mr. CARDOZA, Mrs. MALONEY, Mrs. NAPOLITANO, Mr. BROWN of Ohio, Mr. SCHIFF, Mr. BERRY, Ms. EDDIE BERNICE JOHNSON of Texas, Ms. LEE, Ms. KILPATRICK of Michigan, Mr. FORD, Mr. PRICE of North Carolina, Mr. MCDERMOTT, Ms. ROYBAL-ALLARD, Mr. BRADY of Pennsylvania, Mr. BISHOP of Georgia, and Mr. WU) introduced the following bill; which was referred to the Committee on Homeland Security

APRIL 28, 2006

Reported with an amendment and referred to the Committee on Transportation and Infrastructure for a period ending not later than May 1, 2006, for consideration of such provisions of the bill and amendment as fall within the jurisdiction of that committee pursuant to clause 1(r), rule X

[Strike out all after the enacting clause and insert the part printed in italic]

MAY 1, 2006

Additional sponsors: Mr. LINDER, Mr. FOLEY, Mrs. JO ANN DAVIS of Virginia, Mr. PLATTS, Mr. BACHUS, Mr. WELDON of Pennsylvania, Mrs. MYRICK, Mr. KLINE, Mr. CUMMINGS, Ms. BERKLEY, Mr. WEINER, Mr. MCNULTY, Ms. WASSERMAN SCHULTZ, Mr. SCOTT of Virginia, Mr.

Figure 32.8A. Reported Bill in the House (First Two Pages Only)

CASE, Mrs. TAUSCHER, Mr. BAIRD, Mr. SWEENEY, Mr. GEORGE MILLER of California, Mr. INSLEE, Mrs. CHRISTENSEN, Mr. BISHOP of New York, Mr. CROWLEY, Mr. AL GREEN of Texas, Mr. SMITH of New Jersey, Ms. WATSON, Mr. REICHERT, Mr. FOSSELLA, Mrs. DAVIS of California, Mr. ROTHMAN, Mr. TOM DAVIS of Virginia, Mr. KING of New York, Mr. SMITH of Texas, Mr. MOORE of Kansas, and Mr. COSTA

MAY 1, 2006

Committee on Transportation and Infrastructure discharged; committed to the Committee of the Whole House on the State of the Union and ordered to be printed

[For text of introduced bill, see copy of bill as introduced on March 14, 2006]

A BILL

To improve maritime and cargo security through enhanced layered defenses, and for other purposes.

Be it enacted by the Senate and House of Representatives of the United States of America in Congress assembled,

SEC. 1. SHORT TITLE; TABLE OF CONTENTS.

(a) SHORT TITLE.—This Act may be cited as the "Security and Accountability For Every Port Act" or "SAFE Port Act".

(b) TABLE OF CONTENTS.—The table of contents for this Act is as follows:

Figure 32.8A. Continued

The "Ramseyer rule", which was originally proposed by Representative Christian Ramseyer and adopted in 1929, is a requirement in the House rules that whenever a committee reports legislation amending or repealing a provision of existing law (whether the amendment or repeal results from the introduced bill itself or from committee amendments), the accompanying committee report must show the changes by "appropriate typographical devices". Usually this is done by setting forth the existing law with the stricken matter in boldface brackets, the new matter in italics, and the remaining (unchanged) matter in roman type; occasionally it is done by showing the changes in parallel columns. The Senate has a similar requirement, which is known as the "Cordon rule" (although it too is often colloquially referred to as a "Ramseyer"). Compliance with the Ramseyer rule can be a massive job or a simple mechanical one, depending on the number and complexity of the changes in existing law that the bill makes.

(Note that the Ramseyer rule is one of the most important reasons why you should "narrow your target" as recommended in 16.1; read literally it requires that the report show all of any provision of existing law that is changed even slightly. Thus when you want to revise a sentence in paragraph (3) of section 6(b) of some existing law you should start off by saying "The third sentence in section 6(b)(3) [of the ABC Act] is amended...", rather than "Section 6 of [the ABC Act] is amended...", even though either could do the job, because in the latter case [in theory at least] the Ramseyer would have to show gratuitously a great deal of unchanged language from section 6 in addition to the target sentence itself.)

Figure 32.8B shows the first two pages of the report on H.R. 4954, setting forth the beginning of the committee's amendment. (Note that the front page reflects three types of "views" submitted by Members (minority, dissenting, and additional). Committee reports can be quite lengthy. This one consists of 155 pages of small, single-spaced typeface.

A few final comments deserve to be made on the subject of committees and reported bills:

(1) When a subcommittee reports a bill to its full committee, no official printing of the bill occurs. However, if the subcommittee has made amendments, an informal intermediate version with the amendments in place, or a detailed summary of the subcommittee's actions, is usually prepared for the full committee's convenience.

(2) If the introduced bill was referred to more than one committee, as often happens in the case of major bills that are broad in scope, there may be special problems for the drafter and others. When the bill is taken up on the floor, can one committee amend another committee's amendments? Indeed, how do you distinguish one committee's amendments from another's on the face of the bill? The variations are infinite. Suffice it to say that the procedures to be followed in any particular case will be determined by the parliamentarian of the House involved on an ad hoc basis, and you should be very sure of what those procedures are before beginning work on committee amendments.

(3) The committee amendments shown in a reported bill are only proposed amendments. Even though they may have more "steam" behind them (since they represent the collective product of an established body of specialized legislators), they still have to be offered and adopted on the floor just like any other amendments. To the extent that they have more dignity than amendments offered on the floor by individual Members, it is only because (A) they are actually printed in the reported bill, and (B) they are generally taken up (often en bloc) before the individual Members' amendments (they are usually made in order (in the House) under the ad hoc rule accompanying the bill's consideration on the floor), which may give them a tactical advantage.

(4) Published committee hearings are not legislative vehicles in the sense in which we have been using that term. Hearings, studies, and oversight reports may have real value for the policymakers, but they seldom concern the drafter directly.

109TH CONGRESS } HOUSE OF REPRESENTATIVES { REPT. 109–447
2d Session } { Part 1

SECURITY AND ACCOUNTABILITY FOR EVERY PORT ACT

APRIL 28, 2006.—Ordered to be printed

Mr. KING of New York, from the Committee on Homeland Security, submitted the following

REPORT

together with

MINORITY, DISSENTING, AND ADDITIONAL VIEWS

[To accompany H.R. 4954]

[Including cost estimate of the Congressional Budget Office]

The Committee on Homeland Security, to whom was referred the bill (H.R. 4954) to improve maritime and cargo security through enhanced layered defenses, and for other purposes, having considered the same, report favorably thereon with an amendment and recommend that the bill as amended do pass.

CONTENTS

The amendment is as follows:

49–006

Figure 32.8B. House Report Showing an Amendment by a Committee (First Two Pages Only)

2

Strike all after the enacting clause and insert the following:

SECTION 1. SHORT TITLE; TABLE OF CONTENTS.

(a) SHORT TITLE.—This Act may be cited as the "Security and Accountability For Every Port Act" or "SAFE Port Act".

(b) TABLE OF CONTENTS.—The table of contents for this Act is as follows:

SEC. 2. FINDINGS.

Congress makes the following findings:

(1) Maritime vessels are the primary mode of transportation for international trade and they carry over 80 percent of international trade by volume.

(2) In 2004, maritime vessels carried approximately 9,700,000 shipping containers into United States seaports at an average of 27,000 containers per day.

(3) The security of the international container supply chain and the maritime transportation system is critical for the prosperity and liberty of all countries.

(4) In its final report, the National Commission on Terrorist Attacks Upon the United States noted, "While commercial aviation remains a possible target, terrorists may turn their attention to other modes of transportation. Opportunities to do harm are as great, or greater in maritime or surface transportation.".

(5) In May 2002, the Brookings Institution estimated that costs associated with United States port closures from a detonated terrorist weapon could add up to $1 trillion from the resulting economic slump and changes in our Nation's inability to trade. Anticipated port closures on the west coast of the United States could cost the United States economy $1 billion per day for the first five days after a terrorist attack.

(6) Significant steps have been taken since the terrorist attacks against the United States that occurred on September 11, 2001:

(A) Congress passed the Maritime Transportation Security Act of 2002 on November 14, 2002.

(B) The Coast Guard issued a comprehensive set of port security regulations on October 22, 2003.

Figure 32.8B. Continued

32.9 Engrossed bills

There may be hundreds of amendments offered to a bill (and adopted) on the floor,[5] or there may be none at all; but when the smoke clears and the bill has been passed it is the function of the enrolling clerk of the House involved to put together the "engrossed bill", which is the third official version of the bill and the only official version of what that House did.

The engrossed bill is prepared by taking the reported bill, eliminating any of the committee amendments that were rejected on the floor, and incorporating into it all the other amendments (committee and individual) that were adopted on the floor. It looks and feels different from either of the earlier versions, and is recognizable by several changes in its form:

(1) Most of the mechanical items at the front of the bill (including the name of the sponsor, the date of introduction, and the material relating to committee reference) have disappeared.

(2) It now describes itself as "AN ACT" instead of as "A BILL" (even though it has of course not yet actually been enacted).

(3) It is printed on heavier stock and, if it is a House bill, on blue paper.

(4) The attestation of the Clerk of the House (or the Secretary of the Senate in the case of a Senate bill) appears at the end.

Note, however, that the final action in the second body always takes the form of an amendment or amendments to the first body's engrossed bill, consisting either of a complete substitute or of cut-and-bite amendments; the resulting document is headed "AMENDMENT" or "AMENDMENTS", without an enacting or resolving clause, and is properly referred to as the "engrossed amendment" (or "engrossed amendments") of that body.

Figure 32.9A (without attempting to reproduce the blue paper) shows the beginning of H.R. 4954 in its engrossed form, with the Clerk's attestation at the end of the bill; figure 32.9B shows the first pages of the Senate's engrossed amendment, with the Secretary of the Senate's attestation at the end.

As a drafter you should ideally use the engrossed version of a bill when working on amendments to the bill in the second body, simply because it is the only official version. This is available on the website *www.congress.gov*. As indicated earlier, the earliest version printed in the second House is a copy of the bill as passed the first House as "messaged over" to the second House, and should be completely reliable.

Note that every bill that passes Congress goes through the same three official printings in both Houses—the introduced, reported, and engrossed versions—at least if you treat the "messaged over" version in the second body as that body's introduced version and the engrossed amendments of the second body as its engrossed bill.

109TH CONGRESS
2D SESSION

H. R. 4954

AN ACT

To improve maritime and cargo security through enhanced layered defenses, and for other purposes.

Be it enacted by the Senate and House of Representatives of the United States of America in Congress assembled,

2

SECTION 1. SHORT TITLE; TABLE OF CONTENTS.

(a) SHORT TITLE.—This Act may be cited as the "Security and Accountability For Every Port Act" or "SAFE Port Act".

(b) TABLE OF CONTENTS.—The table of contents for this Act is as follows:

Figure 32.9A. House Engrossed Bill (First Two Pages Only and Clerk's Attestation)

TITLE I—SECURITY OF UNITED STATES SEAPORTS

Subtitle A—General Provisions

Subtitle B—Grant and Training Programs

Subtitle C—Miscellaneous Provisions

TITLE II—SECURITY OF THE INTERNATIONAL SUPPLY CHAIN

•HR 4954 EH

* * * * *

Passed the House of Representatives May 4, 2006.

Attest:

Clerk.

Figure 32.9A. Continued

32.10 Conference reports

It is not enough that the House and Senate both pass the same bill—they must both pass it in identical form if it is to become law. Unless one body is willing to accept the other's version in its entirety, or a compromise between their two versions can be worked out entirely through amendments adopted on the floor, a committee of conference consisting of Members of the House of Representatives and Senators must be appointed to iron out the differences. Those appointed are called the "conferees", or (more formally) the "managers on the part of the two Houses".

Although most bills are agreed to without the necessity of a conference, major bills will likely go through this stage.

A conference report is simply the document that shows what the conferees on a bill have done. It sets forth the bill in its final form (either verbatim or by reference to the action taken on the individual items in dispute), and is accompanied (in the same document) by a "joint explanatory statement of the committee of conference" explaining what happened and why.

In the Senate of the United States,

September 14, 2006.

Resolved, That the bill from the House of Representatives (H.R. 4954) entitled "An Act to improve maritime and cargo security through enhanced layered defenses, and for other purposes.", do pass with the following

AMENDMENT:

Strike out all after the enacting clause and insert:

SECTION 1. SHORT TITLE; TABLE OF CONTENTS.

(a) SHORT TITLE.—This Act may be cited as the "Port Security Improvement Act of 2006".

Figure 32.9B. Senate Engrossed Amendment (First Two Pages Only and Secretary's Attestation)

(b) TABLE OF CONTENTS.—The table of contents for this Act is as follows:

Sec. 1. Short title; table of contents.
Sec. 2. Definitions.

TITLE I—SECURITY OF UNITED STATES SEAPORTS

Subtitle A—General Provisions

Sec. 101. Area Maritime Transportation Security Plan to include salvage response plan.
Sec. 102. Requirements relating to maritime facility security plans.
Sec. 103. Unannounced inspections of maritime facilities.
Sec. 104. Transportation security card.
Sec. 105. Prohibition of issuance of transportation security cards to convicted felons.
Sec. 106. Long-range vessel tracking.
Sec. 107. Establishment of interagency operational centers for port security.
Sec. 108. Notice of Arrival for foreign vessels on the outer Continental Shelf.

Subtitle B—Port Security Grants; Training and Exercise Programs

Sec. 111. Port Security Grants.
Sec. 112. Port Security Training Program.
Sec. 113. Port Security Exercise Program.

Subtitle C—Port Operations

Sec. 121. Domestic radiation detection and imaging.
Sec. 122. Port Security user fee study.
Sec. 123. Inspection of car ferries entering from Canada.
Sec. 124. Random searches of containers.
Sec. 125. Work stoppages and employee-employer disputes.
Sec. 126. Threat assessment screening of port truck drivers.

TITLE II—SECURITY OF THE INTERNATIONAL SUPPLY CHAIN

Subtitle A—General Provisions

Sec. 201. Strategic plan to enhance the security of the international supply chain.
Sec. 202. Post incident resumption of trade.
Sec. 203. Automated Targeting System.
Sec. 204. Container security standards and procedures.
Sec. 205. Container Security Initiative.

Subtitle B—Customs-Trade Partnership Against Terrorism

Sec. 211. Establishment.
Sec. 212. Eligible entities.
Sec. 213. Minimum requirements.
Sec. 214. Tier 1 participants in C–TPAT.
Sec. 215. Tier 2 participants in C–TPAT.
Sec. 216. Tier 3 participants in C–TPAT.
Sec. 217. Consequences for lack of compliance.
Sec. 218. Revalidation.

Figure 32.9B. Continued

* * * * *

HR 4954 EAS

Attest:

Secretary.

Figure 32.9B. Continued

The terminology here may be a bit confusing. The term "conference report" is popularly used to describe the entire document filed by the conferees, but in a literal sense only the part of the document that contains the legislative language is the "conference report"—the remainder is the "joint statement". It is important to remember that the conference report itself is the bill, not a report like a committee report, and that only the joint statement resembles what would normally be considered a "report".

A few comments about conference organization and procedure may be in order before addressing the conference report itself:

(1) With respect to any particular difference between the House and Senate versions of a bill, either House may surrender to the other, or the two Houses (within parliamentary limitations) may agree upon a compromise provision acceptable to both.

(2) Each House determines for itself the number of conferees it will have. The number makes no difference (one House may have 17 and the other 3) because the conferees from each House collectively cast a single vote on any matter in disagreement, and both the conference report and the joint statement must be signed by a majority of them.

(3) Conferees are usually chosen from the members of the standing committees that had jurisdiction over the bill (although occasionally

a noncommittee member who sponsored an important amendment to it on the floor will be included). They elect their own chairman, who may be from either House; in cases where there are periodic conferences involving similar bills and substantially the same members (such as annual authorization Acts in a particular field), the chairmanship customarily alternates between the two Houses.

(4) Separate conference reports are filed in the House and Senate—identical but each with its own report number—and once filed the conference report must be adopted as is in each House; it may not be amended on the floor. (There is a special procedure in the House for eliminating nongermane matter from a conference report (see 34.8).

The conference stage of a bill is generally considered the most important single stage because the small number of conferees makes it possible to actually address the substantive problems and negotiate the differences, the conferees are usually appointed from among Members who are particularly knowledgeable about the matters involved, and their final product is voted on by both Houses without amendment (and with very limited debate).

The terminology and variations of conference reports could be the subject of an entire book (the most common variations being those involving amendments to the title as well as the text, bills that have bounced back and forth between the two Houses before going to conference, and bills reported in disagreement—all discussed briefly below). Suffice it to say here that every conference report takes one of two forms:

(1) **The complete substitute.** When one House has simply substituted its own text for the entire text of the bill as passed by the other, the conference report will do the same—it will treat the second House's text as a single amendment and will set forth in the report (as a single amendment) its own substitute for the entire text of both the House and Senate versions. This is by far the most common form of conference report, and the simplest; after the front page it is plain bill text (although printed in italic type), just like any other amendment that begins "strike all after the enacting clause and insert the following:".

(2) **Numbered amendments.** When one House has made cut-and-bite amendments at specific places in the bill as passed by the other (rather than adopting a complete substitute), every amendment is assigned a number—there may be anywhere from one to 1,000—and the conference is very different. It must deal separately with each amendment (and may not deal at all, in theory at least, with any part of the bill that is not included within one of the amendments). In this case the conference report will not show the bill as a whole; instead, it will consist of—

(A) a list of the numbers of the specific amendments on which the House surrendered outright;

(B) a list of the numbers of the specific amendments on which the Senate surrendered outright; and

(C) a series of paragraphs (referring to the remaining amendments in numerical order), each of which sets forth the conferees' compromise action on a particular amendment.

This form of conference report, if used at all, would be used on bills from the Ways and Means and Appropriations Committees. It tends to be complicated and largely incomprehensible, is highly technical, and gives the casual reader no clue about what the bill is going to look like when the enrolling clerk gets through putting it together.

(There is a standard format for the front page of a complete-substitute conference report and for the front page of a numbered-amendments conference report. There is also a standard format for the front page of a joint statement. But you would need to know them only if you are responsible for assembling the final product. These formats are the same in both Houses except for any necessary reversals of the terms "House" and "Senate", and are always used.)

Figure 32.10A shows the first and last pages of the complete-substitute conference report on H.R. 4954 (the statement of managers is omitted).

And just for purposes of comparison, Figure 32.10B is an example (entirely unrelated, of course) showing the beginning and end of a numbered-amendments conference report (which is unusual).

Finally, a word about a few of the more common variants that were mentioned a few pages back:

(1) If the conference involves an amendment to the bill's title as well as one or more amendments to its text, the amendment to the title is treated separately—after the text has been disposed of. (Thus if the conference report on H.R. 4954 had included an amendment to the bill's title there would have been two amendments in disagreement, and the introductory language of the report would have referred only to the Senate amendment "to the text of the bill"; the amendment to the title would have been dealt with later—immediately before the conferees' signatures.)

(2) If the bill has bounced back and forth between the two Houses one or more times before going to conference, it is the action of the last House from which it bounced that is the subject of the conference; the conference report might describe itself, for example, as being "on the amendments of the House to the amendments of the Senate to the bill H.R. 1234" instead of just being "on the amendments of the Senate to the bill H.R. 1234".

(3) When the conferees are unwilling or unable to file a report in full agreement, one of three possible situations exists:

(A) The conferees may actually be unable to reach any agreement at all (or to reach agreement on the really basic differences). In this situation they may just allow the bill to die without any formal action, possibly calling for another conference, or they may file a conference report "in disagreement" without addressing any of the issues involved. In the latter case the report simply states that the conferees "have been unable to agree"; and in either case the process reverts to the point to which it had progressed when the conferees were appointed. At this point, however, motions that tend to bring the two Houses of Congress together become privileged and preferential—for example, a motion to recede and concur in the Senate amendment.

(B) With numbered amendments, the conferees may have reached agreement on most of the issues but be unable to reach agreement on all of them. In this case they usually file a normal conference report showing all the amendments that were agreed to, and report the bill with the remaining amendments still in disagreement; the latter are taken up one by one on the floor of each House immediately after it adopts the conference report. (All of the remaining amendments must of course be agreed to in some form before the bill can be said to have passed.)

(C) The conferees may have actually reached a complete agreement among themselves but cannot file a report incorporating that agreement because it would include matter outside the "scope" of the conference and would therefore be subject to a parliamentary challenge on the floor of either House (see 34.8). Here, too, the conference report is filed "in disagreement", but the disagreement is "technical"; it is anticipated that the language the conference committee would have reported (including the offending provisions) will in fact be agreed to in one form or another on the floor of the two Houses (where there would be no problem with scope), and the joint statement accompanying the report will normally make clear both the problem and the expected solution.

Despite all of the procedural issues discussed in (3)(A), (B), and (C), however, parliamentary challenges in the House of Representatives can rarely be raised because conference reports are routinely considered under an ad hoc rule that waives points of order against them.

109TH CONGRESS
2d Session } HOUSE OF REPRESENTATIVES { REPORT
109–711

SAFE PORT ACT

SEPTEMBER 29, 2006.—Ordered to be printed

Mr. KING of New York, from the committee of conference, submitted the following

CONFERENCE REPORT

[To accompany H.R. 4954]

The committee of conference on the disagreeing votes of the two Houses on the amendment of the Senate to the bill (H.R. 4954), to improve maritime and cargo security through enhanced layered defenses, and for other purposes, having met, after full and free conference, have agreed to recommend and do recommend to their respective Houses as follows:

That the House recede from its disagreement to the amendment of the Senate and agree to the same with an amendment as follows:

In lieu of the matter proposed to be inserted by the Senate amendment, insert the following:

SECTION 1. SHORT TITLE; TABLE OF CONTENTS.

(a) SHORT TITLE.—This Act may be cited as the "Security and Accountability For Every Port Act of 2006" or the "SAFE Port Act".

(b) TABLE OF CONTENTS.—The table of contents for this Act is as follows:

49–006

* * * * *

Figure 32.10A. House Complete-Substitute Conference Report (First and Last Pages)

80

(b) REPORT REQUIRED.—The Secretary of the Treasury shall submit an annual report to the Congress on any deliberations between the United States and other countries on issues relating to Internet gambling.

And the Senate agree to the same.

From the Committee on Homeland Security:
PETER KING,
DANIEL E. LUNGREN,
JOHN LINDER,
ROB SIMMONS,
DAVID REICHERT,
MICHAEL T. MCCAUL,
DON YOUNG,
BENNIE G. THOMPSON,
LORETTA SANCHEZ,
JANE HARMAN,
BILL PASCRELL, Jr.,

From the Committee on Energy and Commerce:
JOE BARTON,
FRED UPTON,

From the Committee on Transportation and Infrastructure:
BILL SHUSTER,

From the Committee on Science:
SHERWOOD BOEHLERT,
MIKE SODREL,
CHARLIE MELANCON,

From the Committee on Ways and Means:
WM. THOMAS,
E. CLAY SHAW, Jr.,
Managers on the Part of the House.

From the Committee on Homeland Security and Governmental Affairs:
SUSAN COLLINS,
NORM COLEMAN,
R.F. BENNETT,

From the Committee on Commerce, Science, and Transportation:
TED STEVENS,
TRENT LOTT,
KAY BAILEY HUTCHISON,

From the Committee on Finance:
CHUCK GRASSLEY,
ORRIN HATCH,
MAX BAUCUS,

From the Committee on Banking, Housing, and Urban Affairs:
RICHARD SHELBY,
Managers on the Part of the Senate.

Figure 32.10A. Continued

105TH CONGRESS
1st Session

HOUSE OF REPRESENTATIVES

REPORT
105–337

MAKING APPROPRIATIONS FOR THE DEPARTMENT OF THE INTERIOR AND RELATED AGENCIES, FOR THE FISCAL YEAR ENDING SEPTEMBER 30, 1998, AND FOR OTHER PURPOSES

OCTOBER 22, 1997.—Ordered to be printed

Mr. REGULA, from the committee on conference, submitted the following

CONFERENCE REPORT

[To accompany H.R. 2107]

The committee of conference on the disagreeing votes of the two Houses on the amendments of the Senate to the bill (H.R. 2107) "making appropriations for the Department of the Interior and Related Agencies, for the fiscal year ending September 30, 1998, and for other purposes," having met, after full and free conference, have agreed to recommend and do recommend to their respective Houses as follows:

That the Senate recede from its amendments numbered 4, 6, 7, 13, 28, 30, 35, 40, 54, 61, 91, 95, 106, 131.

That the House recede from its disagreement to the amendments of the Senate numbered 2, 5, 10, 16, 18, 20, 25, 31, 33, 38, 39, 41, 44, 45, 46, 47, 48, 49, 52, 53, 56, 58, 59, 60, 62, 63, 64, 66, 71, 72, 73, 75, 76, 79, 85, 86, 92, 94, 100, 107, 112, 113, 116, 117, 119, 120, 122, 123, 125, 126, 127, 133, 135, 139, 140, 141, 145, 147, 148, 149, 154, 155, 159, 160, and 161; and agree to the same.

Amendment numbered 1:

That the House recede from its disagreement to the amendment of the Senate numbered 1, and agree to the same with an amendment, as follows:

In lieu of the sum proposed by said amendment insert: *$583,270,000*; and the Senate agree to the same.

Amendment numbered 3:

That the House recede from its disagreement to the amendment of the Senate numbered 3, and agree to the same with an amendment, as follows:

In lieu of the sum proposed by said amendment insert: *$583,270,000*; and the Senate agree to the same.

Amendment numbered 8:

43–689

* * * * *

Figure 32.10B. House Numbered-Amendments Conference Report (First and Last Pages)

49

(2) any member of the Miccosukee Tribe as a member of the Tribe.

(c) TAXATION.—

(1) IN GENERAL.—

(A) MONIES.—None of the monies paid to the Miccosukee Tribe under this Act or the Settlement Agreement shall be taxable under Federal or State law.

(B) LANDS.—None of the lands conveyed to the Miccosukee Tribe under this Act or the Settlement Agreement shall be taxable under Federal or State law.

(2) PAYMENTS AND CONVEYANCES NOT TAXABLE EVENTS.—No payment or conveyance referred to in paragraph (1) shall be considered to be a taxable event.

And the Senate agree to the same.

RALPH REGULA,
JOSEPH M. MCDADE,
JIM KOLBE,
JOE SKEEN,
CHARLES H. TAYLOR,
GEORGE R. NETHERCUTT, Jr.,
DAN MILLER,
ZACH WAMP,
BOB LIVINGSTON,
SIDNEY R. YATES,
JOHN P. MURTHA,
NORM DICKS,
DAVID E. SKAGGS,
JAMES P. MORAN,
DAVID OBEY,
Managers on the Part of the House.

SLADE GORTON,
TED STEVENS,
THAD COCHRAN,
PETE V. DOMENICI,
CONRAD BURNS,
ROBERT F. BENNETT,
JUDD GREGG,
BEN NIGHTHORSE CAMPBELL,
ROBERT BYRD,
PATRICK LEAHY,
DALE BUMPERS,
ERNEST HOLLINGS,
HARRY REID,
BYRON DORGAN,
BARBARA BOXER,
Managers on the Part of the Senate.

Figure 32.10B. Continued

32.11 Enrolled bills

When a bill has finally been agreed to by both bodies, it is "enrolled" for presentation to the President by the enrolling clerk of the House in which it originated.

In preparing the enrolled bill the clerk starts with the engrossed bill and the engrossed amendments, and then superimposes on them—

(1) the conference report if there was one (along with the subsequent floor actions if that report was filed in disagreement), or

(2) the post-engrossment actions of the two Houses if their differences were resolved without a conference, in order to give full effect to the final compromise.

An enrolled bill is printed on parchment paper and certified by the Clerk of the House or the Secretary of the Senate before being signed by the presiding officers of the two Houses and sent to the President. There are no other physical copies (except the enrolling clerk's working copies); most longtime Members and staffers have never even seen one. However, you can access an electronic version of the enrolled bill online (on *www.congress. gov*). The first page of a copy of H.R. 4954 in its enrolled form is included in Figure 32.11A.

Figure 32.11B shows the first and last pages of the statute resulting from H.R. 4954 (Public Law 109-347) in its slip law form.

H.R. 4954

One Hundred Ninth Congress of the United States of America

AT THE SECOND SESSION

Begun and held at the City of Washington on Tuesday, the third day of January, two thousand and six

An Act

To improve maritime and cargo security through enhanced layered defenses, and for other purposes.

Be it enacted by the Senate and House of Representatives of the United States of America in Congress assembled,

SECTION 1. SHORT TITLE; TABLE OF CONTENTS.

(a) SHORT TITLE.—This Act may be cited as the "Security and Accountability For Every Port Act of 2006" or the "SAFE Port Act".

(b) TABLE OF CONTENTS.—The table of contents for this Act is as follows:

Figure 32.11A. Enrolled Bill (First Page Only)

120 STAT. 1884 PUBLIC LAW 109–347—OCT. 13, 2006

Public Law 109–347
109th Congress

An Act

Oct. 13, 2006
[H.R. 4954]

To improve maritime and cargo security through enhanced layered defenses, and for other purposes.

Be it enacted by the Senate and House of Representatives of the United States of America in Congress assembled,

Security and Accountability For Every Port Act of 2006.
6 USC 901 note.

SECTION 1. SHORT TITLE; TABLE OF CONTENTS.

(a) SHORT TITLE.—This Act may be cited as the "Security and Accountability For Every Port Act of 2006" or the "SAFE Port Act".

(b) TABLE OF CONTENTS.—The table of contents for this Act is as follows:

* * * * *

Figure 32.11B. Bill as Enacted in Slip Law Form (First and Last Pages)

120 STAT. 1962 PUBLIC LAW 109–347—OCT. 13, 2006

31 USC 5361 note.

SEC. 803. INTERNET GAMBLING IN OR THROUGH FOREIGN JURISDICTIONS.

(a) IN GENERAL.—In deliberations between the United States Government and any foreign country on money laundering, corruption, and crime issues, the United States Government should—

(1) encourage cooperation by foreign governments and relevant international fora in identifying whether Internet gambling operations are being used for money laundering, corruption, or other crimes;

(2) advance policies that promote the cooperation of foreign governments, through information sharing or other measures, in the enforcement of this Act; and

(3) encourage the Financial Action Task Force on Money Laundering, in its annual report on money laundering typologies, to study the extent to which Internet gambling operations are being used for money laundering purposes.

(b) REPORT REQUIRED.—The Secretary of the Treasury shall submit an annual report to the Congress on any deliberations between the United States and other countries on issues relating to Internet gambling.

Approved October 13, 2006.

LEGISLATIVE HISTORY—H.R. 4954 (S. 2008) (S. 2459):

HOUSE REPORTS: Nos. 109–447, Pt. 1 (Comm. on Homeland Security) and 109–711 (Comm. of Conference).

CONGRESSIONAL RECORD, Vol. 152 (2006):

May 4, considered and passed House.

Sept. 7, 8, 11–14, considered and passed Senate, amended.

Sept. 29, House and Senate agreed to conference report.

WEEKLY COMPILATION OF PRESIDENTIAL DOCUMENTS, Vol. 42 (2006):

Oct. 13, Presidential remarks and statement.

Figure 32.11B. Continued

32.12 Last-minute corrections

It may be hard to believe, but occasionally a mistake is made somewhere along the line in the text of a bill, and sometimes that mistake is not discovered until too late to fix it in the conference report. This is usually the result of the haste with which the conference report was developed and filed; an erroneous reference may not have been picked up in the final proofreading, or the report may not accurately reflect some action that was in fact taken by the conferees.

In such a case Congress may, if it acts in time and the mistake is serious enough, adopt a concurrent resolution instructing the enrolling clerk (actually the Clerk of the House or the Secretary of the Senate, who are the officials for whom the enrolling clerks work) to make the necessary corrections.

Figure 32.12 is an example showing a concurrent resolution of this kind.

The mistakes that are correctable in this way are theoretically limited to those of a technical or mechanical nature, but the device has also been used to make substantive additions of compromise language that could not be agreed upon in the time available to the conferees (or deletions of substantive language about which last-minute misgivings have arisen). The concurrent resolution is considered on the floor of the House and Senate immediately after the conference report if it can be made ready in time, but may be considered later if it cannot.

115TH CONGRESS
2D SESSION

H. CON. RES. 149

IN THE SENATE OF THE UNITED STATES

DECEMBER 21, 2018

Received

CONCURRENT RESOLUTION

Directing the Clerk of the House of Representatives to make certain corrections in the enrollment of H.R. 4174.

Resolved by the House of Representatives (the Senate concurring), That in the enrollment of the bill H.R. 4174, the Clerk of the House of Representatives shall make the following corrections:

(1) Page 2, beginning line 13, strike "has the meaning given the term 'Executive agency' under section 105" and insert "means an agency referred to under section 901(b) of title 31".

Figure 32.12. House Concurrent Resolution to Correct Enrollment

2

(2) Page 19, line 13, insert "for data that does not concern monetary policy" after "open data plan".

(3) Page 32, beginning line 6, strike "career" and all that follows through "title 5)" and insert "nonpolitical appointee employee".

Passed the House of Representatives December 21, 2018.

Attest: KAREN L. HAAS,

Clerk.

Figure 32.12. Continued

Thus, if you are involved as a drafter (on a major bill at least), you cannot yet relax when the conference report is filed. Almost immediately, you will often receive requests for enrollment-correcting language; you will often discern errors yourself and suggest a correcting concurrent resolution to the appropriate staff. As a practical matter such a concurrent resolution will not be possible without the prior consent of the leadership and the principal legislative figures involved, and that consent is not always given.

Needless to say, concurrent resolutions to correct the enrollment of bills are very convenient devices and can cover a multitude of sins, since they bypass most of the regular steps in the legislative process, and (being cleared in advance) they are usually adopted without study or debate.

Note that a modified version of this kind of concurrent resolution can be used for the same purposes after the bill has been enrolled (in which case it would have to include language rescinding the enrollment), and even after the bill has been sent to the President (in which case it would request the

President to return the bill and then rescind its enrollment), but these are rare.

32.13 Committee prints

Before leaving the subject of legislative vehicles, it may be worthwhile to mention briefly the committee print, which is a totally informal and unofficial relative of a bill.

When a legislative committee (or a subcommittee or conference committee) is considering major legislation, it is frequently necessary to go through successive revisions over a period of many days, weeks, or even months. Sometimes the various proposals involved can be handled individually, and then all put together at the last minute; but just as often the provisions are too interrelated for that, and the drafters and technicians (not to mention the committee members themselves) simply cannot keep track of where they are at any particular time without an up-to-date revised version of the entire package to work with.

And sometimes a committee wants to junk the bill it started with and begin again from scratch, or is simply considering ideas before any bill at all has been introduced.

In these cases the most effective way to operate is to work from an informal draft (or a series of successive drafts) that incorporates all prior decisions (both final and tentative) as of any given time. The most efficient device for this purpose is the "committee print" in bill form, which looks exactly like a bill but is normally headed "COMMITTEE PRINT" (with a number and date when necessary to indicate its place in the series).

The point is mentioned here because committee prints often develop a life of their own—these totally unofficial documents, rather than the basic bills to which they relate, become the documents that are discussed, quoted, and argued about during the legislative process and even thereafter. Proposals are incorporated into them, debated, and then eliminated, only to reappear in later versions. To the drafter (and to anyone else who is interested in following the progress of the legislation involved) they can be the most important legislative vehicles in the whole process during most of the pre-enactment life of the legislation.[6]

Note that some committees may prepare comparative prints to use when considering important legislation. These committee prints show for comparative purposes both the bill being considered and some other legislative document—either the existing law that the bill amends or another bill that incorporates a different approach to the same problem. The two documents may be shown in side-by-side columns, or they may be made into a single composite that reveals the similarities and differences by variations in typography. Comparative prints can be particularly useful for conference committees (the two documents in this case being the House bill and the Senate amendments or vice versa).

If you are working with one or more pieces of a major bill that is being considered or developed in a committee, you should expect to find that the versions of the bill you most often need to see are the unofficial committee prints. In many cases these are readily available to any legitimately interested person who requests one.

32.14 Tracking a bill through Congress

There are a number of reasons why you might want to follow the course of a bill as it moves through the legislative process. You may be asked to work on it (or write amendments to it), so you need to keep abreast of its progress. Or you may want to follow it just because you are interested in what it does, particularly if it falls within an area in which you regularly work. And sometimes the progress of a related bill already under consideration will determine how you should draft your own.

It is the purpose of 32.14 to help you track a bill through Congress, and to indicate some of the information sources that may be available to you for this purpose.

The two tracking objectives. Most people who want to follow a bill through the legislative process are primarily interested in knowing when and where the various steps in the process will be taken, so they can observe proceedings or only because they are interested in the legislation. This might be called "schedule" tracking, and may be either prospective (to discover where a bill is going) or retrospective (to learn where the bill has been).

As a drafter, however, you will need more than just dates, times, room numbers, summaries, and publicity handouts. Especially if you are (or expect to be) personally involved with the drafting of the bill or amendments to it, you will need literal copies of the bill in each of its forms (plus supporting documents) in addition to the schedule.

The basic information sources. If you are "on the scene" and have congenial contacts all over Capitol Hill, you should normally have no problem in finding out what you need to know. Otherwise, the information you need to keep abreast of happenings on Capitol Hill is widely available on *www.congress.gov*, on GPO's website (*www.govinfo.gov*), and on the websites of the House, the Senate, and the committees of Congress. These sites contain links to the following important sources (which are also available in printed form):

(1) **The *Congressional Record*.** This is the all-purpose information source, published daily while Congress is in session. It is widely available, including online (on *www.congress.gov*), and anyone can subscribe to it. Among many other things it includes each day—

(A) a list of all bills introduced or reported in each body;

(B) the full text of all bills taken up on the floor and of any amendments offered to those bills;

(C) the full text of all conference reports;

(D) a list of projected committee meetings; and

(E) a *Daily Digest*, summarizing what has happened that day and indicating what is expected to happen on the next.

The *Record* is useful for substantive tracking as well as schedule tracking, subject to the caveat (discussed earlier) that you cannot rely on it for the niceties of form and style because of its format and typography (and, regrettably, because its overnight printing tends to result in typographical errors).

(2) **The Calendars.** The House and Senate each publish an official Calendar, which is brought up to date daily and is available on the respective websites of the House and Senate, as well as on *www.congress.gov* and *www.govinfo.gov*. The Calendars list every bill of the current Congress on which any post-introduction action has been taken and give its legislative history to date, identify all bills that are scheduled for conference, in conference, or through conference, and contain a great deal of other information of various kinds.

The Calendars are easier to use than the *Record* but since they do not show the text of any bill or amendment, their use is largely limited to schedule tracking.

(Most committees publish their own calendars as well.)

(3) **Loose-leaf services**. There are several companies that publish loose-leaf volumes (some general and some limited to particular fields) expressly aimed at helping people track bills through Congress. They are updated regularly and are very complete, although they rarely show any actual bill text. *The Congressional Index* (put out by Commerce Clearing House), for example, lists all introduced bills and resolutions with complete legislative histories, along with other information such as committee memberships, hearings, voting records, and companion bills.

(4) **Broader nongovernmental services**. There are nongovernmental organizations that provide across-the-board tracking services, such as CQ (*www.info.cq.com*). Websites such as CQ also offer "action alerts" (through e-mail) to subscribers who want up-to-the-minute information on particular subjects.

The number of bill tracking websites seems to be proliferating; however, it is safest to start with the government sources, like *congress.gov* and *govinfo.gov*.

Two other publications deserve to be mentioned in this subdivision, not because they are tracking sources in the strict sense but because they are invaluable sources of background information that no tracker should be without:

The *Congressional Directory* is the best available (and only official) source of general information about who's who and what's what in Congress—the names, office locations, and telephone numbers of all the Members of Congress, Senators, committees, and major congressional staff members (along with the corresponding information for all Federal agencies and their officers), the membership of all congressional committees, and a vast amount of other useful information (even including maps of the various levels in the Capitol building). It is available online (*www.govinfo.gov*) and can be purchased from the Government Publishing Office (or that website).

And the *U.S. Code Congressional & Administrative News* (USCCAN, a monthly publication of the West Publishing Company) not only gives you the text of all new laws as they are enacted, in the literal form in which they will appear in the Statutes at Large—it contains cumulative tables that show the Code classification of each provision of law enacted during the current Congress and all Code sections (both positive and nonpositive law) that are mentioned in or affected by those provisions, along with recently issued Executive orders, Presidential messages, Federal regulations, and Federal court rules. USCCAN contains major committee reports and sometimes Presidential signing statements as part of its Legislative History section for the public laws.

All of the publications and services mentioned in this subdivision are useful, of course, but you may still want to know someone to contact for last-minute information. When you need a time, place, or schedule, there is almost always someone, somewhere, who knows it and will be happy to tell you if you ask; and when you need a document there is always someone who has physical or electronic copies and will usually be willing to give you one, let you reproduce it, or tell you how to get a copy of your own. Crucial legislative events happen fast, and schedules are always subject to change—often with little or no notice—and you could miss something crucial. Make it your business to know whom to call and arrange your contacts in advance if you can.

Tracking at different stages of the process. Needless to say, your ability to track a bill in Congress effectively (and the usefulness of the various information sources) will vary widely from stage to stage of the legislative process. In addition, special circumstances at any stage can sometimes make the task easy when it would normally be hard, and hard when it would normally be easy. The following offers a few brief comments about what your expectations should be at each stage.

Until a bill is introduced there is of course no way of knowing precisely what will be in it, or even (unless you somehow learn about the sponsor's plans in advance) of knowing that something worth inquiring about is going to surface. If you need to see the literal text of the bill or obtain a copy—and as a drafter, you should never rely on anything else to tell you what it contains—you may have to wait a few days until it is available (online or in printed form). A printed bill may be obtained from the House and Senate document rooms, from the committee to which the bill was referred, from the sponsor's office, or from the Government Publishing Office. Note that a bill can be printed from *www.congress.gov* in PDF format and in 2 editable formats.

The websites of the different committees will contain a schedule of their hearings and markups (as will *congress.gov*), and many of these meetings are webcast.

The committee stage is one stage at which personal observation is a real plus. Almost all committee meetings are open to the public; if you cannot observe the meeting electronically, and if you can afford the time (and are a good notes-taker), you should try to be on the scene when the committee is "marking up" the bill; you will understand better what is happening, and your physical presence has the additional advantage of allowing you to get copies of amendments and committee prints that will be hard to find later.

The committee stage really includes two separate stages—subcommittee and full committee. Tracking is often difficult when a bill is at the subcommittee stage, because the scheduling is "iffier" and because the actions taken (being often informal and tentative) are less widely reported and sometimes harder to pin down. And you should remember that there are two separate staffs involved; when the bill in which you are interested is in subcommittee, it is the subcommittee staff that you should contact—the full committee staff may not even be aware of what the subcommittee is doing.

Committee hearings (though they may be of great interest to casual observers) are of little value to a drafter; professional drafters rarely go to them. You should concentrate on the committee markup sessions, which are where the action is; all of the committee's legislative and scheduling decisions are made in those sessions. Though the hearings often generate amendments proposed for the markup sessions, you can always consult the hearing testimony, if necessary, to better understand the basis for those amendments.

In the House the first concrete action on the floor is the adoption of the "rule" on the bill (see 34.3), which normally happens just before the bill is called up. You are not likely to have any interest in this except as an indication that the real floor action will soon begin (although bargains struck in the Rules Committee as a condition of its clearance can occasionally require some redrafting of the bill or the drafting of some agreed-upon amendments to be offered on the floor). The Senate has no corresponding step.

Several of the listed sources manage to keep their subscribers in touch with what is happening on the floor and what is expected to happen there and provide summaries of the amendments offered—a few also provide the literal text of any amendments adopted. But for most people the best source is still the *Congressional Record,* which provides a verbatim transcript of the proceedings, including the complete text of the bill and of all amendments offered (with a summary in the *Daily Digest*). Personal observation from the House or Senate galleries (or C-Span), though an occasionally pleasant spectator sport, is not likely to be of any value to you as a drafter or tracker.

As indicated earlier, the committee and floor stages in the second House are substantially the same as those in the first, although they may vary in their procedural details; and the information sources available to the tracker are also the same.

Sometimes, of course, the second House passes its own version of the bill (with its own number) rather than amending the first House's bill; parallel bills of this kind can help to get some of the early spadework done but they cannot produce a law, since sooner or later one House must take up and pass the other's bill or the process dies.

Sometimes, when the second House approves the first House's bill with changes, the easiest way to resolve the differences is to do so directly, by amendments offered on the floor of one or both Houses. Unfortunately, the compromise is usually worked out by informal negotiations between the leadership and relevant committee chairmen of the two Houses, and the floor actions necessary to adopt it are just "fitted in" where convenient. In most cases, there is simply no way of learning from publicly available sources just what is in the offing and when it will happen.

(You should check the proceedings in the *Congressional Record* each morning after the process starts; in a situation like this the majority leader in each House is often called upon by Members—usually toward the close of the day's session—to explain what is being planned for the next day, and the majority leader responds if the answer is known.)

Normally, however, when the House and Senate, after passing a major bill in different forms, have reached the "stage of disagreement" (a complicated parliamentary concept describing the point at which it becomes clear that the disputes cannot be settled directly as described earlier), a committee of conference is appointed to work out the differences.

As noted earlier, the conference stage is the most critical stage in the whole process. Unfortunately, though, it is also the most difficult stage to keep up with. Conference committees have no rooms of their own and conferees have their regular duties to perform, so the meetings must often be held wherever vacant space can be found and whenever the conferees (or at least most of them) have some free time. This causes problems for the tracker.

Many conferences do meet at regularly scheduled times and in obvious places (such as the main committee room of the standing committee of the House or Senate most directly concerned); in such cases, you would usually have advance notice. But it would be equally typical for a conference (after a few hasty phone calls to summon the conferees) to meet at 10 a.m. in the Capitol attic, recess until 1:15 p.m., and reconvene in one of the House or Senate lunchrooms (hoping that the tables will have been cleared by then); and even the conferees and their staffs have trouble keeping up with all of this.

The negotiations in a conference committee invariably involve a lot of private conversations between conferees, and a lot of caucusing behind closed doors to work out offers and counteroffers, so that nobody knows what is happening. Your best bet is just to stay in touch with someone on the scene who is personally involved, remembering that even that individual may have no advance notice until a few minutes before the gavel falls.

Once the conference report is filed it will be printed in the next day's *Congressional Record,* whether or not the report itself is available. Here again there are difficulties; conference reports are "in order at any time" on the floor—they do not have to be scheduled in advance like a bill or resolution—and they are customarily "fitted in" among the bills that are scheduled. But there is really no more tracking to do, since a conference report is presented to each House on a take-it-or-leave-it basis, and once passed by both Houses is enrolled for the President to sign. This is not trackable; there is literally no way for you to find out just when the enrollment will occur. The only possible complication arises when a concurrent resolution making corrections in the enrollment (see 32.12) is needed; but resolutions of this kind are not trackable either, since they do not go through committee and are almost always adopted (before they are even printed) along with the conference report itself.

The signing of the bill by the President is a tracking stage in a sense, but when and how it is done is somewhat beyond the scope of this subdivision. Unless the President chooses to have a formal signing ceremony, it is highly unlikely that you could discover the time and place, or that you would be interested in it anyway.

Notes

1 In recent Congresses, it is rare for a short bill to go through each stage of the legislative process: introduced bill, reported bill, engrossed bill, Senate-passed amendment to the bill, and conference report. In many cases both Houses agree to language before it passes one House, so that the other can accept the language without sending it back to the first House. In other cases, any disagreements between the Houses of Congress are generally resolved by amendments sent back and forth between the Houses until agreement is reached. This bill (H.R. 4954) is quite long, so only the first couple of pages are shown.

2 Both the House and the Senate, by December 2000, adopted XMetal (commercial eXtensible Markup Language [XML] software) as the primary standard for the exchange of legislative documents between the House, the Senate, and other legislative branch agencies. Information about this program is available at *http://xml.house.gov*.

3 A list of the names of House Members is available from the website of the Office of the Clerk (*https://clerk.house.gov*).

4 Woodrow Wilson, *Congressional Government: A Study in American Politics*, 15th ed. (Boston: Houghton Mifflin, 1900), p. 79.

5 As will be seen in chapter 34, the ad hoc rules that accompany the consideration of bills on the House floor for the most part restrict the amendments that can be offered to a short list provided for in the rule.

6 In the digital age, a bill is converted to a committee print by merely inserting "Committee Print" at the top in a computer-generated copy. Before the widespread use of computers, a "committee print" was produced by the Government Printing [now Publishing] Office and therefore had more of the imprimatur of an official document.

33. Federal Drafting Styles

33.1 Preliminary comments

Although what you do before you put pen to paper is generally more important than what you do afterward, this chapter will, for many readers, constitute the core of the book. After all, thinking about and analyzing a problem is a familiar operation for anyone, but actually writing a bill is not. And the mystery is compounded by the fact that there are several different drafting styles in concurrent use at the Federal level with many others, obviously, being employed at the State and local levels.

"Drafting style" is the term used to describe the external characteristics of legislative language, and has nothing to do (directly) with what that language does or how the bill as a whole is organized. Some styles may be better than others for various reasons, a fact that will be discussed more fully in the succeeding subdivisions; but any legislative proposal could be legitimately expressed in any one of the currently accepted styles. You have no choice and must follow one of these styles if your sponsor is a Representative or Senator, of course, and you would be well advised to do the same when drafting Federal legislation for a noncongressional sponsor if you do not want some other drafter deciding how the final version should be written.

For these purposes, bills will be treated as stylistically divisible into three parts:

(1) *Sections*—the basic building blocks of a bill. All bills have them.

(2) *Inferior subdivisions*—the subsections, paragraphs, subparagraphs, clauses, subclauses, items, and subitems into which the sections are divided. Most sections have inferior subdivisions; and most of the differences between the various Federal drafting styles involve them.

(3) *Senior components*—the broader divisions (titles, subtitles, chapters, subchapters, parts, and subparts) into which most major bills are broken down and of which the sections are a part.

The bulk of this chapter will be devoted to an examination of the basic section and its subdivisions in each of the four principal Federal drafting styles (33.2 through 33.5). In the case of each such style the examination focuses on the same characteristics (headings, designation, and indentation), discussing in detail the specifications for the style involved and either setting forth an example of a section written in that style or indicating what it would look like by a comparative reference to one of the other styles.

The discussion of the various ways in which senior components and superior headings are handled under the four Federal styles (along with a detailed tabular comparison) is reserved for 33.6, since the differences between them are largely trivial.

After addressing a few collateral considerations in 33.7, the chapter then concludes (in 33.8) with a comparison and critique of the four styles.

Note that amendments are not regarded as a special case or treated separately. The vehicular portion of an amendatory provision in a bill is written in the same drafting style as the rest of the bill, while the amendment itself is written in the drafting style of the law being amended (usually: see chapter 8 and 33.2)—the two are usually but not always the same—and the vehicular language always takes the same form (see chapters 15 and 16) regardless of the drafting style or styles otherwise involved.

And remember, as you consider the descriptions contained in this chapter, that a section or inferior subdivision consists of two or three separate parts—its heading (if it has one), its designation, and its text. Any unqualified reference to a "section", "subsection", or other inferior subdivision encompasses them all; so if you wish to address one without addressing the others you must be explicit about it.

Two other preliminary comments about this chapter:

(1) Differences in drafting style are largely a matter of typography, and in describing drafting styles this chapter uses a number of typographical terms that are not found in everyday conversation. These terms were discussed in detail in chapter 30, and examples of some of their descriptive uses were given in chapter 20.

(2) In discussing each of the four Federal drafting styles, the example or comparative reference is given first to indicate how the style involved actually looks, and a statement of the detailed specifications for that style follows. To help you compare the four styles, the same section is used in each example; it is based on section 3121(u) of the Internal Revenue Code of 1986, which has however been rearranged, paraphrased, and shortened in order to focus on the purely stylistic aspects.

33.2 The traditional or classic style

More existing statutes are written in the traditional style than in any other, largely because they were originally enacted before the other three styles came into widespread use (although amendments to these laws can be written in revenue or modified revenue style—see chapter 8 [the Roman rule, modified]). This style is the least demanding of all the accepted Federal styles, in that it has the fewest arbitrary technical requirements. As seen in chapter 8, the Offices of the Legislative Counsel of the House of Representatives and the Senate abandoned using traditional style in the drafting of bills in favor of revenue or modified revenue style. And amendments to a statute drafted in traditional style can be written in revenue or modified revenue style as well.

See below for an example of a section written in the traditional style.

MEDICARE COVERAGE OF GOVERNMENT EMPLOYEES

SEC. 123.(a) For purposes of chapter 21 of the Internal Revenue Code of 1986, the term "medicare qualified government employment" means service which—

(1) is employment (as defined in that chapter) with the application of subsection (b), but

(2) would not be employment (as so defined) without the application of that subsection.

(b)(1) For purposes of the taxes imposed by sections 3101(b) and 3111(b) of such Code, section 3121(b) of such Code shall be applied without regard to paragraph (5) thereof.

(2) For purposes of such taxes—

(A) except as provided in subparagraph (B), section 3121(b) of such Code shall be applied without regard to paragraph (7) thereof; and

(B) service shall not be treated as employment by reason of subparagraph (A) if—

(i) it is included under an agreement under section 218 of the Social Security Act, or

(ii) it is performed by an individual who is employed by a State or political subdivision to relieve the individual from unemployment.

Headings. Section headings are optional in the traditional style (subject to the Roman rule) but are desirable for the reasons given in 20.5. If a heading is included, it is centered, appears on a line of its own, and is printed in regular (lightface) small caps.

The inferior subdivisions are not usually given headings. The occasional subsection heading is centered on a line of its own and printed in regular (lightface) caps and lowercase letters (with only the key words capitalized).

Designations. The section designation ("SEC. 123.", for example) is paragraphed on the first line of the text (the line immediately below the section heading if there is one), and is set in caps and small caps— that is, the "S" is a large cap and the remaining letters are small caps. The section number is always an Arabic numeral. The text itself begins immediately after the designation and is run in—it is not dropped down to the next line.

The designation of the inferior subdivisions follows the standard practice (see 20.3), with each such designation consisting simply of a letter or number enclosed in parentheses—"(a)" for a subsection, "(1)" for a paragraph, "(A)" for a subparagraph, "(i)" for a clause, "(I)" for a subclause, and (to be avoided) "(aa)" for an item, and "(AA)" for a subitem—and being followed immediately by the first word of the subdivision's text.

When a section is broken down into subsections, the designation of the first subsection ("(a)") is run in immediately after the section designation, not dropped down onto a new line. And the same principle—that the designation of an inferior subdivision is treated as part of the text of its parent and run in immediately after the parent's designation—applies when a subsection is broken down into paragraphs (or when any other inferior subdivision is further broken down). Note the designations "SEC. 123.(a)" and "(b)(1)" in the example.

Indentation. Inferior subdivisions are set full measure, just as the matter involved would be if the section had not been subdivided at all; each is paragraphed and given a designation, but it is not cut in (indented as a whole). Thus every section, except for its heading, its first line, and the first lines of its various paragraphed components, is set flush to the left-hand margin in its entirety, no matter how extensively it is broken down and subdivided.

And this applies to the paragraphed components within sections—the subsections, paragraphs, and paragraphed clauses—as well as to the sections themselves. But it does not apply, of course, to paragraphed components that are parts of a tabulated list or series or a tabulated sentence (see 23.4 and 23.5)—these are always cut in two ems more than their lead-in language—or to run-in clauses.

33.3 United States Code style

As its name suggests, this style originated with the compilers of the United States Code and is the style used in all the titles of the Code (both positive law and nonpositive law). It is not—currently at least—a bill-drafting style, since bills are always written in, preferably, revenue or modified revenue styles; even in a bill that consists of nothing but amendments to the Code, the vehicular language and overall format are in revenue or modified revenue style, and only the amendments themselves reflect the Code style.

But Code style deserves an equal place among the accepted Federal drafting styles for two reasons. First, a substantial part of the Federal law is already embodied in positive-law titles of the United States Code, and the drafting of amendments to the Code has become a significant part of every drafter's work. Second, there is a good chance that the Law Revision Counsel's objective of converting all of the Federal statutory law into positive-law titles of the Code will be successfully achieved at some time in the future, and if and when that happens it is quite possible that Code style will become the only style, even for vehicular language and for freestanding bills.

The full example will not be repeated here, and it is not necessary to go through the detailed specifications again, because Code style is exactly the same as traditional style in all respects but two:

(1) Every section must have a heading, which appears on a line of its own but

(A) is set flush to the left-hand margin rather than being centered,

(B) is printed in boldface lowercase letters with only the first word capitalized, and

(C) is combined with the section designation, which uses a boldface "twist mark" before the Arabic numeral instead of "SEC." or "SECTION".

(Thus when the section is broken down into subsections, the designation of the first subsection ["(a)"] cannot be run in immediately after the section designation as in the traditional style but appears instead on the next line at the beginning of the text.)

(2) In the past, headings for subsections were seldom used, and headings for subdivisions below the subsection level were never given headings. However, as with amendments to laws drafted in traditional style, amendments to positive-law titles of the Code can have headings for subsections and inferior subdivisions. Such a heading is run in between the subsection (or other subdivision) designation and the first word of the text, and is printed in lightface caps and small caps followed by a period and a dash, as in revenue style (see 33.4).

If the example given in 33.2 were written in Code style, its first few lines would read as follows:

---

§123. Medicare coverage of government employees

(a) For purposes of chapter 21 of the Internal Revenue Code of 1986...

or

(a) MEDICARE QUALIFIED GOVERNMENT EMPLOYMENT DEFINED.—For purposes of chapter 21 of the Internal Revenue Code of 1986...

And the remaining provisions may have headings as in revenue style.

33.4 Revenue style

As its name suggests, "revenue" style is the style in which the tax laws of the United States (the Internal Revenue Code of 1986 and its predecessors) have been written for many years. It is a very disciplined style, and without question the most intricate and demanding of all the accepted Federal drafting styles. And with its mandatory use of headings for all subdivisions and its mandatory use of progressively increasing indentations below the section level, it is very different from the traditional style.

The example below sets forth the section shown in 33.2 as it would be written in revenue style (which of course is the style in which it was originally written). Note especially the headings and indentations.

SEC. 123. MEDICARE COVERAGE OF GOVERNMENT EMPLOYEES.

(a) MEDICARE QUALIFIED GOVERNMENT EMPLOYMENT DEFINED.—For purposes of chapter 21 of the Internal Revenue Code of 1986, the term "medicare qualified government employment" means service which—

(1) is employment (as defined in that chapter) with the application of subsection (b), but

(2) would not be employment (as so defined) without the application of that subsection.

(b) APPLICATION OF HOSPITAL INSURANCE TAX TO FEDERAL, STATE, AND LOCAL EMPLOYMENT.—

(1) FEDERAL EMPLOYMENT.—For purposes of the taxes imposed by sections 3101(b) and 3111(b) of such Code, section 3121(b) of such Code shall be applied without regard to paragraph (5) thereof.

(2) STATE AND LOCAL EMPLOYMENT.—For purposes of such taxes—

(A) IN GENERAL.—Except as provided in subparagraph (B), section 3121(b) of such Code shall be applied without regard to paragraph (7) thereof.

(B) EXCEPTION FOR CERTAIN SERVICES.—Service shall not be treated as employment by reason of subparagraph (A) if—

(i) it is included under an agreement under section 218 of the Social Security Act, or

(ii) it is performed by an individual who is employed by a State or political subdivision to relieve the individual from unemployment.

Headings. Every revenue-style section has a heading, which is set flush to the left-hand margin rather than being centered, appears on a line of its own in combination with the section designation, and is printed in boldface 10-point caps with a period at the end.

All inferior subdivisions also have headings, no matter how far down the scale you go—subsections, paragraphs, subparagraphs, and paragraphed clauses and subclauses (and, to be avoided, items and subitems), except for those that are parts of a tabulated list or series or a tabulated sentence—although some drafters do violate the rule and omit them occasionally in the more trivial lower subdivisions. The mandatory use of headings for all inferior subdivisions is the first of the two major differences between revenue style and the others.

The heading of any inferior subdivision is "run in" between the subdivision's designation and the first word of its text. In the case of a subsection, it is printed in caps and small caps (with the former being used for the first letters of the key words), and in the case of a paragraph or other lower-level component it is printed entirely in small caps except for an initial large cap on the first word, followed immediately (in either case) by a period and a dash.

The dash leads directly into the text if the component involved is not further subdivided, but leads only into thin air if the component *is* further subdivided, because in revenue style—as explained below—each successive level of subdivision has to be "dropped down" and further indented.

Designations. As indicated in the preceding paragraph, the section designation in revenue style is printed in 10-point boldface caps and combined with the heading on a separate line, set flush to the left-hand margin.

The designation of the inferior subdivisions follows the standard practice (see 20.3), as in the other two styles, with each such designation consisting simply of a letter or number enclosed in parentheses—"(a)" for a subsection, "(1)" for a paragraph, "(A)" for a subparagraph, "(i)" for a clause, and "(I)" for a subclause (and, if necessary, "(aa)" for an item and "(AA)" for a subitem)—and being followed immediately by the heading.

If the section is not broken down into subsections, the text begins (paragraphed on the line just below the section heading) without a designation, as in the case of United States Code style.

But when a subsection is broken down into paragraphs (or any other inferior component is further broken down), the designation of the first such paragraph (or other lower-level component) is not treated as part of the text of its parent and run in immediately after the parent's designation as in the case of the other two styles.

Instead, it is dropped down onto a new line (and indented two ems, or two additional ems); thus there can never be two designations juxtaposed in any component in revenue style. This produces the second major stylistic difference between revenue style and the others, and its discussion is continued in the following paragraphs.

Indentation. In revenue style, inferior subdivisions below the subsection level are progressively indented ("cut in") by multiples of two ems as you go down the scale; and none of the comments made about indentation in 33.2 and 33.3 will apply.

Thus all subsections are set full measure, all paragraphs are cut in two ems, all subparagraphs are cut in four ems, all clauses (other than run-in clauses) are cut in 6 ems, and so forth. And, of course, each of them has to be given a heading (see above).

The following sequence may serve to depict the progression more graphically:

SECTION 1. IMPOSITION AND RATE OF TAX.

(a) RATE OF TAX.—[subsection, full measure]

(1) IN GENERAL.—[paragraph, cut in 2 ems]

(A) SPECIAL RULES.—[subparagraph, cut in 4 ems]

(i) EXCEPTIONS.—[clause, cut in 6 ems]

(I) EFFECTIVE DATE.—[subclause, cut in 8 ems]

Note that units below subclauses (items [cut in 10 ems] and subitems [cut in 12 ems]) should be avoided.

33.5 Modified revenue style

As discussed in chapter 8, there has been a concerted effort, spearheaded by the Legislative Counsel's Offices in the House of Representatives and the Senate, to adopt a uniform drafting style that incorporates the acknowledged virtues of revenue style without including what some people regard as its drawbacks (for these virtues and drawbacks see 33.8). The result is best described as "modified revenue style", which permits many of the characteristics of "full" revenue style to be either included or not included, at the drafter's option.

The full example will not be repeated here, and it is not necessary to go through the detailed specifications again, because modified revenue style is simply the old familiar revenue style (as described in 33.4) with three possible modifications:

(1) Subsection headings are still required, but headings for the lower-level subdivisions—paragraphs, subparagraphs, clauses, sub-clauses (and below)—are optional.

(2) The lower-level subdivisions need not be progressively indented as in revenue style, but can be set full measure as in the traditional

and Code styles so long as they are not given headings. If this were done, the first subdivision designation at any level would immediately follow the parent's designation (and heading if any).

(3) The revenue-prescribed hierarchy of superior headings (which will be discussed in 33.6) can be modified as appropriate considering the nature and overall structure of the bill. For instance, the bill's titles could be set in 14-point caps and broken down into parts if 18-point caps and subtitles seem too ostentatious for the job at hand.

If the example set forth in 33.4 were written in modified revenue style rather than in "full" revenue style, it could conceivably differ in various ways—it might, for example, omit the paragraph and subparagraph headings in subsection (b) (and run in paragraph (1) immediately after the subsection heading)—but all the other specifications for full revenue style would apply. (For what it is worth, the authors' preference would be to stay with full revenue style, since none of the extremes of that style—see 33.8—are present in the example.)

Whether you should adopt any of the modifications described in this subdivision or just go with straight revenue style is a matter of judgment, depending upon the size, scope, and nature of the bill and the context in which you are working. But if you do choose to adopt one of them in writing a particular bill you should use it consistently.

33.6 Superior headings

When a bill is broken down into senior components—titles, subtitles, parts, subparts, chapters, or subchapters—their headings are always centered, and set in various combinations of different-sized lightface or boldface caps, small caps, and lowercase letters so as to distinguish them from each other and from the section headings.

Each of the four accepted Federal drafting styles has its own hierarchy of senior components, with its own typefaces and its own system of designation and headings.

Fortunately, however, the four hierarchies are very similar, and can be thought of as simply four variations of a single standard arrangement. The designations and headings reflect a mixture of Roman numerals, Arabic numerals, and capital letters, and the typefaces often differ (revenue style uses only boldface type while the others use lightface [with a few exceptions], and revenue style ranks chapters above parts while the others do not). And except for title and subtitle headings (18-point), part and subpart headings (12-point), and section headings (10-point) in revenue style, and section headings (12-point) in United States Code style, all superior headings (like inferior headings and bill text) are set in 14-point type.

In revenue style the established system for naming and designating senior components, and for setting their headings in type, is faithfully and consistently followed. And in modified revenue style the revenue-style system for senior components is faithfully followed unless a specific modification is consciously adopted.

In the traditional style, however, the prescribed system is honored more in the breach than in the observance. The first breakdown of a bill into senior components is always into titles, of course; but if a further breakdown is necessary there is very little discernible consistency in actual practice (see chapter 20).

And in United States Code style (which otherwise faithfully follows its prescribed system) there are a couple of special considerations:

(1) The chapter is the basic senior component in the Code, and every title is broken down into chapters even if that means omitting several of the intermediate levels that are otherwise prescribed.

(2) At several levels of senior components in the Code there is a choice or potential choice between using Roman numerals or capital letters as designations. This choice in any given case is distributive—it depends upon what other senior components are included in the title involved and what form of designation is available taking into account the needs of those components. Accordingly, you should always look first at the particular title you are proposing to amend and follow its style.

Table 33.6 shows in tabular form the accepted hierarchies of all the components under the various Federal drafting styles (with modified revenue style being treated as a part of revenue style for this purpose), along with their designations and the kinds of type in which they are set. Figure 33.6 gives literal examples of the superior headings in each drafting style as they would appear in a bill.

33.7 Maverick styles

It should come as no surprise that sometimes bills are drafted and introduced (and even enacted) in a style that bears little resemblance to any of the four Federal styles discussed in this chapter. This can happen in several ways.

There are cases in which whoever drafted the bill paid no attention to style at all, and simply wrote down the ideas as they surfaced without regard to form or arrangement, as if taking notes at a lecture. This is inexcusable, of course, but seldom has any permanent bad effect. It most often happens when a Member introduces a constituent's draft without having had it reviewed by an experienced drafter; and, if it were actually taken seriously, it would be reviewed.

There are cases in which the drafter clearly paid a great deal of attention to style, but elected for some reason to invent and use unusual stylistic features. In the Atomic Energy Act of 1954, for example, the subsection and paragraph designations were not enclosed in parentheses but each included a period—thus "a." or "1." instead of the more familiar "(a)" or "(1)"—which was perhaps tolerable in the designations themselves but a disaster in the cross-references (since it resulted in periods being scattered about in the middle of sentences). Why it was done this way is open to speculation; but it may be significant that the Joint Committee on Atomic Energy never used on-the-scene drafters (except as after-the-fact editors, when it was too late to make sweeping stylistic changes) since the drafters never seemed to have the required security clearance.

And there are cases in which the drafter followed one of the accepted styles but incorporated into it one or more features of another style. The Congressional Budget Act of 1974, for example, was written in the traditional style, but included revenue-style subsection headings; this happened because the desirability of the headings did not occur to the committees' professional staffs (or the drafter) until too late in the game for a general stylistic overhaul. There is nothing really wrong with this kind of stylistic combination (although it would have been better if the bill had been written in revenue or modified revenue style in the first place).

Table 33.6 Superior Headings

Traditional Style	U.S. Code Style	Revenue Style
Title I, II, III . . .	**Title** 1, 2, 3 . . .	**Title** I, II, III . . .
14-pt caps	14-pt caps	18-pt bf caps
Subtitle A, B, C . . .	**Subtitle** I, II, III . . . (or A, B, C . . .)	**Subtitle** A, B, C . . .
14-pt c + lc	14-pt c + lc	18-pt bf c + lc
Part 1, 2, 3 . . .	**Part** I, II, III . . .	**Chapter** 1, 2, 3 . . .
14-pt c + sc	14-pt c + sc	14-pt bf caps
Subpart A, B, C . . .	**Subpart** A, B, C . . .	**Subchapter** A, B, C . . .
14-pt c + lc	14-pt c + lc	14-pt bf c + lc
Chapter 1, 2, 3 . . .	**Chapter** 1, 2, 3 . . .	**Part** I, II, III . . .
14-pt bf caps	14-pt bf caps	12-pt bf caps
Subchapter I, II, III . . .	**Subchapter** I, II, III . . .	**Subpart** A, B, C . . .
14-pt caps	14-pt caps	12-pt bf c + lc
Section 1, 2, 3 . . .	**Section** 1, 2, 3 . . .	**Section** 1, 2, 3 . . .
14-pt sc ctr	12-pt bf lc fl	10-pt bf caps fl
Subsection (a), (b) . . .	**Subsection** (a), (b) . . .	**Subsection** (a), (b) . . .
14-pt c + lc ctr	14-pt c + sc run-in	14-pt c + sc run-in
		Par., etc. (1), (2) . . .
		14-pt sc run-in

Traditional style

TITLE II—TITLE HEAD
Subtitle A—Subtitle Head
PART 3—PART HEAD
Subpart A—Subpart Head
CHAPTER 2—CHAPTER HEAD
SUBCHAPTER II—SUBCHAPTER HEAD

United States Code style

“TITLE 10—TITLE HEAD
“Subtitle II—Subtitle Head
“PART II—PART HEAD
“Subpart A—Subpart Head
“CHAPTER 2—CHAPTER HEAD
“SUBCHAPTER II—SUBCHAPTER HEAD

Revenue (and modified revenue) style

TITLE II—TITLE HEAD
Subtitle A—Subtitle Head
CHAPTER 2—CHAPTER HEAD
Subchapter A—Subchapter Head
PART II—PART HEAD
Subpart A—Subpart Head

Figure 33.6. Literal Examples of Superior Headings

A similar case arises when, as discussed in chapter 8 and earlier in this chapter, new material is being added to an existing law drafted in traditional (or original Code style) and the drafter chooses elements of revenue style for the new material. Continuing the example given in the preceding paragraph, when two new titles were added to the Congressional Budget Act in 1990 they were drafted in full revenue style despite the fact that the existing titles of that Act were written in (slightly modified) traditional style.

One final comment: as mentioned earlier (12.13), the most common (and most important) example of a major bill that uses a maverick style is the typical general appropriations bill, which is sometimes described by uncharitable persons as having no style at all. It has some superior headings (which are not used consistently and follow no consistent typographical pattern even when they are), but the bulk of it—everything except the miscellaneous provisions that appear toward the end of the bill—does not even have section numbers. Such bills are exhausting to read and, even with a search function, can be difficult to find anything in. Fortunately, it is unlikely that you will ever have to work on one.

33.8 Comparison and critique

If you have a choice, which of the four styles should you use?

Again, there is nothing really wrong with any of the four styles; their purely typographical differences are largely trivial. The differences that matter have to do with the way in which the various elements of a bill's sections are set apart from each other and their place in the hierarchy of ideas identified. On the basis of these differences (and the experience of the Offices of the Legislative Counsel of the House of Representatives and the Senate), it is the authors' judgment that—

(1) revenue style and modified revenue style should be preferred over the traditional and United States Code styles, other things being equal; and

(2) modified revenue style has advantages over straight revenue style because it is more flexible and usually more readable.

The traditional style and the "old" Code style (that is, where subdivision headings are not used) are relatively bland; the inferior subdivisions are set apart from each other only by their designations, and they are otherwise written as a more or less continuous narrative in the style of everyday prose composition. There are very few technicalities to learn.

Revenue style, on the other hand, makes extensive use of technical devices such as headings and indentations to set the inferior subdivisions apart from each other and indicate their place in the hierarchy. As indicated earlier, these devices (along with the more typographically prominent section headings) not only help you as a drafter to organize your thoughts, to unearth gaps, overlaps, and other problems, and in general to handle complicated assignments efficiently—they also help sponsors and staffs to find their way through the maze. And the slight additional effort needed to master them is well worth it even if you will normally be using another style.

Modified revenue style has all the virtues of straight revenue style, without some of its faults:

(1) The headings required by straight revenue style for all inferior subdivisions of a section are sometimes counterproductive in the case of the lower-level components. A heading for a two-line clause that simply clarifies some minor point made in the preceding provisions of its parent subparagraph, for example, often appears artificially technical and can make the subparagraph harder rather than easier to read and comprehend. Modified revenue style allows such headings to be omitted when the parent provision can best be read smoothly as a unified whole—without the distracting pauses that result from the too many minor headings.

(2) The progressive indentation required by straight revenue style for lower-level subdivisions is sometimes counterproductive for the same reasons. A section containing several levels of inferior subdivisions can have a very odd appearance; a page from a tax bill can often

> be recognized from clear across the room by the large amount of empty space it contains (which may explain the fervor with which tax drafters claim to abhor clauses and subclauses even while using them liberally). Modified revenue style allows the lower-level subdivisions to be set full measure, as in the traditional or Code style, when that will make the overall text read more naturally.

To paraphrase *HOLC* (page 53), modified revenue style ("office style") provides you with more options and flexibility than any other, with the widest range and variety of drafting tools and conventions. On the one hand, it can be used full-bore (straight revenue style) to promote the clear expression of complex policies, and on the other, it can be applied in a limited way (modified style) in the expression of less complex policies.

Modified revenue style quickly became the style of choice in the two Legislative Counsel's Offices following its introduction in the late 1980s.

At any rate, you should know how to use any of the four accepted styles when the occasion calls for it. And when there is no reason (Roman rule or otherwise) to choose one style over the others, you should use the one you are most comfortable with. But if you like to "go with the flow," you should use the revenue and modified revenue styles, which are without question the Federal drafting styles of the future.

34. Federal Parliamentary Considerations

34.1 Preliminary comments

Parliamentary pitfalls abound in every legislative setting. You cannot wish them out of existence, of course, and you cannot control what other people do with your product after you have turned it loose, but you are not doing your job unless you consciously do everything you can to avoid them. Many a beautifully drafted bill comes to naught because the drafter was unaware of (or just plain forgot) some parliamentary obstacle that could have been circumvented or some parliamentary requirement that could have been met.

This does not mean, however, that you should try (or expect) to become a full-blown parliamentarian. In the first place, every legislature has one of those, whose word is law on parliamentary points and whose rulings may be technically appealable but as a practical matter are almost never successfully challenged. And in the second place, it would be a futile effort; the subject is so broad and complicated that only a person who has studied it full-time over a period of many years could claim real expertise.

What it does mean is that you must always be aware of the potential for such problems. You should know and understand the most common ones and you should know where to go for information on the others. And you must always warn the sponsor of any parliamentary problems you can foresee. Sponsors can usually live with losing on the merits but are understandably piqued when their proposals are unexpectedly shot down on technicalities.

The restrictions and prohibitions that parliamentary requirements impose come primarily from three sources (in addition to the ad hoc rules that apply in particular cases—see 34.3):

(1) The published rules of the legislative body involved (the Rules of the House of Representatives and the Standing Rules of the Senate, at the Federal level). Note that *Jefferson's Manual*, dating from 1797, still governs the House to the extent it is not inconsistent with the regular rules, and is printed in the same volume as the House Rules. These rules may either flatly prohibit the consideration of certain kinds of bills or limit the circumstances under which certain kinds of bills may be considered.

(2) Statutes (such as the Congressional Budget Act of 1974 and the Trade Act of 1974, which contain many similar prohibitions and limitations). Note that the procedural provisions of these statutes are treated as rules of the two Houses (see 12.14) even when they are not cast in that form.

(3) The precedents of the legislative body involved—that is, the sum total of all the rulings made and interpretations given over the years by its parliamentarians. In theory these are nothing but explanations of

> what the rules mean, but they "fill in the chinks" in cases where the application of the rules is not clear, and the chinks are often large enough to give the precedents a very important life of their own.

Of course, parliamentary rulings and interpretations are actually made by the presiding officer of the House involved—not by the parliamentarian—but the presiding officer always acts on the basis of the parliamentarian's recommendations if the case is clear-cut and relies on the parliamentarian's advice when there are conflicting precedents and strategic reasons might dictate choosing one over the other.

Compliance with parliamentary requirements is usually enforced through parliamentary means. That is, the rule involved simply says that "it shall not be in order" to consider a bill or take a specified action if the requirement has not been complied with; any single Member, however deeply embedded in the minority, can prevent that action by simply raising a point of order against it. When a more direct form is used (as when the rule or statute says that "no bill [of a specified type] shall be considered unless…"), the proscription is absolute on its face, and the chair may apply the rule on the initiative of the chair.

It may be true (as you are doubtless well aware) that almost any parliamentary requirement can be waived by unanimous consent, suspension of the rules, or special order and that possible points of order are sometimes overlooked (or voluntarily withheld for one reason or another). But such things are totally unpredictable, and you should never proceed on the assumption that they will happen.

This chapter makes no pretense of being exhaustive; it merely endeavors to alert you to the kinds of parliamentary proscriptions that bear upon what a drafter does at the Federal level, and to familiarize you with some of the most commonly arising requirements. It uses the House of Representatives primarily as its model because the House (largely because of its 435 Members) must adhere much more strictly to parliamentary procedures than the Senate (with only 100 Members) in order to function effectively as a legislative body. However, the parliamentary rules in different legislative bodies resemble each other to a surprising extent.

34.2 Committee referral and jurisdiction

Before 1975, an introduced bill (in the House of Representatives) was referred to a single committee on a "predominance of jurisdiction" standard, regardless of how many different subject matters were involved.

Bills today are referred to the committee or committees legitimately concerned with their subject matter, and you cannot avoid this. The relevant provision in the House Rules (clause 2 of Rule XII) provides as follows:

> 2. (a) The Speaker shall refer each bill, resolution, or other matter that relates to a subject listed under a standing committee named in clause 1 of rule X in accordance with the provisions of this clause.
>
> (b) The Speaker shall refer matters under paragraph (a) in such manner as to ensure to the maximum extent feasible that each committee that has jurisdiction under clause 1 of rule X over the subject matter of a provision thereof may consider such provision and report to the House thereon …
>
> (c) In carrying out paragraphs (a) and (b) with respect to the referral of a matter, the Speaker—
>
> > (1) shall designate a committee of primary jurisdiction (except where [the Speaker] determines that extraordinary circumstances justify review by more than one committee as though primary);
> >
> > (2) may refer the matter to one or more additional committees for consideration in sequence, either initially or after the matter has been reported by the committee of primary jurisdiction;
> >
> > (3) may refer portions of the matter reflecting different subjects and jurisdictions to one or more additional committees;
> >
> > (4) may refer the matter to a special, ad hoc committee appointed by the Speaker with the approval of the House, and including members of the committees of jurisdiction, for the specific purpose of considering that matter and reporting to the House thereon;

(5) may subject a referral to appropriate time limitations; and

(6) may make such other provision as may be considered appropriate.

What this means is that if your sponsor wishes to have a bill referred to a particular committee, you must try to draft it in a way that clearly invokes an established jurisdictional basis of that committee (and you should always read the listing of that committee's jurisdiction in the Rules of the House involved before you begin drafting).

Note that the rule requires the Speaker to designate a committee of primary jurisdiction. The bill may also be referred initially to additional committees. Although the Speaker may impose a time limit within which the committee of primary jurisdiction must report the bill, this is rarely done. The result is that the committee of primary jurisdiction controls when the bill is reported and when it will be sequentially referred to other committees.[1] However, the referral of bills to committees, even the committee of primary jurisdiction, is limited "in each case for consideration of such provisions as fall within the jurisdiction of the committee concerned". As a result, an attempt in a committee to extend its consideration to matters in the bill within the jurisdiction of another committee is subject to a point of order in the committee making the attempt.

In the Senate, legislation is referred to the committee that has jurisdiction over "subject matter which predominates" (Rule XVII, paragraph 1). Although multiple referrals are allowed in the Senate by joint motion of the Senate Majority and Minority Leaders (Rule XVII, paragraph 3), in practice multiple referrals are done by unanimous consent and are rare; they are far more common in the House than in the Senate.

Sometimes there is nothing you can do to influence a bill's referral. However, the way you characterize the things you are doing, by the careful and repeated use of key jurisdictional words and phrases (taken from the Rules), can often get the desired result.

If the sponsor would like to have the bill considered first by a particular subcommittee—each committee can divide its jurisdiction among whatever subcommittees it chooses to establish—you should draft the bill with similar emphasis on matters within the jurisdiction of that subcommittee.

The thing to remember is that if you include anything at all that impinges on the jurisdiction of another committee, the bill may also be referred (concurrently or sequentially) to that committee. If the impingement is minor or only technical, referral to the other committee is usually made only when formally requested by the other committee; but if it is clear-cut and obviously significant (and there are quite a few areas in which two or more committees are expressly given overlapping jurisdiction by the Rules), the referral to the other committee will be made automatically, at the time the bill is introduced.

Finally, it is worth mentioning that a number of committees have rules that bar the consideration of specified types of bills referred to them—usually to avoid discrimination or on the grounds that adequate administrative or judicial remedies are available. (The Rules of both the House and the Senate flatly prohibit even the introduction of private bills of several kinds and [under House Rules] of commemorations [bills designating a specified period of time for a remembrance, celebration, or the like].) It is the drafter's job to be aware of these obstacles and to warn the sponsor so that the sponsor will not unexpectedly run into a stone wall after having made promises to constituents.

34.3 Procedure generally (on the floor and in committee)

Floor procedure. The rules that determine how a bill is considered on the floor are numerous, often complicated, and occasionally obscure. Their details are beyond the scope of this book, and the parliamentarians of the House and Senate will not advise the public gratuitously (although they can advise Members who are making inquiries on behalf of others), so you should try to maintain contact with some person experienced in parliamentary procedure to whom you can turn when you need advice.

A few general comments about the usual floor procedure in the House of Representatives may be helpful, however. Bear in mind that variations are possible, and that the special ad hoc rule on the bill (see below) will normally determine many of the details.

When a typical bill is called up for consideration (after the adoption of the rule on the bill), the House resolves itself into the "Committee of the Whole House on the State of the Union", which is chaired by a Member appointed by the Speaker. The bill then goes through three stages.

The first stage consists of general debate, in which Members are supposed to discuss the bill in general terms but which they often use to talk about the specific amendments they plan to offer later. The amount of time allowed for general debate (for and against the bill) is always specified in the rule; it can range from one hour to 50 hours.

Upon completion of general debate, the bill is read for amendment (the second stage). All amendments (except amendments to the title and, in the case of resolutions, to the "preamble" [whereas clauses that precede the matter after the resolving clause]) are offered and dealt with in the Committee of the Whole, and their consideration is made easier because in that Committee it takes only 100 Members (instead of 218) to make a quorum. The bill is customarily read section by section, or title by title, under the five-minute rule (which technically limits debate on each side of any amendment to five minutes but is easily circumvented by the use of pro forma amendments[2]); once a particular section or title is finished, it cannot be returned to, except by unanimous consent. When all amendments have been acted on, the Committee reports the bill as amended to the full House and "rises"; and the Speaker resumes the chair.

The bill with its amendments is now "back in the House" (the third stage). After considering and acting on usually one motion to recommit (see below), the House approves the bill; this constitutes final passage of the bill. Amendments to the title are considered after passage of the bill.[3]

Several aspects of this procedure deserve special mention for their parliamentary implications:

(1) **The "rule".** If you are interested in knowing how a particular bill is going to be handled on the floor, you should find out what the special ad hoc rule on that bill (usually just called the "rule" on the bill) provides. Rules are public documents—ordinary simple House resolutions—but they spring full-blown from the Committee on Rules without ever having been introduced. However, the Rules Committee posts the rule on its website shortly after the rule's adoption by the Committee.

The rule prescribes the floor procedure to be followed, and the bill cannot be considered until the rule is adopted.[4] The rule not only specifies the procedures that are to be followed (as described above and elsewhere)—it will frequently also waive or modify particular parliamentary requirements, making amendments possible when they would otherwise be forbidden by the House Rules or forbidding amendments that would otherwise be in order. Rules that forbid amendments altogether are called "closed rules"; the jargon to describe rules that permit only specified amendments has changed as this type of rule has become prevalent in the House—from "modified open"[5] to "structured"[6] rules. Closed rules are common in the tax area; structured rules are the norm in almost every other subject area.[7]

There is nothing like this procedure in the Senate. Because each Senator has the right to unlimited debate, measures on the Senate floor can move forward only by unanimous consent agreements and invocation of cloture.[8]

Some rules are short and simple, consisting almost entirely of boilerplate, while others are long and complicated—it depends on the nature of the legislation involved and on tactical considerations. Figure 34.3 provides two examples. The first (from the 101st Congress) is an example of one that is somewhat complex; note that this example allows any Member to offer an amendment and is an open rule, which has become rare to nonexistent. The second example, H. Res. 806, is from the 109th Congress; note that no amendments are in order under this rule except those printed in the report accompanying this resolution. This means that only those amendments that have been approved in advance by the Committee on Rules may be offered on the floor. The difference between the two examples is substantial; the consequence under the second example is that debate on the floor is highly constrained.

Methods are available for discharging the Rules Committee and bringing to the floor a bill that is "bottled up" in that committee, but they very seldom work and are rarely even tried.

(2) **Order of amendments.** The order in which amendments to a given provision may be offered and considered, as discussed more fully in 34.4, can be tactically significant. It can prevent your amendment from being offered at all if your sponsor is not sufficiently alert, and (because it determines what other amendments your own will become entangled with) it materially affects the odds for success. Make sure you understand it.

(3) **Recommittals**. A motion to recommit usually represents the last gasp of the losing side—it has to be made by someone opposed to the bill—but it is sometimes a politically attractive alternative to a "no" vote on final passage (and sometimes succeeds for that reason) because it can be viewed as a technical device that simply returns the bill to the committee from which it came (presumably for further consideration there) rather than actually killing it. Adopting a simple motion to recommit (without instructions) does effectively defeat the bill, and as a practical matter is equivalent to a "no" vote on final passage; but a motion to recommit with instructions sometimes has a better chance of success because it is selective about its targets—isolating and attacking the weakest links—and permits the bill (with those targets destroyed) to be passed immediately.

House Calendar No. 62

101ST CONGRESS
1ST SESSION

H. RES. 255

[Report No. 101–267]

Providing for the consideration of the bill (H.R. 1495) to amend the Arms Control and Disarmament Act to authorize appropriations for the Arms Control and Disarmament Agency, and for other purposes.

IN THE HOUSE OF REPRESENTATIVES

OCTOBER 3, 1989

Mr. DERRICK from the Committee on Rules, reported the following resolution; which was referred by the House Calendar and ordered to be printed

RESOLUTION

Providing for the consideration of the bill (H.R. 1495) to amend the Arms Control and Disarmament Act to authorize appropriations for the Arms Control and Disarmament Agency, and for other purposes.

Resolved, That at any time after the adoption of this resolution the Speaker may, pursuant to clause 1(b) of rule XXIII, declare the House resolved into the Committee of the Whole House on the State of the Union for the consideration of the bill (H.R. 1495) to amend the Arms Control and Disarmament Act to authorize appropriations for the Arms Con-

Figure 34.3. "Special Rule" for Consideration of a Bill in the House

trol and Disarmament Agency, and for other purposes, and the first reading of the bill shall be dispensed with. After general debate, which shall be confined to the bill and which shall not exceed one hour, with thirty minutes to be equally divided and controlled by the chairman and ranking minority member of the Committee on Foreign Affairs, and with thirty minutes to be equally divided and controlled by the chairman and ranking member of the Committee on Armed Services, the bill shall be considered for amendment under the five-minute rule by titles instead of by sections and each title shall be considered as having been read. All points of order against the bill for failure to comply with the provisions of clause 5(a) of rule XXI are hereby waived. It shall be in order to consider en bloc as amendments to title II the amendments recommended by the Committee on Armed Services now printed in the bill. At the conclusion of the consideration of the bill for amendment, the Committee shall rise and report the bill to the House with such amendments as may have been adopted, and the previous question shall be considered as ordered on the bill and amendments thereto to final passage without intervening motion except on motion to recommit.

Figure 34.3. Continued

House Calendar No. 174

109TH CONGRESS
2D SESSION

H. RES. 806

[Report No. 109–459]

Providing for consideration of the bill (H.R. 5122) to authorize appropriations for fiscal year 2007 for military activities of the Department of Defense, to prescribe military personnel strengths for fiscal year 2007, and for other purposes.

IN THE HOUSE OF REPRESENTATIVES

MAY 9, 2006

Mr. COLE, from the Committee on Rules, reported the following resolution; which was referred to the House Calendar and ordered to be printed

---

RESOLUTION

Providing for consideration of the bill (H.R. 5122) to authorize appropriations for fiscal year 2007 for military activities of the Department of Defense, to prescribe military personnel strengths for fiscal year 2007, and for other purposes.

Resolved, That at any time after the adoption of this resolution the Speaker may, pursuant to clause 2(b) of rule XVIII, declare the House resolved into the Committee of the Whole House on the state of the Union for consideration of the bill (H.R. 5122) to authorize appropriations

Figure 34.3. Continued

2

for fiscal year 2007 for military activities of the Department of Defense, to prescribe military personnel strengths for fiscal year 2007, and for other purposes. The first reading of the bill shall be dispensed with. All points of order against consideration of the bill are waived. General debate shall be confined to the bill and shall not exceed one hour equally divided and controlled by the chairman and ranking minority member of the Committee on Armed Services. After general debate the bill shall be considered for amendment under the five-minute rule. It shall be in order to consider as an original bill for the purpose of amendment under the five-minute rule the amendment in the nature of a substitute recommended by the Committee on Armed Services now printed in the bill. The committee amendment in the nature of a substitute shall be considered as read. All points of order against the committee amendment in the nature of a substitute are waived. Notwithstanding clause 11 of rule XVIII, no amendment to the committee amendment in the nature of a substitute shall be in order except those printed in the report of the Committee on Rules accompanying this resolution. Each such amendment may be offered only in the order printed in the report, may be offered only by a Member designated in the report, shall be considered as read, shall be debatable for the time specified in the report equally divided

Figure 34.3. Continued

3

and controlled by the proponent and an opponent, shall not be subject to amendment, and shall not be subject to a demand for division of the question in the House or in the Committee of the Whole. All points of order against such amendments are waived. After disposition of the amendments printed in the report of the Committee on Rules, the Committee of the Whole shall rise without motion. No further consideration of the bill shall be in order except pursuant to a subsequent order of the House.

Figure 34.3. Continued

The traditional form for a motion to recommit without instructions is as follows:

> Mr. [Ms.] ________ moves to recommit the bill (H.R. 1234) to the Committee on ____________.

A motion to recommit with instructions simply adds a few words, followed by whatever amendments to the bill the offeror of the motion chooses to include—one or two short amendments or many pages of them. Thus:

> Mr. [Ms.] ________ moves to recommit the bill (H.R. 1234) to the Committee on ____________ with instructions to report the bill back to the House [promptly] [forthwith] with the following amendment [or amendments]:... .[9]

The amendments are written in the usual form (like other amendments to bills as described in 14.6 and 32.7). The drafter has to be aware of (and have copies of) the necessary amendments in order to incorporate them into the motion to recommit. The effect of using the word "forthwith" in the motion is that the chairman reports at once without awaiting action by the committee, if the motion to recommit is agreed to.[10] Motions to recommit are rarely agreed to, but it does happen.

You should understand the uses and forms of these motions (whether or not you ever have to write one) simply because they are legislative vehicles in every sense, requiring (in the case of a motion with instructions) the same drafting skills as ordinary amendments.

Note that a motion to recommit with instructions to report the bill back to the House "promptly" (which sends the bill back to the committee) is a way to avoid certain points of order under the Budget Act that would lie against "amendments". (The budget points of order apply to bills and amendments, but not to motions).

(4) **Suspensions**. One frequently used parliamentary shortcut that you ought to be aware of is the passage of bills in the House "under suspension of the rules". The procedure is activated by a motion made on the floor; adoption of the motion requires a two-thirds vote and the procedure is only available at specified times, but it has real advantages when a bill that could easily pass is having trouble finding a time-slot sufficient for its full-scale consideration.

A bill taken up "under suspension" can have as many amendments in it as the sponsor desires, already included in the copy of the bill that accompanies the motion. No amendments to it can be offered on the floor, and debate is limited to 40 minutes, evenly divided between the pros and cons, or between the managers of the bill who represent the committee (in most cases, of primary jurisdiction) to which the bill was referred upon introduction. And all parliamentary requirements that would otherwise apply are waived. This sounds as though it would invite widespread abuse; however, because of the required two-thirds majority to pass a measure, in practice the procedure is usually limited to noncontroversial measures of relatively limited cost.

To prepare a motion to suspend the rules is relatively simple:

(A) Prepare a version of the bill (the starting point is usually the bill as reported by the relevant committee) that incorporates any additional amendments proposed by the sponsor. If you are not proposing a complete substitute text that simply incorporates all proposed changes, all changes to the bill *as introduced* need to be clearly indicated and noted on the front page of the document. Note that preparing the bill for suspension as a complete substitute text allows the drafter the opportunity to make technical corrections in the bill (with the approval of the sponsor). Otherwise, under regular procedure, these technical changes would have to be offered as amendments on the floor.

(B) The first page of the document should have a heading indicating what is being done, for instance, "Suspend the Rules and Pass the Bill, H.R. 1234, With [an Amendment] [Amendments]". If the printed bill does not contain all the amendments to be included in the bill to be considered, clearly show any matter being stricken from the introduced bill, and clearly show any matter added. An amendment to the title is stated at the end of the bill (just as it is when a bill is reported from a committee).

On the top of the first page, also indicate what the changes are; for example, "The amendment[s] strike[s] all after the enacting clause and insert[s] a new text [and a new title]," or indicate the page and line numbers of the changes.

(C) You may also want to prepare the motion itself for the sponsor, as in the following:

> Mr. [Ms.] ________ moves to suspend the rules and pass the bill H.R. 1234 [as amended]:

You should ensure that the sponsor knows how many copies of the finished product are necessary for distribution to House officials and representatives of both the majority and the minority on the floor (usually four or five copies).

Unanimous consent. In the House of Representatives, bills can be brought up by unanimous consent. (Remember that in the Senate this is standard operating procedure.) However, as a practical matter, a Member would not be recognized for such a request without the agreement of committee and floor leadership on both sides of the aisle. The form of the bill, which the drafter may be called upon to prepare, would be whatever was agreed upon.

Committee procedure. The Rules of the House "are the rules of its committees and subcommittees so far as applicable", with minor exceptions (in Rule XI, clause 1), and subcommittees are subject to the rules of their parent committees "so far as applicable". Each committee has its own rules and, in most parliamentary respects, they follow the Rules of the parent body closely.

But in fact there are many differences between House procedures and committee procedures; committees only partially resemble the "Committee of the Whole House on the State of the Union"; they have no designated general debate on a measure (although the "opening statements" of Members who are recognized by committee chairmen for that purpose are comparable); they do, however, use the five-minute rule to limit debate on amendments.[11] There is no definitive body of parliamentary law on what "so far as applicable" means in this context; when a question arises on the floor about the validity (under the Rules) of some committee action, the presiding officer in the House decides.

To the best of the authors' knowledge, no one has ever tried to enforce complete procedural conformity among committees (although most committees do insist on conformity among their subcommittees). The only thing that can be safely said is that committee rules and procedures bear a noticeable resemblance to those of the parent body but tend to be a good deal looser in actual practice. You usually can assume that committee chairmen will impose the same requirements and interpret the rules in the same way as their House (or Senate) counterparts, but you should not entirely rely on that assumption. And you should, of course, have a copy of the rules of any committee you deal with regularly.

It should be mentioned again that the Rules of the House require all committee reports on bills to include a number of specific items; among them are various budgetary findings, oversight summaries, and economic statements as well as the "Ramseyer" (see 32.8). Preparing most of these items is up to the committee staff (although the Ramseyer is normally left to the drafter), but if you are responsible for assembling the final report you should remember to make sure that all the pieces are there. The bill may be subject to a point of order on the floor if they are not.

34.4 Amendments

Degree. Both in committee and on the floor, there is a limitation on the number and kind of proposed amendments to a provision of a bill that may be pending at any one time. It is usually put this way: amendments in the "first degree" and "second degree" are permissible, while amendments in the "third degree" (or any higher degree) are not.

Under this limitation there can be as many as four amendments pending at the same time:

(1) An amendment to the text of the bill (first degree). This can be either a simple amendment or an amendment "in the nature of a substitute".

(2) A substitute for that amendment (also treated as first degree). This must be called a substitute—headed either "Substitute Offered by Mr. [Ms.] Y for the Amendment Offered by Mr. [Ms.] X" or "Amendment in the Nature of a Substitute Offered by Mr. [Ms.] Y to the Amendment Offered by Mr. [Ms.] X".

(3) An amendment to the original amendment (second degree)—"Amendment Offered by Mr. [Ms.] Z to the Amendment Offered by Mr. [Ms.] X".

(4) An amendment to the substitute (also second degree)—"Amendment Offered by Mr. [Ms.] Z to the Substitute Offered by Mr. [Ms.] Y".

In addition, if the first amendment is a motion to strike only (that is, no new text is to be inserted), then this motion will be held in abeyance while other "perfecting" amendments (that is, amendments to strike text and insert new text) are disposed of first. Any amendment offered to either of amendments (3) and (4) would be "in the third degree", and would be out of order.

Committee amendments included in the printed bill as reported are counted as amendments on the floor, so that if there is a committee amendment to a particular section of the bill, only three additional floor amendments to that section can be pending at any one time. It should be noted, however, that when a committee has reported a bill, whether as an amendment in the nature of a complete substitute (striking out the entire text of the bill and inserting a new text), or as a series of "cut-and-bite" amendments to the introduced bill, the House resolution providing the rule for considering the bill on the House floor frequently provides that the committee amendments are to be treated as the original text for purposes of amendment, which restores the four-amendment possibility.

When the time comes to act on the four pending amendments, the first one voted on is the amendment to the amendment (clause (3)), followed in order by the amendment to the substitute (clause (4)), the substitute itself (clause (2)), and the original amendment (clause (1)). Members waiting in the wings with amendments that would have been in the third degree can offer them as soon as slots become available; for example, a Member who has another amendment to the substitute can offer it as soon as the first amendment to the substitute has been disposed of.

Needless to say, all of this poses real problems for the absentee drafter (and even for an on-the-scene drafter), who must tailor amendments to fit a scenario that changes by the minute. And when the smoke clears it may be too late to offer them. However, as a practical matter, complex amendment scenarios do not arise often.

The rules governing amendments in committee and on the floor have been simplified and condensed in what is sometimes called the basic amendment tree (see figure 34.4).

Germaneness. Any amendment offered to a bill in committee or on the floor must be "germane" to that bill and to the particular provision or provisions affected. The dictionary defines germaneness as the quality of being "closely related, appropriate, pertinent, to the point, akin, relevant". The Rules of the House (Rule XVI, clause 7) put it this way: "No motion or proposition on a subject different from that under consideration shall be admitted under color of amendment".

The requirement is absolute and must be complied with, but you do not have to be a genius to recognize that "germaneness" is an elusive term. How far afield can you go before your amendment can be said to involve "a subject different from that under consideration"?

If the bill involved, for example, is one that increases widows' insurance benefits under the Social Security program, an amendment to change the amount of the increase is clearly germane, and an amendment to provide military assistance to Pakistan is clearly not. But what about an amendment to decrease widows' benefits instead, or to change the amount of other types of benefits, or to change eligibility requirements for widows, or to improve related administrative procedures? What if it goes further and increases disability benefits, or benefits under the SSI program? All of these contain subject matter that could be characterized, in varying degrees, either as "related to" or "different from" the bill.

You might take a sabbatical and read the several thousand existing precedents on the subject of germaneness, starting with the parliamentarian's notes following the cited clause in the bound volume of the House Rules. The authors would not recommend this, although the parliamentarian's notes (which could be read through and digested in an hour or so) would give you a good feel for the subject and might be worth the effort. The parliamentarian's task is a difficult one; in the case of precedents that appear to be conflicting, the parliamentarian must study the texts involved to draw the distinction between them, and apply the precedents to the language under debate.

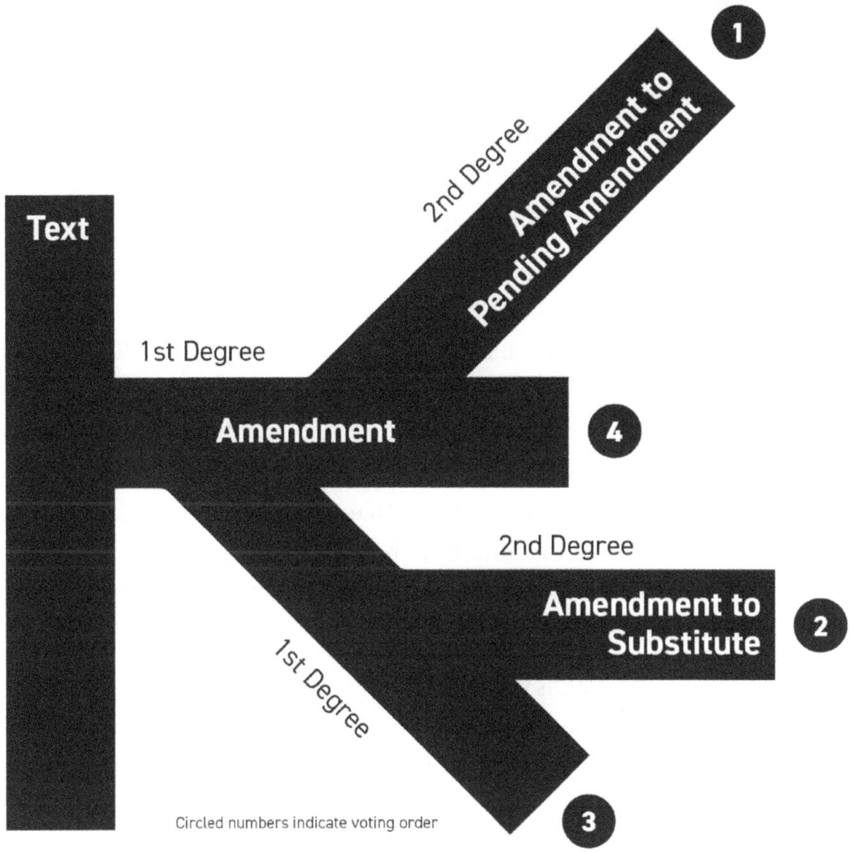

Figure 34.4. Basic Amendment Tree

In most cases, however, it is not really that difficult—after all, the meaning of the term is clear in a general sense even if its application to particular cases can sometimes be troublesome. And in any event, there are several considerations that may be helpful:

(1) In dealing with questions of germaneness you should apply four basic tests—the subject matter, the breadth or scope of the bill (or provision) being amended, the fundamental purposes of the bill (or provision) and of the amendment, and the jurisdiction of the

committee that is considering or has reported the bill. These tests are not exclusive.

(2) To the extent possible, in doubtful cases, you should look for ways to tie your amendment to what is already in the bill—make it look like an exception, a special rule, or a conforming change, rather than like a freestanding and apparently separate provision.

(3) If you are responsible for the bill, and the sponsor (for tactical reasons) wants to make it harder for others to amend, keep its scope and apparent purpose narrow, and include language reflecting that narrowness wherever possible. A bill "to amend section 202(e)(2)(A) of the Social Security Act to provide a 10 percent increase in widow's insurance benefits" is better in this respect (though unnecessarily cumbersome for most purposes) than a bill "to amend title II of the Social Security Act to improve the benefit structure of the OASDI program"; and either is better than a bill "to provide greater financial security for aged individuals".

Since the parliamentarian is the expert on germaneness, you, as the drafter, should always advise the sponsor to consult the parliamentarian on this question, requesting (if it is the sponsor's wish) that the communication be confidential.

In the Senate, points of order for germaneness can be raised only on certain budget measures (including reconciliation bills), and on other measures only after cloture is invoked. In the latter case, germaneness is applied so that no amendment can amend a bill in more than one place. The end result is a bill that has provisions at the end of it that in effect amend earlier provisions in the bill, a result that may make the bill very difficult to piece together.

34.5 Prohibited Appropriations

The Rules of the House prohibit appropriations in two types of cases that occasionally rise up to trouble well-intentioned legislators. You will probably never have to draft a bill making appropriations, but if you are called upon to draft an amendment doing that you should understand what is involved so you can advise your sponsor properly.

Appropriations without previous authorization. An appropriation cannot be made unless it has been authorized in a previously enacted statute. The pertinent language is in House Rule XXI, clause 2(a)(1): "An appropriation may not be reported in a general appropriation bill, and may not be in order as an amendment thereto, for an expenditure not previously authorized by law...". This requirement was discussed in 12.5. (Note that the requirement does not apply to so-called continuing resolutions [that is, bills to continue funding for government programs in the short term in the absence of the enactment of general appropriations bills for those programs].)[12]

Most bills creating major programs include a provision explicitly authorizing appropriations in specified amounts and for specified periods. When confusion arises it is usually because the program involved does not include such a provision, which sometimes makes sponsors nervous about whether or not the program can be funded. But it is well established that any law that creates a function or requires an action to be taken is in and of itself an authorization of whatever appropriations may be necessary for that function or action, without limit as to amount or time.

Thus an explicit authorization of appropriations is necessary only to place limitations upon the amount of the appropriations or the period for which they can be made. The prohibition against unauthorized appropriations is aimed at appropriations in amounts or for periods exceeding those limitations, or for programs or functions that have not yet been created at all. (A related provision of the Rules prohibits reappropriations, in a general appropriations bill, of unexpended balances from prior years, except for the continuation of public works.)

Appropriations in legislative bills. An appropriation cannot be included in a "legislative" bill (that is, in a bill not originating in the Committee on Appropriations), or in any amendment to such a bill. The pertinent language is in House Rule XXI, clause 4: "A bill or joint resolution carrying an appropriation may not be reported by a committee not having jurisdiction to report appropriations, and an amendment proposing an appropriation shall not be in order during the consideration of a bill or joint resolution reported by a committee not having that jurisdiction.".[13]

For the most part this is an easy requirement to comply with, since appropriations are usually recognizable as such on their face.

There are a couple of situations, however, in which the prohibition applies, but the offending provision may not be recognizable on its face as an appropriation.

One is when funds have been properly appropriated for a specified purpose, a legislative bill that subsequently makes a sufficiently basic change in that purpose may sometimes be viewed as diverting the previously authorized and previously appropriated funds from the old purpose to a totally new one. If it is so viewed (whether or not the bill explicitly says that the existing funds are to be available for the new purpose), it will be treated as constituting a new appropriation, and requires a new authorization, unless the bill's language makes it clear that the availability of the funds for the new purpose is subject to a subsequent appropriation.

Obviously, the dividing line between a completely new purpose and a merely modified or expanded one is not always easy to spot. Adding new features to an existing program or increasing its size is everyday stuff for the drafter, of course, and creates no problems; but substituting an entirely new program for the old one (using the money already available) will fall before a point of order every time, unless the use of the money is made subject to a subsequent appropriation. And any overhaul of the old program may be suspect if it is extensive enough to constitute a basic change in the program's purpose.

You should be alert to these possibilities, and if you think you have a problem (after reading the operating and funding provisions of both the existing law and the proposed bill as well as the previous appropriation), you should raise with the sponsor the possible necessity of explicitly writing the bill as an authorization only (like any other bill establishing a new program) and obtaining the funding through new appropriations in a separate bill to be enacted later.

Another case in which a legislative bill appropriates money (although it may not be obvious) is when a legislative bill establishes a fee and then permits the collecting agency to use the funds collected (usually for a specified purpose). This in essence is an appropriation of Federal funds that will raise a point of order against the bill. It is cured by making the funds available to the agency "in such amounts as are provided in appropriations Acts".

34.6 Legislation in appropriations bills

The other side of the coin is that the House Rules also prohibit the inclusion of "legislation" in a general appropriations bill. The pertinent language is in Rule XXI, clause 2(b) and (c): "A provision changing existing law may not be reported in a general appropriation bill ... [and] [an] amendment to a general appropriations bill shall not be in order if changing existing law, including an amendment making the availability of funds contingent on the receipt or possession of information not required by existing law for the period of the appropriation.". (There are limited exceptions to these prohibitions [for example, "germane provisions which retrench expenditures by the reduction of amounts of money covered by the bill" and rescissions of appropriations contained in appropriations Acts]).[14]

If the prohibition against changing existing law were uniformly applied according to its terms, your options would be clear, and appropriations riders—the devices commonly used to legislate in appropriations Acts (see 12.13)—could hardly exist. In fact, however, it can be circumvented.

Principle of limitation. The most important method of getting around the prohibition is based on the so-called principle of "limitation". That principle (which is well known to all Members of Congress but perhaps not fully understood) provides in essence that since Congress is not obliged to appropriate anything just because there is an authorization of appropriations on the books, it is permissible for Congress to limit the use of any appropriation it does make. The limitation is usually accomplished by simply providing that no part of the appropriation involved in the bill shall be used for certain specified purposes. The limitation, however, must not impose new duties on officials who are to carry out the prohibition.

Assume, for example, that the Appropriations Committee disapproves of an agency's (legally authorized) practice of awarding contracts in some cases to persons who were not the low bidders. If the Committee added a provision in that agency's annual appropriations bill that "no part of any amount appropriated for a project in this Act shall be used to carry out a contract with a person who was not the low bidder on that project", that may not be in order; if an official has to decide who the "low bidder" is, and that decision is not already authorized by law in those exact terms (in other words, the official is authorized by law to determine who is the "low bidder"), the limitation may be ruled out of order as legislation.

The long-established practice of Treasury borrowing to finance major Federal programs ("backdoor spending"), which was finally put to death by the Congressional Budget Act of 1974, was actually brought to a grinding halt around 1960 by a rider (placed in every general appropriations bill) that simply said, in effect, "No part of any amount appropriated in this Act for salaries and expenses shall be used to pay the salary or expenses of any officer or employee who is engaged in carrying out a program or activity funded in whole or in part from sources other than appropriations".

Such a limitation does not literally terminate the offending program or activity, of course; it only cuts off the funds. The officials involved could theoretically continue the program or activity and pay for it out of their own pockets, but somehow they never do.

The question of what constitutes a permissible "limitation" is a very complicated one, and there are hundreds of precedents that bear on it. But if the language does not give affirmative directions, does not impose new duties, and does not directly interfere with anyone's discretionary authority—that is, if the job can be done by a simple negative on the use of the appropriation—the device can be (and regularly is) used freely. However, the prohibition has become increasingly difficult to overcome. The offeror of a limitation amendment will have the burden of defending its legitimacy. Note that the phrase (in House Rule XXI, clause 2(c)) barring a provision making the availability of funds contingent on the receipt or possession of information not required by existing law (added in the 105th Congress) put an end to limitation amendments barring the use of funds by an official when specified circumstances became "known" by the official, unless it was the official's duty to know these circumstances under existing law.

Case study: A limitation amendment. It bears repeating that the limitation amendment is often a lawmaker's most potent legislative tool (see 12.13), but drafting it to survive parliamentary scrutiny is challenging. Consider the following case, which occurred in the 109th Congress. Note the involvement of the same statute that was discussed in the case study in chapter 27, although this predated the Dubai Ports World controversy.

In June of 2005, amid the omnipresent concern over energy supplies, the press reported the proposed acquisition of Unocal, a United States oil and gas company, by the Chinese National Offshore Oil Company (CNOOC), a company owned by the government of the People's Republic of China. The message that the public gleaned from this report was that some U.S. energy supplies would be controlled by China. The annual bill making appropriations to the Department of the Treasury (among other departments and agencies)[15] was scheduled for consideration on the floor of the House of Representatives in late June. A request from the legislative director of a Member of Congress was referred to the author to "discuss an idea" for an amendment to the Transportation, Treasury Appropriations bill.[16] The idea was to express a "sense of the House of Representatives" that the Treasury Department expend the necessary resources to have the Committee on Foreign Investment in the United States conduct a complete review of the proposed acquisition, including an assessment of the economic and national security implications of the acquisition. The legislative director also wanted to explore ways of strengthening the proposal.

On its face, even a "sense of the House of Representatives" provision would be legislating in an appropriations bill; in this case it expresses a policy of how funds should be expended. After this point was raised with the legislative director, he asked the author to prepare a limitation amendment that would have the effect of stopping the acquisition.

The key to a limitation amendment is to tie the limitation on use of funds in the bill to a function for which the funds can be used. After researching the state of the law, the author came up with the following amendment: "None of the funds made available in this Act to the Department of the Treasury may be used to recommend approval of the sale of Unocal Corporation to CNOOC Ltd. of China.". The legislative director consulted the Office of the Parliamentarian on whether the amendment would be in order on the floor. The parliamentarian's office asked for the statutory citation that gave the Treasury Department the authority to approve the proposed acquisition. The following was the author's response, which encapsulated the research that was necessary to approach this amendment:

> The President has the authority to investigate, suspend, or prohibit any acquisition, merger, or takeover of a person engaged in interstate commerce, under section 721 of the Defense Production Act of 1950 (50 U.S.C. App. 2170)[17]. By interim directive dated October 26, 1988 (53 F.R. 43999), the President delegated to the Secretary of the Treasury the authority to carry out section 721 of the Defense Production Act of 1950. Executive Order 11858, as amended (15 U.S.C. 78b note), established the Committee on Foreign Investment in the United States (CFIUS) (on which the Secretary of the Treasury serves) and delegated to it the authority to conduct investigations under section 721(a), and to make reports to the President with recommendations. The Chairman of the Committee (the Secretary of the Treasury) is delegated the authority to issue regulations to carry out section 721 of the Defense Production Act. The President retains the authority to act on the recommendation, unless the memorandum noted above is still active. But it seems clear that the Secretary of the Treasury (as the Chairman of CFIUS) has authorities (to recommend approval of an acquisition) under that section, as delegated by the President.

This short amendment shows the effort that can be involved in drafting a limitation amendment that passes parliamentary muster. Writing the words took a couple of minutes. Doing the legwork to back it up took many hours. In the end, it was the opinion of the parliamentarian that the amendment would pass parliamentary muster; no point of order against the amendment was raised on the House floor and the amendment passed. Most significantly, this "powerful legislative tool" achieved the desired result. Even though the amendment could not directly stop the approval of the merger (since the Secretary of the Treasury lacked the clear legal authority to do so), in the face of the political pressure, CNOOC withdrew its bid to acquire Unocal.

The changes in the House Rules in recent Congresses (intended to discourage appropriations riders by imposing restrictions on when and how they can be offered [limitation amendments offered on the floor are to be offered at the end of the bill, before the short title[18]] and by giving the majority leader the right to effectively prevent their consideration in some cases [Rule XXI, clause 2(d)]) have cut down on the practice but have not eliminated it. If you are called upon to write an appropriations rider you should have no misgivings about it; just be sure that the sponsor is aware of the practical difficulties and *in every case* recommend that the parliamentarian review the amendment before it is offered.

34.7 The budget process

The Congressional Budget Act of 1974 (titles I through IX of the Congressional Budget and Impoundment Control Act of 1974) imposes a number of limitations on the way in which (and the times at which) bills and amendments having budgetary impact may be considered. Some of these limitations must be taken into account in the actual drafting process; the rest do not directly concern you as a drafter but are important nonetheless, because you will often be called upon to advise your sponsor on the best legislative route to take and on the obstacles that route is likely to contain.

This body of law—the Budget Act and its confederates (the Budget Enforcement Act of 1990, and a few others)—makes up a tapestry that is far too complicated and mysterious to address in detail here. But the limitations that are likely to concern you as a drafter are reasonably clear; and without attempting anything exhaustive it is the purpose of this subdivision to remind you of a few of the more important provisions as they currently exist—new ones are added and old ones changed on a regular basis):

(1) No bill or amendment having budgetary impact in any fiscal year can be considered in either House until the budget resolution for that year has been agreed to (section 303 of the Budget Act [2 U.S.C. 634]). For this purpose "budgetary impact" means new budget authority,[19] changes in revenues, changes in the public debt limit, and (in the Senate) new entitlement authority or changes in outlays.

(2) After the budget resolution for any fiscal year has been agreed to, no bill or amendment can be considered in either House if it would have the effect of increasing budget authority, within any committee or subcommittee allocation, beyond the applicable levels permitted by that allocation (section 302 of the Budget Act [2 U.S.C. 633]).

(3) No amendment to a reconciliation bill can be considered if it would have the effect of increasing outlays or reducing revenues, unless it makes offsetting reductions in other outlays or offsetting increases in other revenues (section 310 of the Budget Act [2 U.S.C. 641]).

(4) After the budget resolution for any fiscal year has been agreed to, no bill or amendment can be considered in either House if it would have the effect of increasing budget authority or outlays or reducing revenues beyond the level specified in the resolution (section 311 of the Budget Act [2 U.S.C. 642]).

(5) No bill or amendment providing Treasury borrowing authority or advance contract authority, or providing new credit authority, can be considered in either House unless it also specifically provides that such authority "is to be effective for any fiscal year only to the extent or in the amounts provided in advance in appropriation Acts" (section 401(a) of the Budget Act [2 U.S.C. 651(a)]). (This allows the practice but maintains control within the appropriations process.)

(6) No bill or amendment can be considered in either House if it provides entitlement authority that would become effective before the first day of the upcoming fiscal year (section 401(b)(1) of the Budget Act [2 U.S.C. 651(b)(1)]).

(7) In the Senate, any matter "extraneous" to a reconciliation bill is deemed stricken from the bill (section 313 of the Budget Act [the so-called "Byrd" rule; 2 U.S.C. 644]); section 313(b) defines what is and is not "extraneous"; in general, material is extraneous if it does not achieve the purpose of reducing outlays in accordance with the reconciliation instructions, or if it includes any recommendations with respect to Social Security.

(8) Though not in the Budget Act, there are Pay-As-You-Go (PAYGO) provisions in law (The Statutory Pay-As-You-Go Act of 2010) and House and Senate Rules establishing points of order against legislation having the net effect of increasing the deficit over either the following six-year or 11-year fiscal-year period.

Bear in mind that this list is provided only to help you understand the kinds of parliamentary obstacles your bills will face on the budgetary front. There are other points of order, and procedural ways of overcoming them. A complete mastery of the budget field is more than the authors would try to impose on anyone. Any problems you may have in this area will most likely involve uncertainty about the meaning of the key terms; you should read the definitions carefully and consult an expert if you can find one, but actually reading the entire Budget Act and its confederates is something you should do only as a last resort if you hope to maintain your sanity.

34.8 Conference limitations

Every drafter should be aware, in general terms at least, of just how far conferees can go in resolving differences between the two Houses.

The basic rule in the House, which is stricter than the corresponding rule in the Senate (and governs in any case, as a practical matter, because both

Houses must be able to agree to whatever the conferees come up with), is found in Rule XXII, clause 9:

> Whenever a disagreement to an amendment has been committed to a conference committee, the Managers on the part of the House may propose a substitute that is a germane modification of the matter in disagreement. The introduction of any language presenting specific additional matter not committed to the conference committee by either House does not constitute a germane modification of the matter in disagreement. Moreover, a conference report may not include matter not committed to the conference committee by either House and may not include a modification of specific matter committed to the conference committee by either or both Houses if that modification is beyond the scope of that specific matter as committed to the conference committee.

As in the case of most major parliamentary problems, the questions that arise in the conference area can often be answered in different ways by different people, and there are hundreds of precedents that bear upon what is permissible and what is not. But it is in the application of the parliamentary requirements to particular cases that the difficulties arise—the requirements themselves are fairly straightforward.

This subdivision will not attempt to address all the intricacies but will limit itself to a few of the more fundamental considerations that every drafter should understand.

Complete substitutes versus numbered amendments. As indicated earlier, a conference report can take one of two forms:

(1) If the Senate amendment was a complete substitute for the House bill (or vice versa), the conference report will be a complete substitute for both of them. The entire document will have been committed to the conferees, as a single amendment in disagreement, and is "in conference".

(2) If the Senate instead made "cut-and-bite" amendments at specific points in the House bill (or vice versa), each of those individual

amendments is given a number, and only the numbered amendments are "in conference".

The requirements of germaneness and scope apply equally in either case. The conferees have no power to consider anything that is not before them ("in conference"). What is before them are the differences between the House and Senate bills. Thus if the same provision appeared in both the House and Senate bills, it would not be before the conferees and could not be stricken.

Germaneness. Whether or not one proposition is "germane" to another is, of course, a matter of subjective judgment in close cases. Enough has been said about the elusiveness of the concept (see 34.4); but you should remember that it is an absolute requirement in conference reports.

Under the Rules of the House, not only must every conference action be germane to the provisions of either the House or Senate version of the bill when that action is taken during the conference, but when the conference report is subsequently considered in the House, all of its provisions (including, for example, any Senate provisions that were agreed to by the conferees) must meet the same test of germaneness as they would have if they had been offered as amendments to the bill when it was originally being considered on the House floor. There is a special House procedure for voting on eliminating nongermane matter included in a conference report and then adopting the rest of the report; therefore, if a point of order for germaneness were sustained, and a motion to reject the nongermane matter were made and not adopted, the matter in question would stay in the conference report. If the motion to reject were adopted, what is before the House then is the remainder of the conference report.

As a practical matter, when a conference report is brought up on the floor of the House of Representatives, a special rule providing for the consideration of the conference report will almost certainly waive points of order against the conference report, so germaneness will never be raised. The same is true of issues of scope.

Scope. Under the Rules of the House, conferees may not adopt matters beyond the "scope" of the conferees' powers. When the difference between the House and Senate versions of a particular provision is measurable on some objective scale, the conferees must adopt one of the two versions or come down somewhere between them.

Thus if one House authorized $1,000,000 for benefits to be paid in or after 2025 to individuals age 65 or over, and the other House authorized $3,000,000 for benefits in or after 2027 to individuals age 62 or over, the conferees could agree upon an authorization of $1,000,000 or $3,000,000 or any figure in between, upon a starting date of 2025, 2026, or 2027, and upon an age limit of 62, 63, 64, or 65 (and they could do this in any combination unless the three differences were regarded [for parliamentary purposes] as part of an indivisible whole). But they would have no power to go higher than $3,000,000 or lower than $1,000,000, or to start earlier than 2025 or later than 2027, or to specify an age above 65 or below 62—if they did, a point of order would lie against their entire report.

Obviously, most scope measurements are not this easy. Usually the two versions are at least comparable in substance, however, and the conferees must try to find the outer limits of each in order to comply with the scope requirement. In the relatively rare cases where they are not comparable at all—for example, a House provision imposing capital punishment for some crime, replaced in the Senate by a provision for the appointment of additional judges to hear cases of the kind involved—it would be futile to try and measure the scope of the difference without consulting the parliamentarians (to adopt both provisions would be beyond the scope of the conference, because no position "between" the two provisions would have resulted). The "compromise" would also be subject to the germaneness rule.

If you become involved in very many conferences you will soon have your fill of scope and germaneness questions, many with no clear-cut answers. Just be alert for them, and hope that someone at the conference has the ear of the official parliamentarians (who will advise the presiding official ruling on such matters) so that these questions can be settled on the spot; waiting for a ruling until after the conference report has been filed is unsatisfactory for obvious reasons.

It bears repeating that because conference reports are routinely considered in the House under a special rule waiving points of order against them, issues of germaneness and scope (and budgetary points of order) are moot. Since the Senate does not bring matters to the floor of the Senate subject to rules, any waiver of points of order would have to be done by unanimous consent.[20]

Notes

1 Before the 104th Congress, a bill could be jointly referred to more than one committee of primary jurisdiction. Joint referrals caused procedural complications in reporting and on the floor, and also invited obstruction of the primary objective on unrelated grounds. In the 104th Congress, the rules were modified to require the designation of only one committee of primary jurisdiction.

2 A "pro forma" amendment is an amendment to "strike the last word" or to "strike the requisite number of words" and provides additional opportunities to speak on a substantive amendment that is pending.

3 Technically the preamble of a resolution would also be voted on after passage of the text of the resolution, but this issue almost never arises because resolutions are almost always brought up under suspension of the rules.

4 In some limited cases involving a "privileged" matter, a bill can be considered without a rule.

5 A "modified open" rule would allow amendments to be offered that are printed beforehand in the *Congressional Record;* amendments to those amendments would not be required to be preprinted.

6 A "structured" rule would in most cases specify in the Rules Committee report accompanying the rule those amendments that may be offered, but bar any amendments to those amendments, and allow one motion to recommit (see point (3) in this list).

7 This was not always the case; open rules were common before the 1990s. And general appropriations bills often have open rules, although the strictures that apply to appropriations bills greatly limit the amendments that are in order to such a bill.

8 Cloture is the only procedure by which the Senate can vote to place a time limit on consideration of a bill or other matter, and thereby overcome a filibuster. Under the cloture rule (Rule XXII), the Senate may limit consideration of a pending matter to 30 additional hours, but only by vote of three-fifths of the full Senate, normally 60 votes.

9 The bill that is being recommitted is the bill with all amendments agreed to on the floor.

10 A motion to recommit with instructions that the committee report the bill back "promptly" instead of "forthwith" in effect sends the bill back to committee for an uncertain future.

11 Under the Rules of the House, the committees are to follow the procedure of the "House as in the Committee of the Whole", which has its own set of procedures under the Rules; one example is that under this procedure a Member does not need to obtain unanimous consent to withdraw an amendment that the Member offered (unanimous consent is otherwise required).

12 The comparable provision in the Standing Rules of the Senate that prohibits unauthorized provisions in appropriations bills appears in Rule XVI, clause 1, but it has exceptions. For example, the Appropriations Committee or the committee with legislative jurisdiction over the matter in question can by motion include such a provision in an appropriations bill.

13 The Senate Rules do not prohibit appropriations in authorizing legislation.

14 Rule XVI of the Standing Rules of the Senate (clauses 2 and 4) contains comparable restrictions on legislating in appropriations bills.

15 The Transportation, Treasury, Housing and Urban Development, the Judiciary, the District of Columbia, and Independent Agencies Appropriations Act, 2006.

16 Gene Fisher (then Legislative Director and [in the 110th Congress] Chief of Staff of the Hon. Carolyn Kilpatrick), who requested that this amendment be drafted, gave his permission to discuss this case.

17 As discussed in 27.8, section 721 of the Defense Production Act of 1950 was amended extensively after the proposed acquisition of a U.S. port by a foreign entity, and this section was later reclassified by Law Revision Counsel to 50 U.S.C. 4565.

18 In appropriations bills, the short title appears at the very end.

19 Budget authority means any authority provided by Federal law to incur financial obligations, including borrowing and contract authority (section 3 of the Congressional Budget and Impoundment Control Act of 1974 [2 U.S.C. 622]).

20 The Senate's concept of "scope" is broader than that of the House. Rule XXVIII, clause 2 of the Standing Rules of the Senate provides as follows:

> Conferees shall not insert in their report matter not committed to them by either House, nor shall they strike from the bill matter agreed to by both Houses....

As mentioned in 34.4, points of order for germaneness in the Senate can be raised only on certain budget matters, and on other measures only after cloture is invoked.

PART IX

STATE AND REGULATORY DRAFTING CONSIDERATIONS

35. Drafters of Nonfederal Law

35.1 Preliminary comments

One of the basic tenets of this book is that good drafting principles can be applied to any legal document a drafter is asked to prepare. The purpose of this chapter is to highlight some issues that may arise for the drafter of legislation for a State or subdivision of a State. The obvious difficulty in attempting to do so is that every jurisdiction is different. The challenge for the drafter is to know the idiosyncrasies of that jurisdiction.

In addition to any law library, the constitutions and laws of the States and the District of Columbia can for the most part be found online on the websites of the individual jurisdictions. A valuable website for the drafter of State or local legislation is the website of the National Conference of State Legislatures (*www.ncsl.org*). The website organizes links by subject areas, and a researcher can compare the laws of the States on an issue. For example, under "ethics", you can compare issues like "gifts" and "lobbying" in all the jurisdictions. Another website, *www.statenet.com* (a LexisNexis database), tracks bills in the 50 States and the District of Columbia. Other useful websites include *www.findlaw.com*; *www.law.cornell.edu/states/listing.html*; and *www.llsdc.org/sourcebook*, which has links to resources on legislation and drafting.

As with any source you use, you will need to check the official version (whether in a codification or not) of the laws in the jurisdiction in which you are working to ensure the accuracy of the text you are using as a reference.

35.2 Constitutional requirements

While the United States Constitution imposes some procedural requirements regarding the enactment of laws—for example, revenue bills must originate in the House of Representatives, bills must pass both Houses of Congress and be signed by the President to become law, presidential vetoes can be overridden by a two-thirds vote of each House of Congress—the Constitution allows each House to prescribe its own rules for conducting its business. Some requirements regarding bills are codified in title 1 of the United States Code (specifying the enacting and resolving clauses (1 U.S.C. 101, 102), requiring each section to be numbered and contain "as nearly as may be" a single proposition of enactment (1 U.S.C. 104), and specifying the title of an appropriation Act (1 U.S.C. 105); however, the other particulars of enacting a bill into law are left to the rules of the two Houses of Congress.

By contrast, the States have many procedural requirements for enacting laws that are specified in their constitutions. Regardless of their origin, they appear to serve the purpose of maximizing the transparency of the legislative process through mechanisms to provide notice of a bill's contents and to ensure careful consideration of legislation by the legislature.

Diverse procedural provisions in the States. In Pennsylvania, for example, the provisions of Article III of the State constitution prohibiting bills from being altered or amended so as to change their original purpose (section 1), prohibiting the consideration of bills unless "referred to a committee, printed for use of the members and returned therefrom" (section 2), limiting a bill to a single subject reflected in its title (section 3), requiring every bill to be considered on three different days in each House (section 4), and requiring all amendments adopted be printed for the use of the members before the final vote on passage of the bill is taken (section 4) were adopted "to place restraints on the legislative process and encourage an open, deliberative and accountable government," *Stilp v. Commonwealth of Pennsylvania,* 588 Pa. 539, 595–596, 905 A.2d 918, 952 (2006), quoting *City of Philadelphia v. Com.,* 575 Pa. 542, 573, 838 A.2d 566, 585 (2003) (internal citation omitted).

Many State constitutions (Maryland, Minnesota, North Dakota, Texas, Washington, and Wyoming are included in this group) impose requirements to prevent the enactment of laws in a hurried fashion by prohibiting bills, or certain types of bills (for example, appropriations bills), from being introduced during the final days of a session or after the legislature has been in session for a certain period of time, or by prohibiting bills from being considered unless they have been introduced or acted on within a specified time before consideration. The exceptions to the rules in the States are a matter of public record, for example by special message of the governor or by a supermajority or unanimous consent of the legislature or house (as in an appropriations measure).

Some State constitutions (Georgia, Louisiana, Tennessee, and Texas, for example) prohibit the consideration of a bill containing the same substance of a bill already rejected in that session. (In some cases, the prohibition can be overruled by special vote of the legislature.)

Many State constitutions (Alabama, Arkansas, California, Idaho, Kentucky, Louisiana, Maryland, Mississippi, New Jersey, New Mexico, and Texas, for example) prohibit amending a law by the cut-and-bite approach, or by reference only to the title or section of the law being amended; in other words, the provision of law being amended must be shown as it would read as amended, or must be shown indicating the matter stricken and inserted. Likewise, a law that is to be revived must be restated in full. Some

State constitutions (Arkansas, Louisiana, New Jersey, and North Dakota, for example) prohibit enactments by reference; in other words, the provisions of another law being incorporated must be restated in the law being enacted.

Many States (California, Idaho, Maryland, and Mississippi are examples) require that bills be read a specified number of times (three) in each House before final passage and on different days. This rule may be dispensed with usually by a vote of a supermajority (for example, two-thirds).

Most States have requirements limiting bills to a single subject, and require the subject to be reflected in the title; the constitutions of many States specify that a subject not expressed in the title is void. Some constitutions prohibit amending a bill that would change its original purpose or scope. (There are exceptions in some States for appropriations bills and bills containing a codification or general revision of the laws.)

Some States prohibit the consideration of bills not referred to and reported from committee.

Most States have constitutional provisions specifying what the effective date of a law will be, usually after its publication or at some specified period after enactment, subject to special exceptions to address emergency situations.

Generally, emergency measures that override constitutional procedural restrictions will require a separate vote of the legislature, usually by a supermajority, to determine whether a measure is an "emergency", and will require that the emergency be expressed in the bill.

Most State constitutions prohibit "special laws"—private relief bills that grant an exemption from the law or some other monetary or other benefit to a particular person. An issue here for the drafter in one of these States may be whether a "general" law that is drafted in such a way as to apply to only one person (or very few persons) is a special law within that jurisdiction.

And then, like the Federal Constitution, there are procedures governing presentment to the governor of the State and veto override.

Court challenges. While many of these procedural provisions will not affect the drafter in composing legislation, the inclusion of procedural requirements in a State constitution that apply to a bill's contents raises the stakes for the drafter because the consequence of violating the restrictions that apply to the drafting of a bill would render it unconstitutional.

Court challenges to State laws can be brought by persons who would not meet the requirements for standing in Federal court (for example, the need for the litigant to show harm). Indeed, the standing requirements seem to recognize the unlikelihood of legislators bringing such a court challenge. In Pennsylvania, for example, a taxpayer has standing to bring a constitutional challenge to a statute if "(1) the governmental action would otherwise go unchallenged; (2) those directly and immediately affected by the complained-of matter are beneficially affected and not inclined to challenge the action; (3) judicial relief is appropriate; (4) redress through other channels is unavailable; and (5) no other persons are better situated to assert the claim." *Stilp v. Commonwealth of Pennsylvania,* 588 Pa. 539, 593, 905 A.2d 918, 950 (2006). A drafter of State law, therefore, should be aware that standing rules can be different on the State level from Federal standing rules.

Single-subject provisions have been the basis of court challenges to legislative proposals, including proposed amendments to the constitution of a State that address social issues. In both Georgia and Florida, requirements in the respective constitutions of those States that proposed amendments to the Constitution on which the public will vote by referendum deal with only one subject were the basis of court challenges to proposed amendments to those constitutions banning same-sex marriage.[1]

The drafter, then, aside from having the responsibility of knowing the procedural mandates of the constitution of the State, needs to know how the courts of that State are likely to apply those mandates in a constitutional challenge.

35.3 Statutes on statutory construction

Rules of statutory construction, as well as across-the-board definitions, are codified in many States. Many of these attempt to ease the drafter's task by removing ambiguity before it arises. Consider the issue of computing a number of months. In drafting a Federal statute, providing that a law become effective "6 months after the date of enactment" creates an ambiguity about how to calculate "months": Is it the succession of months that follows the enactment, regardless of the number of days in the month? Is it the same calendar day as the date of enactment in the sixth month after enactment? State Codes address this issue head on. But compare section 645.14 of the Minnesota statutes, which provides as follows:

> **645.14 Time; computation of months**
>
> When, in any law, the lapse of a number of months before or after a certain day is required, such number of months shall be computed by counting the months from such day, excluding the calendar month in which such day occurs, and including the day of the month in the last months so counted having the same numerical order as the day of the month from which the computation is made, unless there be not so many days in the last month so counted, in which case the period computed shall expire with the last day of the month so counted.

with section 1.45 of the Ohio Revised Code:

> **§1.45. Computation of time.**
>
> If a number of months is to be computed by counting the months from a particular day, the period ends on the same numerical day in the concluding month as the day of the month from which the computation is begun, unless there are not that many days in the concluding month, in which case the period ends on the last day of that month.

Both provisions appear to reflect the same policy, yet Ohio's provision manages to state it in a more concise, understandable way. The purpose of the provision is to avoid ambiguity in computing "months", yet Minnesota's is confusing. Consider the phrase "including the day of the month in the last months so counted *having the same numerical order as the day of the month from which computation is made*".

What does the italicized phrase mean? It looks as if it modifies "last months so counted". Are there months that do not have the same numerical order, that is, 1, 2, 3 (which is absurd), or are you supposed to skip months that do not have the same number of days in them as the beginning month has (equally absurd)? If it modifies "the day of the month", then a day "having the same numerical order" as another day is still nonsensical. Substituting "same numerical day" as in the Ohio statute, or simply "same day" would eliminate the confusion. Note also that there appears to be an erroneous plural: "including the day of the last months so counted", when the provision makes sense only if a single "last month" is counted. In addition, note the archaic "unless there be not so many days", as compared with the clearer "unless there are not that many days" in the Ohio law.

States codify the canons of construction discussed in chapter 28. For example, a State may have provisions dealing with inconsistent enactments—for instance, the particular provision controls the general, and if provisions are irreconcilable, the later enactment prevails. But there are inevitably wrinkles in these provisions of which the drafter in the jurisdiction should be aware. As with the canons of construction themselves, some of these codified rules of construction may be inconsistent. Consider the following two provisions from the Minnesota Statutes:

645.38 Effect of reenactment on intervening law

A law which reenacts the provisions of an earlier law shall not be construed to repeal an intermediate law which modified such earlier law. Such intermediate law shall be construed to remain in force and to modify the reenactment in the same manner as it modified the earlier law.

645.39 Implied repeal by later law

When a law purports to be a revision of all laws upon a particular subject, or sets up a general or exclusive system covering the entire subject matter of a former law and is intended as a substitute for such former law, such law shall be construed to repeal all former laws upon the same subject. When a general law purports to establish a uniform and mandatory system covering a class of subjects, such law shall be construed to repeal preexisting

> local or special laws on the same class of subjects. In all other cases, a later law shall not be construed to repeal an earlier one unless the two laws are irreconcilable.

Section 645.38 talks about a law that "reenacts" provisions of an "earlier" law not repealing an "intermediate" law. The use of fuzzy terms like "earlier" and "intermediate" makes it difficult to follow the sequence of enactments here. It looks as if the legislature passes a law that amends an existing law, and then passes another law that "reenacts" that same existing law, apparently unaware of the first law passed; the first law passed is construed to amend the reenacted law. One must suppose that "reenactment" means passing in identical form. But what if a law is reenacted with technical improvements? How is the first law passed going to be construed to amend the reenacted law if it is modified, even slightly, from the original?

Section 645.39 looks like a State version of Federal preemption; that is, a law "preempting the field" nullifies other laws on the subject. Section 645.39 seems to say that if a law is a *revision* of all laws on a subject, then all former laws on the subject are repealed. Under this section, the "intermediate" law described in section 645.38 would be repealed. One wonders what the difference is between a "revision" and a "reenactment". The relationship between 645.38 and 645.39 is not clear.

And finally, there is section 645.42, which provides as follows:

> When a law repeals any provision of a law incorporated into a code adopted at the same session of the legislature, the law repealing the provisions so incorporated into the code shall be construed to effect a repeal of the corresponding provision of the code.

This provision seems to say that even if you have a general revision or reenactment of a field of law, a repeal of a provision of the law prior to the revision or reenactment is not "preempted", but is deemed to repeal the corresponding provision of the revised or reenacted code if all this happens in the same session of the legislature. Because the drafting of sections 645.38, 645.39, and 645.42 is imprecise, it is difficult to harmonize these three provisions, which seems to defeat the purpose of this chapter on statutory construction. Consequently, the drafter should check to see how the courts of the jurisdiction have interpreted the statutes on statutory interpretation.

Rules of construction necessitated by constitutional requirements. It is worth noting that issues of statutory construction arise because of requirements in State constitutions that laws proposing amendments to existing law must restate the entire law, with amendments incorporated and indicated in the text of that law, even though there is no intent to modify the entire law. The laws of Texas address resolving inconsistent provisions in this context (title 3, subtitle B of the Government Code):

> Sec. 311.025. IRRECONCILABLE STATUTES AND AMENDMENTS.
>
> .....
>
> (c) In determining whether amendments are irreconcilable, text that is reenacted because of the requirement of Article III, Section 36, of the Texas Constitution is not considered to be irreconcilable with additions or omissions in the same text made by another amendment. Unless clearly indicated to the contrary, an amendment that reenacts text in compliance with that constitutional requirement does not indicate legislative intent that the reenacted text prevail over changes in the same text made by another amendment, regardless of the relative dates of enactment.

The provision in the Texas Constitution referred to requires the restatement of all provisions of law revived or amended:

> No law shall be revived or amended by reference to its title; but in such case the act revived, or the section or sections amended, shall be reenacted and published at length.

35.4 General defined terms

As in the Federal arena, the States have lists of defined terms that apply universally to the laws of that State. Be aware of what they are, but beware of their weaknesses as well. The introductory language preceding these lists generally says that the definitions apply "unless the context requires otherwise". The problem with this language is that it is saying "the following words mean what the definitions say they mean, but maybe they do not".[2] As a drafter you need to be sure that the general definitions are intended to apply to the case you are addressing; if there will be any ambiguity, you should clarify that they do or do not apply.

Some definitions are not helpful. For example, section 1.02 of the Ohio Revised Code provides the following:

> As used in this Revised Code, unless the context otherwise requires:
>
> ...
>
> (D) "Bond" includes an undertaking.
>
> (E) "Undertaking" includes a bond.
>
> ...
>
> (F) "And" may be read "or", and "or" may be read "and" if the sense requires it.
>
> ...
>
> (G) "Registered mail" includes "certified mail", and "certified mail" includes registered mail.

These definitions are circular; one does not know what a "bond" or an "undertaking" is, only that each term includes the other. The same is true of (G). And it looks like (F) may be anticipating drafting errors: a court in 1972 held that, in an ordinance prohibiting "dumping of refuse or waste matter and burning of such…", "and" may be read as "or in accordance with RC section 1:02(F), since otherwise liability could be avoided by having one person dump and another burn the same refuse, and also the reference to 'dumping' would be mere surplusage". (*State v. Kenmore Demolition Co. Inc.*, 34 Ohio App.2d 19, 20, 295 N.E.2d 416, 417 [1972]).[3]

Note also that these defined terms are capitalized, even though they would not be within the statute, which itself violates the precision required with defined terms. This is avoided by stating, for example, "the term 'bond' means".

States may define the term "person" or "whoever" to include governmental entities (this is not true at the Federal level). Consequently, issues of sovereign immunity may arise when statutes are drafted that impose duties or prohibitions; they are likely to start out by saying "any person who" or "whoever". Even though there will be a presumption in favor of sovereign immunity, it is better to resolve the issue directly. Texas has done so in its Code Construction Act (title 3, subtitle B, chapter 311 of the Government Code):

> Sec. 311.034. WAIVER OF SOVEREIGN IMMUNITY.
>
> In order to preserve the legislature's interest in managing state fiscal matters through the appropriations process, a statute shall not be construed as a waiver of sovereign immunity unless the waiver is effected by clear and unambiguous language. In a statute, the use of "person," as defined by Section 311.005 to include governmental entities, does not indicate legislative intent to waive sovereign immunity unless the context of the statute indicates no other reasonable construction. Statutory prerequisites to a suit, including the provision of notice, are jurisdictional requirements in all suits against a governmental entity.

35.5 Preemption

Chapter 13 (13.5) addressed preemption as an issue in Federal legislation. Needless to say, the drafter at the State or local level must be aware of the extent to which Federal statutes and regulations may preempt State and local law in a given area. Research is your best bet here, which can start with a web search of preemption in State laws.

35.6 Summing up

The laws and rules among State and local jurisdictions that affect the drafting of legislation obviously vary widely. But sound drafting principles can be applied in any jurisdiction, because those principles require the drafter to learn the idiosyncrasies of the jurisdiction and figure out how to accommodate them. It is hoped that this chapter begins to guide the drafter toward that goal.

Notes

1 In the Georgia case (*Perdue v. O'Kelley*, 280 Ga. 732, 632 S.E.2d 110 [2006]), a lower court judge had found that the proposed amendment violated the single-subject rule in the Georgia Constitution because the amendment dealt with both the definition of marriage and the treatment of same-sex marriage under the laws of Georgia. However, the Supreme Court of Georgia applied a broader "germaneness" test and held the proposed amendment to pass constitutional muster because the amendment had only one objective, namely reserving marriage and its benefits to unions between a man and a woman.

2 It is encouraging to see some evidence of abandoning the "unless the context requires otherwise" formula. In 2005, the State of North Carolina amended its lobbying laws. The 1995 law (Session Law 2005-456) showed the changes to existing law that were made and, in the definitions section (defining, among other terms, "lobbying"), the words "unless the context clearly indicates a different meaning" were stricken.

3 See chapter 28 on statutory construction. What is referenced here is the canon that the courts assume every word used by the legislature has a purpose; this is the rule against "mere surplusage".

36. Considerations in Drafting Regulations

36.1 Introduction

This book has concentrated its discussion of drafting principles on legislative drafting. But these same principles can be used in drafting any legal document. This chapter focuses on a few elements of regulatory drafting.

At the Federal level, the National Archives and Record Administration (NARA) (*www.archives.gov/federal-register*) has published a number of resources to be used in drafting documents for publication in the *Federal Register*, the repository of all orders issued by the President and regulations issued Federal agencies. These include the *Document Drafting Handbook* and the *Incorporation by Reference (IBR) Handbook*. Final regulations are then included in the next publication of the Code of Federal Regulations (CFR), where all Federal regulations are recodified. NARA has also published the *Regulatory Drafting Guide* and the *Federal Plain Language Guidelines*, the latter implementing the Plain Writing Act of 2010 (Public Law 111-274; 5 U.S.C. 301 note). The purpose of the Plain Writing Act is to direct agencies to use "plain language" in their published documents that do *not* include regulations. Plain writing is defined as writing that is "clear, concise, well-organized, and follows other best practices appropriate to the subject or field and intended audience".[1] The *Regulatory Drafting Guide* sets forth a number of drafting principles, many of which are addressed in this book.[2]

Comparable documents may be available for regulatory drafters at the State or local level as well. The flexibility that the drafter may have in drafting regulations will be constrained by the extent to which these documents require that regulations be drafted in a certain way. But these requirements should not interfere with the process by which the drafter composes a legal document, namely, getting the policy right and ensuring that the work product carries out that policy effectively.

36.2 Document Drafting Handbook

The *Document Drafting Handbook* prescribes one detailed set of requirements for drafting proposed rules and another one for drafting final rules.[3] These obviously promote uniformity in how all regulations appear in the *Federal Register;* examples are requirements governing the placement of tables of contents, headings, the citation of legal authority for the regulations, and the system of designation used in the Code of Federal Regulations. Some of these requirements, however, do not necessarily promote clarity.

All subdivisions within a section are referred to as "paragraphs", as opposed to a hierarchical structure (subsection, paragraph, subparagraph, and so forth) designed to clarify cross-references. As a result, one cannot refer internally to "this paragraph" without creating ambiguity as to which paragraph in the section the reference applies.[4] Subdivisions are not progressively indented to clarify the relationship of the paragraphs to one another.

Many of the terms that the Handbook directs agencies to use when proposing amendments to regulations can be confusing to readers. The term "add" is used to insert language in an existing regulation without specifying exactly where the language is to be inserted. The term "republish" is used to indicate the restatement of a provision without change "for the convenience of the reader", and the term "revise" is used to indicate that an existing CFR unit is replaced in its entirety. However, it is not clear where to draw the line between one and the other; if a provision is "revised", it at times includes language that is unchanged. The term "redesignate" is used to "transfer" a CFR unit to a "vacant" position and assign it a new designation, yet when a unit is "removed", it is to be "reserved"—leaving a gap in numbering. It is unclear when redesignations are permitted.

Cross-references to any other agency rules are permitted only in limited situations and are subject to an approval process. The *Incorporation By Reference Handbook* (IBR) sets out the rules for incorporation by reference.

These factors are idiosyncrasies that may be confusing to a reader unfamiliar with the terminology used in regulatory drafting. In addition, it is interesting to note that each agency bears the cost of publication of its regulations in the *Federal Register*. It is possible that in the quest to save money an agency may, in drafting regulations, sacrifice clarity by condensing ideas to the point where economy of expression leads to confusion.

36.3 A closer look at regulations

As already stated, regardless of the form prescribed for regulations in any jurisdiction, the drafting principles can still be applied in composing the language. With this in mind, what follows are some observations on one set of regulations.

Foreign Narcotics Kingpin sanctions regulations. In 1999, the Foreign Narcotics Kingpin Designation Act (title VIII of Public Law 106-120) was enacted. The purpose of this Act was to hinder international narcotics traffickers by freezing their assets in, for example, bank accounts over which the United States has jurisdiction. Under the provisions of this Act, property "owned or controlled" by "significant foreign narcotics traffickers" (identified by the President) and of other foreign persons identified by the Secretary of the Treasury because of their involvement in international narcotics trafficking is "blocked",[5] and transactions in the blocked property are prohibited. "United States persons" are subject to the prohibitions. The Act includes definitions and penalties, and the Secretary of the Treasury is given broad authority to enforce the prohibitions through regulations.

The regulations of the Secretary of the Treasury appear in part 598 of title 31, Code of Federal Regulations. The regulations use the term "specially designated narcotics trafficker" to include all the persons whose property is blocked by the statute (that is, the "significant foreign narcotics traffickers" and the other persons involved in narcotics trafficking, described in the preceding paragraph).

The regulations block (in section 598.202) all "property" and "interests in property" "*of*" a specially designated narcotics trafficker and prohibit (in section 598.203) transactions in that property or interests in that property. The word "of" does not define the relationship between the property and the trafficker. The definition of "blocked account" and "blocked property" in section 598.301 refer to an account or property subject to the prohibitions in section 598.202, so that "of" remains undefined and ambiguous. A concept such as property "owned or controlled" by a specially designated national could be a way of describing the relationship.

Note also that section 598.202 refers only to "property" and "interests in property", not accounts:

> The terms *property* and *property interest* include but are not limited to money, checks, drafts, bullion, bank deposits, savings accounts, debts, indebtedness, obligations, notes, guarantees, debentures, stocks, bonds, coupons, any other financial instruments, bankers acceptances, mortgages, pledges, liens or other rights in the nature of security, warehouse receipts, bills of lading, trust receipts, bills of sale, any other evidences of title, ownership, or indebtedness, letters of credit and any documents relating to any rights or obligations thereunder, powers of attorney, goods, wares, merchandise, chattels, stocks on hand, ships, goods on ships, real estate mortgages, deeds of trust, vendors' sales agreements, land contracts, leaseholds, ground rents, real estate and any other interest therein, options, negotiable instruments, trade acceptances, royalties, book accounts, accounts payable, judgments,

> patents, trademarks or copyrights, insurance policies, safe deposit boxes and their contents, annuities, pooling agreements, services of any nature whatsoever, contracts of any nature whatsoever, and any other property, real, personal, or mixed, tangible or intangible, or interest or interests therein, whether present, future, or contingent.

The definition of "property" and "property interest" includes savings accounts and any other financial instrument. Therefore, as discussed below, the definition of "blocked account" is unnecessary and confusing since "account" is included in the definition of "property' and "property interest".[6]

Note also that the definition in section 598.312 defines "property" and "property interest", although "interest in property" is what is actually used in the provisions establishing the prohibitions sections 598.202 and 598.205.

Since the terms "property" and "property interest" both have the same meaning, and since the definition includes any "interest" in the long laundry list of items, only the term "property" is necessary. Then the use of the variant terms "interest in property" or property in which a trafficker has an "interest", and the ambiguity created by the "elegant variation" discussed in 7.4, could be avoided.

This definition begins with "include but are not limited to". As discussed in 22.15, the phrase "but not limited to" is unnecessary and can create ambiguity. More importantly, since the catchall belts-and-suspenders phrase at the end ("any other property, real, personal, or mixed, tangible or intangible, or interest or interests therein, whether present, future, or contingent") leaves nothing else out there, "include" should be replaced with "mean".

There is also a separate definition of "interest" in section 598.307 as follows:

> Except as otherwise provided in this part, the term *interest* when used with respect to property (e.g., *an interest in property*) means an interest of any nature whatsoever, direct or indirect.

This definition would seem to apply to the variant descriptions of interests in property in the chapter, but does it also define "interest" in the definition of "property" and "property interest"? What does the introductory phrase

"Except as otherwise provided in this part" address? It is such a general cross-reference that it is not much help to the reader who wants to know when the definition applies. That issue aside, if the phrase "property interest" were dropped from the definition of property, and the variant references to "interest in property" or property in which a trafficker has an "interest" were dropped throughout the chapter (since the definition of property includes interests in property), the confusion disappears. The ambiguity created by the "elegant variation" would be avoided. And the definition of "interest" is then limited to the reference to "interest" in the definition of property.

Prior to May 17, 2021, section 598.204 (Evasions, attempts, and conspiracies) of the regulations provided as follows:

> Except to the extent provided in regulations, orders, instructions, licenses, or directives issued pursuant to this part, and notwithstanding any contract entered into or any license or permit granted prior to the effective date, any transaction or dealing by any United States person, or within the United States, that evades or avoids, or has the effect of evading or avoiding, and any endeavor, attempt, or conspiracy to violate any of the prohibitions set forth in this part is prohibited.

This sentence is problematic. It is difficult to parse; at the very least, a comma should appear after "conspiracy to violate" to clarify that the last phrase goes with everything that precedes it (this comma *does* appear in the statute). It is unclear what the effect of the "notwithstanding" clause is. Does it mean that any contract, license, or permit granted before the effective date of the prohibition ("effective date" is defined in section 598.302) is no longer valid, or is it the opposite? The confusion results from an exception and a "notwithstanding" clause appearing next to each other, before the reader gets to the main message. If the policy is to nullify those contracts, licenses, and permits, it would be clearer to redraft this provision as follows:

> (a) *Prohibition.*—The following is prohibited:
>
> (1) Any transaction or dealing by any United States person, or within the United States, that evades or avoids, or has the effect of evading or avoiding, any of the prohibitions set forth in this part.

(2) Any endeavor, attempt, or conspiracy to violate any of the prohibitions set forth in this part.

(b) *Exception.*—The prohibitions in paragraph (a) do not apply to the extent that a regulation, order, instruction, license, or directive issued pursuant to this part provides otherwise.

(c) *Cancellation of prior contracts, licenses, etc.*—Any contract entered into, or any license or permit granted, before the effective date is not effective on and after the effective date to the extent the contract, license, or permit would allow an activity prohibited under paragraph (a).

This now lays out the general rule, followed by an exception, followed by a clear statement of the effects of the general rule on prior contracts, and so forth.

As it turned out, the regulation was simplified to an even greater degree to read as follows (effective May 17, 2021):

§ 598.204 Evasions; attempts; conspiracies.

(a) Any transaction on or after the effective date that has the purpose of evading or avoiding, causes a violation of, or attempts to violate any of the prohibitions set forth in this part is prohibited.

(b) Any conspiracy formed to violate the prohibitions set forth in this part is prohibited.

Section 598.205 deals with the effect of transfers (of property or property interests) violating the prohibitions in the regulations. Paragraph (a) begins "Any transfer … is null and void and shall not be the basis for the assertion…". Paragraph (b) begins "No transfer … shall be the basis for the assertion…". Both should be stated the same way, beginning "any transfer", thereby avoiding the "no … shall" construction discussed in 22.2. The expression of a prohibition should be "may not" rather than "shall not". The words "null and" are unnecessary, although the expression "null and void" is so commonly used to express invalidity that using only half of the phrase may raise questions as to its meaning.

Section 598.206 requires that blocked funds be held in interest-bearing accounts. Funds in such an account "may not be invested in instruments the maturity of which exceeds 180 days". To avoid ambiguity as to whether the 180 days applies to each instrument or to all instruments combined, the directive should be stated in the singular: "an instrument the maturity of which exceeds 180 days".

Sections 598.301 to 598.319 contain definitions.

As mentioned above, section 598.301 defines "blocked account" and "blocked property":

> The terms *blocked account* and *blocked property* shall mean any account or property subject to the prohibitions in § 598.202 held in the name of a specially designated narcotics trafficker, or in which such person has an interest, and with respect to which payments, transfers, exportations, withdrawals, or other dealings may not be made or effected except pursuant to a license or other authorization from OFAC [Office of Foreign Assets Control] expressly authorizing such action.

This paragraph is confusing: it is unclear how the different phrases are connected because there is both an "or" and an "and" connecting three phrases, and the sentence lacks parallelism. In addition, the reference to a license or authorization "from" OFAC is imprecise. The relationships between the phrases could be clarified if a few changes (shown in bold) are made as follows:

> The terms *blocked account* and *blocked property* mean any account or property subject to the prohibitions in § 598.202—
>
> **(a) which is** held in the name of a specially designated narcotics trafficker, or in which a specially designated narcotics trafficker has an interest; and
>
> **(b)** with respect to which payments, transfers, exportations, withdrawals, or other dealings may not be made or ~~effected~~ **carried out** except pursuant to a license or authorization ~~from~~ **that is issued by** the OFAC **and that authorizes** ~~authorizing~~ such action.

(The words “carried out” were substituted for the less commonly used “effected”.) This definition says the terms “shall mean” rather than simply “mean”, which is used in the other definitions. The language should be consistent.

It is also unclear why most of the definition is necessary. Section 598.202 blocks the property and prohibits transactions in the property, except as otherwise provided in regulations, licenses, or authorizations in the chapter. Since a bank account is included in the definition of “property”, using the term “blocked account” here would seem to be unnecessary. If the reference is to section 598.206 (which deals with holding funds in interest-bearing accounts), it creates confusion, because the term “blocked interest-bearing account” is the defined term used in section 598.206. It appears as though the definition in section 598.301 could be simplified by saying that “the term ‘blocked property’ means any property blocked under section 598.202”. By operation of section 298.202, transactions in the property are automatically blocked, so that fact need not be repeated here.

Section 598.302 defines “effective date” as follows:

> The term *effective date* refers to the effective date of the applicable prohibitions and directives of this part, which is December 3, 1999, or, in the case of specially designated narcotics traffickers designated after that date, the earlier of the date on which actual or constructive notice of such designation is received.

The word “refers to” instead of “means” raises the question of why different words are used here than in the other definitions. The first phrase (“the effective date of the applicable prohibitions and directives of this part”) appears to be unnecessary and should therefore be omitted. Referring to specially designated narcotics traffickers “designated” after the date is not precise (and should be in the singular, since each trafficker will have a different effective date); the definition (in section 598.314) of “specially designated narcotics trafficker” includes a “significant foreign narcotics trafficker” who is “identified” by the President in the underlying statute. The use of the passive voice in the last phrase raises an ambiguity regarding the notice; the provision should specify who gets the notice. A possible rewrite might be the following:

> The term *effective date* ~~refers to the effective date of the applicable prohibitions and directives of this part, which is~~ **means** December 3, 1999, or, in the case of **a foreign person who is designated or publicly identified (as the case may be) as a** specially designated narcotics trafficker~~s designated~~ after that date, the earlier of the date on which **the foreign person receives** actual or constructive notice of such designation **or identification** ~~is received~~.

It is also unclear what constitutes "constructive notice", which in turn creates an ambiguity about which day will actually be the effective date.

The definition of "foreign person" (section 598.305) "means any citizen or national of a foreign state or any entity not organized under the laws of the United States, but does not include a foreign state". It is unclear whether the term also includes an entity that is owned or controlled by a foreign state. This definition is in the statute, but presumably the regulations could clarify this issue.

Section 598.318 defines "United States person" as "any United States citizen or national, permanent resident alien, an entity organized under the laws of the United States (including its foreign branches), or any person within the United States". There should be an "a" before "permanent resident alien" (every other noun has an article before it). The definition of "U.S. financial institution" follows; it is defined as any "U.S. entity" ... engaged in the business of accepting deposits..." and includes "U.S. holding companies, U.S. affiliates, or U.S. subsidiaries". However, one cannot tell what makes an entity, holding company, affiliate, or subsidiary a "U.S." entity; if the term "United States person" had been used instead, one would know that the entity is either organized under the laws of the United States or is in the United States. One also does not know what determines whether an entity is an "affiliate" or "subsidiary" of another entity.

One last point. Under subpart D (Interpretations) is the following provision (in section 598.403):

> (a) Whenever a transaction licensed pursuant to this part results in the transfer of property (including any property interest) away from a specially designated narcotics trafficker, the transferred property will no longer be considered property in which that person has or has had an interest. Provided no other specially designated narcotics trafficker has any interest in the transferred property following the transfer, the transferred property will no longer be considered property blocked pursuant to § 598.202.

This paragraph addresses transfers of property of specially designated narcotics traffickers. The phrase "property (including any property interest)" does not fit exactly with the definitions; as mentioned already, the term "property" and "property interest" are defined as meaning the same thing; therefore, one is not included in the other. The phrase "transfer … away from" seems to describe a physical distance between property and its owner rather than a legal relationship between the two.

In addition, the phrase "the transferred property will no longer be considered property in which that person has or has had an interest" looks like a statement negating the trafficker's interest in the property for purposes other than these regulations; no language limits the phrase, and the addition of the words "or has had an interest" seems to look to all time predating the transfer. The question becomes whether this language could be used to challenge a person's interest in property in some legal forum unrelated to the subject of the regulations. A possible rewrite could be the following:

> (a) ~~Whenever~~ **If** a transaction licensed pursuant to this part results in the transfer of **ownership or control** of property ~~(including any property interest) away~~ from a specially designated narcotics trafficker **to another person, then after such transfer—**
>
> (1) the ~~transferred~~ property will ~~no longer~~ **not** be considered**, for purposes of this part, to be** property in which that person has [or has had] an interest; **and**
>
> **(2)** the **property will not be considered to be property blocked pursuant to §598.202,** ~~Provided~~ **if** no other specially designated narcotics trafficker has any interest in the ~~transferred~~ property ~~following the transfer,~~

> ~~the transferred property will no longer be considered property blocked pursuant to Sec. 598.202~~.

The meaning of the bracketed phrase "[or has had]" would have to be clarified by the sponsor.

In conclusion. The points discussed regarding these regulations are not the result of a detailed analysis of these regulations, and they may seem trivial, but stiff civil and criminal penalties attach to violating the prohibitions under the regulations; precision ensures that the people affected have adequate notice of what the prohibitions are and to whom they apply. It is hoped that the discussion illustrates the kind of things the drafter looks for or, rather, is on the lookout for in the drafting process.

Notes

1 It is noteworthy that section 6 of the Plain Writing Act of 2010 (5 U.S.C. 301 note) bars judicial review of compliance or noncompliance with any provision of that Act; otherwise the judicial review provisions of the Administrative Procedure Act (5 U.S.C. 701 et seq.) would apply and potentially cause a spike in lawsuits over what constitutes "plain language".

2 Drafting principles include the arrangement of provisions (for example, general before specific), word usage and grammar (using the active voice, list of preferred words), avoiding ambiguity, and rules for using definitions.

3 Under the administrative procedure provisions of title 5, United States Code, Federal agencies follow a process involving notice and comment for a proposed rule and the publication of the final rule at the conclusion of the process.

4 The Handbook has a table specifying how to refer to the different paragraphs within a paragraph, but it would seem that the potential for error is increased when everything under the level of section is a paragraph.

5 The term "blocked" is used to stop access to property; the term is used in connection with prohibitions on transactions in the blocked property.

6 This inconsistency appears in the statute as well.

Appendix

A Quick Guide to *The Legislative Drafter's Desk Reference*

This guide is intended to lay out some of the basic principles of this book. However, it is an overview only, and should not be the only part of this book a drafter uses in tackling a drafting project. Rather, it should serve as a checklist from which the reader can consult the relevant sections of the book (references in this guide) that address each subject in depth.

Overview of the Drafting Process (Chapters 1–5)

1. **Terminology**

   (a) **Bill.** Proposed legislation, whether a bill, joint resolution, or resolution.

   (b) **Sponsor.** The individual or entity who requests the drafter to prepare the bill, who determines its policy, and who will be responsible for proposing or introducing it.

   (c) **Policy.** The sponsor's basic objective in a bill (the "main thrust"), including the sponsor's intent with respect to any subsidiary or collateral questions that may be involved in achieving the basic objective.

   (d) **Setting and context.** The situations in which drafters operate (procedural, constitutional, institutional, stylistic) that determine drafting choices.

(e) **Audience.** The people or entities to which a bill is primarily directed.

2. **Steps in the drafting process**

(a) Understanding the problems leading to the sponsor's request for legislative relief.

(b) Understanding the sponsor's policy to deal with those problems. Exploring with the sponsor possible ways of achieving the goal.

(c) Identifying and dealing with legal and other problems involved, including subsidiary and collateral questions (see **chapter 5**), effect on existing law, and unintended consequences.

(d) Deciding upon the approach (general or narrow, self-executing or delegating to administrative agencies) and organization of the bill.

(e) Taking into account the legislative context—the legislative vehicle to be used and any parliamentary or constitutional restrictions.

(f) Writing the bill.

(g) Carrying out steps (a) through (f) with impartiality.

General Guidelines in Preparing to Write a Bill (Chapters 6–10)

1. **Decide how to organize the bill**

(a) Example of a **model bill**.

SECTION 1. SHORT TITLE; TABLE OF CONTENTS; REFERENCES.

SEC. 2. FINDINGS AND PURPOSES.

SEC. 3. DEFINITIONS.

SEC. 4. BASIC PROGRAM AUTHORITY OR ESTABLISHMENT OF OFFICE.

SEC. 5. ADMINISTRATIVE PROVISIONS.

SEC. 6. REGULATIONS.

SEC. 7. CIVIL PENALTIES.

SEC. 8. CRIMINAL PENALTIES.

SEC. 9. REPORTS.

SEC. 10. AUTHORIZATION OF APPROPRIATIONS.

SEC. 11. CONFORMING AMENDMENTS.

SEC. 12. TRANSITION RULES AND SAVINGS PROVISIONS.

SEC. 13. EFFECTIVE DATE (AND TERMINATION OF AUTHORITY, IF APPLICABLE).

(b) Use **modular construction** generally, that is, each component and subdivision of a bill should be dedicated to a **single** subject and contain all the substantive provisions readers need to understand the subject.

(c) **Split provisions and amendments** are an exception to modular construction, as when an amendment to a law appears in one place in a bill and the effective date of the amendment is in another.

2. **General principles in drafting**

   (a) Use **everyday English** in (preferably) short sentences.

   (b) Use a **consistent style** and an **organization** that gets the message across.

   (c) Apply the **Roman rule**, but not at the expense of clarity (see **chapter 8**).

   (d) **Maximize readability, but clarity is paramount**. For complex concepts, consider using **tables, tabulated sentences**, and **incorporations by reference (9.4; see chapter 23)**.

(e) Know the accepted **statutory format** of the jurisdiction in which you are working.

(f) Be aware of **parliamentary restrictions** in different legislative settings.

(g) **Models** can be useful as a starting point.

Writing Specific Provisions (Chapters 11–13)

1. **Introductory provisions**

   The long title, enacting (or resolving) clause, first section, short title.

2. **Definitions**

   (a) Use definitions for any word that may be unfamiliar, unclear, ambiguous, or used in a way different from its dictionary meaning (for forms and cautions, see **11.7**).

   (b) **Avoid** putting **substantive rules** in the definitions.

   (c) **Avoid artificial definitions.**

   (d) Be aware of **across-the-board statutory definitions (19.5; 35.3).**

3. **Central provisions**

   (a) The **key operating provisions**, that carry out the bill's principal objective, or state the "**general rule**".

   (b) **Exceptions** to the general rule, and **special rules** for applying the general rule to specific circumstances. Ensure that the relationship between the general rule and the exceptions and special rules is clear (through, e.g., placement or cross-references) (see **12.3** and **22.4**).

   (c) Any **structural changes** to agencies carrying out the bill's policy (**12.4**).

   (d) **Funding (12.5)**.

   (e) Any **entitlements** (**12.6**).

(f) **Reporting requirements (12.8).**

(g) **Administrative and judicial review** provisions. **Rulemaking, adjudications,** authority to issue rules; applicability of **administrative procedure** and other provisions of title 5, U.S.C. to agencies generally **(12.9).**

(h) **Sanctions (12.10).**

  (1) **Criminal.** Who is subject to the provision, what is unlawful, what is the penalty, and what is the state of mind? Avoid using "willful".

  (2) **Civil.** Clarify who is to impose civil penalties; constitutional issues if the penalty is criminal in nature.

  (3) **Termination or withholding of funds.**

(i) **Technical and conforming amendments.**

(j) **Substantive amendments to other laws.**

(k) Provisions **modifying congressional procedures (12.14).**

(l) Special rules apply to **appropriations bills and riders (12.13** and **34.5–34.6).**

4. **The Caboose**

(a) **Authorization of appropriations.**

(b) **Effective-date provisions.**

  (1) Unnecessary if there is a **default effective date** (e.g., date of enactment) **(13.2).**

  (2) **Delayed effective dates (26.2).**

  (3) **Retroactive effective dates (26.3).**

  (4) **Event-related effective dates (26.4).**

  (5) **Hybrids (26.5).**

  (6) **Internal effective dates (26.8).**

  (7) Effective dates for **amendments (16.5).**

(c) **Transitional provisions (13.3).**

(d) **Savings clauses (13.4).**

   (e) **Preemption provisions (13.5)** (express, conflict, field preemption).
   (f) **Sunset provisions (13.6).**
   (g) **Severability clauses (13.7).**
5. **Check the Bill for Sources of Ambiguity (see 13.8 for a checklist).**

Drafting Amendments (Chapters 14–18)

1. **Amendatory provisions**
   (a) There are 2 parts to every amendment—the **vehicular** language ("The ABC Act is amended by inserting after section 4 the following new section"), and the language constituting the amendment (i.e., the new section inserted).
   (b) In a bill, early amendments should not anticipate later ones, but later amendments should assume the enactment of earlier ones (**14.4**).
   (c) Rules for amending a bill in Congress. Use the **imperative mood;** describe the target by page and line numbers if available (**14.6**).
2. **Amendatory tools**
   (a) **Cut-and-bite** approach **(15.2).**
   (b) **Amendment by restatement** (**15.3**).
   (c) **Repealers (15.5).**
3. **Amendatory form and style**
   (a) **Amendatory terminology**. Use "**striking**" and "**inserting**"; try to narrow the target; be precise in describing amended material; use a **consolidated reference** if there are many amendments to one law (**16.1**).
   (b) Use the correct amendatory **punctuation** (**quotation marks** have special rules) (**16.2**).
   (c) **Be literal.** The material must appear exactly as it will look in

the law, with correct punctuation and margins (**16.3–16.4**).

(d) There are special usages for long and short titles, and tables of contents, for amendatory bills (**16.5**).

4. **Make sure amendments have an orderly arrangement (17).**

5. **Amendatory cautions**

(a) **Redesignations** and the need for precision (**18.1**).

(b) **Implied amendments** and their risks (**18.2**); avoid **"notwithstanding any other provision of law".**

(c) **Amend an amendatory law only in specific circumstances** (**18.3**).

(d) **Do not amend a nonpositive-law title of the U.S. Code.**

Style, Form, and Usage (Chapters 19–27)

1. **Drafting principles**

(a) Be **consistent.**

(1) Use the same style and form throughout the bill.

(2) Use the same words to describe the same concept throughout the bill.

(3) Use rules of construction, if necessary, to achieve consistency (**19.5**).

(b) Avoid **ambiguity** (words or context that is capable of more than one interpretation) (**19.4**).

(1) Beware using **vague** or **general** terms (uncertainty arising from the use of a broad term) (19.4).

(2) Avoid using **undefined adjectives**.

2. **Architecture (20)**

(a) The numbered **section** is the fundamental division of all statutes.

(b) **Senior components** (divisions larger than sections).

[Division A, B, C], title (I, II, III), [subtitle A, B, C], [chapter 1, 2, 3], [subchapter A, B, C], [part I, II, III], [subpart A, B, C] [bracketed items are optional]; components vary by drafting style (see **table 33.6**).

(c) **Section subdivisions.** Subsection ((a), (b), (c)), paragraph ((1), (2), (3)), subparagraph ((A), (B), (C)), clause ((i), (ii), (iii)), subclause ((I), (II), (III)), [item ((aa), (bb), (cc))], [subitem ((AA), (BB), (CC))] [avoid bracketed items].

(d) Use **headings** for each senior component, and for **section** and (to the maximum extent possible) **its subdivisions.**

3. **Grammar**

(a) Use the **singular,** in the **present tense** (but certain uses of "shall" are okay (**21.3**)), in the **active voice** and **indicative mood** (but certain uses of "shall" are okay (**21.5**).

(b) Use ordinary rules of **punctuation**, including the **serial comma**, but note special rules for using colons and dashes (with lists), and (in amendatory legislation) periods and quotation marks (**21.6**).

(c) **Capitalization** (**21.7**) of certain terms varies among jurisdictions.

(d) **"That"** is defining; **"which"** is nondefining and informative (**21.8**).

(e) Use **"who"** and **"whose"** to refer to persons, with certain exceptions (**21.9**).

(f) Use of **"and"** and **"or"** must be clear from the context (**21.10**).

(g) **Split infinitives** and **sentence-ending prepositions** are usually okay to use (**21.11**).

4. **Word usage**

(a) Use **shall** to require an action, and **may** to **authorize** it; avoid **ambiguity** by the **context** (**22.2**).

(b) Use **may not** to prohibit an act. Say "A person **may not** do X", rather than **"No** person **may** do X"; **"shall not"** can be ambiguous (**22.2**).

(c) Do not use **"shall"** if there is no duty to act (**22.2**).

(d) Use of **"such"** to refer to something previously mentioned is okay, but **"that"** is less archaic (**22.3**).

(e) Use **cross-references** to clarify relationships between provisions (**22.4**).

(f) Use **modifiers** and **explanatory phrases** with caution (22.5).

(g) **Vest functions** in the **head** of the agency, not the agency itself (**22.6**).

(h) **"Person"** includes **corporations** and other **entities** as well as **individuals** (**22.7**).

(i) Be precise in describing **time periods** (**22.9**). Do not say "from", "to", "until", or "by" a certain date or "between" one date and another; say "during the period beginning on" X date "and ending on" Y date.

(j) Use **"deeming"** only to create a legal fiction; use **"treating"** to establish a rule of law; use **"considering"** to indicate an exercise of judgment or discretion (**22.11**).

(k) Use **live** words instead of gerunds, participles, or noun forms, e.g., "consider" instead of "give consideration to" (**22.12**).

(l) Do not use duplicative pairs of words, like **"each and every"**, **"force and effect"**, **"null and void"**, or pairs of words where one includes the other, like **"means and includes"** (**22.13**).

(m) Use **"means"** when one thing is identical or synonymous with the other; use **"includes"** when the second thing is part of the first; avoid **"includes, but is not limited to"**, because the second phrase is redundant of the meaning of "includes" (22.15).

(n) Use **"if"** rather than **"when"** or **"where"** to express a condition (**22.18**).

(o) Avoid archaic usages like **"herein"**, **"thereto"**, **"whereof"**, **"aforementioned"**; others (like **"thereafter"**) are acceptable. (**22.19** has a list).

(p) **"Respectively"** and **"as the case may be"** are important to express relationships between lists (**22.20**).

(q) Do not use **"above"**, **"below"**, or **"hereafter"** to direct the reader to another place in the bill (**22.21**).

(r) Use **"percent"** instead of **"per centum"**. Put the negative in the right place (**22.23**).

(s) If you divide a thing into two parts, do not leave out the piece in the middle (e.g., if you say that rule X applies "before May 1" and the rule Y applies "after May 1", you have left no rule to apply *on* May 1) (**22.23**).

5. **Devices to deal with complexity**

   (a) **Definitions** (**23.2**).

   (b) **Incorporation by reference,** but there is some ambiguity in incorporating another law (**23.3**).

   (c) **Tabulated lists** (**23.4**).

   (d) **Tabulated sentences** (**23.5**).

   (e) **Parenthetical expressions** (**23.6**).

   (f) **Tables, formulas, and other graphic aids** (**23.7**).

6. **References to statutory provisions**

   (a) Refer directly to **positive-law titles of the United States Code** (**24.2**).

   (b) If a law is **not in a positive-law** title—

      (1) refer to its **short title** (**24.3**); or

      (2) if there is no short title, refer to its **long title, Public Law number,** or **enactment date** (**24.4**).

(c) Do not add **"as amended"** after naming an Act (**24.5**).

(d) Use **U.S. Code** citations for informational purposes (**24.6**).

(e) When referring to another unit **within an Act or section,** do not add "of this Act" or "of this section" (**24.7**).

(f) Use **composite references** (section 5(b) (2) (A)) rather than strung out references (subparagraph (A) of paragraph (2) of subsection (b) of section 5), with some exceptions (**24.8–24.9**).

(g) Use a **consolidated reference** if making many amendments to one law (**24.10**).

(h) **Abbreviated references** (**"such", "that"**) to provisions already referred to are useful (**24.11; 27.7**).

7. **References to nonstatutory provisions (Executive orders, regulations, treaties, legislative rules, other public documents) (see 25.1–25.5).**

8. **Other usages**

(a) When **referring** to **numerals**, use figures rather than words (with some exceptions) (27.1).

(b) Do not use **provisos** (with limited exceptions) (**27.2**).

(c) Use **gender-neutral** terms (**27.3**).

(d) Do not use **abbreviations** (but parenthetical U.S. Code citations are okay) (**27.4**).

(e) Be careful when expressing the **rounding** of numbers (**27.5**).

(f) An **"Act"** refers to something enacted into law; a "bill" remains a bill until enacted; a "joint resolution" is always referred to as that.

The Role of the Courts (Chapters 28 and 29)

1. **Statutory construction; canons of statutory construction (28.1–28.10)**

   (a) **Textual** canons (based on the words of the statute) (**28.4**).
   (b) **Extrinsic source** canons (based on sources outside the statute) (**28.5**).
   (c) **Substantive** canons (based on common law, other statutes, the Constitution) (**28.6**).
   (d) **Statutory conflicts, precedent, reenactment** (**28.7**).
   (e) Canons and **appropriations Acts** (**28.8**).

2. **Constitutional and other considerations**
   (a) Limitations of the **Commerce Clause** as a justification for Federal legislation **(29.3)**.
   (b) The **Spending Power** and its limitations (**29.4**).
   (c) Limitations on **applicability of Federal statutes to State governments** (**29.5**).
   (d) Other **separation of powers** issues (**29.6**).
      (1) **Legislative vetoes** are unconstitutional.
      (2) The President alone has the **power to appoint officers**; the President's **power to dismiss officers** of independent agencies is limited.
      (3) The Supreme Court is the arbiter of the **constitutionality of statutes.**
   (e) The court will defer to **agency interpretations of statutes** under the Administrative Procedure Act and *Skidmore* (**29.7**).

Uniquely Federal Forms (Chapters 30–34)

1. **Typography (30.1–30.8)**
   (a) Typography terminology. **Full measure, paragraphed, flush, cut-in, run-in, dropped-down** (**30.2**).
   (b) Type characteristics (**30.3**).
   (c) Marking copy (**30.8**).

2. **Locations and forms of existing law**

   (a) **Slip laws.** First official publication of a statute; of limited usefulness to determine the current state of the law (**31.2**).

   (b) **Statutes at Large.** Permanent chronologic collection of the laws; also of limited usefulness to determine the current state of the law (**31.3**).

   (c) United States Code.

      (1) **Positive-law titles.** Enacted by Congress; can be referred to and amended directly (**31.4**).

      (2) **Nonpositive-law titles.** Not an official source of the law and cannot be amended; useful for amendment history of statutes (**31.5**).

   (d) **Compilations of laws.** An **invaluable** tool for the drafter, who needs to know the current state of the law (**31.6**).

   (e) **Interim sources before publication of public law. Enrolled** bill, **engrossed** versions as passed either House of Congress, available online (*www.congress.gov*) (**31.7**).

   (f) Tracking **omnibus budget** and **appropriations** bills is more difficult (**31.8**).

   (g) **Federal regulations**. Changes are published daily in the **Federal Register**; codified in the **Code of Federal Regulations** (31.9).

3. **Legislative vehicles in Congress**

   (a) **Bills, joint resolutions, concurrent resolutions, simple resolutions** (32.2–32.5).

   (b) **Amendments to bills** (32.7).

   (c) **Reported bills. Ramseyer rule** (showing changes to existing law); parliamentary procedure needs to be determined in the case of bills referred to and reported from more than one committee (**32.8**).

(d) **Engrossed bill.** Bill as passed by the House or the Senate (**32.9**).

(e) **Conference report.** Report of a conference committee to address differences between House and Senate versions of a bill, including language agreed upon and matters reported in disagreement (**32.10**).

(f) **Enrolled bill.** Version presented to the President for signature or veto (**32.11**).

(g) **Correcting resolutions.** Concurrent resolutions directing that, in enrolling a bill, specified errors be corrected (**32.12**).

(h) **Tracking a bill through Congress.** *www.congress.gov*, committee websites, *Congressional Record, Daily Digest,* official Calendars, nongovernmental sources (**32.14**).

4. **Federal drafting styles: traditional, United States Code, revenue, modified revenue, maverick (33.1–33.8)**

5. **Federal parliamentary considerations**

   (a) Subject to subsection (b), parliamentary rules affect how to draft a proposal, including the following matters:

   (1) Referral of a bill to committee (**34.2**).

   (2) Committee procedure (**34.3**).

   (3) The **"rule"** under which a bill is to be considered on the House floor (**34.3**).

   (4) Preparation of a **motion to recommit** (**34.3**).

   (5) Preparation of a **motion to suspend the rules** (**34.3**).

   (6) Preparation and form of **amendments** (no amendments in the third degree are permissible) and when they can be offered; amendments in committee and the floor must be **germane** (**34.4**).

   (7) **Rules affecting appropriations** (**34.5–34.6**), for example—

   (A) an appropriation requires a previous authorization;

(B) a legislative bill cannot include an appropriation or reappropriation;

(C) a general appropriations bill cannot include legislation; and

(D) an amendment limiting the use of funds is permitted, if it does not change existing law.

(8) Points of order under the **Budget Act** can be raised (**34.7**).

(9) Points of order against a conference report can be raised if the language is not **germane** to the underlying bill or is beyond the **scope** of the conference (**34.8**).

(b) The parliamentary issues in subsection (a) are usually moot **on the floor of the House of Representatives, because points of order are usually waived in the ad hoc rule that determines the consideration of the bill or conference report on the House floor.**

State and Regulatory Drafting (Chapters 35 and 36)

1. **Drafters of nonfederal law**

(a) **State constitutional requirements** dictate the form and consideration of legislation, including **single subject** requirements, requirements for the **title** of bills, requirements relating to **publication** before consideration and **consideration** on separate days (**35.2**).

(b) **Rules of statutory construction** (**35.3**) and **definitions** (**35.4**) are codified in many States.

(c) Whether or not State law is **preempted** by Federal law must always be considered.

2. **Regulatory drafting (36)**

Legislative drafting principles can be applied to the drafting of regulations, even if a different format is prescribed (as in the *Document Drafting Handbook*).

List of Cases Cited

Index

A

B

C

D

E

I

M

N

O

P

S

T

U

V

W

X

Y

About the Authors

Sandra L. Strokoff has more than forty years of legislative drafting experience in the Office of the Legislative Counsel of the U.S. House of Representatives. In 2009 she was appointed by the Speaker of the House of Representatives as the Legislative Counsel of the House of Representatives, the first woman to hold that position since the Office of the Legislative Counsel was established in 1919. Her areas of expertise have included intellectual property, federal court jurisdiction, international trade and relations, and ethics laws. She has been a Professorial Lecturer in Law at the George Washington University Law School for 15 years. She is also a solo, chamber music, and orchestral violinist.

Lawrence E. Filson had over forty years of legislative drafting experience. He was Deputy Legislative Counsel in the Office of the Legislative Counsel of the U.S. House of Representatives, where he drafted bills on Social Security, RICO, Medicare, housing, foreign affairs, budgets, and other policy issues.

www.ingramcontent.com/pod-product-compliance
Ingram Content Group UK Ltd.
Pitfield, Milton Keynes, MK11 3LW, UK
UKHW020202290926
15471UKWH00005B/1019

9 798989 69922